Handbook of Research on New Investigations in Artificial Life, AI, and Machine Learning

Maki K. Habib
The American University in Cairo, Egypt

A volume in the Advances in Computational Intelligence and Robotics (ACIR) Book Series

Published in the United States of America by
    IGI Global
    Engineering Science Reference (an imprint of IGI Global)
    701 E. Chocolate Avenue
    Hershey PA, USA 17033
    Tel: 717-533-8845
    Fax: 717-533-8661
    E-mail: cust@igi-global.com
    Web site: http://www.igi-global.com

Library of Congress Cataloging-in-Publication Data

Names: Habib, Maki K., 1955- editor.
Title: Handbook of research on new investigations in artificial life, AI,
  and machine learning / Maki Habib, editor.
Description: Hershey, PA : Engineering Science Reference, an imprint of IGI
  Global, [2022] | Includes bibliographical references and index. |
  Summary: "This book provides the latest research, investigation, and
  development in the area of living systems intelligence, human-level
  cognition & artificial systems, nature and bioinspiration, machine
  learning techniques, Deep Learning techniques and applications, and
  systems that exhibit intelligent autonomous behavioral
  characteristics"-- Provided by publisher.
Identifiers: LCCN 2021037979 (print) | LCCN 2021037980 (ebook) | ISBN
  9781799886860 (h/c) | ISBN 9781799886877 (ebook)
Subjects: LCSH: Automatic machinery. | Artificial intelligence--Industrial
  applications. | Affect (Psychology)--Data processing. | Artificial life.
  | Machine learning. | Image processing.
Classification: LCC TJ163.12 .H37 2022 (print) | LCC TJ163.12 (ebook) |
  DDC 670.42/7--dc23/eng/20211004
LC record available at https://lccn.loc.gov/2021037979
LC ebook record available at https://lccn.loc.gov/2021037980

This book is published in the IGI Global book series Advances in Computational Intelligence and Robotics (ACIR) (ISSN: 2327-0411; eISSN: 2327-042X)

British Cataloguing in Publication Data
A Cataloguing in Publication record for this book is available from the British Library.

The views expressed in this book are those of the authors, but not necessarily of the publisher.

For electronic access to this publication, please contact: eresources@igi-global.com.

Advances in Computational Intelligence and Robotics (ACIR) Book Series

Ivan Giannoccaro
University of Salento, Italy

ISSN:2327-0411
EISSN:2327-042X

MISSION

While intelligence is traditionally a term applied to humans and human cognition, technology has progressed in such a way to allow for the development of intelligent systems able to simulate many human traits. With this new era of simulated and artificial intelligence, much research is needed in order to continue to advance the field and also to evaluate the ethical and societal concerns of the existence of artificial life and machine learning.

The **Advances in Computational Intelligence and Robotics (ACIR) Book Series** encourages scholarly discourse on all topics pertaining to evolutionary computing, artificial life, computational intelligence, machine learning, and robotics. ACIR presents the latest research being conducted on diverse topics in intelligence technologies with the goal of advancing knowledge and applications in this rapidly evolving field.

COVERAGE

- Automated Reasoning
- Artificial Life
- Machine Learning
- Algorithmic Learning
- Agent technologies
- Pattern Recognition
- Artificial Intelligence
- Neural Networks
- Computer Vision
- Fuzzy Systems

IGI Global is currently accepting manuscripts for publication within this series. To submit a proposal for a volume in this series, please contact our Acquisition Editors at Acquisitions@igi-global.com or visit: http://www.igi-global.com/publish/.

Titles in this Series

For a list of additional titles in this series, please visit: http://www.igi-global.com/book-series/advances-computational-intelligence-robotics/73674

Applications of Artificial Intelligence in Additive Manufacturing
Sachin Salunkhe (Vel Tech Rangarajan Dr.Sagunthala R&D Institute of Science and Technology, India) Hussein Mohammed Abdel Moneam Hussein (Helwan University, Egypt) and J. Paulo Davim (University of Aveiro, Portugal)
Engineering Science Reference • © 2022 • 240pp • H/C (ISBN: 9781799885160) • US $245.00

Handbook of Research on Lifestyle Sustainability and Management Solutions Using AI, Big Data Analytics, and Visualization
Sailesh Suryanarayan Iyer (Rai University, India) Arti Jain (Jaypee Institute of Information Technology, India) and John Wang (Montclair State University, USA)
Engineering Science Reference • © 2022 • 415pp • H/C (ISBN: 9781799887867) • US $395.00

Socrates Digital™ for Learning and Problem Solving
Mark Salisbury (University of St. Thomas, USA)
Engineering Science Reference • © 2022 • 383pp • H/C (ISBN: 9781799879558) • US $215.00

Regulatory Aspects of Artificial Intelligence on Blockchain
Pardis Moslemzadeh Tehrani (University of Malaya, Malaysia)
Engineering Science Reference • © 2022 • 273pp • H/C (ISBN: 9781799879275) • US $245.00

Genetic Algorithms and Applications for Stock Trading Optimization
Vivek Kapoor (Devi Ahilya University, Indore, India) and Shubhamoy Dey (Indian Institute of Management, Indore, India)
Engineering Science Reference • © 2021 • 262pp • H/C (ISBN: 9781799841050) • US $225.00

Handbook of Research on Innovations and Applications of AI, IoT, and Cognitive Technologies
Jingyuan Zhao (University of Toronto, Canada) and V. Vinoth Kumar (MVJ College of Engineering, India)
Engineering Science Reference • © 2021 • 570pp • H/C (ISBN: 9781799868705) • US $325.00

Decision Support Systems and Industrial IoT in Smart Grid, Factories, and Cities
Ismail Butun (Chalmers University of Technology, Sweden & Konya Food and Agriculture University, Turkey & Royal University of Technology, Sweden)
Engineering Science Reference • © 2021 • 285pp • H/C (ISBN: 9781799874683) • US $245.00

701 East Chocolate Avenue, Hershey, PA 17033, USA
Tel: 717-533-8845 x100 • Fax: 717-533-8661
E-Mail: cust@igi-global.com • www.igi-global.com

List of Contributors

Table of Contents

Detailed Table of Contents

    Katsuyuki Morishita, Nihon University, Japan
    Shinya Kato, Nihon University, Japan
    Yuki Takei, Nihon University, Japan
    Ken Saito, Nihon University, Japan

This chapter presents a receptor cell model that mimics the receptor cell function of living organisms. The receptor cell model converts the signal input of the sensor into an oscillating pulse waveform. Moreover, the oscillation frequency of the receptor cell model varies according to the sensory input intensity. First, the authors constructed a receptor cell model by discrete circuit. In addition, they measured the frequency characteristics using pressure and optical sensors. The results showed that the frequency of the receptor cell model changes according to the intensity of the sensory input. Then, they proposed a receptor cell model based on an integrated circuit. The simulation results showed that the proposed model had the same characteristics as the discrete circuit model. Thus, the proposed receptor cell model is expected to output a vibration pulse waveform that depends on the input intensity of the sensor.

    Yuki Takei, Nihon University, Japan
    Katsuyuki Morishita, Nihon University, Japan
    Ken Saito, Nihon University, Japan

There is still no artificial life with the same adaptability and flexibility as animals. Although artificial life will advance by acquiring nervous systems similar to those of animals, its role and mechanisms remain unknown. The authors have developed a quadruped robot with a bio-inspired gait generation method to realize robots that can behave like animals. The method could generate gaits using pulse-type hardware neuron models (P-HNMs). However, characteristics of the P-HNMs had large scatterings, and the robot could maintain gaits only a few cycles. This chapter explains the method and P-HNM integrated circuits (ICs) developed to improve P-HNMs' characteristics. In addition, dynamic simulations with a simplified method and discussions of the methods and ICs are provided. Although the proposed methods are simple, they could actively generate gaits using interactions between the body and the environment. Therefore, the methods will lead to the realization of a quadruped robot with flexible adaptability.

Duygun Erol Barkana, Yeditepe University, Turkey
Itır Kaşıkçı, Istanbul Commerce University, Turkey
Hatice Kose, Istanbul Technical University, Turkey
Elif Toprak, Yeditepe University, Turkey
Selma Yılar, Cerrahpaşa Medical Faculty, Istanbul University-Cerrahpaşa, Turkey
Dilara Demirpençe Seçinti, Şişli Etfal Research and Training Hospital, Turkey

The chapter aims to classify the physiological data of hearing impaired (HI) and typically developed (TD) children using machine/deep learning techniques 1) to reveal if the physiological data of the HI and TD are distinguishable, 2) to understand which emotions of HI and TD are recognized, and 3) to investigate the effect of computerization in a subset of audiology perception tests. Physiological signals, which are blood volume pulse (BVP), skin conductance (SC), and skin temperature (ST), are collected using a wearable E4 wristband during computerized and conventional tests. Sixteen HI and 18 TD children participated in this study. An artificial neural network (ANN) and a convolutional neural network (CNN) model are used to classify physiological data. The physiological changes of HI and TD children are distinguishable in computerized tests. TD children's positive (pleasant) and negative (unpleasant) emotions (PN) are distinguishable on both computerized and conventional tests. HI children's neutral and negative (unpleasant) (NU) emotions are distinguishable in the computerized tests.

Chapter 4

Batuhan Yılmaz, Boğaziçi University, Turkey
Melih Sen, Marmara University, Turkey
Engin Masazade, Marmara University, Turkey
Vedat Beskardes, Istanbul University-Cerrahpasa, Turkey

Sensing the environment with passive acoustic sensors has been used as a very useful tool to monitor and quantify the status and changes on biodiversity. In this chapter, the authors aim to classify the social calls (biting, feeding, fighting, isolation, mating protest, and sleeping) of a certain bat species, Egyptian fruit bat, which lives in colonies with thousands of others. Therefore, classification of their calls not only helps us to understand the population dynamics but also helps us to offer distinct environmental management procedures. In this work, the authors use the database previously presented in Prat et al. and present the social call classification results under both classical machine learning techniques and a convolutional neural network (CNN). The numerical results show that CNN improves the classification performance up to 20% as compared to the traditional machine learning approaches when all the call classes are considered. It has also been shown that the classes of aggressive calls, which can sound quite close to each other, can be distinguished with CNN.

Chapter 5

Lu Shao, Sanyo-Onoda City University, Japan
Fusaomi Nagata, Sanyo-Onoda City University, Japan
Maki K. Habib, The American University in Cairo, Egypt
Keigo Watanabe, Okayama University, Japan

Previous studies have successfully identified results of searching the desired object in real-time movie frames using a template image prepared in color or shape. In every sample time of 40 ms, the center of gravity (COG) can be consecutively calculated by detecting and identifying the desired object. Hence, it is possible to have visual feedback (VF) control with the quadrotor by referring to the change of the COG as the relative velocity with respect to the desired object. In this chapter, a useful function is developed to enable the detection and counting of desired objects in real-time. This allows the quadrotor to monitor the number of individually selected objects in the frames of a movie such as cars, animals, etc. This supports high-speed counting while avoiding errors due to object overlapping. Also, the proposed VF controller is successfully applied to a pick-and-place robot, in which a transfer learning-based convolutional neural network can estimate object orientation for smooth picking.

Chapter 6

Morteza Mohammadzaheri, Birmingham City University, UK & Sultan Qaboos University, Oman
Hamidreza Ziaiefar, Sultan Qaboos University, Oman
Mojtaba Ghodsi, University of Portsmouth, UK

For many piezoelectric actuators and their areas of operating, charge is proportional to the position of the actuator. Thus, for such actuators, estimation of charge is largely considered as an equivalent to position estimation. That is, a charge estimator may replace a position sensor. Nevertheless, a significant portion of the excitation voltage is wasted for charge estimation. This voltage, not used to deform the actuator, is called voltage drop. A class of charge estimators of piezoelectric actuators have a resistor in series with the actuator and can only work together with a digital processor. These are called digital charge estimators and have been shown to witness the smallest voltage drop compared to other charge estimators. This chapter first proposes a design guide for digital charge estimators of piezoelectric actuators to maximise the accuracy with the smallest possible voltage drop. The chapter then details the use of five different artificial intelligence (AI) techniques to tackle this design problem and assesses their effectiveness through even-handed comparison.

    Ali Selamat, Universiti Teknologi Malaysia, Malaysia
    Shilan S. Hameed, Universiti Teknologi Malaysia, Malaysia
    Liza Abdul Latiff, Universiti Teknologi Malaysia, Malaysia
    Shukor A. Razak, Universiti Teknologi Malaysia, Malaysia
    Ondrej Krejcar, Hradec Kralove University, Czech Republic
    Marek Penhaker, VŠB Technical University of Ostrava, Czech Republic

Smart telemetry medical devices do not have sufficient security measures, making them weak against different attacks. Machine learning (ML) has been broadly used for cyber-attack detection via on-gadgets and on-chip embedded models, which need to be held along with the medical devices, but with limited ability to perform heavy computations. The authors propose a real-time and lightweight fog computing-based threat detection using telemetry sensors data and their network traffic in NetFlow. The proposed method saves memory to a great extent as it does not require retraining. It is based on an incremental form of Hoeffding Tree Naïve Bayes Adaptive (HTNBA) and Incremental K-Nearest Neighbors (IKNN) algorithm. Furthermore, it matches the nature of sensor data which increases in seconds. Experimental results showed that the proposed model could detect different attacks against medical sensors with high accuracy ($\gg$100%), small memory usage (<50 MB), and low detection time in a few seconds.

    Mario Versaci, University "Mediterranea" of Reggio Calabria, Italy
    Francesco Carlo Morabito, University "Mediterranea" of Reggio Calabria, Italy

In the AI framework, edge detection is an important task especially when images are affected by uncertainties and/or inaccuracies. Thus, usual edge detectors are unsuitable, so it is necessary to exploit fuzzy tools as Versaci-Morabito edge detector proposing a procedure to adaptively construct fuzzy membership functions. In this chapter, the authors reformulate this approach exploiting a new formulation for adaptively fuzzy membership functions but characterized by a more reduced computational load making the approach more attractive for any real-time applications. Furthermore, the chapter provides new mathematical results not yet proven in previous works.

    Lorna Uden, Staffordshire University, UK
    Shijie Guan, Shenyang Ligong University, China

AI can even outperform humans in many tasks such as winning games like Go and poker as well as engaging in creative endeavours in writing novels and music. Despite this, it is still a long way from building artificial human intelligence. Current AIs are only designed to excel in their intended functions and cannot generate knowledge to new tasks and situations. For AI to achieve artificial human intelligence requires us to study and understand the human brain. Neuroscience is the study of the anatomy and physiology of the human brain. It provides us interesting insights into how the brain works to develop better AI systems. Conversely, better AI systems can help drive neuroscience forward and further unlock the secrets of the brain. Neuroscience and AI are closely related. The synergy of the two will benefit each other. Besides the benefits of neuroscience for AI research, neuroscience also has important implications for machine learning. This chapter discusses the implications of neuroscience for general artificial intelligence and the benefits of AI for neuroscience research.

Chapter 10

Marco Castellani, University of Birmingham, UK

Luca Baronti, University of Birmingham, UK

Yuanjun Laili, Beihang University, China

Duc Truong Pham, University of Birmingham, UK

The bees algorithm is a popular intelligent optimisation algorithm inspired by the foraging behaviour of honeybees. This chapter describes the application of two combinatorial variants of the bees algorithm to the optimisation of manufacturing processes. The first variant was created for minimisation of printed circuit board assembly times, whilst the second was devised for fast replanning of robotic disassembly of mechanical parts. In both cases, the bees-inspired paradigm proved effective in efficiently solving complex engineering optimisation problems. Compared to a number of state-of-the-art combinatorial optimisation algorithms, the bees algorithm excelled in terms of efficiency of the solutions.

Chapter 11

Sajid Nazir, Glasgow Caledonian University, UK

Shushma Patel, De Montfort University, UK

Dilip Patel, London South Bank University, UK

Deep neural networks provide good results for computer vision tasks. This has been possible due to a renewed interest in neural networks, availability of large-scale labelled training data, virtually unlimited processing and storage on cloud platforms and high-performance clusters. A convolutional neural network (CNN) is one such architecture better suited for image classification. An important factor for a better CNN performance, besides the data quality, is the choice of hyperparameters, which define the model itself. The model or hyperparameter optimisation involves selecting the best configuration of hyperparameters but is challenging because the set of hyperparameters are different for each type of machine learning algorithm. Thus, it requires a lot of computational time and resources to determine a better performing machine learning model. Therefore, the process has a lot of research interest, and currently a transition to a fully automated process is also underway. This chapter provides a survey of the CNN model optimisation techniques proposed in the literature.

Chapter 12

Tomohiro Yamaguchi, Nara College, National Institute of Technology (KOSEN), Japan

Yuto Kawabuchi, Nara College, National Institute of Technology (KOSEN), Japan

Shota Takahashi, Nara College, National Institute of Technology (KOSEN), Japan

Yoshihiro Ichikawa, Nara College, National Institute of Technology (KOSEN), Japan

Keiki Takadama, The University of Electro-Communications, Tokyo, Japan

The mission of this chapter is to formalize multi-objective reinforcement learning (MORL) problems where there are multiple conflicting objectives with unknown weights. The objective is to collect all Pareto optimal policies in order to adapt them for use in a learner's situation. However, it takes huge learning costs in previous methods, so this chapter proposes the novel model-based MORL method by reward occurrence probability (ROP) with unknown weights. There are three main features. First one is that average reward of a policy is defined by inner product of the ROP vector and a weight vector. Second feature is that it learns the ROP vector in each policy instead of Q-values. Third feature is that Pareto optimal deterministic policies directly form the vertices of a convex hull in the ROP vector space. Therefore, Pareto optimal policies are calculated independently with weights and just one time by Quickhull algorithm. This chapter reports the authors' current work under the stochastic learning environment with up to 12 states, three actions, and three and four reward rules.

Chapter 13

Daniela Lopez De Luise, CI2S Labs, Argentina

Natural language is a rich source of information, with a complex structure and a kaleidoscope of contents. This arises from the flexibility that living languages exhibit in order to reflect the speaker's intention, and also due to communication needs. From computational linguistics, multiple strategies have been developed that allow detecting and interpreting textual contents, but there is an uncovered margin, an interpretive range that remains outside the scope of automatic processing, and that requires rethinking the scope and perspectives of these tools. This chapter aims to show this gap and its implications, exploring dialectical and technical reasons. It also proposes a new perspective of interpretation and scope of textual processing, a sort of thermodynamics of productions that involve the communication of certain types. As part of the scope, there is a bibliographic analysis and a statistical and heuristic exploration of the proposal applied to 20Q game.

Chapter 14

Siti Dianah, Universiti Teknologi Malaysia, Malaysia
Ali Selamat, Universiti Teknologi Malaysia, Malaysia
Ondrej Krejcar, Hradec Kralove University, Czech Republic

In higher education institutions (HEI), the ability to predict student grades as an early warning system is one of the important areas that gained attention to improve educational outcomes. Over the years, machine learning techniques have facilitated and successfully addressed student grade prediction for identifying the potentially weak students in a particular course. However, dealing with an imbalanced multiclass classification dataset is challenging due to biased results towards predicting the minority class. Therefore, this chapter proposes a method that can increase the classification performance by using a modified synthetic minority oversampling technique and feature selection (MSMOTE-FS). The experiments tested the proposed method's effectiveness by utilizing four oversampling techniques and six standard classification algorithms. This finding indicated that the proposed method gives promising results to improve the accuracy in multiclass classification of student grade prediction.

Chapter 15

Kamisah Osman, Universiti Kebangsaan Malaysia, Malaysia

Recent studies have revealed that the existing measurement methods related to computational thinking (CT) pivot on gauging thinking skills, recommending an extended understanding of CT as disposition. Disposition reflects inclination towards learning CT and indicates the interest to think intelligently about issues confronting them. Hence, the aim of this chapter is to assess students' affection towards learning CT as problem solving tool that can transform knowledge more productively. In the context of the affective domain, attitudes and beliefs can be regarded of as generic responses to something, the core quality of an emotion, feeling, mood, or temperament, and hence as affective mental activities. The framework of the CT disposition proposed in this chapter was developed based on tripartite classification of mental activities known as of trilogy of mind: cognitive, affective, and conative. The basic tenet of this chapter is aligned with the theoretical underpinnings of thinking dispositions which is expected to suit different contexts and needs.

Chapter 16

Goran Klepac, Hrvatski Telekom d.d., Croatia & Algebra University College, Croatia
Leo Mršić, Algebra University College, Croatia
Robert Kopal, Algebra University College, Croatia

The chapter will propose a novel approach that combines the traditional machine learning approach in churn management and customer satisfaction evaluation, which unite traditional machine learning approach and expert-based approach, which leans on event-based management. The core of the proposed framework is hybrid fuzzy expert system, which can contain a variety of data mining predictive models responsible for some specific areas as additions to traditional rule blocks. It can also include social network analysis metrics based on linguistic variables and incorporated within rule blocks. The chapter will introduce how revealed patterns can be applied for continual portfolio management improvement. The proposed solution unites advanced analytical techniques with the decision-making process within a holistic self-learning framework.

Chapter 17

Dhanushka Chamara Liyanage, Tallinn University of Technology, Estonia
Mart Tamre, Tallinn University of Technology, Estonia
Robert Hudjakov, Tallinn University of Technology, Estonia

Product quality assurance is a vital component in any manufacturing process. With the advancement of machine vision, the product quality inspection has been vastly improved. This couldn't be achieved with human inspection otherwise when it comes to consistency, accuracy, and the speed. The advance sensor technologies and image processing algorithms are ensuring the product and process quality in various industries including pharmaceutical manufacturing, food production, agriculture, and waste sorting. In contrast to the RGB imaging technology, multispectral and hyperspectral imaging technologies carry more information about the objects under inspection. With the help of both spectral and spatial information, it is possible to discriminate the quality indices of various products with higher accuracy than RGB imaging methods. This chapter discusses the state-of-the-art product quality inspection applications using hyperspectral imaging and multispectral imaging using modern machine learning and other statistical algorithms.

Chapter 18

    Rogério Sales Gonçalves, Federal University of Uberlândia, Brazil
    Guilherme Salomão Agostini, Federal University of Uberlândia, Brazil
    Reinaldo A. C. Bianchi, Centro Universitario FEI, Brazil
    Rafael Zimmermann Homma, CELESC, Brazil
    Daniel Edgardo Tio Sudbrack, CELESC, Brazil
    Paulo Victor Trautmann, CELESC, Brazil
    Bruno Cordeiro Clasen, CELESC, Brazil

Insulators are power transmission line components responsible for two key tasks: the first one is to support the mechanical stress originated by the weight of the cables and devices, and the second one is to avoid electrical dissipation from the cables to the tower structure. Even though the shape and material of the insulator is made in such a way as to avoid the conduction of electrical current on its surface, if some types of dirty accumulates excessively, the insulator can still conduct an electric arc to the tower, causing damage to the power grid. This chapter first presents the state-of-the-art power line insulator cleaning methods and the techniques used to identify insulators that require cleaning. Then, this chapter describes an algorithm that makes use of machine learning, deep learning, and computer vision technics, which can be used embedded in an unmanned aerial vehicle, to support the energy company in the assessment of the levels of dirt on the insulators. Finally, experimental results are presented showing the challenges and the open problems.

Preface

Artificial Intelligence (AI), Artificial Life (ALife), and Machine Learning (ML) are very hot and highly progressing topics that impact daily human lives, businesses, the economy, health, ecosystems, and industry.

As technology spreads globally, researchers and scientists continue developing and studying the strategy behind creating artificial life. This research field is ever-expanding, and it is essential to stay current in the contemporary trends in artificial life, artificial intelligence, and machine learning.

This research and development direction demands the creation. It develops new ideas by understanding how the human brain analyzes and solves problems and builds efficient and complex techniques, models, and algorithms. Besides, it is also essential to know the fundamentals of life, how life in nature has evolved, and how researchers can be inspired by nature as a reference model and the integrated ecosystems to develop new ideas, technologies, techniques, and algorithms that facilitate and demonstrate learning capabilities.

The latest development in AI, ALife, and ML aims to automate and enhance the accuracy of the decision-making capabilities and are featured by the continuous ability to interact, learn from experience, reason, predict, estimate, adapt, recommend, decide, and take effective practical actions. It is essential to mention that the ALife overlaps with biology and chemistry while integrating interdisciplinary knowledge to facilitate life research and development.

The *Handbook of Research on New Investigations in Artificial Life, AI, and Machine Learning* covers critical topics that motivate researchers and scientists to advance and inspire industry leaders for new applications. The book provides concepts, theories, systems, technologies, techniques, algorithms, and procedures that exhibit any living system or human's properties, phenomena, or abilities. In addition, the handbook presents the most up-to-date research and new application developments. Besides, the book investigates the latest progress in the field of AI, ALife, and ML

This handbook includes 18 chapters contributing to the state-of-art on research advancement in AI, ALife, and ML. The chapters provide relevant theoretical knowledge, practices, behavior classification, quality control, medical diagnosis and devices, and new findings. Furthermore, the handbook helps prepare engineers and scientists looking for innovative development, challenging, intelligent, bioinspired systems, and value-added ideas for autonomous and intelligent interdisciplinary products and techniques to meet today and future most pressing challenges.

The book serves as an essential resource for researchers, graduate students, academicians, stakeholders, practitioners, scientists studying Alife, AI, biological inspiration, machine learning, and more.

ORGANIZATION OF BOOK

Chapter 1: This chapter presents a receptor cell model that mimics the receptor cells' function of living organisms. The receptor cell model converts the signal input of the sensor into an oscillating pulse waveform. Moreover, the oscillation frequency of the receptor cell model varies according to the sensory input intensity. First, we constructed a receptor cell model by discrete circuit. In addition, we measured the frequency characteristics using pressure and optical sensors. The results showed that the frequency of the receptor cell model changes according to the intensity of the sensory input. Then, we proposed a receptor cell model based on an integrated circuit. The simulation results showed that the proposed model had the same characteristics as the discrete circuit model. Thus, the proposed receptor cell model is expected to output a vibration pulse waveform that depends on the input intensity of the sensor.

Chapter 2: There is still no artificial life with the same adaptability and flexibility as animals. Although artificial life will advance by acquiring nervous systems similar to those of animals, its role and mechanisms remain unknown. The authors have developed a quadruped robot with a bio-inspired gait generation method to realize robots that can behave like animals. The method could generate gaits using pulse-type hardware neuron models (P-HNMs). However, characteristics of the P-HNMs had large scatterings, and the robot could maintain gaits only a few cycles. This chapter explains the method and P-HNM integrated circuits (ICs) developed to improve P-HNMs' characteristics. In addition, dynamic simulations with a simplified method and discussions of the methods and ICs are provided. Although the proposed methods are simple, they could actively generate gaits using interactions between the body and the environment. Therefore, the methods will lead to the realization of a quadruped robot with flexible adaptability.

Chapter 3: The chapter aims to classify the physiological data of hearing impaired (HI) and typically developed (TD) children using machine/deep learning techniques i) to reveal if the physiological data of the HI and TD are distinguishable, ii) to understand which emotions of HI and TD are recognized and iii) to investigate the effect of computerization in a subset of audiology perception tests. Physiological signal, which are blood volume pulse (BVP), skin conductance (SC), skin temperature (ST), are collected using a wearable E4 wristband during computerized and conventional tests. 16 HI and 18 TD children participated to this study. An artificial neural network (ANN) and a Convolutional Neural Networks (CNN) model are used to classify physiological data. The physiological changes of HI and TD children are distinguishable in computerized tests. TD children's positive (pleasant) and negative (unpleasant) emotions (PN) are distinguishable in both computerized and conventional tests. HI children's neutral and negative (unpleasant) (NU) emotions of are distinguishable in the computerized tests.

Chapter 4: Sensing the environment with passive acoustic sensors has been used as a very useful tool to monitor and quantify the status and changes on biodiversity. In this chapter, the authors aim to classify the social calls (biting, feeding, fighting, isolation, mating protest and sleeping) of a certain bat species, Egyptian fruit bat which lives in colonies with thousands of others. Therefore, classification of their calls not only helps us to understand the population dynamics but also helps us to offer distinct environmental management procedures. In this work, the authors use the database previously presented in Prat et al. and present the social call classification results under both classical machine learning techniques and a convolutional neural network (CNN). The numerical results show that CNN improves the classification performance up to 20% as compared to the traditional machine learning approaches when all the call classes are considered. It has also been shown that the classes of aggressive calls which can sound quite close to each other can be distinguished with CNN.

Chapter 5: In previously reported successfully identified results of searching the desired object in real-time movie frames using a template image prepared in color or shape. In every sample time of 40 ms, the center of gravity (COG) can be consecutively calculated by detecting and identifying the desired object. Hence, it is possible to have visual feedback (VF) control with the quadrotor by referring to the change of the COG as the relative velocity with respect to the desired object. In this chapter, a useful function is developed to enable the detection and counting of desired objects in real-time. This allows the quadrotor to monitor the number of individually selected objects in the frames of a movie such as cars, animals, etc. This supports high-speed counting while avoiding errors due to object overlapping. Also, the proposed VF controller is successfully applied to a pick and place robot, in which a transfer learning-based convolutional neural network can estimate objects' orientation for smooth picking.

Chapter 6: For many piezoelectric actuators and their areas of operating, charge is proportional to the position of the actuator. Thus, for such actuators, estimation of charge is largely considered as an equivalent to position estimation. That is, a charge estimator may replace a position sensor. Nevertheless, a significant portion of the excitation voltage is wasted for charge estimation. This voltage, not used to deform the actuator, is called voltage drop. A class of charge estimators of piezoelectric actuators have a resistor in series with the actuator and can only work together with a digital processor. These are called digital charge estimators and have been shown to witness the smallest voltage drop compared to other charge estimators. This chapter first proposes a design guide for digital charge estimators of piezoelectric actuators to maximise the accuracy with the smallest possible voltage drop. The chapter then details the use of five different artificial intelligence (AI) techniques to tackle this design problem and assess their effectiveness through even-handed comparison.

Chapter 7: Smart telemetry medical devices do not have sufficient security measures, making them weak against different attacks. Machine learning (ML) has been broadly used for cyber-attack detection via on-gadgets and on-chip embedded models, which need to be held along with the medical devices, but with limited ability to perform heavy computations. We propose a real-time and lightweight fog computing-based threat detection using telemetry sensors data and their network traffic in NetFlow. The proposed method saves memory to a great extend as it does not require retraining. It is based on an incremental form of Hoeffding Tree Naïve Bayes Adaptive (HTNBA) and Incremental K-Nearest Neighbors (IKNN) algorithm. Furthermore, it matches the nature of sensor data which increases in seconds. Experimental results showed that our proposed model could detect different attacks against medical sensors with high accuracy ($\gg$100%), small memory usage (<50 MB) and low detection time in few seconds.

Chapter 8: In the AI framework, edge detection is an important task especially when images are affected by uncertainties and/or inaccuracies. Thus, usual edge detectors are unsuitable, so it is necessary to exploit fuzzy tools as Versaci-Morabito edge detector proposing a procedure to adaptively construct fuzzy membership functions. In this chapter, we reformulate this approach exploiting a new formulation for adaptively fuzzy membership functions but characterized by a a more reduced computational load making the approach more attractive for any real-time applications. Furthermore, the chapter provides new mathematical results not yet proven in previous works.

Chapter 9: AI can even outperform humans in many tasks such as winning games like Go and poker, as well as engaging in creative endeavours in writing novels and music. Despite this, it is still a long way from building artificial human intelligence. Current AIs are only designed to excel in their intended functions and cannot generate knowledge to new tasks and situations. For AI to achieve artificial human intelligence requires us to study and understand the human brain. Neuroscience is the study of the anatomy and physiology of the human brain. It provides us interesting insights into how the brain works to develop better AI systems. Conversely, better AI systems can help drive neuroscience forward and further unlock the secrets of the brain. Neuroscience and AI are closely related. The synergy of the two will benefit each other. Besides the benefits of neuroscience for AI research, neuroscience also has important implications for machine learning. This chapter discusses the implications of neuroscience for general artificial intelligence and the benefits of AI for neuroscience research.

Chapter 10: The Bees Algorithm is a popular intelligent optimisation algorithm inspired by the foraging behaviour of honeybees. This paper describes the application of two combinatorial variants of the Bees Algorithm to the optimisation of manufacturing processes. The first variant was created for minimisation of printed circuit board assembly times, whilst the second was devised for fast replanning of robotic disassembly of mechanical parts. In both cases, the bees-inspired paradigm proved effective in efficiently solving complex engineering optimisation problems. Compared to a number of state-of-the-art combinatorial optimisation algorithms, the Bees Algorithm excelled in terms of efficiency of the solutions.

Chapter 11: Deep neural networks provide good results for computer vision tasks. This has been possible due to a renewed interest in neural networks, availability of large-scale labelled training data, virtually unlimited processing and storage on cloud platforms and high-performance clusters. A Convolutional Neural Network (CNN) is one such architecture better suited for image classification. An important factor for a better CNN performance, besides the data quality, is the choice of hyperparameters, which define the model itself. The model or hyperparameter optimisation involves selecting the best configuration of hyperparameters, but is challenging because the set of hyperparameters are different for each type of machine learning algorithm. Thus, it requires a lot of computational time and resources to determine a better performing machine learning model. Therefore, the process has a lot of research interest and currently a transition to a fully automated process is also underway. This paper provides a survey of the CNN model optimisation techniques proposed in the literature.

Chapter 12: The mission of this chapter is to formalize multi-objective reinforcement learning (MORL) problems where there are multiple conflicting objectives with unknown weights. The objective is to collect all Pareto optimal policies in order to adapt them for use in a learner's situation. However, it takes huge learning costs in previous methods, so this chapter proposes the novel model-based MORL method by reward occurrence probability (ROP) with unknown weights. There are three main features. First one is that average reward of a policy is defined by inner product of the ROP vector and a weight vector. Second feature is that it learns the ROP vector in each policy instead of Q-values. Third feature is that Pareto optimal deterministic policies directly form the vertices of a convex hull in the ROP vector space. Therefore, Pareto optimal policies are calculated independently with weights and just one time by Quickhull algorithm. This chapter reports the authors' current work under the stochastic learning environment with up to twelve states, three actions and three and four reward rules.

Chapter 13: Natural Language is a rich source of information, with a complex structure and a kaleidoscope of contents. This arises from the flexibility that living languages exhibit in order to reflect the speaker's intention, and also due to communication needs. From computational linguistics, multiple strategies have been developed that allow detecting and interpreting textual contents, but there is an uncovered margin, an interpretive range that remains outside the scope of automatic processing, and that requires rethinking the scope and perspectives of these tools. This chapter aims to show this gap and its implications, exploring dialectical and technical reasons. It also proposes a new perspective of interpretation and scope of textual processing, a sort of thermodynamics of productions that involve the communication of certain types. As part of the scope, there is a bibliographic analysis and a statistical and heuristic exploration of the proposal applied to 20Q game.

Chapter 14: In higher education institutions (HEI), the ability to predict student grades as an early warning system is one of the important areas that gained attention to improve educational outcomes. Over the years' machine learning techniques have facilitated and successfully addressed student grade prediction for identifying the potentially weak students in a particular course. However, dealing with an imbalanced multiclass classification dataset is challenging due to biased results towards predicting the minority class. Therefore, this paper proposes a method that can increase the classification performance by using a modified synthetic minority oversampling technique and feature selection (MSMOTE-FS). The experiments tested the proposed method's effectiveness by utilizing four oversampling techniques and six standard classification algorithms. This finding indicated that the proposed method gives promising results to improve the accuracy in multiclass classification of student grade prediction.

Chapter 15: Recent studies have revealed that the existing measurement methods related to Computational Thinking (CT) pivot on gauging thinking skills, recommending an extended understanding of CT as disposition. Disposition reflects inclination towards learning CT and indicates the interest to think intelligently about issues confronting them. Hence, the aim of this chapter is to assess students' affection towards learning CT as problem solving tool that can transform knowledge more productively. In the context of the affective domain, attitudes and beliefs can be regarded of as generic responses to something, the core quality of an emotion, feeling, mood, or temperament, and hence as affective mental activities. The framework of the CT disposition proposed in this chapter was developed based on tripartite classification of mental activities known as of trilogy of mind: cognitive, affective and conative. Basic tenet of this chapter is aligned with the theoretical underpinnings of thinking dispositions which is expected to suit different contexts and needs

Chapter 16: Chapter will propose novel approach which combine traditional machine learning approach in churn management and customer satisfaction evaluation which unite traditional machine learning approach and expert based approach which leans on event-based management. Core of the proposed framework is hybrid fuzzy expert system which can contain variety data mining predictive models responsible for some specific areas as addition to traditional rule blocks. It can also include social network analysis metrics based on linguistic variables and incorporated within rule blocks. Chapter will introduce permanent monitoring and self-learning approach-based o mentioned approach with workflow how revealed patterns can be applied for continual portfolio management improvement. Proposed solution unite advanced analytical techniques with decision making process within holistic self-learning framework.

Chapter 17: Product quality assurance is a vital component in any manufacturing process. With the advancement of machine vision, the product quality inspection has been vastly improved. This couldn't be achieved with human inspection otherwise when it comes to consistency, accuracy, and the speed. The advance sensor technologies, image processing algorithms are ensuring the product and process quality in various industries including pharmaceutical manufacturing, food production, agriculture, and waste sorting. In contrast to the RGB imaging technology, multispectral and hyperspectral imaging technologies carry more information about the objects under inspection. With the help of both spectral and spatial information, it is possible to discriminate the quality indices of various products with higher accuracy than RGB imaging methods. This book chapter discusses the state-of-the-art product quality inspection applications using hyperspectral imaging and multispectral imaging using modern machine learning and other statistical algorithms.

Chapter 18: Insulators are power transmission lines components responsible for two key tasks: the first one is to support the mechanical stress originated by the weight of the cables and devices, and the second one is to avoid electrical dissipation from the cables to the tower structure. Even though the shape and material of the insulator is made in such a way as to avoid the conduction of electrical current on its surface, if some types of dirty accumulates excessively, the insulator can still conduct an electric arc to the tower, causing damage to the power grid. This chapter first presents the state-of art power lines insulators cleaning methods and the technics used to identify insulator that require cleaning. Then, this chapter describes an algorithm that makes use of machine learning, deep learning, and computer vision technics, which can be used embedded in an unmanned aerial vehicle, to support the energy company in the assessment of the levels of dirt on the insulators. Finally experimental results are presented showing the challenges and the open problems.

Maki K. Habib
The American University in Cairo, Egypt

Chapter 1
Development of a Receptor Cell Model for Artificial Life

Katsuyuki Morishita
Nihon University, Japan

Shinya Kato
Nihon University, Japan

Yuki Takei
Nihon University, Japan

Ken Saito
Nihon University, Japan

ABSTRACT

This chapter presents a receptor cell model that mimics the receptor cell function of living organisms. The receptor cell model converts the signal input of the sensor into an oscillating pulse waveform. Moreover, the oscillation frequency of the receptor cell model varies according to the sensory input intensity. First, the authors constructed a receptor cell model by discrete circuit. In addition, they measured the frequency characteristics using pressure and optical sensors. The results showed that the frequency of the receptor cell model changes according to the intensity of the sensory input. Then, they proposed a receptor cell model based on an integrated circuit. The simulation results showed that the proposed model had the same characteristics as the discrete circuit model. Thus, the proposed receptor cell model is expected to output a vibration pulse waveform that depends on the input intensity of the sensor.

INTRODUCTION

Autonomous robots play a crucial role in various fields, such as medicine and agriculture (Cheein & Carelli, 2013). In addition, there is a need to reduce contact with other people due to the global outbreak of the novel coronavirus disease 2019. Therefore, the demand for autonomous robots is expected to increase in fields such as package delivery. The increase in the demand for autonomous robots increases

DOI: 10.4018/978-1-7998-8686-0.ch001

the need for high-performance autonomous robots. An example of a high-performance autonomous robot is Boston Dynamics' "BigDog" (Raibert, Blankespoor, Nelson & Playter, 2008). "BigDog" is a quadrupedal robot that can move smoothly while maintaining its balance on unstable footholds, such as mountain paths. Furthermore, this robot can walk while maintaining its balance to avoid falling over under disturbance, such as being pushed. Therefore, the development of high-performance autonomous robots is expected to expand the field of autonomous robotics. However, it is challenging to realize robots that can surpass the superior functions of living organisms.

As one method to improve the performance of autonomous robots, researches are being conducted to use systems that mimic the structure of animals (e.g., El Daou, Salumäe, Ristolainen, Toming, Listak & Kruusmaa, 2011; Phan, Aurecianus, Kang & Park, 2019). As part of the research is that mimics animal-nervous systems to control robots. The nervous system of animals can achieve high levels of environmental adaptability with low-energy consumption. For example, animals can generate patterned movements, such as walking and breathing, with simple neural circuits in the spinal cord (e.g., Delcomyn, 1980; Dick, Oku, Romaniuk & Cherniack, 1993; Cazalets, Borde & Clarac, 1995). Additionally, quadrupeds like horses and cats can move efficiently by switching their gait according to their movement speed and the environment (Hoyt & Taylor, 1981; McMahon, 1985; Bhatti, Waqas, Mahesar, & Karbasi, 2017). Therefore, systems that mimic the mechanisms of the animal nervous system can provide robots with a high degree of autonomy like animals. Various types of robots that mimic the nervous system of animals have been developed, including quadruped robots (e.g., Kimura & Fukuoka, 2004; Fukuoka & Kimura, 2009), hexapod robots (e.g., Zhong, Zhang, Xu, Zhou, Fang & Li, 2018; Minati, Frasca, Yoshimura & Koike, 2018), and snake-like robots (e.g., Crespi, Badertscher, Guignard & Ijspeert, 2005; Ijspeert & Crespi, 2007). These robots are controlled using software models of the nervous system. Software models have been used in many studies because the models are relatively easy to implement in robots. However, software models are different with nervous system of organisms; therefore, a model more similar to living organisms was desired. In addition to software models, electronic circuit models are used to mimic the nervous system of animals (Simoni, Cymbalyuk, Sorensen, Calabrese & DeWeerth, 2004; Arthur & Boahen, 2010). The electronic circuit model is not as easy to implement as the software model; however, it has advantages, such as the high speed of analog circuits and the possibility of min-iaturizing the system using integrated circuit technology.

We develop an autonomous control system mimicking the animal nervous system with analog circuits (e.g., Saito, Ohara, Abe, Kaneko & Uchikoba, 2017; Kurosawa, Sasaki, Usami, Kato, Sakaki, Takei, Kaneko, Uchikoba & Saito, 2021; Sasaki, Kurosawa, Usami, Kato, Sakaki, Takei, Kaneko, Uchikoba & Saito, 2021). As part of our research, we apply the hardware neuron model (HNM), which mimics the functions of animal neurons in analog electronic circuits, to control robots by mimicking the functions of the animal nervous system.

Figure 1 shows a quadruped robot equipped with HNMs. In conventional programming-based robots, a huge amount of computation is required to make the robot walk according to the environment. In our developed robot, independent HNM controls each foot, and the oscillation period of the HNM is changed by the feedback of the toe pressure sensor. Despite the simple control of this robot, we found that the robot actively generates a mammalian gait. We also showed that the robot could generate different gait patterns by varying the basal velocity of its foot movements (Takei, Morishita, Tazawa & Saito, 2021; Takei, Morishita, Tazawa, Katsuya & Saito, 2021). However, the current robot has only one pressure sensor on each sole. Some mammals use the entire sole of their foot to walk. Installing multiple micro-sensors (e.g., Angiulli, Jannelli, Morabito & Versaci, 2018; Versaci, Jannelli, Morabito & Angiulli,

2021) on the sole can help investigate the effect of the distribution of pressure on the sole on walking. Also, to realize autonomous functions similar to those of animals in the future, sensors different from pressure sensors need to be installed to capture exterior and external information. In our control system, a microcontroller, Arduino, sends signals from the sensors as input to the HNM. Therefore, the amount of information processing increases as the number of sensors increases and, the robot will have difficulty processing sensor signals in parallel in real time like an animal.

Figure 1. Quadruped robot equipped with HNMs

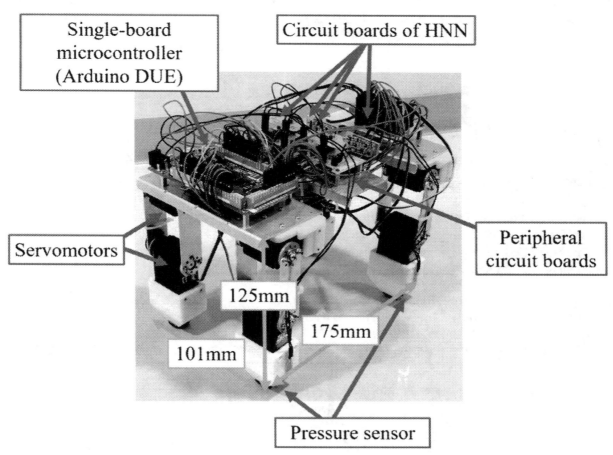

We developed a receptor cell model that mimics the function of receptor cells, which are the input parts of sensory organs in the body, using discrete elements. This receptor cell model vibrates by applying an input signal to the sensor, and the number of vibrations varies depending on the intensity of the input (Morishita, Kato, Sasaki, Takei, Saito, 2021).

We present the measurement of the characteristics of a sensor connected to a receptor cell model by discrete elements developed earlier. We also report the measurement of the characteristics of a newly developed receptor cell model by integrated circuits.

RECEPTOR CELL MODEL

Animals acquire sensory information through receptor cells. These receptor cells respond to specific stimuli, such as light and vibration (e.g., Johansson & Vallbo, 1983; Schneeweis & Schnapf, 1995). We developed a receptor cell model that mimics the properties of receptor cells. A receptor cell model is an analog electronic circuit that mimics a receptor cell. This receptor cell model is a circuit designed based on the cell body model that we previously developed. The cell body model is an analog electronic circuit that mimics a neuron (Saito, Ohara, Abe, Kaneko & Uchikoba, 2017). Additionally, a cell body model oscillates similarly to the firing of a biological neuron. It also mimics the threshold and refractory periods of biological neurons. The receptor cell model has the property that the oscillation characteristics of the receptor cell model change by the input of a signal to the sensor.

RECEPTOR CELL MODEL BY DISCRETE ELEMENTS

Circuit Structure of Receptor Cell Model by Discrete Elements

Figure 2 shows the circuit diagram of a receptor cell model by discrete elements. A receptor cell model is a circuit in which a sensor replaces the resistor in the cell body model. A receptor cell model consists of a supply voltage V_A, resistors R_G, R_M, and R_1, capacitors C_G and C_M, MOSFETs M_1 and M_2, and a sensor (resistance-change type) R_{sensor}. V_A, M_1, M_2, C_G, and R_G constitute a negative resistance circuit containing equivalent inductance. R_L represents the leakage resistance, and C_M represents the membrane capacitance. The voltage divider circuit composed of R_1 and R_{sensor} generates the gate voltage of M_2. Therefore, the gate voltage of M_2 changes as the value of R_{sensor} changes.

Figure 2. Circuit diagram of a receptor cell model by discrete elements

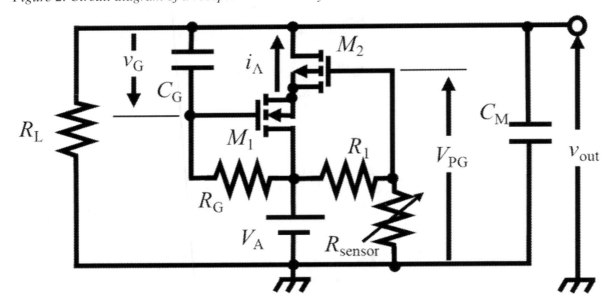

Operating Principles of Receptor Cell Model by Discrete Elements

The operation of the receptor cell model by discrete elements is shown below. Initially, the capacitor C_G is charged from V_A through the resistor R_G. As the C_G is charged, the voltage v_G increases and exceeds the threshold of M_1; thus, causing the current i_A to flow. The current i_A is charged to the capacitor C_M, and the voltage v_{out} becomes larger. Furthermore, as the voltage v_{out} becomes larger, v_G becomes smaller, and the magnitude of i_A becomes smaller. Therefore, the charge accumulated in C_M is discharged through the resistor R_L, and the voltage v_{out} becomes smaller. The receptor cell model oscillates by repetition of these actions.

Figure 3 shows the characteristics of i_A versus v_{out} under the conditions of $v_G = 2.2$, 2.6, and 3.0 V. The solid line shows the characteristics for $V_{PG} = 1.1$ V, and the dotted line shows the characteristics for $V_{PG} = 1.7$ V. The figure shows that as V_{PG} becomes larger, i_A becomes smaller. Furthermore, as i_A becomes smaller, the time required to charge the C_M becomes longer, and the oscillation characteristics of the receptor cell model change. Therefore, the oscillation ON/OFF and the oscillation frequency of the receptor cell model can be changed by changing V_{PG}.

Figure 3. Characteristics of i_A by varying v_{out} (simulation result)

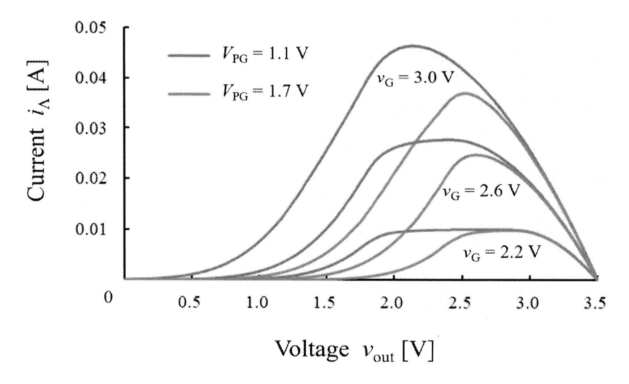

Simulation Results of Receptor Cell Model by Discrete Elements

We implemented a receptor cell model by discrete elements. First, we simulated circuit operation using a circuit simulator. Then, we used PSpice from Cadence Design Systems as the simulator. The circuit constants are $R_G = 75$ kΩ, $R_L = 3.3$ kΩ, $C_G = 10$ nF, $C_M = 1.0$ nF, and $V_A = 3.5$ V. We also used SSM3K17FU for M_1 and BSH203 for M_2.

Figure 4 shows an example of the oscillation of the receptor cell model through simulation. Figures 4 (a) and (b) show the waveforms for V_{PG} of 1.05 and 1.80 V, respectively. As shown in Figure 4, the oscillation frequency of the receptor cell model changes with the change in V_{PG}.

Figure 5 shows the oscillation frequency characteristics of the receptor cell model relative to V_{PG}. As shown in the figure, the receptor cell model oscillates in the range of V_{PG} from 1.05 V to 1.80 V, and the oscillation frequency varies from about 1000 Hz to 380 Hz. The oscillation frequency decreases as V_{PG} increases. The measurement results show that the receptor cell model changes the oscillation ON/OFF and oscillation frequency depending on the size of V_{PG}.

Figure 6 shows the simulation results of the frequency change of the receptor cell model for R_{Sensor}. We simulated R_1 at 20 and 30 kΩ. Comparison of simulation results of R_1 for 20 and 30 kΩ show that R_1 increases as the threshold of R_{Sensor}, at which the receptor cell model oscillates, increases. Furthermore, the range of resistance in which the receptor cell model oscillates becomes wider. This result shows that the threshold and range of oscillation of the receptor cell model changes by varying R_1.

Figure 4. Examples of output waveform of the receptor cell model (simulation result)

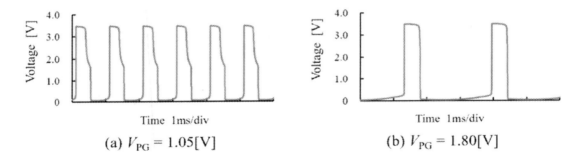

(a) $V_{PG} = 1.05$[V] (b) $V_{PG} = 1.80$[V]

Figure 5. Characteristic of output frequency by varying V_{PG} (simulation result)

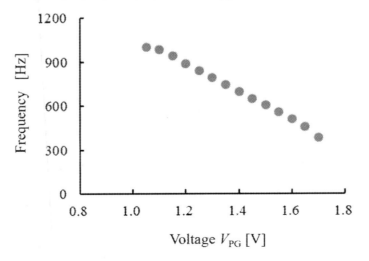

Figure 6. Characteristic of output frequency by varying R_{Sensor} (simulation result)

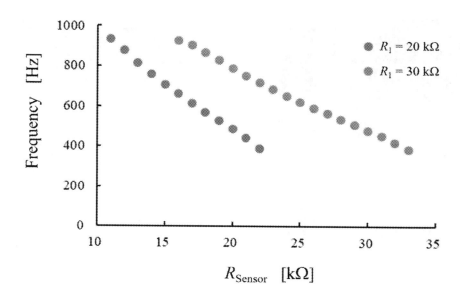

Measurement Results of Receptor Cell Model by Discrete Elements

We constructed a receptor cell model by discrete elements and measured its characteristics based on the simulation results. The circuit is a simplified receptor cell model similar to the circuit used in the simulation. The constants of the elements were the same as in the simulation, and only the supply voltage V_A was changed to 4.5 V.

Figure 7 shows an example of the output waveform of the receptor cell model consisting of discrete elements. Figures 7 (a) and (b) show the waveforms for V_{PG} of 0.75 and 1.40 V, respectively. As shown in Figure 5, the oscillation frequency of the receptor cell model changes as V_{PG} changes, as in our simulation.

Figure 8 shows the oscillation frequency characteristics of the receptor cell model in relation to V_{PG}. The figure shows that the receptor cell model oscillates in the range of V_{PG} from 0.75 V to 1.40 V and the oscillation frequency varies from about 630 Hz to 270 Hz. As in the simulation, the oscillation frequency decreases as V_{PG} increases.

Figure 7. Examples of output waveform of the receptor cell model (experimental results)

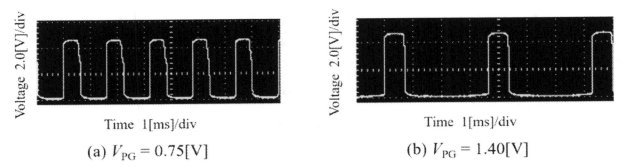

(a) $V_{PG} = 0.75[V]$ (b) $V_{PG} = 1.40[V]$

Figure 8. Characteristic of the output frequency by varying V_{PG} (experimental results)

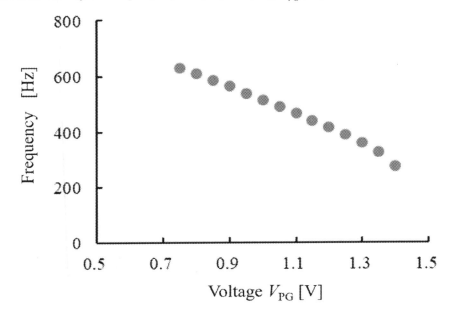

Measurement Results with a Pressure Sensor

The receptor cell model is designed to be used in a quadruped robot that we have previously developed, in which independent HNM controls each leg. Therefore, we measured the characteristics of the receptor cell model with a pressure sensor. We used the same pressure sensor used in the quadruped robot. Each robot's foot is controlled so that the speed of the foot varies according to the magnitude of the load applied to the pressure sensor mounted on the toe.

Figure 9 shows the oscillation characteristics of the receptor cell model in response to pressure. The circuit constants are $R_G = 75$ kΩ, $R_L = 3.3$ kΩ, $C_G = 10$ nF, $C_M = 1.0$ nF, and $V_A = 3.7$ V. We also used SSM3K17FU for M_1 and BSH203 for M_2 and used FSR402 from Interlink Electronics as the pressure sensor. The resistance value of the pressure sensor varies from 1 kΩ to 6 kΩ under the condition that the load applied to the sensor is between 1000 g and 100 g. Furthermore, we measured the characteristics of the receptor cell model at $R_1 = 20$ kΩ and 30 kΩ. The pressure sensor used has low resistance and a low V_{PG} by applying a load. Therefore, the greater the load applied, the higher the frequency of oscillation of the receptor cell model. The range of oscillation of the receptor cell model varies under the condition of different R_1. Finally, we confirmed that by varying R_1, the load range at which the receptor cell model oscillates varied.

Measurement Results with an Optical Sensor

We also measured the characteristics of the receptor cell model equipped with sensors different from the pressure sensor to confirm the applicability to robot systems other than the quadruped robot controlled by HNM. As a sensor different from the pressure sensor, we installed an optical sensor in the receptor cell model and measured its characteristics. We used a CdS cell (VT90N2) as the optical sensor. The resistance of the CdS cell is 24 kΩ (typical value) under 10 lux conditions and 500 kΩ (minimum value) in the dark. The circuit constants were the same as those of the receptor cell model with the pressure sensor, except for V_A and R_1, where $V_A = 4.5$ V and $R_1 = 21$ kΩ.

Figure 10 shows the oscillation characteristics of the receptor cell model as a function of light intensity. The receptor cell model equipped with a CdS cell oscillates in the range of 2 klx to 8 klx light intensity input to the sensor. Similar to the experiment of the receptor cell model equipped with the pressure sensor, the frequency increases with the amount of light input because the V_{PG} decreases as the signal is input.

Figure 9. Characteristic of the output frequency by a strength of sensor input (pressure sensor)

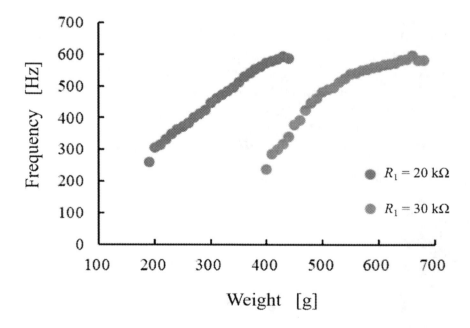

Figure 10. Characteristic of the output frequency by a strength of sensor input (optical sensor)

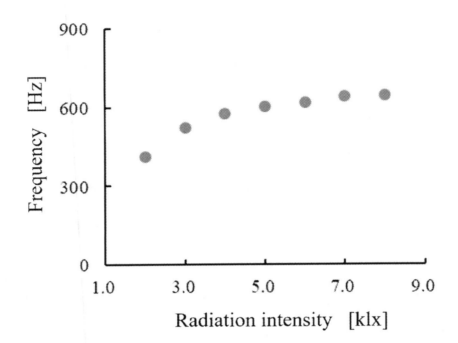

RECEPTOR CELL MODEL BY INTEGRATED CIRCUITS

Circuit Structure of Receptor Cell Model by Integrated Circuits

We integrated the receptor cell model by integrated circuits. Figure 11 shows the circuit diagram of the receptor cell model by integrated circuits. The model consists of a supply voltage V_A, resistor R_1, capacitors C_G and C_M, MOSFETs M_L, M_G, M_1 and M_2, and a sensor (resistance-change type) R_{sensor}. To make integrated circuits of the receptor cell model, we changed resistors R_G and R_L to MOSFETs M_G and M_L. Also, we configured a voltage divider circuit composed of resistors R_1 and R_{sensor} outside the integrated circuits.

Figure 11. Circuit diagram of the receptor cell model by integrated circuits

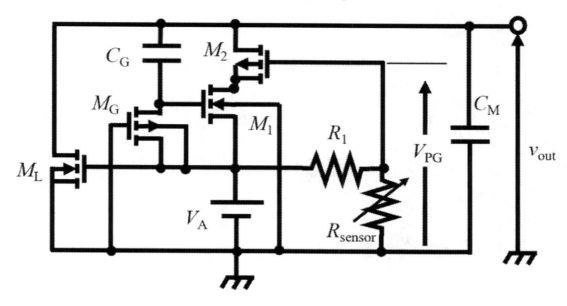

Figure 12. Examples of the output waveform of the receptor cell model (simulation result)

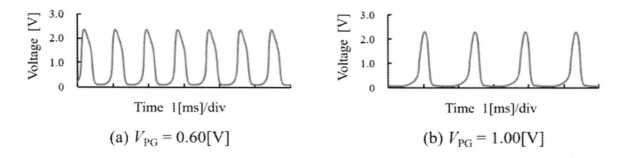

(a) $V_{PG} = 0.60[V]$ (b) $V_{PG} = 1.00[V]$

Simulation Results of Receptor Cell Model by Integrated Circuits

For the simulation, we used HSPICE. The circuit constants are M_1 = W/L = 10 μm /1.2 μm, M_2 = 21 μm /1.0 μm, M_G = 1.2 μm /10 μm, M_L = 3μm /10 μm, C_G = 3.3 nF, C_M = 1.8 nF. The supply voltage is V_A = 3.6 V. Figure 12 shows examples of the simulation results of the output waveform of the receptor cell model. Figures 12 (a) and (b) show the output waveforms for V_{PG} of 0.60 and 1.00 V, respectively. As shown in Figure 12, the oscillation frequency of the receptor cell model changes by changing V_{PG}, similar to the receptor cell model consisting of discrete elements.

Figure 13 shows the oscillation characteristics of the receptor cell model by integrated circuits for V_{PG}. The receptor cell model oscillates only in the range of V_{PG} between 0.60 and 1.00 V, and the oscillation frequency varies from about 1000 Hz to 700 Hz. We also observed that the oscillation frequency decreases with increasing V_{PG}, similar to the discrete element receptor cell model.

Figure 13. Characteristic of the output frequency by varying V_{PG} (simulation result)

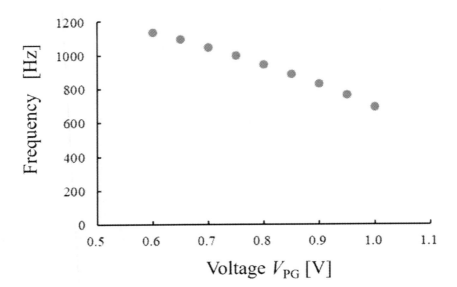

Layout of Receptor Cell Model by Integrated Circuits

Based on the simulation results, a prototype of the integrated circuit model of the receptor cell was developed. Figure 14 shows the fabricated chip of the receptor cell model by integrated circuits. The capacitors C_G and C_M of the receptor cell model are large (3.3 and 1.8 nF, respectively); thus, terminals are provided for external connections. We also designed terminals on the V_{PG} to directly apply V_{PG} from the supply voltage. Therefore, we can measure the change in the vibration characteristics of the receptor cell model in response to the input to the sensor by configuring an external voltage divider circuit of a sensor and a resistive element and by applying the divided voltage at the terminals of the V_{PG}. We also designed cell body and synaptic models (Saito, Ohara, Abe, Kaneko & Uchikoba, 2017) previously developed to conduct experiments to apply the receptor cell model to neural network models in the future.

We designed four receptor cell models with different W/L of M_2 in the chip. Additionally, we designed W/L of M_2 as 15 μm /1.0 μm, 21 μm /1.0 μm, 27 μm /1.0 μm, and 33 μm /1.0 μm, respectively, in the order of (1) to (4) in the figure.

Figure 14. Layout of the receptor cell model by integrated circuits

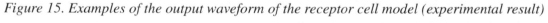

Measurement Results of Receptor Cell Model by Integrated Circuits

We performed measurements on the prototype receptor cell model by integrated circuits. The circuit constants are the same as those of the receptor cell model used in the simulation. Figure 15 shows an example of the output waveform of the receptor cell model.

Figures 15 (a) and (b) show the output waveform for V_{PG} = 0.10 and 0.75 V, respectively. As shown in Figure 15, the oscillation frequency of the receptor cell model changes as V_{PG} changes.

Figure 16 shows the oscillation characteristics of the receptor cell model in response to V_{PG}. We confirmed that the receptor cell model oscillates only in the range of V_{PG} from 0.10 V to 0.75 V, and the oscillation frequency varies from about 890 Hz to 370 Hz. Similar to the simulation results, the oscillation frequency of the receptor cell model decreases with increasing V_{PG} within the oscillation range.

Figure 15. Examples of the output waveform of the receptor cell model (experimental result)

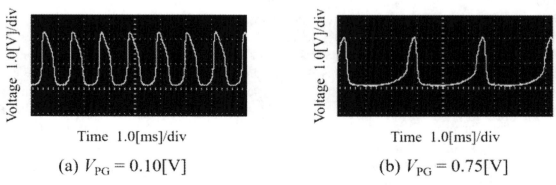

Figure 16. Characteristic of the output frequency by varying V_{PG} (experimental result)

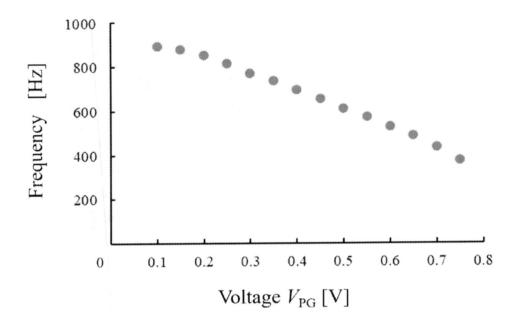

CONCLUSION

In this chapter, we developed a receptor cell model that mimics the function of receptor cells in sensory organs. The receptor cell model oscillates as input signals are applied to the sensor, and the oscillation frequency depends on the strength of the input signal. In the receptor cell model by discrete elements, V_{PG} oscillates in the range of 0.75 V to 1.40 V and the oscillation frequency varies from 630 Hz to 270 Hz. We also observed that the oscillation frequency of the receptor cell model equipped with pressure and optical sensors changed depending on the input intensity to the sensor. From the results, we consider that the proposed receptor cell model has sufficient performance to be installed in our robot system. Additionally, we developed the receptor cell model by integrated circuits. The receptor cell model by integrated circuits was constructed by changing some of the resistive elements to MOSFETs. The circuit simulation shows that the receptor cell model oscillates only in the range of V_{PG} between 0.60 and 1.00 V, and the oscillation frequency varies from about 1100 Hz to 700 Hz. Furthermore, the oscillation frequency varies from about 1100 Hz to 700 Hz, and the receptor cell model's oscillation frequency decreases as V_{PG} increases. We fabricated a prototype of the integrated circuit model of the receptor cell and measured its oscillation characteristics. The measurement results confirmed that the receptor cell model oscillates in the range of 0.10 V to 0.75 V V_{PG}, and the oscillation frequency varies from 890 Hz to 370 Hz. Similar to the simulation, the higher the V_{PG}, the lower the oscillation frequency of the receptor cell model. The measurement results of the integrated circuit show the same characteristics as the receptor cell model by discrete elements. Therefore, we consider that the receptor cell model mounted on the robot can be made a smaller system.

In future studies, we will implement the receptor cell model by integrated circuits into the robot system. In addition, the current receptor cell model can only be equipped with sensors that change resistance. In the future, we plan to develop a receptor cell model that responds to changes in capacitance. By developing a receptor cell model that responds to changes in capacitance, we can equip the receptor cell model with sensors such as membrane micro-sensors.

ACKNOWLEDGMENT

This work was supported by Nihon University Multidisciplinary Research Grant for (2020) and supported by Research Institute of Science and Technology Nihon University College of Science and Technology Leading Research Promotion Grant. Also, the part of the work was supported by JSPS KAKENHI Grant Number JP18K04060. The VLSI chip has been fabricated by Digian Technology, Inc. This work is supported by VLSI Design and Education Center (VDEC), the University of Tokyo in collaboration with Synopsys, Inc., Cadence Design Systems, Inc. and Mentor Graphics, Inc. The VLSI chip in this study has been fabricated in the chip fabrication program of VLSI Design and Education Center (VDEC), the University of Tokyo in collaboration with On-Semiconductor Niigata, and Toppan Printing Corporation. Also, we appreciate the Nihon University Robotics Society.
The authors would like to thank Enago (www.enago.jp) for the English language review.

REFERENCES

Angiulli, G., Jannelli, A., Morabito, F. C., & Versaci, M. (2018). Reconstructing the membrane detection of a 1 D electrostatic-driven MEMS device by the shooting method: Convergence analysis and ghost solutions identification. *Computational & Applied Mathematics*, *37*(4), 4484–4498. doi:10.100740314-017-0564-4

Arthur, J. V., & Boahen, K. A. (2010). Silicon-neuron design: A dynamical systems approach. *IEEE Transactions on Circuits and Systems. I, Regular Papers*, *58*(5), 1034–1043. doi:10.1109/TCSI.2010.2089556 PMID:21617741

Bhatti, Z., Waqas, A., Mahesar, A. W., & Karbasi, M. (2017). Gait analysis and biomechanics of quadruped motion for procedural animation and robotic simulation. *Bahria University Journal of Information & Communication Technologies*, *10*(2), 1–7.

Cazalets, J. R., Borde, M., & Clarac, F. (1995). Localization and organization of the central pattern generator for hindlimb locomotion in newborn rat. *The Journal of Neuroscience: The Official Journal of the Society for Neuroscience*, *15*(7), 4943–4951. doi:10.1523/JNEUROSCI.15-07-04943.1995 PMID:7623124

Cheein, F. A. A., & Carelli, R. (2013). Agricultural robotics: Unmanned robotic service units in agricultural tasks. *IEEE Industrial Electronics Magazine*, *7*(3), 48–58. doi:10.1109/MIE.2013.2252957

Crespi, A., Badertscher, A., Guignard, A., & Ijspeert, A. J. (2005). AmphiBot I: An amphibious snake-like robot. *Robotics and Autonomous Systems*, *50*(4), 163–175. doi:10.1016/j.robot.2004.09.015

Delcomyn, F. (1980). Neural basis of rhythmic behavior in animals. *Science*, *210*(4469), 492–498. doi:10.1126cience.7423199 PMID:7423199

Dick, T. E., Oku, Y., Romaniuk, J. R., & Cherniack, N. S. (1993). Interaction between central pattern generators for breathing and swallowing in the cat. *The Journal of Physiology*, *465*(1), 715–730. doi:10.1113/jphysiol.1993.sp019702 PMID:8229859

El Daou, H., Salumäe, T., Ristolainen, A., Toming, G., Listak, M., & Kruusmaa, M. (2011, June). A biomimetic design and control of a fish-like robot using compliant structures. In *2011 15th International Conference on Advanced Robotics (ICAR)* (pp. 563-568). IEEE.

Fukuoka, Y., & Kimura, H. (2009). Dynamic locomotion of a biomorphic quadruped 'Tekken'robot using various gaits: Walk, trot, free-gait and bound. *Applied Bionics and Biomechanics*, *6*(1), 63–71. doi:10.1155/2009/743713

Hoyt, D. F., & Taylor, C. R. (1981). Gait and the energetics of locomotion in horses. *Nature*, *292*(5820), 239–240. doi:10.1038/292239a0

Ijspeert, A. J., & Crespi, A. (2007, April). Online trajectory generation in an amphibious snake robot using a lamprey-like central pattern generator model. In *Proceedings 2007 IEEE International Conference on Robotics and Automation* (pp. 262-268). IEEE. 10.1109/ROBOT.2007.363797

Johansson, R. S., & Vallbo, Å. B. (1983). Tactile sensory coding in the glabrous skin of the human hand. *Trends in Neurosciences*, *6*, 27–32. doi:10.1016/0166-2236(83)90011-5

Kimura, H., & Fukuoka, Y. (2004, September). Biologically inspired adaptive dynamic walking in outdoor environment using a self-contained quadruped robot: 'Tekken2'. In *2004 IEEE/RSJ International Conference on Intelligent Robots and Systems (IROS) (IEEE Cat. No. 04CH37566)* (Vol. 1, pp. 986-991). IEEE. 10.1109/IROS.2004.1389481

Kurosawa, M., Sasaki, T., Usami, Y., Kato, S., Sakaki, A., Takei, Y., Kaneko, M., Uchikoba, F., & Saito, K. (2021). Neural networks integrated circuit with switchable gait pattern for insect-type microrobot. *Artificial Life and Robotics*, *26*(2), 297–303. doi:10.100710015-021-00678-y

McMahon, T. A. (1985). The role of compliance in mammalian running gaits. *The Journal of Experimental Biology*, *115*(1), 263–282. doi:10.1242/jeb.115.1.263 PMID:4031769

Minati, L., Frasca, M., Yoshimura, N., & Koike, Y. (2018). Versatile locomotion control of a hexapod robot using a hierarchical network of nonlinear oscillator circuits. *IEEE Access: Practical Innovations, Open Solutions*, *6*, 8042–8065. doi:10.1109/ACCESS.2018.2799145

Morishita, K., Kato, S., Sasaki, T., Takei, Y., & Saito, K. (2021, January). Development of receptor cell model converting sensor inputs into pulse waveforms. *The Twenty-Sixth International Symposium on Artificial Life and Robotics 2021*.

Phan, H. V., Aurecianus, S., Kang, T., & Park, H. C. (2019). KUBeetle-S: An insect-like, tailless, hover-capable robot that can fly with a low-torque control mechanism. *International Journal of Micro Air Vehicles*, *11*, 11. doi:10.1177/1756829319861371

Raibert, M., Blankespoor, K., Nelson, G., & Playter, R. (2008). Bigdog, the rough-terrain quadruped robot. *IFAC Proceedings Volumes*, *41*(2), 10822-10825.

Saito, K., Ohara, M., Abe, M., Kaneko, M., & Uchikoba, F. (2017). *Gait generation of multilegged robots by using hardware artificial neural networks. In Advanced Applications for Artificial Neural Networks.* INTEC.

Sasaki, T., Kurosawa, M., Usami, Y., Kato, S., Sakaki, A., Takei, Y., Kaneko, M., Uchikoba, F., & Saito, K. (2021). Development of neural networks chip generating driving waveform for electrostatic motor. *Artificial Life and Robotics*, *26*(2), 222–227. doi:10.100710015-020-00669-5

Schneeweis, D. M., & Schnapf, J. L. (1995). Photovoltage of rods and cones in the macaque retina. *Science*, *268*(5213), 1053–1056. doi:10.1126cience.7754386 PMID:7754386

Simoni, M. F., Cymbalyuk, G. S., Sorensen, M. E., Calabrese, R. L., & DeWeerth, S. P. (2004). A multiconductance silicon neuron with biologically matched dynamics. *IEEE Transactions on Biomedical Engineering*, *51*(2), 342–354. doi:10.1109/TBME.2003.820390 PMID:14765707

Takei, Y., Morishita, K., Tazawa, R., Katsuya, K., & Saito, K. (2021). Non-programmed gait generation of quadruped robot using pulse-type hardware neuron models. *Artificial Life and Robotics*, *26*(1), 109–115. doi:10.100710015-020-00637-z

Takei, Y., Morishita, K., Tazawa, R., & Saito, K. (2021). *Active Gaits Generation of Quadruped Robot Using Pulse-Type Hardware Neuron Models. In Biomimetics.* IntechOpen.

Versaci, M., Jannelli, A., Morabito, F. C., & Angiulli, G. (2021). A Semi-Linear Elliptic Model for a Circular Membrane MEMS Device Considering the Effect of the Fringing Field. *Sensors (Basel)*, *21*(15), 5237. doi:10.339021155237 PMID:34372474

Zhong, B., Zhang, S., Xu, M., Zhou, Y., Fang, T., & Li, W. (2018). On a CPG-based hexapod robot: AmphiHex-II with variable stiffness legs. *IEEE/ASME Transactions on Mechatronics*, *23*(2), 542–551. doi:10.1109/TMECH.2018.2800776

Chapter 2
Quadruped Robots With Bio-Inspired Gait Generation Methods Using Sole Pressure Sensory Feedback

Yuki Takei
Nihon University, Japan

Katsuyuki Morishita
Nihon University, Japan

Ken Saito
Nihon University, Japan

ABSTRACT

There is still no artificial life with the same adaptability and flexibility as animals. Although artificial life will advance by acquiring nervous systems similar to those of animals, its role and mechanisms remain unknown. The authors have developed a quadruped robot with a bio-inspired gait generation method to realize robots that can behave like animals. The method could generate gaits using pulse-type hardware neuron models (P-HNMs). However, characteristics of the P-HNMs had large scatterings, and the robot could maintain gaits only a few cycles. This chapter explains the method and P-HNM integrated circuits (ICs) developed to improve P-HNMs' characteristics. In addition, dynamic simulations with a simplified method and discussions of the methods and ICs are provided. Although the proposed methods are simple, they could actively generate gaits using interactions between the body and the environment. Therefore, the methods will lead to the realization of a quadruped robot with flexible adaptability.

DOI: 10.4018/978-1-7998-8686-0.ch002

INTRODUCTION

Artificial life is being studied in various fields, broadly categorized as soft, hard, and wet, and is becoming increasingly interdisciplinary (Aguilar, Santamaría-Bonfil, Froese, & Gershenson, 2014; Habib, 2011; Habib, Watanabe, & Izumi, 2007). The main topic of this chapter is control methods for legged robots, but since these methods are bio-inspired, they apply also to soft and wet fields.

Modern legged robots can perform advanced movements and are used in many applications (Biswal & Mohanty, 2020). For example, some of them can patrol in response to their surroundings using optical devices and other equipment. However, even though their mobility is already comparable to that of animals, none of them can act as autonomously as animals. One of the reasons is that responding autonomously to myriad situations is an arduous task for modern robot control methods. Legged robots need to complete the task as soon as possible. These robots achieve their robustness through advanced control systems that use many sensors (e.g., Raibert, Blankespoor, Nelson, & Playter, 2008; Fankhauser, Bjelonic, Bellicoso, Miki, & Hutter, 2018). The computation costs required to develop a robot that can act autonomously as animals will be incomparable to current ones. Although robots will gradually improve as computers become more powerful, as we have seen in the past, there is a significant capability gap between robots and animals. This problem arises because the computer, the robot's brain, has to perform all calculations to expand its capabilities.

On the other hand, animals behave autonomously with seeming ease. The significant difference between robots and animals is whether the brain processes all behaviour or not. For example, animals unconsciously generate respiration, chewing, walking, and so on (e.g., Marder & Bucher, 2001; Selverston & Ayers, 2006). Particularly, since walking is one of the most important movements for both legged animals and robots, the knowledge about the generating mechanism will solve the problems limiting current robot control methods. Quadrupeds are the most common of legged animals, and there are many studies on their walking behaviour. These studies have shown that they have several locomotion patterns (gaits) that they switch depending on the situation (Bhatti, Waqas, Mahesar, & Karbasi, 2017; McMahon, 1985; Taylor, 1985). Findings on the relationship between horses' locomotion speed and oxygen consumption are well known (Hoyt & Taylor, 1981). In addition, neurophysiology experiments have provided insights into the relationships of the nervous system to gait generation (e.g., Duysens & Pearson, 1980; Grillner, 1975; Orsal, Cabelguen, & Perret, 1990). The theory that quadruped animals unconsciously generate gaits by interacting with the central pattern generator (CPG) and sensory inputs is currently widely accepted (Bellardita & Kiehn, 2015; Frigon & Rossignol, 2006; Grillner & Zangger, 1979). Despite many discussions on animals' gait generation mechanisms, much remains unknown (e.g., Arshavsky, Deliagina, & Orlovsky, 2016; Delcomyn, 1980).

Developing models that simulate CPGs and analyzing their behaviour have been studied (e.g., Ito, Yuasa, Luo, Ito, & Yanagihara, 1998; Kukillaya, Proctor, & Holmes, 2009; Yuasa & Ito, 1990). Furthermore, experiments with robot systems using CPG models to generate locomotion have shown advantages such as efficiency, adaptability, and stability (e.g., Habu, Yamada, Fukui, & Fukuoka, 2018; Ishii, Masakado, & Ishii, 2004; Li, Wang, & Yi, 2016; Liu, Jia, & Bi, 2017). However, these results do not necessarily solve the problem of robot control because the structure of animals' CPGs and the function of sensory inputs are unknown.

Owaki, Kano, Nagasawa, Tero, and Ishiguro (2013) proposed a quadruped robot system with active joints controlled by decoupled mathematical oscillators and sensory feedback. The oscillators were designed based on an active rotator model (Shinomoto & Kuramoto, 1986). The quadruped robot's legs were controlled depending on the oscillator's phase individually. The robot system generated phase differences (i.e., gait) by feeding back each foots' pressures to the oscillators to accelerate or decelerate the joints' angular velocities. The generated gait had characteristics of animals' gait. In addition, another robot system using the same method generated and switched the gaits according to its locomotion speed (Owaki & Ishiguro, 2017). These results suggest that using the difference in pressure on each foot to generate gaits is effective. Although they did not design the oscillator they used to control the joint on a biological basis, the suggestion that the reaction force received by the leg from the floor is closely related to the gait is consistent with the results of physiological experiments (Frigon & Rossignol, 2006).

The authors have developed a quadruped robot system that implements a bio-inspired gait generation method using pulse-type hardware neuron models (P-HNMs), based on the finding that it is an effective way to feedback the sole pressure to the angular velocity of the joints individually. Based on the results of walking machines that could generate gait patterns when they were placed on slopes without active joint controlling systems, the authors designed the method that does not use phases of legs to feedback the pressure of soles to the joints' angular velocity (McGeer, 1990; Nakatani, Sugimoto, & Osuka, 2009; Sugimoto, Yoshioka, & Osuka, 2011). As a result of experiments, the authors confirmed that the robot system could actively generate quadrupeds' gaits (Takei, Morishita, Tazawa, & Saito, 2021; Takei, Morishita, Tazawa, Katusya, & Saito, 2021). However, the robot system could maintain gaits only for tens of seconds in the experiments. The authors speculate that the cause was the mechanical and electrical disturbance elements. Therefore, the authors imported the robot's structure into a dynamic simulator as a robot model to simulate its behaviour in an ideal space by applying an alternative method to the model (Takei, Tazawa, Kaimai, Morishita, & Saito, 2021). Besides, the authors developed a P-HNM integrated circuit (IC) chip to realize circuits with small characteristic scatterings. This chapter explains the gait generation methods and P-HNM ICs. In addition, this chapter provides comprehensive discussions of both methods and ICs.

QUADRUPED ROBOT SYSTEM

Figure 1 shows the quadruped robot system. This section explains the quadruped robot system's components, gait generation method, and experimental results.

Body Structure and Electrical Components

The quadruped robot system is composed of the body structure and electrical components. The body structure is constructed by assembling a body frame and four-leg units, as shown in Figure 2. Each leg unit has two joints using servomotors KRS-2552RHV ICS (Kondo Kagaku Co., Ltd.), Parts A, B, and C. The robot system has degrees of freedom only in the leg units to focus on gait generation through leg movements. The body frame and Part B were machined from aluminium alloy sheets using a computerized numerical control machining system and bender. Parts A and C are formed using a three-dimensional printer. The entire weight of the quadruped robot system is approximately 1.1 kg.

The electrical components of the robot system are P-HNM circuit boards, a peripheral circuit board, pressure sensors FSR402 (Interlink Electronics, Inc. see key terms section for more information), and a single board microcontroller Arduino DUE (see key terms section for more information). The pressure sensors are attached between Part C and the rubber sole (see Figure 3). In addition, the quadruped robot system has a battery and Bluetooth module for experimentation without the need for physical connections for power supply and data logging.

Figure 1. Overview of the quadruped robot system

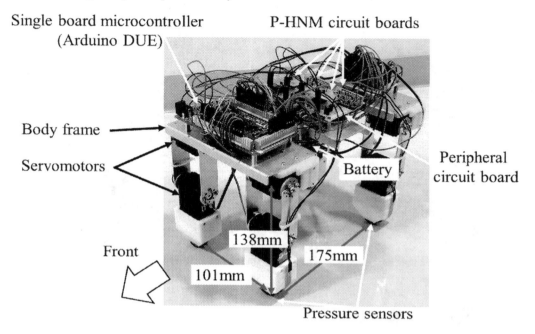

Figure 2. Body structure of the quadruped robot system

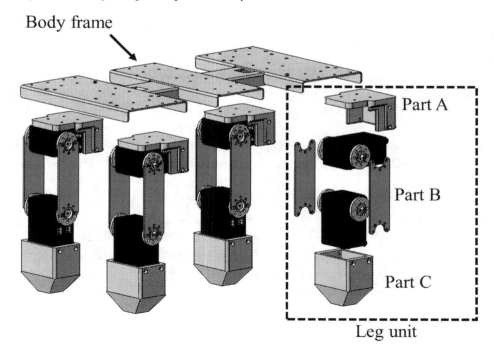

Figure 3. Detail of the sole's structure

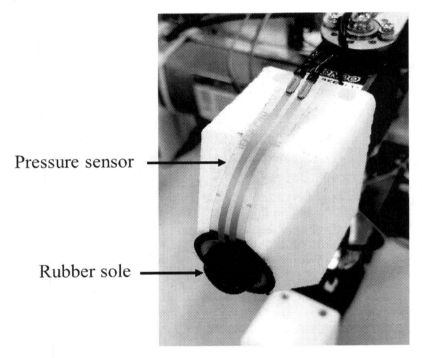

Pulse-Type Hardware Neuron Model

The P-HNM consists of a cell body model and an inhibitory synaptic model. Figure 4 depicts the P-HNM's circuit diagram. The cell body model includes a voltage control-type negative resistance, an equivalent inductance, resistors R_1 and R_2, and a membrane capacitor C_M. The voltage control-type negative resistance circuit with equivalent inductance consists of an n-channel MOSFET M_1, a p-channel MOSFET M_2, a voltage source V_A, a leak resistor R_L, a resistor R_G, and a capacitor C_G. The cell body model generates oscillating patterns of electrical activity v_{out}. More detail of the cell body model is described by Saito, Ohara, Abe, Kaneko, and Uchikoba (2017).

The inhibitory synaptic model comprises simple current mirror circuits. The inhibitory synaptic model inhibits the cell body model's pulse generation by pulling out current from the cell body model. MOSFET M_5 in the inhibitory synaptic model controls the current that the inhibitory synaptic model pulls from the cell body model. Therefore, voltage v_w applied to M_5 represents the strength of inhibition.

Figure 5 displays the simulation result of the waveform output by the P-HNM. The authors modified v_w in the middle of this simulation to explain how the pulse period varies. The circuit constants are C_{IS} = 3.3 μF, C_G = 47 pF, C_M = 10 pF, R_1 = 15 kΩ, R_2 = 20 kΩ, R_G = 8.2 MΩ, and R_L = 10 kΩ. The MOS-FETs are $M_{1, 5, 6, 7, 8}$: BSS83 and $M_{2, 3, 4}$: BSH205. The power sources are V_{DD} = 5.0 V and V_A = 3.5 V.

Figure 6 shows measuring results of pulse period characteristics of four P-HNM circuit boards mounted on the robot system by discrete elements. Figure 6A shows an example of the measured relation between the pulse period T and the synaptic weight control voltage v_w. Figure 6A indicates the P-HNM circuit board has a characteristic that the pulse period varies by a factor of about two between v_w of 0.9

V to 1.2 V. The characteristic of T for v_w in this area can be approximated by Equation (1). Equation (1) indicates that the pulse period varies quadratically with v_w.

$$T = 5.0v_w^{\,2} - 8.0v_w + 3.9\,. \tag{1}$$

Since the P-HNM circuit boards were made by implementing discrete elements on separate circuit boards, there are scattering in their characteristics, as shown in Figures 6B and C. No. 1 to No. 4 in the figures denote the results for each P-HNM circuit board.

Figure 6B shows pulse period characteristics against V_A at $V_{DD} = 0$ V and $v_w = 0$ V for each circuit board. The circuit boards do not generate pulses outside of the plot's continuous area. The characteristics between circuit boards significantly differ, as shown in Figure 6B. In addition, it shows that there is only an area between about $V_A = 2.8$ to 2.9 V in which all circuit boards generate pulses when V_A is common to all circuit boards.

Figure 6C shows pulse period characteristics against v_w for each circuit board in the area ($V_A = 2.9$ V). Figure 6C displays that the results of No. 3 and No. 4 show a significant variation in the pulse period against v_w, while No. 1 and No. 2 display almost no variation. The reason for this characteristics difference is that within the range of V_A over which the circuit board generates pulses shown in Figure 6B, the lower the voltage V_A, the greater the extension of the pulse period relative to the voltage v_w, and the higher the V_A, the smaller the variation in the pulse period.

The characteristic scatterings directly relate to differences in the legs' behaviours. Therefore, the authors made adjustments described in the next section to match the characteristics shown in Figure 6A.

Figure 4. Schematic diagram of P-HNM by discrete elements

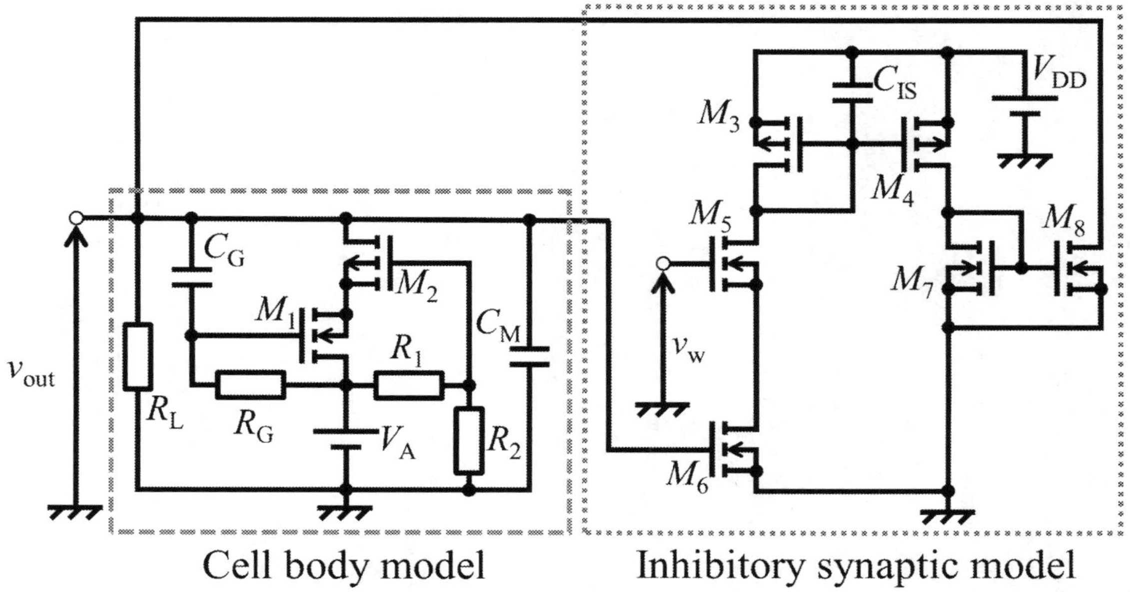
C_{IS}
V_{DD}
M_3
M_4
M_5
M_8
M_7
C_G
M_2
M_1
C_M
R_1
v_w
v_{out}
R_L
R_G
V_A
R_2
M_6
Cell body model
Inhibitory synaptic model

Figure 5. Example of P-HNM's output waveform (simulation result)

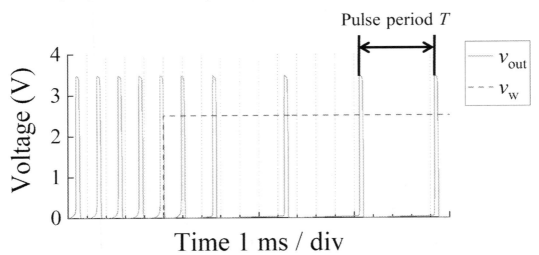

Figure 6. Measuring results of pulse period characteristics of P-HNM circuit boards. A: Example of pulse period characteristics against v_w, B: pulse period characteristics against V_A and C: pulse period characteristics against v_w

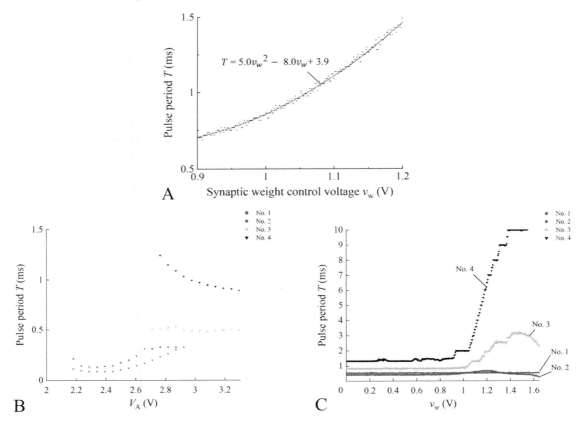

Gait Generation Method

The authors connected four-leg controlling systems to the microcontroller. The microcontroller links each P-HNM to each leg and controls the legs individually. Figure 7 depicts the peripheral circuit and one of the leg controlling system's schematic diagrams. The peripheral circuits comprise integrator, buffers, and voltage dividers. The peripheral circuits' constants were $C_F = 3.3$ µF, $R_F = 11$ kΩ, $R_{D1, D2, D3} = 11$ kΩ, and $U_{1, 2}$: LMC6032. The overview of the entire peripheral circuit board and the P-HNM circuit board is described in Figure 8.

The pressure sensor is a polymer thick film device that outputs the pressure applied to the surface as the electrical resistance. The resistance reduces in proportion to the increase in pressure. The microcontroller reads the output of the pressure sensor as voltage v_{pressi} using the voltage divider R_{D3}. Therefore, v_{pressi} decreases in proportion to the pressure. The P-HNM circuit board receives v_w from the microcontroller's pulse width modulation (PWM) waveform output through the integrator R_F and C_F, buffer U_1, and voltage dividers R_{D1} and R_{D2}. Equation (2) describes the relationship between v_{pressi} and v_w. The subscript i in the following equations denotes the parameter for the ith leg. Thus, i ranges from 1 to 4, namely, left fore, left hind, right fore, and right hind leg, respectively.

$$v_{wi} = \sigma v p_{ressi.}$$ (2)

where σ represents the feedback gain. The microcontroller sends signals to the servomotors so that the sole passes through four target points in the order shown in Figure 9. Figure 9 also shows the phases of the target points. Each P-HNM outputs v_{out} to the microcontroller's interrupt pins through the buffer U_2. The microcontroller changes the servomotors' angle by a constant angle θ each time v_{out} exceeds the microcontroller's interrupt trigger voltage (approximately 1.7 V). Therefore, the joints' angular velocity can be described as the following equation:

$$\omega_i = \frac{\theta}{T_i},$$ (3)

where T represents the pulse period. The robot's locomotion speed depends on θ. The following equation describes the joints' angular velocity from Equations (1) and (3).

$$\omega_i = \frac{\theta}{5.0v_w^2 - 8.0v_w + 3.9}.$$ (4)

This equation indicates that the pressure at the sole reduces the angular velocity of moving the leg. In addition, the weight supported by each leg tip changes the joints' angular velocities, generating phase differences between the legs.

There are differences in characteristics between circuit boards, as mentioned in the previous section. Therefore, the authors adjusted θ and σ for each circuit board to match the characteristics in Figure 6A in experiments.

Figure 7. Schematic diagram of the peripheral circuit board and one of leg controlling system

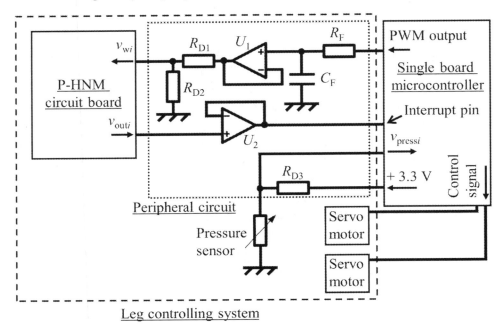

Figure 8. Overview of P-HNM circuit boards and the peripheral circuit board. A: P-HNM circuit board and B: peripheral circuit board

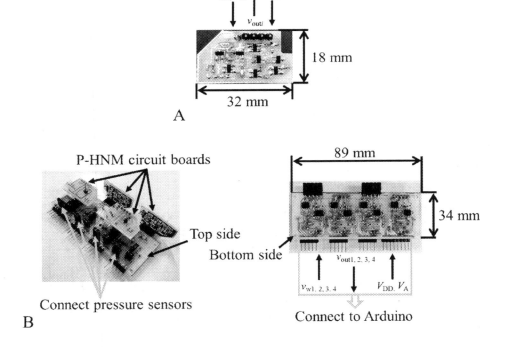

Figure 9. Sole trajectory and phases of target points

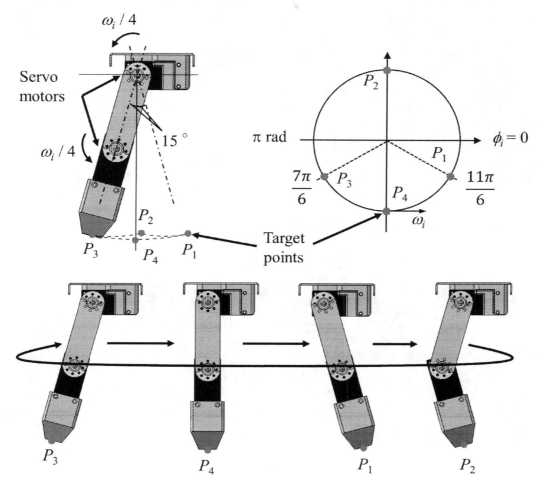

Experimental Results

The authors placed the quadruped robot system on a flat floor and allow it to move around. The experimental conditions were low and high locomotion speeds for the robot. The authors changed θ to change the locomotion speed. Nevertheless, other values were the same in both experiments. The initial phase of each leg is $3\pi/2$, and the legs start moving simultaneously.

Although the authors show transitions of phase differences, the robot system did not recognize and used them to control its legs, as described above. Figure 10 depicts the transitions of the legs' phase at low-speed locomotion. The borders in Figure 10 indicate one cycle of gait. Figure 10 shows that the quadruped robot system actively generates each leg's phase differences approximately 90° (0.5π rad) three steps after it begins to locomote. Furthermore, the order of moving the legs was left fore (LF), right hind (RH), right fore (RF), and left hind (LH), indicating that this gait is the same as horses' walk gait. In this experiment, the legs' angular velocity when the legs were not on the floor, i.e., v_w is zero, was approximately 30°/s (0.52 rad/s).

Figure 11 shows the result of high-speed locomotion. Figure 11 depicts how the quadruped robot system generated phase differences approximately 180° (π rad) for each leg four steps after it began to locomote. In addition, the order of moving the legs is LF and RH, RF and LH, which means that this is the same as the horses' trot gait. In this experiment, the legs' angular velocity when v_w is zero, was approximately 51°/s (0.89 rad/s).

These results show that the quadruped robot system could actively generate gaits by reducing the legs' angular velocity depending on the pressure on the sole. In addition, the robot system could generate different gaits depending on the locomotion speed. Furthermore, the characteristics of the generated gaits were consistent with horses' gaits. The control method limits the change factor in each leg's speed to feedback using weight-bearing balance. Therefore, the authors conclude that the trigger for the break in the initial phase symmetry differed in the robot's weight that is supported by the legs.

Figure 10. Transition of legs' phase difference at low-speed locomotion. A: Walking quadruped robot system and B: transition of legs' phase difference

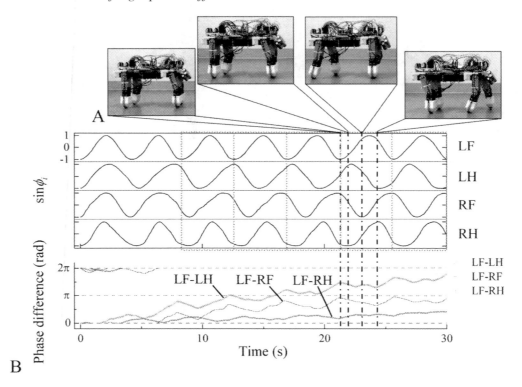

Figure 11. Transition of legs' phase difference at high-speed locomotion. A: Trotting quadruped robot system and B: transition of legs' phase difference

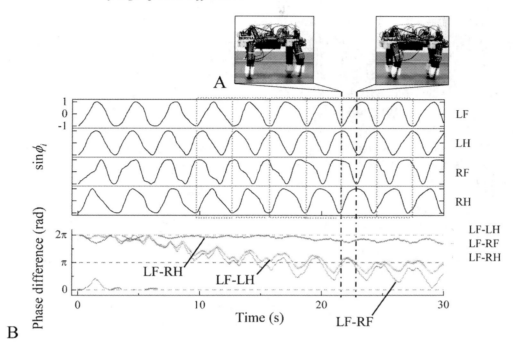

Pulse-Type Hardware Neuron Model by Integrated Circuits

The hand-made fabrication is prone to characteristic scatterings, as shown in Figure 6. Therefore, the authors developed a P-HNM IC chip to realize circuits with small characteristic scatterings. P-HNMs implemented in the IC chip replace resistors in a P-HNM shown in Figure 4 with MOSFETs. Figure 12 shows the schematic diagram of P-HNM by ICs. The W/L ratio which is the ratio of the channel width to the channel length of MOSFETs are $M_{C1} = W/L = 3/10$, $M_{C2} = W/L = 1.2/10$, $M_{C3,4} = W/L = 10/1.2$, $M_{IS1,5}: W/L = 10/100$, $M_{IS2,6}: W/L = 40/2$, $M_{IS3}: W/L = 10/10$, $M_{IS4}: W/L = 20/2$. The circuit constants are $C_{IS} = 100$ pF, $C_G = 10$ nF, $C_M = 20$ pF. C_Gs are placed outside of the IC chip because of the capacitance size.

Figures 13A and 13B depict layout patterns of the entire IC chip and single P-HNM circuit, respectively. The authors implemented four P-HNMs, the number required for the quadruped robot system in the IC chip. Figure 14 shows a picture of the bare chip. The size of the bare chip is 2.4×2.4 mm. The authors packaged the IC chip as a QFP80 using external foundries. The size of the packaged IC chip is 17×17 mm.

Figure 15 shows measured pulse period characteristics of four P-HNM ICs implemented in an IC chip. Figure 15A shows pulse period characteristics against V_A at $V_{DD} = 0$ V and $v_w = 0$ V for each circuit in the IC chip. Figure 15A displays that the characteristic scatterings between the circuits are very small compared to the results in Figure 6B. In addition, there is almost no scattering in the range of $V_A = 2.6$ V and above.

Figure 15B shows pulse period characteristics against v_w at $V_A = 2.89$ V and $V_{DD} = 3.30$ V for each circuit in the IC chip. Figure 15A displays that there are characteristic scatterings between the circuits. However, ranges in which the pulse period varies are around 1 ms to 2 ms; therefore, the characteristics scatterings of the circuits against v_w are smaller than the results in Figure 6C. In addition, since the pulse periods at $v_w = 0$ V are consistent, the V_A applied to the circuits can be unified.

The main factors of characteristic scattering that affect the implementation in the robot system are the v_w at which the pulse period starts to vary and the slope of the variation. Therefore, the authors consider that a quadruped robot system with the IC chip could generate gaits like the robot system with P-HNMs by discrete elements by adjusting σ. Although there is still some characteristic scattering among circuits, the characteristics against V_A are aligned. Therefore, there are fewer parameters that need to be adjusted. Thus, the authors assume that a quadruped robot system with the IC chip can maintain gaits for more extended cycles.

Figure 12. Schematic diagram of P-HNM by ICs

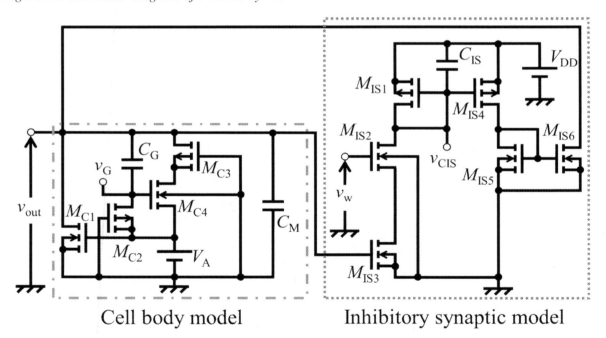

Cell body model   Inhibitory synaptic model

Figure 13. Layout pattern of the IC. A: Entire layout pattern and B: layout pattern of single P-HNM circuit

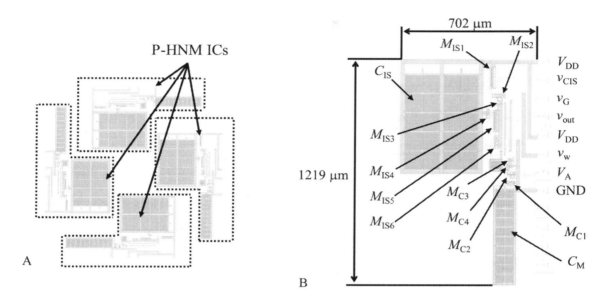

Figure 14. Picture of the bare chip

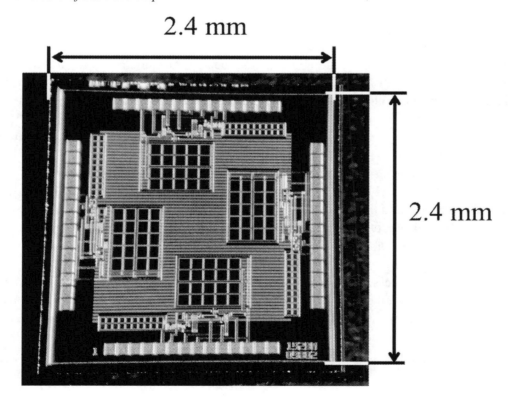

Figure 15. Measuring results of P-HNM ICs' pulse period characteristics. A: Pulse period characteristics against V_A, B: pulse period characteristics against v_w

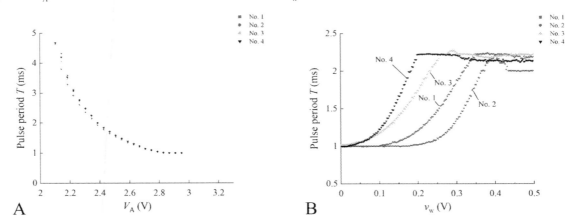

DYNAMIC SIMULATION OF QUADRUPED ROBOT MODEL

The authors built the quadruped robot model on the dynamic simulator CoppeliaSim (Coppelia Robotics AG, see key terms section for more information). This section explains the quadruped robot model and simulation results.

Quadruped Robot Model

Figure 16 shows the quadruped robot model. The authors imported the parts' data of the quadruped robot system in STL format, except for a few structures. The excluded structures are mainly the microcontroller, peripheral circuit board, and P-HNM circuit boards. The simulator converts STL data into structures called random shapes. Although random shapes can represent any mesh, using them makes the simulation slow and unstable. The fastest and most stable way to simulate is to use structures celled pure shapes. However, it also means that a significant portion of the robot system's shape is lost. On the other hand, structures called convex shapes can represent more general shapes than pure shapes. Therefore, the authors morphed random shapes into convex shapes to develop the quadruped robot model resembling the robot system's structure.

The quadruped robot model is composed of a body structure and leg units similar to the quadruped robot system. Figure 17 shows the body structure's detail. Some passively moving parts were deemed a single structure. The body structure has four joints and a cubic weight to tune the centre of mass. Figure 18 shows the detail of the leg unit's structure. Each leg unit has a joint, Parts 1, 2, 3, and a force sensor. Although Part 1 consists of two structures separated by space, it performs as a single structure. The force sensor measures the pressure between Parts 2 and 3 in the same way as the quadruped robot system does. The leg modules rotate around the body structure's joints; Parts 2 and 3 and the force sensor rotate around the leg units' joints. The joints' positions are on the axis of the servomotors' structures. The mechanical properties of each structure are the same as those of the quadruped robot system. Table 1 shows the mechanical properties. The robot model's entire mass is 1.0 kg.

Figure 16. Quadruped robot model

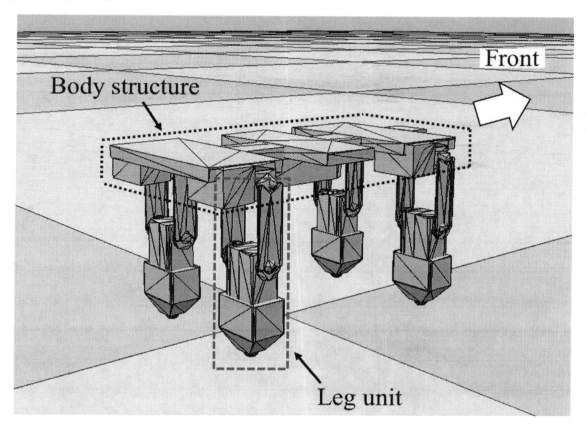

Figure 17. Detail of the body structure

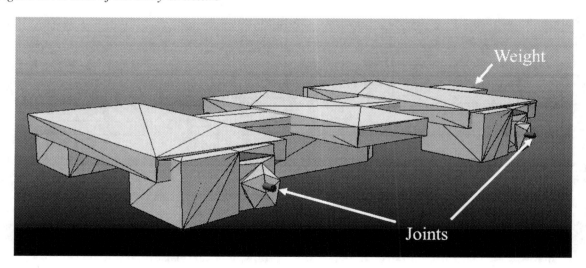

Figure 18. Detail of leg unit's structure

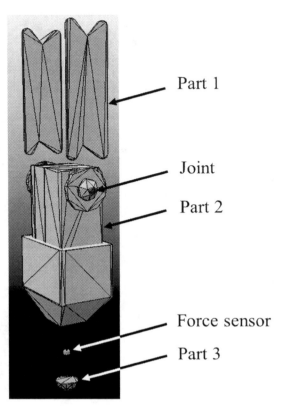

Part 1

Joint

Part 2

Force sensor

Part 3

Table 1. Parts' mechanical parameters

Name	Mass
Body structure	525 g
Part 1	7.0 g
Part 2	83 g
Part 3	1.0 g
Weight	92 g

Alternative Gait Generation Method

Since the simulator does not simulate electrical circuits, the authors programmed an alternative gait generation method that does not use P-HNMs in simulation. Nevertheless, the method reduces the joints' angular velocities depending on the pressure on the soles as the same as the method using the P-HNMs.

Figure 19 shows the programmed simulator's operations, which consist of an initializing process, a sensing process, and an actuation process. The initializing process sets initial values of joint actuation periods, joints' angles, and feedback gains. The initial actuation periods were zero, and the joints' angles were set to angles at which the robot model stands upright, as shown in Figure 16. The sensing process first checks the existence of legs for which the simulation time from the last time the legs moved to the times when this process exceeds the drive cycles. Then, it calculates the target angles at which the upcoming actuation process should drive the joints' angles of the relevant legs. The target angles are calculated to be a constant amount θ away from the current angles so that the soles follow the trajectory shown in Figure 9. The individual actuation periods for each leg depending on the soles' pressures are calculated at the end of the sensing process.

Figure 19. Dynamic simulator's operations

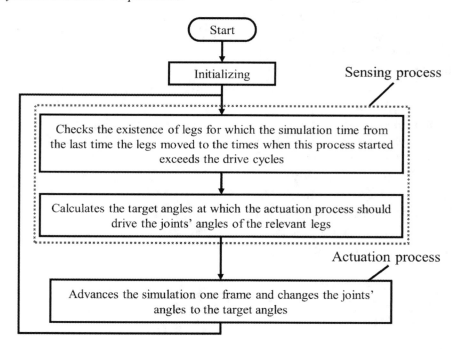

The simulator advances the simulation one frame and changes the joints' angles to the target angles in the actuation process. Since the simulator defines every actuation period as 0 s in an initializing process, the joints immediately move in the first actuation process. Furthermore, the simulator continues to simulate as long as the simulation time does not exceed a predefined limit.

The following equations describe parameters with primes to distinguish them from the quadruped robot system's gait generation method. Each leg's joint actuation period $T\phi$ can be described as follows:

$$T'_i = T_I + N_i \sigma',$$

(5)

where T_I represents a constant value corresponding to the P-HNM's pulse period when the pressure and v_w are zero in Equation (4). N represents the pressure that the sole received from the floor. $\sigma\phi$ represents a constant value representing the effect of the pressure. The robot model rotates the joints by the constant angle $\theta\phi$ in each actuation period. Therefore, $\theta\phi$ represents the locomotion speed. Hence, the joint's angular velocity $\omega\phi$ is given by

$$\omega'_i = \frac{\theta'}{T_I + N_i\sigma'} .$$
(6)

Simulation Results

The authors simulated the quadruped robot model's behaviour in each condition by changing $\theta\phi$ from $0.20°$ to $1.4°$ in increments of $0.01°$ while keeping the constant values T_1 and $\sigma\phi$. The constants were $T_1 = 20$ ms and $\sigma\phi = 8.0$. Each leg's initial phases were $3\pi/2$, and the authors allowed the quadruped robot model to move its legs simultaneously on a sufficiently wide plane.

The quadruped robot model actively generated different gaits depending on the locomotion speed, as the quadruped robot system. Figures 20 and 21 show examples of phase differences' transitions that the quadruped robot model generated. In the 5000-s simulation, these are the simulation results in which the quadruped robot model generated each gait the fastest. In addition, these results confirm that the quadruped robot model maintained the gaits for the longest time. The vertical axes in Figures 20 and 21 represent the phase differences from the LF leg to the other legs. $\theta\phi$ values in the simulations in Figures 16 and 17 were $0.99°$ and $1.09°$, respectively. The phase differences that the quadruped robot model generated in Figure 20 were approximately $90°$ (0.5π rad). In addition, the legs' moving order was LF, RH, RF, and LH; therefore, this was the walk gait. The phase differences generated by the robot model in Figure 21 were approximately $180°$ (π rad). Furthermore, the legs' moving order was LF and RH, RF and LH; therefore, this was the trot gait.

Figure 20. Example of generated gait by quadruped robot model (walk gait)

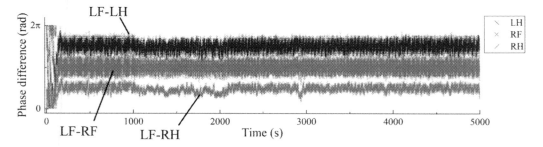

Figure 21. Example of generated gait by quadruped robot model (trot gait)

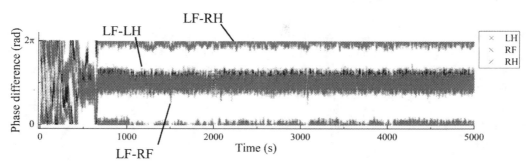

DISCUSSION

The authors proposed a gait generation method using P-HNM. In addition, the authors developed a quadruped robot system that implements the method and showed that the system could actively generate gaits due to experiments. The authors' goal is to realize a robot system that can behave autonomously by artificial nervous systems like animals. Previously, the authors developed a CPG model that could stably generate gait patterns, albeit passively. The authors intend to develop artificial nervous systems that incorporate this method of active gait generation into the CPG model in the future. Since high response speed is important for mobile robots, the authors used P-HNMs with high response speeds to realize the artificial nervous systems and configured a significant part of the robot system using electrical circuits. Although the authors used the microcontroller in the robot system, there are only three roles:

1. Input voltage depending on the pressure to P-HNMs
2. Send signals to servomotors to move legs along the trajectory
3. Record data during the locomotion.

Each of these roles can be accomplished without a microcontroller as follows:

1. Input the outputs of pressure sensors directly to P-HNMs
2. Use actuators to drive the mechanical structure that generates the leg trajectory instead of servomotors to drive joints
3. Monitor the walking robot from the outside.

However, to confirm the gait generation by our methods and analyze the robot's behaviour, abolishing the microcontroller will only make experiments and analyses pointlessly inconvenient.

The proposed method is based on the method proposed by other researchers (Owaki & Ishiguro, 2017) to feedback pressure to four decoupled phase oscillators individually. Their method used the oscillators' phases as leg motions' phases. The following equation describes the oscillator:

$$\dot{\phi}_i = \omega + \sigma N_i cos\phi_i \tag{7}$$

where ω denotes intrinsic angular velocity, σ denotes feedback gain, and ϕ denotes oscillator's phase. Therefore, the left side of Equation (7) denotes the angular velocity of oscillation. Thus, the strength of the feedback to the oscillators varies according to the phase. In addition, the feedback accelerates or decelerates the angular velocity according to the leg phase. It is characteristic of their method that each oscillator has a stable equilibrium point at which the right side of Equation (7) is zero, and the oscillators behave toward the point. In contrast, our method does not use the leg phase to vary the angular velocity. Our method feeds back the pressure that the sole receives to the P-HNM to decrease the angular velocity of the joint while not accelerating it. Therefore, our method does not recognize and use the leg motions' phases to generate gaits. Thus, the experimental results indicate that the robot system could generate gaits by interacting with the other legs by the body, without each leg recognizing the phase of its motion. Since even a walking machine without arbitrary systems to control legs could generate gaits (Nakatani, Sugimoto, & Osuka, 2009), the authors speculate that analyzing the robot system implementing our method will reveal essential elements necessary for gait generation.

Besides, the robot system could maintain gaits only for tens of seconds in the previous experiments. The authors speculate that the cause was the mechanical and electrical disturbance elements. Therefore, the authors developed P-HNM ICs to realize circuits with small characteristic scatterings. As a result of measurements, the authors confirmed that the characteristics of the ICs were pretty consistent compared to characteristic scatterings of the circuits, which was a problem in P-HNM by discrete elements. Although there is still some characteristic scattering among circuits, the results suggest that a quadruped robot system with the IC chip can maintain gaits for more extended cycles.

Furthermore, the authors confirmed that a robot model built in a dynamic simulator generated gaits like the robot system. The simulation results show that the robot model started locomotion with random footsteps and then generated animals' gaits and maintained them for many cycles. The cycles of random footsteps were greater than the experiment results of the robot system. The authors attributed this because the simulator defined all the structures as rigid, allowing vibrations and shocks to remain. They were absorbed by the rubber soles and rattling of parts in the robot system. The authors implemented a simplified version of the quadratic function described in Equation (1) to a linear function described in Equation (5) in the robot model. Since the simpler method should be closer to the principle of gait generation, the authors expect to discover the principle by further analyzing the behaviour of the robot model with the simplified method. However, the calculational cost will increase for adding functions other than gait generation (e.g., posture control and direction change) to the robot model. Therefore, it will increase calculation time like current robot control methods. Thus, the authors assume that developing animal-like neural systems that extend the P-HNM-based method is necessary to realize a robot that can perform advanced walking like an animal.

The authors experimentally determined θ and σ in experiments and simulations. Since θ, σ, and mechanical parameters (e.g., the body structure and the leg trajectory) are deeply involved in gait generation, referring to animals' data is necessary to understand animals' gait generation methods using our methods. For example, developing a robot based on animals' body size, gait cycle, and leg trajectory are needed.

CONCLUSION

This chapter explained quadruped robots with bio-inspired gait generation methods. The authors applied the method using P-HNMs and the robot's soles' pressures to a quadruped robot system. The experimental results showed that the quadruped robot system could actively generate typical gaits of quadruped animals. The novelty of this method is that the quadruped robot can generate gaits by feeding back sole pressures to P-HNMs without using phases of legs. In addition, the authors developed P-HNM ICs to realize circuits with small characteristic scatterings. As a result of measurements, the authors confirmed that the characteristics of the ICs were pretty consistent compared to characteristic scatterings of the circuits, which was a problem in P-HNM by discrete elements.

Furthermore, the quadruped robot system was simulated using a dynamic simulator. The simulator implemented an alternative gait generation method based on simple mathematics instead of P-HNMs. In contrast to using P-HNMs, implementing this alternative method in a real robot would require a high-computing processor to include more functionalities, as in the traditional method. However, the simulation results suggest the innovative finding that the robot model can generate gaits even with the simpler method using P-HNM.

On the other hand, although our methods are based on biology, the quadruped robots' behaviours differ from quadruped animals. For example, the robots may move one leg for one cycle, whereas the other leg moves for two cycles. This phenomenon occurs because the methods do not manage or limit the phase of each leg. To determine whether this phenomenon is biologically plausible, progress in the biological understanding of the animal's gait generation method is required. The authors speculate that because the P-HNMs do not have many functions, as animals' neurons, they may need to be connected to other nervous systems to generate sophisticated animal-like movements.

ACKNOWLEDGMENT

This research was supported by the JSPS KAKENHI [grant number JP18K04060]; the Nihon University Multidisciplinary Research Grant for (2020); the Research Institute of Science and Technology Nihon University College of Science and Technology Leading Research Promotion Grant. The VLSI chip has been fabricated by Digian Technology, Inc. This work is supported by VLSI Design and Education Center (VDEC), the University of Tokyo in collaboration with Synopsys, Inc., Cadence Design Systems, Inc. and Mentor Graphics, Inc. The VLSI chip in this study has been fabricated in the chip fabrication program of VLSI Design and Education Center (VDEC), the University of Tokyo in collaboration with On-Semiconductor Niigata, and Toppan Printing Corporation. Also, we appreciate the Nihon University Robotics Society.

The authors would like to thank Enago (www.enago.jp) for the English language review.

REFERENCES

Aguilar, W., Santamaría-Bonfil, G., Froese, T., & Gershenson, C. (2014). The past, present, and future of artificial life. *Frontiers in Robotics and AI*, *1*(8), 1–15. doi:10.3389/frobt.2014.00008

Arshavsky, Y. I., Deliagina, T. G., & Orlovsky, G. N. (2016). Central pattern generators: Mechanisms of operations and their role in controlling automatic movements. *Neuroscience and Behavioral Physiology*, *46*(6), 696–718. doi:10.100711055-016-0299-5

Bellardita, C., & Kiehn, O. (2015). Phenotypic characterization of speed-associated gait changes in mice reveals modular organization of locomotor networks. *Current Biology, 25*(11), 1426–1436. doi:10.1016/j. cub.2015.04.005 PMID:25959968

Bhatti, Z., Waqas, A., Mahesar, A. W., & Karbasi, M. (2017). Gait analysis and biomechanics of quadruped motion for procedural animation and robotic simulation. *Bahria University Journal of Information & Communication Technologies, 10*(2), 1–7.

Biswal, P., & Mohanty, P. K. (2021). Development of quadruped walking robots: A review. *Ain Shams Engineering Journal, 12*(2), 2017–2031. doi:10.1016/j.asej.2020.11.005

Delcomyn, F. (1980). Neural basis of rhythmic behavior in animals. *Science, 210*(4469), 492–498. doi:10.1126cience.7423199 PMID:7423199

Duysens, J., & Pearson, K. G. (1980). Inhibition of flexor burst generation by loading ankle extensor muscles in walking cats. *Brain Research, 187*(2), 321–332. doi:10.1016/0006-8993(80)90206-1 PMID:7370733

Fankhauser, P., Bjelonic, M., Bellicoso, B. C., Miki, T., & Hutter, M. (2018). Robust rough-terrain locomotion with a quadrupedal robot. In *2018 IEEE International Conference on Robotics and Automation (ICRA)* (pp. 5761-5768). IEEE. 10.1109/ICRA.2018.8460731

Frigon, A., & Rossignol, S. (2006). Experiments and models of sensorimotor interactions during locomotion. *Biological Cybernetics, 95*(6), 607–627. doi:10.100700422-006-0129-x PMID:17115216

Grillner, S. (1975). Locomotion in vertebrates: Central mechanisms and reflex interaction. *Physiological Reviews, 55*(2), 247–304. doi:10.1152/physrev.1975.55.2.247 PMID:1144530

Grillner, S., & Zangger, P. (1979). On the central generation of locomotion in the low spinal cat. *Experimental Brain Research, 34*(2), 241–261. doi:10.1007/BF00235671 PMID:421750

Habib, M. K. (2011). Biomimetics: Innovations and robotics. *International Journal of Mechatronics and Manufacturing Systems, 4*(2), 113–134. doi:10.1504/IJMMS.2011.039263

Habib, M. K., Watanabe, K., & Izumi, K. (2007). The sociotechnical nature of mobile computing work: Evidence from a study of policing in the United States. *International Journal of Technology and Human Interaction, 1*(3), 1–14.

Habu, Y., Yamada, Y., Fukui, S., & Fukuoka, Y. (2018). A simple rule for quadrupedal gait transition proposed by a simulated muscle-driven quadruped model with two-level CPGs. In *2018 IEEE International Conference on Robotics and Biomimetics (ROBIO)* (pp. 2075-2081). IEEE.

Hoyt, D. F., & Taylor, C. R. (1981). Gait and the energetics of locomotion in horses. Nature, 292, 239–240.

Ishii, T., Masakado, S., & Ishii, K. (2004). Locomotion of a quadruped robot using CPG. In *2004 IEEE International Joint Conference on Neural Networks* (vol. 4, pp. 3179-3184). IEEE. 10.1109/ IJCNN.2004.1381184

Ito, S., Yuasa, H., Luo, Z., Ito, M., & Yanagihara, D. (1998). A mathematical model of adaptive behavior in quadruped locomotion. *Biological Cybernetics, 78*(5), 337–347. doi:10.1007004220050438 PMID:9691263

Kukillaya, R., Proctor, J., & Holmes, P. (2009). Neuromechanical models for insect locomotion: Stability, maneuverability, and proprioceptive feedback. *Chaos (Woodbury, N.Y.), 19*(026107), 1–15. doi:10.1063/1.3141306 PMID:19566267

Li, X., Wang, W., & Yi, J. (2016). Foot contact force of walk gait for a quadruped robot. In *2016 IEEE International Conference on Mechatronics and Automation (ICMA)* (pp. 659-664). IEEE. 10.1109/ICMA.2016.7558641

Liu, H., Jia, W., & Bi, L. (2017). Hopf oscillator based adaptive locomotion control for a bionic quadruped robot. In *2017 IEEE International Conference on Mechatronics and Automation (ICMA)* (pp. 949-954). IEEE. 10.1109/ICMA.2017.8015944

Marder, E., & Bucher, D. (2001). Central pattern generators and the control of rhythmic movements. *Current Biology, 11*(23), 986–996. doi:10.1016/S0960-9822(01)00581-4 PMID:11728329

McGeer, T. (1990). Passive dynamic walking. *The International Journal of Robotics Research, 9*(2), 62–82. doi:10.1177/027836499000900206

McMahon, T. A. (1985). The role of compliance in mammalian running gaits. *The Journal of Experimental Biology, 115*(1), 263–282. doi:10.1242/jeb.115.1.263 PMID:4031769

Nakatani, K., Sugimoto, Y., & Osuka, K. (2009). Demonstration and analysis of quadruped passive dynamic walking. *Advanced Robotics, 23*(5), 483–501. doi:10.1163/156855309X420039

Owaki, D., & Ishiguro, A. (2017). A quadruped robot exhibiting spontaneous gait transitions from walking to trotting to galloping. *Scientific Reports, 7*(277), 1–10. doi:10.103841598-017-00348-9 PMID:28325917

Owaki, D., Kano, T., Nagasawa, K., Tero, A., & Ishiguro, A. (2013). Simple robot suggests physical interlimb coordination is essential for quadruped walking. *Journal of the Royal Society, Interface, 10*(78), 20120669. doi:10.1098/rsif.2012.0669 PMID:23097501

Raibert, M., Blankespoor, K., Nelson, G., & Playter, R. (2008). BigDog, the rough-terrain quadruped robot. In *IFAC Proceedings Volumes* (vol. 41, pp. 10822-10825). Elsevier. 10.3182/20080706-5-KR-1001.01833

Saito, K., Ohara, M., Abe, M., Kaneko, M., & Uchikoba, F. (2017). *Gait generation of multilegged robots by using hardware artificial neural networks. In Advanced Applications for Artificial Neural Networks*. INTEC.

Selverston, A. I., & Ayers, J. (2006). Oscillations and oscillatory behavior in small neural circuits. *Biological Cybernetics, 95*(6), 537–554. doi:10.100700422-006-0125-1 PMID:17151878

Shinomoto, S., & Kuramoto, Y. (1986). Phase transitions in active rotator systems. *Progress of Theoretical Physics, 75*(5), 1105–1110. doi:10.1143/PTP.75.1105

Shinomoto, S., & Kuramoto, Y. (1986). Cooperative phenomena in two-dimensional active rotator systems. *Progress of Theoretical Physics, 75*(6), 1319–1327. doi:10.1143/PTP.75.1319

Sugimoto, Y., Yoshioka, H., & Osuka, K. (2011). Development of super-multi- legged passive dynamic walking robot "Jenkka-III". In *SICE Annual Conference 2011* (pp, 576-579). IEEE.

Takei, Y., Morishita, K., Tazawa, R., Katsuya, K., & Saito, K. (2021). Non-programmed gait generation of quadruped robot using pulse-type hardware neuron models. *Artificial Life and Robotics*, *26*(1), 109–115. doi:10.100710015-020-00637-z

Takei, Y., Morishita, K., Tazawa, R., & Saito, K. (2021). *Active Gaits Generation of Quadruped Robot Using Pulse-Type Hardware Neuron Models. In Biomimetics*. IntechOpen.

Takei, Y., Tazawa, R., Kaimai, T., Morishita, K., & Saito, K. (2021, January). *Dynamic simulation of non-programmed gait generation of quadruped robot* [Paper presentation]. The Twenty-Sixth International Symposium on Artificial Life and Robotics 2021.

Taylor, C. R. (1980). Force development during sustained locomotion: A determinant of gait, speed and metabolic power. *The Journal of Experimental Biology*, *115*(1), 253–262. doi:10.1242/jeb.115.1.253 PMID:4031768

Yuasa, H., & Ito, M. (1990). Coordination of many oscillators and generation of locomotory patterns. *Biological Cybernetics*, *63*(3), 177–184. doi:10.1007/BF00195856

KEY TERMS AND DEFINITIONS

Arduino DUE: A single board microcontroller using ARM CPU. It has 12 PWM output pins and 12 analogue inputs. Although it also has two digital-to-analogue converters (DACs), the authors used the PWM output pins and the peripheral circuits because the number of the DAC is not enough for the quadruped robot system.

CoppeliaSim: A dynamic simulator that supports several application programming interfaces (APIs) and remote APIs. The CoppeliaSim also supports four different dynamics engines: the Bullet physics library, the Open Dynamics Engine, Vortex Studio engine, and the Newton Dynamics engine. The authors simulated the quadruped robot model using the Newton Dynamics engine.

FSR402: A force-sensing resistor. The authors used FSR402 with a voltage divider to use as a pressure sensor. The detailed characteristics are available online at: https://www.interlinkelectronics.com/fsr-402.

Gait: Phase differences between the legs during locomoting. Walk, trot, and gallop gait are typical gaits in quadrupedal locomotion. For example, in the walk gait, LF, LH, RF, and RH move in 90° phase difference, and in the trot gait, the diagonal legs move in 180° phase difference in synchronization.

KRS-2552RHV ICS: A common servomotor that can be controlled by serial or PWM mode. The authors controlled them with PWM mode using Arduino DUE.

Pulse Width Modulation (PWM): A method the microcontroller outputs voltages. Outputs a voltage by alternately turning on / off, and by integrating the output voltage, it can generate any voltage between on and off. The authors used this method to vary the output from the microcontroller in increments of approximately 0.8 mV.

Pulse-Type Hardware Neuron Model (P-HNM): A kind of artificial neuron model that emulates biological neurons' functions by analogue electrical circuits. There are other artificial neuron models by mathematical equations.

Chapter 3

Deep Learning Models for Physiological Data Classification of Children During Computerized Auditory Tests:
Deep Learning–Based Emotion Recognition in Child–Computer Interaction

Duygun Erol Barkana
https://orcid.org/0000-0002-8929-0459
Yeditepe University, Turkey

Itır Kaşıkçı
Istanbul Commerce University, Turkey

Hatice Kose
https://orcid.org/0000-0003-4796-4766
Istanbul Technical University, Turkey

Elif Toprak
Yeditepe University, Turkey

Selma Yılar
Cerrahpaşa Medical Faculty, Istanbul University-Cerrahpaşa, Turkey

Dilara Demirpençe Seçinti
Şişli Etfal Research and Training Hospital, Turkey

ABSTRACT

The chapter aims to classify the physiological data of hearing impaired (HI) and typically developed (TD) children using machine/deep learning techniques 1) to reveal if the physiological data of the HI and TD are distinguishable, 2) to understand which emotions of HI and TD are recognized, and 3) to investigate the effect of computerization in a subset of audiology perception tests. Physiological signals, which are blood volume pulse (BVP), skin conductance (SC), and skin temperature (ST), are collected using a wearable E4 wristband during computerized and conventional tests. Sixteen HI and 18 TD children participated in this study. An artificial neural network (ANN) and a convolutional neural network (CNN) model are used to classify physiological data. The physiological changes of HI and TD children are distinguishable in computerized tests. TD children's positive (pleasant) and negative (unpleasant) emotions (PN) are distinguishable on both computerized and conventional tests. HI children's neutral and negative (unpleasant) (NU) emotions are distinguishable in the computerized tests.

DOI: 10.4018/978-1-7998-8686-0.ch003

INTRODUCTION

In the time of COVID-19 pandemics, there has been a rise in the use of tablet and computer-based versions of conventional education and health applications. As a result, computer-based intervention systems are becoming particularly important, especially for pediatric populations.

Most of the computer-based interventions developed for pediatric populations aim to evaluate cognitive abilities (Akshoomoff et al., 2014), to screen for related pathologies (Luciana, 2003), and even to provide therapeutic use (Kollins et al., 2020). Compared to these studies, a few computerized tests have previously been developed to evaluate perceptive capacities as vision and audition (Eisenberg et al., 2007; Herdman et al., 1998).

Children with hearing loss are a group that requires special attention and equipment. Early intervention is important so that these children develop similarly to their peers and become productive individuals. Regular assessment of children's auditory skills is necessary to set rehabilitation goals. If the auditory tests are fun and designed to prolong children's attention spans, they will be more successful. Unfortunately, it is not possible to keep children away from technology today. Therefore, demonstrating the effectiveness of a computerized assessment method will contribute positively to the development of children with hearing loss and the field of audiology. Thus, it has previously been mentioned that evaluating the comparability between computerized and conventional tests (Hassler Hallstedt & Ghaderi, 2018; Neumann & Neumann, 2019).

The study presented in this chapter is a part of a project that aimed to computerize and evaluate two subtests of the developmental test of auditory perception (DTAP) used for children in audiology clinics (Uluer, 2020). This chapter first presents how a computerized version of a developmental test of auditory perception (DTAP) for hearing impaired children is developed. Then, physiological data collected from participating children during a clinical trial has been classified using machine and deep learning methods to understand i) if the physiological data of the two groups of children (HI and TD) is distinguishable, ii) if the computerized/conventional, in other words, effects of technology, can be extracted, and iii) if the children's emotions can be classified.

BACKGROUND

Auditory Perception

Auditory perception is the recognition and interpretation of auditory stimuli and is especially important for speech and language development in children (Cole, 2007). Furthermore, auditory maturation is the basic component in the development of auditory perception (Saffran, 2006), and children with hearing loss are at risk in the development of auditory perception. For this reason, evaluation of the auditory perception skills of children with hearing loss is also necessary for typical development.

Auditory perception tests are screening or diagnostic evaluation tools used to identify deficiencies, especially auditory discrimination skills. Therefore, it is essential to evaluate auditory perception skills, especially preschool and school-age children (Hull, 1999). developmental test of auditory perception (DTAP) is a comprehensive auditory perception test battery previously used and validated in a study done with Turkish typically developed children (Cinar, 2021).

DTAP consists of five subtests to evaluate auditory perception: environmental sounds, word discrimination, phonemes in isolation, tonal pattern, and rhyming sounds. In this chapter, environmental sounds and tonal patterns are used to evaluate the auditory perception skills of children with hearing loss and are presented in two different media (computerized and conventional), and the results were evaluated.

Emotion Recognition

Emotion recognition is becoming increasingly a very active research area. The emotions are modeled in two ways. The discrete emotion model (Ekman, 1992; Izard, 2009; Plutchik, 2001) defines emotions in a non-continuous manner and represents them in different states as happy, angry, bored, and so forth. In contrast, the two-dimensional emotion model places other emotions in different data points on a Cartesian plane with two continuous dimensions: arousal and valence (Lang, 1995). This chapter aims to understand if the children feel positive (pleasant), negative (unpleasant), or neutral during their computerized and conventional tests. Thus, the valence dimension property of the two-dimensional emotion model is selected.

The emotional states of people can be understood using different parameters such as facial expression (Grabowski et al., 2019; Lang, 1995), speech, and electroencephalography (EEG) (Gonuguntla et al., 2015; Liu & Sourina, 2014). Physiological signals such as skin conductance (SC), blood volume pulse (BVP), and skin temperature (ST) have also been commonly used to recognize emotions (Bruno et al., 2017; J. S. Choi et al., 2015; Dissanayake et al., 2019; Greco et al., 2016; Khezri et al., 2015; Marin-Morales et al., 2018; Yin et al., 2017). A survey about the sensors used to recognize emotions has been presented (Dzedzickis et al., 2020). Physiological signals such as EEG, BVP, SC, and ST have previously been used to recognize the emotions of adults (Gumuslu et al., 2020). However, while facial expressions, speech, EEG, and physiological signals have been widely used in studies with adult subjects to recognize emotions, studies in children have rarely been done.

Disgust, fear, happiness, sadness, and surprise emotions have been recognized for typically developed children using Infrared Thermal Imaging (IRTI) (Goulart et al., 2019). Audio signals and children's heart rate have been detected using a wearable device to understand the children's stress (Y. Choi et al., 2017). iCalm has been used to detect the stress of children (Fletcher et al., 2010). Electrodermal activity (EDA) signals have been used to classify emotions in children (Feng & Golshan, 2018). SC, BVP, and ST are used to recognize the children's emotions (Garbarino et al., 2014).

Various machine and deep learning methods have been used to classify the emotions of people using physiological signals. Support vector machine (SVM), K-Nearest Neighborhood (KNN), Naive Bayes (NB), Linear Discriminant Analysis (LDA), Radial Basis Function (RBF), Multi-class Support Vector Machine (ML-SVM), Least Squares Support Vector Machine (LS-SVM), Quadratic Discriminant Analysis (QDA), Multi-Layer Perception Back Propagation (MLP-BP) are the most commonly used methods to classify the emotions physiological signals (Dzedzickis et al., 2020). Several deep learning approaches have also been studied and used for emotion classification because of the high-dimensional physiological features (Supratak et al., 2016; Rim et al., 2020; Yin et al., 2017). A machine learning algorithm called Gradient Boosting Machines (GBM) and a deep learning algorithm called Convolutional Neural Networks (CNN) have been used to classify pleasant, unpleasant, and neutral emotions from the recorded EEG and physiological signals of adults (Gumuslu et al., 2020). Aspects of machine learning in emotion detection systems and physiological data are comprehensively overviewed (Panicker & Gayathri, 2019). The emotions have previously been identified using the heart activity, skin conductance, and physical activity signals recorded by the E4 wristband (Bulagang et al., 2020; Can et al., 2019; Gouverneur et al., 2017; Jalan, 2020; Kikhia et al., 2016; Ollander, 2015). Machine learning and deep learning algorithms have previously been used to classify emotions from EEG and physiological signals of adults (Gumuslu et al., 2020).

The study presented in this chapter first presents the computerized version of a developmental test of auditory perception (DTAP) for hearing impaired children. Then, physiological data are collected from children. Later, machine/deep learning methods are used for physiological data classification of children during computerized auditory tests. This classification is first done to investigate if the physiological data of the two groups of children (HI and TD) are separable. Furthermore, the effects of technology are also extracted in both computerized and conventional audiology tests. Finally, the classification is done to understand which emotions of HI and TD can be classified in audiology tests.

MATERIALS AND METHODS

Participants

Thirty-four children (18 F, 16 M; mean age 6.14±0.97) participated in the study. There were 16 hearing impaired (HI) children (10 F, 6 M; mean age 6.12±0.78) and 18 children (8 F, 10 M; mean age 6.16±1.11) in the typically developed (TD) group. HI children were the patients followed by Cerrahpasa Medical Faculty, Department of Audiology, and their hearing was corrected by either using hearing aids (N=6) or cochlear implants (N=10). Among those 34, BVP, SC, and ST physiological data of all TD children (18) and 6 HI children (4 F, 2 M; mean age 6.67±0.47) were included in the analysis of the emotion recognition using the physiological data.

Hearing development is better in older children than in younger children, and the endpoint of maturation is between 6 and 12 years of age (1,2). Therefore, the assessment of auditory development was considered in this age range. Children using hearing aids or cochlear implants were included in the research. These children have normal or near-normal hearing with hearing aids. The cochlear implant is a hearing prosthesis applied to children with severe to profound hearing loss. Children with cochlear implants were implanted under the age of 3 in this study. Children who use hearing aids have moderate hearing loss. All children receive special education support. None of the children with hearing loss has any pathology other than hearing loss.

HI children were first invited to Istanbul Technical University, Faculty of Computer and Informatics Engineering, for the computerized tests in February 2020 as a part of the RoboRehab Project activities. Unfortunately, due to the extraordinary pandemic, the data collection had to be postponed to September 2020, and only six children out of 16 participated at Cerrahpasa Medical Faculty, Department of Audiology. TD children were recruited from the relatives of the Şişli Etfal Hospital workers between August and October 2020. The ethical committee approved the study of Istanbul Technical University and Istanbul University Cerrahpasa Medical Faculty.

The participants were evaluated by a clinical audiologist and a child psychiatrist to exclude any possible cause of the performance difference between the two groups. Children's developmental milestones in both groups were by their age, and they were not treated by the child and adolescent psychiatrists beforehand. There were no significant differences in the groups regarding gender and age (p<0.05).

Conventional Tests and Application

Two subtests of the DTAP, environmental sounds, and tonal patterns, were used with permission from the test developers (Reynolds et al., 2008). The environmental sounds and tonal patterns tests were selected because they do not require high-level verbal reasoning or high memory capacity. Thirty test items consisted of environmental sounds that exist in nature in the environmental sounds test.

The child heard two environmental sounds presented consecutively and determined whether these sounds were the same or different. Thirty test items consisted of consecutive tonal patterns presented at the same frequency and intensity in the tonal patterns test. The child heard the two tonal patterns consecutively and determined whether they were the same or different. The tests were carried out individually with the child in a quiet room where the background noise was below 35 dBA. The facial expressions of the children were videotaped simultaneously. Children's physiological data (BVP, SC, and ST) were recorded using the E4 wristband. The researcher had a short conversation with the children before applying the tests about the same-different concepts in the conventional test (Figure 1).

Figure 1. Conventional test setup

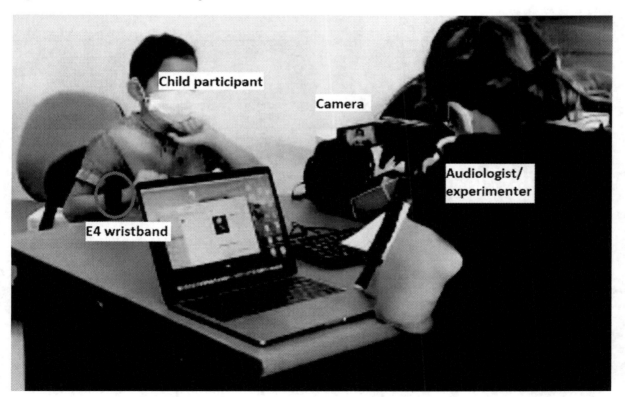

Test Computerization and Application

The conventional tests were gamified and converted into digital media, then presented to the children via tablet interface. For example, the "same" and "different" concepts were represented in the computerized test using cartoons of cupcakes and ice creams with two identical images of cupcakes representing "same" whereas one cupcake with one ice cream image representing "different" (Figure 2).

The initial screen of the test software asked for the demographic information (age and gender) of the children and provided a selection menu for the test to be applied (environmental sounds or tonal patterns). The tablet was right in the child's hands in the application, and the experimenter was sitting near the child during the test (Figure 3). The test platform software and the test interface were prepared using the Unity Game engine installed on a tablet computer. The software provided all audio outputs, feedback, and instructions on the tablet. All instructions in the tablet test were given through voice recordings and written and visual directions to allow minimum intervention from the researcher. The voice is generated by text-to-speech, and modifications on the parameters of voice signals are done to make them as natural and understandable as possible for the children.

Figure 2. Tablet screen

Figure 3. Computerized test setup

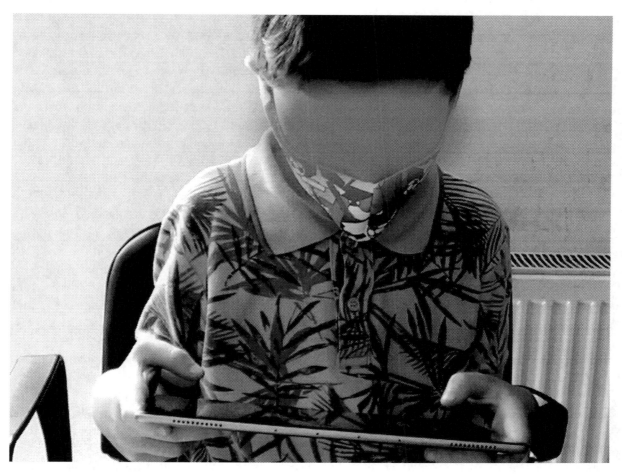

Physiological Data Collection and Processing

Physiological data were collected using the E4 wristband worn on the wrist (Figure 1). Blood volume pulse (BVP) data was acquired with a photoplethysmography (PPG) sensor with a sampling rate of 64 Hz, skin conductivity (SC) data with an electrodermal activity (EDA) sensor at 4 Hz, and skin temperature (ST) data with an infrared thermopile at 4 Hz. SC and ST data were upsampled to 64 samples per second so that the number of samples of all data was equal. MATLAB's interp1 function was used for upsampling (The MathWorks, 2020). The data from all sensors were epoched into 1-second slices. Multisensor data fusion at the data level is used to fuse EDA, ST, and BVP sensors resulting in 64x2 vectors for each one-second slice.

Classification Methods

First of all, the physiological data of HI and TD children were classified using machine learning techniques to reveal if the data of the two groups are distinguishable. Then, the data samples were labeled TD and HI for environmental sounds and tonal patterns for computerized and conventional tests.

After that, the computerized versus conventional test-related physiological data were classified using machine/deep learning to understand if the test, in other words, effects of technology, can be extracted from the physiological data (Figure 4). Data samples were labeled considering the test media: computerized (T, for tablet) versus conventional (C) for the environmental sounds test, tonal patterns test, and both tests taken together. Computerized- conventional (TC) classifications were calculated for TD and HI children.

Lastly, in addition to the mere classification of computerized versus conventional, it is aimed to classify the children's emotions depending on the test (Figure 4). Therefore, the data samples were labeled considering the children's emotional states (Pleasant-P, Unpleasant-U, and Neutral-N) during the experiments assigned by a psychologist. Thus, the pleasant-unpleasant (PU), pleasant-neutral (PN), neutral-unpleasant (NU), and pleasant-neutral- unpleasant (PNU) emotions were classified.

In all three classification attempts given above, the training and test sets were prepared for three-fold cross-validation. It is observed that there was an unbalanced number of samples for each class (TD, HI for classification 1; T, C for classification 2; P, N, U for classification 3) of the classification tasks (TD, HI for classification 1; T, C for classification 2; PU, PN, NU, and PNU for classification 3). Hence, the training datasets in all classification applications were augmented using the random oversampling method.

A classical neural network (ANN) was used for all classifications as the machine learning algorithm (Figure 4). The neural network architecture consists of only one hidden layer with 64 units using the sigmoid function. A fully connected dense layer, which uses the softmax function, was added. The loss function was selected as binary cross-entropy for binary classifications, and categorical cross-entropy is used for the multi-class classifications. Furthermore, a convolutional neural network (CNN) was used for classification (Figure 4). CNN model consists of one convolutional layer with 8 filters that have kernel sizes of 8-by-2. A maximum pooling layer followed with a pool size of 64-by-1. The same arrangement was set as the classical neural network at the last layer because binary and multi-class classification tasks exist.

Figure 4. Work flow of classification task using physiological signal

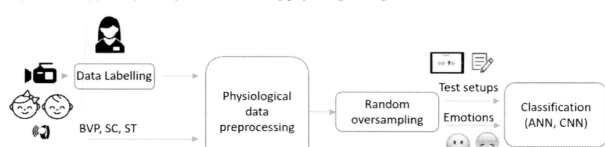

RESULTS

Video Labeling

The emotions of the children were labeled as pleasant (P), unpleasant (U), or neutral (N) using the Video Labeling Tool (VLT) (Uluer et al., 2020). There were 6 children in HI, 18 children in the TD group. Labeled HI group data was not enough for comparison due to the small group size. TD group VLT label results are given in Table 1 as percentages. These values were calculated by dividing the time labeled as P, U, or N by the total time labeled in that given condition (P+U+N).

Classifications using ANN and CNN

Different emotional states (P, N, U) were analyzed by looking at the classification performance using physiological data for hearing impaired (HI) and typically developed (TD) children, computerized (T), and conventional (C) tests. Since the number of samples belonging to different classes in the test sets remained unbalanced, the f1-score, recall, precision, specificity, Matthew's correlation coefficient (MCC), the geometric mean of sensitivity (recall) and precision (GSP), the geometric mean of sensitivity (recall), and specificity (GSS) and Kappa statistics besides classification accuracies for emotion classifications were also presented. The results for the classification of TD and HI are given in Table 2. 81% accuracy (Kappa=0.62) was obtained for classifying the HI and TD children for environmental sounds when CNN was used in computerized tests (Table 2). Similarly, 84% accuracy (Kappa=0.68) was obtained in tonal patterns for ANN.

Test (TC) classification results were given in Table 3 for TD children and in Table 4 for HI children. When classifiers were examined in terms of performance, we assessed the results of the classifiers that had a greater value than 0.61 in terms of Kappa statistics. While 0.61 to 0.81 corresponded to the substantial agreement, values greater than 0.81 corresponded to an almost good agreement. Thus, only those results (greater than 0.61 in terms of Kappa statistics) were presented in this chapter.

86% (Kappa=0.64) and 94% (Kappa=0.87) accuracies were obtained for ANN and CNN, respectively, in computerized tests. Furthermore, 95% (Kappa=0.89) and 92% (Kappa=83) accuracy results were obtained for ANN and CNN, respectively in conventional tests. As a result, tonal patterns of TD children could be assessed for emotion classification (task=PN) in both computerized and conventional setups (Table 5). 96% accuracy (Kappa=0.91) and 98% accuracy (Kappa=0.95) for ANN and CNN, respectively, were obtained for environmental sounds. Moreover, 97% accuracy (Kappa=0.92) was obtained for CNN for tonal patterns. Computerized tests could be assessed in terms of emotion classification (task=NU) for HI children from Table 6.

Table 1. Video labeling

Typically Developed	P	N	U
Computerized - Environmental Sounds (TE) (N=12)	46.75	52.93	0.32
Computerized - Tonal Patterns (TT) (N=15)	4.34	95.66	0.00
Conventional - Environmental Sounds (CE) (N=8)	20.77	78.18	1.05
Conventional - Tonal Patterns (CT) (N=7)	19.26	80.74	0.00

Table 2. Classification results for HI children vs. TD children

Item Set	Metric	ANN	CNN	Item Set	Metric	ANN	CNN
Computerized - Environmental Sounds (TE)	Accuracy	0.80	0.81	**Conventional - Environmental Sounds (CE)**	Accuracy	0.75	0.72
	Precision	0.81	0.84		Precision	0.75	0.72
	Recall	0.80	0.81		Recall	0.75	0.72
	F1-score	0.79	0.81		F1-score	0.75	0.72
	Specificity	0.80	0.81		Specificity	0.75	0.72
	GSP	0.80	0.82		GSP	0.75	0.72
	GSS	0.79	0.80		GSS	0.75	0.72
	MCC	0.61	0.65		MCC	0.50	0.45
	Kappa	0.60	0.62		Kappa	0.50	0.45
Computerized - Tonal Patterns (TT)	Accuracy	0.84	0.75	**Conventional - Tonal Patterns (CT)**	Accuracy	0.73	0.68
	Precision	0.84	0.75		Precision	0.74	0.69
	Recall	0.84	0.75		Recall	0.73	0.68
	F1-score	0.84	0.75		F1-score	0.73	0.68
	Specificity	0.84	0.75		Specificity	0.73	0.68
	GSP	0.84	0.75		GSP	0.73	0.68
	GSS	0.84	0.75		GSS	0.73	0.67
	MCC	0.68	0.49		MCC	0.47	0.37
	Kappa	0.68	0.49		Kappa	0.47	0.36

Table 3. Classification results of computerized-conventional (TC) of TD children

Item Set	Metric	ANN	CNN	Item Set	Metric	ANN	CNN
Environmental Sounds	Accuracy	0.59	0.56	**Tonal Patterns**	Accuracy	0.75	0.66
	Precision	0.62	0.57		Precision	0.75	0.67
	Recall	0.59	0.56		Recall	0.75	0.66
	F1-score	0.57	0.54		F1-score	0.75	0.66
	Specificity	0.59	0.56		Specificity	0.75	0.66
	GSP	0.59	0.55		GSP	0.75	0.66
	GSS	0.55	0.52		GSS	0.75	0.66
	MCC	0.21	0.13		MCC	0.49	0.33
	Kappa	0.19	0.12		Kappa	0.49	0.33

Table 4. Classification results of computerized-conventional (TC) of HI children

Item Set	Metric	ANN	CNN	Item Set	Metric	ANN	CNN
Environmental Sounds	Accuracy	0.76	0.74	Tonal Patterns	Accuracy	0.70	0.78
	Precision	0.78	0.78		Precision	0.70	0.79
	Recall	0.76	0.74		Recall	0.70	0.78
	F1-score	0.76	0.73		F1-score	0.69	0.78
	Specificity	0.76	0.74		Specificity	0.70	0.78
	GSP	0.76	0.74		GSP	0.70	0.78
	GSS	0.75	0.71		GSS	0.69	0.78
	MCC	0.54	0.52		MCC	0.40	0.57
	Kappa	0.52	0.48		Kappa	0.40	0.56

Table 5. Emotion classification results of TD children in computerized and conventional setups

Item Set	Metric	ANN	CNN	Item Set	Metric	ANN	CNN
Computerized - Environmental Sounds (TE)	Accuracy	0.77	0.77	Conventional - Environmental Sounds (CE)	Accuracy	0.75	0.60
	Precision	0.78	0.78		Precision	0.73	0.60
	Recall	0.77	0.77		Recall	0.74	0.62
	F1-score	0.77	0.77		F1-score	0.73	0.59
	Specificity	0.77	0.77		Specificity	0.74	0.62
	GSP	0.77	0.77		GSP	0.73	0.60
	GSS	0.77	0.76		GSS	0.74	0.61
	MCC	0.55	0.55		MCC	0.46	0.22
	Kappa	0.55	0.54		Kappa	0.46	0.20
Computerized - Tonal Patterns (TT)	Accuracy	0.86	0.94	Conventional - Tonal Patterns (CT)	Accuracy	0.95	0.92
	Precision	0.90	0.95		Precision	0.94	0.90
	Recall	0.79	0.93		Recall	0.96	0.93
	F1-score	0.81	0.93		F1-score	0.95	0.91
	Specificity	0.79	0.93		Specificity	0.96	0.93
	GSP	0.83	0.94		GSP	0.95	0.91
	GSS	0.76	0.92		GSS	0.96	0.93
	MCC	0.68	0.87		MCC	0.90	0.83
	Kappa	0.64	0.87		Kappa	0.89	0.83

Table 6. Emotion classification results of HI children in computerized and conventional setups

Item Set	Metric	ANN	CNN	Item Set	Metric	ANN	CNN
Computerized - Environmental Sounds (TE)	Accuracy	0.96	0.98	Conventional - Environmental Sounds (CE)	Accuracy	0.75	0.79
	Precision	0.96	0.98		Precision	0.81	0.85
	Recall	0.95	0.98		Recall	0.75	0.79
	F1-score	0.95	0.98		F1-score	0.74	0.77
	Specificity	0.95	0.98		Specificity	0.75	0.79
	GSP	0.95	0.98		GSP	0.76	0.80
	GSS	0.95	0.98		GSS	0.72	0.75
	MCC	0.91	0.96		MCC	0.55	0.63
	Kappa	0.91	0.95		Kappa	0.50	0.57
Computerized -Tonal Patterns (TT)	Accuracy	0.84	0.97	Conventional - Tonal Patterns (CT)	Accuracy	0.72	0.56
	Precision	0.91	0.98		Precision	0.57	0.54
	Recall	0.76	0.95		Recall	0.63	0.55
	F1-score	0.78	0.96		F1-score	0.60	0.53
	Specificity	0.76	0.95		Specificity	0.63	0.55
	GSP	0.81	0.96		GSP	0.60	0.54
	GSS	0.71	0.95		GSS	0.46	0.47
	MCC	0.65	0.93		MCC	0.26	0.09
	Kappa	0.59	0.92		Kappa	0.26	0.08

CONCLUSION

The study presented in this chapter is a part of the RoboRehab project, aiming to design and develop an affectively aware social robot and a gamified tablet interface to assist children with hearing impairment (Uluer et al., 2020). The tablet setup was used to display the computerized and gamified auditory tests, and the children's physiological data were collected to investigate i) if the physiological data of the HI and TD are separable, ii) if there is an effect of technology in audiology tests and iii) if emotions (positive, negative and neutral) emotions of HI and TD can be recognized. To the best of our knowledge, the research on the evaluation with machine and deep learning classification using physiological data of TD and HI children for computerized vs conventional audiology tests has not been done before.

Two subsets of the test, environmental sounds and tonal patterns were applied to hearing impaired (HI) and typically developed (TD) children in conventional and computerized setups. Machine learning and deep learning models were used to classify the physiological data collected during these tests. It has been noticed that HI and TD children are only distinguishable for the environmental sounds when CNN was used, and tonal pattern tests when ANN was used in computerized tests. Therefore, the emotion classification accuracies for HI and TD groups were calculated separately. The results revealed that TD children's positive and negative emotions (PN) were distinguished when performing the tonal pattern tests in both computerized and conventional setups. On the other hand, the negative and neutral emotions of HI children were distinguishable in environmental sound tests and tonal patterns tests in the computerized test.

In the time of COVID-19 pandemics, there has been a rise in the use of tablet and computer-based versions of otherwise paper-based education and health applications (Uluer et al. 2021). Especially in pandemics, such technology-assisted approaches supported by machine learning methods for rehabilitation will be very helpful for the vulnerable user groups.

Further validation studies with larger samples are needed to evaluate the reliability of these results in future studies. Finally, we aim to extend the use of this system on assistive robots and in clinical settings.

ACKNOWLEDGMENT

This work was supported by the Turkish Academy of Sciences in the scheme of the Outstanding Young Scientist Award (TÜBA-GEBİP); and The Scientific and Technological Research Council of Turkey (TÜBİTAK) [grant number 118E214]. The authors would like to thank collaborating audiologists Talha Cogen and Busra Gokce from Istanbul University Cerrahpasa Medical Faculty, and the computer engineers Koray Oz and Turgut Can Aydinalev from Istanbul Technical University, Game Technologies and Interaction Program who designed and developed the VLT tool, and the computerized test interface for this study and Pınar Uluer from Galatasaray University for their contributions to this study.

REFERENCES

Akshoomoff, N., Newman, E., Thompson, W. K., McCabe, C., Bloss, C. S., Chang, L., Amaral, D. G., Casey, B. J., Ernst, T. M., Frazier, J. A., Gruen, J. R., Kaufmann, W. E., Kenet, T., Kennedy, D. N., Libiger, O., Mostofsky, S., Murray, S. S., Sowell, E. R., Schork, N., ... Jernigan, T. L. (2014). The NIH toolbox cognition battery: Results from a large normative developmental sample (PING). *Neuropsychology*, *28*(1), 1–10. doi:10.1037/neu0000001

Bruno, P., Melnyk, V., & Völckner, F. (2017). Temperature and emotions: Effects of physical temperature on responses to emotional advertising. *International Journal of Research in Marketing*, *34*(1), 302–320. doi:10.1016/j.ijresmar.2016.08.005

Bulagang, A. F., Mountstephens, J., & Wi, J. T. T. (2020). Tuning support vector machines for improving four-class emotion classification in virtual reality (VR) using heart rate features. *Journal of Physics: Conference Series*, *1529*, 052069.

Can, Y. S., Chalabianloo, N., Ekiz, D., & Ersoy, C. (2019). Continuous stress detection using wearable sensors in real life: Algorithmic programming contest case study. *Sensors (Basel)*, *19*(8), 1849. doi:10.3390/s19081849

Choi, J. S., Bang, J. W., Heo, H., & Park, K. R. (2015). Evaluation of fear using nonintrusive measurement of multimodal sensors. *Sensors (Basel)*, *15*(7), 17507–17533. doi:10.3390/s150717507

Choi, Y., Jeon, Y. M., Wang, L., & Kim, K. (2017). A biological signal-based stress monitoring framework for children using wearable devices. *Sensors (Basel)*, *17*(9), 1936. doi:10.3390/s17091936

Cinar Satekin, M., Polat, Z., Çögen, T., Yılar, S., & Cangökçe Yaşar, Ö. (2021). Preliminary Results of the Adaptation of Developmental Test of Auditory Perception (DTAP) to Turkish with Normal Hearing Children and Adolescents. *Archives of Health Science and Research*, *8*(1), 3–9. doi:10.5152/ArcHealthSciRes.2021.20112

Cole, E. B., & Flexer, C. (2007). *Children with Hearing Loss: Developing Listening and Talking Birth to Six* (1st ed.). Plural Publishing Inc.

Dissanayake, T., Rajapaksha, Y., Ragel, R., & Nawinne, I. (2019). An ensemble learning approach for electrocardiogram sensor based human emotion recognition. *Sensors (Basel)*, *19*(20), 4495. doi:10.3390/s19204495

Dzedzickis, A., Kaklauskas, A., & Bucinskas, V. (2020). Human emotion recognition: Review of sensors and methods. *Sensors (Basel)*, *20*(3), 592. doi:10.3390/s20030592

Eisenberg, L. S., Martinez, A. S., & Boothroyd, A. (2007). Assessing auditory capabilities in young children. *International Journal of Pediatric Otorhinolaryngology*, *71*(9), 1339–1350. doi:10.1016/j.ijporl.2007.05.017

Ekman, P. (1992). An argument for basic emotions. *Cognition and Emotion*, *6*(3-4), 169–200. doi:10.1080/02699939208411068

Feng, H., Golshan, M. H., & Mahoor, M. H. (2018). A wavelet-based approach to emotion classification using EDA signals. *Expert Systems with Applications*, *112*, 77–86. doi:10.1016/j.eswa.2018.06.014

Fletcher, R. R., Dobson, K., Goodwin, M. S., Eydgahi, H., Wilder-Smith, O., Fernholz, D., Kuboyama, Y., Hedman, E., Poh, M.-Z., & Picard, R. W. (2010). Icalm: Wearable sensor and network architecture for wirelessly communicating and logging autonomic activity. *IEEE Transactions on Information Technology in Biomedicine*, *14*(2), 215–223. doi:10.1109/TITB.2009.2038692

Garbarino, M., Lai, B. D. M., Picard, R., & Tognetti, S. (2014). Empatica e3 - a wearable wireless multi-sensor device for real-time computerized biofeedback and data acquisition. In 2014 EAI 4th International Conference on Wireless Mobile Communication and Healthcare (MOBIHEALTH) *(pp. 39-42). Academic Press.*

Gonuguntla, V., Shafiq, G., Wang, Y., & Veluvolu, K. C. (2015). Overlapping community detection via bounded nonnegative matrix trifactorization. In 2015 37th Annual International Conference of the IEEE Engineering in Medicine and Biology Society (EMBC) *(pp. 2896-2899). IEEE.*

Goulart, C., Valadao, C., Delisle-Rodriguez, D., Caldeira, E., & Bastos, T. (2019). Emotion analysis in children through facial emissivity of infrared thermal imaging. *PLoS One*, *14*(3), e0212928. doi:10.1371/journal.pone.0212928

Gouverneur, P., Jaworek-Korjakowska, J., Koping, L., Shirahama, K., Kleczek, P., & Grzegorzek, M. (2017). Classification of physiological data for emotion recognition. In International Conference on Artificial Intelligence and Soft Computing *(pp. 619-627). Springer. doi:10.1007/978-3-319-59063-9_55*

Grabowski, K., Rynkiewicz, A., Lassalle, A., Baron-Cohen, S., Schuller, B., Cummins, N., Baird, A., Podgórska-Bednarz, J., Pieniążek, A., & Lucka, I. (2019). Emotional expression in psychiatric conditions: New technology for clinicians. *Psychiatry and Clinical Neurosciences, 73*(2), 50–62. doi:10.1111/pcn.12799

Greco, A., Lanata, A., Citi, V. N. L., Valenza, G., & Scilingo, E. P. (2016). Skin admittance measurement for emotion recognition: A study over frequency sweep. *Electronics (Basel), 5*(3), 46. doi:10.3390/electronics5030046

Gumuslu, E., Barkana Erol, D., & Kose, H. (2020). Emotion recognition using eeg and physiological data for robot-assisted rehabilitation systems. In Proceedings of the 2020 International Conference on Multimodal Interaction, *(pp. 379-387). Academic Press.*

Hassler Hallstedt, M., & Ghaderi, A. (2018). Tablets instead of paper-based tests for young children? Comparability between paper and tablet versions of the mathematical heidelbergerrechen test 1-4. *Educational Assessment, 23*(3), 195–210. doi:10.1080/10627197.2018.1488587

Herdman, S. J., Tusa, R. J., Blatt, P., Suzuki, A., Venuto, P. J., & Roberts, D. (1998). Computerized dynamic visual acuity test in the assessment of vestibular deficits. *Otology & Neurotology, 19*(6), 790–796

Hull, R. (1999). *Aural rehabilitation serving children and adults* (4th ed.). Singular Publishing Group Inc.

Izard, C. E. (2009). Emotion theory and research: Highlights, unanswered questions, and emerging issues. *Annual Review of Psychology, 60*(1), 1–25. doi:10.1146/annurev.psych.60.110707.163539

Jalan, U. (2020). Four-class emotion classification using electrocardiography (ECG) in virtual reality (VR). *International Journal of Advanced Science and Technology, 29*(6), 1523–1529.

Khezri, M., Firoozabadi, M., & Sharafat, A. R. (2015). Reliable emotion recognition system based on dynamic adaptive fusion of forehead biopotentials and physiological signals. *Computer Methods and Programs in Biomedicine, 122*(2), 149–164. doi:10.1016/j.cmpb.2015.07.006

Kikhia, B., Stavropoulos, T. G., Andreadis, S., Karvonen, N., Kompatsiaris, I., Sävenstedt, S., Pijl, M., & Melander, C. (2016). Utilizing a wristband sensor to measure the stress level for people with dementia. *Sensors (Basel), 16*(12), 1989. doi:10.3390/s16121989

Kollins, S. H., DeLoss, D. J., Cañadas, E., Lutz, J., Findling, R. L., Keefe, R. S., & Faraone, S. V. (2020). A novel digital intervention for actively reducing severity of paediatric adhd (stars-adhd): A randomised controlled trial. The Lancet. *Digital Health, 2*(4), 168–178. doi:10.1016/S2589-7500(20)30017-0

Lang, P. J. (1995). The emotion probe: Studies of motivation and attention. *The American Psychologist, 50*(5), 372–385. doi:10.1037/0003-066X.50.5.372

Liu, Y., & Sourina, O. (2014). Transactions on Computational Science XXIII: Special Issue on Cyberworlds (Lecture Notes in Computer Science, 8490) *(2014 ed.). Springer.*

Luciana, M. (2003). Practitioner review: computerized assessment of neuropsychological function in children: clinical and research applications of the Cambridge Neuropsychological Testing Automated Battery (CANTAB). *Journal of Child Psychology and Psychiatry, and Allied Disciplines, 44*(5), 649–663. doi:10.1111/1469-7610.00152

Marin-Morales, J., Higuera-Trujillo, J. L., Greco, A., Guixeres, J., Llinares, C., Scilingo, E. P., Alcañiz, M., & Valenza, G. (2018). Affective computing in virtual reality: Emotion recognition from brain and heartbeat dynamics using wearable sensors. *Scientific Reports*, 8(1), 1–15. doi:10.1038/s41598-018-32063-4

Moore, D. R., Cowan, J. A., Riley, A., Edmondson-Jones, A. M., & Ferguson, M. A. (2011). Development of auditory processing in 6- to 11-yr-old children. *Ear and Hearing*, 32(3), 269–285. doi:10.1097/AUD.0b013e318201c468

Neumann, M. M., & Neumann, D. L. (2019). Validation of a touch screen tablet assessment of early literacy skills and a comparison with a traditional paper-based assessment. *International Journal of Research & Method in Education*, 42(4), 385–398. doi:10.1080/1743727X.2018.1498078

Ollander, S. (2015). Wearable sensor data fusion for human stress estimation *[Ph.D. thesis]. Linköping University.*

Panicker, S. S., & Gayathri, P. (2019). A survey of machine learning techniques in physiology based mental stress detection systems. *Biocybernetics and Biomedical Engineering*, 39(2), 444–469. doi:10.1016/j.bbe.2019.01.004

Plutchik, R. (2001). The nature of emotions: Human emotions have deep evolutionary roots, a fact that may explain their complexity and provide tools for clinical practice. *American Scientist*, 89(4), 344–350. doi:10.1511/2001.4.344

Reynolds, C. R., Voress, J. K., Pearson, A., N. (2008). Developmental test of auditory perception. *Examiner's Manual, PRO-ED.*

Rim, B., Sung, N., Min, S., & Hong, M. (2020). Deep learning in physiological signal data: A survey. *Sensors (Basel)*, 20(4), 969. doi:10.3390/s20040969

Saffran, J. R., Werker, J. F., & Werner, L. A. (2006). In D. Kuhn, R. S. Siegler, D. William, & R. M. Lerner (Eds.), *The infant's auditory world: Hearing, speech and the beginnings of language* (6th ed., pp. 58–108). Handbook of Child Psychology. John Wiley and Sons.

Sanes, D. H., & Woolley, S. M. (2011). A behavioral framework to guide research on central auditory development and plasticity. *Neuron*, 72(6), 912–929. doi:10.1016/j.neuron.2011.12.005

Supratak, A., Wu, D. H. C., Sun, K., & Guo, Y. (2016). Survey on feature extraction and applications of biosignals. In *Machine Learning for Health Informatics* (pp. 161–182). Springer., doi:10.1007/978-3-319-50478-0_8.

The MathWorks. (2020). Matlab (version (r2020a)) [computer software]. https://www.mathworks.com/

Uluer, P., Kose, H., Landowska, A., Zorcec, T., Robins, B., Barkana Erol, D. (2021). Child-robot interaction studies during covid-19 pandemic. *Academic Press.*

Uluer, P., Kose, H., Oz, B. K., & Aydinalev, C. (2020). Towards an affective robot companion for audiology rehabilitation: How does pepper feel today? In 2020 29th IEEE International Conference on Robot and Human Interactive Communication (RO-MAN), *(pp. 567-572). IEEE.*

Van Rossum, F. L., & Drake, G. (2009). *Python 3 reference manual*. Createspace.

Yin, Z., Zhao, M., Wang, Y., Yang, J., & Zhang, J. (2017). Recognition of emotions using multimodal physiological signals and an ensemble deep learning model. *Computer Methods and Programs in Biomedicine*, *140*, 93–110. doi:10.1016/j.cmpb.2016.12.005

KEY TERMS AND DEFINITIONS

Auditory Perception: The ability to identify, interpret, and attach meaning to the sound that is heard.

Classification: Recognizing the states of the categorized objective to solve a grouping, detecting, or stratifying problem.

Computerized Test: A conventional test designed and developed as a computer program via a digitized interface.

Conventional Test: The traditional tests that are manually done with paper-and-pencil formats.

Emotion: The automatically evoked regulation system of the body when a situation is encountered relating to ones' well-being.

Hearing Loss: The partial or complete disability to hear the sound by one or both of ones' ears.

Physiological Signals: Biological markers such as heat, heartbeat, or skin moisture that are collected via sensors on the skin and that change according to people's emotional states.

Chapter 4
Behavior Classification of Egyptian Fruit Bat (Rousettus aegyptiacus) From Calls With Deep Learning

Batuhan Yılmaz
(iD) https://orcid.org/0000-0001-6698-6050
Boğaziçi University, Turkey

Melih Sen
Marmara University, Turkey

Engin Masazade
(iD) https://orcid.org/0000-0002-1871-2378
Marmara University, Turkey

Vedat Beskardes
Istanbul University-Cerrahpasa, Turkey

ABSTRACT

Sensing the environment with passive acoustic sensors has been used as a very useful tool to monitor and quantify the status and changes on biodiversity. In this chapter, the authors aim to classify the social calls (biting, feeding, fighting, isolation, mating protest, and sleeping) of a certain bat species, Egyptian fruit bat, which lives in colonies with thousands of others. Therefore, classification of their calls not only helps us to understand the population dynamics but also helps us to offer distinct environmental management procedures. In this work, the authors use the database previously presented in Prat et al. and present the social call classification results under both classical machine learning techniques and a convolutional neural network (CNN). The numerical results show that CNN improves the classification performance up to 20% as compared to the traditional machine learning approaches when all the call classes are considered. It has also been shown that the classes of aggressive calls, which can sound quite close to each other, can be distinguished with CNN.

DOI: 10.4018/978-1-7998-8686-0.ch004

INTRODUCTION

The bats had separated from other mammals towards the end of the Cretaceous period (~70 million years ago). But main diversification had occurred around 52 million years ago. They are an important order of mammals that have gained the ability to fly like birds and that recognized about 1386 species all over the world with that the second largest order of the mammals (Dietz et al., 2009, Burgin et al., 2018). Bats have ecologically and economically important roles in the ecosystem as predators, prey for vertebrates, hosts for parasites, pollination, seed dispersal, soil fertility, and nutrient distribution, bioindicators, and they serve as a biological control agent for pests (Kasso & Balakrishnan, 2013). Because of ecological and economic importance, all bat species are protected according to Bern Convention in appendices II and III, and some of their conservation statuses are evaluated near threatened, vulnerable, endangered, or critically endangered in the IUCN (International Union for Conservation Nature).

There are 39 bat species living in Turkey (Özkurt & Bulut, 2020). Among 39 bat species in Turkey, there is a special one because of its foraging type. As its name suggests, the Egyptian fruit bat feeds on fruits and it differs from the other 38 insectivorous species. Egyptian fruit bats are considered as important agents for the ecological balance due to their diet. Their preferred meals are seeded fruits and flower nectars such as figs, cherry, plum, Persian lilac, apricots, peaches, apples, citrus plants, bananas, as well as mulberries and dates. In winters, they eat the leaves of carob and figs as well. Egyptian fruit bats have a minor role in pollination, however, when they travel through different locations, they play important role in seed dispersal of their food plants. They leave feces with undigested plant seeds, increasing the spread of plants with enhanced fertility, and impacting the preservation of plant species positively (Al-bayrak et al., 2008; Dietz et al., 2009). Egyptian fruit bats are important for the biodiversity of Turkey, because of being Afro-tropical species reaching the northernmost of its distribution (Benda et al., 2012), and regarding as a separate, endemic in terms of 10% mtDNA divergence from sub-Saharan Populations (DelVaglio et al., 2011). Egyptian fruit bats use echolocation and sights to find their ways or foods during the flights. If the light is sufficient, orientation takes place by sight. Echolocation calls are short-paired clicks and emitted between frequencies from 12 to 70 kHz, and duration 0.3 – 0.5 milliseconds long. Echolocation calls provide much information about bats' ecology and behavior. Furthermore, Egyptian fruit bats are social animals: the colonies may comprise from 50 to 500 individuals in some caves. Thus, that will help us to understand the habitat preference, social relationships, foraging, reproduction, mobility and migration, the anomalies in colonies such as diseases, food shortage, underpopulation, and overpopulation. In this chapter, the authors aim to detect the important behaviors of bats by utilizing deep learning methods on their calls, rather than only finding different species. The obtained results have the potential to enlighten the path for understanding the bats' or other animals' vocal communication and their social interaction.

The rest of this chapter is organized as follows. The next section presents a literature review on classification based on animal calls. Then, the contributions of the chapter with respect to the previous literature are given. After the explanation of the database used in this work and its data processing, two classification approaches are introduced. First, conventional machine learning approaches based on the one-dimensional (1D) features generated from the bat calls are investigated. Then, for the same purpose a deep learning method, i.e., convolutional neural network (CNN) is also considered. Upon the performance comparison between classical machine learning and deep learning techniques, the chapter is finalized with conclusions and a short discussion of future research directions.

BACKGROUND

In general, animal calls are produced on purpose, just like in human communication. Studies show that animals that communicate with sound use their vocal capabilities to create social bonds, threatening an enemy and alerting a threat (Janik & Slater, 2000). To elaborate the meanings of animal calls, environmental sound classification techniques (Blumstein et al., 2011), (Salamon, 2017a), (Mushtaq & Su, 2020) are being increasingly used in many animal studies. The main goal of environmental sound classification is to find out the distinctive sound sources from the complex audio input, such as car engines, sirens; including even some domestic animals in a city: dogs, birds, etc. Environmental sound classification becomes critically important in the industry to improve the efficiency of operations. For example, considering the livestock industry, Bishop et al. (2019) extracted features from environmental sounds and classify the sources around a barn to assess animal welfare. As a context-centric approach, Jung et al. (2021) utilized a CNN-based model for tracking the current situation of cattle, with respect to four main categories of actions.

In the literature, different approaches for animal sound classification are available (Kvsn et al., 2020; Molnar et al., 2008; Lee et al., 2015). The first and conventional method is machine learning which is broadly used in speech recognition, anomaly detection, and image classification which relies on features generated from the time and frequency domain representations of sounds of interest. As an early example (Molnar et al., 2008), used machine learning to classify the context of Hungarian sheepdog barks, divided into seven situations, such as "Stranger", "Play", "Fight" etc. (Lee et al., 2015) utilized support vector machines (SVM) to find out stress state of laying hens by the help of extracted sound features in both time and frequency. As state-of-the-art methods suggest, extracting different types of features may provide more distinct classification and less redundancy, such as log spectrogram, mel-spectrogram, mel-frequency cepstral coefficients (MFCC), gammatone frequency cepstral coefficients (GFCC) (Blumstein et al., 2011). For bird species classification, advanced feature extraction methods from bird calls or bird songs and classifiers were presented in (Umapathy et al., 2007; Jancovic & Köküer, 2019; Somervuo et al., 2006; Kim et al., 2015, Bastas, 2012, Mirzaei et. al., 2012, Vidaña-Vila, 2020).

Recently, deep learning methods were also adopted in animal call classification due to their high accuracy rates and adaptability. With convolutional neural networks (CNN), it is possible to get rid of the curse of dimensionality, solving more complex communication between features (Kuo & Sloan, 2005). In CNN, the model is typically trained with different combinations of preprocessed spectrogram images as features to increase the extraction efficiency. As an example, to detect whale calls, deep learning algorithms based on CNN have been proposed in (Ibrahim, 2018), (Lu et.al., 2020), (Vickers et.al., 2020). Furthermore, using CNN, classification of bird species based on their calls or songs have also been presented in (Salamon, 2017b), (Stowell, 2019), (Lostanlen et al., 2019), (Xie et.al., 2019), (Narasimhan, 2017), (Bold et. al., 2019), (Chandu et. al., 2020), (Incze et. al., 2018), (Huang & Basanta, 2021). Note that the above literature considers the availability of the audio files at a central processor for classification. On the other hand, the work presented in (Nagy, et. al., 2020) and (Disabato, 2021) enables CNN classification on edge devices as well.

Rather than the classification of interested species, there are additional studies that detect animal behavior based on vocal activity. In (Stowell, 2017), feature extraction and classification using a Hidden Markov Model (HMM) was presented to classify 19 different activities of Eurasian jackdaws. In (Thiebault, 2019), four different actions (on water, taking off, flying, before diving) of a foraging seabird were classified with a Random Forest classifier. Determination of bird behaviors (danger, feeding, etc.)

from their call pattern in the spectrogram was shown for the North American bird species (Pieplow, 2019). The studies which involve behavior characterization have been typically performed for domesticated animals such as cattle, sheep, cats, and dogs, which have little or no interaction with wilderness (Jung et al., 2021; Bishop et al., 2019; Pandeya et al., 2018; Kim et al., 2018, Ntalampiras, 2021). As an example, in (Ntalampiras, 2021), individual vocalizations were classified to determine the mood of a cat (i.e., boredom, anger, etc.) using a CNN-based deep learning model.

Specifically, for bat species classification, state-of-the-art feature extraction and classification methods have been using echolocation calls for a long time (Herr et al. (1997) and Mirzaei et al. (2011, 2012); Parsons, 2000; Armitage, 2010). Recently, CNN models have also been used to classify different bat species based on their echolocation calls as well (Aodha et al., 2018; Hu et al., 2020; Paumen, 2021; Chen et. al., 2020; Beauvois & Dierckx, 2021; Tabak et. al., 2021; Schwab et al., 2021). Rather than using a centralized processor to classify bat species, in (Zualkernan et al., 2020a), (Zualkernan et al., 2020b) implementation of the CNN classifiers on edge devices were also presented.

Due to the importance of training data in machine learning, dataset studies are equivalently important to have a better inference performance. There are several studies for creating an audio dataset. For instance, Piczak et al. (2015) published a 50-class dataset of environmental sounds by the means of three general groups: transient, harmonically strong, and harmonically less structured sounds. Another example is the CLO-43SD dataset by Lostanlen et al. (2019), also used by BirdVoxDetect, which is a large dataset for avian flight calls including meaningful context about birds.

THE IDEA BEHIND BAT BEHAVIOUR CLASSIFICATION

For bat studies, despite that the echolocation calls have been studied for a long time, social calls are different, and they have been neglected so far as compared to echolocation calls (Vernes et al., 2019). Echolocation calls can be emitted at frequencies as high as 200 kHz whereas social calls can have a frequency as low as 1 kHz (Vernes et al., 2019). Like humans, birds, or elephants, bats are also highly social species and exhibit various degrees of social complexity. Such social calls can be emitted for reproduction, feeding, parent-offspring union, territorial defense, or maintaining group integration. The ability to classify bat behavior automatically based on their social calls without human intervention provides researchers invaluable information to monitor the entire population, to understand the population dynamics, and opens new opportunities to propose effective environment management or protection strategies (Winifred et al., 2020). As an example, the ability to differentiate nestling bats from their parents indicates that the bat population has been reproductive, and the environment is self-sufficient to support necessary conditions for reproduction. Furthermore, bats may emit aggressive calls to find space, capture food, or for reproduction. Therefore, the ability to segregate aggressive calls such as mating protest and fighting helps the researchers better understand the instant population dynamics. Additionally, the ability to detect feeding calls from the other calls may indicate that the population habitat is rich in food resources, therefore the fighting calls may originate from mating desire or space capturing.

Since bats, birds, elephants, whales, humans, etc. are all social species, understanding animal communication can teach us to understand the human language (Vernes et al., 2019). Further understanding animal behavior may indirectly help us to understand human actions better. On the other hand, understanding human behavior (or emotions) from a speech signal is a completely different and emerging body of research area (Wang et al., 2015; Deshmukh et al., 2019; Xie et al., 2019; (Mustaqeem et al., 2020;

Lotfian et al., 2019; Sun et al., 2020) and out of the scope of this chapter. The purpose of this chapter is to understand bat behaviors from their social calls to help humans to be cautious of some situations beforehand. As an example, if the sleeping calls of bats can be separated from other calls, it can be concluded that the bat population has a safe shelter (i.e., cave). Therefore, before a road construction or a mining project, such caves need to be well preserved. Furthermore, in a habitat rich in food resources, the bats may emit more feeding calls and less aggressive calls. A decline in feeding calls and an increase in aggressive calls may indicate a food shortage in the habitat and there might be a risk that the entire population may leave their habitat soon. Note that bats are important in the food chain and most of the bat species typically consume insects which can be harmful to agricultural products. Since Egyptian fruit bats consume fruits, they play important role in seed dispersal of their food plants and hence increase the spread of plants with enhanced fertility. Furthermore, like manure, guano is a highly effective fertilizer due to its exceptionally high content of nitrogen, phosphate, and potassium which are the key nutrients essential for plant growth. If the bat population leaves its habitat, there can be serious consequences on the agricultural production of the vicinity. Therefore, interpreting bat behavior based on their social calls has a great benefit to making proactive decisions in agricultural planning.

In this work, rather than classifying the bat species based on their echolocation calls, behaviors of a certain bat species, i.e., Egyptian fruit bat have been classified. In the work of Gadziola (2012), four different behaviors (low aggression, medium aggression, high aggression, and appeasement) of Big Brown Bats were classified using features generated from bat calls and Electrocardiogram monitoring. The purpose of this chapter is to understand whether the calls of Egyptian fruit bats under different behaviors (biting, feeding, fighting, isolation, mating protest, sleeping) are separable or not using both conventional machine learning and a recent deep learning approach, CNN. Classification of such behaviors provides the opportunity of understanding deeper context semantics from the bat sounds and helps researchers to better understand population dynamics such as nesting conditions, gender balance, fertility and reproductivity, and feeding. The authors hope that this work will help paving the way to preserve the wildlife with more ingenuine decision-making instead of empirical work. Moreover, humans would use fewer resources to take action and interfere less with other species while a specific one is being ameliorated. Consequently, this work is expected to have the potential assisting zoologists or other people in similar disciplines by putting deep learning technology into a good use.

In this work, the Egyptian fruit bat (Rousettus aegyptiacus) database presented in (Prat et al., 2017) is used. The dataset involves approximately 90,000 annotated bat call recordings with thirteen different contexts, including additional pre-vocalization and post-vocalization actions of the roost members individually (Prat et al., 2017). The bat call audio data generally consists of a few seconds with different lengths, and it is sampled with a frequency of 250 kHz (Prat et al., 2017). As the first approach, 1-D features from raw bat social calls are considered as input, such as zero-crossing rate, root-mean-square energy spectral centroid, etc. Since the extracted one-dimensional features consist of noncomplex variables, simple classifiers are applied as a first step. For this purpose, common machine learning (ML) algorithms have been employed in favor of acquiring rapid results, such as logistic regression, k-nearest neighbors (KNN, with K=5), AdaBoost, support vector machines (SVM), naïve Bayes, and linear discriminant analysis (LDA) (Wright, 1995; Kramer et al., 2013; Schapire, 2013; Hearst et al., 1998; Rish, 2001; Izenman, 2013). Further steps include putting a CNN model into use and comparing it with the initially obtained ML results, with the help of a different feature: spectrogram. The main reason for using a spectrogram image is to widen the span of obtainable low-level features. In this work, the CNN model has been adopted from the "CNN Fast pipeline" previously presented by Aodha et al (2018), which was used to detect bat echolocation calls in noisy audio recordings.

The experiments are performed in Google Colab platform, which provides suitable computing and coding environment. In this work, two different configurations for Colab have been used. The 1-D models utilized CPU-based runtime (Intel(R) Xeon(R) CPU @ 2.20GHz), whereas the CNN model has been put GPU session into use (Nvidia K80/T4).

Data Preparation and Preprocessing

In this section, it is presented that how the data is processed to be used for classification pipelines. In the dataset, labels are divided into thirteen different classes of behavior context. In Table 1, a list of classes with pre-vocalization and post-vocalization actions are shown as follows:

Table 1. List of contexts and behaviors with their numbers (Prat et al., 2017). Used classes in this work are indicated with "*".

ID	Context/Behavior	Number of recordings
Context		
0	Unknown	640
1	Separation	504
2	Biting*	1788
3	Feeding*	6683
4	Fighting*	7963
5	Grooming	383
6	Isolation*	5714
7	Kissing	362
8	Landing	16
9	Mating protest*	2338
10	Threat-like	1065
11	General	29627
12	Sleeping*	33997
Pre-vocalization action		
0	Unknown	13553
1	Fly in	3909
2	Present	158164
3	Crawl in	6534
Post-vocalization action		
0	Unknown	13437
1	Cower	77
2	Fly away	6745
3	Stay	155485
4	Crawl away	6416

Figure 1. Visualization of raw sound waves. The contexts are stated as follows: biting (a), feeding (b), fighting (c), isolation (d), mating protest (e), sleeping (f).

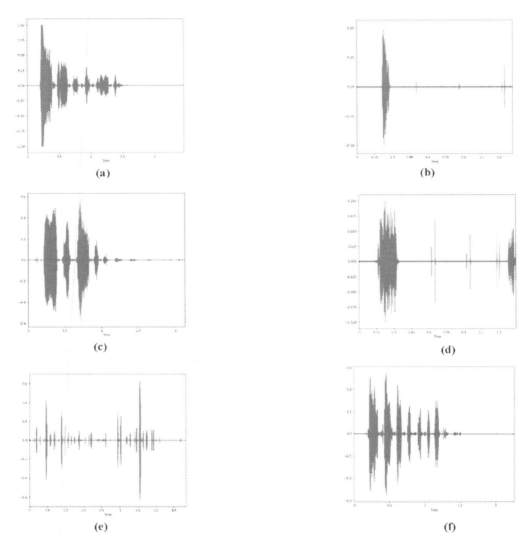

In Figure 1, several waveforms of sound examples from different classes are shown. At first glance, there is no significant difference between the sound data for human perception. The decision of choosing the right classes is given with respect to two aspects. The first one is the relevancy of comparison. Due to the different scenarios of classification, the most usable classes are needed to be selected for real-life conditions. For instance, if it is too little or no isolation sounds are present from the colony, there would be a risk of population decline or it means that some factors may negatively affect the reproduction success of adult members of the colony, which can be also supported with the occurrence of mating protest actions (Dasman, 1981). Additionally, if feeding sounds are emitted less than expected and biting/fighting action is relatively high, it would indicate a famine through the colony. The next topic is choosing a proper data distribution for classification tasks. If a generalized learning scheme is desired, each class should have a sufficient number of samples and the total number of samples from each class needs to be as close as possible. Relying on this purpose, when a classification procedure is being evaluated, the class with the lowest number of samples defines the number of samples from the other classes. The selected classes give us information about the population dynamics. For example, biting, feeding, and fighting are related to interspecific competition in the colony. Mating protests also show us competition for reproduction (Dietz et al., 2009).

As a result of considerations for possible use cases such as low-level acquisition systems, sound samples are picked, trimmed, and clipped to fit 1.5 seconds for providing fixed-size input to the system. To preserve the equal size for each input data, the sound data have been zero-padded to match the number of 375,000 (where 1.5 sec is the call duration and 250 kHz is the sampling rate) samples. This approach enables the CNN model to benefit from more data from the dataset Since the original data was captured under isolated conditions and necessary noise cancellation processes were completed, it is not needed to add further denoising in the pipeline in this work (Prat et al., 2017).

Feature Extraction

Low-level features of audio data are highly dependent on mathematical derivations of the input signals. In this work, several linear and spectral features have been examined.

The first and the most basic feature is zero-crossing rate (ZCR). As the name implies, the output is the number of times that the sound waves intersect with zero line. The next feature is root mean square energy (RMSE). It is a simple function of the energy of the signal x, with N is the number of samples as,

$$RMSE(x) = \sqrt{\frac{1}{N} \sum_n |x[n]|^2} \tag{1}$$

Additionally, spectral features are attached to the 1-D data pipeline. Table 2 shows the parameters used for short-time Fourier transform (STFT).

Table 2. Parameters for FFT

Entity	Value
Sampling rate	250000
Number of FFTs	2048
Hop length	512
Window length	1024

Spectral centroid is highly correlated with the "brightness" of the audio signal, which would represent distinct information about different types of bat actions (Grey & Gordon, 1978). $x(n)$ and $f(n)$ indicate weighted frequency value and the center frequency of bin n respectively. Then, spectral centroid can be basically defined as a weighted mean of signal frequencies as,

$$Centroid(x) = f_c = \frac{\sum_{n=0}^{N-1} f(n)x(n)}{\sum_{n=0}^{N-1} x(n)} \qquad (2)$$

Spectral bandwidth is the difference between the lowest and the highest frequencies, which is expected to give the difference of the vocal range of Egyptian fruit bats (Genzel et al., 2019). Spectral bandwidth can be computed from,

$$Bandwidth = \left(\sum_n S(n)\left(f(n) - f_c\right)^p \right)^{\frac{1}{p}} \qquad (3)$$

where $S(n)$ indicates the spectral magnitude. It should be noted that p is selected as 2.

Finally, the spectral roll-off shows the frequency value of which a specified percentage of the overall spectral energy. In this work, the roll-off threshold is adjusted to 85%. Appendix 1 further presents the visualizations of the features under different classes.

Figure 2. Diagram for 1-D feature classification pipeline

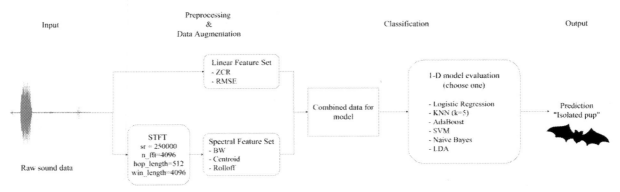

In Figure 2, the proposed model for 1-D feature evaluation and classification is shown as follows.

Getting Data Ready

To make the data usable for the machine learning models, means of spectral features are calculated over the entire 1.5-seconds of the audio file. The main reason for this adjustment is to reduce the amount of data as much as possible, thus reducing computational complexity, training, and evaluation speed.

Towards the decision of which classes are separable using the 1-D low features, i.e., ZCR, RMSE, spectral centroid, spectral bandwidth and spectral roll-off, principal component analysis (PCA) is used (Jolliffe, 2005). The PCA has been held both for 2-D and 3-D projections as shown in Figure 3 and Figure 4 respectively. The labels have approximately 1000 data each.

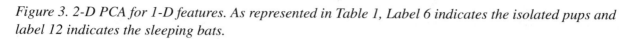

Figure 3. 2-D PCA for 1-D features. As represented in Table 1, Label 6 indicates the isolated pups and label 12 indicates the sleeping bats.

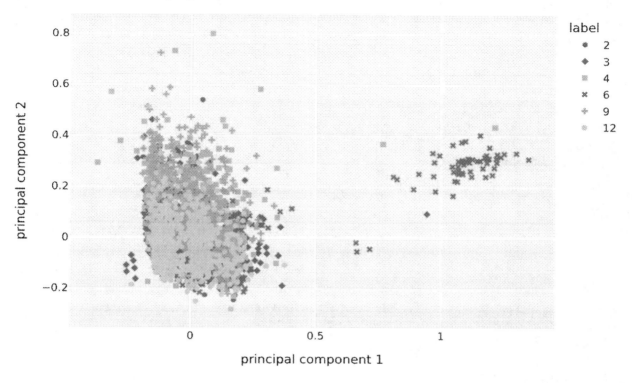

Figure 4. 3-D PCA for 1-D features

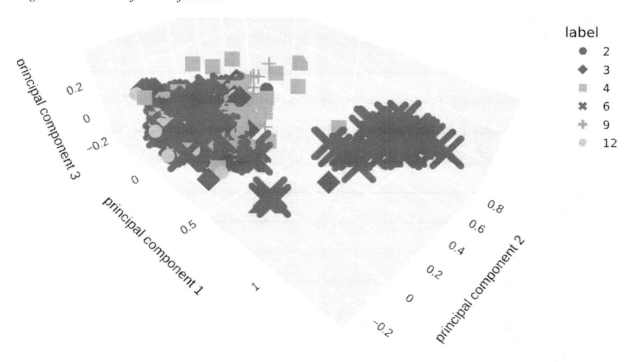

Numerical results in Figure 3 and Figure 4 indicate that PCA gives the result of significant discrimination of pups in an isolated environment, meaning that the model has a better distinction ability to choose between a newborn pup and an adult bat. Thus, it is expected from the model that the performance of finding juvenile bats is better than the others. This phenomenon can be explained by the vocal capabilities of juvenile bats (Genzel et al., 2019) On the other hand, it is not straightforward to infer the distinction of other classes which motivate the need for advanced learning structures. As an example, sleeping action can be different than other aggressive attitude actions. Aggressive behavior is a pattern that generally arises from the sharing of resources (mate, food, place, nesting area, etc.) among individuals of the same species (Öber, 2007). Behaviors, for which the dataset has the most data for evaluation, such as biting, feeding, fighting, and mating protests; include mostly aggressive ones. Naturally, those sounds can be perceived quite close to each other.

Spectrogram

Getting a valid classification result from the given data is important. To fulfill this purpose, getting the most out of the information plays a fundamental role in the way of achieving better accuracy. There are several practices that use spectrograms to classify different audio sources (Pavan, 2008). With the help of CNN, it is possible to find out the specific features of specific entities, which is saving time and effort to determine the entries manually. Under the consideration of fast and reliable generation of spectrogram data, the effort has been handled with the help of Python libraries Librosa and SPAFE (McFee et al., 2015; SPAFE).

Obtaining Spectrogram

As a first step, depending on the spectrogram type, the magnitude of short-time Fourier transform (STFT) is calculated to extract the spectral features with different parameters. Besides, for all spectrogram types, Hanning type windowing is used.
In Table 3, the STFT parameters for the calculations of every type of spectrogram are given.

Table 3. STFT parameters used for spectrogram types

	Linear spectrogram	Power spectrogram	Power spectrogram w/ TE	Mel-spectrogram
Sampling rate (treatment)	250000	250000	2500	250000
Number of FFTs	512	4096	4096	4096
Hop length	256	512	512	512
Window length	512	4096	4096	4096
Number of mel-filter banks	-	-	-	150

The sampling rate of each raw audio file in the dataset is 250 kHz. Nevertheless, to perform a time expansion operation, the sampling rate is treated as the fraction of 100 of the actual value.

An audio wave example is picked from an isolation group to show the similarities and differences between the spectrogram options. In Figure 5, different spectrogram images of the example specimen are shown, and in Figure 6, the CNN structure including the preprocessing steps is shown.

Figure 5. Visualization of spectrograms ('files101/120603001628934346.WAV'). The contexts are stated as follows: Linear Spectrogram (a), Power Spectrogram (b), Power Spectrogram \w Time Expansion (c), Mel-spectrogram (d). It should be noted that the black regions are the result of zero-padding for equalizing the sample numbers for every input.

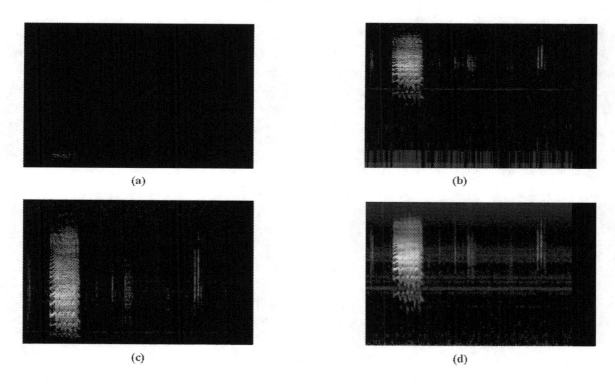

Figure 6. Flowchart of the operations used in the deep learning approach

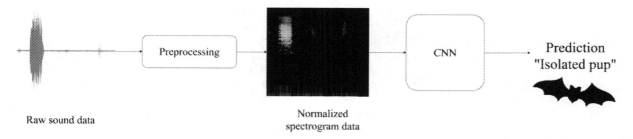

The final outputs of both the 1-D ML and the CNN models are given as one-hot encoded vectors of classes. It should be noted that the output is not given as an image, but the detected behavior is in a binary vector form with the detected class as 1 and all the other classes are 0. With this method, the evaluation of the output will become more expressive and understandable. In Appendix 2, different spectrogram types (linear spectrogram, power spectrogram, power spectrogram with time expansion, and mel-spectrogram) are presented for the six classes considered in this work.

Spectrogram Images and CNN Structure

Due to the limited resources of computation, data acquisition and feature extraction pipelines take significant computational resources. In order to overcome the bottleneck of heavy feature extraction and data preprocessing, one of the measures is saving the data in Pandas data frames, which is a database library, as clusters of pickle (.pkl) files to provide faster access to the variables.

In Table 4, a comparison for elapsed spectrogram image extraction time for a single sample audio is presented, where extracting the Mel-spectrogram is the fastest one compared to the other spectrogram types.

Table 4. Comparison of feature extraction time for different spectrogram types

	Linear spec.	Power spec.	Power spec. w/ TE	Mel–spec.
Time per image	0.42 seconds	1.75 seconds	1.77 seconds	0.35 seconds

Figure 7 shows the preprocessing operations. After the spectrogram image conversion, images are represented in four channels, (144,144,4) due to the nature of the conversion function "savefig", which saves the spectrogram into a PNG file (Hunter, 2007). It should also be noted that the image is saved with Viridis colormap. Despite that, the concerns of the size of the model and memory are valid. To fit the needs of the proposed CNN layer structure, the shape of the image has been formed into a square. The size of the image is specified as (144,144) where it is observed that slight changes in image size do not affect the classification performance. Hence, the number of channels has been reduced to convert the image into grayscale, saving one-fourth of the required storage.

Figure 7. Flowchart of the operations used in the preprocessing block before feeding into CNN

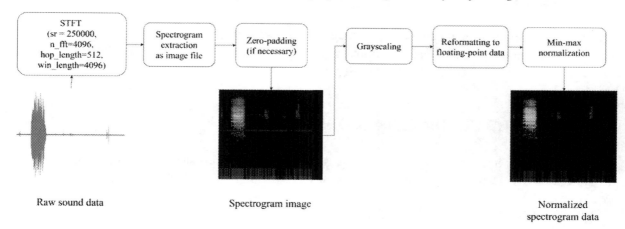

In the proposed CNN block, there are 9 layers in total, including 2-D convolution, max-pooling, dropout, dense, and flattening layers. The detailed CNN structure is shown in Figure 8 below

Figure 8. CNN Structure

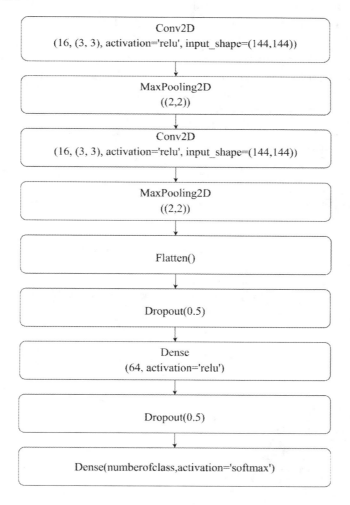

Train-Test Split

The optimum training-validation split has been defined as 80% for training and 20% for validation where it is also observed that slight changes on training-validation split do not affect the classification performance. Further performance comparison of a different distribution has been discussed in Results section.

SOLUTIONS AND RECOMMENDATIONS

In this section, the authors present the classification results based on conventional machine learning with low-level 1-D features and deep learning with spectrogram images. Calls of the following actions are classified:

- **Biting (2), Feeding (3), Fighting (4), Isolation (6), Mating Protest (9), Sleeping (12):** Evaluation of all selected classes, which results in the most generalized classifier.
- **Biting (2), Feeding (3), Fighting (4), Isolation (6), Mating Protest (9):** Selected to find out the differences between all non-sleeping actions among the Egyptian fruit bat colony excluding the sleeping class.
- **Biting (2), Feeding (3), Fighting (4), Isolation (6):** Selected to find out the differences between calls without mating-protest ones, where mating protest is typically emitted by females.
- **Biting (2), Feeding (3), Fighting (4):** Selected to find out the differences between aggression calls of adult bats.
- **Biting (2) vs. Feeding (3):** Selected to find out the difference between biting and feeding calls,
- **Biting (2) vs. Isolation (6):** Selected to find out the difference between biting and isolation calls, where biting is an aggressive call, and isolation is emitted by juveniles.
- **Biting (2) vs. Mating Protest (9):** Selected to find out the difference between biting and mating protest actions where male bats can bite females before the mating request (Dowd, 2020).
- **Fighting (4) vs. Mating Protest (9):** Selected to find out the difference between mating protest and fighting, which are both aggressive acts where fighting is mostly emitted by male, where mating protest is mostly emitted by females.
- **Sleeping (12) vs. other five actions:** Selected to understand the sleeping and nonsleeping activeness of the colony.

Train-Test Split

Three different data distributions have been tested upon both 1-D and CNN inference accuracy. In Table 5, the results of 70-30, 80-20, and 90-10 are shown as follows:

Table 5. Comparison of accuracy results of different train-test data ratio

		Train-test split		
		70-30	**80-20**	**90-10**
KNN	**Accuracy**	0.429	0.424	0.424
CNN	**Loss**	1.048	1.048	1.012
	Accuracy	0.617	0.620	0.619

Results in Table 5 show no significant effect of a different distribution. Additionally, 80%-20% train-test data distribution has been experimented as the common practice within the literature (Schwab et al., 2021). To generalize the results, audio samples are shuffled to randomly change the input distribution of samples.

Classification Results with 1-D Features

In this section, the classification performance of the machine learning models using low-level 1-D features are investigated. The experiments for the models are handled with a different selection of behavior classes. Except for the sleeping versus all classification, each label has approximately 1000 individual data. Additionally, the effect of the labeled previous and post vocalization actions of the bats are also incorporated. In Table 6, the obtained results are presented.

Table 6. Results of ML models on extracted one-dimensional features

	Accuracy											
	Logistic Regression		KNN		AdaBoost		SVM		Naïve Bayes		LDA	
Classes (See Table 1)	w/o pre+post voc.	With pre+post voc.	w/o pre+post voc.	With pre+post voc.	w/o pre+post voc.	With pre+post voc.	w/o pre+post voc.	with pre+post voc.	w/o pre+post voc.	with pre+post voc.	w/o pre+post voc.	with pre+post voc.
2-3-4-6-9-12	0.328	0.408	0.349	0.424	0.367	0.422	0.291	0.429	0.295	0.360	0.323	0.414
2-3-4-6-9	0.432	0.514	0.474	0.561	0.431	0.549	0.377	0.433	0.392	0.472	0.411	0.516
2-3-4-6	0.461	0.628	0.576	0.657	0.555	0.648	0.533	0.624	0.396	0.554	0.453	0.620
2-3-4	0.573	0.564	0.618	0.632	0.624	0.607	0.587	0.579	0.581	0.528	0.555	0.574
2-3	0.712	0.743	0.771	0.812	0.743	0.800	0.557	0.733	0.674	0.731	0.743	0.786
2-6	0.547	0.824	0.827	0.919	0.778	0.907	0.740	0.895	0.559	0.898	0.632	0.821
2-9	0.760	0.700	0.756	0.723	0.782	0.733	0.675	0.634	0.773	0.481	0.768	0.707
4-9	0.569	0.648	0.561	0.676	0.604	0.622	0.529	0.575	0.556	0.557	0.579	0.601
12-non12	0.566	0.629	0.597	0.626	0.615	0.643	0.444	0.426	0.521	0.593	0.575	0.633

The results show that the KNN model has the best perception ability with the extracted low-level features. Therefore, in further sections, KNN is used as a benchmark to compare the classification accuracy of the CNN model. Numerical results in Table 6 also show that including the pre-vocalization and post-vocalization actions has a significant improvement on the performance of the classification model.

In Table 7, evaluation results on KNN are elaborated in detail for all the six classes considered in this work. The first distinctive result is that, as can be seen from the F1 score, the isolation class is the best perceptible class among the other ones. This result matches with the previous PCA results, justifying that bat pups develop a spectrally different sound signal which is easier to separate from adult bat sounds (Genzel et al., 2019). On the other hand, the determination of sleeping cluster by this 1-D model is the worst one as the perception of other classes.

Table 7. KNN results for all available classes in the prepared dataset

	Biting	Feeding	Fighting	Isolation	Mating Protest	Sleeping
Biting	75	21	18	3	18	34
Feeding	29	93	18	17	26	14
Fighting	40	39	73	3	51	16
Isolation	9	27	6	158	5	8
Mating Protest	37	29	37	0	74	15
Sleeping	79	40	23	9	19	34
Precision	0.279	0.373	0.417	0.832	0.383	0.281
Recall	0.444	0.472	0.329	0.742	0.385	0.167
F1 Score	0.342	0.417	0.368	0.784	0.384	0.209
Accuracy	0.424					

Since the sounds emitted by sleeping bats are the hardest ones to distinguish, performing a more distinguished binary classification scheme for sleeping and non-sleeping bat sounds would provide a wider resolution of the signals. The total number of samples are increased by treating the other labels as non-sleeping instances. Before the train-test split, the sleeping class and the others consist of approximately 5000 instances each. In Table 8, the findings of the experiment are shown. The results indicate that the detection of a sleeping cluster changes positively, but still does not help to find the dormant bat sounds in an effective way. In the CNN part, the same experiment is expected to give better classification results.

Table 8. Results for sleeping and non-sleeping bat sounds

	Sleeping	Non-sleeping
Sleeping	577	453
Non-sleeping	347	606
Precision	0.572	0.624
Recall	0.636	0.560
F1 Score	0.602	0.591
Accuracy	0.597	

Further results about the confusion matrices and evaluation metrics between different classes using KNN have been given in Appendix 3.

Classification Results with Spectrogram Features - All Classes

Since the decision of the type of spectrogram plays a fundamental role in increasing accuracy, the best spectrogram type should be decided first for the rest of the experiments. In Table 9, the results for different spectral image types are shown.

Table 9. Comparison of CNN accuracy including confusion matrices, for all available actions

Classes		Biting	Feeding	Fighting	Isolation	Mating Protest	Sleeping
Linear Spectrogram	Precision	0.237	0.65	0.708	0.968	0.594	0
	Recall	0.934	0.131	0.263	0.934	0.303	0
	F1 Score	0.378	0.218	0.383	0.951	0.401	0
	Loss	1.224					
	Accuracy	0.428					
Power Spectrogram	Precision	0.318	0.765	0.707	0.958	0.655	0.459
	Recall	0.741	0.623	0.572	0.919	0.459	0.174
	F1 Score	0.445	0.687	0.632	0.938	0.540	0.253
	Loss	1.074					
	Accuracy	0.583					
Power Spectrogram (TE)	Precision	0.345	0.731	0.673	0.954	0.657	0.475
	Recall	0.761	0.588	0.552	0.954	0.494	0.194
	F1 Score	0.475	0.652	0.606	0.954	0.564	0.276
	Loss	1.003					
	Accuracy	0.592					
Mel-Spectrogram	Precision	0.365	0.744	0.779	0.968	0.605	0.571
	Recall	0.782	0.643	0.619	0.944	0.540	0.185
	F1 Score	0.498	0.690	0.689	0.956	0.570	0.279
	Loss	1.004					
	Accuracy	0.620					

When the classification results are examined, all spectrogram extraction methods except linear spectrogram share relatively close results, and mel-spectrogram surpasses the others by the means of accuracy and loss. It should be noted that the mel-spectrogram provides better accuracy than the others. Moreover, as previously stated in Table 4, extraction of mel-spectrogram is the fastest option, which leads the proposed work on top of this feature.

Table 10. CNN results for all available classes in the prepared dataset

	Biting	Feeding	Fighting	Isolation	Mating Protest	Sleeping
Biting	154	10	3	1	19	10
Feeding	50	128	4	3	10	4
Fighting	37	13	120	1	15	8
Isolation	9	1	1	187	0	0
Mating Protest	69	7	10	0	107	5
Sleeping	103	13	16	1	26	36
Precision	0.365	0.744	0.779	0.969	0.605	0.571
Recall	0.781	0.643	0.619	0.944	0.540	0.185
F1 Score	0.498	0.690	0.690	0.957	0.571	0.279
Loss	1.00					
Accuracy	0.620					

Table 10 shows that when all six classes are considered, biting, feeding, fighting and isolation are mostly correctly classified, and the number of correctly classified samples are increased as compared to KNN, which has been given in Table 7. On the other hand, numerical results also show that some of the mating protest calls and most of the sleeping calls are incorrectly classified as biting. Nevertheless, for all the considered classes, the accuracy of CNN is obtained as 0.620 whereas in Table 7, the accuracy of KNN is seen as only 0.424.

Classification Results with Spectrogram Features - Sleeping vs. Non-Sleeping

As mentioned in the 1-D evaluation section and Table 10, the accuracy of finding sleeping bats is harder to maintain. The corresponding CNN model is run on the same data distribution as in the 1-D classification task. In this case, mel-spectrogram of the raw data is put into the evaluation pipeline. About 5000 sleeping class data is used versus biting, feeding, fighting, isolation, and mating protest classes are labeled as non-sleeping class, which are also about 5000 mel-spectrogram data in total. In Table 11, the results are introduced as follows.

Table 11. CNN evaluation results for sleeping and non-sleeping classes.

	Non-sleeping	Sleeping
Non-sleeping	688	298
Sleeping	224	752
Precision	0.754	0.716
Recall	0.698	0.770
F1 Score	0.725	0.742
Loss	0.503	
Accuracy	0.734	

The CNN results show that the accuracy of the sleeping class is relatively better than the results of the 1-D classification. Thus, it can be said that choosing between the dormant and the non-dormant bats provides more reasonable results with this CNN method. Nevertheless, among the 2-class classification tasks, it has the least accuracy.

Comparison of Results

All stated classification tasks are performed on both one-dimensional lower-level features and more sophisticated mel-spectrogram images with their suitable decision-making algorithms. The main comparison has been held with CNN and the best performing machine learning model, KNN. In Table 12, both methods are put in one-to-one comparison with respect to different combinations of vocalization actions. When the sleeping class (class 12) is excluded, the classification accuracies of the other classes are significantly improved in CNN as compared to KNN. The success of the classification model is highly prone to vocalization classes that are hard to distinguish, such as sleeping. These classes pull down the precision of the generalized model. The other subsequent results have been procured to create more specific classifiers to find out the contribution of the classes individually. Thus, it would be more reasonable that considering the two-class classification results within the scope of usability on more specific tasks.

Table 12. Comparative table for KNN and CNN results

	Accuracy		
	1-D ML (KNN)	**CNN**	**Improvement (%)**
2-3-4-6-9-12	0.424	0.620	+19.6
12 – (2,3,4,6,9)	0.597	0.734	+13.7
2-3-4-6-9	0.561	0.742	+18.1
2-3-4-6	0.657	0.822	+16.5
2-3-4	0.632	0.803	+17.1
2-3	0.812	0.881	+6.9
2-6	0.919	0.977	+5.8
2-4	0.798	0.898	+10.0
3-9	0.775	0.892	+11.7
2-9	0.723	0.782	+5.9
4-9	0.676	0.832	+15.6

When all behaviors are included in the model (i.e.: 2,3,4,6,9,12), the success of distinguishing the behavior may seem relatively low as compared to other selections. On the other hand, when the increment of accuracy from KNN to CNN is taken under consideration, the greatest impact is achieved when all six-class models are considered. For the large number of classes, it is hard to find features to distinguish different classes, on the other hand, CNN determines the best filter and neural network weights based on the training data. Therefore, the improvement of CNN with respect to KNN is achieved 19.6%. When the sleeping class is compared with a combination of other non-sleeping classes, the performance of CNN is still relatively low (0.734). On the other hand, CNN still improves the performance with respect to KNN by 13.7%. When the sleeping call is discarded from other active calls, (i.e.: 2,3,4,6,9) that is when the bats are awake, defined 1D features cannot fully capture the difference behind five classes and like the first case, CNN improves the classification accuracy by 18.1%.

Note that classes biting (2), feeding (3), fighting (4), mating protest (9) may reflect aggressive behavior, and isolation (6) is mostly emitted by juvenile bats. Isolation provides clear information about the juveniles and the degree of development of the population. For example, a decrease in the number of sounds in isolation indicates a declining population, whereas an increase can be considered as a sign of a developing population. Furthermore, Class 9 (mating protest) is typically emitted by females. When mating protest is excluded from the group, CNN still yields relatively accurate results (0.822) and outperforms KNN by 16.5%.

When three different aggressive calls are compared with each other (biting (2), feeding (3), fighting (4)), CNN yields relatively accurate results (0.803) and outperforms KNN by 17.1%. It is interesting to note that, an aggressive call, biting (2) and a less aggressive call, feeding (3) are still separable even using 1D features with KNN (0.812). Therefore, the improvement of CNN is only 6.9% with respect to KNN. Similarly, since the call frequencies of juveniles are different than adults, isolation calls (6) can be detected easily from the aggressive call biting (2) using 1D features with KNN (0.919). Therefore, the improvement of CNN with respect to KNN is also limited (5.8%).

When aggressive calls biting (2) and fighting (4) are compared within each other, CNN yields accurate results (0.898) and outperforms KNN by 10%. Similarly, when feeding (3), and mating protest (9) are compared within each other, CNN still yields accurate results (0.892) and outperforms KNN with 11.7%. On the other hand, when biting (2), and mating protest (9) are compared within each other, the performance of CNN drops down to 0.782 and CNN outperforms KNN by only 5.9%. This might happen because, in Table 10, a significant portion of mating protest calls is incorrectly classified as biting. Lastly, when mating protest (9) is compared with the aggressive call fighting (4), CNN yields accurate results (0.832) with a significant improvement of 15% as compared to KNN.

Appendix 4 further presents in-detail comparisons with different class groupings.

FUTURE RESEARCH DIRECTIONS

The authors aim to develop this work in further studies within the aspect of three topics. The first goal is to optimize the models and their perception of data. For this purpose, a deeper model would be used without increasing the computational effort tremendously. Additionally, although the data acquisition is fast enough, further parallelization techniques can be adopted for optimizing the complexity of the pipeline. The results obtained from the 1-D models show that adding pre and post-vocalization actions to the input data boost the accuracy and the corresponding metrics of the pipeline. Then, it becomes possible that using a hybrid model allowing multiple types of inputs can lead to better inference performance. If the spectrogram and other 1-D features would be desired to work simultaneously in a deep learning model, data should be merged with common labels, which Pandas provides the flexibility for combining separate data.

The second objective is to make the most out of the dataset. Since audio waves constitute time series data, using a decision-making model which learns from a sequence would be feasible. Thus, all parts of an individual sound data will contribute to the classification pipeline. For instance, a long-short term memory (LSTM) model will be able to learn the early and late vocalization characteristics of an action (Greff et al., 2016).

Another approach would be taking the advantage of probabilistic approaches. Most of the living creatures have randomness in their actions. This fact creates probabilistic distributions that can be learned with functions. Hidden Markov models (HMM) and Gaussian mixture models (GMM) can be brought into practice to guess the distributions of the features for acquiring the context of the bat calls (Brown & Smaragdis, 2009).

CONCLUSION

In this preliminary study, vocalization actions of Egyptian fruit bats were investigated and being classified upon the separability of call spectrum images, over a considerably large dataset. Classification results showed that the CNN method using mel-spectrogram performed with better accuracy as compared to the KNN method using 1D features with an improvement of 20% when all the classes were considered. This was because the defined 1D features could not fully represent each behavior content, and CNN captured the best model weights based on the available training data. Similarly, it was also observed that the different combinations of aggressive call classes which may sound quite close to each other (i.e., biting, mating protest, fighting), were distinguished well with CNN as compared to KNN with an improvement of at least 10%. It was also observed that when all the classes were considered, most of the classes were classified correctly where the lowest performance was obtained while recognizing the sleeping cluster. Therefore, new features need to be generated to distinguish the sleeping class from the rest of the individual classes, or a hierarchical model could be proposed which first checks the roosts whether the members of it hibernate or not. Such a smaller model to classify sleeping versus nonsleeping would still have enough performance to fulfill this task. Lastly, calls of isolated pups', had already given better discernibility results with KNN in binary comparisons. The authors state that the main underlying reason for this phenomenon is linked to the fact that the vocal capabilities of isolated bat pups are not mature enough as adult bats' vocal patterns (Prat et al., 2015).

The outcomes of this research can be used in fields such as the agricultural industry. Therefore, the existence of a bat colony near an agricultural field brings critical benefits. Since the Egyptian fruit bats are important agents for the ecological balance due to their fruit consuming diet, they play important role in seed dispersal of their food plants and hence increase the spread of plants with enhanced fertility. Monitoring, the bat colony based on their calls with passive unattended sensors provides invaluable information about the overall progress of the colony. As example, if there are pups or juveniles in the colony, isolation calls will be heard. Feeding calls indicate the environment is rich in food resources. Fighting and biting calls further indicate that the colony is reproductive. When an anomaly is detected in one or more social call classes may indicate the bat habitat might be in danger and the entire colony may die or leave the shelter soon. So, an acoustic bat monitoring system that can detect different bat behaviors has the potential to intervene proactively before a serious threat to the colony and consequently to agricultural production arises.

REFERENCES

Albayrak, İ., Aşan, N., & Yorulmaz, T. (2008). The natural history of the Egyptian fruit bat, Rousettus aegyptiacus, in Turkey (Mammalia: Chiroptera). *Turkish Journal of Zoology*, *32*(1), 11–18.

Armitage, D. W., & Ober, H. K. (2010). A comparison of supervised learning techniques in the classification of bat echolocation calls. *Ecological Informatics*, *5*(6), 465–473. doi:10.1016/j.ecoinf.2010.08.001

Beauvois, M., Dierckx, L., Bonaventure, O., & Nijssen, S. (2021). *Automated detection of bat species in Belgium.* http://hdl.handle.net/2078.1/thesis:30594

Bastas, S., Majid, M. W., Mirzaei, G., Ross, J., Jamali, M. M., Gorsevski, P. V., ... Bingman, V. P. (2012, May). A novel feature extraction algorithm for classification of bird flight calls. In *2012 IEEE International Symposium on Circuits and Systems (ISCAS)* (pp. 1676-1679). IEEE. 10.1109/ISCAS.2012.6271580

Benda, P., Vallo, P., Hulva, P., & Horáček, I. (2012). The Egyptian fruit bat Rousettus aegyptiacus (Chiroptera: Pteropodidae) in the Palaearctic: Geographical variation and taxonomic status. *Biologia*, *67*(6), 1230–1244. doi:10.247811756-012-0105-y

Bishop, J. C., Falzon, G., Trotter, M., Kwan, P., & Meek, P. D. (2019). Livestock vocalisation classification in farm soundscapes. *Computers and Electronics in Agriculture, 162*, 531–542. doi:10.1016/j.compag.2019.04.020

Blumstein, D. T., Mennill, D. J., Clemins, P., Girod, L., Yao, K., Patricelli, G., Deppe, J. L., Krakauer, A. H., Clark, C., Cortopassi, K. A., Hanser, S. F., McCowan, B., Ali, A. M., & Kirschel, A. N. (2011). Acoustic monitoring in terrestrial environments using microphone arrays: Applications, technological considerations and prospectus. *Journal of Applied Ecology, 48*(3), 758–767. doi:10.1111/j.1365-2664.2011.01993.x

Bold, N., Zhang, C., & Akashi, T. (2019, October). Bird Species Classification with Audio-Visual Data using CNN and Multiple Kernel Learning. In *2019 International Conference on Cyberworlds (CW)* (pp. 85-88). IEEE. 10.1109/CW.2019.00022

Brown, J. C., & Smaragdis, P. (2009). Hidden Markov and Gaussian mixture models for automatic call classification. *The Journal of the Acoustical Society of America, 125*(6), EL221–EL224. doi:10.1121/1.3124659 PMID:19507925

Chandu, B., Munikoti, A., Murthy, K. S., Murthy, G., & Nagaraj, C. (2020, January). Automated Bird Species Identification using Audio Signal Processing and Neural Networks. In *2020 International Conference on Artificial Intelligence and Signal Processing (AISP)* (pp. 1-5). IEEE. 10.1109/AISP48273.2020.9073584

Cramer, J., Wu, H. H., Salamon, J., & Bello, J. P. (2019, May). Look, listen, and learn more: Design choices for deep audio embeddings. In *ICASSP 2019-2019 IEEE International Conference on Acoustics, Speech and Signal Processing (ICASSP)* (pp. 3852-3856). IEEE.

Cramer, J., Lostanlen, V., Farnsworth, A., Salamon, J., & Bello, J. P. (2020, May). Chirping up the right tree: Incorporating biological taxonomies into deep bioacoustic classifiers. In *ICASSP 2020-2020 IEEE International Conference on Acoustics, Speech and Signal Processing (ICASSP)* (pp. 901-905). IEEE.

Dasman, R. F. (1981). *Wildlife Biology* (2nd ed.). John Wiley & Sons, Inc.

Del Vaglio, M. A., Nicolaou, H., Bosso, L., & Russo, D. (2011). Feeding habits of the Egyptian fruit bat Rousettus aegyptiacus on Cyprus island: A first assessment. *Hystrix, 22*(2), 281–289.

Dietz, C., von Helversen, O., Nill, D., Lina, P. H., & Hutson, A. M. (2009). *Bats of Britain, Europe and Northwest Africa*. A & C Black.

Disabato, S., Canonaco, G., Flikkema, P. G., Roveri, M., & Alippi, C. (2021, August). Birdsong Detection at the Edge with Deep Learning. In *2021 IEEE International Conference on Smart Computing (SMARTCOMP)* (pp. 9-16). IEEE. 10.1109/SMARTCOMP52413.2021.00022

Dowd, B. (2020). *What are the Mating Habits of Bats?* Online available: https://www.skedaddlewildlife.com/blog/what-are-the-mating-habits-of-bats/

Frick, W. F., Kingston, T., & Flanders, J. (2020). A review of the major threats and challenges to global bat conservation. *Annals of the New York Academy of Sciences, 1469*(1), 5–25. doi:10.1111/nyas.14045 PMID:30937915

Gadziola, M. A., Grimsley, J. M., Faure, P. A., & Wenstrup, J. J. (2012). *Social vocalizations of big brown bats vary with behavioral context.* Academic Press.

Genzel, D., Desai, J., Paras, E., & Yartsev, M. M. (2019). Long-term and persistent vocal plasticity in adult bats. *Nature Communications, 10*(1), 1–12. doi:10.103841467-019-11350-2 PMID:31358755

Greff, K., Srivastava, R. K., Koutník, J., Steunebrink, B. R., & Schmidhuber, J. (2016). LSTM: A search space odyssey. *IEEE Transactions on Neural Networks and Learning Systems, 28*(10), 2222–2232. doi:10.1109/TNNLS.2016.2582924 PMID:27411231

Grey, J. M., & Gordon, J. W. (1978). Perceptual effects of spectral modifications on musical timbres. *The Journal of the Acoustical Society of America, 63*(5), 1493–1500. doi:10.1121/1.381843

Hearst, M. A., Dumais, S. T., Osuna, E., Platt, J., & Scholkopf, B. (1998). Support vector machines. *IEEE Intelligent Systems & their Applications, 13*(4), 18–28. doi:10.1109/5254.708428

Herr, A., Klomp, N. I., & Atkinson, J. S. (1997). Identification of bat echolocation calls using a decision tree classification system. *Complexity International, 4,* 1–9.

Hu, J., Huang, W., Su, Y., Liu, Y., & Xiao, P. (2020, June). BatNet++: A Robust Deep Learning-Based Predicting Models for Calls Recognition. In *2020 5th International Conference on Smart Grid and Electrical Automation (ICSGEA)* (pp. 260-263). IEEE.

Huang, Y. P., & Basanta, H. (2021). Recognition of Endemic Bird Species Using Deep Learning Models. *IEEE Access: Practical Innovations, Open Solutions, 9,* 102975–102984. doi:10.1109/AC-CESS.2021.3098532

Hunter, J. D. (2007). Matplotlib: A 2D graphics environment. *Computing in Science & Engineering, 9*(03), 90–95. doi:10.1109/MCSE.2007.55

Ibrahim, A. K., Zhuang, H., Erdol, N., & Ali, A. M. (2018, December). Detection of north atlantic right whales with a hybrid system of cnn and dictionary learning. In *2018 International Conference on Computational Science and Computational Intelligence (CSCI)* (pp. 1210-1213). IEEE. 10.1109/CSCI46756.2018.00232

Incze, A., Jancsó, H. B., Szilágyi, Z., Farkas, A., & Sulyok, C. (2018, September). Bird sound recognition using a convolutional neural network. In *2018 IEEE 16th International Symposium on Intelligent Systems and Informatics (SISY)* (pp. 295-300). IEEE. 10.1109/SISY.2018.8524677

Izenman, A. J. (2013). Linear Discriminant Analysis. In *Modern Multivariate Statistical Techniques. Springer Texts in Statistics.* Springer. doi:10.1007/978-0-387-78189-1_8

Jancovic, P., & Köküer, M. (2019). Bird species recognition using unsupervised modeling of individual vocalization elements. *IEEE/ACM Transactions on Audio, Speech, and Language Processing, 27*(5), 932–947. doi:10.1109/TASLP.2019.2904790

Janik, V. M., & Slater, P. J. (2000). The different roles of social learning in vocal communication. *Animal Behaviour, 60*(1), 1–11. doi:10.1006/anbe.2000.1410 PMID:10924198

Jolliffe, I. (2005). *Principal component analysis.* Encyclopedia of statistics in behavioral science.

Jung, D. H., Kim, N. Y., Moon, S. H., Jhin, C., Kim, H. J., Yang, J. S., Kim, H. S., Lee, T. S., Lee, J. Y., & Park, S. H. (2021). Deep Learning-Based Cattle Vocal Classification Model and Real-Time Livestock Monitoring System with Noise Filtering. *Animals (Basel), 11*(2), 357. doi:10.3390/ani11020357 PMID:33535390

Kim, J., Caire, G., & Molisch, A. F. (2015). Quality-aware streaming and scheduling for device-to-device video delivery. *IEEE/ACM Transactions on Networking, 24*(4), 2319–2331. doi:10.1109/TNET.2015.2452272

Kim, Y., Sa, J., Chung, Y., Park, D., & Lee, S. (2018). Resource-efficient pet dog sound events classification using LSTM-FCN based on time-series data. *Sensors (Basel), 18*(11), 4019. doi:10.339018114019 PMID:30453674

Kramer, O. (2013). K-nearest neighbors. In *Dimensionality reduction with unsupervised nearest neighbors* (pp. 13–23). Springer. doi:10.1007/978-3-642-38652-7_2

Kuo, F. Y., & Sloan, I. H. (2005). Lifting the curse of dimensionality. *Notices of the American Mathematical Society, 52*(11), 1320–1328.

Kvsn, R. R., Montgomery, J., Garg, S., & Charleston, M. (2020). Bioacoustics data analysis–A taxonomy, survey and open challenges. *IEEE Access: Practical Innovations, Open Solutions, 8*, 57684–57708. doi:10.1109/ACCESS.2020.2978547

Lee, J., Noh, B., Jang, S., Park, D., Chung, Y., & Chang, H. H. (2015). Stress detection and classification of laying hens by sound analysis. *Asian-Australasian Journal of Animal Sciences, 28*(4), 592–598. doi:10.5713/ajas.14.0654 PMID:25656176

Lostanlen, V., Salamon, J., Farnsworth, A., Kelling, S., & Bello, J. P. (2019). Robust sound event detection in bioacoustic sensor networks. *PLoS One, 14*(10), e0214168. doi:10.1371/journal.pone.0214168 PMID:31647815

Lostanlen, V., Salamon, J., Farnsworth, A., Kelling, S., & Bello, J. P. (2018, April). Birdvox-full-night: A dataset and benchmark for avian flight call detection. In *2018 IEEE International Conference on Acoustics, Speech and Signal Processing (ICASSP)* (pp. 266-270). IEEE. 10.1109/ICASSP.2018.8461410

Lu, Z., Zhang, B., Sun, L., Fan, L., & Zhou, J. (2020, October). Whale-Call Classification Based on Transfer Learning and Ensemble Method. In *2020 IEEE 20th International Conference on Communication Technology (ICCT)* (pp. 1494-1497). IEEE. 10.1109/ICCT50939.2020.9295729

Mac Aodha, O., Gibb, R., Barlow, K. E., Browning, E., Firman, M., Freeman, R., Harder, B., Kinsey, L., Mead, G. R., Newson, S. E., Pandourski, I., Parsons, S., Russ, J., Szodoray-Paradi, A., Szodoray-Paradi, F., Tilova, E., Girolami, M., Brostow, G., & Jones, K. E. (2018). Bat detective—Deep learning tools for bat acoustic signal detection. *PLoS Computational Biology, 14*(3), e1005995. doi:10.1371/journal.pcbi.1005995 PMID:29518076

Mac Aodha, O., Gibb, R., Barlow, K. E., Browning, E., Firman, M., Freeman, R., Harder, B., Kinsey, L., Mead, G. R., Newson, S. E., Pandourski, I., Parsons, S., Russ, J., Szodoray-Paradi, A., Szodoray-Paradi, F., Tilova, E., Girolami, M., Brostow, G., & Jones, K. E. (2018). Bat detective—Deep learning tools for bat acoustic signal detection. *PLoS Computational Biology*, *14*(3), e1005995. doi:10.1371/journal.pcbi.1005995 PMID:29518076

McFee, B., Raffel, C., Liang, D., Ellis, D. P., McVicar, M., Battenberg, E., & Nieto, O. (2015, July). librosa: Audio and music signal analysis in python. In *Proceedings of the 14th python in science conference* (Vol. 8, pp. 18-25). 10.25080/Majora-7b98e3ed-003

Mirzaei, G., Majid, M. W., Ross, J., Jamali, M. M., Gorsevski, P. V., Frizado, J. P., & Bingman, V. P. (2012, May). The BIO-acoustic feature extraction and classification of bat echolocation calls. In *2012 IEEE International Conference on Electro/Information Technology* (pp. 1-4). IEEE. 10.1109/EIT.2012.6220700

Mirzaei, G., Majid, M. W., Bastas, S., Ross, J., Jamali, M. M., Gorsevski, P. V., ... Bingman, V. P. (2012, November). Acoustic monitoring techniques for avian detection and classification. In *2012 Conference Record of the Forty Sixth Asilomar Conference on Signals, Systems and Computers (ASILOMAR)* (pp. 1835-1838). IEEE. 10.1109/ACSSC.2012.6489353

Mirzaei, G., Majid, M. W., Jamali, M. M., Ross, J., Frizado, J., Gorsevski, P. V., & Bingman, V. (2011, July). The application of evolutionary neural network for bat echolocation calls recognition. In *The 2011 International Joint Conference on Neural Networks* (pp. 1106-1111). IEEE. 10.1109/IJCNN.2011.6033347

Molnár, C., Kaplan, F., Roy, P., Pachet, F., Pongrácz, P., Dóka, A., & Miklósi, Á. (2008). Classification of dog barks: A machine learning approach. *Animal Cognition*, *11*(3), 389–400. doi:10.100710071-007-0129-9 PMID:18197442

Mushtaq, Z., & Su, S. F. (2020). Environmental sound classification using a regularized deep convolutional neural network with data augmentation. *Applied Acoustics*, *167*, 107389. doi:10.1016/j.apacoust.2020.107389

Nagy, K., Cinkler, T., Simon, C., & Vida, R. (2020, October). *Internet of Birds (IoB): Song Based Bird Sensing via Machine Learning in the Cloud: How to sense, identify, classify birds based on their songs?* In *2020 IEEE Sensors*. IEEE.

Narasimhan, R., Fern, X. Z., & Raich, R. (2017, March). Simultaneous segmentation and classification of bird song using CNN. In *2017 IEEE International Conference on Acoustics, Speech and Signal Processing (ICASSP)* (pp. 146-150). IEEE. 10.1109/ICASSP.2017.7952135

Ntalampiras, S., Kosmin, D., & Sanchez, J. (2021, July). Acoustic classification of individual cat vocalizations in evolving environments. In *2021 44th International Conference on Telecommunications and Signal Processing (TSP)* (pp. 254-258). IEEE. 10.1109/TSP52935.2021.9522660

Öber, A. (2007). *Hayvan Davranışları (Temel Ögeler)*. Nobel Yayın Dağıtım Lt. Şti.

Pandeya, Y. R., Kim, D., & Lee, J. (2018). Domestic cat sound classification using learned features from deep neural nets. *Applied Sciences (Basel, Switzerland)*, *8*(10), 1949. doi:10.3390/app8101949

Parsons, S., & Jones, G. (2000). Acoustic identification of twelve species of echolocating bat by discriminant function analysis and artificial neural networks. *The Journal of Experimental Biology, 203*(17), 2641–2656. doi:10.1242/jeb.203.17.2641 PMID:10934005

Paumen, Y., Mälzer, M., Alipek, S., Moll, J., Lüdtke, B., & Schauer-Weisshahn, H. (2021). Development and test of a bat calls detection and classification method based on convolutional neural networks. *Bioacoustics*, 1–12. doi:10.1080/09524622.2021.1978863

Pavan, G. (2008). Short field course on bioacoustics. Taxonomy Summer School, 1-15.

Piczak, K. J. (2015, October). ESC: Dataset for environmental sound classification. In *Proceedings of the 23rd ACM international conference on Multimedia* (pp. 1015-1018). 10.1145/2733373.2806390

Pieplow, N. (2019). *Peterson Field Guide to Bird Sounds of Western North America*. Peterson Field Guides.

Prat, Y., Taub, M., & Yovel, Y. (2015). Vocal learning in a social mammal: Demonstrated by isolation and playback experiments in bats. *Science Advances, 1*(2), e1500019. doi:10.1126ciadv.1500019 PMID:26601149

Prat, Y., Taub, M., Pratt, E., & Yovel, Y. (2017). An annotated dataset of Egyptian fruit bat vocalizations across varying contexts and during vocal ontogeny. *Scientific Data, 4*(1), 1–7. doi:10.1038data.2017.143 PMID:28972574

Rish, I. (2001, August). An empirical study of the naive Bayes classifier. In IJCAI 2001 workshop on empirical methods in artificial intelligence (Vol. 3, No. 22, pp. 41-46). Academic Press.

Ruiz, A. T., Jung, K., Tschapka, M., Schwenker, F., & Palm, G. (2017). *Automated identification method for detection and classification of neotropical bats*. Academic Press.

Thiebault, A., Charrier, I., Pistorius, P., & Aubin, T. (2019). At sea vocal repertoire of a foraging seabird. *Journal of Avian Biology, 50*(5), jav.02032. Advance online publication. doi:10.1111/jav.02032

Schapire, R. E. (2013). Explaining adaboost. In *Empirical inference* (pp. 37–52). Springer. doi:10.1007/978-3-642-41136-6_5

Salamon, J., & Bello, J. P. (2017). Deep convolutional neural networks and data augmentation for environmental sound classification. *IEEE Signal Processing Letters, 24*(3), 279–283. doi:10.1109/LSP.2017.2657381

Salamon, J., Bello, J. P., Farnsworth, A., & Kelling, S. (2017, March). Fusing shallow and deep learning for bioacoustic bird species classification. In 2017 IEEE international conference on acoustics, speech and signal processing (ICASSP) (pp. 141-145). IEEE. doi:10.1109/ICASSP.2017.7952134

Schwab, Pogrebnoj, Freund, & Flossmann, Vogl, & Frommolt. (2021). Automated Bat Call Classification using Deep Convolutional. *Neural Networks*.

Şişli, N. (1999). *Ekoloji (Çevre Bilim)*. Gazi Büro Kitabevi Tic. Ltd. Şti.

Somervuo, P., Harma, A., & Fagerlund, S. (2006). Parametric representations of bird sounds for automatic species recognition. *IEEE Transactions on Audio, Speech, and Language Processing, 14*(6), 2252–2263. doi:10.1109/TASL.2006.872624

SPAFE. (n.d.). *Simplified Python audio features extraction.* https://spafe.readthedocs.io

Stowell, D., Benetos, E., & Gill, L. F. (2017). On-bird sound recordings: Automatic acoustic recognition of activities and contexts. *IEEE/ACM Transactions on Audio, Speech, and Language Processing, 25*(6), 1193–1206. doi:10.1109/TASLP.2017.2690565

Stowell, D., Wood, M. D., Pamuła, H., Stylianou, Y., & Glotin, H. (2019). Automatic acoustic detection of birds through deep learning: The first Bird Audio Detection challenge. *Methods in Ecology and Evolution, 10*(3), 368–380. doi:10.1111/2041-210X.13103

Tabak, M. A., Murray, K. L., Lombardi, J. A., & Bay, K. J. (2021). Automated classification of bat echolocation call recordings with artificial intelligence. bioRxiv. doi:10.1101/2021.06.23.449619

Umapathy, K., Krishnan, S., & Rao, R. K. (2007). Audio signal feature extraction and classification using local discriminant bases. *IEEE Transactions on Audio, Speech, and Language Processing, 15*(4), 1236–1246. doi:10.1109/TASL.2006.885921

Vernes, S. C., & Wilkinson, G. S. (2020). Behaviour, biology and evolution of vocal learning in bats. *Philosophical Transactions of the Royal Society B, 375*(1789), 20190061.

Vickers, W., Milner, B., Gorpincenko, A., & Lee, R. (2021, January). Methods to Improve the Robustness of Right Whale Detection using CNNs in Changing Conditions. In *2020 28th European Signal Processing Conference (EUSIPCO)* (pp. 106-110). IEEE. 10.23919/Eusipco47968.2020.9287565

Vidaña-Vila, E., Navarro, J., Alsina-Pages, R. M., & Ramirez, A. (2020). A two-stage approach to automatically detect and classify woodpecker (Fam. Picidae) sounds. *Applied Acoustics, 166*, 107312. doi:10.1016/j.apacoust.2020.107312

Wright, R. E. (1995). *Logistic regression.* Academic Press.

Xie, J., Hu, K., Zhu, M., Yu, J., & Zhu, Q. (2019). Investigation of different CNN-based models for improved bird sound classification. *IEEE Access: Practical Innovations, Open Solutions, 7*, 175353–175361. doi:10.1109/ACCESS.2019.2957572

Chen, X., Zhao, J., Chen, Y. H., Zhou, W., & Hughes, A. C. (2020). Automatic standardized processing and identification of tropical bat calls using deep learning approaches. *Biological Conservation, 241*, 108269.

Zualkernan, I., Judas, J., Mahbub, T., Bhagwagar, A., & Chand, P. (2020, September). A Tiny CNN Architecture for Identifying Bat Species from Echolocation Calls. In *2020 IEEE/ITU International Conference on Artificial Intelligence for Good (AI4G)* (pp. 81-86). IEEE.

Zualkernan, I., Judas, J., Mahbub, T., Bhagwagar, A., & Chand, P. (2021, January). An AIoT System for Bat Species Classification. In *2020 IEEE International Conference on Internet of Things and Intelligence System (IoTaIS)* (pp. 155-160). IEEE.

KEY TERMS AND DEFINITIONS

Deep Learning: Is a class of broader machine learning algorithms which uses multiple layers to gradually extract higher-level features from the raw input data.

Egyptian Fruit Bat (Egyptian rousette, *Rousettus aegyptiacus*)**:** Is a megabat species that can be found in the Middle East, the Mediterranean, the Indian subcontinent, and Africa.

Feature Extraction: Is a process of dimensionality reduction which defines manageable resources to describe an initial large raw data set.

Machine Learning: Imitates the way the human learns with the use of algorithms and data, and learning accuracy improves automatically through experience.

Mel-Spectrogram: Is a type of spectrogram calculation. It can be acquired by rendering frequencies logarithmically, with a certain corner frequency (threshold).

MtDna: Is an abbreviation of Mitochondrial DNA.

One-Hot Encoding: Is one of the ways for representing a categorical information with a vector which has binary resolution. The main intention is to elaborate data for processing pipelines and/or understanding the behavior.

Spectrogram: Is a visual representation of the signal frequency spectrum over time.

APPENDIX 1

In this section, 1D features generated from illustrative bat calls are represented in Figure 9.

Figure 9a. The contexts are stated as follows: biting (a,b,c), feeding (d,e,f), fighting (g,h,i), isolation (j,k,l), mating protest (m,n,o), sleeping (p,q,r). Feature types are as follows: spectral centroid, (a,d,g,j,m,p) spectral bandwidth (b,e,h,k,n,q), spectral rolloff (c,f,i,l,o,r).

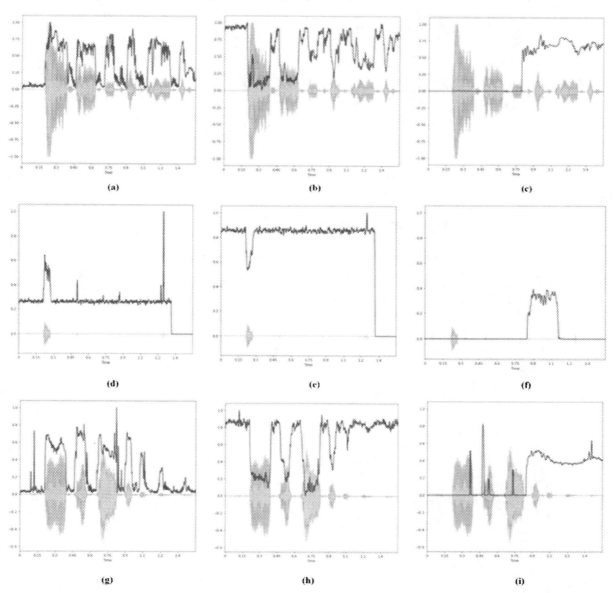

Figure 9b. The contexts are stated as follows: biting (a,b,c), feeding (d,e,f), fighting (g,h,i), isolation (j,k,l), mating protest (m,n,o), sleeping (p,q,r). Feature types are as follows: spectral centroid, (a,d,g,j,m,p) spectral bandwidth (b,e,h,k,n,q), spectral rolloff (c,f,i,l,o,r).

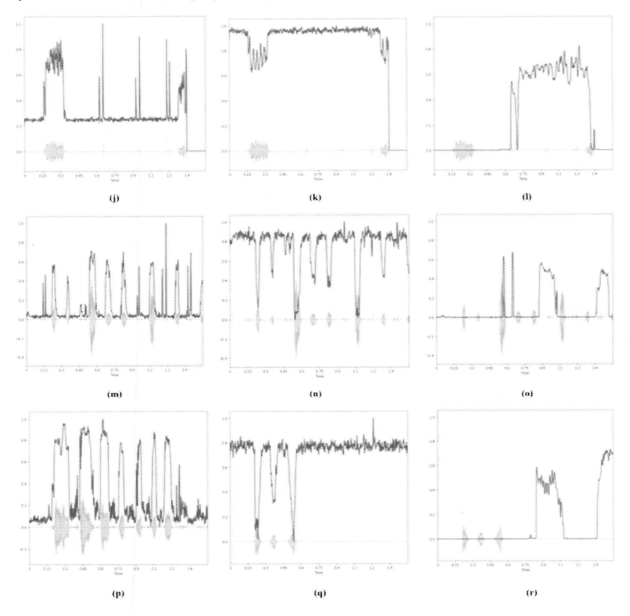

APPENDIX 2

Figure 10. Linear spectrograms. The contexts are stated as follows: biting (a), feeding (b), fighting (c), isolation (d), mating protest (e), sleeping (f).

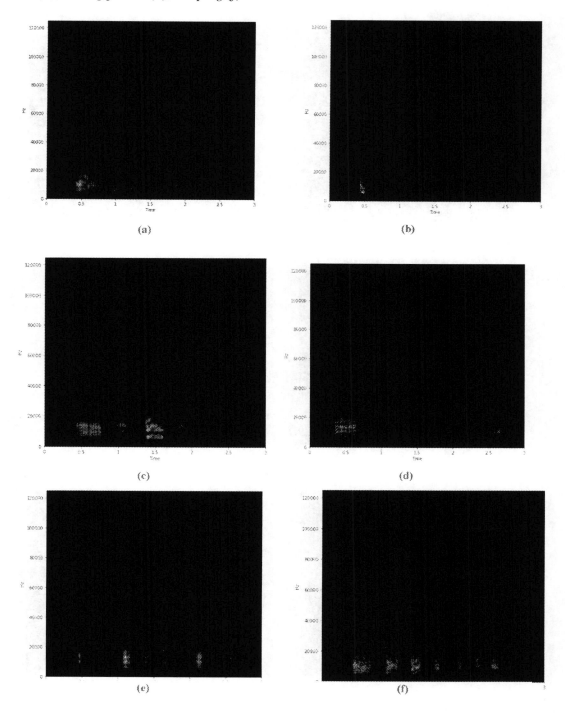

Figure 10 shows the linear spectrograms from call samples biting, feeding, fighting, isolation, mating protest and sleeping.

Figure 11. Power spectrograms. The contexts are stated as follows: biting (a), feeding (b), fighting (c), isolation (d), mating protest (e), sleeping (f).

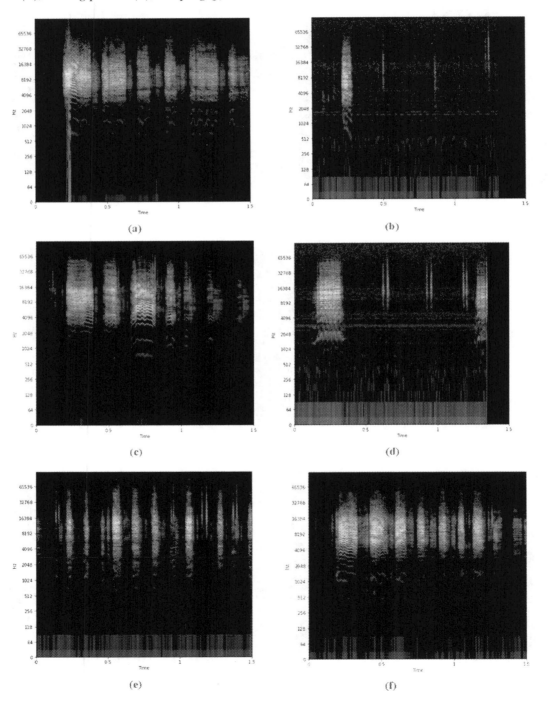

Figure 11 shows the power spectrograms from call samples biting, feeding, fighting, isolation, mating protest and sleeping.

Figure 12. Power spectrograms with time expansion with 1/100th of sampling rate. The contexts are stated as follows: biting (a), feeding (b), fighting (c), isolation (d), mating protest (e), sleeping (f).

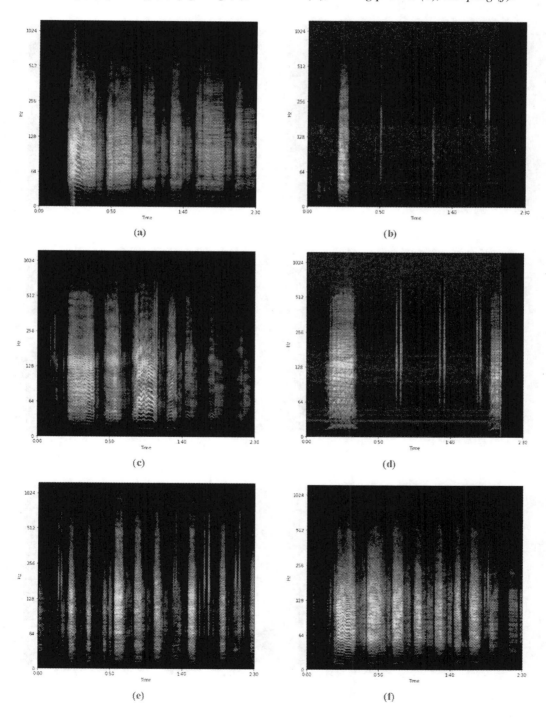

Figure 12 shows the power spectrograms with time expansion from call samples biting, feeding, fighting, isolation, mating protest and sleeping.

Figure 13. Mel-based spectrograms. The contexts are stated as follows: biting (a), feeding (b), fighting (c), isolation (d), mating protest (e), sleeping (f).

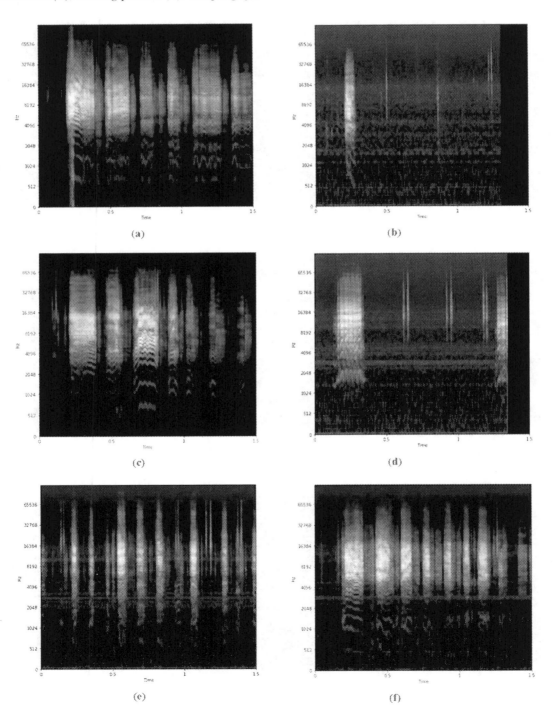

Figure 13 shows the Mel-spectrograms call samples biting, feeding, fighting, isolation, mating protest and sleeping.

APPENDIX 3

Table 13 represents the KNN results with pre-post actions for biting, feeding, fighting, isolation and mating protest.

Table 13. KNN results with pre-post actions for biting, feeding, fighting, isolation and mating protest.

	Biting	**Feeding**	**Fighting**	**Isolation**	**Mating Protest**
Biting	126	19	23	5	28
Feeding	47	108	25	14	15
Fighting	29	40	83	3	35
Isolation	10	16	8	164	0
Mating Protest	44	33	43	1	79
Precision	0.492	0.500	0.456	0.877	0.503
Recall	0.627	0.517	0.437	0.828	0.395
F1 Score	0.551	0.508	0.446	0.852	0.443
Accuracy	0.561				

Table 14 represents the KNN results with pre-post actions for biting, feeding, fighting, and isolation.

Table 14. KNN results with pre-post actions for biting, feeding, fighting, and isolation

	Biting	**Feeding**	**Fighting**	**Isolation**
Biting	130	26	30	3
Feeding	43	116	38	18
Fighting	37	41	112	3
Isolation	3	22	10	166
Precision	0.610	0.566	0.589	0.874
Recall	0.688	0.540	0.580	0.826
F1 Score	0.647	0.552	0.585	0.849
Accuracy	0.657			

Table 15 represents the KNN results with pre-post actions for biting, feeding, and fighting.

Table 15. KNN results with pre-post actions for biting, feeding, and fighting

	Biting	Feeding	Fighting
Biting	151	33	31
Feeding	46	131	23
Fighting	40	47	96
Precision	0.637	0.621	0.640
Recall	0.702	0.655	0.525
F1 Score	0.668	0.637	0.577
Accuracy	0.632		

Table 16 represents KNN results with pre-post actions for two classes classifications such as biting vs isolation, biting vs feeding, biting vs mating, fighting vs mating protest, biting vs fighting and feeding vs mating protest.

Table 16. KNN results with pre-post actions for two classes classifications such as biting vs isolation, biting vs feeding, biting vs mating, fighting vs mating protest, biting vs fighting and feeding vs mating protest.

	Biting	Isolation		Biting	Feeding
Biting	180	8	Biting	172	38
Isolation	26	206	Feeding	41	169
Precision	0.874	0.963	Precision	0.808	0.816
Recall	0.957	0.888	Recall	0.819	0.805
F1 Score	0.914	0.924	F1 Score	0.813	0.811
Accuracy	0.919		Accuracy	0.812	
	Biting	Mating-protest		Fighting	Mating protest
Biting	158	56	Fighting	117	70
Mating-protest	53	126	Mating protest	55	144
Precision	0.749	0.692	Precision	0.680	0.673
Recall	0.738	0.704	Recall	0.626	0.724
F1 Score	0.744	0.698	F1 Score	0.652	0.697
Accuracy	0.723		Accuracy	0.676	
	Biting	Fighting		Feeding	Mating protest
Biting	170	43	Feeding	154	53
Fighting	42	165	Mating protest	36	152
Precision	0.802	0.793	Precision	0.811	0.741
Recall	0.798	0.797	Recall	0.744	0.809
F1 Score	0.8	0.795	F1 Score	0.776	0.774
Accuracy	0.798		Accuracy	0.775	

APPENDIX 4

Table 17 represents the CNN results for biting, feeding, fighting, isolation and mating protest.

Table 17. CNN results with mel-spectrogram for biting, feeding, fighting, isolation and mating protest

	Biting	Feeding	Fighting	Isolation	Mating Protest
Biting	143	13	8	1	32
Feeding	29	136	10	6	18
Fighting	25	20	124	2	23
Isolation	3	4	2	188	1
Mating Protest	31	13	13	0	141
Precision	0.619	0.731	0.789	0.954	0.656
Recall	0.725	0.683	0.639	0.949	0.712
F1 Score	0.668	0.706	0.706	0.952	0.683
Loss	0.762				
Accuracy	0.742				

Table 18 represents the CNN results for biting, feeding, fighting, and isolation.

Table 18. CNN results with mel-spectrogram for biting, feeding, fighting and isolation

	Biting	Feeding	Fighting	Isolation
Biting	162	16	18	1
Feeding	35	154	10	0
Fighting	22	19	152	1
Isolation	7	8	3	180
Precision	0.717	0.782	0.831	0.989
Recall	0.822	0.774	0.784	0.909
F1 Score	0.766	0.778	0.806	0.947
Loss	0.483			
Accuracy	0.822			

Table 19 represents the CNN results for biting, feeding, and fighting.

Table 19. CNN results with mel-spectrogram for biting, feeding, and fighting

	Biting	Feeding	Fighting
Biting	173	10	14
Feeding	31	158	10
Fighting	29	22	143
Precision	0.742	0.832	0.856
Recall	0.878	0.794	0.737
F1 Score	0.804	0.812	0.792
Loss	0.533		
Accuracy	0.803		

Table 20 represents the CNN results with mel-spectrogram for two classes classifications such as biting vs isolation, biting vs feeding, biting vs mating protest, fighting vs mating protest, biting vs fighting and feeding vs mating protest.

Table 20. CNN results with mel-spectrogram for two classes classifications such as biting vs isolation, biting vs feeding, biting vs mating protest, fighting vs mating protest, biting vs fighting and feeding vs mating protest

	Biting	Isolation		Biting	Feeding
Biting	197	0	**Biting**	189	8
Isolation	9	189	**Feeding**	39	160
Precision	0.956	1	**Precision**	0.829	0.952
Recall	1	0.954	**Recall**	0.959	0.804
F1 Score	0.977	0.976	**F1 Score**	0.889	0.872
Loss	0.092		**Loss**	0.339	
Accuracy	0.977		**Accuracy**	0.881	
	Biting	**Mating-protest**		**Fighting**	**Mating protest**
Biting	148	49	**Fighting**	155	39
Mating-protest	37	161	**Mating protest**	27	171
Precision	0.8	0.766	**Precision**	0.852	0.814
Recall	0.751	0.813	**Recall**	0.799	0.864
F1 Score	0.775	0.789	**F1 Score**	0.824	0.838
Loss	0.487		**Loss**	0.486	
Accuracy	0.782		**Accuracy**	0.832	
	Biting	**Fighting**		**Feeding**	**Mating protest**
Biting	173	24	**Feeding**	177	22
Fighting	16	178	**Mating protest**	21	177
Precision	0.915	0.881	**Precision**	0.894	0.889
Recall	0.878	0.918	**Recall**	0.889	0.894
F1 Score	0.896	0.899	**F1 Score**	0.892	0.892
Loss	0.355		**Loss**	0.353	
Accuracy	0.898		**Accuracy**	0.892	

Chapter 5
Visual Feedback Control Through Real-Time Movie Frames for Quadcopter With Object Count Function and Pick-and-Place Robot With Orientation Estimator

Lu Shao
Sanyo-Onoda City University, Japan

Fusaomi Nagata
Sanyo-Onoda City University, Japan

Maki K. Habib
https://orcid.org/0000-0001-8088-8043
The American University in Cairo, Egypt

Keigo Watanabe
Okayama University, Japan

ABSTRACT

Previous studies have successfully identified results of searching the desired object in real-time movie frames using a template image prepared in color or shape. In every sample time of 40 ms, the center of gravity (COG) can be consecutively calculated by detecting and identifying the desired object. Hence, it is possible to have visual feedback (VF) control with the quadrotor by referring to the change of the COG as the relative velocity with respect to the desired object. In this chapter, a useful function is developed to enable the detection and counting of desired objects in real-time. This allows the quadrotor to monitor the number of individually selected objects in the frames of a movie such as cars, animals, etc. This supports high-speed counting while avoiding errors due to object overlapping. Also, the proposed VF controller is successfully applied to a pick-and-place robot, in which a transfer learning-based convolutional neural network can estimate object orientation for smooth picking.

DOI: 10.4018/978-1-7998-8686-0.ch005

INTRODUCTION

There are growing demands in developing robot technologies that enable advanced functions, such as enhancing flexibility, agility, and support friendly interaction with the environment, other robots, and human beings in many different application domains. During the last decade, the technologies supporting the development of Unmanned Ariel Vehicles (UAV) such as quadrotors have remarkably progressed. Hence, many promising applications tried to contribute new results. For example, Lu et al. developed remote control and monitoring system using a quadrotor to enable an operator to remotely control the quadcopter and monitor its operational surroundings using an iOS device. Primary handlers for obtaining compass information, controlling a gimbal, autopilot function for landing or emergency intervention, photo and video preview, photoshoot, and movie video recording have been developed and implemented. The developed functionalities were implemented, evaluated, and confirmed through experiments (Lu et al., 2017a). Koziar et al. discussed a quadrotor design for outdoor air quality monitoring. They were described that monitoring air quality to prevent environmental pollution and improve human quality of life is essential. One of the most promising directions in ecological applications is measurements with UAVs which has a significant advantage over ground vehicles like high maneuverability and easy deployment (Koziar et al., 2019). Rosario et al. applied an image processing technique to detect cars in a specific parking lot together with a UAV that can hover above the parking lot (Rosario et al., 2020). Also, Allen and Mazumder proposed an integrated system concept for autonomously surveying and planning emergency response for areas impacted by natural disasters, which was composed of a network of ground stations and autonomous aerial vehicles interconnected by an ad hoc emergency communication network (Allen & Mazumder, 2020). More research covered the development of using multiple UAVs as a subset of multi robotic systems, which represents an important step to support communication coordination and cooperation that facilitate applying such technology for a wide range of tasks. The advantages of such research directions cover flexibility, reliability, cooperation, complementarity, time efficiency, and cost.

For the developed technology in this chapter that focuses on image processing technology, various applications using consumer cameras and smartphones are being implemented and used. For example, detecting people by surveillance cameras has already been realized. Also, to support autonomous driving of cars, image processing techniques supported by different machine learning techniques are now being developed and quickly progressing. Developing an effective autonomous navigation system requires recognizing the road environment around the automobile and avoiding any possible clash. Hence, image recognition technology is applied to movies obtained by a camera used as primary sensors (Hattori, 2008). Cameras, movie frames, and image processing techniques are used in association with the functions of UAVs for different purposes. Serizawa et al. developed a video system that rotates and translates a stereo camera mounted on a flying robot to synchronize the operator's head movement (Serizawa et al., 2019). Otsuka et al. developed a small UAV localization technique in a GPS-unavailable indoor environment using dropping type AR (Augmented Reality) markers (Ostuka, et al., 2015). Saito et al. proposed a method to measure how the movement of a person can be captured and recognized. Setting multiple markers on the ground made it possible to estimate a UAV's position by capturing those markers' images using a camera integrated with the UAV body and supported by analyzing algorithms. Concurrently, the trajectory of a person is monitored successfully by estimating his position on the ground in the same images. Reducing the measurement in position error was the focus of Saito's research team. This was achieved by using Kalman filter (Saito et al., 2018). Lu et al. developed two software programs for rounding around a target object and executing a mission planning function with multiple flight tasks. These functions were implemented and integrated with a quadrotor (Lu et al., 2017b; Lu et al., 2018).

Gomez-Avila et al. developed an algorithm that uses visual feedback to control a quadrotor to track a ground vehicle. The quadcopter used an onboard monocular vision system integrated with the used quadrotor. The transpose of the interaction matrix is used instead of the pseudo-inverse matrix to facilitate the tracking. This technique has the advantage of reducing the calculation complexity and the avoidance of singularities (Gomez-Avila et al., 2018). Also, Yang et al. proposed a method to track a static target by UAV using an image-based visual servo control algorithm. For this aim, the centroid coordinates of the target object are extracted for the input images. At the same time, the control output is calculated to adjust the heading direction by the image Jacobian model (Yang et al., 2019). Sheng et al. suggested an observer-based model predictive control scheme for the image-based visual servoing of a quadrotor. The developed control scheme aims to reduce the feature loss due to significant rotation and improve visibility. In addition, a high gain observer was designed to facilitate the estimation ability of the linear velocity even though a global positioning system is not available (Sheng et al., 2019).

Moreover, Cao et al. introduced an image dynamics-based visual servoing for quadrotors to realize successful tasks related to stable hovering and tracking. Four types of perspective image moments are used as visual features to control all the degrees of freedom of a quadrotor independently. The complicated interaction matrix is simplified by projecting an original image on the virtual image plane (Cao et al., 2019).

Besides these technological and software advancements in the field, there is limited relevant research using visual servoing techniques to enhance the control performance for different types of UAVs. However, to the best of the author's knowledge, there seems to be almost no work that includes the availability of practical functions that enable iOS based devices such as iPhone to control a UAV and monitor its surroundings directly. Considering the fact that the iOS application can utilize the calculated results obtained in real-time by the robust multi-paradigm numerical computing environment. In the previously presented report by the authors, an iOS application of quadrotor mission planning using a smartphone and GPS signals was proposed (Shao et al., 2019). Besides, the authors constructed a highly functional and value-added system that can automatically recognize an object existing in the images or video frames acquired by a quadrotor with a surveillance camera and utilize it for visual feedback control to track objects in the scene without using GPS signals. The visual feedback control was realized by automatic object recognition based on image processing technologies. The center of gravity (COG) in the image coordinate system can be calculated from color or shape information (Shao et al., 2020a; Shao et al., 2020b). The COG can be used as the current position in image coordinate frame. In the proposed VF controller by the authors, the value of COG is controlled to be at just the center of the captured image frames.

The literature survey shows that many practical research results in the field have been introduced utilizing various UAVs. However, expanding them to conduct environmental monitoring, object detecting, counting functions, and developing a smartphone-based user interface that facilitates such requirements. In this chapter, besides the VF controller, an additional helpful function is considered for counting the number of target objects in image frames of a movie. Such capability makes it possible to monitor the number of individuals such as animals, persons, cars, and other objects in a natural environment. Not only it is difficult for human eyes to conduct high-speed counting of such objects, but also counting errors may occur due to, e.g., overlapping of target objects. The authors are developing an environmental monitoring system using a quadrotor, which can be controlled with a smartphone while solving its problems. In addition, the proposed VF controller is applied with a pick and place robot. A transfer learning-based convolutional neural network is proposed to estimate the orientation of objects for smooth picking.

EXPERIMENTAL SYSTEM

For testing and validating the development covered by this chapter, the experiments were designed using Matrice 100-DJI quadrotor (Dji, 2021) shown in Fig. 1 (a) and (b), and its technical specifications are listed in Table 1. The used quadcopter is featured with good stability and flexibility. More advanced types of Matrice quadcopters are also available commercially, such as Matrice 300 RTK. The flight control and image processing software were developed using Xcode and MATLAB, respectively. Figure 2 shows the overall system software structure, in which three software development kits (SDKs) provided by DJI and the authors developed color-based and shape-based object tracking functions are included. The Mobile SDK for MacOS Xcode allows us to build a customized mobile application for iOS devices such as a smartphone. For example, a smartphone application that executes hovering, target lock, and distance control functions can be implemented. API functions provided in DJI Onboard and Guidance SDKs are used in the embedded unit (Windows OS) to remotely monitor and control the flight movement, e.g., for a built-in smart navigation mode to autonomously follow preset routes. This paper presents a smartphone application that works as a user interface for quadrotors provided by DJI. The application is a visual feedback flight controller included in Fig. 2, enabling a quadrotor to track a target object in real-time. The software development language used for this quadcopter is Swift.

1. The Matrice 100-DJI quadrotor while flying. (Dji, 2021)
2. Matrice 100-DJI with remote control interactive experiment

Figure 1. Quadrotor matrice 100-DJI used in visual feedback control experiments.

Table 1. The main technical specifications list of matrice 100 DJI

Diagonal Wheelbase distance	650 mm	Maximum Speed of Ascent	5 m/s	Power Supply	Built-in Battery
Maximum Takeoff Weight	3600 g	Maximum Speed of Descent	4 m/s	Standard Battery	TB47D 4500 mAh LiPo 6S 600 g
Weigh (with TB47D) with no load	2355 g	Maximum Speed	22 m/s (ATTI mode, no payload, no wind). 17 m/s (GPS mode, no payload, no wind).	Output Power	9 W
Weigh (with TB48D) with no load	2431 g	Maximum Wind Resistance	10 m/s	Mobile Device Holder	Supports smartphones and tablets
Zenmuse X3 Gimbal with Camera Weight	247 g	Hovering Accuracy (P-Mode With GPS	Vertical: 0.5 m, Horizontal: 2.5 m	Max Mobile Device Width	170 mm
Maximum Angular Velocity	Pitch: 300°/s, Yaw: 150°/s	Operating Frequency	5.725~5.825 GHz		
Maximum Tilt Angle	35°	Transmission Distance (free of interference)	3.5 to 5 km		
Operating Temperature	-10 to 40 C °	Video Output	USB, Mini-HDMI		

Figure 2. The quadcopter software development environment based on three SDKs provided by DJI and MATLAB for video and image processing.

Hereafter, the data flow in the application under consideration is explained. When operating a smartphone, commands given by an operator are sent to the C1 controller via wireless or serial communication. The C1 controller, which works as a repeater, is designed to handle the quadrotors provided by DJI. The C1 controller repeats the commands from the smartphone to the small computer embedded in the quadrotor with wireless communication (bandwidth: 922.7-927.7 MHz, output power: 9 W, baud rate: 15 Mbps, maximum communication distance: 5 km). Reversely, position and altitude information obtained by a GPS sensor and distances to obstacles measured by five ultrasonic sensors feedback their activities to the smartphone via the C1 controller. The practical, measurable distance of the ultrasonic sensors is about 7 m. Furthermore, the height from the ground to the quadrotor is measured using a laser distance sensor fixed to the underside of the quadrotor so that a simple feedback controller can be implemented to keep the height at the desired value. The maximum height to be measured by the sensor is about 20 m.

IMAGE PROCESSING FUNCTION DEVELOPED ON MATLAB

MATLAB is a high-level programing language that provides an interactive environment for algorithm development, data analysis, visualization, and numerical calculations. Besides, This applied to image processing and video analysis. This section describes image processing software developed using MATLAB. Images or videos taken by an onboard camera integrated with the quadrotor are sent to the Mac computer for deeper analysis, as shown in Fig. 2. For example, the calculated center of gravity (COG) of a detected object is based on the information of color or shape by using the proposed image processing software. By referring to the variation of the COG position as the quadrotor's motion, some visual feedback controllers can be designed.

1. Extraction of Object COG Using Color Information

a. Connectivity for Forming an Object in an Image

This section introduces finding the centric coordinates (x, y) of an object in the target image by specifying red, green, blue, white, or black colors. Figure 3 shows a user-friendly image analysis tool developed using MATLAB to extract objects in images and video frames sent from the quadrotor to the supporting land computer. This tool extracts the COG position of an object based on color or shape in a captured frame. To detect a target object specified by red, green, or blue color, it is necessary to separate R, G, and B channels with 256 gradations from an original RGB image. Each channel is viewed with 256 grayscale resolution.

Figure 3. MATLAB application developed for object detection and counting in images or video frames.

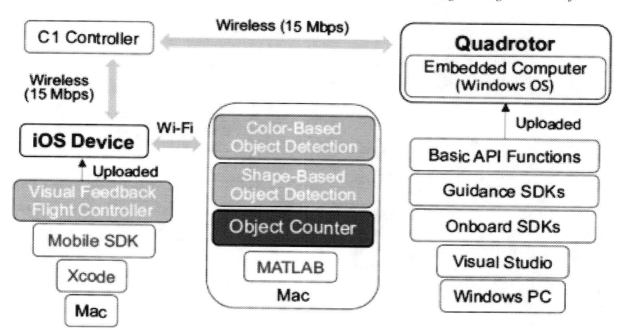

In the developed tool, lower and upper thresholds Th1 and Th2 ($0 <$ Th1 $<$ Th2 < 1) are required to be set in advance. For example, the binarized R channel based on Th2 is set to RB if a red object is searched. Similarly, the binarized G and B channels based on Th1 are set to GB and BB, respectively. Then, pixels having a value set to 1 in the RB channel and simultaneously 0 in both the GB and BB channels are set to 1, and the remaining ones are set to 0 so that a new binary image BW is generated. This BW identifies object candidates based on the two-dimensional connectivity specified by 4-connection or 8-connection, as shown in Fig. 4. Accordingly, the COG of the object with the largest area can be calculated. For example, in the case of 8-connection, pixels, whose edges or corners are touching, are connected to shape an object. Two adjacent pixels become a part of the same object if they are connected along the horizontal, vertical, or diagonal direction. In this experiment, a method with 8-connection is used. Once a green or blue object is specified, it is possible to obtain the COG position associated with the largest object following the same procedure.

Also, if a white object is specified, then pixels with values 1 in all RB, GB, and BB are set to 1; if a black object is specified, then pixels with 0 in all RB, GB, and BB are set to 0. Consequently, a new binary image BW can be generated for COG calculation. Object candidates are nominated based on the two-dimensional connectivity obtained by 8-connection in this BW image, then the largest object is selected and its COG $[G_x(t)G_y(t)]^T$ is finally determined. The COG position is the output from the image processing.

Figure 4. Two-dimensional connectivity called 4- connected and 8-connected, respectively.

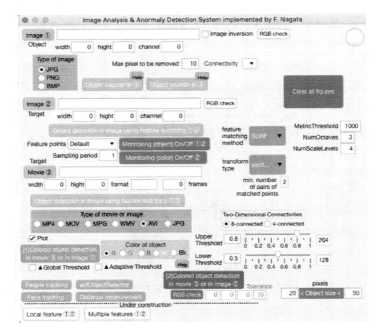

b. Calculation of an Object COG in Image Coordinate System

In the constructed binary image BW, each pixel in the object region has a value of 1, and that in the remaining region has a value of 0.

The COG $[G_x(t)G_y(t)]^T$ of the target object in this BW is calculated using the following equations.

$$G_x(t) = \frac{\sum_{x=1}^{X}\sum_{y=1}^{Y} xf(x,y)}{S} \ldots\ldots \tag{1}$$

$$G_y(t) = \frac{\sum_{x=1}^{X}\sum_{y=1}^{Y} yf(x,y)}{S} \ldots\ldots \tag{2}$$

Where (X, Y) are the width and height of the image and (x, y) are the variables of column and row in the image. Also, f (x, y) is the binary value of a pixel specified by the x and y coordinate, i.e., either 1 or 0. The S represents the area of the extracted object, which means the total number of pixels with a value of 1 forming the object. The quadrotor can track the object by setting the time-varying COG position to $[G_x(t)G_y(t)]^T$ in the feedback, the controller is given by Eqns. (3) and (4). Object detection in image frames can be done by specifying the color and the shape template discussed below.

2. Function to Extract Object COG by Shape

Another object detection method based on the shape of objects is developed. In a preliminary comparative experiment, the target tracking function provided in the Mobile SDK is used to detect the movement based on the object's shape in a video. The quadrotor searched for a rectangular tracking target, locked it after recognizing it, and automatically started tracking it while maintaining the desired altitude. Several experiments were conducted to assess the performance of the tracking function. Consequently, as a severe drawback of the SDK, it was found that the SDK could not recognize shapes other than a rectangle or a circle.

In order to improve the functionality, two types of shape-based object detection methods are developed using MATLAB to track an object with an arbitrary shape. This function can be executed through the mobile application using an iOS device. The first object detection method is executed by specifying a target template image. The template image is raster-scanned pixel by pixel from the upper left to the lower right in a scene frame image. The highest matched region with the template in the scene image is extracted based on the correlation coefficient. Since each movie recorded every sampling period can be divided into multiple frames (still images), the still image processing to calculate COG described in A.2 can be applied similarly. However, this object detection method is not robust to changing the orientation of objects and scale.

The performance of arbitrarily set orientation and scale is enhanced by considering the second shape-based object detection using functions provided by MATLAB. First of all, feature points called interest points in both of the target template images and the scene frame image, containing information about speeded-up robust features (SURF) (Bay et al., 2008), are severally detected. Then, feature vectors called descriptors, and their corresponding positions are extracted from each grayscaled image. The feature vectors are derived from pixels surrounding interest points. Next, matched feature points are obtained based on pairwise distances between feature vectors found in the template and scene frame images. Finally, taking an average of the matched feature points can lead to obtaining the COG position of the target object in the scene frame image.

3. Visual Feedback Control of a Quadrotor

A visual feedback flight control is realized using COG information in consecutive scene frame images. The velocity vector $v(t) = [v_x(t) v_y(t)]^T$ for the manipulated variable needed to control a quadrotor is given by,

$$v(t) = -k_p e(t) - k_i \int e(t) dt \ldots \ldots$$

(3)

where k_p and k_i are the feedback gains for Proportional (P) and Integral (I) control components. Error $e(t) = [e_x(t) e_y(t)]^T$ in the image coordinate system viewed from the quadrotor is given by

$$\begin{pmatrix} e_x(t) \\ e_y(t) \end{pmatrix} = \begin{pmatrix} \dfrac{X}{2} \\ \dfrac{Y}{2} \end{pmatrix} - \begin{pmatrix} G_x(t) \\ G_y(t) \end{pmatrix} \ldots \ldots$$

(4)

where $[G_x(t)G_y(t)]^T$ is the current COG position of the target object, while $\left[\dfrac{X}{2}\ \dfrac{Y}{2}\right]^T$ represents the desired target position, i.e., the center of the captured image. The configuration of this description is shown in Fig. 5.

Figure 5. Camera coordinate system viewed from the quadrotor.

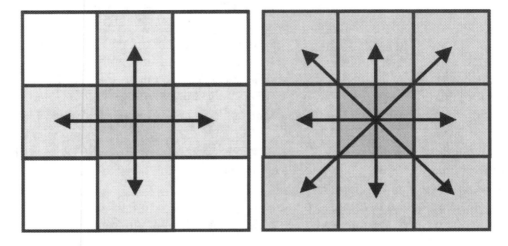

Figure 5 shows the camera (image) coordinate system viewed from the endoscope camera in VF control mode. The VF controller flexibly and steadily performs to get the quadrotor to approach just above the object. Hence, the Vf control mode makes it possible to control the norm of the error vector between the center of the captured image and the object COG to zero. Figure 6 shows a real successful experimental scene of the target tracking function, in which the VF control laws given by Eqns. (3) and (4) are applied with a sampling period of 40 ms. Note that the aspect ratio (X, Y) of the target scene frame is changed to a typical 1280×720 from the original size of 1310×600 to make it easier to see

Figure 6. A real successful experimental scene of the shape-based target tracking function.

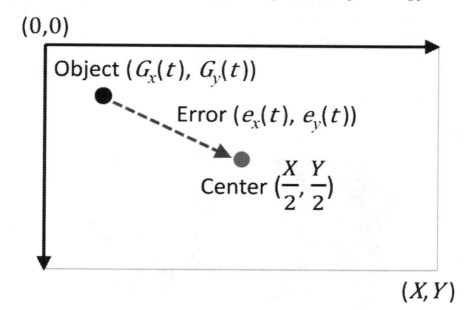

4. Object Counting Function

A function needs to be developed to count the number of target objects available in an image to fulfill the target object counting task. Figure 7 shows a test image of (860×726) used to evaluate the proposed counting function. First, in Fig. 8, the opening operation defines a disk-shaped structured element with a radius of 15 pixels. The objects that are completely contained in this structured element (objects to be counted) are deleted.

Figure 7. Test image for evaluating the counting function

Then, subtracting the adjusted background image in Fig. 8 from the original image in Fig. 7 gives an image like Fig. 9. By unifying the background color to black, it is possible to facilitate post-process and analysis. In addition, the function named "imadjust()" is used to increase the contrast of the processed image by saturating the pixel values in Fig. 9 with their lower 1% and upper 1%. Consequently, a clear image like Fig. 10 is obtained. Since the pixel values of target objects correspond to the upper 1% of all the pixel values in Fig. 9, they can be displayed in brighter white, as shown in Fig. 10.

Figure 8. After processing by using a disk-shaped structuring element.

Figure 9. After subtracting the background color in Fig. 8 from Fig. 7.

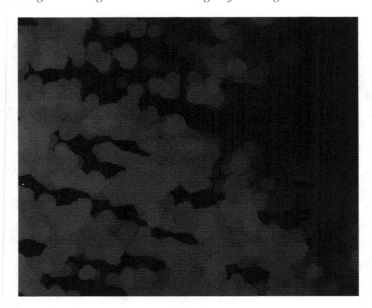

Figure 10. After enhancing the contrast of Fig. 9.

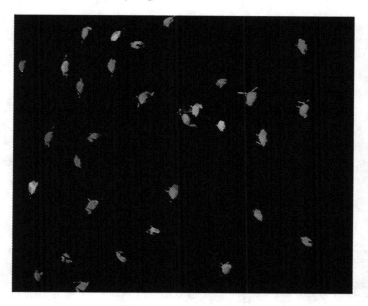

Finally, the MATLAB image processing function named "imbinarize()" is used to convert a grayscale image to a binary image, which enables the analysis by the function "bwareaopen()". The "bwareaopen()" has a function to delete small objects that should not be counted in the binary image, and at this time, the objects with an area of less than 160 in terms of the total number of pixels are deleted. Figure 11 shows the coordinates and the area of each object detected in the binarized image. In this experiment, 31 objects were detected and counted.

Figure 11. After binarizing Fig. 7 to identify target objects effectively.

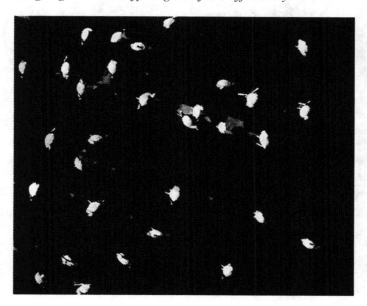

APPLICATION OF VF CONTROLLER TO A PICK AND PLACE ROBOT

In this chapter, a quadrotor was controlled using a smartphone, and its application to environmental monitoring was our principle motivating development. In addition, the VF controller was applied to a pick and place robot. The authors developed convolutional neural networks (CNN) to efficiently construct transfer learning-based CNNs that can classify images of products into several categories as non-defect or defects, such as crack, burr, chipping, and so on (Nagata et al., 2021). BY using the CNN design application, the construction of a transfer learning-based CNN to estimate the orientation of objects is shown in Fig. 12, which illustrates the redesigned replaced part. In the transfer learning-based CNN design, the last fully connected layers are replaced for orientation detection. A total of 12 labels are set every 15 degrees.

Figure 12. Structure of a transfer learning-based CNN for estimating the orientation of objects.

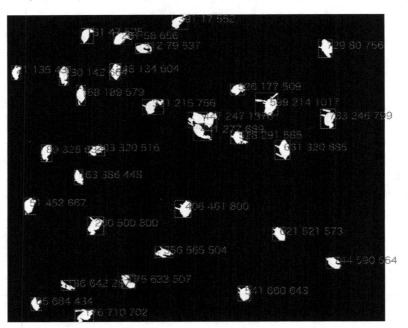

After the training of the CNN, the generalization ability was checked by classifying several test images of pen-type objects. Figure 13 shows the classification result. As can be seen, the CNN could well detect the orientation. The CNN is applied to a pick and place robot, as shown in Fig. 14. The VF controller is also incorporated to omit the complicated calibration process concerning camera and robot coordinate systems (Nagata et al., 2020). Figure 14 shows the experimental setup based on a DOBOT magician with an endoscope camera. The endoscope camera is used and fixed close to the gripper to snapshot the top of the working table.

Figure 13. Classification results of test images using the transfer learning-based CNN to estimate object orientation.

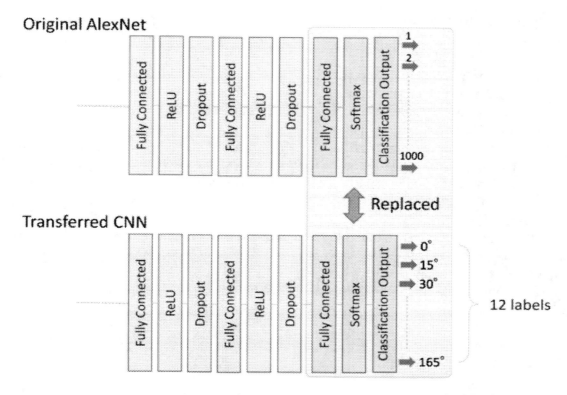

Figure 14. Pick and place robot utilizing a VF controller and a CNN-based orientation estimator.

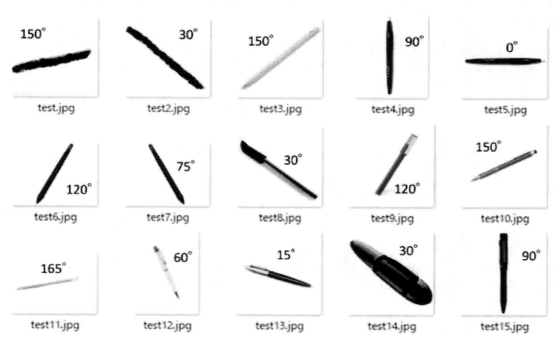

CONCLUSION

This chapter successfully presented the application development using quadcopter and visual feedback through real-time movie frames. The quadrotor can automatically recognize the existence of a target object within the scene and count them successfully. It is possible to use color or shape information to facilitate automatic recognition of desired objects in the video frames to extract the COG of each object and in each frame successfully. Such development was applied to the visual feedback control for automatic tracking without using GPS signals. Consequently, promising visual feedback flight control using a smartphone could be easily realized.

Besides the VF controller, another useful function to count the number of target objects has also been considered. Experiments to count the birds in test frames show that this function enables the quadrotor to monitor the number of individual objects available in movie frames, such as animals, cars, and others. In future work, AI techniques such as convolutional neural networks are planned to enhance identification and counting performance.

In addition, another application of the VF controller has been introduced for a pick and place robot. A convolutional neural network (CNN) to estimate the orientations of resin molded articles can be successfully incorporated. In future work, promising CNNs to identify counted objects are planned to be designed and implemented in the quadrotor. The CNNs will enhance the performance of the quadrotor-based environment monitoring system.

REFERENCES

Allen, R., & Mazumder, M. (2020). Toward an Autonomous Aerial Survey and Planning System for Humanitarian Aid and Disaster Response. *2020 IEEE Aerospace Conference*, 1-11. 10.1109/AERO47225.2020.9172766

Bay, H., Ess, A., Tuytelaars, T., & Gool, L. V. (2008). SURF: Speeded Up Robust Features. *Computer Vision and Image Understanding, 110*(3), 346–359. doi:10.1016/j.cviu.2007.09.014

Cao, Z., Chen, X., Yu, Y., Yu, J., Liu, X., Zhou, C., & Tan, M. (2020). Image Dynamics-Based Visual Servoing for Quadrotors Tracking a Target with a Nonlinear Trajectory Observer. *IEEE Transactions on Systems, Man, and Cybernetics. Systems, 50*(1), 376–384. doi:10.1109/TSMC.2017.2720173

Dji. (2021). *Matrice 100.* https://www.dji.com/matrice100/

Gomez-Avila, J., Lopez-Franco, C., Alanis, A. Y., Arana-Daniel, N., & Lopez-Franco, M. (2018). Ground Vehicle Tracking with a Quadrotor using Image Based Visual Servoing. *IFAC Papers OnLine, 2nd IFAC Conference on Modelling, Identification and Control of Nonlinear Systems MICNON 2018, 51*(13), 344–349. 10.1016/j.ifacol.2018.07.302

Hattori, H. (2008). Stereo Vision Technology for Automotive Applications. *IEEE Intelligent Vehicles Symposium, 63*(5), 48–51.

Koziar, Y., Levchuk, V., & Koval, A. (2019). Quadrotor Design for Outdoor Air Quality Monitoring. *2019 IEEE 39th International Conference on Electronics and Nanotechnology (ELNANO),* 736-739.

Lu, Z., Nagata, F., & Watanabe, K. (2017a). Development of iOS application handlers for quadrotor UAV remote control and monitoring. *2017 IEEE International Conference on Mechatronics and Automation (ICMA)*, 513-518. 10.1109/ICMA.2017.8015870

Lu, Z., Nagata, F., & Watanabe, K. (2018). Mission Planning of iOS Application for a Quadrotor UAV. *Artificial Life and Robotics*, 23(3), 428–433. doi:10.100710015-018-0432-3

Lu, Z., Nagata, F., Watanabe, K., & Habib, M. K. (2017b). iOS Application for Quadrotor UAV Remote Control – Implementation of Basic Functions with iPhone. *Artificial Life and Robotics*, 22(3), 374–379. doi:10.100710015-017-0372-3

Nagata, F., Habib, M. K., & Watanabe, K. (2021). Design and Implementation of Convolutional Neural Network based SVM Technique for Manufacturing Defect Detection. *International Journal of Mechatronics and Automation*, 8(2), 53–61.

Nagata, F., Miki, K., Otsuka, A., Yoshida, K., Watanabe, K., & Habib, M. K. (2020). Pick and Place Robot Using Visual Feedback Control and Transfer Learning-Based CNN. *Procs. of the 2020 IEEE International Conference on Mechatronics and Automation (ICMA 2020)*, 850-855.

Otsuka, H., Yajima, R., Nagatani, K., & Kubo, D. (2015). Localization of a Small Multi-Rotor UAV Using Dropping AR Markers. *Procs. of the 2015 JSME Conference on Robotics and Mechatronics*, 2A2-G02.

Rosario, J.R.B., Azarraga, E.J.C., Chiu, M.J.C., Del Rosario, A.J.C., Jarabelo, A.B.S., & Bandala, A.A. (2020). Development of a Vision Based Parking Monitoring System Using Quadrotor UAV. *Proc. Of the 2020 IEEE 12th International Conference on Humanoid, Nanotechnology, Information Technology, Communication and Control, Environment, and Management (HNICEM)*, 1-6.

Saito, H., Takubo, T., Ueno, A., Cai, K., Miyamoto, R., & Hara, S. (2018). Recognizing Own UAV Position and Measuring Position of a Person Using Camera Image. *Procs. of the 2018 JSME Conference on Robotics and Mechatronics*, 1P1-C08. 10.1299/jsmermd.2018.1P1-C08

Serizawa, K., Ladig, R., & Shimonomura, K. (2019). Movable Camera and Stereoscopic Image System for Teleoperation of Aerial Robot Working in High Place. *Procs. of the 2019 JSME Conference on Robotics and Mechatronics*, 1P2-N08. 10.1299/jsmermd.2019.1P2-N08

Shao, L., Nagata, F., Ochi, H., Otsuka, A., Ikeda, T., Watanabe, K., & Maki, K. H. (2020). Visual Feedback Control of Quadrotor by Object Detection in Movies. *Procs. of 25th International Symposium on Artificial Life and Robotics*, 624–628. 10.100710015-020-00609-3

Shao, L., Nagata, F., Ochi, H., Otsuka, A., Ikeda, T., Watanabe, K., & Maki, K. H. (2020). Visual Feedback Control of Quadrotor by Object Detection in Movies. *Artificial Life and Robotics*, 25(3), 488–494. doi:10.100710015-020-00609-3

Shao, L., Nagata, F., & Watanabe, K. (2019). Remote Control Application for a Quadrotor Supporting iOS and Android. *Procs. of the 2019 JSME Conference on Robotics and Mechatronics*, 1P1–N06.

Sheng, H., Shi, E., & Zhang, K. (2019). Image-Based Visual Servoing of a Quadrotor with Improved Visibility Using Model Predictive Control. *Procs. Of the 2019 IEEE 28th International Symposium on Industrial Electronics (ISIE)*, 551–556. 10.1109/ISIE.2019.8781212

Yang, L., Liu, Z., & Wang, X. (2019). A New Image-Based Visual Servo Control Algorithm for Target Tracking Problem of Fixed-Wing Unmanned Aerial Vehicle. *Procs. Of the 2019 Chinese Control Conference (CCC),* 8142-8147. 10.23919/ChiCC.2019.8865341

Chapter 6
Digital Charge Estimation for Piezoelectric Actuators:
An Artificial Intelligence Approach

Morteza Mohammadzaheri

 https://orcid.org/0000-0002-8187-6375

Birmingham City University, UK & Sultan Qaboos University, Oman

Hamidreza Ziaiefar

Sultan Qaboos University, Oman

Mojtaba Ghodsi

University of Portsmouth, UK

ABSTRACT

For many piezoelectric actuators and their areas of operating, charge is proportional to the position of the actuator. Thus, for such actuators, estimation of charge is largely considered as an equivalent to position estimation. That is, a charge estimator may replace a position sensor. Nevertheless, a significant portion of the excitation voltage is wasted for charge estimation. This voltage, not used to deform the actuator, is called voltage drop. A class of charge estimators of piezoelectric actuators have a resistor in series with the actuator and can only work together with a digital processor. These are called digital charge estimators and have been shown to witness the smallest voltage drop compared to other charge estimators. This chapter first proposes a design guide for digital charge estimators of piezoelectric actuators to maximise the accuracy with the smallest possible voltage drop. The chapter then details the use of five different artificial intelligence (AI) techniques to tackle this design problem and assesses their effectiveness through even-handed comparison.

DOI: 10.4018/978-1-7998-8686-0.ch006

INTRODUCTION

Piezoelectricity, the inter-convertibility of mechanical and electrical quantities in so-called piezoelectric materials was discovered in 19th century by Curie brothers (Jayesh Minase et al., 2010). Currently, quartz and other crystals, ferroelectric polycrystalline ceramics, piezoceramics (e.g. barium titanate) and most commonly lead zirconate titanate (PZT) are used to produce piezoelectric materials (Aggrey et al., 2020; Izyumskaya et al., 2007; Jayesh Minase et al., 2010; Yang et al., 2020).

In piezoelectric materials, electrons are distributed asymmetrically in ions (Sabek et al., 2015). Therefore, mechanical force, which moves ions, provides energy to electrons, and this results in electrical voltage. In addition, electrical voltage, through pushing electrons, moves ions and generates deformation. The latter case is known as inverse piezoelectricity (Chopra, 2002). Devices, made of piezoelectric materials and deliberately produced to employ inverse piezoelectricity, are called piezoelectric actuators(Rios & Fleming, 2014). Piezoelectric actuators have applications in energy harvesting (Hou et al., 2021), vibration control (Singh et al., 2021) and precise positioning (Flores & Rakotondrabe, 2021) including micro/nanopositioning.

Piezoelectric actuators are both the most compact and the most precise actuators in micro/nanopositioning (Mohammadzaheri & AlQallaf, 2017). Micro/nanopositioning aims at precise position control of matter at micro/nanometre scale (Morteza Mohammadzaheri et al., 2021), which is not necessarily equivalent to the development of micrometric scale actuators or sensors, e.g. in (Versaci et al., 2021; Xu et al., 2019). Fine machining (Hu et al., 2021), manipulation of biological cells (Deng et al., 2021), scanning probe microscopy (Szeremeta et al., 2021) and precise robotic surgery (Meinhold et al., 2020) are among applications of micro/nanopositioning with piezoelectric actuators or piezo-actuated micro/nanopositioning .

The key task in piezo-actuated micro/nanopositioning is precise position control of (an unfixed point/surface of) the actuator (Miri et al., 2015). The origin of the position of (a point/surface on) a piezoelectric actuator is its position at relaxed state, when the actuator has not been subject to any electrical or mechanical excitation for a considerably long period of time (e.g. some minutes). That is, position of a piezoelectric actuator is its displacement from the relaxed state. Experiments have indicated that charge of a piezoelectric actuator is proportional to its position for a wide area of operating (Bazghaleh et al., 2010; M Bazghaleh et al., 2013; J. Minase et al., 2010; Yi & Veillette, 2005). Consequently, a charge estimator can replace a costly and demanding position/displacement sensor. This has been a prominent motivation for design and built of charge estimators for piezoelectric actuators (Liu et al., 2018; Mohammadzaheri & AlQallaf, 2017; Yang et al., 2017).

All existing charge estimators need electrical element(s) (e.g. resistor(s) or capacitor(s)) in series with the piezoelectric actuator. Such elements take/waste a portion of the excitation voltage (Bazghaleh et al., 2018) . This squandered voltage does not deform the actuator, and is commonly known as "voltage drop"(J. Minase et al., 2010). It has been reported that, among existing charge estimators of piezoelectric actuators, estimators with a sensing resistor witness the smallest voltage drop (M Bazghaleh et al., 2013). These estimators, unlike others, cannot be implemented without digital processors. Hence, they are broadly named "digital charge estimators" (Mohammadzaheri, Emadi, et al., 2019).Such digital charge estimators are the focus of this book chapter.

The sensing resistor of digital charge estimators often either has a fixed resistance, e.g. in (Mohsen Bazghaleh, Steven Grainger, et al., 2013; M Bazghaleh et al., 2013; Mohsen Bazghaleh, Morteza Mohammadzaheri, et al., 2013) or a few intuitively selected resistances (M Bazghaleh et al., 2013). This book chapter shows that such estimators lead to either a considerable voltage drop or a noticeable impreciseness in wide operating areas. The chapter shows that the aforementioned dilemma can be appropriately resolved, if a varying resistance is employed and the resistance is correctly found for different operating areas. Analytical approach to find the apt resistance has been shown to suffer from inherent defects (Mohammadzaheri, Emadi, et al., 2019). This book chapter, instead, employs artificial intelligence (AI) techniques to find the apt resistance for the sensing resistor.

As detailed in "Problem Statement", the chapter particularly requires AI techniques to identify a mathematical function out of experimental input-output data. Data-driven system modelling (or regression) methods based on supervised learning suit such a purpose (Sen et al., 2020). To the best of authors' knowledge, only five existing AI methods in this category are universal approximators, with verified ability for data-driven modelling: radial basis function networks, RBFNs (both exact and efficient types), neurofuzzy networks, multi-layer perceptions (MLPs), and fully connected cascade, FFC, networks. (Chen & Chen, 1995; Morteza Mohammadzaheri, Lei Chen, et al., 2012; Mohammadzaheri, Ghodsi, et al., 2018; Park & Sandberg, 1993; Ying, 1998). All these methods are examined in this chapter to tackle the stated problem, and their performance is compared.

The parameters of employed AI models are normally identified with one of the following general approaches or a combination of them: (i) transformation of the parameter identification problem to a matrix equation and solving the matrix equation, widely used in linear modelling and support vector machines e.g. (Azimi-Pour et al., 2020) and (ii) defining an error function and minimising/optimising this function iteratively through a derivative-based optimisation method. RBFNs are often (and in this research) identified with approach (i) and MLP and FFC networks with approach (ii). A hybrid approach is commonly used to identify the parameters of neuro-fuzzy networks. Antecedent parameters are iteratively tuned with a gradient method (approach ii), but at each iteration, the parameters of the consequent are identified through the method of least square of errors, based on matrix calculations, (approach iii). Detailed information on the employed AI models in this research and their parameter identification methods is presented in section "Artificial Intelligence Approach to Approximate the Sensing Resistor"

Digital Charge Estimators of Piezoelectric Actuators

Figure 1 depicts a schematic of a digital charge estimator. V_e is the 'excitation voltage'. V_S is the voltage across the sensing resistor, R_S, or the 'sensing voltage', and f_c is the cut-off frequency of the high-pass filter in Hz. The estimator is composed of (i) a digital part, inside the computer, (ii) an analogue to digital (A/D) converter, and (iii) an analogue part including a piezoelectric actuator and a sensing resistor.

The sensing resistor, R_S, is grounded; thus, almost all the current passing through the actuator, i_P, moves along R_S. Therefore, i_P is nearly equal to the current passing R_S, i.e. i_R. In addition, as to Kirchhoff voltage law, $V_S = i_R R_S$. Hence,

$$i_P \simeq i_R = \frac{V_S}{R_S}. \tag{1}$$

Figure 1. A schematic of digital charge estimator. The estimator includes integral and high pass filter in a computer software or program (digital part), a grounded sensing resistor and the actuator (analogue part) and an A/D convertor to connect the analogue part to the digital part.

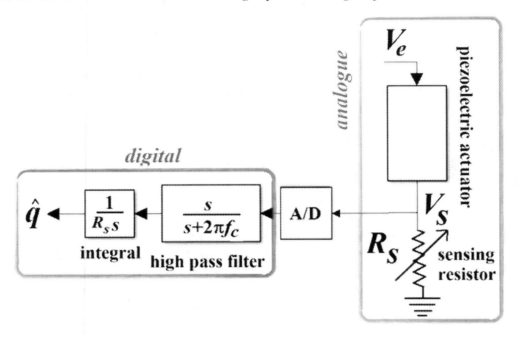

Theoretically, integral of i_p is the charge of the actuator. However, such an integration has complications. The reason is that the A/D converter, in practice, adds a miniscule offset voltage to electrons. This offset voltage besides dielectric voltage leakage of the piezoelectric actuator create a low frequency (nearly constant) tiny bias voltage, V_b. Therefore, the voltage of the current entering A/D is $V_S + V_b$, in reality. V_b is integrated together with V_S, as shown in (2), and adversely affects estimation accuracy. In summary, the estimated charge, $\hat{q}_P$, is not equal to the actual charge of the actuator, q_p:

$$\hat{q}_P = \int \frac{V_S + V_b}{R_s} \, dt \neq \int \frac{V_S}{R_s} \, dt \simeq q_P. \tag{2}$$

This discrepancy is known as drift (Mohsen Bazghaleh, Morteza Mohammadzaheri, et al., 2013). A high-pass filter, e.g. the one in Fig.1, can subdue low frequency voltage signals including V_b and accordingly prevent drift. This filter, however, suppresses low frequency components of V_S either. Consequently, digital charge estimators do not suit low frequency applications.

PROBLEM STATEMENT

Considering Fig.1, with a known A/D convertor and actuator, the main task in design/optimisation of a digital charge estimator for a piezoelectric actuator is to choose the sensing resistance, R_S. Dual rough design objectives of O1 and O2 are taken into account for this purpose:

- O1- high precision
- O2- low voltage drop

The A/D converter plays a critical role in the selection of R_S so as to meet the aforementioned design objectives, particularly O1. Each A/D unit has n bits resolution (e.g. 8 or 12 bits) and one or a number of range(s) for its input voltage (e.g. ± 1 V, ± 5 V and ± 10 V). After discretisation, the input range of choice is presented by uniformly distributed 2^n digital numbers (Gray, 2006). For any given input range of the A/D converter, a wider coverage of the range by the input voltage (e.g. V_S in Fig.1) means that the input voltage is presented by more digital numbers (maximum 2^n). For example, let us assume in two digital estimators, half and full of the input range is covered by V_S. Then, V_S is presented by 2^{n-1} and 2^n digital numbers respectively. In the latter case (full coverage of the input range), each digital number refers to 50% smaller value of V_S. This simply means a higher precision. Thus, for any given resolution/input range in digital charge estimators, maximum precision is attained, if an input range of the A/D is fully covered by V_S. In other words, in order to achieve O1, R_S should be selected so as the range of V_S equals an input range of the A/D.

Voltage drop, the portion of V_e not used for actuator deformation, equals V_S. Therefore, V_S can replace voltage drop in O2, and O2 can be re-expressed as V_S should be as small as possible.

In summary, for a digital estimator with a given A/D, design objectives of O1 and O2 may result in the following design recommendations:

i- The range of V_S should be equal to an input range of the A/D.
ii- V_S should be as small as possible.

Both abovementioned recommendations, with prioritising the precision, can be merged as «Design Guide: the range of V_S should be equal to the smallest input range of the A/D».

This guide assures the maximum precision at the smallest possible voltage drop. The value(s) of R_S, in Fig. 1, meeting the aforementioned design guide are called 'apt' in this chapter, $\tilde{R}_S$.

Figure 2 depicts V_S for the digital estimator of Fig.1, where the actuator is a $5\times5\times36$ mm^3 piezoelectric stack actuator (PiezoDrive, 2021) and $R_S = 44$ Ω. The excitation voltage is a triangular function of time with the peaks 0 and 20 V and frequencies of 20 Hz and 60 Hz. The smallest input range of the A/D converter is ± 0.625 V. Figure 2 shows that, with the excitation frequency of 60 Hz, the smallest input range of the A/D (± 0.625 V) is almost fully covered by V_S, and the design guide is satisfied. However, with the frequency of 20 Hz, more than half of the minimum input range of the A/D is not used; that is, the design guide is not satisfied.

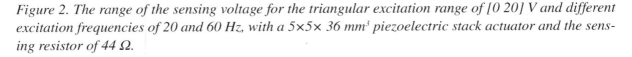

Figure 2. The range of the sensing voltage for the triangular excitation range of [0 20] V and different excitation frequencies of 20 and 60 Hz, with a 5×5× 36 mm³ piezoelectric stack actuator and the sensing resistor of 44 Ω.

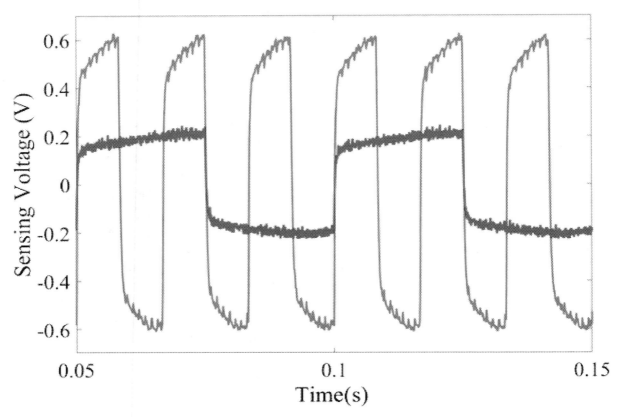

Figure 2 indicates that a digital charge estimator with a fixed R_S cannot satisfy the design guide for an extensive area of operating. While, reported digital charge estimators of piezoelectric actuators mostly use one (Mohsen Bazghaleh, Steven Grainger, et al., 2013; Mohsen Bazghaleh, Morteza Mohammadzaheri, et al., 2013) or a few intuitively selected values of R_S (M Bazghaleh et al., 2013). This chapter, alternatively, proposes an adaptive digital charge estimator with a varying R_S so as to satisfy the design guide for different operating areas. Such a digital charge estimator needs a formula (*F* in (3)) to approximate $\tilde{R}_S$ at various values of operating factors:

$$R_S^* = F(\text{operating factors}): \text{range of } V_S = \text{smallest input range of the A/D} \tag{3}$$

where operating factors are amplitude (in V), waveform and frequency (in Hz) of the excitation voltage (V_e in Fig.1). R_S^* denotes an approximated value of $\tilde{R}_S$.

This chapter addresses operating areas with either sinusoidal or triangular excitation voltages, in which their use have been frequently reported in micro/nanopositioning (Morteza Mohammadzaheri, Steven Grainger, et al., 2012b; Mohammadzaheri et al., 2013; M. Mohammadzaheri et al., 2012). For either sinusoidal or triangular excitation voltage functions, operating factors are range, r, and frequency, f, of the excitation voltage:

$$\begin{cases} \widehat{R}_{SS} = F_S(r, f) : r = \min(\text{input ranges of the A/D}) & \text{sinusoidal excitation} \\ \widehat{R}_{ST} = F_T(r, f) : r = \min(\text{inpput ranges of the A/D}) & \text{triangualr excitation} \end{cases} \quad (4)$$

where F_S, R_{SS}, F_T and R_{ST} are the equivalents of F and R_S in (3) for sinusoidal or triangular excitation voltages respectively. This chapter focuses on identification of F_S and F_T, in order to approximate $\tilde{R}_S$. Identification of F_S and F_T, with a physics-based analytical approach has been tried and shown to be inaccurate (Mohammadzaheri, Emadi, et al., 2020; Mohammadzaheri, Emadi, et al., 2019; Moham-madzaheri; et al., 2019). This chapter employs five different artificial intelligence methods to identify F_S and F_T, compares them and interprets the findings.

EXPERIMENTAL DATA COLLECTION

Figure 3 depicts the excitation voltages used in experiments. The values of r were set to 10, 15, 20, 25, 30 and 35 V for sinusoidal excitations, and 10, 20, 30, 40 and 50 V for triangular excitations. In both cases, the values of f were 20, 30, 40, 50, 60, 70 and 80 Hz . As a result, 35 and 42 experiments were conducted for triangular and sinusoidal excitations, respectively.

The utilised piezoelectric actuator is a 5×5×36 mm³, detailed in (PiezoDrive, 2021) . An Aetechron 7114 voltage amplifier and an Advantech PCI-1710U input/output (I/O) card were also used in experiments. The aforementioned card has A/D units with the resolution of 12 bits and five input ranges: ±10, ±5, ±2.5, ±1.25 and ±0.625 V. Moreover, MATLAB 8.6 /Simulink 8.6 software including Simulink Real-Time Desktop Toolbox 5.1 were used to generate excitation signals and observe the sensing voltages.

In each experiment, partly depicted in Fig.4, for any given excitation voltage, the sensing resistor was tuned so that the sensing voltage range became as close as possible to ±0.625 V, the smallest input range of the A/D. Such a resistance is apt ($\tilde{R}_S$) or satisfies the design guide presented in section Problem Statement. Thus, the outputs of F_S or F_T in (4) should ideally match these values of experimental $\tilde{R}_S$.

Figure 3. A cycle of excitation voltage

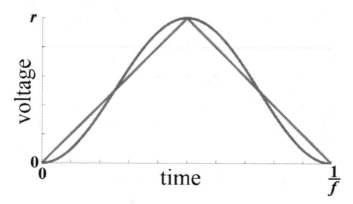

Figure 4. Parts of the experimental setup

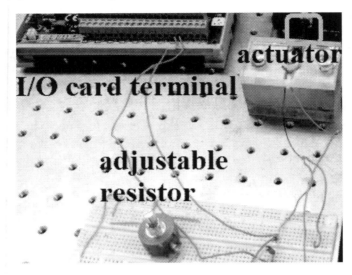

Figure 5 shows the trend of the apt sensing resistors with change of frequency (f) for three ranges of voltage (r). It is evident that for the same f and r, triangular excitation demands a higher $\tilde{R}_S$.

Figure 5. Voltage range (r) versus frequency (f) versus the apt sensing resistance ($\tilde{R}_S$) for some of experimental data for sinusoidal and triangular excitations

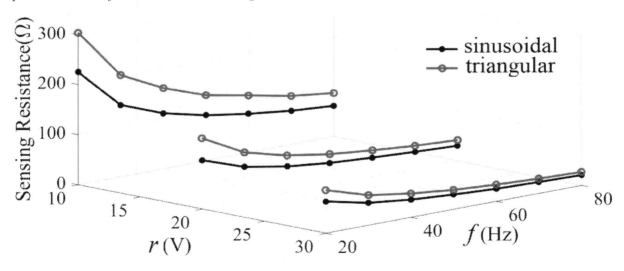

Artificial Intelligence Approach to Approximate the Sensing Resistor

This section reports the development of artificial intelligence models to approximate F_T and F_S in (4) with use of the collected experimental data. The employed types of models are RBFNs (both exact and efficient types), neurofuzzy networks, MLPs and FFC networks. All these models are universal approximators with proven capability to model any system when adequate data are accessible (Chen & Chen, 1995; Morteza Mohammadzaheri, Lei Chen, et al., 2012; Mohammadzaheri, Ghodsi, et al., 2018; Park & Sandberg, 1993; Ying, 1998). The models were developed through programming in MATLAB 9.4 with occasional use of commands from Neural Network Toolbox Version 11.1 and Fuzzy Logic Toolbox Version 2.3.1 of the software package.

Three series of data were employed for model developments: modelling, validation and test data. Modelling data were used to identify the mathematical structure of the model and/or to identify the model parameters. Validation data were used to avoid overfitting. Overfitting refers to excessive focus on matching the model to the modelling data, which lessens the generality of the model (Cawley & Talbot, 2010; Mohammadzaheri et al., 2007). Test data were merely used to cross-validate the model in the end. In this chapter, hold-out or one round cross-validation was used, which simply requires the accuracy of the model with the test data to be acceptable (Lendasse et al., 2003). In this research, for each excitation function and r, seven different values of $\tilde{R}_S$ are available, one per excitation frequency (f). Amongst these seven pieces of data, five were randomly assigned to the modelling data, one to the validation data and one to the test data, as depicted in Figs.6 and 7. As to these figures, the collected experimental data are dense (Mohammadzaheri, Ziaeifar, et al., 2019; Zhang & Wang, 2016).

In all modelling methods, presented in this chapter, the aim is to minimise an error function, E, representing the discrepancy between the experimental and the approximated apt sensing resistors, $\tilde{R}_S$ and R_S' (Mohammadzaheri, Emadi, et al., 2020). Mean of squared errors, defined in (5), was used as the error function in this research, as a popular option for similar problems (Mohammadzaheri, Akbarifar, et al., 2020; Mohammadzaheri, Firoozfar, et al., 2019):

Figure 6. Voltage range (r) and frequency (f) information of modelling, validation and tests data for triangular excitation

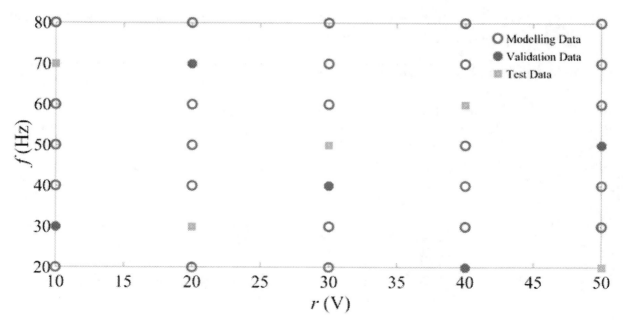

Figure 7. Voltage range (r) and frequency (f) information of modelling, validation and tests data for sinusoidal excitation

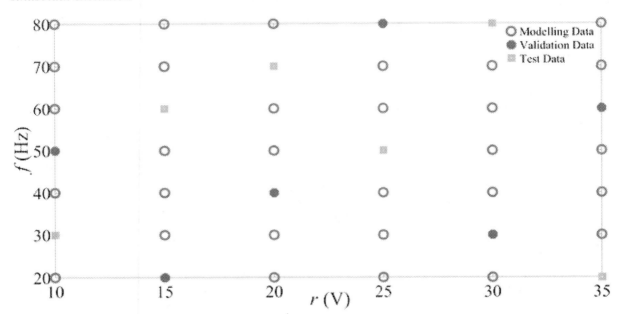

$$E = \frac{\sum_{i=1}^{n_d}\left(R_{Si}^E - \tilde{R}_{Si}\right)^2}{n_d}. \tag{5}$$

where n_d is the number of samples in a data series, e.g. modelling, validation or test data. The following subsections detail different artificial intelligence techniques used in this research.

Radial Basis Function Networks (RBFNs)

An RBFN is a combination of (6) and (7). A vector of inputs, $\mathbf{U}$, with m pairs of r and f is fed into an RBFN, and the model estimates an output vector $\hat{\mathbf{Y}}$, with up to m values of R_S^*. Maximum value of m is the number of data sets within the modelling data, n_m (25 for triangular and 30 for sinusoidal excitation); which is also the maximum value of i and k in (6).

$$\ddot{\mathbf{Y}}_{ik} = \exp\left(-\left(\frac{0.8326}{S}\underbrace{\sum_{j=1}^{2}\left(\mathbf{A}_{ij} - \mathbf{U}_{jk}\right)^2}_{\text{distance between input and weight arrays}}\right)^2\right) \tag{6}$$

$$\hat{\mathbf{Y}}_{1\times m} = \mathbf{B}_{1\times m}\times\mathbf{O}_{m\times m} + \mathbf{C}_{1\times m}. \tag{7}$$

where all elements of $\mathbf{C}$ are same. As to (6), the range of $\mathbf{O}$ elements is [0 1], and the condition of $\mathbf{A}_{ij}=\mathbf{U}_{jk}$ maximises $\mathbf{O}_{ik}$.

In RBFN modelling, arrays of $\mathbf{A}$, $\mathbf{B}$ and $\mathbf{C}$ and the scalar of S namely 'spread' should be defined or identified. At model development stage, $\mathbf{U}_{\mathbf{M}}$ and $\mathbf{Y}_{\mathbf{M}}$, arrays of inputs/outputs of the modelling data were used instead of $\mathbf{U}$ and $\hat{\mathbf{Y}}$. In addition, n_m was used instead of m. Then, it was considered that

$$\mathbf{A}=\mathbf{U}_{\mathbf{M}}^{\mathrm{T}} \quad (8),$$

where T refers to transpose. Thus, all $\mathbf{O}$ elements equalled to 1. Moreover, (9) was replaced with (7) during model development:

$$\mathbf{Y}_{\mathbf{M}\,1\times n_m} =\begin{bmatrix}\mathbf{B} & \mathbf{C}\end{bmatrix}_{1\times 2n_m}\begin{bmatrix}\mathbf{O}\\ \mathbf{I}\end{bmatrix}_{2n_m\times n_m}. \quad (9)$$

$\mathbf{B}$ and $\mathbf{C}$, as the only unknowns of (9), were calculated. Afterwards, S was selected so as to minimise E (as defined in (5)) calculated with the validation data, also known as the validation error, VE. The values of 23 and 141 was opted for S in exact RBFNs approximating F_S and F_T of (4), respectively. Here is the utilised pseudo-algorithm of exact RBFN modelling to find $\mathbf{A}$, $\mathbf{B}$, $\mathbf{C}$ and S using $\mathbf{U}_{\mathbf{M}}$ and $\mathbf{Y}_{\mathbf{M}}$:

Step 1: Set $\mathbf{A}= \mathbf{U}_{\mathbf{M}}^{\mathrm{T}}$
Step 2: Set $\mathbf{O}_{nm\times nm}=\mathrm{ones}(n_m\times n_m)$
Step 3: Form and solve (9) with $\mathbf{Y}_{\mathbf{M}}$ and $\mathbf{O}$ to find $\mathbf{B}$ and $\mathbf{C}$
Step 4: Find S, with trial and error, so as to minimise the validation error of the developed RBFN

The developed exact RBFN model has $3n_m+2$ paraments (scalers or the elements of arrays) to be identified. An alternative with fewer parameters is an efficient RBFN model. In development of these models, a number of (p) columns of $\mathbf{U}_{\mathbf{M}}$ were chosen and transposed to form $\mathbf{A}$(Mohammadzaheri, Ghodsi, et al., 2018). Therefore, the number of $\mathbf{A}$ rows is $p \leq n_m$, and (10) replaced (9):

$$\mathbf{Y}_{\mathbf{M}\,1\times p} =\begin{bmatrix}\mathbf{B} & \mathbf{C}\end{bmatrix}_{1\times 2p}\begin{bmatrix}\mathbf{O}\\ \mathbf{I}\end{bmatrix}_{2p\times p}. \quad (10)$$

RBFN modelling was started with picking a spread, S, and a target error, E_t. For each pair of S and E_t, every single column of $\mathbf{U}_{\mathbf{M}}$ was transposed and considered as a single-row $\mathbf{A}$. Then, $\mathbf{B}$ and $\mathbf{C}$ were calculated from (10), where $p=1$. The column of $\mathbf{U}_{\mathbf{M}}$ resulting in the smallest modelling error, ME, was transposed and set as the first row of $\mathbf{A}$. ME was calculated with (5) and the modelling data. Subsequently, other columns of $\mathbf{U}$ were examined to detect the column in which addition of its transpose to $\mathbf{A}$ resulted in the largest decrease of ME. Such a column was then transposed and appended to $\mathbf{A}$. This procedure continued until ME reached E_t. The whole procedure to identify $\mathbf{A}$ was repeated for different pairs of S and E_t. The pair resulted in the lowest VE was opted. Based on similar research, the search space for S and E_t were all integers between 50 and 100 and the numbers between 1 and 10 Ω^2 with an increment of 0.1, respectively. Here is the pseudo-algorithm of efficient RBFN modelling:

Step 1: $\mathbf{A}$=null, $\mathbf{U}_{rem}$= $\mathbf{U}_{\mathbf{M}}$, $\mathbf{U}_{opt}$=null, p=1, EX=VEX=10000 (a large number), $^T\mathbf{A}$=null (temporary weight matrix)

Step 2: Loop 1, for all values of E_t, from 0 to 10 with the increment of 0.1

Step 3: Loop 2, for all values of S, from 50 to 100 with the increment of 1

Step 4: Loop 3, while $EX>E_t$ *and* $p<n_m$, $p=p+1$

Step 5: Loop 4 for all values of k, from 1 to n_m-p with the increment of 1

Step 6: Add transpose of kth column of $\mathbf{U}_{rem}$ to $\mathbf{A}$ to form $^T\mathbf{A}$

Step 7: Calculate $\mathbf{O}$ from (6) with $\mathbf{U}_{rem}$, $^T\mathbf{A}_{p\times n}$ and S

Step 8: Solve (10) to find $\mathbf{B}$ and $\mathbf{C}$ ($\mathbf{Y}_{\mathbf{M}}$ and $\mathbf{O}$ are available from the modelling data and step 7)

Step 9: Find the modelling error, ME (the model should be run more than once if $p< n_m$).

Step 10: If $ME<EX$, then $EX=ME$ and $\mathbf{U}_{opt}=\mathbf{U}_k$

Step 11: End of Loop 4

Step 12: Remove $\mathbf{U}_{opt}$ from $\mathbf{U}_{rem}$ and add it to $\mathbf{A}$

Step 13: End Loop 3

Step 14: Find the validation error, VE

Step 15: If $VE<VEX$ then $VEX=VE$, $SX=S$, $E_tX=E_t$, and store $\mathbf{A}$, $\mathbf{B}$ and $\mathbf{C}$

Step 16: End of Loop 2

Step 17: End of Loop 1

Neurofuzzy Networks

Neurofuzzy networks, fairly similar to the ones used in (Ahmadpour Khanghashlaghi et al., 2009; Angiulli & Versaci, 2002; Lin & Chen, 2005; Mohammadzaheri, AlQallaf, et al., 2018; Morteza Mohammadzaheri, Amirhosein Amouzadeh, Mojtaba Doustmohammadi, Mohammadreza Emadi, Ehsan Jamshidi, Mojtaba Ghodsi, et al., 2021)were employed in this research. Such a neurofuzzy network, unlike RBFNs, receive single sets of inputs, i.e. a pair of r and f, and produces its associate R_s. These neurofuzzy networks have n_r rules, each with two membership functions, one for r and one for f. Each input to the model, u_i, (either r of f), in j^{th} rule, goes through a Gaussian membership function of (11), which results in a membership grade,μ_{ij} (Mehrabi et al., 2017):

$$\mu_{ij} = \exp\left(-\frac{(u_i - \mathbf{D}_{ij})^2}{2\mathbf{E}_{ij}^{\ 2}}\right). \tag{11}$$

The product of dual membership grades of a rule is considered as the weight of the rule, a real number between zero and one. The output of a rule is a linear combination of its inputs, as presented in the numerator of (12). The output of the neurofuzzy network is the weighted sum of rule outputs, similar to the model in (Mehrabi et al., 2017):

$$\widehat{R}_S = \frac{\displaystyle\sum_{j=1}^{n_r}\left(\overbrace{\left(\sum_{i=1}^{2}\mathbf{F}_{ij}u_i+\mathbf{G}_j\right)}^{j^{th}\ rule\ output}\prod_{i=1}^{2}\mu_{ij}\right)}{\displaystyle\sum_{j=1}^{n_r}\underbrace{\prod_{i=1}^{2}\mu_{ij}}_{j^{th}\ rule\ weight}}.$$ (12)

The number of rules of the neurofuzzy model, n_r in (12) and 7 in Fig.8, as well as an initial version of the model were estimated with the modelling data through subtractive clustering algorithm. The employed subtractive algorithm is similar to the one explained in subsection 2-3 of (Morteza Mohammadzaheri, Steven Grainger, et al., 2012a). In both neurofuzzy models, for sinusoidal and triangular excitation voltages, the following parameters were used in subtractive clustering, influence range=0.5, squash factor =1.25, accept ratio=0.5 and reject ratio=0.15.

After finding n_r, the elements of **D**, **E**, **F** and **G**, as the parameters of the model, in (12), were tuned with the modelling data through an iterative algorithm. At each iteration, elements of **D** and **E** were adjusted with gradient descent error back propagation method, and the elements of **F** and **G** were found with least square of errors (LSE) method (Jang et al., 2006; Mohammadzaheri, AlQallaf, et al., 2018). The aforementioned algorithm normally leads to a continuously decreasing modelling error, *ME*. The validation error, *VE*, was calculated too at each iteration. Rise of *VE*, while *ME* keeps decreasing, was perceived as a sign of overfitting. In the case of such an event, aforesaid iterative algorithm was stopped.

Figure 8. Rules of the neurofuzzy network for sinusoidal excitation, an approximation of F_S in (4). The values of 22.5, 50 and 37.5 show an example of pair of inputs and the estimated output.

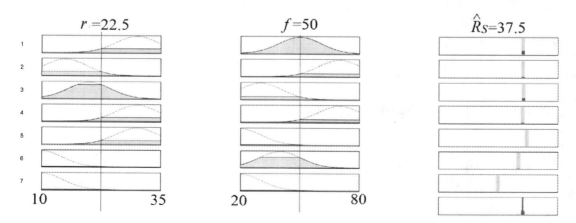

Multi-Layer Perceptrons (MLPs)

The employed MLPs, (13), receive a set of inputs, u_i |i=1 and 2 (*r* and *f*) . The MLP models of this research have one hidden layer of neurons with the activation function ϕ, presented in (14), to fit to the conditions of a universal approximator (Sifaoui et al., 2008). Kolmogorov's theorem suggests that, in MLPs with a single hidden layer, the number of neurons of the hidden layer is 2×(number of inputs)+1 (Hecht-Nielsen, 1987; Morteza Mohammadzaheri, Amirhosein Amouzadeh, Mojtaba Doustmohammadi, Mohammadreza Emadi, Ehsan Jamshidi, Mojataba Ghodsi, et al., 2021; Morteza Mohammadzaheri, Lei Chen, et al., 2012). Thus, the number of hidden layer neurons is 2×2+1=5.

$$\widehat{R}_S = \sum_{j=1}^{5} \mathbf{H}_j \phi \left(\sum_{i=1}^{2} \mathbf{I}_{ij} u_i + \mathbf{J}_i \right) + \mathbf{J}_{i+1}, \tag{13}$$

$$\phi(x) = \frac{2}{1 + \exp(-2x)} - 1. \tag{14}$$

The activation function of (14) is nearly a hyperbolic tangent function. This activation function has been shown to outperform other renowned activation functions such as uni-polar and bi-polar sigmoid, radial basis function (RBF) and conic section in terms of providing the MLP with a higher recognition accuracy (Karlik & Olgac, 2011; Morteza Mohammadzaheri, Amirhosein Amouzadeh, Mojtaba Doustmohammadi, Mohammadreza Emadi, Ehsan Jamshidi, Mojataba Ghodsi, et al., 2021).

Nguyen-Widrow algorithm was employed to find initial values for model parameters, $\mathbf{H}$, $\mathbf{I}$ and $\mathbf{J}$ elements; more details of this algorithm can be found in (Mohammadzaheri et al., 2016; Nguyen & Widrow, 1990). Then, error back propagation with Levenberg-Marquardt algorithm was utilised to minimise the modelling error iteratively and to identify MLP parameters; this algorithm has been explained in (Mohammadzaheri & Chen, 2010). Parameter identification was stopped with the same procedure used for neurofuzzy networks to avoid overfitting.

As a drawback, with some initial values of MLP parameters, the employed parameter identification algorithm is trapped in so called local minima of the modelling error. This results in lack of model accuracy. Accordingly, for approximation of any model of (4) with an MLP, parameter identification was 10 times replicated with different initial parameters. The model with the smallest validation error was opted as the MLP of choice.

Fully Connected Cascade (FCC) Networks

The utilised FCC networks, in terms of mathematical structure, are MLPs with extra parameters ($\mathbf{N}$ elements) which directly connect the inputs to the output, as presented in (15) and Fig.9:

$$\widehat{R}_S = \sum_{j=1}^{5} \mathbf{K}_j \phi \left(\sum_{i=1}^{2} \mathbf{L}_{ij} u_i + \mathbf{M}_i \right) + \sum_{i=1}^{2} \mathbf{N}_i u_i + \mathbf{M}_{i+1}. \tag{15}$$

Figure 9. The schematic of an FCC used in this research. An MLP is similar to an FCC without connections which directly link the inputs to the summation function (Σ).

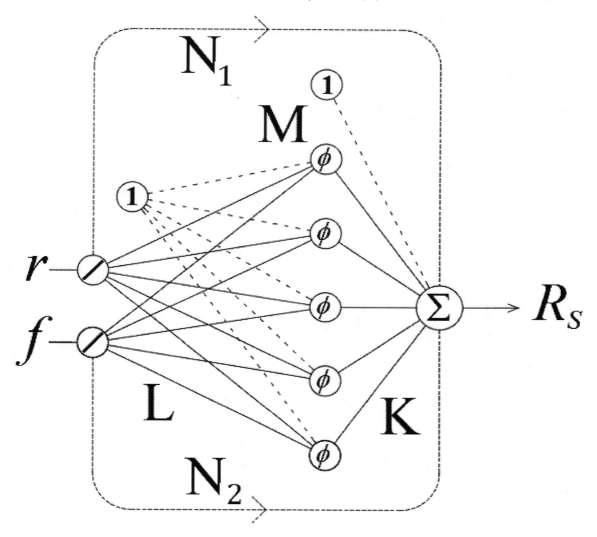

FCC networks use the same inputs, number of layers/neurons and activation functions as the MLPs, as well as same parameter initialisation and parameter identification algorithms. The capability of FCC networks in tackling some non-engineering benchmarks has been presented (Hunter et al., 2012), so that they have been claimed to have the most powerful architecture for system identification (Hunter et al., 2012).

RESULTS AND DISCUSSION

Figures 10 and 11 exhibit the test results, including the values of experimental $\tilde{R}_s$ and R_s approximated by different models for the tests data, never been involved in model developments reported in the previous section. For sinusoidal excitation, exact RBFN and the neurofuzzy network, each, result in an $\hat{R}_{SS}$ obviously distant from $\tilde{R}_{SS}$, shown with *; the second S in the index refers to sinusoidal, as mentioned in (4). In addition, the neurofuzzy network, both RBFNs and the FCC network produce one approximated $\hat{R}_{SS}$ recognisably distant from $\tilde{R}_{SS}$. For triangular excitations, Fig.11, all model outputs are fairly close to $\tilde{R}_{ST}$, shown with *; the second T in the index refers to triangular. However, the neurofuzzy network and both RBFNs have two values of $\hat{R}_{ST}$ detectably distant from $\tilde{R}_{ST}$; the FCC network has such an $\hat{R}_{ST}$ too.

Prior to further analysis of test results of the models, the serious risk associated with overestimation of the apt sensing resistor, $\tilde{R}_S$, needs to be clarified. From figure 1, the relationship between the excitation and the sensing voltages can be found as (16) (Morteza Mohammadzaheri et al., 2021):

$$\frac{V_S(s)}{V_e(s)} = \frac{R_S C_P s}{R_S C_P s + 1}. \tag{16}$$

As a result, (17) demonstrates the relationship between the magnitudes of the two voltages:

$$\frac{|V_S(\omega)|}{|V_e(\omega)|} = \frac{R_S C_P \omega}{\sqrt{R_S^2 C_P^2 \omega^2 + 1}}. \tag{17}$$

where ω is the excitation frequency in rad/s. For a given ω, C_p and $|V_e|$, the greater the R_S, the higher $|V_S|$. Therefore, if a R_S larger than $\tilde{R}_S$ is used, $|V_S|$ exceeds its pre-defined value, i.e. 0.625 V in this research. That is, at occasions, V_S lays outside the selected input range of the A/D converter. Thus, V_S is not correctly transferred to the digital processor, or V_S is saturated. Hence, there is a great risk in overestimation of $\tilde{R}_S$, while underestimation of $\tilde{R}_S$ (i.e. too small $\hat{R}_S$) only reduces the precision, as detailed in Problem Statement section.

Figure 10. Test results for sinusoidal excitation

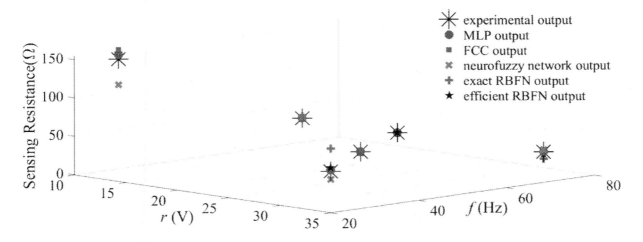

Figure 11. Test results for triangular excitation

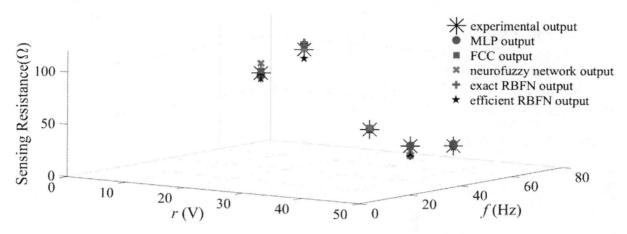

Let us assume error, e, and error bias, b, as

$$\begin{cases} e = \widehat{R}_S - \tilde{R}_S, \\[2mm] b = \dfrac{\displaystyle\sum_{i=1}^{n_t} e_i}{n_t}, \end{cases} \tag{18}$$

where n_t is the number of data sets in the test data. With use of test data and considering a Gaussian distribution for e, it can be concluded that by the chance of 97%, $-3\sigma \le e\text{-}b \le 3\sigma$, (19), where σ is the standard deviation of e (Montgomery & Runger, 2017).
As a result of (19),

$$-3\sigma \le e - b \le 3\sigma \Rightarrow -3\sigma \le \widehat{R}_S - \tilde{R}_S - b \le 3\sigma$$

$$\Rightarrow -3\sigma - \widehat{R}_S + b \le -\tilde{R}_S \le 3\sigma - \widehat{R}_S + b \Rightarrow \widehat{R}_S + 3\sigma - b \ge \tilde{R}_S \ge \widehat{R}_S - 3\sigma - b$$

Thus, by the chance of 97%,

$$\tilde{R}_S \ge \widehat{R}_S - 3\sigma - b. \tag{20}$$

In order to avoid saturation of V_S, a sensing resistance of $R_S^*\text{-}3\sigma\text{-}b$ is recommended to be used, rather than R_S^*. Therefore, a large σ results in too small values of R_S and sacrifice of precision in A/D conversion of V_S. Hence, the models with lower error standard deviation are particularly preferred.

Tables 1 and 2 provide more detailed insight into the performance of the AI models. As to both tables, MLPs clearly outperform other models and provide better results in all criteria except for the error bias. The MLPs have the smallest number of parameters amongst the models, 21, while they still fully meet the requirements of Kolmogorov's theorem. Relatively low number of parameters can play a major role in their performance, considering the fact that the modelling data could be as small as 25 data sets. For sinusoidal excitations, efficient RBFN is the second-best model with a noticeably low error standard deviation. Although, disadvantageously, the number of parameters of this model is more than two times greater than the number of MLP or FCC parameters. For triangular excitations, detailed in Table 2, in terms of commonly accepted criteria of mean of squared errors and mean of absolute errors, the FCC is the second-best model after the MLP. However, the efficient RBFN is the second-best in terms of error standard deviation and maximum absolute error. In general, this research shows the claims about superiority of FCC networks, e.g. in (Hunter et al., 2012), are not valid for the problem proposed and tackled in this chapter.

Table 1. Assessment of different models to estimate the apt sensing resistance with different criteria, for sinusoidal excitations

Sinusoidal Excitation	RBFN Exact	RBFN Efficient	Neurofuzzy	MLP	FCC
Mean of Absolute Errors (Ω)	8.278156	1.884255	8.516957	**1.292185**	2.808868
Max Absolute Error (Ω)	29.38565	7.889629	33.40893	**5.845352**	12.33573
Mean of Squared Errors (Ω^2)	170.7362	11.10937	207.4555	**5.979151**	26.31438
Error Standard Deviation (Ω)	11.98713	2.869653	12.58472	**2.100265**	4.292393
Error Variance (Ω^2)	143.6913	8.234907	158.3751	**4.411114**	18.42464
Error Bias (Ω)	-5.20048	-1.69542	7.005739	**-1.25221**	-2.80887
Number of Parameters	92	50	49	**21**	23

Table 2. Assessment of different models to estimate the apt sensing resistance with different criteria, for triangular excitations

Triangular Excitation	RBFN Exact	RBFN Efficient	Neurofuzzy	MLP	FCC
Mean of Absolute Errors (Ω)	3.350581	4.498346	3.467672	**2.038999**	2.710431
Max Absolute Error (Ω)	9.381276	8.511782	9.401186	**4.619328**	9.02141
Mean of Squared Errors (Ω^2)	26.61291	31.34458	23.0949	**6.44773**	17.58085
Error Standard Deviation (Ω)	5.139481	3.333085	4.540334	**2.326708**	4.095632
Error Variance (Ω^2)	26.41427	11.10946	20.61463	**5.413569**	16.7742
Error Bias (Ω)	0.44569	4.498346	-1.57489	**-1.01694**	0.898133
Number of Parameters	78	50	49	**21**	23

CONCLUSION

This chapter first briefly introduced digital charge estimators of piezoelectric actuators. With given A/D converter and processor, the only adjustable element of these estimators is the resistance of their so called sensing resistor. A design guide was proposed to adjust the aforementioned resistance to maximise charge estimation accuracy with the smallest possible voltage drop. Reported experimental results showed the sensing resistance should adapt itself to the operating condition to meet the design guide.

In order to adapt the sensing resistance, a formula is needed to relate the sensing resistance to the operating conditions. The operating conditions include the relationship of excitation voltage and time (e.g. voltage is a sinusoidal and triangular function of time in this research) as well as the range and the frequency of excitation voltage. It was also shown that overestimation of the sensing resistance is seriously risky, and a method was presented to avoid it, even at the cost of some accuracy loss in charge estimation.

Accurate identification of the formula, mentioned in the previous paragraph, leads to development of highly accurate charge/position estimators with slight voltage drop. Such estimators can replace bulky and expensive position sensors and open new horizons to nanopositioning. Analytical models have already failed to accurately identify the aforementioned formula. Alternatively, five different artificial intelligence methods were utilised to identify the aforementioned formulae: exact and efficient radial basis functions (RBFNs), neurofuzzy networks, multi-layer perceptions (MLPs) and fully connected cascade (FCC) networks. All these methods were employed even-handedly and with appropriate use of randomly chosen modelling, validation and test data, identical for all methods. MLPs show highly accurate estimation and absolute superiority over other methods. Efficient RBFN and FCC are the second-best models for different excitations/criteria. Neurofuzzy network and exact RBFN show occasional significant inaccuracy ($>20\Omega$) in test. In summary, the results support that the MLP is a reliable option to estimate the sensing resistance and to design/optimise digital charge estimators.

REFERENCES

Aggrey, P., Salimon, A., & Korsunsky, A. (2020). Diatomite inspired nanostructured quartz as a piezoelectric material. *Limnology and Freshwater Biology*, (4), 828–829. doi:10.31951/2658-3518-2020-A-4-828

Ahmadpour Khanghashlaghi, M., Yue, W. L., & Mohammadzaheri, M. (2009). *Neuro-fuzzy modelling of workders trip production* The 32nd Austalasian Transport Research Forum, Auckland, New Zealand.

Angiulli, G., & Versaci, M. (2002). A Neuro-Fuzzy Network for the design of circular and triangular equilateral microstrip antennas. *International Journal of Infrared and Millimeter Waves*, 23(10), 1513–1520. doi:10.1023/A:1020333704205

Azimi-Pour, M., Eskandari-Naddaf, H., & Pakzad, A. (2020). Linear and non-linear SVM prediction for fresh properties and compressive strength of high volume fly ash self-compacting concrete. *Construction & Building Materials*, 230, 117021. doi:10.1016/j.conbuildmat.2019.117021

Bazghaleh, M., Grainger, S., Cazzolato, B., & Lu, T.-f. (2010, December). *An innovative digital charge amplifier to reduce hysteresis in piezoelectric actuators*. Australian Robotics and Automation Association (ACRA), Brisbane, Australia.

Bazghaleh, M., Grainger, S., Mohammadzaheri, M., Cazzolato, B., & Lu, T. (2013). A digital charge amplifier for hysteresis elimination in piezoelectric actuators. *Smart Materials and Structures*, 22(7), 075016. doi:10.1088/0964-1726/22/7/075016

Bazghaleh, M., Grainger, S., Mohammadzaheri, M., Cazzolato, B., & Lu, T.-F. (2013). A novel digital charge-based displacement estimator for sensorless control of a grounded-load piezoelectric tube actuator. *Sensors and Actuators. A, Physical, 198*, 91–98. doi:10.1016/j.sna.2013.04.021

Bazghaleh, M., Grainger, S., & Mohammadzaheri, M. J. J. I. M. S. (2018). A review of charge methods for driving piezoelectric actuators. *Journal of Intelligent Material Systems and Structures, 29*(10), 2096–2104. doi:10.1177/1045389X17733330

Bazghaleh, M., Mohammadzaheri, M., Grainger, S., Cazzolato, B., & Lu, T. F. (2013). A new hybrid method for sensorless control of piezoelectric actuators. *Sensors and Actuators. A, Physical, 194*, 25–30. doi:10.1016/j.sna.2013.01.043

Cawley, G. C., & Talbot, N. L. (2010). On over-fitting in model selection and subsequent selection bias in performance evaluation. *Journal of Machine Learning Research, 11*(Jul), 2079–2107.

Chen, T. P., & Chen, H. (1995). Approximation capability to functions of several variables, nonlinear functionals, and operators by radial basis function neural networks. *IEEE Transactions on Neural Networks, 6*(4), 904-910.

Chopra, I. (2002). Review of state of art of smart structures and integrated systems. *AIAA Journal, 40*(11), 2145–2187. doi:10.2514/2.1561

Deng, J., Liu, S., Liu, Y., Wang, L., Gao, X., & Li, K. (2021). A 2-DOF Needle Insertion Device Using Inertial Piezoelectric Actuator. *IEEE Transactions on Industrial Electronics*.

Flores, G., & Rakotondrabe, M. (2021). Robust nonlinear control for a piezoelectric actuator in a robotic hand using only position measurements. *IEEE Control Systems Letters*. Advance online publication. doi:10.1109/LCSYS.2021.3136456

Gray, N. (2006). ABCs of ADCs. N. Semiconductor.

Hecht-Nielsen, R. (1987). Kolmogorov's mapping neural network existence theorem. *Proceedings of the International Conference on Neural Networks*.

Hou, W., Zheng, Y., Guo, W., & Pengcheng, G. (2021). Piezoelectric vibration energy harvesting for rail transit bridge with steel-spring floating slab track system. *Journal of Cleaner Production, 291*, 125283.

Hu, C., Shi, Y., & Liu, F. (2021). Research on Precision Blanking Process Design of Micro Gear Based on Piezoelectric Actuator. *Micromachines, 12*(2), 200. doi:10.3390/mi12020200 PMID:33672013

Hunter, D., Yu, H., Pukish, M. S. III, Kolbusz, J., & Wilamowski, B. M. (2012). Selection of proper neural network sizes and architectures—A comparative study. *IEEE Transactions on Industrial Informatics, 8*(2), 228–240. doi:10.1109/TII.2012.2187914

Izyumskaya, N., Alivov, Y., Cho, S. J., Morkoc, H., Lee, H., & Kang, Y. S. (2007). Processing, structure, properties, and applications of PZT thin films. *Critical Reviews in Solid State and Material Sciences, 32*(3-4), 111–202. doi:10.1080/10408430701707347

Jang, J. R., Sun, C., & Mizutani, E. (2006). *Neuro-Fuzzy and Soft Computing*. Prentice-Hall of India.

Karlik, B., & Olgac, A. V. (2011). Performance analysis of various activation functions in generalized MLP architectures of neural networks. *International Journal of Artificial Intelligence and Expert Systems*, *1*(4), 111–122.

Lendasse, A., Wertz, V., & Verleysen, M. (2003). Model selection with cross-validations and bootstraps—application to time series prediction with RBFN models. *Artificial Neural Networks and Neural Information Processing—ICANN/ICONIP 2003*, 174-174.

Lin, C.-J., & Chen, C.-H. (2005). Identification and prediction using recurrent compensatory neuro-fuzzy systems. *Fuzzy Sets and Systems*, *150*(2), 307–330. doi:10.1016/j.fss.2004.07.001

Liu, S.-T., Yen, J.-Y., & Wang, F.-C. (2018). Compensation for the Residual Error of the Voltage Drive of the Charge Control of a Piezoelectric Actuator. *Journal of Dynamic Systems, Measurement, and Control*, *140*(7), 1–9. doi:10.1115/1.4038636

Mehrabi, D., Mohammadzaheri, M., Firoozfar, A., & Emadi, M. (2017). A fuzzy virtual temperature sensor for an irradiative enclosure. *Journal of Mechanical Science and Technology*, *31*(10), 4989–4994. doi:10.100712206-017-0947-x

Meinhold, W., Martinez, D. E., Oshinski, J., Hu, A.-P., & Ueda, J. (2020). A direct drive parallel plane piezoelectric needle positioning robot for MRI guided intraspinal injection. *IEEE Transactions on Biomedical Engineering*, *68*(3), 807–814. doi:10.1109/TBME.2020.3020926 PMID:32870782

Minase, J., Lu, T.-F., Cazzolato, B., & Grainger, S. (2010). A review, supported by experimental results, of voltage, charge and capacitor insertion method for driving piezoelectric actuators. *Precision Engineering*, *34*(4), 692–700. doi:10.1016/j.precisioneng.2010.03.006

Minase, J., Lu, T. F., Cazzolato, B., & Grainger, S. (2010). A review, supported by experimental results, of voltage, charge and capacitor insertion method for driving piezoelectric actuators. *Precision Engineering*, *34*(4), 692–700. doi:10.1016/j.precisioneng.2010.03.006

Miri, N., Mohammadzaheri, M., & Chen, L. (2015). An enhanced physics-based model to estimate the displacement of piezoelectric actuators. *Journal of Intelligent Material Systems and Structures*, *26*(11), 1442–1451. doi:10.1177/1045389X14546648

Mohammadzaheri, M., Akbarifar, A., Ghodsi, M., Bahadur, I., AlJahwari, F., & Al-Amri, B. (2020). *Health Monitoring of Welded Pipelines with Mechanical Waves and Fuzzy Inference Systems* [Paper presentation]. *International Gas Union Research Conference*, Muscat, Oman.

Mohammadzaheri, M., & AlQallaf, A. (2017). Nanopositioning systems with piezoelectric actuators, current state and future perspective. *Science of Advanced Materials*, *9*(7), 1071–1080. doi:10.1166/sam.2017.3088

Mohammadzaheri, M., AlQallaf, A., Ghodsi, M., & Ziaiefar, H. (2018). Development of a Fuzzy Model to Estimate the Head of Gaseous Petroleum Fluids Driven by Electrical Submersible Pumps. *Fuzzy Information and Engineering*, *10*(1), 99–106. doi:10.1080/16168658.2018.1509523

Mohammadzaheri, M., AlSulti, S., Ghodsi, M., Bahadur, I., & Emadi, M. (2021). Assessment of capacitor-based charge estimators for piezoelectric actuators. *2021 IEEE International Conference on Mechatronics (ICM)*.

Mohammadzaheri, M., Amouzadeh, A., Doustmohammadi, M., Emadi, M., Jamshidi, E., & Ghodsi, M. (2021). *Fault Diagnosis of an Automobile Cylinder Block with Neural Process of Modal Information*. *Academic Press*.

Mohammadzaheri, M., Amouzadeh, A., Doustmohammadi, M., Emadi, M., Jamshidi, E., Ghodsi, M., & Soltani, P. (2021). Fuzzy Analysis of Resonance Frequencies for Structural Inspection of an Engine Cylinder Block. *Fuzzy Information and Engineering*, 1-11. https://www.tandfonline.com/doi/pdf/10.10 80/16168658.2021.1908819

Mohammadzaheri, M., & Chen, L. (2010). Intelligent predictive control of a model helicopter's yaw angle. *Asian Journal of Control*, *12*(6), 667–679. doi:10.1002/asjc.243

Mohammadzaheri, M., Chen, L., & Grainger, S. (2012). A critical review of the most popular types of neuro control. *Asian Journal of Control*, *16*(1), 1–11. doi:10.1002/asjc.449

Mohammadzaheri, M., Emadi, M., Ghodsi, M., Bahadur, I. M., Zarog, M., Saleem, A. J. I. J. A. I., & Learning, M. (2020). Development of a Charge Estimator for Piezoelectric Actuators: A Radial Basis Function Approach. *International Journal of Artificial Intelligence and Machine Learning*, *10*(1), 31–44. doi:10.4018/IJAIML.2020010103

Mohammadzaheri, M., Emadi, M., Ghodsi, M., Jamshidi, E., Bahadur, I., Saleem, A., & Zarog, M. (2019). A variable-resistance digital charge estimator for piezoelectric actuators: An alternative to maximise accuracy and curb voltage drop. *Journal of Intelligent Material Systems and Structures*, *30*(11), 1699–1705. doi:10.1177/1045389X19844011

Mohammadzaheri, M., Emadi, M., Ziaiefar, H., Ghodsi, M., Bahadur, I., Zarog, M., & Saleem, A. (2019). Adaptive Charge Estimation of Piezoelectric Actuators, a Radial Basis Function Approach. *20th International Conference on Research and Education in Mechatronics Wels*, Austria.

Mohammadzaheri, M., Firoozfar, A., Mehrabi, D., Emadi, M., & Alqallaf, A. (2019). Temperature Estimation for a Point of an Infrared Dryer Using Temperature of Neighbouring Points: An Artificial Neural Network Approach. *Journal of Engineering Research*, *7*(4).

Mohammadzaheri, M., Ghodsi, M., & AlQallaf, A. (2018). Estimate of the Head Produced by Electrical Submersible Pumps on Gaseous Petroleum Fluids, a Radial Basis Function Network Approach. *International Journal of Artificial Intelligence Applications*, *9*(1).

Mohammadzaheri, M., Grainger, S., & Bazghaleh, M. (2012). Fuzzy modeling of a piezoelectric actuator. *International Journal of Precision Engineering and Manufacturing*, *13*(5), 663–670. doi:10.100712541-012-0086-3

Mohammadzaheri, M., Grainger, S., & Bazghaleh, M. (2013). A system identification approach to the characterization and control of a piezoelectric tube actuator. *Smart Materials and Structures*, *22*(10), 105022. doi:10.1088/0964-1726/22/10/105022

Mohammadzaheri, M., Grainger, S., Bazghaleh, M., & Yaghmaee, P. (2012). *Intelligent modeling of a piezoelectric tube actuator. International Symposium on Innovations in Intelligent Systems and Applications (INISTA)*, Trabzon, Turkey. 10.1109/INISTA.2012.6246980

Mohammadzaheri, M., Mirsepahi, A., Asef-afshar, O., & Koohi, H. (2007). Neuro-fuzzy modeling of superheating system of a steam power plant. *Applied Mathematical Sciences*, *1*, 2091–2099.

Mohammadzaheri, M., Tafreshi, R., Khan, Z., Franchek, M., & Grigoriadis, K. (2016). An intelligent approach to optimize multiphase subsea oil fields lifted by electrical submersible pumps. *Journal of Computational Science*, *15*, 50–59. doi:10.1016/j.jocs.2015.10.009

Mohammadzaheri, M., Ziaeifar, H., Bahadur, I., Zarog, M., Emadi, M., & Ghodsi, M. (2019). *Data-driven Modelling of Engineering Systems with Small Data, a Comparative Study of Artificial Intelligence Techniques. 5th Iranian Conference on Signal Processing and Intelligent Systems (ICSPIS)*, Semnan, Iran. 10.1109/ICSPIS48872.2019.9066058

Montgomery, D. C., & Runger, G. (2017). *Probability and Statistics for Engineers*. Wiley.

Nguyen, D., & Widrow, B. (1990). *Improving the learning speed of 2-layer neural networks by choosing initial values of the adaptive weights. International Joint Conference on Neural Networks*, San Diego, CA.

Park, J., & Sandberg, I. W. (1993). Approximation and radial-basis-function networks. *Neural Computation*, *5*(2), 305–316. doi:10.1162/neco.1993.5.2.305 PMID:31167308

PiezoDrive. (2021). *Piezoelectric Actuators*. https://www.piezodrive.com/actuators/

Rios, S., & Fleming, A. (2014). *Control of Piezoelectric Benders Using a Charge Drive*. Proc. Actuator.

Sabek, W., Al-mana, A., Siddiqui, A. R., Assadi, B. E., Mohammad-khorasani, M., Mohammadzaheri, M., & Tafreshi, R. (2015). Experimental Investigation of Piezoelectric Tube Actuators Dynamics. *2nd International Conference on Robotics and Mechatronics*, Madrid, Spain.

Sen, P. C., Hajra, M., & Ghosh, M. (2020). Supervised classification algorithms in machine learning: A survey and review. In *Emerging technology in modelling and graphics* (pp. 99–111). Springer. doi:10.1007/978-981-13-7403-6_11

Sifaoui, A., Abdelkrim, A., & Benrejeb, M. (2008). On the use of neural network as a universal approximator. *Int. J. Sci. Tech. Control Comput. Eng*, *2*, 386–399.

Singh, K., Sharma, S., Kumar, R., & Talha, M. (2021). Vibration control of cantilever beam using poling tuned piezoelectric actuator. *Mechanics Based Design of Structures and Machines*, 1–24. doi:10.1080/15397734.2021.1891934

Szeremeta, W. K., Harniman, R. L., Bermingham, C. R., & Antognozzi, M. (2021). Towards a Fully Automated Scanning Probe Microscope for Biomedical Applications. *Sensors (Basel)*, *21*(9), 3027. doi:10.339021093027 PMID:33925843

Versaci, M., Jannelli, A., Morabito, F. C., & Angiulli, G. (2021). A Semi-Linear Elliptic Model for a Circular Membrane MEMS Device Considering the Effect of the Fringing Field. *Sensors (Basel)*, *21*(15), 5237. doi:10.339021155237 PMID:34372474

Xu, Y., Hu, X., Kundu, S., Nag, A., Afsarimanesh, N., Sapra, S., Mukhopadhyay, S. C., & Han, T. (2019). Silicon-based sensors for biomedical applications: A review. *Sensors (Basel)*, *19*(13), 2908. doi:10.339019132908 PMID:31266148

Yang, C., Li, C., & Zhao, J. (2017). A Nonlinear Charge Controller With Tunable Precision for Highly Linear Operation of Piezoelectric Stack Actuators. *IEEE Transactions on Industrial Electronics*, *64*(11), 8618–8625. doi:10.1109/TIE.2017.2698398

Yang, X., Li, Z., Fei, C., Liu, Y., Li, D., Hou, S., ... Zhou, Q. (2020). High frequency needle ultrasonic transducers based on Mn doped piezoelectric single crystal. *Journal of Alloys and Compounds*, *832*, 154951. doi:10.1016/j.jallcom.2020.154951

Yi, K. A., & Veillette, R. J. (2005). A charge controller for linear operation of a piezoelectric stack actuator. *IEEE Transactions on Control Systems Technology*, *13*(4), 517–526. doi:10.1109/TCST.2005.847332

Ying, H. (1998). *General Takagi-Sugeno fuzzy systems are universal approximators*. Academic Press.

Zhang, X., & Wang, J.-L. (2016). From sparse to dense functional data and beyond. *Annals of Statistics*, *44*(5), 2281–2321. doi:10.1214/16-AOS1446

Chapter 7

A Fog-Based Threat Detection for Telemetry Smart Medical Devices Using a Real-Time and Lightweight Incremental Learning Method

Ali Selamat
iD https://orcid.org/0000-0001-9746-8459
Universiti Teknologi Malaysia, Malaysia

Shilan S. Hameed
Universiti Teknologi Malaysia, Malaysia

Liza Abdul Latiff
iD https://orcid.org/0000-0002-5652-5477
Universiti Teknologi Malaysia, Malaysia

Shukor A. Razak
Universiti Teknologi Malaysia, Malaysia

Ondrej Krejcar
iD https://orcid.org/0000-0002-5992-2574
Hradec Kralove University, Czech Republic

Marek Penhaker
VŠB Technical University of Ostrava, Czech Republic

ABSTRACT

Smart telemetry medical devices do not have sufficient security measures, making them weak against different attacks. Machine learning (ML) has been broadly used for cyber-attack detection via on-gadgets and on-chip embedded models, which need to be held along with the medical devices, but with limited ability to perform heavy computations. The authors propose a real-time and lightweight fog computing-based threat detection using telemetry sensors data and their network traffic in NetFlow. The proposed method saves memory to a great extent as it does not require retraining. It is based on an incremental form of Hoeffding Tree Naïve Bayes Adaptive (HTNBA) and Incremental K-Nearest Neighbors (IKNN) algorithm. Furthermore, it matches the nature of sensor data which increases in seconds. Experimental results showed that the proposed model could detect different attacks against medical sensors with high accuracy (»100%), small memory usage (<50 MB), and low detection time in a few seconds.

DOI: 10.4018/978-1-7998-8686-0.ch007

INTRODUCTION

Today is the era of smart and intelligent systems such as Cyber-Physical Systems (CPS) and Internet of Things (IoT) (Gatouillat et al., 2018). IoT has been applied in different domains, including industry, healthcare, military, and energy (Rahman & Mohsenian-Rad, 2012; Xu et al., 2019; Zhou et al., 2019). The emergence of 5G technology (Ahad et al., 2019), big data (Sollins, 2018), and advances in Artificial Intelligence (AI) (Ma et al., 2017) brings the world to the Internet of Everything and Internet of skills. Nevertheless, these technology sprouts will bring more security issues and gaps that need attention before developing them(Mosenia & Jha, 2016).

Smart medical systems such as the Internet of Medical Things (IoMT) and Medical Cyber-Physical System (MCPS) is a branch of the Internet of thing (Gatouillat et al., 2018) which is getting popularised by using simple fitness devices that connects athletes with their mobile devices and cloud system (Pandey & Litoriya, 2020). However, the IoMT is a comprehensive technology that includes many applications and systems such as implantable devices, elderly care wearable devices (telemetry devices) for monitoring(Uddin et al., 2018), internet-connected hospital devices, and remote surgery systems(Shilan S Hameed, Wan Haslina Hassan, Liza Abdul Latiff, et al., 2021). Etc.

It is not deniable; such systems made life healthier and helped in having longer life with improved caring systems(Gatouillat et al., 2018; Wei et al., 2020). However, most of the devices used in hospitals and personal medical devices are vulnerable to different threats(S. Gupta et al., 2020; Shilan S Hameed, Wan Haslina Hassan, Liza Abdul Latiff, et al., 2021; Jaigirdar et al., 2019). This is due to some weaknesses, such as the lack of security measures in small medical devices and having outdated operating systems and vulnerable applications installed on hospital devices(Jaigirdar et al., 2019; Sun et al., 2019). These software and hardware faults increase the risk of different malware attacks and other cyber-attacks in such systems(Goud, 2020). It is not always possible to have such updated operating systems, and hackers are continuously developing new cyber-attacks (Landau et al., 2020). A wide range of attacks jeopardize the patient's life and stop the smart medical system(Shilan S Hameed, Wan Haslina Hassan, Liza Abdul Latiff, et al., 2021). This urges us to develop defensive systems such as threat intelligence and intrusion detection systems that use machine learning technology. Machine learning (ML) has been used for attack detection in different ways (Xiao et al., 2018; Zuhair et al., 2020), and its performance has been approved by giant companies and leading businesses (Pannu, 2015). However, machine learning techniques may not perform well on tiny smart devices with limited power and processing units (Shilan S Hameed, Wan Haslina Hassan, Liza Abdul Latiff, et al., 2021). Therefore, it has been used with cloud computing attack detection for medical devices (Kintzlinger et al., 2020; Kumar et al., 2021). Cloud computing is associated with delay and centralized architecture that are less effective for critical systems such as IoMT. Sometimes ML techniques are tested on external devices that need to be protected and at the time changing the data, the model on such devices need to be retrained on other efficient devices (Abdaoui et al., 2020; Rathore et al., 2018), making them not viable for ever-increasing medical data. Therefore, fog-based threat detection is recently being adopted, which has merit in overcoming the delay and centralized architecture of the cloud (Alrashdi et al., 2019; Shilan S Hameed, Wan Haslina Hassan, & Liza Abdul Latiff, 2021). Few studies have used fog-based threat detection, especially for medical IoT(Alrashdi et al., 2019; Shilan S Hameed, Wan Haslina Hassan, & Liza Abdul Latiff, 2021). They are not real-time nor lightweight as these two features are essential for fog devices due to their critical position in the IoMT architecture and the big stream data nature of such devices, which needs real-time attack detection(Cisco, 2015; Sudqi Khater et al., 2019; Tabassum et al., 2021).

Furthermore, the model's setting of using few Megabytes and low CPU time made it a lightweight approach. Therefore, in this study, a fog-computing computing-based threat detection system is proposed for medical devices which use incremental learning techniques in a real-time fashion. The model uses new IIoT telemetry sensor data, which consists of seven datasets representing the medical sensor stream data and the NetFlow data of the network traffic of such telemetry system. By this, the system will be applicable for immediate threat and attack detection in lightweight fog devices.

Therefore, the contributions of this study are as follows:

1. The proposed machine learning technique uses incremental K-NN (IKNN) and Hoeffding Tree Naïve Bayes Adaptive (HTNBA), which incrementally uses data and avoids the batch setting that needs the data to be collected and stored in memory to be processed later by the ML techniques. This makes it more compatible with real-world scenarios of ever-increasing sensor data that arrive at fog devices in a streaming way.
2. The model has been tested on devices whose memory has been set to a minimum limit to be compatible with those fog devices that have a shortage of memory.
3. For validation and experimental analysis, we have used sensor telemetry data and their NetFlow instead of using one type of data. Furthermore, the proposed model had better performances than previously reported studies.

BACKGROUND AND LITERATURE REVIEW

Smart Medical Systems

In the Internet of Medical Things (IoMT), four categories of medical devices can be found depending on the devices' proximity to the patient's body (Nanayakkara et al., 2019) as follow:

1. Implantable sensor devices are implanted in human organs such as hip implants, cardiac pacemakers, and implanted insulin pumps.
2. Wearable sensor devices: These devices are worn by humans like a smartwatch, fitness devices, etc.
3. Ambient sensor devices: These devices are for monitoring human behaviors, such as telemetry devices for patient and remote elderly monitoring.
4. Stationary medical devices These devices are used inside hospitals, such as imaging devices with connectivity like X-rays and lab devices (Nanayakkara et al., 2019).

The Food and Drug Administration (FDA) (FDA, 2021) classifies IoMT devices according to the device's risk. The high risky devices such as implantable sensors need to be certified by the FDA. The rest of the devices that do not need to be implanted hold low risk (Jaigirdar et al., 2019).

Medical biosensing devices capture the human vitals and transmit massive amounts of unprocessed biodata in real-time, such as heartbeat, brainwaves, body temperature, and blood sugar levels (Dang et al., 2019). Later, this data will arrive at devices such as personal databases like cellphones and laptops or far devices like routers and access points to be aggregated and pre-processed. (Newaz et al., 2020).

Usually, low power networks such as Bluetooth Low Energy (BLE), and Zigbee are used to communicate between the sensors and private server (Newaz et al., 2020; Sun et al., 2019). The pre-processed data by the personal serves and gateways are landed in the hospital databases. Long-range wireless topologies Wi-Fi and GSM are commonly utilized for communication among private and hospital servers. The architecture of the IoMT and its components are illustrated in Figure 1.

Figure 1. The entities and components of medical IoT architecture

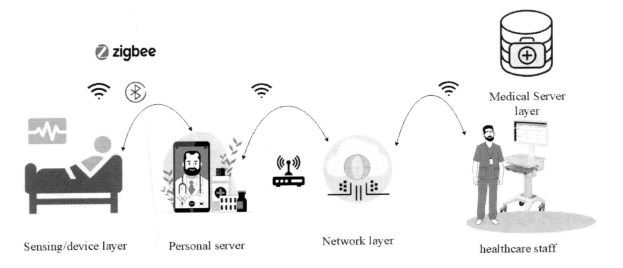

Furthermore, cloud nodes are usually used for computing processes. Recently, fog computing was introduced to overcome the issues of the cloud. Hence, fog nodes can handle some of the cloud works at the edge of the network. Therefore, the application of fog computing is important for a time-critical and distributed system of the IoMT (Dang et al., 2019; Firouzi et al., 2018; Rahmani et al., 2018).

Fog Computing in Smart Medical Systems

Fog computing can quickly process the huge data gathered from medical devices (Prabavathy et al., 2018). The fog nodes should have computing and storage capability. Examples of fog nodes are gateways, routers, and personal servers. (Cisco, 2015).

Furthermore, a fog node may function as the first security point for tiny devices with no security measures (Group, 2017). From Figure 2, we can depict that fog architecture consists of one head cluster, followed by a lower layer of more than one sub-head cluster until it reaches the edge devices. Additionally, whenever we dive from top to below the architecture, the analytical ability decreases while raw data increases.

Figure 2. The proposed architecture of fog based medical IoT

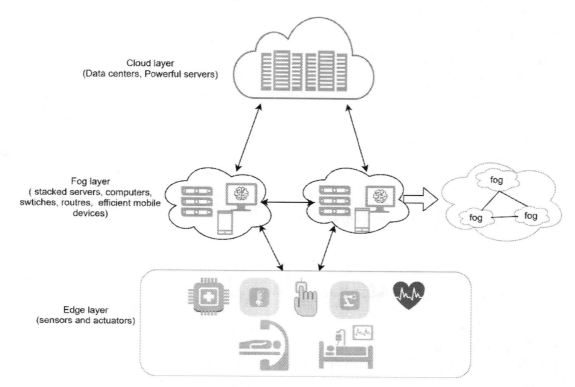

Fog nodes can be used for analytical and reactive purposes. The fundamental principle is that computational ability is maximum in the upper layers of the hierarchy, and it decreases while approaching the edge devices. Machine learning algorithms can be run on fog nodes with the computing power to perform the task at that layer (Moh & Raju, 2018). Complex machine learning models are developed at nodes near the cloud or inside the cloud itself. While less complex techniques can be used at the lower nodes, the generated model in the higher fog layer can be fetched and re-used at the lower nodes. One can use the training of the models at the upper layer and predication and classification at the less computationally intensive nodes (Kumar et al., 2021; Samy et al., 2020). The data gathered at fog nodes are enormous to be handled by current ML techniques. Hence, new techniques are required.

Threat Detection in Smart Medical Devices Using Fog Computing

Threats on Medical Devices

To achieve an optimal secure IoMT system, the whole parts and components of the system should be secured. The most critical layer to be initially secured is the devices themselves. The most repeatable and known attacks against the device and sensing layer of a smart medical system are shown in Table 1.

Table 1. The attack targeted sensors and devices of the smart medical system.

Attacks	Reference
Physical Sensor/ Node tampering	(Xing et al., 2010)
False data Injection	(Bostami et al., 2019; Farroha, 2019; Newaz et al., 2020; Rahman & Mohsenian-Rad, 2012)
Resource Depletion Attacks (Battery drain, Sleep deprivation, Buffer overflow)	(Hei et al., 2010), (Mosenia & Jha, 2016), (S. Gupta et al., 2020)
Side-channel	(Newaz et al., 2020; Zhang et al., 2013)
Hardware Trojan	(Mosenia & Jha, 2016; Qu & Yuan, 2014)
Eavesdropping	(R. Gupta et al., 2020) (McMahon et al., 2017)

Threat Detection in Smart Medical Devices

The use of data-hungry and heavy machine learning techniques for threat detection in tiny smart medical devices is a challenging task. Therefore, some efforts have been made to solve this issue, such as using external gadgets and embedded electrical chips. In a study (Zhang et al., 2013), a multi-layer threat detection was installed on an external device for detecting Radio Frequency signals received and sent by the medical devices. Additionally, other authors (Sehatbakhsh et al., 2018) used a statistical-based system on an external hardware device to detect code injection attacks. Nevertheless, these external devices should be held everywhere, and there is a risk of being stolen. In some other studies, edge devices such as Raspberry Pi3 and deep learning are used for detecting false data injection in implantable brain devices (Abdaoui et al., 2020). However, DL techniques are heavy low-power devices. In another study, MLP and FPGA chips are used for attack detection in insulin pumps (Rathore et al., 2018). Nevertheless, these devices need lightweight models, and by the time they will stop working because of too much computation.

Furthermore, using mobile computing, authors in (Ben Amor et al., 2020) have used PCA and Correlation Coefficient feature selection for detecting false sensor readings. On the other hand, in some studies, cloud computing is used to detect attacks against medical devices; for example, in (Kintzlinger et al., 2020), authors suggested a cloud method for detecting and preventing resource depletion assaults an implanted cardioverter-defibrillator (ICD). The system was separated into six sub-layers, one of which was dedicated to the machine learning approach utilizing one-class SVM. Because of inadequate attacking examples, the studies on real healthcare data revealed that one class SVM was unable to obtain a higher detection rate.

Nevertheless, attack detection at the cloud is characterized by delay, and it is not distributed, making it less effective for distributed systems like medical IoT. This is because it will not use the medical devices themselves for heavy computation. Furthermore, it is much closer to the medical devices which makes instant response when there is an attack in a distributed manner. Therefore, a fog-based threat detection that is distributed and closer to the edge network will solve the above limitations.

Threat Detection Using Fog Computing

Alrashdi et al. (Alrashdi et al., 2019) proposed a fog computing-based Intrusion Detection System attack using an online sequential extreme learning machine (EOS-ELM) for a smart medical system. They proved that their distributed fog-based architecture is better than cloud-computing-based architecture as it has a lower detection time and higher detection rate. Furthermore, researchers (Kumar et al., 2021) developed an IDS for medical IoT by using a fog-cloud framework. To differentiate an attack from typical network data, they employed an ensemble of Decision Tree, Naive Bayes, and Random Forest to build XGBoost, while binary categorization was performed. Because their model was too large for fog devices, they recommended using cloud computing for training and fog computing for testing. In another study, an ensemble incremental learning classification technique was proposed for network attack detection at the fog devices in medical IoT (Shilan S. Hameed et al., 2021).

Nevertheless, the used dataset was not a new IoT dataset. In another study, researchers (Sudqi Khater et al., 2019) created a light model at the fog layer leveraging Multi-layer Perceptron (MLP) and network traffic data. The model, however, was not intended for use in medical devices, and its accuracy has to be improved.

METHODS

Dataset and Attacks

In this study, we are using two new IoT and IIoT cyber-attack datasets. The first dataset is sensors data of IoT devices consisting of seven sub-datasets. The second dataset is the network traffic data for the same system. In developing the testbed for generating the datasets, seven different sensors and telemetry services are used, making the dataset heterogeneous. Furthermore, in the sensors' datasets, there are seven IoT cyber-attacks with normal data. Each dataset has different features of the devices. The total samples of all datasets are 401,119 (fridge: 59944, Garage door: 59587, GPS: 58960, Modbus: 51106, Motion light: 59488, Thermostat: 52774, Weather: 59260). The attacks in the sensors' datasets are (backdoor, Distributed Denial of Service (DDoS), injection, password, ransomware, scanning, Cross Site Scripting (xss)). The dataset has been gathered from the original researcher and generator (Moustafa, 2019). Furthermore, the second dataset, which is the system's network traffic packets, is transformed to NetFlow format. The NetFlow data represents the metadata features of the infected traffic. The generated NetFlow data is also used for attack detection representing the data at the network layer. This dataset consists of 14 features and 1,379,274 samples. The dataset includes all the attacks which exist in its sensor telemetry datasets such as (backdoor, Distributed Denial of Service (DDoS), injection, Scanning, password, ransomware, Cross Site Scripting (xss)) with another two attacks of (Denial of Service (DoS), Man in the Middle (MiM)) which mainly target the network layer. The features of each sensor data of the seven sensors and the NetFlow are different; we will not discuss them here to avoid detailed discussion. However, the definition of each attack is given as follow:

Backdoor Attack: A backdoor attack is one in which intruders use deception and adequate concealment to payload malware that can bypass the usually required security procedures of the IoMT system.

DoS and DDoS: In DoS attack, the hacker attempts to stop the systems and services and make them inaccessible to the users, while DDoS attack is distributed form of DoS, in which the hacker floods many systems and networks at the same time with DoS attacks.

Injection: In this attack, the hacker injects the sensors with false data and injects the databases with SQL queries to alter them accordingly.

Scanning: Is the process of scanning the network and the system for any vulnerability to attack the system through that entry point.

Password: Is the process of hacking or stealing the users' passwords and credentials.

Ransomware: Is a type of malware attack which either encrypts the files to demand ransom or locks IoT devices.

Cross Site Scripting (xss): This injection form wherein malevolent JavaScript codes are inserted into websites.

Man in the Middle (MiM): In this attack, Attackers appear to be both genuine parties after getting "in the midst" of a conversation to eavesdrop.

Proposed Fog Computing-Based Threat Detection

From Figure 3, which illustrates the overview of the proposed system, we can see that the sensors and devices at the edge layer are vulnerable to multiple threats due to lacking security measures at that layer. The red unlocked icon indicates missing security protocols. As a result, the hacker will simply breach the system and attack it with various attacks, such as (ransomware, DDoS, DoS, injection, Man in the middle attack.). Therefore, the data which transfers to the fog devices will be contaminated by such attacks. The data flow from the edge sensors arrives at the fog nodes in a matter of seconds. These data accumulate over time and generate massive data, while fog devices are inefficient at storing them. Additionally, the attack detection system should be able to process such increasing data. As a result, it would be preferable to utilize the data progressively than retrain it. The suggested model is applied to the sensors and network data in an online learning approach using a sliding window configuration to accomplish this goal. The memory will reset whenever a batch of new examples arrives, and they will be assigned to a sliding window. The sliding window is set to the minimum number of samples per window, which was 1000 samples per window. However, the sampling frequency is set to 5 thousand records. Based on the experimental analysis, these settings were chosen to minimize the complexity of the system.

This means that once the first 5 thousand records are processed, they will be deleted in the memory and substituted by the new ones. Consequently, the benefit of this technique is twofold; the threats will be detected as soon as they come, and the threat detection system will use a short memory. The machine learning techniques used in this study are Incremental K-Nearest Neighbour (IKNN), and Hoeffding Tree Naïve Bayes Adaptive (HTNBA). The main reason for choosing these techniques is that the KNN method is a well-known simple technique, while the HTNBA method is a new modified technique which is fast and accurate, making them suitable for our study objective.

Incremental K-Nearest Neighbour (IKNN): is an incremental version of the original K-Nearest Neighbour, a supervised machine learning approach for classification and regression applications. Based on the concept of similarities (also known as distance), the IKNN technique implies that similar objects are near together. To put it in another way, related items are close together. The K-value, the number of nearest neighbors used to determine if an example belongs to their class, is one of the variables that must be supplied into this approach. The numerical approach for determining the distance is another variable. The value of N is fixed to 10 in this study, and the numerical technique is a linear equation. Figure 4 depicts how IKNN predicts new examples as they come into the system. If we choose a smaller circle with a K value of five, the labels of the five closest samples will be inspected. The class of the new example will then be determined based on the most repeatable class. As a result, when K is five in the smaller circle, the arriving example is regarded a threat since the threat nearby samples is at least three. However, assuming the K value is 11, as illustrated in the larger circle, the new incoming example will be classified as normal since six typical examples surround it.

Figure 3. The proposed system and methods, consisting of edge medical devices sending stream data to fog devices, implement the proposed methodology.

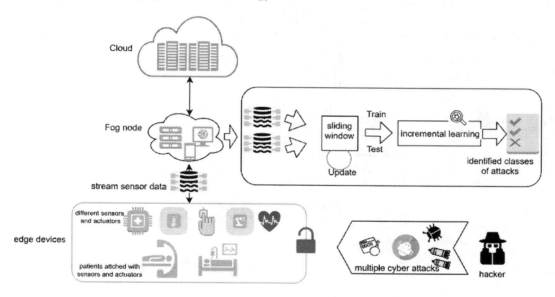

Figure 4. The IKNN method predicts new data as a threat or normal based on different K-value and distance equations.

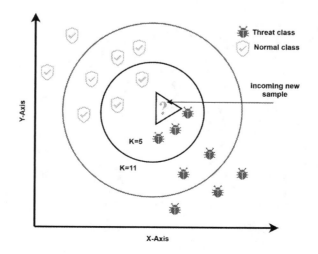

Hoeffding Tree Naïve Bayes Adaptive (HTNBA)

Typical tree-based classifiers can only utilize a small number of examples to train their models because they assume that all of the data should be kept in memory all at once (Muallem et al., 2017). Hoeffding Tree (HT) is a fast and straightforward tree-based classifier built specifically for massive stream data. The Hoeffding Tree has a theoretically appealing feature that other incremental tree-based learners do not have because it guarantees reliable efficiency. The original HT relies on the majority class approach to determine the classes on the tree's branches. Other approaches are being used at the HT leaves to enhance the classifier's accuracy. Another method to improve the accuracy of the HT classification is to use Naive Bayes classifiers at the leaves instead of the majority class classifier. However, noisy data HT with Naive Bayes on leaves reported to be not much better than the HT with majority class. Therefore, a combination of majority class and Naïve Bayes is proposed to overcome both techniques' shortcomings, called Hoeffding Tree Naïve Bayes Adaptive (HTNBA)(Holmes et al., 2005). The HTNBA method uses Naïve Bayes Adaptive to classify the instances based on their discriminative features. It uses the Gain value to decide about the class of the incoming instances. The Hoeffding Tree algorithm is given in Figure 5.

Figure 5. Hoeffding Tree algorithm
Source: (Domingos & Hulten, 2000)

Inputs: S is a sequence of examples,
          $\mathbf{X}$ is a set of discrete attributes,
          $G(.)$ is a split evaluation function,
          δ is one minus the desired probability of
            choosing the correct attribute at any
            given node.
Output: HT is a decision tree.

Procedure HoeffdingTree $(S, \mathbf{X}, G, \delta)$
Let HT be a tree with a single leaf l_1 (the root).
Let $\mathbf{X}_1 = \mathbf{X} \cup \{X_\emptyset\}$.
Let $\overline{G}_1(X_\emptyset)$ be the $\overline{G}$ obtained by predicting the most
    frequent class in S.
For each class y_k
    For each value x_{ij} of each attribute $X_i \in \mathbf{X}$
       Let $n_{ijk}(l_1) = 0$.
For each example $(\mathbf{x}, y_k)$ in S
    Sort $(\mathbf{x}, y)$ into a leaf l using HT.
    For each x_{ij} in $\mathbf{x}$ such that $X_i \in \mathbf{X}_l$
       Increment $n_{ijk}(l)$.
    Label l with the majority class among the examples
       seen so far at l.
    If the examples seen so far at l are not all of the same
       class, then
          Compute $\overline{G}_l(X_i)$ for each attribute $X_i \in \mathbf{X}_l - \{X_\emptyset\}$
            using the counts $n_{ijk}(l)$.
          Let X_a be the attribute with highest $\overline{G}_l$.
          Let X_b be the attribute with second-highest $\overline{G}_l$.
          Compute ϵ using Equation 1.
          If $\overline{G}_l(X_a) - \overline{G}_l(X_b) > \epsilon$ and $X_a \neq X_\emptyset$, then
            Replace l by an internal node that splits on X_a.
            For each branch of the split
               Add a new leaf l_m, and let $\mathbf{X}_\mathbf{m} = \mathbf{X} - \{X_a\}$.
               Let $\overline{G}_m(X_\emptyset)$ be the $\overline{G}$ obtained by predicting
                 the most frequent class at l_m.
               For each class y_k and each value x_{ij} of each
                 attribute $X_i \in \mathbf{X}_\mathbf{m} - \{X_\emptyset\}$
                 Let $n_{ijk}(l_m) = 0$.
Return HT.

Evaluation Metrics

Average accuracy is the average of all the sliding windows' accuracies at the end of the analysis. In incremental learning, accuracy is not calculated the same as in batch learning because there is a high possibility that all the samples in one sliding window belong to one class only.

$$\text{Average accuracy} = \frac{\sum_i acc}{N}$$

acc is the accuracy for the samples in each *i* sliding window over *N* total of the sliding windows while *acc* can be defined as follow:

$$acc = \frac{Cc}{M}$$

Where *Cc* is the correctly classified instances.

Average Time (s): It is the average CPU time taken by the incremental learning method for each sliding window dataset's training and evaluation process.

Average Memory (MiB): The incremental learning technique takes the average memory to do the operations and save each sliding window dataset.

RESULTS AND DISCUSSION

After setting up our experimental tools and datasets, we have achieved the results of applying the techniques on the datasets online. It can be seen in Table 2 that the accuracy of the proposed methods is almost 100 for all the datasets using both methods. Additionally, the average CPU time was HTNBA between 1.05 to 11 s for all the datasets using the HTNBA method and between 8.38 to 25.96 s for all the datasets using the IKNN method. Furthermore, the average memory usage was between 0.48 MiB to 0.95 MiB for all the datasets using the HTNBA method, while for the IKNN method, the memory usage was between 2.46 MiB to 3.16 MiB. These results indicate that our proposed model uses a maximum of 4 MiB with a few seconds of CPU time, making it suitable for the lightweight and Real-time feature of the fog devices. Nevertheless, as we can see from Table 2, the bold values mean better performance, and it can be concluded that the HTNBA method had better performance than the IKNN method.

Table 2 shows the average accuracy, average CPU time, and memory usage by each incremental learning method in the ToNT-IoT dataset.

Individual datasets	Method	Average accuracy (%)	Average time (s)	Average memory (MiB)
IoT-fridge	IKNN	99.72	8.96	2.8
	HTNBA	**99.92**	**2.04**	**0.61**
Garage door	IKNN	99.80	9.08	2.51
	HTNBA	**99.96**	**2.28**	**0.71**
GPS tracker	IKNN	**99.79**	**9.32**	2.46
	HTNBA	99.76	25.96	**0.79**
Modbus	IKNN	100.00	9.85	3.16
	HTNBA	100.00	**1.05**	**0.48**
Motion light	IKNN	99.80	**10.59**	3.04
	HTNBA	**99.87**	11.78	**0.95**
Thermostat	IKNN	99.90	8.38	3.00
	HTNBA	**100.00**	**1.90**	**0.72**
Weather	IKNN	99.82	9.51	2.75
	HTNBA	**99.97**	**1.58**	**0.54**

It is known that by default, increasing the number of instances, the CPU time will increase. As we can see from Figure 6, once the learning instances have arrived incrementally, the methods time increases. This can be seen in IKKN more than the HTNBA method, and this may relate to the fact that the IKNN method may slow down when it faces more incoming samples (Bhatia, 2010).

Figure 6. The CPU time difference between HTNBA and IKKN methods for the dataset of modbus sensor while its samples increase incrementally

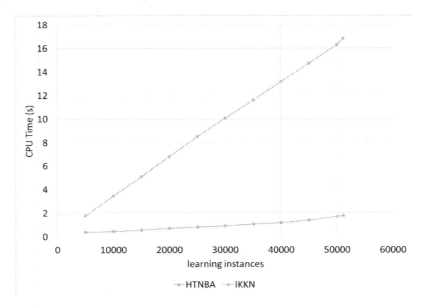

To compare the time and space complexity of the two proposed methods once they are used for all the datasets, Figure 7 has been sketched. It was seen that the HTNBA method has less average memory usage (space complexity) than the IKNN method for all datasets. Furthermore, the HTNBA method took a lesser average CPU time (time complexity) than the IKNN method except for two sensor data (motion light and GPS tracker). These results are compatible with the theoretical complexity of each method. The computational complexity of both IKNN and HT is $O(n*f)$, in which n is the number of samples (examples), indicating that it increases with increasing the number of test instances (García-Martín et al., 2018; Trisal & Kaul, 2019).

Additionally, f is the number of features that are constant in our experiment. However, the drawback of IKNN is that it adds up the instances once they arrive to update its model. Therefore, its complexity is gradually increased over time.

Figure 7. The average time (CPU time) and Average memory usage by the IKNN and HTNBA method for all datasets

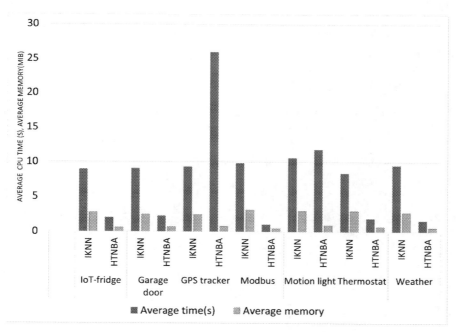

After that, the NetFlow-ToNIoT dataset, which collects network traffic of all the sensors, is used in NetFlow format. They are fed to our model to see its performance. From Table 3, the average accuracy of the proposed models is 100 for the HTNBA method and 99.79 for the IKNN method. The average memory usage was 0.08 MiB for HTNBA and 1.15 MiB for IKNN. This assures us that the network analysis of the attacks only took less than 2 MiB, making it compatible with very lightweight devices. On the other hand, the average CPU time for detecting all attacks was only 5.02 s for the HTNBA method. However, time was higher for the IKNN method.

Table 3. An average accuracy of each incremental learning method, CPU time, and memory usage in the NetFlow-ToNIoT dataset.

Individual datasets	Method	Average accuracy (%)	Average time (s)	Average memory (MiB)
NetFlow-ToNIoT	IKNN	99.79	184.69	1.15
	HTNBA	**100.00**	**5.02**	**0.08**

As stated previously, that the accuracy of the classifiers was high. However, HTNBA was more accurate than IKNN. To demonstrate the accuracy of each classifier when the data was received by the system incrementally, one should look at Figure 8. We can see that the IKNN classifier performed well for all the sliding windows, and it had its worst accuracy at only 1.7 percent maximum difference with its best sliding window accuracy. Furthermore, the HTNBA classifier had a stable accuracy during all the sliding windows making it a reliable method.

Figure 8. The accuracy of the IKNN and HTNBA method for all datasets for each subset of data samples per (slide window).

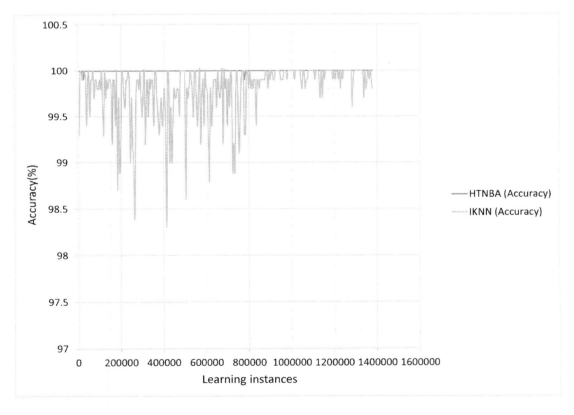

Comparison with previous studies in the literature shows that our methodology and results outperform their reported ones. As one sees from Table 4, our proposed model is lightweight and real-time, and we have proved this by using complexity measurement techniques such as (memory usage and CPU time). Furthermore, the device performance of our study is much less than that of the previous study, which indicates the more compatibility of our study with less efficient devices at the fog layer, as can be seen in Table 4. Furthermore, our study achieved the highest accuracy of 100.00% for the sensor telemetry and NetFlow data. Additionally, in our research, incremental learning is utilized compared to batch learning. Moreover, the complexity metrics are considered in the current study.

Table 4. The comparison between this study and previous study in the literature

Reference	Architecture	Lightweight	Realtime	Device specs	Type of data	Best testing accuracy (%)	Type of learning	Complexity metrics	Splitting method
(Kumar et al., 2021)	Cloud-Fog	No	No	CPU 2.20 GHz (10 cores, 13.75 MB L3 Cache), and 128 GB RAM	Telemetry	96.35	batch	Not considered	Train-test (80:20)
This work	Fog	yes	yes	CPUs »2.2GHz (4 cores, 3 MB L3 Cache), and 8GB RAM	Telemetry and NetFlow	100.00	incremental	considered	windowing (test-train)

CONCLUSION

The components and architecture of smart medical systems, also known as IoMT, are discussed in the current work. Furthermore, threats against IoMT sensors and devices with their detection systems using machine learning techniques at cloud, fog, and external gadgets are discussed with particular attention to fog computing. Likewise, we have proposed a lightweight and real-time machine learning technique composed of incremental classifiers of IKNN and HTNBA for different types of threat detection at fog devices of a smart telemetry system using sensor datasets and their NetFlow traffic. It was concluded that both techniques provide a high accuracy near 100% for all datasets. However, the HTNBA technique was seen to use less memory and CPU time compared to IKNN. Furthermore. The detection time, which is also CPU time, has remained at some seconds, and the memory usage was less than a few Megabytes, making the proposed model good working on lightweight fog devices. Furthermore, the proposed model was better than its predecessors' performance, architecture, and complexity.

ACKNOWLEDGMENT

The authors wish to thank Universiti Teknologi Malaysia (UTM) for its support under Research University Grant Vot-20H04, Malaysia Research University Network (MRUN) Vot 4L876, and the Fundamental Research Grant Scheme (FRGS) Vot (FRGS/1/2018/ICT04/UTM/01/1) supported by the Ministry of Higher Education Malaysia.

REFERENCES

Abdaoui, A., Al-Ali, A., Riahi, A., Mohamed, A., Du, X., & Guizani, M. (2020). Secure medical treatment with deep learning on embedded board. In *Energy Efficiency of Medical Devices and Healthcare Applications* (pp. 131–151). Elsevier. doi:10.1016/B978-0-12-819045-6.00007-8

Ahad, A., Tahir, M., & Yau, K. A. (2019). 5G-Based Smart Healthcare Network: Architecture, Taxonomy, Challenges and Future Research Directions. *IEEE Access: Practical Innovations, Open Solutions, 7,* 100747–100762. doi:10.1109/ACCESS.2019.2930628

Alrashdi, I., Alqazzaz, A., Alharthi, R., Aloufi, E., Zohdy, M. A., & Ming, H. (2019). *FBAD: Fog-based attack detection for IoT healthcare in smart cities. 2019 IEEE 10th Annual Ubiquitous Computing, Electronics & Mobile Communication Conference.* UEMCON.

Ben Amor, L., Lahyani, I., & Jmaiel, M. (2020). AUDIT: AnomaloUs data Detection and Isolation approach for mobile healThcare systems. *Expert Systems: International Journal of Knowledge Engineering and Neural Networks, 37*(1), e12390.

Bhatia, N. (2010). *Survey of nearest neighbor techniques.* arXiv preprint arXiv:1007.0085.

Bostami, B., Ahmed, M., & Choudhury, S. (2019). False Data Injection Attacks in Internet of Things. In *Performability in Internet of Things* (pp. 47–58). Springer. doi:10.1007/978-3-319-93557-7_4

Cisco, C. (2015). *Fog computing and the Internet of Things: extend the cloud to where the things are.* https://www. cisco. com/c/dam/en_us/solutions/trends/iot/docs/computing-overview. pdf

Dang, L. M., Piran, M., Han, D., Min, K., & Moon, H. (2019). A survey on internet of things and cloud computing for healthcare. *Electronics (Basel), 8*(7), 768. doi:10.3390/electronics8070768

Domingos, P., & Hulten, G. (2000). Mining high-speed data streams. *Proceedings of the sixth ACM SIGKDD international conference on Knowledge discovery and data mining.*

Farroha, J. (2019). Security Analysis and Recommendations for AI/ML Enabled Automated Cyber Medical Systems. In F. Ahmad (Ed.), *Big Data: Learning, Analytics, and Applications* (Vol. 10989). Spie-Int Soc Optical Engineering. doi:10.1145/347090.347107

FDA. (2021). https://www.fda.gov/

García-Martín, E., Lavesson, N., Grahn, H., Casalicchio, E., & Boeva, V. (2018). Hoeffding Trees with nmin adaptation. *2018 IEEE 5th International Conference on Data Science and Advanced Analytics (DSAA).*

Gatouillat, A., Badr, Y., Massot, B., & Sejdic, E. (2018, Oct). Internet of Medical Things: A Review of Recent Contributions Dealing With Cyber-Physical Systems in Medicine. *IEEE Internet of Things Journal, 5*(5), 3810-3822. doi:10.1109/jiot.2018.2849014

Goud, N. (2020). *Malware and ransomware attack on Medical Devices.* Retrieved 28/4/2021 from https://www.cybersecurity-insiders.com/malware-and-ransomware-attack-on-medical-devices/

Group, O. C. A. W. (2017). OpenFog reference architecture for fog computing. *OPFRA001, 20817,* 162.

Gupta, R., Tanwar, S., Tyagi, S., & Kumar, N. (2020). Machine learning models for secure data analytics: A taxonomy and threat model. *Computer Communications, 153*, 406–440.

Gupta, S., Venugopal, V., Mahajan, V., Gaur, S., Barnwal, M., & Mahajan, H. (2020). *HIPAA, GDPR and Best Practice Guidelines for preserving data security and privacy-What Radiologists should know.* Academic Press.

Hameed, S. S., Hassan, W. H., & Latiff, L. A. (2021). An Efficient Fog-Based Attack Detection Using Ensemble of MOA-WMA for Internet of Medical Things. In F. Saeed, F. Mohammed, & A. Al-Nahari (Eds.), Innovative Systems for Intelligent Health Informatics. Springer.

Hameed, S. S., Hassan, W. H., & Latiff, L. A. (2021). An Efficient Fog-Based Attack Detection Using Ensemble of MOA-WMA for Internet of Medical Things. In *Innovative Systems for Intelligent Health Informatics. IRICT 2020* (Vol. 72, pp. 774-785). Springer. doi:https://doi.org/10.1007/978-3-030-70713-2_70

Hameed, S. S., Hassan, W. H., Latiff, L. A., & Ghabban, F. (2021). A systematic review of security and privacy issues in the internet of medical things; the role of machine learning approaches. *PeerJ. Computer Science, 7*, e414.

Hei, X., Du, X., Wu, J., & Hu, F. (2010). Defending resource depletion attacks on implantable medical devices. *2010 IEEE global telecommunications conference GLOBECOM 2010.*

Holmes, G., Kirkby, R., & Pfahringer, B. (2005). Stress-testing hoeffding trees. *European conference on principles of data mining and knowledge discovery.*

Jaigirdar, F. T., Rudolph, C., & Bain, C. (2019). Can I Trust the Data I See? A Physician's Concern on Medical Data in IoT Health Architectures. *Proceedings of the Australasian Computer Science Week Multiconference.*

Kintzlinger, M., Cohen, A., Nissim, N., Rav-Acha, M., Khalameizer, V., Elovici, Y., Shahar, Y., & Katz, A. (2020). CardiWall: A Trusted Firewall for the Detection of Malicious Clinical Programming of Cardiac Implantable Electronic Devices. *IEEE Access: Practical Innovations, Open Solutions, 8*, 48123–48140.

Kumar, P., Gupta, G. P., & Tripathi, R. (2021). An ensemble learning and fog-cloud architecture-driven cyber-attack detection framework for IoMT networks. *Computer Communications, 166*, 110–124. https://doi.org/10.1016/j.comcom.2020.12.003

Landau, O., Cohen, A., Gordon, S., & Nissim, N. (2020). Mind your privacy: Privacy leakage through BCI applications using machine learning methods. *Knowledge-Based Systems*, 105932.

Ma, Y., Wang, Y., Yang, J., Miao, Y., & Li, W. (2017). Big Health Application System based on Health Internet of Things and Big Data. *IEEE Access: Practical Innovations, Open Solutions, 5*, 7885–7897. https://doi.org/10.1109/ACCESS.2016.2638449

McMahon, E., Williams, R., El, M., Samtani, S., Patton, M., & Chen, H. (2017). Assessing medical device vulnerabilities on the Internet of Things. *2017 IEEE International Conference on Intelligence and Security Informatics (ISI).*

Moh, M., & Raju, R. (2018). Machine Learning Techniques for Security of Internet of Things (IoT) and Fog Computing Systems. *2018 International Conference on High Performance Computing & Simulation (HPCS)*.

Mosenia, A., & Jha, N. K. (2016). A comprehensive study of security of internet-of-things. *IEEE Transactions on Emerging Topics in Computing*, *5*(4), 586–602.

Moustafa, N. (2019). *TON_IOT Datasets*. doi:10.21227/fesz-dm97

Muallem, A., Shetty, S., Pan, J. W., Zhao, J., & Biswal, B. (2017). Hoeffding tree algorithms for anomaly detection in streaming datasets: A survey. *Journal of Information Security*, *8*(4).

Nanayakkara, N., Halgamuge, M., & Syed, A. (2019). Security and Privacy of Internet of Medical Things (IoMT) Based Healthcare Applications. *RE:view*.

Newaz, A., Sikder, A. K., Rahman, M. A., & Uluagac, A. S. (2020). *A Survey on Security and Privacy Issues in Modern Healthcare Systems: Attacks and Defenses*. arXiv preprint arXiv:2005.07359.

Pandey, P., & Litoriya, R. (2020). Elderly care through unusual behavior detection: A disaster management approach using IoT and intelligence. *IBM Journal of Research and Development, 64*(1/2), 15:11-15:11. doi:10.1147/JRD.2019.2947018

Pannu, A. (2015). Artificial intelligence and its application in different areas. *Artificial Intelligence*, *4*(10), 79–84.

Prabavathy, S., Sundarakantham, K., & Shalinie, S. M. (2018). Design of cognitive fog computing for intrusion detection in Internet of Things. *Journal of Communications and Networks (Seoul)*, *20*(3), 291–298.

Qu, G., & Yuan, L. (2014). *Design THINGS for the Internet of Things—An EDA perspective. In 2014 IEEE/ACM international conference on Computer-Aided Design*. ICCAD.

Rahman, M. A., & Mohsenian-Rad, H. (2012). False data injection attacks with incomplete information against smart power grids. *2012 IEEE Global Communications Conference (GLOBECOM)*.

Rahmani, A. M., Gia, T. N., Negash, B., Anzanpour, A., Azimi, I., Jiang, M., & Liljeberg, P. (2018). Exploiting smart e-Health gateways at the edge of healthcare Internet-of-Things: A fog computing approach. *Future Generation Computer Systems*, *78*, 641–658.

Rathore, H., Wenzel, L., Al-Ali, A. K., Mohamed, A., Du, X., & Guizani, M. (2018). Multi-layer perceptron model on chip for secure diabetic treatment. *IEEE Access: Practical Innovations, Open Solutions*, *6*, 44718–44730.

Samy, A., Yu, H., & Zhang, H. (2020). Fog-Based Attack Detection Framework for Internet of Things Using Deep Learning. *IEEE Access: Practical Innovations, Open Solutions*, *8*, 74571–74585. https://doi.org/10.1109/access.2020.2988854

Sehatbakhsh, N., Alam, M., Nazari, A., Zajic, A., & Prvulovic, M. (2018). *Syndrome: Spectral analysis for anomaly detection on medical iot and embedded devices. In 2018 IEEE international symposium on hardware oriented security and trust*. HOST.

Sollins, K. R. (2018). *IoT Big Data Security and Privacy vs. Innovation. IEEE Internet Things J.*

Sudqi Khater, B., Wahab, A., Bin, A. W., Idris, M. Y. I. B., Abdulla Hussain, M., & Ahmed Ibrahim, A. (2019). A lightweight perceptron-based intrusion detection system for fog computing. *Applied Sciences (Basel, Switzerland), 9*(1), 178.

Sun, Y., Lo, F. P.-W., & Lo, B. (2019). Security and Privacy for the Internet of Medical Things Enabled Healthcare Systems: A Survey. *IEEE Access: Practical Innovations, Open Solutions, 7,* 183339–183355.

Tabassum, A., Erbad, A., Mohamed, A., & Guizani, M. (2021). Privacy-Preserving Distributed IDS Using Incremental Learning for IoT Health Systems. *IEEE Access: Practical Innovations, Open Solutions, 9,* 14271–14283.

Trisal, S. K., & Kaul, A. (2019). K-RCC: A novel approach to reduce the computational complexity of KNN algorithm for detecting human behavior on social networks. *Journal of Intelligent & Fuzzy Systems, 36*(6), 5475–5497.

Uddin, M. A., Stranieri, A., Gondal, I., & Balasubramanian, V. (2018). Continuous Patient Monitoring With a Patient Centric Agent: A Block Architecture. *IEEE Access: Practical Innovations, Open Solutions, 6,* 32700–32726. https://doi.org/10.1109/ACCESS.2018.2846779

Wei, K., Zhang, L., Guo, Y., & Jiang, X. (2020). Health Monitoring Based on Internet of Medical Things: Architecture, Enabling Technologies, and Applications. *IEEE Access: Practical Innovations, Open Solutions, 8,* 27468–27478. https://doi.org/10.1109/ACCESS.2020.2971654

Xiao, L., Wan, X., Lu, X., Zhang, Y., & Wu, D. (2018). IoT security techniques based on machine learning: How do IoT devices use AI to enhance security? *IEEE Signal Processing Magazine, 35*(5), 41–49.

Xing, K., Srinivasan, S. S. R., Jose, M., Li, J., & Cheng, X. (2010). Attacks and countermeasures in sensor networks: a survey. In *Network security* (pp. 251–272). Springer.

Xu, G., Lan, Y., Zhou, W., Huang, C., Li, W., Zhang, W., Zhang, G., Ng, E. Y. K., Cheng, Y., Peng, Y., & Che, W. (2019). An IoT-Based Framework of Webvr Visualization for Medical Big Data in Connected Health. *IEEE Access: Practical Innovations, Open Solutions, 7,* 173866–173874. https://doi.org/10.1109/ACCESS.2019.2957149

Zhang, M., Raghunathan, A., & Jha, N. K. (2013). MedMon: Securing medical devices through wireless monitoring and anomaly detection. *IEEE Transactions on Biomedical Circuits and Systems, 7*(6), 871–881. https://ieeexplore.ieee.org/document/6507636/

Zhou, L., Guo, H., & Deng, G. (2019). A fog computing based approach to DDoS mitigation in IIoT systems. *Computers & Security, 85,* 51–62. https://doi.org/10.1016/j.cose.2019.04.017

Zuhair, H., Selamat, A., & Krejcar, O. (2020). A Multi-Tier Streaming Analytics Model of 0-Day Ransomware Detection Using Machine Learning. *Applied Sciences (Basel, Switzerland), 10*(9). https://doi.org/10.3390/app10093210

Chapter 8
Joint Use of Fuzzy Entropy and Divergence as a Distance Measurement for Image Edge Detection

Mario Versaci
University "Mediterranea" of Reggio Calabria, Italy

Francesco Carlo Morabito
University "Mediterranea" of Reggio Calabria, Italy

ABSTRACT

In the AI framework, edge detection is an important task especially when images are affected by uncertainties and/or inaccuracies. Thus, usual edge detectors are unsuitable, so it is necessary to exploit fuzzy tools as Versaci-Morabito edge detector proposing a procedure to adaptively construct fuzzy membership functions. In this chapter, the authors reformulate this approach exploiting a new formulation for adaptively fuzzy membership functions but characterized by a more reduced computational load making the approach more attractive for any real-time applications. Furthermore, the chapter provides new mathematical results not yet proven in previous works.

INTRODUCTION

Edge detection marks points in a digital image where light intensity changes abruptly. Abrupt changes in the properties of an image are symptom of events or changes in the physical world of which the images are the representation. These changes can be: discontinuity in depth and orientation of surfaces, modification of material properties and variations in lighting from the surrounding environment. Outline recognition is a research field of image processing, in particular of the branch of feature extraction.

DOI: 10.4018/978-1-7998-8686-0.ch008

The contour recognition generates images containing much less information than the original ones, since it eliminates most of the details not relevant to the identification of the contours, while preserving the essential information to describe the shape and structural and geometric characteristics of the objects represented. As first step it is possible to use the gradient of the image which will have a low value in correspondence of areas with few changes in intensity. By applying a threshold to the latter, one is able to generate a new image containing only the outlines of the object depicted, ignoring any disturbances.

There are many other methods for recognizing contours groupable into two categories: search-based and zero-crossing methods. Search-based methods recognize boundaries by looking for the maxima/minima of the I- derivative of the image, looking for the direction where the maximum local gradient occurs. Zero-crossing methods look for points where the II- derivative passes through zero, usually the Laplacian function or a differential expression of a non-linear function. More systematically, the standard edge detection procedures can be classified into I and II order procedures. For example, the gradient operator technique, together the procedure elaborated by Roberts Prewitt and Sobel belong to I order procedures; while the Laplacian of Gaussian technique and the Zero Cross Operator are II order procedures. In 1986 the American John F. Canny designed an algorithm for the recognition of the contours that is now defined as the gold standard in this field.

However, the images can be affected by uncertainties and/or inaccuracies so the usual edge detection techniques fail or, at best, do not provide optimal results. Therefore, it is necessary to use fuzzy techniques which, notoriously, manage the problem with high levels of performances: on the one hand, makes the approach more "readable" ever by non-experts and, on the other hand, favors its updating through the expert knowledge. Many researchers are actively engaged in research activities concerning fuzzy edge detection with highly competitive results. Among these, the work published in (Versaci & Morabito, 2021) based on fuzzy entropy computations, presented results almost comparable to the results achieved by the Canny procedure. However, in (Versaci & Morabito, 2021) many mathematical statements have only been intuitively verified without rigorous mathematical proof. Furthermore, the adaptive construction procedure of the fuzzy membership functions used there required a considerable computational effort that hardly conciles with any real-time applications. So, the goal of this chapter is twofold: to complete what is presented in (Versaci & Morabito, 2021) by a set of Propositions with rigorous proofs that fill in the aforementioned gaps; to propose a new procedure for the adaptive construction of fuzzy membership functions with reduced computational complexity (replacing the one proposed in (Versaci & Morabito, 2021)) without experiencing appreciable drops in performance (testing the procedure on a larger database of images than stated in (Versaci & Morabito, 2021)). Finally, for the sake of completeness, the chapter also offers a broader description of the more well-known edge detection techniques currently in use than those reported in (Versaci & Morabito, 2021).

LITERATURE REVIEW

Some methodologies for edge detection (ED) exploit techniques of thresholding (Di Martino & Sessa, 2020), grouping (Pont-Tuset, Arbelaez, Barron, Marquez, & Malik, 2017) (Li, et al., 2013) (Xia, Gu, & Zhang, 2020), compression (Qasim, Din, & Alyousuf, 2020), (Krishnaraj, Elhoseny, Thenmozhi, & et al., 2020), variational approaches (Combettes & Pesquet, 2011), (Clerici & et al., 2020), graph partitions (Peng, Zhang, & Zhang, 2013), (Bejar & et al., 2020), or analytical procedures based on partial differential equations as well as multi-scale approaches (Hay, Castilla, Wulder, & Ruiz, 2005) (Sharon,

Brandt, & Basri, 2020), (Cui, 2021), (Sinha & Dolz, 2021), and many others reliable techniques (Russ & Brent Neal, 2018) (Zhang, Zhang, Wang, Tian, & Yang, 2018) (Cao, Chen, Wang, & Tian, 2018), (Qui, Li, Liu, Zhou, & Sun, 2020). Yet, the techniques are characterized by significant computational costs; hence, their use in real-time applications is often inhibited. However, several applications only require the ED as the first step of the segmentation. Therefore, if suitable edge detectors highlight any discontinuity in the features (Russ & Brent Neal, 2018), (Pattanaik, Mishra, & Rana, 2015), than they simplifies the analysis of an image as the data to be processed are considerably reduced (Chaira & Ray, 2010), (Chaira, 2015). There are many ED procedures used that exhibit effectiveness and efficiency. However, the enormous variety of fields where they are used requires a constant commitment by researchers to develop innovative and competitive edge detectors capable of interfacing with sophisticated and increasingly smaller technologies (Zhou & et al., 2020), (Pradeep Kumar Reddy & Nagaraju, 2019), (Mittal & et al., 2019), (Ma, et al., 2018),, (Wang & et al., 2019). Historically, EDs using operators based on I-order derivative are the procedures of Roberts, Prewitt, and Sobel exploiting templates convoluted with the image. Looking for the intensity of edges after the local maxima are computed is common among these techniques (Hagara & Kubinek, 2018) (Sekehravani, Babulak, & Masoodi, 2020) (Nanda & et al., 2018). Obviously, operators based on the II-order derivatives can also be exploited (Russ & Brent Neal, 2018). However, given the presence of the II-order derivative, this operator is very sensitive to noise, and, in addition, it could produce double edges and incomplete segmentation without considering the problems that arise from not considering any dispersion of the information content in the images (Sonka & et al., 2001), (Pattanaik, Mishra, & Rana, 2015). This led to the idea of using entropy concepts in ED, as they offered formulations with reduced computational load. In this context, it was formalized, on the one hand, by Albuquerque and his team idea that introduced the maximum entropy principle using the Tallis's formulation (Albuquerque, Esquef, & Gesualdi Mello, 2004), and, on the other hand, by Sahoo and Arona who proposed the 2D Renyi entropy formulated through the use of 2D histogram, established by the gray value of the pixels and their local average (Sahoo & Arora, 2004).

Starting from these pioneering works, numerous other scientific works have been proposed about EDs based, for example, on the use of multi-thresholds. Furthermore, the scientific literature is rich about EDs based on entropic formulations, for example, Chavart and Shannon's entropy for EDs, which was built with highly sophisticated techniques based on entropy combined with particle swarm optimization. The fact that the edges are often not clearly delineated as they are affected by uncertainties and/or inaccuracies, so the use of usual edge detectors would result in failure. In these cases, it is necessary to use soft computing techniques based on fuzzy logic (FL), as they are highly suitable for managing data affected by ambiguities, uncertainties, and/or inaccuracies. An image, particularly, can contain vagueness, uncertainties, and/or inaccuracies that can be easily managed by introducing a suitable adaptive membership function (MF) (Chaira & Ray, 2010). EDs based on FL make fuzzy templates (FTs), convoluted with the image under study. For example, Sobel's procedure calculates the gradient by combining special a trial-and-error method. If the pixels showed high differences in their gray levels (with respect to the neighborhood region), they would be classified as belonging to a fuzzy edge region; otherwise, they would be classified as belonging to the fuzzy smooth region. Hence, the boundaries of the two regions are determined by four threshold values derived from a difference histogram, calculated from the maximum difference in the gray level of each pixel in all eight directions. Then, as specified in (Kenneth, Ohnishi, & Ohnishi, 1995), the FTs are mathematically convoluted with the image to be analyzed; thus, suitable fuzzy similarities are evaluated between each pixel of the image and each pixel of each template, highlighting, with "ad hoc" procedures, the presence of any edges by combining the fuzzy similarities obtained and highlighting the edges more by suitable operators. A consolidated approach in the literature, which is based on this principle, is the Chaira-Ray method, which, starting from Sobel's fuzzy procedure, proposed 16 FTs by formulating the distances between the pixels of the FTs and the image by a known formulation of fuzzy divergence (FD) in matrices, without proving that the FD used represented (in a suitable metric space) a distance function (Chaira & Ray, 2010). The Chaira-Ray method, even if it is one of the most popular approaches for fuzzy ED, does not consider that the images could be the site of uncertainties and/or inaccuracies, which can only be assessed by quantifying their entropic content. Unlike the Chaira-Ray method, in (Versaci & Morabito, 2021) the concept of fuzzy entropy (FE) was exploited to present a new fuzzy ED (FED), by quantifying the uncertainty contained in an image via the calculation of the value of certainty of a dataset, satisfying the requirement of the edge pixels, thus realizing an effective detection of the edges. Particularly, starting from (Silva, Senra Filho, Fazan, Felipe, & Murta Junior) where a $2D$ entropy formulation was exploited for assessing the image texture by irregularity, in (Versaci & Morabito, 2021), a formulation of FE based on FD, measuring the distance between the first image and the second one, and vice versa, was presented. Furthermore, the fuzzification of each image was performed in (Versaci & Morabito, 2021) by an "ad-hoc" S-shaped fuzzy MF, adaptively built by exploiting both FE minimization and noise reduction for the optimal localization of MF on its universe of discourse. However, the application of the approach proposed in (Versaci & Morabito, 2021) required the evaluation of the fuzziness content in each image to be processed. Therefore, four indexes of fuzziness (IoFs) based on the FD computation were built and performed achieving interesting results if compared with other well-established ED I- and II-order approaches (Kaur & Kayr, 2014) exploiting formulations presented there where distances among images were computed by FD formulation. Moreover, two well-known non-reference quality assessment metrics (QAMs) were exploited to confirm the results achieved by the metrics.

In this chapter we present a complete and comprehensive extension of (Versaci & Morabito, 2021) which is expressed in the following points:

1. a broader and more detailed description of the steps that led to the definition of the approach starting from the Chaira-Ray approach;
2. a proof concerning the formulation of the entropy and the optimal threshold proposed in (Versaci & Morabito, 2021);
3. a new and more complete proof of the fact that FD in (Versaci & Morabito, 2021) is a distance between images in a suitable functional space;
4. a proof concerning the commutativity of the FD formulation;
5. a broader description of the first and second order operators best known in the literature;
6. a proof concerning the limitations of the IoFs formulated in (Versaci & Morabito, 2021);

Moreover, in this chapter important innovations are introduced with respect to (Versaci & Morabito, 2021). Particularly, a new procedure for the adaptive construction of fuzzy MFs with lower computational load than proposed in (Versaci & Morabito, 2021);
The approach, in this chapter, has been tested on:

1. gray-level experimental ECs maps subjecting steel plates to biaxial loads (as in (Versaci & Morabito, 2021)); moreover, ECs maps achieved without applying loads have been analyzed.

2.   two typologies of gray-level thermal camera IR images for ballistic uses (only one type of images was analyzed in (Versaci & Morabito, 2021)).

3.   gray-level electro-spinning images with and without defects (in (Versaci & Morabito, 2021) only free-defect images were analyzed).

BASIC FL CONCEPTS

Fuzzy logic (FL) with vagueness in the membership of each element *u* to a given set *A,* ranging on [0 … 1] by a membership function (MF) managing its fuzziness (Chaira & Ray, 2010). Defining the universe of discourse *U* as the set of all possible values defining *A,* we build a MF on *U* ranging over [0 … 1], defining the membership of *u*∈*U* to *A*. Fuzzy IP, usually, is structured in three steps: fuzzification (maps an image from the pixel plane to the fuzzy plane), inference engine and defuzzification (maps the inverse process).

Definition 1 - Crisp Image as a Matrix (Gray-Level Image)

A 2D gray-level image is a matrix, **I**, constituted by *M* rows and *N* columns, with *N*×*M* elements *(i,j),* *i=1,…,M, j=1,…,N* (pixels of **I**). To each *(i,j),* we associate its gray-level $a_{ij} \in [0,255]$, which represents its brightness.

Definition 2 – Fuzzy Image (Special Matrix)

Let us consider $\mathbf{I}_{norm}$ as a new image where each pixel has its related gray level

$$\widehat{a_{ij}} = \left(a_{ij} / 255 \right) \in [0,1].$$
(1)

On $\mathbf{I}_{norm}$, a fuzzy MF,

$$m_{\mathrm{I}_{norm}} \left(\widehat{a_{ij}} \right) : \mathbf{I}_{norm} \rightarrow [0,1]$$
(2)

formalizes how much fuzzily $\widehat{a_{ij}}$ belongs to $\mathbf{I}_{norm}$. If $m_{\mathrm{I}_{norm}} \left(\widehat{a_{ij}} \right) = 1$, $\widehat{a_{ij}}$ totally belongs to $\mathbf{I}_{norm}$; if $m_{\mathrm{I}_{norm}} \left(\widehat{a_{ij}} \right) = 0$, $\widehat{a_{ij}}$ does not totally belong to $\mathbf{I}_{norm}$; finally, if $m_{\mathrm{I}_{norm}} \left(\widehat{a_{ij}} \right) \in (0,1)$, $\widehat{a_{ij}}$ partially belongs to $\mathbf{I}_{norm}$. Let us consider $F(\mathbf{I}_{norm})$ as the fuzzified image of $\mathbf{I}_{norm}$ whose pixels represent $m_I \left(\widehat{a_{ij}} \right)$, *i=1,…,M* and *j=1,…,N.*

Since the new fuzzy edge detection procedure (FED), proposed in (Versaci & Morabito, 2021) and here improved, derives from the Chaira-Ray fuzzy approach, we introduce it, starting from the well-known fuzzy Sobel procedure.

FED: SOBEL AND CHAIRA-RAY APPROACHES

Fuzzy Sobel ED Procedure

By this approach (Khamy & et al., 2000), the image is convolved with two 3×3 templates, calculating the gradient in two directions, computing the final gradient by combining the two achieved results, detecting the edges using a dependent thresholding procedure following a trial-and-error method by the user. **I** is divided into two regions: if the pixels are having high (low) gray-level difference with their neighborhood region, then they are classified in a fuzzy edge (smooth) region. The boundary between two regions is achieved from four threshold values (low threshold, high limit, low limit, and high threshold) deriving from difference histogram calculated by the maximum difference in the gray-level value of each pixel in all the eight directions:

$$diff\left(x,y\right) = max\left(I\left(x,y\right) = I\left(x+i,y+j\right)\right) \tag{3}$$

$(i,j= -1,0,1)$; $I(x,y)$ is the gray level of the image at (x,y) and $I(x+i, y+j)$ is the gray level of the image in the eight directions. The values of the difference histogram do not range from *0* to *255* while the range in the difference histogram, in which peak values decay more or less than *20%*, is highlighted. The lower (higher) value of the range is assigned as low (high) threshold region. In addition, since the distances between the thresholds are considered equal, the upper and limits are obtained accordingly. Exploiting the above four threshold values, fuzzy smooth and edge regions are constructed. The gradient of **I**, $G(\mathbf{I})$, is achieved exploiting Sobel operator, and the output of the modified FED is obtained by fuzzy reasoning. If $G(\mathbf{I})$ is greater (lower) than high (low) threshold, then $\mathbf{I}(i,j)=255 \parallel (\mathbf{I(i,j)}=0)$. Otherwise,

$$\mathbf{I}\left(i,j\right) = G\left(\mathbf{I}\left(i.j\right)\right) \cdot \max\left(m_{\mathbf{I}_{smooth}}\left(i,j\right), m_{\mathbf{I}_{edgeregion}}\left(i,j\right)\right), \tag{4}$$

where $m_{\mathbf{I}_{smooth}}\left(i,j\right)$ and $m_{\mathbf{I}_{edgeregion}}\left(i,j\right)$ are the MFs of the image smooth and edge regions, respectively. Be

FD IN ED: THE CHAIRA-RAY APPROACH

Definition 3 – Fuzzy Divergence Measurement between Fuzzy Images

On *U* let *FS(U)* be the set of all fuzzified images. The following non-negative mapping *D*:

$$D: FS(U) \times FS(U) \rightarrow [0,1] \tag{5}$$

can be a measure of FD *iff*, for each fuzzified image *A* and *B,* the following conditions holds:

$$1: D(A,B) = D(B,A); \tag{6}$$

$2: D(A,A) = 0;$ (7)

$3: D(A \cap C, B \cap C) \leq D(A,B), \forall C \in FS(U);$ (8)

$4: D(A \cup C), B \cup C) \leq D(A,B), \forall C \in FS(U).$ (9)

Starting from Subsection 3.1, Chaira-Ray used FD between the image window and each of the following set of sixteen 3×3 templates (the edge profiles of different types):

$$\begin{pmatrix} 0 & .8 & .3 \\ 0 & .8 & .3 \\ 0 & .8 & .3 \end{pmatrix} \begin{pmatrix} .3 & .3 & .3 \\ 0 & 0 & 0 \\ .8 & .8 & .8 \end{pmatrix} \begin{pmatrix} .3 & .3 & .8 \\ .8 & .8 & 0 \\ .8 & 0 & 0 \end{pmatrix} \begin{pmatrix} .8 & .8 & .8 \\ 0 & 0 & 0 \\ .3 & .3 & .3 \end{pmatrix} \begin{pmatrix} .8 & .3 & .3 \\ 0 & .8 & .3 \\ 0 & 0 & .8 \end{pmatrix} \begin{pmatrix} .8 & .3 & 0 \\ .8 & .3 & 0 \\ .8 & .3 & 0 \end{pmatrix} \begin{pmatrix} .3 & 0 & .8 \\ .3 & 0 & .8 \\ .3 & 0 & .8 \end{pmatrix} \begin{pmatrix} 0 & 0 & 0 \\ .8 & .8 & .8 \\ .3 & .3 & .3 \end{pmatrix}$$ (10)

$$\begin{pmatrix} .3 & .3 & .3 \\ .8 & .8 & .8 \\ 0 & 0 & 0 \end{pmatrix} \begin{pmatrix} .3 & .8 & 0 \\ .3 & .8 & 0 \\ .3 & .8 & 0 \end{pmatrix} \begin{pmatrix} 0 & 0 & 0 \\ .3 & .3 & .3 \\ .8 & .8 & .8 \end{pmatrix} \begin{pmatrix} 0 & .3 & .8 \\ 0 & .3 & .8 \\ 0 & .3 & .8 \end{pmatrix} \begin{pmatrix} .8 & .8 & .8 \\ .3 & .3 & .3 \\ 0 & 0 & 0 \end{pmatrix} \begin{pmatrix} .8 & 0 & .3 \\ .8 & 0 & .3 \\ .8 & 0 & .3 \end{pmatrix} \begin{pmatrix} .8 & 0 & 0 \\ .3 & .8 & 0 \\ .3 & .3 & .8 \end{pmatrix} \begin{pmatrix} 0 & 0 & 8 \\ 0 & .8 & .3 \\ .8 & .3 & .3 \end{pmatrix}.$$ (11)

0.3 and 0.8 have been chosen ensuring good ED, as other values belonging to (0,1) did not improve the performance. Therefore, the center of each template was located at each *(i,j)* position over $\mathbf{I}_{norm}$. Indicating by $(\mathbf{I}_{norm})_w$ through the chosen window in the test image (with the same size as that of the FT), FD is definable as (Chaira, 2015):

$$D(i,j) = \max_{\#templates} \left[\min_9 \left(Div\left((\mathbf{I}_{norm})_w, FT \right) \right) \right]$$ (12)

in which $Div((\mathbf{I}_{norm})_w, FT)$ is the divergence between $(\mathbf{I}_{norm})_w$ and FT, evaluated by computing the FD between each of the elements $(\mathbf{I}_{norm})_w (\widehat{a}_{ij})$ and FT(i,j) of $(\mathbf{I}_{norm})_w$, respectively.

To formulate the fuzzy divergence between $(\mathbf{I}_{norm})_w$ and FT, one must consider how much $(\mathbf{I}_{norm})_w$ *"fuzzily diverges"* from FT and vice-versa. Indicating by $\bar{D}\left((\mathbf{I}_{norm})_w, FT \right)$ and $\bar{D}\left(FT, (\mathbf{I}_{norm})_w \right)$, respectively, the *"total divergence"* $D((\mathbf{I}_{norm})_w, FT)$ between $(\mathbf{I}_{norm})_w$ and FT is evaluable as follows, (Versaci, La Foresta, Morabito, & Angiulli, A Fuzzy Divergence Approach for Solving Electrostatic Identification Problems for NDT Applications, 2018), (Versaci & Morabito, 2021):

$$D\left((\mathbf{I}_{norm})_w, FT \right) = \bar{D}\left((\mathbf{I}_{norm})_w, FT \right) + \bar{D}\left(FT, (\mathbf{I}_{norm})_w \right)$$ (13)

where

$$\overline{D}\left(\left(\mathbf{I}_{\text{norm}}\right)_w, \text{FT}\right) == \sum_{i=1}^{M} \sum_{j=0}^{N} \left(1 - \left(1 - m_{\left(\mathbf{I}_{\text{norm}}\right)_w\left(\widehat{a}_{ij}\right)}\right) e^{m_{\left(\mathbf{I}_{\text{norm}}\right)_w\left(\widehat{a}_{ij}\right)} - m_{\text{FT}(i,j)}} - m_{\left(\mathbf{I}_{\text{norm}}\right)_w\left(\widehat{a}_{ij}\right)} e^{m_{\text{FT}(i,j)} - m_{\left(\mathbf{I}_{\text{norm}}\right)_w\left(\widehat{a}_{ij}\right)}}\right)$$

(14)

$$\overline{D}\left(\text{FT}, \left(\mathbf{I}_{\text{norm}}\right)_w\right) == \sum_{i=1}^{M} \sum_{j=1}^{N} \left(1 - \left(1 - m_{\text{FT}(i,j)}\right) e^{m_{\text{FT}(i,j)} - m_{\left(\mathbf{I}_{\text{norm}}\right)_w\left(\widehat{a}_{ij}\right)}} - m_{\text{FT}(i,j)} e^{m_{\left(\mathbf{I}_{\text{norm}}\right)_w\left(\widehat{a}_{ij}\right)} - m_{\text{FT}(i,j)}}\right).$$

(15)

Remark 1

As proved in (Chaira & Ray, 2010), (14) and (15) satisfy the axioms, which define a FD measurement (see (5), (6), (7), (8) and (9)). Moreover, in (Versaci & Morabito, 2021) it has not been proved that (13) satisfies the following statement:

$$0 < D((\mathbf{I}_{\text{norm}})_w, \text{FT}) < 1.$$

(16)

The following Proposition fills this gap.

Proposition 1

$D((\mathbf{I}_{\text{norm}})_w, \text{FT})$, as defined by (13), satisfies the condition (16).

Proof

By definition, $D((\mathbf{I}_{\text{norm}})_w, \text{FT}) > 0$. Furthermore, if absurdly

$$D\left(\left(\mathbf{I}_{\text{norm}}\right)_w, \text{FT}\right) = \left(1 - \left(1 - m_{\left(\mathbf{I}_{\text{norm}}\right)_w\left(\widehat{a}_{ij}\right)}\right) e^{m_{\left(\mathbf{I}_{\text{norm}}\right)_w\left(\widehat{a}_{ij}\right)} - m_{\text{FT}(i,j)}} - m_{\left(\mathbf{I}_{\text{norm}}\right)_w\left(\widehat{a}_{ij}\right)} e^{m_{\text{FT}(i,j)} - m_{\left(\mathbf{I}_{\text{norm}}\right)_w\left(\widehat{a}_{ij}\right)}}\right)$$
$$+ \left(1 - \left(1 - m_{\text{FT}(i,j)}\right) e^{m_{\text{FT}(i,j)} - m_{\left(\mathbf{I}_{\text{norm}}\right)_w\left(\widehat{a}_{ij}\right)}} - m_{\text{FT}(i,j)} e^{m_{\left(\mathbf{I}_{\text{norm}}\right)_w\left(\widehat{a}_{ij}\right)} - m_{\text{FT}(i,j)}}\right) > 1,$$

(17)

It follows

$$2 > \left(1 - m_{\left(\mathbf{I}_{\text{norm}}\right)_w\left(\widehat{a}_{ij}\right)} + m_{\text{FT}(i,j)} e^{m_{\left(\mathbf{I}_{\text{norm}}\right)_w\left(\widehat{a}_{ij}\right)} - m_{\text{FT}(i,j)}}\right) + \left(1 - m_{\text{FT}(i,j)} + m_{\left(\mathbf{I}_{\text{norm}}\right)_w\left(\widehat{a}_{ij}\right)}\right) e^{m_{\text{FT}(i,j)} - m_{\left(\mathbf{I}_{\text{norm}}\right)_w\left(\widehat{a}_{ij}\right)}} + 1.$$

(18)

In the most stringent case, we will have

$$2 > 2e^{-1} + 2e^{-1} + 1 = 2.46$$

(19)

which is absurd. Therefore, $D((\mathbf{I}_{norm})_w, FT)<1$. ∎

Remark 2

In (Chaira & Ray, 2010), the threshold technique has not been specified. So, in (Versaci & Morabito, 2021) a new approach to thresholding by a FE formulation, to fuzzily consider the measure of any loss of information content or, conversely, the measure of any fuzzy information gained exploiting fuzzy constructs.

FORM THE CHAIRA-RAY APPROACH TO THE ALGORITHM IN (Versaci & Morabito, 2021)

Definition 4 – Fuzzy Entropy

Let X be a fuzzy set. The map

$$FE: F(2^X) \rightarrow [0,1] \tag{20}$$

is a fuzzy set defined on fuzzy sets; it represents a measure *iff* it satisfies (Chaira & Ray, 2010):

$$FE(A)=0 \; iff A \in 2^X \; (A \text{ non-fuzzy set}); \tag{21}$$

$$FE(A)=1 \; iff \, m_A(x_i)=0.5, \forall i \tag{22}$$

$FE(A) \leq FE(B)$ if $m_A \leq m_B(x)$ when $m_B(x) \leq 0.5$

and $m_A(x)^3 m_B(x)$ when $m_B(x)>0.5$, $(A,B \text{ non-fuzzy sets})$ $\qquad(23)$

$$FE(A) = FE(A^c) \tag{24}$$

(A^c is the fuzzy complementary of A). The approach in (Versaci & Morabito, 2021) almost overlaps with the Chaira-Ray approach, except for the thresholding procedure of the FD matrix, which exploits a new formulation based on both FE and FD (see below).

The FED Procedure

Step 1: At each (i,j), we apply a FT over $\mathbf{I}_{norm}$ so that the center of the FT coincides with (i,j).
Step 2: As in (13), (14) and (15), FD between each of the elements of $(\mathbf{I}_{norm}\mathbf{I}_{norm})_w$ and the FT is computed, to select the minimum value.

Step 3: To consider each possible direction of the edge, repeat Step 1 and Step 2 for all the 16 FTs ((10) and (11)).

Step 4: Step 3 provides 16 minimum FD values. Among them, select the maximum value.

Step 5: On (i,j), associate the maximum value achieved by the Step 4.

Step 6: To repeat from step 2 to step 5, for all the pixels positions, to construct a new divergence matrix.

Step 7: To threshold the FD matrix achieved. Here, a new entropic *2D* fuzzy thresholding approach, exploiting the FE minimization and FD has been proposed in (Versaci & Morabito, 2021).

Computed the FD matrix, for each threshold $T \in [0\|1]$, a reduced square matrix, $A^{\sigma}_{\bar{i},\bar{j}}(T)$ is set, centered on $(\bar{i},\bar{j})$. Moreover, another reduced square window, $A^{\sigma}_{h,k}(T)$, located on another pixel *(h,k)*, is considered Therefore, the distance between $A^{\sigma}_{\bar{i},\bar{j}}(T)$ and $A^{\sigma}_{h,k}(T)$, $D^{\sigma}_{\bar{i},\bar{j},h,k}$, is computable by

$$D^{\sigma}_{\bar{i},\bar{j},h,k} = D\left(A^{\sigma}_{\bar{i},\bar{j}}(T), A^{\sigma}_{h,k}(T)\right). \tag{25}$$

The mean value of all the FDs achieved by the (25) by moving *(h,k)* in all possible locations in the image is computed. And again, we calculate the mean value achieved by moving $(\bar{i},\bar{j})$ in all possible locations, which we indicate by $\chi^{\sigma}(T)$. Thus, this procedure is repeated for all the $\sigma+1$ square windows obtainable, achieving $\chi^{\sigma+1}(T)$. As known, FE is the -*ln* of the conditional probability that two "*similar*" σ-dimensional patterns remain similar for $\sigma+1$. Then:

$$FE(T) = -\ln\left(\frac{\chi^{\sigma+1}(T)}{\chi^{\sigma}(T)}\right) = \ln\left(\frac{\chi^{\sigma}(T)}{\chi^{\sigma+1}(T)}\right) \tag{26}$$

so,

$$T_{\text{optimum}} = \arg\|\min_T \left\{\|FE(T)\|\right\} = \arg\|\min_T \left\{\left\|\ln\left(\frac{\chi^{\sigma}(T)}{\chi^{\sigma+1}(T)}\right)\right\|\right\}. \tag{27}$$

(27) makes sense, if $\chi^{\sigma+1}(T) > \chi^{\sigma}(T)$ and $\chi^{\sigma+1}(T) \neq 0$. In (Versaci & Morabito, 2021) this verification has not been presented. This chapter fills this gap with the following Proposition.

Proposition 2

Let us tw fuzzy images $F(\mathbf{I}_{\text{norm}})_j$, *j*=1,2, with MF values $\widehat{a_{ij}}$, $\widehat{b_{ij}} \in X$. Then,

$$\chi^{\sigma+1}(T) > \chi^{\sigma}(T), \tag{28}$$

$$\chi^{\sigma+1}(T) \neq 0 \tag{29}$$

and

$$0 \leq FE(T) \leq 1. \tag{30}$$

Proof

(28) follows from the definition of χ.

To prove (29), taking into account (13) (14) and (15), we must prove that

$$\left(1 - m_{F(I_{\text{norm}})_1}\left(\widehat{a_{ij}}\right)\right) e^{m_{F(I_{\text{norm}})_1}\left(\widehat{a_{ij}}\right) - m_{F(I_{\text{norm}})_2}\left(\widehat{b_{ij}}\right)} - m_{F(I_{\text{norm}})_1}\left(\widehat{a_{ij}}\right) e^{m_{F(I_{\text{norm}})_2}\left(\widehat{b_{ij}}\right) - m_{F(I_{\text{norm}})_1}\left(\widehat{a_{ij}}\right)}$$
$$+ 1 - \left(1 - m_{F(I_{\text{norm}})_2}\left(\widehat{b_{ij}}\right)\right) e^{m_{F(I_{\text{norm}})_2}\left(\widehat{b_{ij}}\right) - m_{F(I_{\text{norm}})_1}\left(\widehat{a_{ij}}\right)} - m_{F(I_{\text{norm}})_2}\left(\widehat{b_{ij}}\right) e^{m_{F(I_{\text{norm}})_1}\left(\widehat{a_{ij}}\right) - m_{F(I_{\text{norm}})_2}\left(\widehat{b_{ij}}\right)} \neq 0 \tag{31}$$

If absurdly

$$\left(1 - m_{F(I_{\text{norm}})_1}\left(\widehat{a_{ij}}\right)\right) e^{m_{F(I_{\text{norm}})_1}\left(\widehat{a_{ij}}\right) - m_{F(I_{\text{norm}})_2}\left(\widehat{b_{ij}}\right)} - m_{F(I_{\text{norm}})_1}\left(\widehat{a_{ij}}\right) e^{m_{F(I_{\text{norm}})_2}\left(\widehat{b_{ij}}\right) - m_{F(I_{\text{norm}})_1}\left(\widehat{a_{ij}}\right)}$$
$$+ 1 - \left(1 - m_{F(I_{\text{norm}})_2}\left(\widehat{b_{ij}}\right)\right) e^{m_{F(I_{\text{norm}})_2}\left(\widehat{b_{ij}}\right) - m_{F(I_{\text{norm}})_1}\left(\widehat{a_{ij}}\right)} - m_{F(I_{\text{norm}})_2}\left(\widehat{b_{ij}}\right) e^{m_{F(I_{\text{norm}})_1}\left(\widehat{a_{ij}}\right) - m_{F(I_{\text{norm}})_2}\left(\widehat{b_{ij}}\right)} = 0 \tag{32}$$

we achieve

$$\left(1 - m_{F(I_{\text{norm}})_1}\left(\widehat{a_{ij}}\right)\right) e^{m_{F(I_{\text{norm}})_1}\left(\widehat{a_{ij}}\right) - m_{F(I_{\text{norm}})_2}\left(\widehat{b_{ij}}\right)} - m_{F(I_{\text{norm}})_1}\left(\widehat{a_{ij}}\right) e^{m_{F(I_{\text{norm}})_2}\left(\widehat{b_{ij}}\right) - m_{F(I_{\text{norm}})_1}\left(\widehat{a_{ij}}\right)}$$
$$= -\left(1 - \left(1 - m_{F(I_{\text{norm}})_2}\left(\widehat{b_{ij}}\right)\right) e^{m_{F(I_{\text{norm}})_2}\left(\widehat{b_{ij}}\right) - m_{F(I_{\text{norm}})_1}\left(\widehat{a_{ij}}\right)} - m_{F(I_{\text{norm}})_2}\left(\widehat{b_{ij}}\right) e^{m_{F(I_{\text{norm}})_1}\left(\widehat{a_{ij}}\right) - m_{F(I_{\text{norm}})_2}\left(\widehat{b_{ij}}\right)}\right) \tag{33}$$

so

$$\left(1 - m_{F(I_{\text{norm}})_1}\left(\widehat{a_{ij}}\right)\right) e^{m_{F(I_{\text{norm}})_1}\left(\widehat{a_{ij}}\right) - m_{F(I_{\text{norm}})_2}\left(\widehat{b_{ij}}\right)} - m_{F(I_{\text{norm}})_1}\left(\widehat{a_{ij}}\right) e^{m_{F(I_{\text{norm}})_2}\left(\widehat{b_{ij}}\right) - m_{F(I_{\text{norm}})_1}\left(\widehat{a_{ij}}\right)}$$
$$= -1 + \left(1 - m_{F(I_{\text{norm}})_2}\left(\widehat{b_{ij}}\right)\right) e^{m_{F(I_{\text{norm}})_2}\left(\widehat{b_{ij}}\right) - m_{F(I_{\text{norm}})_1}\left(\widehat{a_{ij}}\right)} + m_{F(I_{\text{norm}})_2}\left(\widehat{b_{ij}}\right) e^{m_{F(I_{\text{norm}})_1}\left(\widehat{a_{ij}}\right) - m_{F(I_{\text{norm}})_2}\left(\widehat{b_{ij}}\right)} \tag{34}$$

and again

$$2 - \left(1 - \left(m_{F(\mathbf{I}_{\text{norm}})_1}\left(\widehat{a}_{ij}\right) + m_{F(\mathbf{I}_{\text{norm}})_2}\left(\widehat{b}_{ij}\right)\right)\right)e^{m_{F(\mathbf{I}_{\text{norm}})_1}\left(\widehat{a}_{ij}\right) - m_{F(\mathbf{I}_{\text{norm}})_2}\left(\widehat{b}_{ij}\right)} - \left(2 - m_{F(\mathbf{I}_{\text{norm}})_2}\left(\widehat{b}_{ij}\right)\right)e^{m_{F(\mathbf{I}_{\text{norm}})_2}\left(\widehat{b}_{ij}\right) - m_{F(\mathbf{I}_{\text{norm}})_1}\left(\widehat{a}_{ij}\right)} = 0 . \tag{35}$$

Therefore, from (35)

$$2 - \left(1 - \left(m_{F(\mathbf{I}_{\text{norm}})_1}\left(\widehat{a}_{ij}\right) + m_{F(\mathbf{I}_{\text{norm}})_2}\left(\widehat{b}_{ij}\right)\right)\right)e^{m_{F(\mathbf{I}_{\text{norm}})_1}\left(\widehat{a}_{ij}\right) - m_{F(\mathbf{I}_{\text{norm}})_2}\left(\widehat{b}_{ij}\right)} = \left(2 - m_{F(\mathbf{I}_{\text{norm}})_2}\left(\widehat{b}_{ij}\right)\right)e^{m_{F(\mathbf{I}_{\text{norm}})_2}\left(\widehat{b}_{ij}\right) - m_{F(\mathbf{I}_{\text{norm}})_1}\left(\widehat{a}_{ij}\right)} \tag{36}$$

so

$$2 = e^{m_{F(\mathbf{I}_{\text{norm}})_1}\left(\widehat{a}_{ij}\right) - m_{F(\mathbf{I}_{\text{norm}})_2}\left(\widehat{b}_{ij}\right)}$$
$$+ \left(m_{F(\mathbf{I}_{\text{norm}})_1}\left(\widehat{a}_{ij}\right) + m_{F(\mathbf{I}_{\text{norm}})_2}\left(\widehat{b}_{ij}\right)\right)e^{m_{F(\mathbf{I}_{\text{norm}})_1}\left(\widehat{a}_{ij}\right) - m_{F(\mathbf{I}_{\text{norm}})_2}\left(\widehat{b}_{ij}\right)} + \left(2 - m_{F(\mathbf{I}_{\text{norm}})_2}\left(\widehat{b}_{ij}\right)\right)e^{m_{F(\mathbf{I}_{\text{norm}})_2}\left(\widehat{b}_{ij}\right) - m_{F(\mathbf{I}_{\text{norm}})_1}\left(\widehat{a}_{ij}\right)} . \tag{37}$$

But

$$\min\left\{e^{m_{F(\mathbf{I}_{\text{norm}})_1}\left(\widehat{a}_{ij}\right) - m_{F(\mathbf{I}_{\text{norm}})_2}\left(\widehat{b}_{ij}\right)}\right\} = \min\left\{e^{-1}\right\} = e^{-1}, \tag{38}$$

and

$$\min\left\{\left(m_{F(\mathbf{I}_{\text{norm}})_1}\left(\widehat{a}_{ij}\right) + m_{F(\mathbf{I}_{\text{norm}})_2}\left(\widehat{b}_{ij}\right)\right)e^{m_{F(\mathbf{I}_{\text{norm}})_1}\left(\widehat{a}_{ij}\right) - m_{F(\mathbf{I}_{\text{norm}})_2}\left(\widehat{b}_{ij}\right)}\right\} = \min\left\{-e^{-1}\right\} = -e^{-1}. \tag{39}$$

Concerning

$$min\left\{\left(2 - m_{F(\mathbf{I}_{\text{norm}})_2}\left(\widehat{b}_{ij}\right)\right)e^{m_{F(\mathbf{I}_{\text{norm}})_2}\left(\widehat{b}_{ij}\right) - m_{F(\mathbf{I}_{\text{norm}})_1}\left(\widehat{a}_{ij}\right)}\right\} \tag{40}$$

we construct the function

$$f\left(m_{F(\mathbf{I}_{\text{norm}})_1}\left(\widehat{a}_{ij}\right), m_{F(\mathbf{I}_{\text{norm}})_2}\left(\widehat{b}_{ij}\right)\right) = \left(2 - m_{F(\mathbf{I}_{\text{norm}})_2}\left(\widehat{b}_{ij}\right)\right)e^{m_{F(\mathbf{I}_{\text{norm}})_2}\left(\widehat{b}_{ij}\right) - m_{F(\mathbf{I}_{\text{norm}})_1}\left(\widehat{a}_{ij}\right)} . \tag{41}$$

Therefore

$$\begin{cases} \dfrac{\partial f\left(m_{F(\mathbf{I}_{\text{norm}})_1}\left(\widehat{a}_{ij}\right), m_{F(\mathbf{I}_{\text{norm}})_2}\left(\widehat{b}_{ij}\right)\right)}{\partial m_{F(\mathbf{I}_{\text{norm}})_1}\left(\widehat{a}_{ij}\right)} = 0 \\[4mm] \dfrac{\partial f\left(m_{F(\mathbf{I}_{\text{norm}})_1}\left(\widehat{a}_{ij}\right), m_{F(\mathbf{I}_{\text{norm}})_2}\left(\widehat{b}_{ij}\right)\right)}{\partial m_{F(\mathbf{I}_{\text{norm}})_2}\left(\widehat{b}_{ij}\right)} = 0 \end{cases} \tag{42}$$

achieving $m_{F(\mathbf{I}_{\text{norm}})_2}\left(\widehat{b}_{ij}\right) = 2$. Thus,

$$min\left\{\left(2 - m_{F(\mathbf{I}_{\text{norm}})_2}\left(\widehat{b}_{ij}\right)\right)e^{m_{F(\mathbf{I}_{\text{norm}})_2}\left(\widehat{b}_{ij}\right) - m_{F(\mathbf{I}_{\text{norm}})_1}\left(\widehat{a}_{ij}\right)}\right\} = 0 \tag{43}$$

Achieving from (37) the absurd 2=0. Therefore, (29) is true.
Finally, from (28), since (29) holds, we can write

$$0 < \frac{\chi^{\sigma}(T)}{\chi^{\sigma+1}(T)} < 1 \tag{44}$$

and applying the natural logarithm operator the chain of inequalities, (30) yields. ∎

Remark 3

To apply (13), in (Versaci & Morabito, 2021), the functional space, $C(\Omega=[0,1], D)$, has been defined (if X is the set of all real-valued MFs, $m_{I_{norm}}\left(\widehat{a}_{ij}\right)$, $\mathbf{I}_{\text{norm}}$ on $\widehat{a}_{ij}$ defined and continuous on closed/bounded Ω) and, on it, (13) represents a distance (i.e., D satisfies the axioms of metric spaces). This has been proved in (Versaci & Morabito, 2021) but by a procedure unsuitable for computer implementations. Here, we present a new and more complete proof that meet these requirements.

Proposition 3

Let us $F(\mathbf{I}_{\text{norm}})_j$, $j=1,2,3$, with MF values are $\widehat{a}_{ij}, \widehat{b}_{ij}, \widehat{c}_{ij} \in X$. Then, (13) satisfies:

$$D\left(F\left(\mathbf{I}_{\text{norm}}\right)_1, F\left(\mathbf{I}_{\text{norm}}\right)_2\right) \geq 0. \tag{45}$$

$$D\left(F\left(\mathbf{I}_{\text{norm}}\right)_1, F\left(\mathbf{I}_{\text{norm}}\right)_2\right) = 0 \Leftrightarrow F\left(\mathbf{I}_{\text{norm}}\right)_1 = F\left(\mathbf{I}_{\text{norm}}\right)_2. \tag{46}$$

$$D\left(F\left(\mathbf{I}_{\text{norm}}\right)_1, F\left(\mathbf{I}_{\text{norm}}\right)_2\right) = D\left(F\left(\mathbf{I}_{\text{norm}}\right)_1, F\left(\mathbf{I}_{\text{norm}}\right)_2\right). \tag{47}$$

$$D\left(F\left(\mathbf{I}_{\text{norm}}\right)_1, F\left(\mathbf{I}_{\text{norm}}\right)_2\right) \leq D\left(F\left(\mathbf{I}_{\text{norm}}\right)_1, F\left(\mathbf{I}_{\text{norm}}\right)_3\right) + D\left(F\left(\mathbf{I}_{\text{norm}}\right)_3, F\left(\mathbf{I}_{\text{norm}}\right)_2\right). \tag{48}$$

Proof

$d(F(\mathbf{I}_{\text{norm}})_1, F(\mathbf{I}_{\text{norm}})_2)$, $d(F(\mathbf{I}_{\text{norm}})_2, F(\mathbf{I}_{\text{norm}})_3)$ and $d(F(\mathbf{I}_{\text{norm}})_3, F(\mathbf{I}_{\text{norm}})_1)$ can be written a:

$$d\left(F\left(\mathbf{I}_{\text{norm}}\right)_1, F\left(\mathbf{I}_{\text{norm}}\right)_2\right) = \left(2 - \left(1 - \left(m_{F(\mathbf{I}_{\text{norm}})_1}\left(\widehat{a}_{ij}\right) - m_{F(\mathbf{I}_{\text{norm}})_2}\left(\widehat{b}_{ij}\right)\right)\right)\right) e^{m_{F(\mathbf{I}_{\text{norm}})_1}\left(\widehat{a}_{ij}\right) - m_{F(\mathbf{I}_{\text{norm}})_2}\left(\widehat{b}_{ij}\right)}$$
$$- \left(1 + \left(m_{F(\mathbf{I}_{\text{norm}})_1}\left(\widehat{a}_{ij}\right) - m_{F(\mathbf{I}_{\text{norm}})_2}\left(\widehat{b}_{ij}\right)\right)\right) e^{-\left(m_{F(\mathbf{I}_{\text{norm}})_1}\left(\widehat{a}_{ij}\right) - m_{F(\mathbf{I}_{\text{norm}})_2}\left(\widehat{b}_{ij}\right)\right)} \tag{49}$$

$$d\left(F\left(\mathbf{I}_{\text{norm}}\right)_2, F\left(\mathbf{I}_{\text{norm}}\right)_3\right) = \left(2 - \left(1 - \left(m_{F(\mathbf{I}_{\text{norm}})_2}\left(\widehat{b}_{ij}\right) - m_{F(\mathbf{I}_{\text{norm}})_3}\left(\widehat{c}_{ij}\right)\right)\right)\right) e^{\left(\beta m_{F(\mathbf{I}_{\text{norm}})_2}\left(\widehat{b}_{ij}\right) - m_{F(\mathbf{I}_{\text{norm}})_3}\left(\widehat{c}_{ij}\right)\right)}$$
$$- \left(1 + \left(m_{F(\mathbf{I}_{\text{norm}})_2}\left(\widehat{b}_{ij}\right) - m_{F(\mathbf{I}_{\text{norm}})_3}\left(\widehat{c}_{ij}\right)\right)\right) e^{-\left(m_{F(\mathbf{I}_{\text{norm}})_3}\left(\widehat{c}_{ij}\right) - m_{F(\mathbf{I}_{\text{norm}})_1}\left(\widehat{a}_{ij}\right)\right)} \tag{50}$$

$$d\left(F\left(\mathbf{I}_{\text{norm}}\right)_3, F\left(\mathbf{I}_{\text{norm}}\right)_1\right) = \left(2 - \left(1 - \left(m_{F(\mathbf{I}_{\text{norm}})_3}\left(\widehat{c}_{ij}\right) - m_{F(\mathbf{I}_{\text{norm}})_1}\left(\widehat{a}_{ij}\right)\right)\right)\right) e^{m_{F(\mathbf{I}_{\text{norm}})_3}\left(\widehat{c}_{ij}\right) - m_{F(\mathbf{I}_{\text{norm}})_1}\left(\widehat{a}_{ij}\right)}$$
$$- \left(1 + m_{F(\mathbf{I}_{\text{norm}})_3}\left(\widehat{c}_{ij}\right) - m_{F(\mathbf{I}_{\text{norm}})_1}\left(\widehat{a}_{ij}\right)\right) e^{-\left(m_{F(\mathbf{I}_{\text{norm}})_3}\left(\widehat{c}_{ij}\right) - m_{F(\mathbf{I}_{\text{norm}})_1}\left(\widehat{a}_{ij}\right)\right)} \tag{51}$$

If,

$$d\left(F\left(\mathbf{I}_{\text{norm}}\right)_1, F\left(\mathbf{I}_{\text{norm}}\right)_2\right) \geq 0 \tag{52}$$

$$d\left(F\left(\mathbf{I}_{\text{norm}}\right)_1, F\left(\mathbf{I}_{\text{norm}}\right)_2\right) = 0 \Leftrightarrow A = B \tag{53}$$

$$d\left(F\left(\mathbf{I}_{\text{norm}}\right)_1, F\left(\mathbf{I}_{\text{norm}}\right)_2\right) = d\left(F\left(\mathbf{I}_{\text{norm}}\right)_2, F\left(\mathbf{I}_{\text{norm}}\right)_1\right) \tag{54}$$

$$d\left(F\left(\mathbf{I}_{\text{norm}}\right)_1, F\left(\mathbf{I}_{\text{norm}}\right)_2\right) \le d\left(F\left(\mathbf{I}_{\text{norm}}\right)_2, F\left(\mathbf{I}_{\text{norm}}\right)_3\right) + d\left(F\left(\mathbf{I}_{\text{norm}}\right)_3, F\left(\mathbf{I}_{\text{norm}}\right)_1\right) \tag{55}$$

then, applying the double summation operator to (52)-(55), (45)-(48) hold.

We prove (52).

If (52) were true, then

$$d\left(F\left(\mathbf{I}_{\text{norm}}\right)_1, F\left(\mathbf{I}_{\text{norm}}\right)_2\right) = 2 - \left(1 - \left(m_{F(\mathbf{I}_{\text{norm}})_1}\left(\widehat{a}_{ij}\right) - m_{F(\mathbf{I}_{\text{norm}})_2}\left(\widehat{b}_{ij}\right)\right)\right) e^{m_{F(\mathbf{I}_{\text{norm}})_1}\left(\widehat{a}_{ij}\right) - m_{F(\mathbf{I}_{\text{norm}})_2}\left(\widehat{b}_{ij}\right)}$$
$$- \left(1 + m_{F(\mathbf{I}_{\text{norm}})_1}\left(\widehat{a}_{ij}\right) - m_{F(\mathbf{I}_{\text{norm}})_2}\left(\widehat{b}_{ij}\right)\right) e^{-\left(m_{F(\mathbf{I}_{\text{norm}})_1}\left(\widehat{a}_{ij}\right) - m_{F(\mathbf{I}_{\text{norm}})_2}\left(\widehat{b}_{ij}\right)\right)} \ge 0 \tag{56}$$

so,

$$2 \ge \left(1 - \left(m_{F(\mathbf{I}_{\text{norm}})_1}\left(\widehat{a}_{ij}\right) - m_{F(\mathbf{I}_{\text{norm}})_2}\left(\widehat{b}_{ij}\right)\right)\right) e^{m_{F(\mathbf{I}_{\text{norm}})_1}\left(\widehat{a}_{ij}\right) - m_{F(\mathbf{I}_{\text{norm}})_2}\left(\widehat{b}_{ij}\right)}$$
$$+ \left(1 + m_{F(\mathbf{I}_{\text{norm}})_1}\left(\widehat{a}_{ij}\right) - m_{F(\mathbf{I}_{\text{norm}})_2}\left(\widehat{b}_{ij}\right)\right) e^{-\left(m_{F(\mathbf{I}_{\text{norm}})_1}\left(\widehat{a}_{ij}\right) - m_{F(\mathbf{I}_{\text{norm}})_2}\left(\widehat{b}_{ij}\right)\right)}$$
$$= e^{m_{F(\mathbf{I}_{\text{norm}})_1}\left(\widehat{a}_{ij}\right) - m_{F(\mathbf{I}_{\text{norm}})_2}\left(\widehat{b}_{ij}\right)} - \left(m_{F(\mathbf{I}_{\text{norm}})_1}\left(\widehat{a}_{ij}\right) - m_{F(\mathbf{I}_{\text{norm}})_2}\left(\widehat{b}_{ij}\right)\right) e^{m_{F(\mathbf{I}_{\text{norm}})_1}\left(\widehat{a}_{ij}\right) - m_{F(\mathbf{I}_{\text{norm}})_2}\left(\widehat{b}_{ij}\right)}$$
$$+ e^{-\left(m_{F(\mathbf{I}_{\text{norm}})_1}\left(\widehat{a}_{ij}\right) - m_{F(\mathbf{I}_{\text{norm}})_2}\left(\widehat{b}_{ij}\right)\right)} \left(m_{F(\mathbf{I}_{\text{norm}})_1}\left(\widehat{a}_{ij}\right) - m_{F(\mathbf{I}_{\text{norm}})_2}\left(\widehat{b}_{ij}\right)\right) e^{-\left(m_{F(\mathbf{I}_{\text{norm}})_1}\left(\widehat{a}_{ij}\right) - m_{F(\mathbf{I}_{\text{norm}})_2}\left(\widehat{b}_{ij}\right)\right)} \tag{57}$$
$$= \left(e^{m_{F(\mathbf{I}_{\text{norm}})_1}\left(\widehat{a}_{ij}\right) - m_{F(\mathbf{I}_{\text{norm}})_2}\left(\widehat{b}_{ij}\right)} + e^{-\left(m_{F(\mathbf{I}_{\text{norm}})_1}\left(\widehat{a}_{ij}\right) - m_{F(\mathbf{I}_{\text{norm}})_2}\left(\widehat{b}_{ij}\right)\right)}\right)$$
$$- \left(m_{F(\mathbf{I}_{\text{norm}})_1}\left(\widehat{a}_{ij}\right) - m_{F(\mathbf{I}_{\text{norm}})_2}\left(\widehat{b}_{ij}\right)\right) \left(e^{m_{F(\mathbf{I}_{\text{norm}})_1}\left(\widehat{a}_{ij}\right) - m_{F(\mathbf{I}_{\text{norm}})_2}\left(\widehat{b}_{ij}\right)} - e^{-\left(m_{F(\mathbf{I}_{\text{norm}})_1}\left(\widehat{a}_{ij}\right) - m_{F(\mathbf{I}_{\text{norm}})_2}\left(\widehat{b}_{ij}\right)\right)}\right)$$

Therefore,

$$2\cosh\left(m_{F(\mathbf{I}_{\text{norm}})_1}\left(\widehat{a}_{ij}\right) - m_{F(\mathbf{I}_{\text{norm}})_2}\left(\widehat{b}_{ij}\right)\right) - 2\left(m_{F(\mathbf{I}_{\text{norm}})_1}\left(\widehat{a}_{ij}\right) - m_{F(\mathbf{I}_{\text{norm}})_2}\left(\widehat{b}_{ij}\right)\right)\sinh\left(m_{F(\mathbf{I}_{\text{norm}})_1}\left(\widehat{a}_{ij}\right) - m_{F(\mathbf{I}_{\text{norm}})_2}\left(\widehat{b}_{ij}\right)\right) \le 2 \tag{58}$$

from which

$$\cosh\left(m_{F(\mathbf{I}_{\text{norm}})_1}\left(\widehat{a}_{ij}\right) - m_{F(\mathbf{I}_{\text{norm}})_2}\left(\widehat{b}_{ij}\right)\right) - \left(m_{F(\mathbf{I}_{\text{norm}})_1}\left(\widehat{a}_{ij}\right) - m_{F(\mathbf{I}_{\text{norm}})_2}\left(\widehat{b}_{ij}\right)\right)\sinh\left(m_{F(\mathbf{I}_{\text{norm}})_1}\left(\widehat{a}_{ij}\right) - m_{F(\mathbf{I}_{\text{norm}})_2}\left(\widehat{b}_{ij}\right)\right) \le 1. \tag{59}$$

Now, we set:

$$f\left(m_{F(\mathbf{I}_{norm})_1}\left(\widehat{a}_{ij}\right) - m_{F(\mathbf{I}_{norm})_2}\left(\widehat{b}_{ij}\right)\right) =$$
$$\cosh\left(m_{F(\mathbf{I}_{norm})_1}\left(\widehat{a}_{ij}\right) - m_{F(\mathbf{I}_{norm})_2}\left(\widehat{b}_{ij}\right)\right) - \left(m_{F(\mathbf{I}_{norm})_1}\left(\widehat{a}_{ij}\right) - m_{F(\mathbf{I}_{norm})_2}\left(\widehat{b}_{ij}\right)\right)\sinh\left(m_{F(\mathbf{I}_{norm})_1}\left(\widehat{a}_{ij}\right) - m_{F(\mathbf{I}_{norm})_2}\left(\widehat{b}_{ij}\right)\right). \tag{60}$$

so that,

$$f'\left(m_{F(\mathbf{I}_{norm})_1}\left(\widehat{a}_{ij}\right) - m_{F(\mathbf{I}_{norm})_2}\left(\widehat{b}_{ij}\right)\right) = \sinh\left(m_{F(\mathbf{I}_{norm})_1}\left(\widehat{a}_{ij}\right) - m_{F(\mathbf{I}_{norm})_2}\left(\widehat{b}_{ij}\right)\right)$$
$$-\sinh\left(m_{F(\mathbf{I}_{norm})_1}\left(\widehat{a}_{ij}\right) - m_{F(\mathbf{I}_{norm})_2}\left(\widehat{b}_{ij}\right)\right) \tag{61}$$
$$-\left(m_{F(\mathbf{I}_{norm})_1}\left(\widehat{a}_{ij}\right) - m_{F(\mathbf{I}_{norm})_2}\left(\widehat{b}_{ij}\right)\right)\cosh\left(m_{F(\mathbf{I}_{norm})_1}\left(\widehat{a}_{ij}\right) - m_{F(\mathbf{I}_{norm})_2}\left(\widehat{b}_{ij}\right)\right) = 0$$

obtaining

$$\left(m_{F(\mathbf{I}_{norm})_1}\left(\widehat{a}_{ij}\right) - m_{F(\mathbf{I}_{norm})_2}\left(\widehat{b}_{ij}\right)\right)\cosh\left(m_{F(\mathbf{I}_{norm})_1}\left(\widehat{a}_{ij}\right) - m_{F(\mathbf{I}_{norm})_2}\left(\widehat{b}_{ij}\right)\right) = 0. \tag{62}$$

But, $\forall m_{F(I_{norm})_1}\left(\widehat{a}_{ij}\right) - m_{F(I_{norm})_2}\left(\widehat{b}_{ij}\right)$,

$$\boldsymbol{cosh}\left(\boldsymbol{m}_{F(I_{norm})_1}\left(\widehat{a}_{ij}\right) - \boldsymbol{m}_{F(I_{norm})_2}\left(\widehat{b}_{ij}\right)\right) \neq 0, \tag{63}$$

from (62),

$$\boldsymbol{m}_{F(I_{norm})_1}\left(\widehat{a}_{ij}\right) - \boldsymbol{m}_{F(I_{norm})_2}\left(\widehat{b}_{ij}\right) = 0. \tag{64}$$

If

$$\boldsymbol{m}_{F(I_{norm})_1}\left(\widehat{a}_{ij}\right) - \boldsymbol{m}_{F(I_{norm})_2}\left(\widehat{b}_{ij}\right) = 0, \tag{65}$$

thus

$$f\left(m_{F(\mathbf{I}_{norm})_1}\left(\widehat{a}_{ij}\right) - m_{F(\mathbf{I}_{norm})_2}\left(\widehat{b}_{ij}\right)\right) = 1, \tag{66}$$

and if

$$\boldsymbol{m}_{F(I_{norm})_1}\left(\widehat{a}_{ij}\right) - \boldsymbol{m}_{F(I_{norm})_2}\left(\widehat{b}_{ij}\right) = 1, \tag{67}$$

thus

$$f\left(m_{F(\mathbf{I}_{\mathrm{norm}})_1}\left(\widehat{a_{ij}}\right) - m_{F(\mathbf{I}_{\mathrm{norm}})_2}\left(\widehat{b_{ij}}\right)\right) = e^{-1} < 1, \tag{68}$$

so is a point of maximum for
Then, (59) is always true (see Figure 1) so, applying the double summation operator, also (52) holds.

Figure 1. Hyperbolic functions

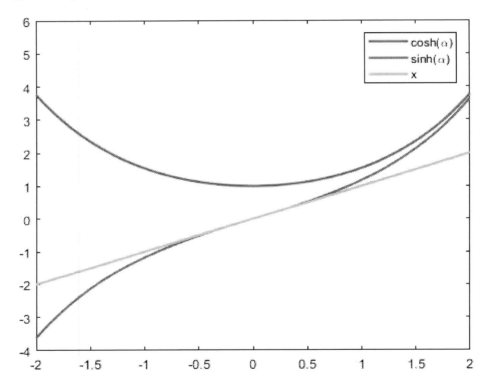

We prove (53).

The sufficient condition is easy to demonstrate. In fact, just if,

$$F(\mathbf{I}_{\mathrm{norm}})_1, F(\mathbf{I}_{\mathrm{norm}})_2, \tag{69}$$

then $m_{F(\mathbf{I}_{\mathrm{norm}})_1}\left(\widehat{a_{ij}}\right) - m_{F(\mathbf{I}_{\mathrm{norm}})_2}\left(\widehat{b_{ij}}\right) = 0,$ so

$$d\left(F\left(\mathbf{I}_{\text{norm}}\right)_1, F\left(\mathbf{I}_{\text{norm}}\right)_2\right) = 2 - \left(1 - \left(m_{F(\mathbf{I}_{\text{norm}})_1}\left(\widehat{a}_{ij}\right) - m_{F(\mathbf{I}_{\text{norm}})_2}\left(\widehat{b}_{ij}\right)\right)\right) e^{m_{F(\mathbf{I}_{\text{norm}})_1}\left(\widehat{a}_{ij}\right) - m_{F(\mathbf{I}_{\text{norm}})_2}\left(\widehat{b}_{ij}\right)}$$
$$- \left(1 + m_{F(\mathbf{I}_{\text{norm}})_1}\left(\widehat{a}_{ij}\right) - m_{F(\mathbf{I}_{\text{norm}})_2}\left(\widehat{b}_{ij}\right)\right) e^{-\left(m_{F(\mathbf{I}_{\text{norm}})_1}\left(\widehat{a}_{ij}\right) - m_{F(\mathbf{I}_{\text{norm}})_2}\left(\widehat{b}_{ij}\right)\right)} = 0 \tag{70}$$

Vice-versa, from $d(F(\mathbf{I}_{\text{norm}})_1, F(\mathbf{I}_{\text{norm}})_2) = 0$,

$$2 = \left(1 - \left(m_{F(\mathbf{I}_{\text{norm}})_1}\left(\widehat{a}_{ij}\right) - m_{F(\mathbf{I}_{\text{norm}})_2}\left(\widehat{b}_{ij}\right)\right)\right) e^{m_{F(\mathbf{I}_{\text{norm}})_1}\left(\widehat{a}_{ij}\right) - m_{F(\mathbf{I}_{\text{norm}})_2}\left(\widehat{b}_{ij}\right)}$$
$$- \left(1 + m_{F(\mathbf{I}_{\text{norm}})_1}\left(\widehat{a}_{ij}\right) - m_{F(\mathbf{I}_{\text{norm}})_2}\left(\widehat{b}_{ij}\right)\right) e^{-\left(m_{F(\mathbf{I}_{\text{norm}})_1}\left(\widehat{a}_{ij}\right) - m_{F(\mathbf{I}_{\text{norm}})_2}\left(\widehat{b}_{ij}\right)\right)} = 0, \tag{71}$$

thus

$$2 = \left(1 - \left(m_{F(\mathbf{I}_{\text{norm}})_1}\left(\widehat{a}_{ij}\right) - m_{F(\mathbf{I}_{\text{norm}})_2}\left(\widehat{b}_{ij}\right)\right)\right) e^{m_{F(\mathbf{I}_{\text{norm}})_1}\left(\widehat{a}_{ij}\right) - m_{F(\mathbf{I}_{\text{norm}})_2}\left(\widehat{b}_{ij}\right)}$$
$$+ \left(1 + m_{F(\mathbf{I}_{\text{norm}})_1}\left(\widehat{a}_{ij}\right) - m_{F(\mathbf{I}_{\text{norm}})_2}\left(\widehat{b}_{ij}\right)\right) e^{-\left(m_{F(\mathbf{I}_{\text{norm}})_1}\left(\widehat{a}_{ij}\right) - m_{F(\mathbf{I}_{\text{norm}})_2}\left(\widehat{b}_{ij}\right)\right)}$$

$$= e^{m_{F(\mathbf{I}_{\text{norm}})_1}\left(\widehat{a}_{ij}\right) - m_{F(\mathbf{I}_{\text{norm}})_2}\left(\widehat{b}_{ij}\right)} - \left(m_{F(\mathbf{I}_{\text{norm}})_1}\left(\widehat{a}_{ij}\right) - m_{F(\mathbf{I}_{\text{norm}})_2}\left(\widehat{b}_{ij}\right)\right) e^{m_{F(\mathbf{I}_{\text{norm}})_1}\left(\widehat{a}_{ij}\right) - m_{F(\mathbf{I}_{\text{norm}})_2}\left(\widehat{b}_{ij}\right)}$$
$$+ e^{-\left(m_{F(\mathbf{I}_{\text{norm}})_1}\left(\widehat{a}_{ij}\right) - m_{F(\mathbf{I}_{\text{norm}})_2}\left(\widehat{b}_{ij}\right)\right)} + \left(m_{F(\mathbf{I}_{\text{norm}})_1}\left(\widehat{a}_{ij}\right) - m_{F(\mathbf{I}_{\text{norm}})_2}\left(\widehat{b}_{ij}\right)\right) e^{-\left(m_{F(\mathbf{I}_{\text{norm}})_1}\left(\widehat{a}_{ij}\right) - m_{F(\mathbf{I}_{\text{norm}})_2}\left(\widehat{b}_{ij}\right)\right)}$$

$$= e^{m_{F(\mathbf{I}_{\text{norm}})_1}\left(\widehat{a}_{ij}\right) - m_{F(\mathbf{I}_{\text{norm}})_2}\left(\widehat{b}_{ij}\right)} + e^{-\left(m_{F(\mathbf{I}_{\text{norm}})_1}\left(\widehat{a}_{ij}\right) - m_{F(\mathbf{I}_{\text{norm}})_2}\left(\widehat{b}_{ij}\right)\right)}$$
$$- \left(m_{F(\mathbf{I}_{\text{norm}})_1}\left(\widehat{a}_{ij}\right) - m_{F(\mathbf{I}_{\text{norm}})_2}\left(\widehat{b}_{ij}\right)\right)\left(e^{m_{F(\mathbf{I}_{\text{norm}})_1}\left(\widehat{a}_{ij}\right) - m_{F(\mathbf{I}_{\text{norm}})_2}\left(\widehat{b}_{ij}\right)} - e^{-\left(m_{F(\mathbf{I}_{\text{norm}})_1}\left(\widehat{a}_{ij}\right) - m_{F(\mathbf{I}_{\text{norm}})_2}\left(\widehat{b}_{ij}\right)\right)}\right)$$
$$- \left(m_{F(\mathbf{I}_{\text{norm}})_1}\left(\widehat{a}_{ij}\right) - m_{F(\mathbf{I}_{\text{norm}})_2}\left(\widehat{b}_{ij}\right)\right)\left(e^{m_{F(\mathbf{I}_{\text{norm}})_1}\left(\widehat{a}_{ij}\right) - m_{F(\mathbf{I}_{\text{norm}})_2}\left(\widehat{b}_{ij}\right)} - e^{-\left(m_{F(\mathbf{I}_{\text{norm}})_1}\left(\widehat{a}_{ij}\right) - m_{F(\mathbf{I}_{\text{norm}})_2}\left(\widehat{b}_{ij}\right)\right)}\right)$$

$$= e^{m_{F(\mathbf{I}_{\text{norm}})_1}\left(\widehat{a}_{ij}\right) - m_{F(\mathbf{I}_{\text{norm}})_2}\left(\widehat{b}_{ij}\right)} + e^{-\left(m_{F(\mathbf{I}_{\text{norm}})_1}\left(\widehat{a}_{ij}\right) - m_{F(\mathbf{I}_{\text{norm}})_2}\left(\widehat{b}_{ij}\right)\right)}$$
$$- \left(m_{F(\mathbf{I}_{\text{norm}})_1}\left(\widehat{a}_{ij}\right) - m_{F(\mathbf{I}_{\text{norm}})_2}\left(\widehat{b}_{ij}\right)\right)\left(e^{m_{F(\mathbf{I}_{\text{norm}})_1}\left(\widehat{a}_{ij}\right) - m_{F(\mathbf{I}_{\text{norm}})_2}\left(\widehat{b}_{ij}\right)} - e^{-\left(m_{F(\mathbf{I}_{\text{norm}})_1}\left(\widehat{a}_{ij}\right) - m_{F(\mathbf{I}_{\text{norm}})_2}\left(\widehat{b}_{ij}\right)\right)}\right)$$

$$= 2\cosh\left(m_{F(\mathbf{I}_{\mathrm{norm}})_1}\left(\widehat{a_{ij}}\right) - m_{F(\mathbf{I}_{\mathrm{norm}})_2}\left(\widehat{b_{ij}}\right)\right)$$
$$-2\left(m_{F(\mathbf{I}_{\mathrm{norm}})_1}\left(\widehat{a_{ij}}\right) - m_{F(\mathbf{I}_{\mathrm{norm}})_2}\left(\widehat{b_{ij}}\right)\right)\sinh\left(m_{F(\mathbf{I}_{\mathrm{norm}})_1}\left(\widehat{a_{ij}}\right) - m_{F(\mathbf{I}_{\mathrm{norm}})_2}\left(\widehat{b_{ij}}\right)\right)$$

(72)

achieving,

$$1 = \cosh\left(m_{F(\mathbf{I}_{\mathrm{norm}})_1}\left(\widehat{a_{ij}}\right) - m_{F(\mathbf{I}_{\mathrm{norm}})_2}\left(\widehat{b_{ij}}\right)\right)$$
$$-\left(m_{F(\mathbf{I}_{\mathrm{norm}})_1}\left(\widehat{a_{ij}}\right) - m_{F(\mathbf{I}_{\mathrm{norm}})_2}\left(\widehat{b_{ij}}\right)\right)\sinh\left(m_{F(\mathbf{I}_{\mathrm{norm}})_1}\left(\widehat{a_{ij}}\right) - m_{F(\mathbf{I}_{\mathrm{norm}})_2}\left(\widehat{b_{ij}}\right)\right).$$

(73)

(73) is verified *iff* $m_{F(\mathbf{I}_{\mathrm{norm}})_1}\left(\widehat{a_{ij}}\right) - m_{F(\mathbf{I}_{\mathrm{norm}})_2}\left(\widehat{b_{ij}}\right) = 0$ (see Figure 1). Then, (53) holds and, applying the double summation operator, also (46) yields.

We prove (53).

Exploiting (49), we can write:

$$d\left(F\left(\mathbf{I}_{\mathrm{norm}}\right)_1, F\left(\mathbf{I}_{\mathrm{norm}}\right)_2\right) = 2 - \left(1 - \left(m_{F(\mathbf{I}_{\mathrm{norm}})_1}\left(\widehat{a_{ij}}\right) - m_{F(\mathbf{I}_{\mathrm{norm}})_2}\left(\widehat{b_{ij}}\right)\right)\right)e^{m_{F(\mathbf{I}_{\mathrm{norm}})_1}\left(\widehat{a_{ij}}\right) - m_{F(\mathbf{I}_{\mathrm{norm}})_2}\left(\widehat{b_{ij}}\right)}$$
$$-\left(1 + m_{F(\mathbf{I}_{\mathrm{norm}})_1}\left(\widehat{a_{ij}}\right) - m_{F(\mathbf{I}_{\mathrm{norm}})_2}\left(\widehat{b_{ij}}\right)\right)e^{-\left(m_{F(\mathbf{I}_{\mathrm{norm}})_1}\left(\widehat{a_{ij}}\right) - m_{F(\mathbf{I}_{\mathrm{norm}})_2}\left(\widehat{b_{ij}}\right)\right)} = 2$$
$$-\left(1 - \left(m_{F(\mathbf{I}_{\mathrm{norm}})_1}\left(\widehat{a_{ij}}\right) - m_{F(\mathbf{I}_{\mathrm{norm}})_2}\left(\widehat{b_{ij}}\right)\right)\right)e^{-\left(m_{F(\mathbf{I}_{\mathrm{norm}})_1}\left(\widehat{a_{ij}}\right) - m_{F(\mathbf{I}_{\mathrm{norm}})_2}\left(\widehat{b_{ij}}\right)\right)}$$
$$-\left(1 + m_{F(\mathbf{I}_{\mathrm{norm}})_1}\left(\widehat{a_{ij}}\right) - m_{F(\mathbf{I}_{\mathrm{norm}})_2}\left(\widehat{b_{ij}}\right)\right)e^{-\left(m_{F(\mathbf{I}_{\mathrm{norm}})_1}\left(\widehat{a_{ij}}\right) - m_{F(\mathbf{I}_{\mathrm{norm}})_2}\left(\widehat{b_{ij}}\right)\right)} = d\left(F\left(\mathbf{I}_{\mathrm{norm}}\right)_2, F\left(\mathbf{I}_{\mathrm{norm}}\right)_1\right).$$

(74)

We prove (54).

Exploiting (49), we achieve

$$d\left(F\left(\mathbf{I}_{\mathrm{norm}}\right)_1, F\left(\mathbf{I}_{\mathrm{norm}}\right)_2\right) = 2 - \left(1 - m_{F(\mathbf{I}_{\mathrm{norm}})_1}\left(\widehat{a_{ij}}\right) - m_{F(\mathbf{I}_{\mathrm{norm}})_2}\left(\widehat{b_{ij}}\right)\right)e^{m_{F(\mathbf{I}_{\mathrm{norm}})_1}\left(\widehat{a_{ij}}\right) - m_{F(\mathbf{I}_{\mathrm{norm}})_2}\left(\widehat{b_{ij}}\right)}$$
$$-\left(1 + m_{F(\mathbf{I}_{\mathrm{norm}})_1}\left(\widehat{a_{ij}}\right) - m_{F(\mathbf{I}_{\mathrm{norm}})_2}\left(\widehat{b_{ij}}\right)\right)e^{-\left(m_{F(\mathbf{I}_{\mathrm{norm}})_1}\left(\widehat{a_{ij}}\right) - m_{F(\mathbf{I}_{\mathrm{norm}})_2}\left(\widehat{b_{ij}}\right)\right)} \leq 2$$
$$-\left(1 - \left(m_{F(\mathbf{I}_{\mathrm{norm}})_2}\left(\widehat{b_{ij}}\right) - m_{F(\mathbf{I}_{\mathrm{norm}})_3}\left(\widehat{c_{ij}}\right)\right)\right)e^{m_{F(\mathbf{I}_{\mathrm{norm}})_2}\left(\widehat{b_{ij}}\right) - m_{F(\mathbf{I}_{\mathrm{norm}})_3}\left(\widehat{c_{ij}}\right)}$$

$$-\left(1+m_{F(\mathbf{I}_{norm})_2}\left(\widehat{b}_{ij}\right)-m_{F(\mathbf{I}_{norm})_3}\left(\widehat{c}_{ij}\right)\right)e^{-\left(m_{F(\mathbf{I}_{norm})_2}\left(\widehat{b}_{ij}\right)-m_{F(\mathbf{I}_{norm})_3}\left(\widehat{c}_{ij}\right)\right)}$$

$$+2-\left(1-\left(m_{F(\mathbf{I}_{norm})_3}\left(\widehat{c}_{ij}\right)-m_{F(\mathbf{I}_{norm})_1}\left(\widehat{a}_{ij}\right)\right)\right)e^{m_{F(\mathbf{I}_{norm})_3}\left(\widehat{c}_{ij}\right)-m_{F(\mathbf{I}_{norm})_1}\left(\widehat{a}_{ij}\right)} \tag{75}$$

$$-\left(1+m_{F(\mathbf{I}_{norm})_3}\left(\widehat{c}_{ij}\right)-m_{F(\mathbf{I}_{norm})_1}\left(\widehat{a}_{ij}\right)\right)e^{-m_{F(\mathbf{I}_{norm})_3}\left(\widehat{c}_{ij}\right)-m_{F(\mathbf{I}_{norm})_1}\left(\widehat{a}_{ij}\right)}$$

from which,

$$d(F(\mathbf{I}_{norm})_1, F(\mathbf{I}_{norm})_2) \le 2$$

$$-\left(1+m_{F(\mathbf{I}_{norm})_1}\left(\widehat{a}_{ij}\right)-m_{F(\mathbf{I}_{norm})_2}\left(\widehat{b}_{ij}\right)+m_{F(\mathbf{I}_{norm})_3}\left(\widehat{c}_{ij}\right)-m_{F(\mathbf{I}_{norm})_1}\left(\widehat{a}_{ij}\right)\right)e^{-\left(m_{F(\mathbf{I}_{norm})_1}\left(\widehat{a}_{ij}\right)-m_{F(\mathbf{I}_{norm})_2}\left(\widehat{b}_{ij}\right)\right)-\left(m_{F(\mathbf{I}_{norm})_3}\left(\widehat{c}_{ij}\right)-m_{F(\mathbf{I}_{norm})_1}\left(\widehat{a}_{ij}\right)\right)}$$

$$-\left(1-\left(m_{F(\mathbf{I}_{norm})_1}\left(\widehat{a}_{ij}\right)-m_{F(\mathbf{I}_{norm})_2}\left(\widehat{b}_{ij}\right)\right)-\left(m_{F(\mathbf{I}_{norm})_3}\left(\widehat{c}_{ij}\right)-m_{F(\mathbf{I}_{norm})_1}\left(\widehat{a}_{ij}\right)\right)\right)e^{m_{F(\mathbf{I}_{norm})_1}\left(\widehat{a}_{ij}\right)-m_{F(\mathbf{I}_{norm})_2}\left(\widehat{b}_{ij}\right)+m_{F(\mathbf{I}_{norm})_3}\left(\widehat{c}_{ij}\right)-m_{F(\mathbf{I}_{norm})_1}\left(\widehat{a}_{ij}\right)}$$

$$+\left(m_{F(\mathbf{I}_{norm})_3}\left(\widehat{c}_{ij}\right)-m_{F(\mathbf{I}_{norm})_1}\left(\widehat{a}_{ij}\right)\right)e^{m_{F(\mathbf{I}_{norm})_1}\left(\widehat{a}_{ij}\right)-m_{F(\mathbf{I}_{norm})_2}\left(\widehat{b}_{ij}\right)+m_{F(\mathbf{I}_{norm})_3}\left(\widehat{c}_{ij}\right)-m_{F(\mathbf{I}_{norm})_1}\left(\widehat{a}_{ij}\right)}$$

$$+2-\left(1-\left(m_{F(\mathbf{I}_{norm})_3}\left(\widehat{c}_{ij}\right)-m_{F(\mathbf{I}_{norm})_1}\left(\widehat{a}_{ij}\right)\right)\right)e^{m_{F(\mathbf{I}_{norm})_3}\left(\widehat{c}_{ij}\right)-m_{F(\mathbf{I}_{norm})_1}\left(\widehat{a}_{ij}\right)} \tag{76}$$

$$-\left(1+m_{F(\mathbf{I}_{norm})_3}\left(\widehat{c}_{ij}\right)-m_{F(\mathbf{I}_{norm})_1}\left(\widehat{a}_{ij}\right)\right)e^{-\left(m_{F(\mathbf{I}_{norm})_3}\left(\widehat{c}_{ij}\right)-m_{F(\mathbf{I}_{norm})_1}\left(\widehat{a}_{ij}\right)\right)}.$$

And by (76),

$$d(F(\mathbf{I}_{norm})_1, F(\mathbf{I}_{norm})_2) \le 2$$

$$-\left(1+m_{F(\mathbf{I}_{norm})_1}\left(\widehat{a}_{ij}\right)-m_{F(\mathbf{I}_{norm})_2}\left(\widehat{b}_{ij}\right)\right)^{-\left(m_{F(\mathbf{I}_{norm})_1}\left(\widehat{a}_{ij}\right)-m_{F(\mathbf{I}_{norm})_2}\left(\widehat{b}_{ij}\right)\right)-\left(m_{F(\mathbf{I}_{norm})_3}\left(\widehat{c}_{ij}\right)-m_{F(\mathbf{I}_{norm})_1}\left(\widehat{a}_{ij}\right)\right)}$$

$$-\left(m_{F(\mathbf{I}_{norm})_3}\left(\widehat{c}_{ij}\right)-m_{F(\mathbf{I}_{norm})_1}\left(\widehat{a}_{ij}\right)\right)e^{-\left(m_{F(\mathbf{I}_{norm})_1}\left(\widehat{a}_{ij}\right)-m_{F(\mathbf{I}_{norm})_2}\left(\widehat{b}_{ij}\right)\right)-\left(m_{F(\mathbf{I}_{norm})_3}\left(\widehat{c}_{ij}\right)-m_{F(\mathbf{I}_{norm})_1}\left(\widehat{a}_{ij}\right)\right)}$$

$$-\left(1-\left(m_{F(\mathbf{I}_{norm})_1}\left(\widehat{a}_{ij}\right)-m_{F(\mathbf{I}_{norm})_2}\left(\widehat{b}_{ij}\right)\right)\right)e^{m_{F(\mathbf{I}_{norm})_1}\left(\widehat{a}_{ij}\right)-m_{F(\mathbf{I}_{norm})_2}\left(\widehat{b}_{ij}\right)+m_{F(\mathbf{I}_{norm})_3}\left(\widehat{c}_{ij}\right)-m_{F(\mathbf{I}_{norm})_1}\left(\widehat{a}_{ij}\right)}$$

$$+\left(m_{F(\mathbf{I}_{norm})_3}\left(\widehat{c}_{ij}\right)-m_{F(\mathbf{I}_{norm})_1}\left(\widehat{a}_{ij}\right)\right)e^{m_{F(\mathbf{I}_{norm})_1}\left(\widehat{a}_{ij}\right)-m_{F(\mathbf{I}_{norm})_2}\left(\widehat{b}_{ij}\right)+3}+2$$

$$-\left(1-\left(m_{F(\mathbf{I}_{norm})_3}\left(\widehat{c}_{ij}\right)-m_{F(\mathbf{I}_{norm})_1}\left(\widehat{a}_{ij}\right)\right)\right)e^{m_{F(\mathbf{I}_{norm})_3}\left(\widehat{c}_{ij}\right)-m_{F(\mathbf{I}_{norm})_1}\left(\widehat{a}_{ij}\right)} \tag{77}$$

$$-\left(1+m_{F(\mathbf{I}_{norm})_1}\left(\widehat{a}_{ij}\right)-m_{F(\mathbf{I}_{norm})_2}\left(\widehat{b}_{ij}\right)\right)e^{-\left(m_{F(\mathbf{I}_{norm})_1}\left(\widehat{a}_{ij}\right)-m_{F(\mathbf{I}_{norm})_2}\left(\widehat{b}_{ij}\right)\right)}.$$

Further, in the right side of (77), adding and subtracting

$$\left(1+m_{F(\mathbf{I}_{\mathrm{norm}})_1}\left(\widehat{a_{ij}}\right)-m_{F(\mathbf{I}_{\mathrm{norm}})_2}\left(\widehat{b_{ij}}\right)\right)e^{-m_{F(\mathbf{I}_{\mathrm{norm}})_1}\left(\widehat{a_{ij}}\right)-m_{F(\mathbf{I}_{\mathrm{norm}})_2}\left(\widehat{b_{ij}}\right)}$$
$$+\left(1-m_{F(\mathbf{I}_{\mathrm{norm}})_1}\left(\widehat{a_{ij}}\right)-m_{F(\mathbf{I}_{\mathrm{norm}})_2}\left(\widehat{b_{ij}}\right)\right)e^{m_{F(\mathbf{I}_{\mathrm{norm}})_1}\left(\widehat{a_{ij}}\right)-m_{F(\mathbf{I}_{\mathrm{norm}})_2}\left(\widehat{b_{ij}}\right)} \tag{78}$$

we achieve,

$$d(F(\mathbf{I}_{\mathrm{norm}})_1, F(\mathbf{I}_{\mathrm{norm}})_2) \le 2$$

$$-\left(1+m_{F(\mathbf{I}_{\mathrm{norm}})_1}\left(\widehat{a_{ij}}\right)-m_{F(\mathbf{I}_{\mathrm{norm}})_2}\left(\widehat{b_{ij}}\right)\right)e^{-\left(m_{F(\mathbf{I}_{\mathrm{norm}})_1}\left(\widehat{a_{ij}}\right)-m_{F(\mathbf{I}_{\mathrm{norm}})_2}\left(\widehat{b_{ij}}\right)\right)}$$

$$-\left(1-\left(m_{F(\mathbf{I}_{\mathrm{norm}})_1}\left(\widehat{a_{ij}}\right)-m_{F(\mathbf{I}_{\mathrm{norm}})_2}\left(\widehat{b_{ij}}\right)\right)\right)e^{m_{F(\mathbf{I}_{\mathrm{norm}})_1}\left(\widehat{a_{ij}}\right)-m_{F(\mathbf{I}_{\mathrm{norm}})_2}\left(\widehat{b_{ij}}\right)}$$

$$+\left(1+m_{F(\mathbf{I}_{\mathrm{norm}})_1}\left(\widehat{a_{ij}}\right)-m_{F(\mathbf{I}_{\mathrm{norm}})_2}\left(\widehat{b_{ij}}\right)\right)e^{-\left(m_{F(\mathbf{I}_{\mathrm{norm}})_1}\left(\widehat{a_{ij}}\right)-m_{F(\mathbf{I}_{\mathrm{norm}})_2}\left(\widehat{b_{ij}}\right)\right)}$$

$$+\left(1-\left(m_{F(\mathbf{I}_{\mathrm{norm}})_1}\left(\widehat{a_{ij}}\right)-m_{F(\mathbf{I}_{\mathrm{norm}})_2}\left(\widehat{b_{ij}}\right)\right)\right)e^{m_{F(\mathbf{I}_{\mathrm{norm}})_1}\left(\widehat{a_{ij}}\right)-m_{F(\mathbf{I}_{\mathrm{norm}})_2}\left(\widehat{b_{ij}}\right)}$$

$$-\left(1+m_{F(\mathbf{I}_{\mathrm{norm}})_1}\left(\widehat{a_{ij}}\right)-m_{F(\mathbf{I}_{\mathrm{norm}})_2}\left(\widehat{b_{ij}}\right)\right)e^{-(m_{F(\mathbf{I}_{\mathrm{norm}})_1}\left(\widehat{a_{ij}}\right)-m_{F(\mathbf{I}_{\mathrm{norm}})_2}\left(\widehat{b_{ij}}\right))}-\left(m_{F(\mathbf{I}_{\mathrm{norm}})_3}\left(\widehat{c_{ij}}\right)-m_{F(\mathbf{I}_{\mathrm{norm}})_1}\left(\widehat{a_{ij}}\right)\right)\}$$

$$-\left(m_{F(\mathbf{I}_{\mathrm{norm}})_3}\left(\widehat{c_{ij}}\right)-m_{F(\mathbf{I}_{\mathrm{norm}})_1}\left(\widehat{a_{ij}}\right)\right)e^{-\left(m_{F(\mathbf{I}_{\mathrm{norm}})_1}\left(\widehat{a_{ij}}\right)-m_{F(\mathbf{I}_{\mathrm{norm}})_2}\left(\widehat{b_{ij}}\right)\right)-\left(m_{F(\mathbf{I}_{\mathrm{norm}})_3}\left(\widehat{c_{ij}}\right)-m_{F(\mathbf{I}_{\mathrm{norm}})_1}\left(\widehat{a_{ij}}\right)\right)}$$

$$-\left(1-\left(m_{F(\mathbf{I}_{\mathrm{norm}})_3}\left(\widehat{c_{ij}}\right)-m_{F(\mathbf{I}_{\mathrm{norm}})_1}\left(\widehat{a_{ij}}\right)\right)\right)e^{m_{F(\mathbf{I}_{\mathrm{norm}})_1}\left(\widehat{a_{ij}}\right)-m_{F(\mathbf{I}_{\mathrm{norm}})_2}\left(\widehat{b_{ij}}\right)+m_{F(\mathbf{I}_{\mathrm{norm}})_3}\left(\widehat{c_{ij}}\right)-m_{F(\mathbf{I}_{\mathrm{norm}})_1}\left(\widehat{a_{ij}}\right)}$$

$$+\left(m_{F(\mathbf{I}_{\mathrm{norm}})_3}\left(\widehat{c_{ij}}\right)-m_{F(\mathbf{I}_{\mathrm{norm}})_1}\left(\widehat{a_{ij}}\right)\right)e^{m_{F(\mathbf{I}_{\mathrm{norm}})_1}\left(\widehat{a_{ij}}\right)-m_{F(\mathbf{I}_{\mathrm{norm}})_2}\left(\widehat{b_{ij}}\right)+m_{F(\mathbf{I}_{\mathrm{norm}})_3}\left(\widehat{c_{ij}}\right)-m_{F(\mathbf{I}_{\mathrm{norm}})_1}\left(\widehat{a_{ij}}\right)}$$

$$+2-\left(1-\left(m_{F(\mathbf{I}_{\mathrm{norm}})_3}\left(\widehat{c_{ij}}\right)-m_{F(\mathbf{I}_{\mathrm{norm}})_1}\left(\widehat{a_{ij}}\right)\right)\right)e^{m_{F(\mathbf{I}_{\mathrm{norm}})_3}\left(\widehat{c_{ij}}\right)-m_{F(\mathbf{I}_{\mathrm{norm}})_1}\left(\widehat{a_{ij}}\right)}$$

$$-\left(1+m_{F(\mathbf{I}_{\mathrm{norm}})_3}\left(\widehat{c_{ij}}\right)-m_{F(\mathbf{I}_{\mathrm{norm}})_1}\left(\widehat{a_{ij}}\right)\right)e^{-\left(m_{F(\mathbf{I}_{\mathrm{norm}})_3}\left(\widehat{c_{ij}}\right)-m_{F(\mathbf{I}_{\mathrm{norm}})_1}\left(\widehat{a_{ij}}\right)\right)} \tag{79}$$

But in (79)

$$2-\left(1+m_{F(\mathbf{I}_{\mathrm{norm}})_1}\left(\widehat{a_{ij}}\right)-m_{F(\mathbf{I}_{\mathrm{norm}})_2}\left(\widehat{b_{ij}}\right)\right)e^{-\left(m_{F(\mathbf{I}_{\mathrm{norm}})_1}\left(\widehat{a_{ij}}\right)-m_{F(\mathbf{I}_{\mathrm{norm}})_2}\left(\widehat{b_{ij}}\right)\right)}$$

$$-\left(1-\left(m_{F(\mathbf{I}_{\mathrm{norm}})_1}\left(\widehat{a_{ij}}\right)-m_{F(\mathbf{I}_{\mathrm{norm}})_2}\left(\widehat{b_{ij}}\right)\right)\right)e^{m_{F(\mathbf{I}_{\mathrm{norm}})_1}\left(\widehat{a_{ij}}\right)-m_{F(\mathbf{I}_{\mathrm{norm}})_2}\left(\widehat{b_{ij}}\right)}=d\left(F\left(I_{norm}\right)_1,F\left(I_{norm}\right)_2\right)\ge 0 \tag{80}$$

and,

$$2 - \left(1 - \left(m_{F(\mathbf{I}_{\text{norm}})_3}\left(\widehat{c_{ij}}\right) - m_{F(\mathbf{I}_{\text{norm}})_1}\left(\widehat{a_{ij}}\right)\right)\right)e^{m_{F(\mathbf{I}_{\text{norm}})_3}\left(\widehat{c_{ij}}\right) - m_{F(\mathbf{I}_{\text{norm}})_1}\left(\widehat{a_{ij}}\right)}$$

$$- \left(1 + m_{F(\mathbf{I}_{\text{norm}})_3}\left(\widehat{c_{ij}}\right) - m_{F(\mathbf{I}_{\text{norm}})_1}\left(\widehat{a_{ij}}\right)\right)e^{-\left(m_{F(\mathbf{I}_{\text{norm}})_3}\left(\widehat{c_{ij}}\right) - m_{F(\mathbf{I}_{\text{norm}})_1}\left(\widehat{a_{ij}}\right)\right)} = d\left(C, A\right) \geq 0. \tag{81}$$

Then (79), considering (80) and (81), becomes:

$$d(F(\mathbf{I}_{\text{norm}})_1, F(\mathbf{I}_{\text{norm}})_2) \leq d(F(\mathbf{I}_{\text{norm}})_1, F(\mathbf{I}_{\text{norm}})_2)$$

$$+ \left(1 + m_{F(\mathbf{I}_{\text{norm}})_1}\left(\widehat{a_{ij}}\right) - m_{F(\mathbf{I}_{\text{norm}})_2}\left(\widehat{b_{ij}}\right)\right)e^{-\left(m_{F(\mathbf{I}_{\text{norm}})_1}\left(\widehat{a_{ij}}\right) - m_{F(\mathbf{I}_{\text{norm}})_2}\left(\widehat{b_{ij}}\right)\right)}$$

$$+ \left(1 - \left(m_{F(\mathbf{I}_{\text{norm}})_1}\left(\widehat{a_{ij}}\right) - m_{F(\mathbf{I}_{\text{norm}})_2}\left(\widehat{b_{ij}}\right)\right)\right)e^{m_{F(\mathbf{I}_{\text{norm}})_1}\left(\widehat{a_{ij}}\right) - m_{F(\mathbf{I}_{\text{norm}})_2}\left(\widehat{b_{ij}}\right)}$$

$$- \left(1 + m_{F(\mathbf{I}_{\text{norm}})_1}\left(\widehat{a_{ij}}\right) - m_{F(\mathbf{I}_{\text{norm}})_2}\left(\widehat{b_{ij}}\right)\right)e^{-\left(m_{F(\mathbf{I}_{\text{norm}})_1}\left(\widehat{a_{ij}}\right) - m_{F(\mathbf{I}_{\text{norm}})_2}\left(\widehat{b_{ij}}\right)\right) - \left(m_{F(\mathbf{I}_{\text{norm}})_3}\left(\widehat{c_{ij}}\right) - m_{F(\mathbf{I}_{\text{norm}})_1}\left(\widehat{a_{ij}}\right)\right)}$$

$$- \left(m_{F(\mathbf{I}_{\text{norm}})_3}\left(\widehat{c_{ij}}\right) - m_{F(\mathbf{I}_{\text{norm}})_1}\left(\widehat{a_{ij}}\right)\right)e^{-\left(m_{F(\mathbf{I}_{\text{norm}})_1}\left(\widehat{a_{ij}}\right) - m_{F(\mathbf{I}_{\text{norm}})_2}\left(\widehat{b_{ij}}\right)\right) - \left(m_{F(\mathbf{I}_{\text{norm}})_3}\left(\widehat{c_{ij}}\right) - m_{F(\mathbf{I}_{\text{norm}})_1}\left(\widehat{a_{ij}}\right)\right)}$$

$$- \left(1 - \left(m_{F(\mathbf{I}_{\text{norm}})_1}\left(\widehat{a_{ij}}\right) - m_{F(\mathbf{I}_{\text{norm}})_2}\left(\widehat{b_{ij}}\right)\right)\right)e^{m_{F(\mathbf{I}_{\text{norm}})_1}\left(\widehat{a_{ij}}\right) - m_{F(\mathbf{I}_{\text{norm}})_2}\left(\widehat{b_{ij}}\right) + m_{F(\mathbf{I}_{\text{norm}})_3}\left(\widehat{c_{ij}}\right) - m_{F(\mathbf{I}_{\text{norm}})_1}\left(\widehat{a_{ij}}\right)}$$

$$+ d(F(\mathbf{I}_{\text{norm}})_3, F(\mathbf{I}_{\text{norm}})_1) \tag{82}$$

reducing the problem to show that,

$$\left(1 + m_{F(\mathbf{I}_{\text{norm}})_1}\left(\widehat{a_{ij}}\right) - m_{F(\mathbf{I}_{\text{norm}})_2}\left(\widehat{b_{ij}}\right)\right)e^{-\left(m_{F(\mathbf{I}_{\text{norm}})_1}\left(\widehat{a_{ij}}\right) - m_{F(\mathbf{I}_{\text{norm}})_2}\left(\widehat{b_{ij}}\right)\right)}$$

$$+ \left(1 - \left(m_{F(\mathbf{I}_{\text{norm}})_1}\left(\widehat{a_{ij}}\right) - m_{F(\mathbf{I}_{\text{norm}})_2}\left(\widehat{b_{ij}}\right)\right)\right)e^{m_{F(\mathbf{I}_{\text{norm}})_1}\left(\widehat{a_{ij}}\right) - m_{F(\mathbf{I}_{\text{norm}})_2}\left(\widehat{b_{ij}}\right)}$$

$$- \left(1 + m_{F(\mathbf{I}_{\text{norm}})_1}\left(\widehat{a_{ij}}\right) - m_{F(\mathbf{I}_{\text{norm}})_2}\left(\widehat{b_{ij}}\right)\right)e^{-\left(m_{F(\mathbf{I}_{\text{norm}})_1}\left(\widehat{a_{ij}}\right) - m_{F(\mathbf{I}_{\text{norm}})_2}\left(\widehat{b_{ij}}\right)\right) - \left(m_{F(\mathbf{I}_{\text{norm}})_3}\left(\widehat{c_{ij}}\right) - m_{F(\mathbf{I}_{\text{norm}})_1}\left(\widehat{a_{ij}}\right)\right)} \tag{83}$$

$$- \left(m_{F(\mathbf{I}_{\text{norm}})_3}\left(\widehat{c_{ij}}\right) - m_{F(\mathbf{I}_{\text{norm}})_1}\left(\widehat{a_{ij}}\right)\right)e^{-\left(m_{F(\mathbf{I}_{\text{norm}})_1}\left(\widehat{a_{ij}}\right) - m_{F(\mathbf{I}_{\text{norm}})_2}\left(\widehat{b_{ij}}\right)\right) - \left(m_{F(\mathbf{I}_{\text{norm}})_3}\left(\widehat{c_{ij}}\right) - m_{F(\mathbf{I}_{\text{norm}})_1}\left(\widehat{a_{ij}}\right)\right)}$$

$$- \left(1 - \left(m_{F(\mathbf{I}_{\text{norm}})_1}\left(\widehat{a_{ij}}\right) - m_{F(\mathbf{I}_{\text{norm}})_2}\left(\widehat{b_{ij}}\right)\right)\right)e^{m_{F(\mathbf{I}_{\text{norm}})_1}\left(\widehat{a_{ij}}\right) - m_{F(\mathbf{I}_{\text{norm}})_2}\left(\widehat{b_{ij}}\right) + m_{F(\mathbf{I}_{\text{norm}})_3}\left(\widehat{c_{ij}}\right) - m_{F(\mathbf{I}_{\text{norm}})_1}\left(\widehat{a_{ij}}\right)} \geq 0.$$

But,

$$\left(1 + m_{F(I_{norm})_1}\left(\widehat{a_{ij}}\right) - m_{F(I_{norm})_2}\left(\widehat{b_{ij}}\right)\right)e^{-\left(m_{F(I_{norm})_1}\left(\widehat{a_{ij}}\right) - m_{F(I_{norm})_2}\left(\widehat{b_{ij}}\right)\right)} \geq 0 \tag{84}$$

and,

$$\left(1 - \left(m_{F(I_{norm})_1}\left(\widehat{a_{ij}}\right) - m_{F(I_{norm})_2}\left(\widehat{b_{ij}}\right)\right)\right)e^{m_{F(I_{norm})_1}\left(\widehat{a_{ij}}\right) - m_{F(I_{norm})_2}\left(\widehat{b_{ij}}\right)} \geq 0. \tag{85}$$

Thus, it remains to be shown that,

$$
\begin{aligned}
&-\left(1 + m_{F(I_{norm})_1}\left(\widehat{a_{ij}}\right) - m_{F(I_{norm})_2}\left(\widehat{b_{ij}}\right)\right)e^{-\left(m_{F(I_{norm})_1}\left(\widehat{a_{ij}}\right) - m_{F(I_{norm})_2}\left(\widehat{b_{ij}}\right)\right) - \left(m_{F(I_{norm})_3}\left(\widehat{c_{ij}}\right) - m_{F(I_{norm})_1}\left(\widehat{a_{ij}}\right)\right)} \\
&-\left(m_{F(I_{norm})_3}\left(\widehat{c_{ij}}\right) - m_{F(I_{norm})_1}\left(\widehat{a_{ij}}\right)\right)e^{-\left(m_{F(I_{norm})_1}\left(\widehat{a_{ij}}\right) - m_{F(I_{norm})_2}\left(\widehat{b_{ij}}\right)\right) - \left(m_{F(I_{norm})_3}\left(\widehat{c_{ij}}\right) - m_{F(I_{norm})_1}\left(\widehat{a_{ij}}\right)\right)} \\
&-\left(1 - \left(m_{F(I_{norm})_1}\left(\widehat{a_{ij}}\right) - m_{F(I_{norm})_2}\left(\widehat{b_{ij}}\right)\right)\right)e^{m_{F(I_{norm})_1}\left(\widehat{a_{ij}}\right) - m_{F(I_{norm})_2}\left(\widehat{b_{ij}}\right) + m_{F(I_{norm})_3}\left(\widehat{c_{ij}}\right) - m_{F(I_{norm})_1}\left(\widehat{a_{ij}}\right)} \\
&+\left(m_{F(I_{norm})_3}\left(\widehat{c_{ij}}\right) - m_{F(I_{norm})_1}\left(\widehat{a_{ij}}\right)\right)e^{m_{F(I_{norm})_1}\left(\widehat{a_{ij}}\right) - m_{F(I_{norm})_2}\left(\widehat{b_{ij}}\right) + m_{F(I_{norm})_3}\left(\widehat{c_{ij}}\right) - m_{F(I_{norm})_1}\left(\widehat{a_{ij}}\right)} \geq 0.
\end{aligned}
\tag{86}
$$

If, absurdly

$$
\begin{aligned}
&-\left(1 + m_{F(I_{norm})_1}\left(\widehat{a_{ij}}\right) - m_{F(I_{norm})_2}\left(\widehat{b_{ij}}\right)\right)e^{-\left(m_{F(I_{norm})_1}\left(\widehat{a_{ij}}\right) - m_{F(I_{norm})_2}\left(\widehat{b_{ij}}\right)\right) - \left(m_{F(I_{norm})_3}\left(\widehat{c_{ij}}\right) - m_{F(I_{norm})_1}\left(\widehat{a_{ij}}\right)\right)} \\
&-\left(m_{F(I_{norm})_3}\left(\widehat{c_{ij}}\right) - m_{F(I_{norm})_1}\left(\widehat{a_{ij}}\right)\right)e^{-m_{F(I_{norm})_1}\left(\widehat{a_{ij}}\right) - m_{F(I_{norm})_2}\left(\widehat{b_{ij}}\right) - \left(m_{F(I_{norm})_3}\left(\widehat{c_{ij}}\right) - m_{F(I_{norm})_1}\left(\widehat{a_{ij}}\right)\right)} \\
&-\left(1 - \left(m_{F(I_{norm})_1}\left(\widehat{a_{ij}}\right) - m_{F(I_{norm})_2}\left(\widehat{b_{ij}}\right)\right)\right)e^{m_{F(I_{norm})_1}\left(\widehat{a_{ij}}\right) - m_{F(I_{norm})_2}\left(\widehat{b_{ij}}\right) + m_{F(I_{norm})_3}\left(\widehat{c_{ij}}\right) - m_{F(I_{norm})_1}\left(\widehat{a_{ij}}\right)} \\
&+\left(m_{F(I_{norm})_3}\left(\widehat{c_{ij}}\right) - m_{F(I_{norm})_1}\left(\widehat{a_{ij}}\right)\right)e^{m_{F(I_{norm})_1}\left(\widehat{a_{ij}}\right) - m_{F(I_{norm})_2}\left(\widehat{b_{ij}}\right) + m_{F(I_{norm})_3}\left(\widehat{c_{ij}}\right) - m_{F(I_{norm})_1}\left(\widehat{a_{ij}}\right)} < 0
\end{aligned}
\tag{87}
$$

we would get:

$$
\begin{aligned}
&\left(m_{F(I_{norm})_3}\left(\widehat{c_{ij}}\right) - m_{F(I_{norm})_1}\left(\widehat{a_{ij}}\right)\right)e^{m_{F(I_{norm})_1}\left(\widehat{a_{ij}}\right) - m_{F(I_{norm})_2}\left(\widehat{b_{ij}}\right) + m_{F(I_{norm})_3}\left(\widehat{c_{ij}}\right) - m_{F(I_{norm})_1}\left(\widehat{a_{ij}}\right)} \\
&< \left(1 + m_{F(I_{norm})_1}\left(\widehat{a_{ij}}\right) - m_{F(I_{norm})_2}\left(\widehat{b_{ij}}\right)\right)e^{-\left(m_{F(I_{norm})_1}\left(\widehat{a_{ij}}\right) - m_{F(I_{norm})_2}\left(\widehat{b_{ij}}\right)\right) - \left(m_{F(I_{norm})_3}\left(\widehat{c_{ij}}\right) - m_{F(I_{norm})_1}\left(\widehat{a_{ij}}\right)\right)} \\
&+ \left(m_{F(I_{norm})_3}\left(\widehat{c_{ij}}\right) - m_{F(I_{norm})_1}\left(\widehat{a_{ij}}\right)\right)e^{-\left(m_{F(I_{norm})_1}\left(\widehat{a_{ij}}\right) - m_{F(I_{norm})_2}\left(\widehat{b_{ij}}\right)\right) - \left(m_{F(I_{norm})_3}\left(\widehat{c_{ij}}\right) - m_{F(I_{norm})_1}\left(\widehat{a_{ij}}\right)\right)}
\end{aligned}
$$

$$+ \left(1 - \left(m_{F(\mathbf{I}_{\text{norm}})_1}\left(\widehat{a}_{ij}\right) - m_{F(\mathbf{I}_{\text{norm}})_2}\left(\widehat{b}_{ij}\right)\right)\right) e^{m_{F(\mathbf{I}_{\text{norm}})_1}\left(\widehat{a}_{ij}\right) - m_{F(\mathbf{I}_{\text{norm}})_2}\left(\widehat{b}_{ij}\right) + m_{F(\mathbf{I}_{\text{norm}})_3}\left(\widehat{c}_{ij}\right) - m_{F(\mathbf{I}_{\text{norm}})_1}\left(\widehat{a}_{ij}\right)}$$

$$= \left(1 + m_{F(\mathbf{I}_{\text{norm}})_1}\left(\widehat{a}_{ij}\right) - m_{F(\mathbf{I}_{\text{norm}})_2}\left(\widehat{b}_{ij}\right) + {}^3\right) e^{-m_{F(\mathbf{I}_{\text{norm}})_1}\left(\widehat{a}_{ij}\right) - m_{F(\mathbf{I}_{\text{norm}})_2}\left(\widehat{b}_{ij}\right) - \left(m_{F(\mathbf{I}_{\text{norm}})_3}\left(\widehat{c}_{ij}\right) - m_{F(\mathbf{I}_{\text{norm}})_1}\left(\widehat{a}_{ij}\right)\right)} \qquad (88)$$

$$+ \left(1 - \left(m_{F(\mathbf{I}_{\text{norm}})_1}\left(\widehat{a}_{ij}\right) - m_{F(\mathbf{I}_{\text{norm}})_2}\left(\widehat{b}_{ij}\right)\right)\right) e^{m_{F(\mathbf{I}_{\text{norm}})_1}\left(\widehat{a}_{ij}\right) - m_{F(\mathbf{I}_{\text{norm}})_2}\left(\widehat{b}_{ij}\right) + m_{F(\mathbf{I}_{\text{norm}})_3}\left(\widehat{c}_{ij}\right) - m_{F(\mathbf{I}_{\text{norm}})_1}\left(\widehat{a}_{ij}\right)}$$

from which,

$$m_{F(\mathbf{I}_{\text{norm}})_3}\left(\widehat{c}_{ij}\right) - m_{F(\mathbf{I}_{\text{norm}})_1}\left(\widehat{a}_{ij}\right) < \left(1 + m_{F(\mathbf{I}_{\text{norm}})_1}\left(\widehat{a}_{ij}\right) - m_{F(\mathbf{I}_{\text{norm}})_2}\left(\widehat{b}_{ij}\right) + m_{F(\mathbf{I}_{\text{norm}})_3}\left(\widehat{c}_{ij}\right)\right.$$

$$\left. - m_{F(\mathbf{I}_{\text{norm}})_1}\left(\widehat{a}_{ij}\right)\right) \frac{e^{-\left(m_{F(\mathbf{I}_{\text{norm}})_1}\left(\widehat{a}_{ij}\right) - m_{F(\mathbf{I}_{\text{norm}})_2}\left(\widehat{b}_{ij}\right)\right) - \left(m_{F(\mathbf{I}_{\text{norm}})_3}\left(\widehat{c}_{ij}\right) - m_{F(\mathbf{I}_{\text{norm}})_1}\left(\widehat{a}_{ij}\right)\right)}}{e^{m_{F(\mathbf{I}_{\text{norm}})_1}\left(\widehat{a}_{ij}\right) - m_{F(\mathbf{I}_{\text{norm}})_2}\left(\widehat{b}_{ij}\right) + m_{F(\mathbf{I}_{\text{norm}})_3}\left(\widehat{c}_{ij}\right) - m_{F(\mathbf{I}_{\text{norm}})_1}\left(\widehat{a}_{ij}\right)}} + \left(1 - \left(m_{F(\mathbf{I}_{\text{norm}})_1}\left(\widehat{a}_{ij}\right) - m_{F(\mathbf{I}_{\text{norm}})_2}\left(\widehat{b}_{ij}\right)\right)\right).$$

$$(89)$$

(89) is always true if

$$\max\left\{m_{F(\mathbf{I}_{\text{norm}})_3}\left(\widehat{c}_{ij}\right) - m_{F(\mathbf{I}_{\text{norm}})_1}\left(\widehat{a}_{ij}\right)\right\}$$

$$min\left(1 + m_{F(\mathbf{I}_{\text{norm}})_1}\left(\widehat{a}_{ij}\right) - m_{F(\mathbf{I}_{\text{norm}})_2}\left(\widehat{b}_{ij}\right)\right) \frac{e^{-\left(m_{F(\mathbf{I}_{\text{norm}})_1}\left(\widehat{a}_{ij}\right) - m_{F(\mathbf{I}_{\text{norm}})_2}\left(\widehat{b}_{ij}\right)\right) - \left(m_{F(\mathbf{I}_{\text{norm}})_3}\left(\widehat{c}_{ij}\right) - m_{F(\mathbf{I}_{\text{norm}})_1}\left(\widehat{a}_{ij}\right)\right)}}{e^{m_{F(\mathbf{I}_{\text{norm}})_1}\left(\widehat{a}_{ij}\right) - m_{F(\mathbf{I}_{\text{norm}})_2}\left(\widehat{b}_{ij}\right) + m_{F(\mathbf{I}_{\text{norm}})_3}\left(\widehat{c}_{ij}\right) - m_{F(\mathbf{I}_{\text{norm}})_1}\left(\widehat{a}_{ij}\right)}} \qquad (90)$$

$$+ \left(1 - \left(m_{F(\mathbf{I}_{\text{norm}})_1}\left(\widehat{a}_{ij}\right) - m_{F(\mathbf{I}_{\text{norm}})_2}\left(\widehat{b}_{ij}\right)\right)\right)\right\}.$$

But,

$$min\left\{1 - m_B\left(b_{ij}\right) - m_A\left(a_{ij}\right)\right\} = 0 \qquad (91)$$

so

$$min\left\{1 + m_{F(\mathbf{I}_{\text{norm}})_1}\left(\widehat{a}_{ij}\right) - m_{F(\mathbf{I}_{\text{norm}})_2}\left(\widehat{b}_{ij}\right) + m_{F(\mathbf{I}_{\text{norm}})_3}\left(\widehat{c}_{ij}\right) - m_{F(\mathbf{I}_{\text{norm}})_1}\left(\widehat{a}_{ij}\right)\right\} = 0 \qquad (92)$$

and,

$$max\left\{\left(\widehat{c}_{ij}\right) - m_{F(\mathbf{I}_{\text{norm}})_1}\left(\widehat{a}_{ij}\right)\right\} = 1 \qquad (93)$$

getting a false inequality. Then, (55) is true and, applying the double summation operator, (48) is verified. ∎

Remark 5

The computational complexity of the proof of Proposition 3 is low, allowing its implementation in high-level languages with reduced effort allowing to compute distances between images or portion between them smoothly. This has already been highlighted in (Versaci & Morabito, 2021) but without, however, being completely evident. The proof above presented allows for such evidence. An opportune choice of the MFs is fundamental in this type of computations.

Remark 6

$D((\mathbf{I}_{\text{norm}})_w, \text{FT})$ satisfies the commutative law, while its addends, $\bar{D}\left((\mathbf{I}_{\text{norm}})_w, \text{FT}\right)$ and $\bar{D}\left(\text{FT}, (\mathbf{I}_{\text{norm}})_w\right)$ respectively, do not satisfy this law. The following Proposition formalizes this assertion.

Proposition 4

$D((\mathbf{I}_{\text{norm}})_w, \text{FT})$ satisfies the commutative law.

Proof

From (13) (14) and (15), it follows

$$
D\left((\mathbf{I}_{\text{norm}})_1, (\mathbf{I}_{\text{norm}})_2\right) = 1 - \left(1 - m_{F(\mathbf{I}_{\text{norm}})_1}\left(\widehat{a_{ij}}\right)\right) e^{m_{F(\mathbf{I}_{\text{norm}})_1}\left(\widehat{a_{ij}}\right) - m_{F(\mathbf{I}_{\text{norm}})_2}\left(\widehat{b_{ij}}\right)}
$$

$$
- m_{F(\mathbf{I}_{\text{norm}})_1}\left(\widehat{a_{ij}}\right) e^{m_{F(\mathbf{I}_{\text{norm}})_2}\left(\widehat{b_{ij}}\right) - m_{F(\mathbf{I}_{\text{norm}})_1}\left(\widehat{a_{ij}}\right)} + 1 - \left(1 - m_{F(\mathbf{I}_{\text{norm}})_2}\left(\widehat{b_{ij}}\right)\right) e^{m_{F(\mathbf{I}_{\text{norm}})_2}\left(\widehat{b_{ij}}\right) - m_{F(\mathbf{I}_{\text{norm}})_1}\left(\widehat{a_{ij}}\right)}
$$

$$
- m_{F(\mathbf{I}_{\text{norm}})_2}\left(\widehat{b_{ij}}\right) e^{m_{F(\mathbf{I}_{\text{norm}})_1}\left(\widehat{a_{ij}}\right) - m_{F(\mathbf{I}_{\text{norm}})_2}\left(\widehat{b_{ij}}\right)} = 2 + \left(m_{F(\mathbf{I}_{\text{norm}})_1}\left(\widehat{a_{ij}}\right) - m_{F(\mathbf{I}_{\text{norm}})_2}\left(\widehat{b_{ij}}\right) - 1\right) e^{m_{F(\mathbf{I}_{\text{norm}})_1}\left(\widehat{a_{ij}}\right) - m_{F(\mathbf{I}_{\text{norm}})_2}\left(\widehat{b_{ij}}\right)}
$$

$$
+ \left(m_{F(\mathbf{I}_{\text{norm}})_2}\left(\widehat{b_{ij}}\right) - m_{F(\mathbf{I}_{\text{norm}})_1}\left(\widehat{a_{ij}}\right) - 1\right) e^{m_{F(\mathbf{I}_{\text{norm}})_2}\left(\widehat{b_{ij}}\right) - m_{F(\mathbf{I}_{\text{norm}})_1}\left(\widehat{a_{ij}}\right)} = D\left((\mathbf{I}_{\text{norm}})_2, (\mathbf{I}_{\text{norm}})_1\right)
$$

$$(94)$$

which proves that (13) is commutative. However, we observe that

$$
\bar{D}\left((\mathbf{I}_{\text{norm}})_1, (\mathbf{I}_{\text{norm}})_2\right) = 1 - \left(1 - m_{F(\mathbf{I}_{\text{norm}})_1}\left(\widehat{a_{ij}}\right)\right) e^{m_{F(\mathbf{I}_{\text{norm}})_1}\left(\widehat{a_{ij}}\right) - m_{F(\mathbf{I}_{\text{norm}})_2}\left(\widehat{b_{ij}}\right)}
$$

$$
- m_{F(\mathbf{I}_{\text{norm}})_1}\left(\widehat{a_{ij}}\right) e^{m_{F(\mathbf{I}_{\text{norm}})_2}\left(\widehat{b_{ij}}\right) - m_{F(\mathbf{I}_{\text{norm}})_1}\left(\widehat{a_{ij}}\right)} \neq \bar{D}\left((\mathbf{I}_{\text{norm}})_2, (\mathbf{I}_{\text{norm}})_1\right)
$$

$$(95)$$

so that (14) and (15) are not commutative. ∎

FE BASED ON FD: A NEW FORMULATION

As in (Silva, Senra Filho, Fazan, Felipe, & Murta Junior) and (Versaci & Morabito, 2021), we consider a $\mathbf{I}_{\text{norm}}$, on which to define $A_{\overline{i},\overline{j}}^{\sigma}$, which represents the pixels of indices ranging from $\overline{i}$ to $\overline{i} + \sigma - 1$ and from column $\overline{j}$ to $\overline{j} + \sigma - 1$:

$$
A_{\overline{i},\overline{j}}^{\sigma} = \begin{pmatrix} \mathbf{I}_{\text{norm}}\left(\widehat{a_{\overline{i},\overline{j}}}\right) & \cdots & \mathbf{I}_{\text{norm}}\left(\widehat{a_{\overline{i},\overline{j}+\tilde{A}-1}}\right) \\ \mathbf{I}_{\text{norm}}\left(\widehat{a_{\overline{i}+1,\overline{j}}}\right) & \cdots & \mathbf{I}_{\text{norm}}\left(\widehat{a_{\overline{i}+1,\overline{j}+\tilde{A}-1}}\right) \\ \cdots & \cdots & \cdots \\ \mathbf{I}_{\text{norm}}\left(\widehat{a_{\overline{i}+\tilde{A}-1,\overline{j}}}\right) & \cdots & \mathbf{I}_{\text{norm}}\left(\widehat{a_{\overline{i}+\tilde{A}-1,\overline{j}+\tilde{A}-1}}\right) \end{pmatrix}.
$$

(96)

Similarly, for $\mathbf{A}_{\overline{i},\overline{j}}^{\tilde{A}+1}$, represents a $\sigma+1$-square window. Further, let us indicate by,

$$
S_{\sigma} = (M - \sigma) \times (N - \sigma)
$$

(97)

the total number of square windows in $\mathbf{I}_{\text{norm}}$ generated for both σ and $\sigma+1$ size. Therefore, for $\mathbf{A}_{\overline{i},\overline{j}}^{\tilde{A}}$ and $\mathbf{A}_{h,k}^{\tilde{A}}$ quantifying their distance, $D_{\overline{i},\overline{j},h,k}^{\tilde{A}}$, as in (13):

$$
D_{\overline{i},\overline{j},h,k}^{\sigma} = D\left(A_{\overline{i},\overline{j}}^{\sigma}, A_{h,k}^{\sigma}\right).
$$

(98)

Unlike (Silva, Senra Filho, Fazan, Felipe, & Murta Junior), (Versaci & Morabito, 2021) introduces a novelty because FD exploits in terms of distance between $\mathbf{A}_{\overline{i}}^{\tilde{A}}$ and $\mathbf{A}_{h,k}^{\tilde{A}}$ to evaluate how far is $\mathbf{A}_{\overline{i}}^{\tilde{A}}$ from $\mathbf{A}_{h,k}^{\tilde{A}}$ and vice-versa.

Therefore, $D_{\overline{i},\overline{j},h,k}^{\sigma}$ is exploited to $\chi_{\overline{i}|\overline{j}}^{\sigma}$ as follows:

$$
\chi_{\overline{i}|\overline{j}}^{\sigma} = \frac{\sum_{h=1,k=1}^{h=M-\sigma,k=N-m} D_{\overline{i},\overline{j},hk}^{\sigma}}{(S_{\sigma} - 1)}
$$

(99)

with $(h,k) \neq (\overline{i},\overline{j})$ to compute:

$$
\chi^{\sigma} = \frac{\sum_{\overline{i}=1,\overline{j}=1}^{\overline{i}=M-\sigma,\overline{j}=N-\sigma} \chi_{\overline{i}|\overline{j}}^{\sigma}}{(S_{\sigma})}.
$$

(100)

Similarly, we compute, $\chi_{\overline{i}|\overline{j}}^{\sigma+1}$ and $\chi^{\sigma+1}$:

$$\chi_{\overline{i}|\overline{j}}^{\sigma+1} = \frac{\sum_{h=1,k=1}^{h=M-\sigma,k=N-\sigma} D_{\overline{i}|\overline{j},hk}^{\sigma+1}}{\left(S_\sigma - 1\right)} \tag{101}$$

$$\chi^{\sigma+1} = \frac{\sum_{\overline{i}=1,\overline{j}=1}^{\overline{i}=M-\sigma,\overline{j}=N-\sigma} \chi_{\overline{i}|\overline{j}}^{\sigma+1}}{S_\sigma}. \tag{102}$$

Finally, by (100) and (102), FE is computed by (26).

Remark 7

To evaluate how far is $\mathbf{A}_{\overline{i}}^{\tilde{A}}$ from $\mathbf{A}_{h,k}^{\tilde{A}}$ and vice-versa by FD is highlighted by its property of commutativity.

ADAPTIVE FUZZY MFS: A SIMPLIFIED PROCEDURE

In (Versaci & Morabito, 2021), an innovative procedure has been proposed to adaptively build fuzzy MFs exploiting S-shaped MFs with three parameters set adaptively using a noise reduction and an entropy maximization procedures jointly. This approach, while providing appreciable results, but, due its high computational load, it does not combine with real-time applications. Here, we present a simplified procedure based on sigmoid with three parameters.

A modified sigmoidal fuzzy MF, $\forall \widehat{a_{ij}}$ in $\mathbf{I}_{\text{norm}}$, is defined as:

$$m_{I_{norm}}\left(\widehat{a_{ij}}\right) = \begin{cases} 0 & \text{if } 0 \leq \widehat{a_{ij}} \leq \min\left\{\widehat{a_{ij}}\right\} \\ 0.001 & \text{if } \widehat{a_{ij}} = \min\left\{\widehat{a_{ij}}\right\} \\ 1 - \dfrac{B}{1 + Ce^{\gamma \widehat{a_{ij}}}} & \text{if } \min\left\{\widehat{a_{ij}}\right\} \leq \widehat{a_{ij}} \leq \min\left\{\widehat{a_{ij}}\right\} \\ 0.999 & \text{if } \widehat{a_{ij}} = \max\left\{\widehat{a_{ij}}\right\} \\ 1 & \text{if } \widehat{a_{ij}} \geq \max\left\{\widehat{a_{ij}}\right\} \end{cases} \tag{103}$$

where B, C and γ are three positive shape parameter obtained by imposing the following three conditions.

- First condition

$$f\left(\min\left\{\widehat{a}_{ij}\right\}=0\right)=0.001 \tag{104}$$

so that

$$1-\frac{B}{1+Ce^{\gamma\min\left\{\widehat{a}_{ij}\right\}}}=0.001 \tag{105}$$

from which

$$B=0.999(1+C). \tag{106}$$

- Second condition

$$f\left(\max\left\{\widehat{a}_{ij}\right\}=1\right)=0.999 \tag{107}$$

achieving

$$1-\frac{B}{1+Ce^{\gamma\max\left\{\widehat{a}_{ij}\right\}}}=0.999 \tag{108}$$

from which

$$\frac{B}{1+Ce^{\gamma}}=0.001. \tag{109}$$

Thus, substituting (106) into (109),

$$\gamma=\ln\left\{\frac{1}{C}\left[\frac{999(1+C)-1}{C}\right]\right\}. \tag{110}$$

- Third Condition

$$f\left(\frac{\left(\min\left\{\widehat{a_{ij}}\right\}=0\right)+\left(\max\left\{\widehat{a_{ij}}\right\}=1\right)}{2}\right)=0.5 \tag{111}$$

achieving

$$1-\frac{B}{1+Ce^{\frac{\gamma}{2}}}=0.5, \tag{112}$$

from which

$$B=\frac{1}{2}\left(1+Ce^{\frac{\gamma}{2}}\right). \tag{113}$$

From (106) (110) and (113),

$$C^2 - 997.004C - 998.004 = 0 \tag{114}$$

and considering just the positive solution

$$\begin{cases} C = 996.51 \\ \gamma = 0.25 \\ B = 997.511. \end{cases} \tag{115}$$

As in (Versaci & Morabito, 2021), the procedure has been qualitative/quantitative evaluated considering the improvements and additions above proposed, exploiting:

1. Gray-level experimental ECs maps obtained at NdT & Electrotechnics Lab, "Mediterranea" University, Reggio Calabria (Italy), subjecting steel plates to biaxial loads. Furthermore, unlike (Versaci & Morabito, 2021), also steel plates without loads are considered;
2. Two typologies of gray-level thermal camera IR images (free download from https://www.flir.com/oem/adas/adas-dataset-form) for ballistic uses, unlike (Versaci & Morabito, 2021) where just one typology has been considered.
   3 Gray-level electro-spinning images (with/without defects) produced at the Laboratory of Chemistry, "Mediterranea" University of Reggio Calabria (Italy). In (Versaci & Morabito, 2021) just gray-level electro-spinning images without defects have been considered.

THE EXPLOITED DATASET

ECs Maps

Steel plates have been subjected to symmetrical bi-axial loads and investigated by ECs. The load imposed biaxially modifies the structure of the steel by modifying its magnetic properties. This degradation was investigated by analyzing the variation of the induced magnetic field by a FLUXSET probe, (Repelianto & Kasai, 2019) whose pick-up voltage provides a measure proportional to the component of the amplitude of the magnetic field, parallel to the longitudinal axis of the sensor (AC sinusoidal exciting field, $1kHz$; electric current, $120mA$ RMS; driving signal, Triangular $100kHz$, $2Vpp$ amplitude). The sensor/probe, assembled to a step-by-step automatic scanning system, moved on the steel plate. Once the load was applied, the plates were investigated, achieving four $2D$ signals (real/imaginary parts; module/amplitude of pick-up voltage [mV]), representing each map as a gray-level image (Figure 2) obtaining 75 images representing the real part of the pick-up voltage. The EC map is significantly different when no load is applied to the plate (Figure 3).

Figure 2. EC map: steel plate subjected to a biaxial load.

Figure 3. EC map: unloaded steel plate.

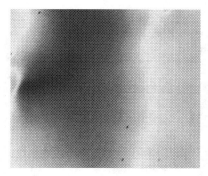

Thermal Camera IR Images

Thermography, a NdT measuring the IR emitted by a body determining its surface temperature, allows to view absolute values and temperature variations of objects, regardless of their illumination in the visible range. The correlation between irradiation and temperature is provided by the Stefan-Boltzmann law:

$$q = \epsilon z S T 4 \tag{116}$$

where σ is the Stefan-Boltzmann constant ($5.6703 \times 10^{-8W} m^{-2K}$-4, ϵ is the emissivity of the emitting surface). Thermography allows the identification of anomalies in the emission of energy and, therefore, with the same emissivity, of thermal anomalies.

Two typologies of IR images for ballistic sciences have been selected:

1. Humans in the thick vegetation (100 images), as in (Versaci & Morabito, 2021);
2. Humans in different actions (100 images), not analyzed in (Versaci & Morabito, 2021). Examples of IR images of both types are shown in Figure 4 and Figure 5.

Figure 4. IR-image (first typology).

Figure 5. IR-image (second typology).

Electro-Spinning Images

ES synthesizes *3*D fibrous structures by controlling the alignment of the fibers with small diameter (Li & et al., 2020) and consists of a high voltage power source, a syringe pump, a syringe, a spinneret and a grounded collection device. The first step loads the polymer solution into the syringe that feeds the die. Through the power source, an electric field is generated between the collection device and the positively charged capillary containing the polymeric solution (Ieracitano & et al., 2020). Under the action of the electric field, a conical drop forms at the tip of the needle. When the electric field exceeds the surface tension of the drop, the cone undergoes an elongation until it emits a thin polymer jet directed towards the collection device. The great speed that the jet reaches allows the solvent to evaporate gradually. The fluid jet is collected in the form of a lattice of polymeric fibers by the collection. Analyzing the morphology of the nanofiber by Phenom Pro-X Scanning Electron Microscope (SEM), gray-level SEM images are produced. The images dataset consists of 75 homogeneous nanofibers (HNF) images and 85 non-homogeneous nanofibers (NHNF) images. Figure 6 and Figure 7 report two examples of HNF and NHNF SEM images, respectively.

Figure 6. A NHF-EMS image.

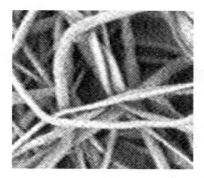

Figure 7. A HNHF-EMS image.

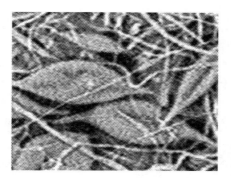

Sections **10** and **11** provide a brief overview of the usual I- and II-order edge detectors exploited in this chapter to compare the results obtained through the proposed approach.

ORDER ED PROCEDURES

Gradient Operator

The most common ED exploits the gradient operator (Gonzales & Woods, 2007) . Thinking of an image as a function with two independent variables:

$$\nabla I = \left[(I)_i \quad (I)_j \right]^T = \left[\frac{\partial I}{\partial i} \quad \frac{\partial I}{\partial j} \right]^T \tag{117}$$

amplitude and direction of an edge in (i,j) (117) points in the direction of greater variation of I on (i,j) and its magnitude,

$$|\nabla I| = \sqrt{\left((I)_i \right)^2 + \left((I)_j \right)^2}, \tag{118}$$

is the rate of change in the direction, $\alpha(i,j)$, of $\tilde{N}I$ computable with respect to the axis i as,

$$\alpha(i,j) = \operatorname{atan}\left[\frac{I_i}{I_j} \right]. \tag{119}$$

The direction of an edge at *(i,j)* is locally orthogonal to $\alpha(i,j)$. To achieve $\tilde{N}I$, one needs to compute a numerical approximation of the partial derivative for each pixel as,

$$(I)_i = I(i + 1, j) - I(i, j) \tag{120}$$

and

$$(I)_j = I(i, j + 1) - I(i, j) \tag{121}$$

implemented for all values of *(i,j)* filtering I by [-1 … 1] and [-1 … 1]^T. If one is interested in the diagonal direction of an edge, one exploits *2D* templates such as in I-order Roberts', Prewitt's and Sobel's operators.

Roberts Edge Detector

It is based on the gradient approximation of an image by the discrete differentiation of the squares of the differences between diagonally adjacent pixels (Gonzales & Woods, 2007). It convolves the original image with:

$$\begin{pmatrix} -1 & 0 \\ 0 & 1 \end{pmatrix} \quad \begin{pmatrix} 0 & -1 \\ 1 & 0 \end{pmatrix}. \tag{122}$$

If $I(i,j)$ is a point of the image and $G_i(I,j)$ and $G_j(I,j)$ are generic points of the images obtained by convolutions with templates respectively, thus:

$$\nabla I(i,j) = G(i,j) = \sqrt{G_i^2 + G_j^2} \tag{123}$$

while:

$$\pm(i,j) = \arctan\left(\frac{G_j(i,j)}{G_j(i,j)}\right) - \frac{3\text{Å}}{4}. \tag{124}$$

Remark 8

Both gradient and Roberts operators do not highlight the correct direction of the edge since they are not symmetrical with respect to the central point. Prewitt and Sobel operators fill this gap.

Prewitt Operator

It computes the gradient in each pixel, indicating the direction of the greatest possible increase from light to dark and the rate of change in that direction showing how the image changes sharply or smoothly at that point, and how the edge is oriented. The following templates are exploited (Chaira & Ray, 2010):

$$\begin{pmatrix} 1 & 0 & -1 \\ 1 & 0 & -1 \\ 1 & 0 & -1 \end{pmatrix} \quad \begin{pmatrix} 1 & 1 & 1 \\ 0 & 0 & 0 \\ -1 & -1 & -1 \end{pmatrix} \tag{125}$$

convolved with **I**:

$$I_i = \begin{pmatrix} 1 & 0 & -1 \\ 1 & 0 & -1 \\ 1 & 0 & -1 \end{pmatrix} * I \qquad (126)$$

and,

$$I_j = \begin{pmatrix} 1 & 1 & 1 \\ 0 & 0 & 0 \\ -1 & -1 & -1 \end{pmatrix} * I. \qquad (127)$$

Therefore, $\tilde{N}I(i,j)$ is computable as in (123), while $\alpha(i,j)$ becomes:

$$\alpha(i,j) = a \tan 2(Gj_, Gi_,). \qquad (128)$$

Sobel Operator

It exploits the same procedure of Prewitt operator except that the template used are (Chaira & Ray, 2010):

$$\begin{pmatrix} 1 & 2 & 1 \\ 0 & 0 & 0 \\ -1 & -2 & -1 \end{pmatrix} \begin{pmatrix} 1 & 0 & -1 \\ 2 & 0 & -2 \\ 1 & 0 & -1 \end{pmatrix}. \qquad (129)$$

(126), (127) and (128) remain valid. Sobel operator can be implemented both via hardware and software: only eight points around each point must be calculate, and the gradient is calculated with simple operations on integer values.

ORDER ED OPERATORS

Marr and Hildreth realized that the intensity variations depend on the image scale requiring the exploitation of operators with higher orders (Gonzales & Woods, 2007). Moreover, sudden intensity change produces either peak along the first derivative or a zero-crossing in the second derivative. Therefore, it is necessary that:

1. The operator must calculate both I and II numerical derivatives at each pixel;
2. It should be adjusted to operate on any type of scale so that large operators act on blurry edges.

Laplacian of Gaussian (LoG) and Zero Cross Operators

After Marr and Hildreth, the best operator respecting both the above conditions 1. and 2. is $\Delta G(i,j)$, where:

$$G\left(i,j\right)=e^{\frac{i^2+j^2}{\text{std}^2}} \tag{130}$$

and *std* represents the standard deviation. Therefore, from (130),

$$\nabla^2 G = \left[\frac{i^2+j^2-2\text{std}^2}{\text{std}^4}\right]e^{-\frac{i^2+j^2}{2\text{std}^2}} \tag{131}$$

that is the LoG operator, whose zero-crossings occurs at $i^2+j^2=2\text{std}^2$ defining a circle centering in the origin. Templates are made sampling $\Delta G(i,j)$ and scaling its coefficients to provide a sum of zero. The sampling of $\Delta G(i,j)$ can also take place at the required size and convolve the results with a Laplacian kernel. It should be borne in mind that the convolution of an image with a Laplacian kernel whose co-efficient give zero sum, we obtain elements which, in turn, provide a sum of zero, also satisfying the need that the sum of the coefficients of the filter LoG is also zero. The algorithm performs the convolution of (131) with the image determining the edge position by computing the zero-crossing by a 3×3 pixel-centered neighborhood so that the signs of at least two of its opposite neighboring pixels must be different. Four cases must be considered: left/right, up/down and the two diagonals, paying attention on the fact that if the values of the filtered image are compared on a line, then not only the sign must be different, but the absolute value of their numerical difference must also exceed a given threshold before being able to confirm that the pixel is zero-crossing.

The Canny Operator

It uses the calculus of variations defining the optima function as the sum of four exponential terms (approximating them by the first derivative of a Gaussian function). For the edge detections, the algorithm uses a filter based on the I-derivative of a Gaussian; therefore, the results produced are disturbed by the noise present in the raw image that must be convoluted with a Gaussian filter obtaining an image with a slight Gaussian blur, where no single pixel is affected by significant noise. An edge of an image can point in any direction; algorithm uses four different filters to detect the horizontal, vertical, and diagonal edges of the image, to which the Gaussian filter was applied. For each resulting pixel, the direction relative to the filter representing the greatest value is assumed to be valid. This direction, combined with the value obtained by applying the filter, corresponds to that in which there is the maximum gradient of brightness in each point of the image. The gradient map provides the value of the light intensity at each point of the image. A strong intensity indicates a strong probability of the presence of a contour. However, this indication is not sufficient to decide whether or not a point corresponds to a contour. Only the points corresponding to local maxima are considered as belonging to an edge and will be taken into consideration by the subsequent processing steps. A local maximum occurs at the point where the derivative of the gradient vanishes. The extraction of the contours from the map generated by the previous step is performed with a procedure called thresholding with hysteresis. Two thresholds are defined, one low and one high, which are compared with the gradient at each point. If the gradient value is below the low threshold, the point is discarded; if it is higher than the high threshold, the point is accepted as part of the edge; if it is between the two thresholds, the point is accepted only if it is contiguous to a previously accepted point. The presence of two thresholds (hence the reference to the hysteresis) is justified by the fact that it is practically impossible to find a single value of the brightness gradient to discriminate whether a point belongs to an edge or not. At the end of this step, a binary image is obtained where each pixel is marked as belonging or not to an edge.

The fuzzy procedure makes sense if the fuzziness content of each image is appreciable. Therefore, in this chapter, we exploit two *IoFs* as defined in (Versaci & Morabito, 2021) proving here two important limitations.

IOFS OF AN IMAGE

In (Versaci & Morabito, 2021), $IoF(F(\mathbf{I}_{norm}))$ has been defined as follows.

Definition 7 – Index of Fuzziness

As in (Versaci & Morabito, 2021), let $D^p\left(F\left(\mathbf{I}_{norm}\right), \overline{F\left(\mathbf{I}_{norm}\right)}\right)$ be the FD between $F(\mathbf{I}_{norm})$ and $\overline{F\left(\mathbf{I}_{norm}\right)}$ powered of $p \in N-\{0\}$, *IoF* defined as:

$$IoF\left(F\left(\mathbf{I}_{norm}\right)\right) = \frac{2\sqrt[p]{D^p\left(F\left(\mathbf{I}_{norm}\right), \overline{F\left(\mathbf{I}_{norm}\right)}\right)}}{\left(M \times N\right)^p}, \quad p \in N-\{0\} \tag{132}$$

where $\overline{F\left(\mathbf{I}_{norm}\right)}$ is the nearest image of $F(\mathbf{I}_{norm})$ whose MF is

$$m_{\overline{F(\mathbf{I}_{norm})}} = \begin{cases} 0 & \text{if } m_{F(\mathbf{I}_{norm})}\left(x_i\right) \leq 0.5 \\ 1 & \text{if } m_{F(\mathbf{I}_{norm})}\left(x_i\right) > 0.5. \end{cases} \tag{133}$$

Moreover, the Yager's Measures has been defined as

$$\left(YM\right)_p = 1 - \frac{2\sqrt[p]{D^p\left(F\left(\mathbf{I}_{norm}\right), \overline{F\left(\mathbf{I}_{norm}\right)}\right)}}{\left(M \times N\right)^p}, \quad p = 1, 2 \tag{134}$$

Unlike (Versaci & Morabito, 2021), here the MF for $F(\mathbf{I}_{norm})$ is (103). However, in (Versaci & Morabito, 2021), no limitation for both *IoFs* have been proved. The following two Propositions fill this gap.

Proposition 5

$IoF(F(\mathbf{I}_{\text{norm}}))$ defined in (132), satisfies

$$0 < IoF(F(\mathbf{I}_{\text{norm}})) < 1. \tag{135}$$

Proof

We observe that

$$0 < \frac{2^p}{\left(M \times N\right)^p} < 1. \tag{136}$$

In fact, by induction, being $M \times N > 2$, we can write as follows. For $p=1$:

$$\frac{2}{M \times N} < 1. \tag{137}$$

Supposing that

$$\frac{2^p}{\left(M \times N\right)^p} < 1 \tag{138}$$

is true, it follows

$$\frac{2^{p+1}}{\left(M \times N\right)^{p+1}} = \frac{2^p}{\left(M \times N\right)^p} \frac{2}{\left(M \times N\right)} < \frac{2}{\left(M \times N\right)} < 1 \tag{139}$$

so $IoF(F(\mathbf{I}_{\text{norm}})) < 1$. Furthermore, we observe that $\dfrac{2^p}{\left(M \times N\right)^p} > 0$. Thus, (136) is verified.

By Proposition 1, we deduce

$$\left(D^p\left(F\left(\mathbf{I}_{\text{norm}}\right), \overline{F\left(\mathbf{I}_{\text{norm}}\right)}\right)\right)^{\frac{1}{p}} < 1 \tag{140}$$

so, being $M \times N > 2$,

$$IoF(F(\mathbf{I}_{\text{norm}})) < 1. \tag{141}$$

Analogously, by **Proposition 1**, it follows

$$\left(D^p \left(F\left(\mathbf{I}_{\text{norm}} \right), \overline{F\left(\mathbf{I}_{\text{norm}} \right)} \right) \right)^{\frac{1}{p}} > 0 \tag{142}$$

thus

$$IoF(F(\mathbf{I}_{\text{norm}})) > 1. \tag{143} \blacksquare$$

Proposition 6

$(YM)_p$ defined in (134) satisfies

$$0 < (YM)_p < 1,\ p = 1, 2. \tag{144}$$

Proof

Exploiting Proposition 5, being $0 < IoF(F(\mathbf{I}_{\text{norm}})) < 1$, (144) follows. $\blacksquare$

Once the FED is applied, the quality of the performance needs to be assessed. For reasons of expediency, we will only present those used in (Versaci & Morabito, 2021).

QUAMS FOR ED PROCEDURES

Reference ED Measures

Mean Square Error (MSE) and Mean Absolute Error (MAE)

Simple statistical indexes are MSE and MAE defined in (Versaci & Morabito, 2021) as follows:

$$MSE = \frac{1}{M \times N} \sum_{i=1}^{N} \sum_{j=1}^{N} \left(D\left(F\left(\mathbf{I}_{\text{norm}} \right)_1 (i,j), F\left(\mathbf{I}_{\text{norm}} \right)_2 (i,j) \right) \right)^2 \tag{145}$$

$$MAE = \frac{1}{M \times N} \sum_{i=1}^{N} \sum_{j=1}^{N} \left| D\left(F\left(\mathbf{I}_{\text{norm}} \right)_1 (i,j), F\left(\mathbf{I}_{\text{norm}} \right)_2 (i,j) \right) \right|. \tag{146}$$

$D(F(\mathbf{I}_{\text{norm}})_1, F(\mathbf{I}_{\text{norm}})_2)$ has been exploited in (145) and (146) to evaluate how far $F(\mathbf{I}_{\text{norm}})_1$ is from $F(\mathbf{I}_{\text{norm}})_2$ and vice-versa.

Structural Similarity Measure (SSIM)

(145) and (146) do not consider the human visual system (HVS) properties. In (Panetta, Gao, Agaian, & Nercessian, 2014), SSIM is based on the fact that HVS extracts structural information, defining the similarity of two images as a function of luminance $l(\mathbf{I}_1,\mathbf{I}_2)$, contrast $c(\mathbf{I}_1,\mathbf{I}_2)$, and structure $s(\mathbf{I}_1,\mathbf{I}_2)$ (for details, see (Versaci & Morabito, 2021)).

Nonreference ED Measures

Yitzhaky's and Peli's Formulation

The approach proceeds with the automatic estimation of the background truth map, by examining a particular curve called the threshold receiver operating characteristics curve, which is obtained starting from a set of detected results. The detection of each single set of parameters is obtained through the map of the edges considered most similar to the estimate background truth edge (Panetta, Gao, Agaian, & Nercessian, 2014), (Versaci & Morabito, 2021).

Panetta's Formulation

Proposed in (Panetta, Gao, Agaian, & Nercessian, 2014) and exploited in (Versaci & Morabito, 2021), it is divided into three steps: 1) generation of a gray-scale edge map; 2) exploitation of reconstruction procedure; 3) application of similarity measure. Starting from an extracted edge map a continuous edge map is developed, exploiting a morphological dilatation to contain information from the image and multiplied with the original image, obtaining a new gray-level edge map. To set a good reconstruction with a good balance and robust to noise, (Panetta, Gao, Agaian, & Nercessian, 2014) exploits a weighted α trimmed. This new image is compared to the original image by a measure of similarity based on GSSIM index (Gradient SSIM).

Finally, introducing a penalty factor, f_p, considering that when more edge pixels exist in an edge map, more information from I is exploited, Panetta's measure is defined as $\left(\text{mean } GSSIM\right) f_p^3$.

Remark 9

Non-reference ED measures need an excellent image taken as a reference. As in (Versaci & Morabito, 2021), the images treated by the Canny procedure are taken as reference images.

SOME NOTABLE RESULTS

Fuzziness Evaluation

Using MatLab R2019a release on a PC Intel Core 2 CPU 1.47 GHz, for each image, $(IoF)_1$, $(IoF)_2$, $(YM)_1$ and $(YM)_2$ values were computed; the results plotted in Figures 2(a), 2(b), 2(c), 2(d) and 2(e), depending on the category to which they belong. As in (Versaci & Morabito, 2021), we note that the indices do not assume trends, suggesting at least qualitatively, that behaviors cannot be linked to each category of images. However, the high values found for each category of images confirmed the high content in fuzziness in each image, encouraging the use of FED procedures, after the proposed approach has been implemented and all images under study edge-detected. The performances obtained can be considered satisfactory as they are almost equivalent with the edge detections achieved by Canny procedure. These results were confirmed by the references/non-reference QAMs. Thus, MFs (simpler to build adaptively) produce, in terms of *IoFs*, the same effect as MFs built as in (Versaci & Morabito, 2021).

Figure 8. IoFs: (a) ECs maps; (b)-(c) IR images; (d)-(e) HNF/NHNF images.

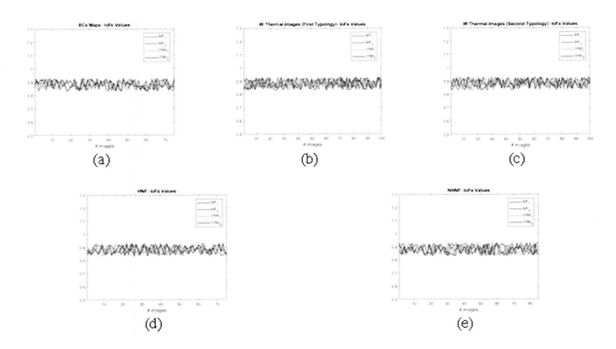

ED of ECs Maps

As in (Versaci & Morabito, 2021), FED identifies the transversal strips, where the most significant pick-up voltage gradients occur, unlike the I-order operators which are unsuccessful. LoG and Zero-Cross identify the main strip of the pick-up voltage gradient, but they are not able to highlight low gradients, highlighting the "state-of-health" of the specimen. Better results are obtained by the Canny operator. However, surprising result is the performance of the FED comparable with that achieved by the Canny operator. Therefore, the procedure proposed here to adaptively construct MFs offers the same performance as the more complex one proposed in (Versaci & Morabito, 2021). Figure 9(a) shows the FED of the ECs map depicted in Figure 2 by the fuzzy operator, showing that the performance is close to the Canny performance (Figure 9(g)). For comparison, as in (Versaci & Morabito, 2021), we highlight how the I-order procedures provide disappointing results (Figures 9(b), 9(c) and 9(d)) while both Figures 9(e) and 9(f) perform LoG and Zero-Cross operators, respectively, confirming a quite good ED but only in relation to the diagonals of the plate subjected to high mechanical stress. Quantitatively, starting from the ECs segmented map achieved by the Canny operator (reference image, as in (Versaci & Morabito, 2021)), all the merit curves obtained from the reference QUAMs have been reported (Figures 10(a), 10(b) and 10(c)) showing that the FED perform almost as the Canny operator. Once again we highlight the good choice of replacing here the adaptive construction procedure of MFs to the advantage of any real-time applications. For completeness, we report the merit curves for the Yitzhaky's and Panetta's measures (Figures 10(d) and 10(e)); hence, the similarity between FED and Canny is once again clearly evident. Finally, we observe that the non-reference QUAMs here proposed (starting from (Versaci & Morabito, 2021) but with the simplest MFs here proposed) operate a better differentiation between the performance of the operators compared to the reference measures which, while showing similarity in performance between the FED and the Canny operator, do not show a clear differentiation capable of evaluating the performance differences of other operators. As for the ECs maps achieved from plates without loads, FEDs perform without highlighting edges. This put in evidence once again that the choice made here to modify the MFs with respect to (Versaci & Morabito, 2021) produce results comparable with those obtained in (Versaci & Morabito, 2021).

Figure 9. ED of Figure 2 treated by (a) FED, (b) Roberts, (c) Prewitt, (d) Sobel, (e) LoG, (f) Zero-Cross, and (g) Canny operators.

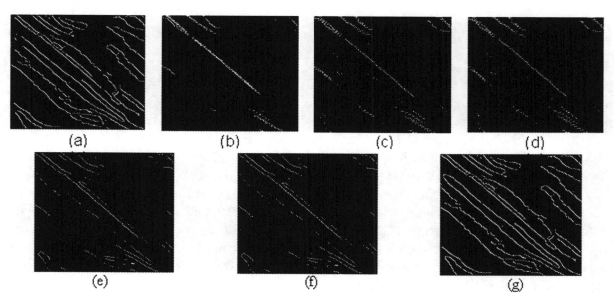

Figure 10. QUAMs for ECs maps: (a) MSE, (b) MAE, (c) SSIM, (d) Yitzhaky's and (e) Panetta's measures.

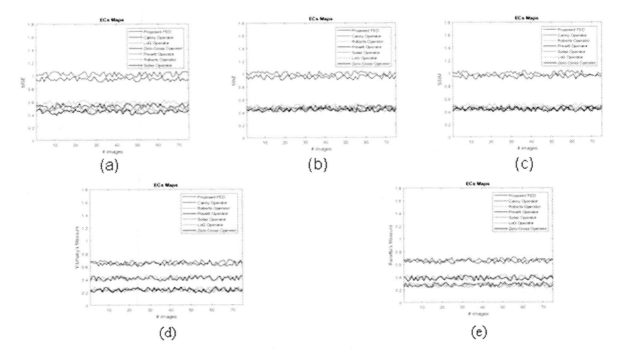

(a) (b) (c)

(d) (e)

ED of IR Images (First Typology)

FED with the MFs here proposed detects humans with details despite the low quality of the starting image where the edges are poorly delineated. As in (Versaci & Morabito, 2021), both Sobel and Prewitt operators fail to detect humans but are quite efficient in delineating the edges. LoG and zero-cross operators certainly perform better than I-order operators, so they detect humans without exhibiting relevant details. Obviously, Canny operator performs optimally providing details even in areas where contrast is lacking. FED performance closely approximates the performance showed in (Versaci & Morabito, 2021): Figure 11 depicts this performance comparable with that achieved by applying the Canny operator (Figure 11(e)). As in (Versaci & Morabito, 2021), Roberts, Prewitt and Sobel operators show poor performance (Figures 11(b), 11(c) and 11(d)), while II-order operators perform much better (Figures 11(e) and 11(f)). Furthermore, the analysis of the merit curves of the reference metrics (Figures 12(a), 12(b), 12(c)) and the non-reference metrics (Figures 12(d) and 12(e)) highlight the similarity of performance of the FED with the Canny operator performance.

ED of IR Images (Second Typology)

FED performance (endowed with the proposed MFs) and the Canny one are qualitatively almost equivalent. The example is shown in Figure 5, whose detection (Figure 12(a)) is almost equivalent to the Canny detection (Figure 13(g)). As for the previous category, Roberts, Prewitt and Sobel procedures offer unacceptable performances (Figures 13(b), 13(c), 13(d)), while LoG and Zero-Cross edge-detectors exhibits performances close to the Canny one (Figures 13(e) and 13(f)). The qualitative analysis was confirmed using the merit curves of the reference/non-reference metrics (Figures 14(a), 14(b), 14(c), 14(d) and 14(e)), highlighting the near equivalence between the performances obtained with the FED and the Canny operator. As for the previous typology, we highlight the strong oscillations in the single curves of merit (detailed images and different panoramic scenarios). Finally, also here, the location of the merit curves in different ranges of metric values once again show the qualitative differences in the performances of the operators. Even for these images, to use simpler MFs did not affect the quality of the procedure proposed in (Versaci & Morabito, 2021).

Figure 11. IR-image (first typology) treated by (a) FED, (b) Roberts, (c) Prewitt, (d) Sobel, (e) LoG, (f) Zero-Cross, and (g) Canny operators.

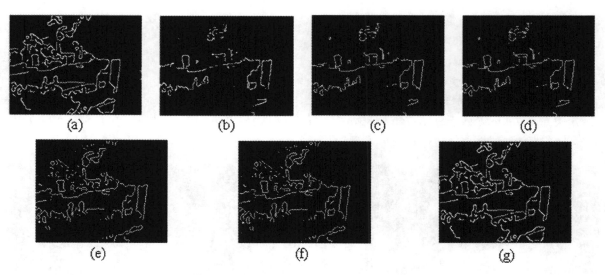

Figure 12. QUAMs for IR-images (first typology): (a) MSE, (b) MAE, (c) SSIM, (d) Yitzhaky's and (e) Panetta's measure.

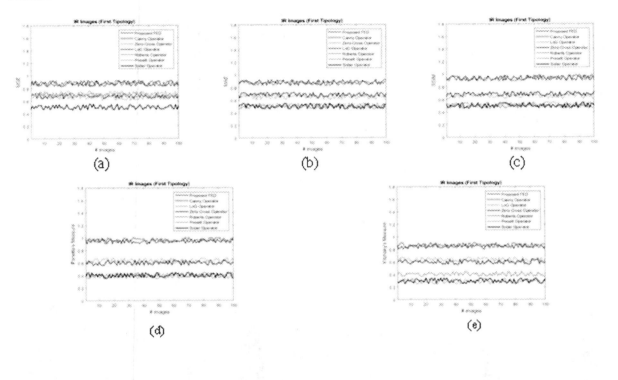

Figure 13. IR-image (second typology) treated by (a) FED, (b) Roberts, (c) Prewitt, (d) Sobel, (e) LoG, (f) Zero-Cross, and (g) Canny operators.

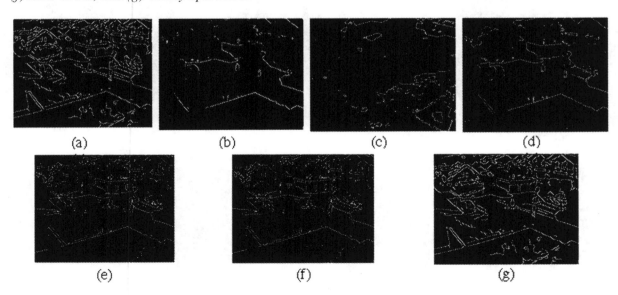

Figure 14. QAMs for IR-images (second typology): (a) MSE, (b) MAE, (c) SSIM, (d) Yitzhaky's and (e) Panetta's measure.

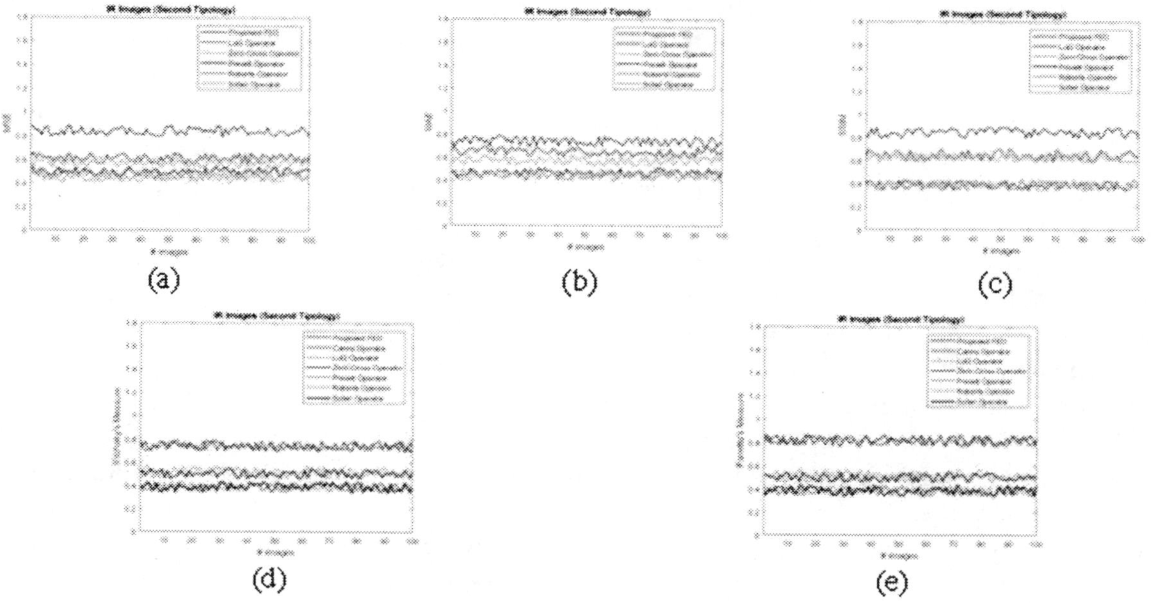

(a)   (b)   (c)

(d)   (e)

ED of HNF/NHNF EMS Images

The details obtained by the FED with the proposed MFs is satisfactory: the detected textures are detailed and almost overlapping to the Canny detected textures (almost equivalence between the performances obtained by the approaches). LoG and zero-cross offer good detection textures, while the I-order techniques offer failed performances. Figure 6 depicts an example of performances highlighting, on the one hand, the near equivalence of the procedure proposed by the Canny operator (Figures 15(a) and 15(g)), and, on the other hand, the unsuitability of I-order procedures for the detection of textures in this type of EMS images (Figures 15(b), 15(c) and 15(d). However, the techniques of II-order offer good results so as to make them still attractive for the ED for these images (Figures 15(e) and 15(f)). The curves of merit (Figures 16(a), 16(b), 16(c), 16(d) and 16(e)) confirm what is highlighted by the qualitative analysis. In fact, they represent the different performances of the operators well, thanks to the fact that the values assumed by the metrics assume defined intervals. Obviously, the erratic trend of each metric is due to the fact that the analyzed images are different from each other. However, the amplitudes of the metric fluctuations are slightly smaller than the values obtained with the IR images (first and second typologies), for the simple reason that the textures of the HNF/NHNF EMS images are quite like each other. Finally, the edge-detectors exploited in this chapter (proposed approach & I- II- orders operators), for the NHNF EMS images, offer performances quite similar to those obtained for the HNF EMS ones as confirmed by merit curves (Figures 18(a), 18(b), 18(c), 18(d) and 18(e)) and from the example processing (Figures 17(a), 17(b), 17(c), 17(d), 17(e), 17(f) and 17(g)).

CONCLUSION

Uncertainty is one of the most compelling problems in the treatment of gray-level images. Therefore, for the image edge detection, fuzzy techniques are required because it considers the characteristics mentioned above. Thus, in this chapter, exploiting the joint use of FE and FD as presented in (Versaci & Morabito, 2021) (reported in this chapter in an extended version with original contributions concerning mathematical properties), the problem was addressed by exploiting a simpler and easier to implement adaptive formulation of MFs (particularly attractive for any real-time applications). In (Versaci & Morabito, 2021), a FD formulation was used which turned out to be also found to be a distance function between images. So, starting with a well-established fuzzy ED formulated by Chaira & Ray and a well-known FE approach, this FED acted on thresholding step, implementing the modified FE, where the distance among gray-level images is evaluated by FD. This formulation of FE by FD allows us to consider how much an image is far from the other one and vice-versa. However, the computational load due to the MFs made such an approach unattractive. Thus, in this chapter, a new computationally lighter formulation of MFs is proposed and tested by three typologies of gray-level images and the achieved edge detected images have been compared with those obtained by well-known operators based on I- and II-order derivatives. The results obtained showed that the performance is qualitatively very close to the performance of Canny's operator. This similarity was confirmed using reference/non-reference quality assessment metrics. This appears more evident for Eddy Currents images because applying different loads different maps are produced and, consequently different merit curves could be used as classifiers of biaxial loads.

Figure 15. NHF-EMS image treated by (a) FED, (b) Roberts, (c) Prewitt, (d) Sobel, (e) LoG, (f) Zero-Cross, and (g) Canny operators

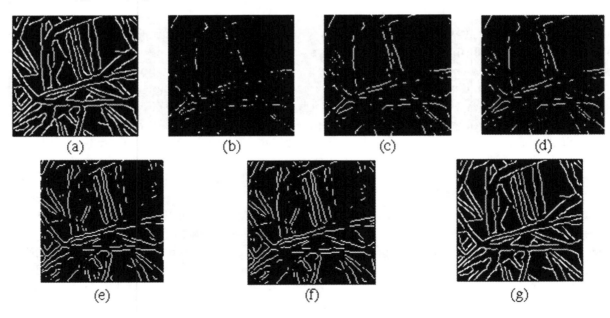

Figure 16. QAMs for HNF-EMS images: (a) MSE, (b) MAE, (c) SSIM, (d) Yitzhaky's and (e) Panetta's measures.

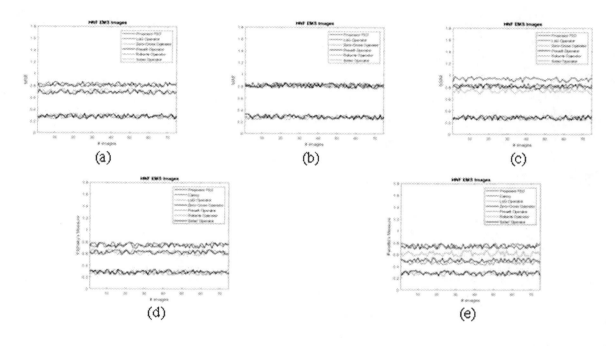

Figure 17. HNHF-EMS image treated by (a) FED, (b) Roberts, (c) Prewitt, (d) Sobel, (e) LoG, (f) Zero-Cross, and (g) Canny operators

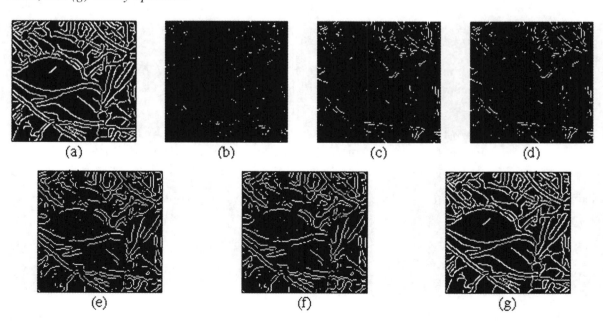

Figure 18. QAMs for NHNF-EMS images: a) MSE, (b) MAE, (c) SSIM, (d) Yitzhaky's and (e) Panetta's measures.

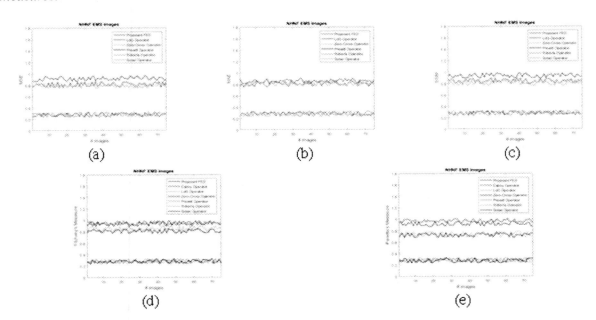

(a) (b) (c)

(d) (e)

REFERENCES

Albuquerque, M. P., Esquef, I., & Gesualdi Mello, A. R. (2004). Image Thresholding Using Tsallis Entropy. *Pattern Recognition Letters*, *25*(9), 1059–1065. doi:10.1016/j.patrec.2004.03.003

Bausys, R., Karakeviciute-Januskeviciene, G., Cavallaro, F., & Usovaite, A. (2020). Algorithm Selection for Edge Detection in Satellite Images by Neutrosophic WASPAS Method. *Sustainability*, *12*(548), 1–12. doi:10.3390u12020548

Bejar, H. H., Ferzoli Guimaraes, S. J., & Miranda, P. A. V. (2020). Efficient hierarchical graph partitioning for imaage segmentation by optimum oriented cuts. *Pattern Recognition Letters*, *131*, 185–192. doi:10.1016/j.patrec.2020.01.008

Cao, J., Chen, L., Wang, M., & Tian, Y. (2018). Implementating a Parallel Image Edge Detection Algorithm Based on the Otsu-Canny Operator on the Hadoop Platform. *Computational Intelligence and Neuroscience*, *2018*, 1–12. doi:10.1155/2018/3598284 PMID:29861711

Chaira, T. (2015). *Medical Image Processing, Advanced Fuzzy Set Theoretic Techniques*. CRC Press. doi:10.1201/b18019

Chaira, T., & Ray, A. K. (2010). *Fuzzy Image Processing and Application with MatLab*. CRC Press.

Chen, S. C., & Chen Chiu, C. C. (2019). Texture Construction Edge Detection Algorithm. *Applied Sciences (Basel, Switzerland)*, *9*, 1–25.

Clerici, F., Ferro, N., Marconi, S., Micheletti, S., Negrello, E., & Perotto, S. (2020). Anisotropic adapted meshes for image segmentation: Application to three-dimensional medical data. *SIAM Journal on Imaging Sciences*, *13*(4), 2189–2212. doi:10.1137/20M1348303

Combettes, P. L., & Pesquet, J. C. (2011). Proximal Splitting Methods in Signal Processing. *Fixed-Point Algorithms for Inverse Problems in Science and Engineering*, 185-212.

Cui, D. (2021). Meta-Heuristic Techniques for Solving Computational Engineering Problems: Challenges and New Research Directions. *Journal of Intelligent & Fuzzy Systems*, *40*(4), 5945–5952. doi:10.3233/JIFS-189434

Di Martino, F., & Sessa, S. (2020, January). PSO image thresholding on images compressed via fuzzy transforms. *Information Sciences*, *506*, 308–324. doi:10.1016/j.ins.2019.07.088

Dougherty, E. R. (Ed.). (2020). *Digital Image Processing Methods*. Dekker, Inc.

Gonzales, R. C., & Woods, R. F. (2007). *Digital Image Processing*. Prentice-Hall.

Hagara, M., & Kubinek, P. (2018). About Edge Detection in Digital Images. *Wuxiandian Gongcheng*, *27*(4), 1–11.

Hay, G. J., Castilla, G., Wulder, M. A., & Ruiz, J. R. (2005). An Automated Object-Based Approach for the Multiscale Image Segmentation of Forest Scene. *International Journal of Applied Earth Observation and Geoinformation*, *7*(4), 339–359. doi:10.1016/j.jag.2005.06.005

Ieracitano, C. (2020). Towards an automatic classification of SEM images of nanomaterial via a deep learning approach. Multidisciplinary approaches to neural computing. *Neural Approaches to Dynamics of Signal Exchanges*, 61-72.

Kaur, D., & Kayr, Y. (2014). Various Image Segmentation Techniques: A Review. *International Journal of Computer Science and Mobile Computing*, *3*(5), 809–814.

Kenneth, H., Ohnishi, H. L., & Ohnishi, N. (1995). *FEDGE-Fuzzy Edge Detection by Fuzzy Categorization and Classification of Edge*. Fuzzy Logic in Artificial Intelligence.

Khamy, E. L. (2000). Modified Sobel Fuzzy Edge Detection. *Proceedings of 17th National Radio Science Conference (NRSC 2000)*, 1-9.

Krishnaraj, N., Elhoseny, M., Thenmozhi, M., Selim, M. M., & Shankar, K. (2020). Deel learning model for real-time imaage compression in Intern Underwater Things (IoUT). *J Real-Time Image PRoc*, *17*(6), 2097–2111. doi:10.100711554-019-00879-6

Li, H. S., Qingxin, Z., Lan, S., Shen, C. Y., Zhou, R., & Mo, J. (2013). Image Storage Retrieval, Compression and Segmentation in a Quantum System. *Quantum Information Processing*, *12*(6), 2269–2290. doi:10.100711128-012-0521-5

Li, X. (2020, March). Gecko-Like Adhesion in the Electrospinning Process. *Results in Physics*, *16*(102899). Advance online publication. doi:10.1016/j.rinp.2019.102899

Ma, X., Liu, S., Hu, S., Geng, P., Liu, M., & Zhao, J. (2018). SAR Image Edge Detection Via Sparse Representation. *Soft Computing*, *22*(8), 2507–2515. doi:10.100700500-017-2505-y

Mittal, M. (2019). *Efficient Edge Detection Approach to Provide Better Edge Connectivity for Image Analysis*. Academic Press.

N., G. I. (2020). Eddy Currents in Multilayer Coils. *American Journal of Physics, 89*(284), 1-24. doi:10.1119/10.0002444

Nanda, A. (2018). Image Edge Detection Using Fractional Calculus with Features and Contrast Enhancement. *Circuits, Systems, and Signal Processing, 37*(9), 3946–3972. doi:10.100700034-018-0751-6

Panetta, K., Gao, C., Agaian, S., & Nercessian, S. (2014). Nonreference Medical Image Edge Map Measure. *International Journal of Biomedical Imaging, 2014*, 1–8. doi:10.1155/2014/937849 PMID:25132844

Pattanaik, A., Mishra, S., & Rana, D. (2015). Comparative Study of Edge Detection Using Renyi Entropy and Differential Evolution. *International Journal of Engineering Research & Technology (Ahmedabad), 4*(3), 1001–1005. doi:10.17577/IJERTV4IS031077

Pavo, J., Gasparics, A., Sebestyen, I., Vertesy, G., Darczi, C. S., & Miya, K. (1996). *Eddy Current Testing with Fluxset Probe*. Applied Electromagnetics and Mechanics.

Peng, B., Zhang, L., & Zhang, D. (2013). A Survey of Graph Theoretical Approaches to Image Segmentation. *Pattern Recognition, 26*(3), 1020–1032. doi:10.1016/j.patcog.2012.09.015

Pont-Tuset, J., Arbelaez, P., Barron, J., Marquez, F., & Malik, J. (2017). Multiscale Combinatorial Grouping for Image Segmentation and Object Proposal Generation. *IEEE Transactions on Pattern Recognition, 39*(1), 128–137. doi:10.1109/TPAMI.2016.2537320 PMID:26955014

Pradeep Kumar Reddy, R., & Nagaraju, C. (2019). Improved Canny Edge Detection Technique Using S-Membership Function. *International Journal of Engineering and Advanced Technology, 8*(6), 43–49. doi:10.35940/ijeat.E7419.088619

Qasim, A. J., Din, R. E., & Alyousuf, F. A. (2020). Review on Techniques and File Formats of Image Compression. *Bulletin of Electrical Engineering and Informatics, 9*(2), 602–610. doi:10.11591/eei.v9i2.2085

Qui, X., Li, K., Liu, P., Zhou, X., & Sun, M. (2020). Deep Attention and Multi-Scale Networks for Accurate Remote Sensing Image Segmentation. *IEEE Access: Practical Innovations, Open Solutions, 8*, 146627–146639. doi:10.1109/ACCESS.2020.3015587

Repelianto, A. S., & Kasai, N. (2019). The Improvement of Flaw Detection by the Configuration of Uniform Eddy Current Probe. *Sensors (Basel), 19*(2), 1–13. doi:10.339019020397 PMID:30669390

Russ, J. C., & Brent Neal, F. (2018). *The Image Processing Handbook*. CRC Press. doi:10.1201/b18983

Sadykova, D., & James, A. P. (n.d.). *Quality Assessment Metrics for Edge Detection and Edge-Aware Filtering: A Tutorial Review*. doi:10.1109/ICACCI.2017.8126200

Sahoo, P. K., & Arora, G. (2004). A Thresholding Method Based on Two-Dimensional Reny's Entropy. *Pattern Recognition, 37*(6), 1149–1161. doi:10.1016/j.patcog.2003.10.008

Sekehravani, E. A., Babulak, E., & Masoodi, M. (2020). Implementing Canny Edge Detection Algorithm for Noisy Image. *Bulleting of Electrical Engioneering and Informatics, 9*(4), 1404–1410. doi:10.11591/eei.v9i4.1837

Sharon, E., Brandt, A., & Basri, R. (2020). Fast Multiscale Image Segmentation. Computer Society Conference on Computer Vision nd. *Pattern Recognition*, *1*, 70–77.

Silva, L. E., Senra Filho, A. C., Fazan, V. P., Felipe, J. C., & Murta Junior, L. O. (n.d.). Two-Dimensional Sample Entropy: Assessing Image Texture Through Irregularity. *Biomedical Physics & Engineering Express*. doi:10.10882057-1976/2/4/045002

Sinha, A., & Dolz, J. (2021). Multi-Scale Self-Guided Attention for Medical Image Segmentation. *Journal of Biomedical and Health Informatics*, *25*(1), 121–130. doi:10.1109/JBHI.2020.2986926 PMID:32305947

Sonka, M. (2001). *Image Processing. Analysis and Machine Vision*. Brooks/Cole Pubisher.

Verma, O. P., & Parihar, A. S. (2017). An Optimal Fuzzy System for Edge Detection in Color Image using Bacterial Foraging Algorithm. *IEEE Transactions on Fuzzy Systems*, *25*(1), 114–127. doi:10.1109/TFUZZ.2016.2551289

Versaci, M., La Foresta, F., Morabito, F. C., & Angiulli, G. (2018). A Fuzzy Divergence Approach for Solving Electrostatic Identification Problems for NDT Applications. *International Journal of Applied Electromagnetics and Mechanics*, *1*(2), 1–14. doi:10.3233/JAE-170043

Versaci, M., La Foresta, F., Morabito, F. C., & Angiulli, G. (2018). Fuzzy Divergence Approach for Solving Electrostatic Identification PRoblems for NDT Applications. *International Journal of Applied Electromagnetics and Mechanics*, *57*(2), 133–146. Advance online publication. doi:10.3233/JAE-170043

Versaci, M., & Morabito, F. C. (2003, May). Fuzzy Time Series Approach for Disruption Prediction in Tokamak Reactors. *IEEE Transactions on Magnetics, 39*(3), 1503-1506.

Versaci, M., & Morabito, F. C. (2021). Image Edge Detection: A New Approach Based on Fuzzy Entropy and Fuzzy Divergence. *International Journal of Fuzzy Systems*, *23*(4), 918–936. doi:10.100740815-020-01030-5

Versaci, M., Morabito, F. C., & Angiulli, G. (2017). Adaptive Image Contrast Enhancement by Computing Distance in a 4-Dimensional Fuzzy Unit Hypercube. *IEEE Access: Practical Innovations, Open Solutions*, *5*, 26922–26931. doi:10.1109/ACCESS.2017.2776349

Vollmer, M., & Mollmann, K. P. (2018). *Infrared Thermal Imaging*. Wiley-YCH Verlag GmbH.

Wang, X., Wang, H., Niu, S., & Zhang, J. (2019). Detection and Localization of Image Forgeries uUsing Improved Mask Regional Convolutional Neural Network. *Mathematical Biosciences and Engineering*, *16*(5), 4581–4593. doi:10.3934/mbe.2019229 PMID:31499678

Xia, K., Gu, X., & Zhang, Y. (2020). Oriented grouping-constrained spectral clustering for medical imaging segmentation. *Multimedia Systems*, *26*(1), 27–36. doi:10.100700530-019-00626-8

Zhang, K., Zhang, Y., Wang, P., Tian, Y., & Yang, J. (2018). An Improvved Sobel Edge Algorithm and FPGA Implementation. *8th International Congress of Information and Comunication Technology, Procedia Computer Science*, 243-248.

Zhang, S., Ma, Z., Zhang, G., Lei, T., & Zhang, R. (2020). Semantinc Image Segmentation with Deep Convolutional Neural Networks and Quick Shift. *Symmetry*, *12*(427), 1–21.

Zhou, G., Lim, Z. H., Qi, Y., & Zhou, G. (2020). Single-Pixel MEMS Imaging Systems. *Micromachines*, *11*(2), 1–24. doi:10.3390/mi11020219 PMID:32093324

Chapter 9
Neuroscience and Artificial Intelligence

Lorna Uden
https://orcid.org/0000-0002-8598-7355
Staffordshire University, UK

Shijie Guan
Shenyang Ligong University, China

ABSTRACT

AI can even outperform humans in many tasks such as winning games like Go and poker as well as engaging in creative endeavours in writing novels and music. Despite this, it is still a long way from building artificial human intelligence. Current AIs are only designed to excel in their intended functions and cannot generate knowledge to new tasks and situations. For AI to achieve artificial human intelligence requires us to study and understand the human brain. Neuroscience is the study of the anatomy and physiology of the human brain. It provides us interesting insights into how the brain works to develop better AI systems. Conversely, better AI systems can help drive neuroscience forward and further unlock the secrets of the brain. Neuroscience and AI are closely related. The synergy of the two will benefit each other. Besides the benefits of neuroscience for AI research, neuroscience also has important implications for machine learning. This chapter discusses the implications of neuroscience for general artificial intelligence and the benefits of AI for neuroscience research.

INTRODUCTION

AI is a buzz word everywhere. It has penetrated all aspects of our life. Today we have the smart speaker, sweeping robot, payment system based on face recognition technology, intelligent voice assistant, etc. It can even outperform humans in many tasks such as winning games like chess, Go and poker, as well as engaging in creative endeavours such as writing novels and music. There is also an emerging trend of AI-powered automation in industries like driverless cars.

DOI: 10.4018/978-1-7998-8686-0.ch009

Artificial Intelligence techniques have traditionally been divided into two categories; Symbolic A.I. and Connectionist A.I. Symbolic A.I. is sometimes referred to as GOFAI (Good Old Fashioned A.I.). It is the classical approach of encoding a model of the problem and expecting the system to process the input data according to this model to provide a solution. The systems in Symbolic A.I often involve deductive reasoning, logical inference, and some search algorithm that finds a solution within the constraints of the specified model. Expert systems are examples of such category.

The connectionist branch of artificial intelligence aims to model intelligence by simulating the neural networks in our brains. Connectionist A.I. is originally from typical network topology that most of the algorithms in this class employ. The most popular technique in this category is the Artificial Neural Network (ANN). This consists of multiple layers of nodes, called neurons, that process some input signals, combine them together with some weight coefficients, and feed them to the next layer. This chapter examines only one aspect of AI: connectionism.

AI has grown from data models for problem-solving to artificial neural networks — a computational model based on the structure and functions of human biological neural networks. It is a key technology in Industry 4.0 because of all the advantages it brings to companies. The advance in AI will bring many benefits: cheaper and better goods and services, medical advances, and new scientific discoveries,

Industry 4.0 and AI

Industry 4.0 is defined as "the current trend of automation and data exchange in manufacturing technologies, including cyber-physical systems, the Internet of things, cloud computing and cognitive computing and creating the smart factory". It is also known as intelligent networking of machines and processes for industry with the help of information and communication technology. From an industry 4.0 point of view, AI technologies can be seen as enablers for systems to perceive their environment, process the data they acquire and solve complex problems, as well as to learn from experience to improve their capability to solve specific tasks. (Peres et al 2020).

Artificial intelligence has revolutionised the management and business models of organisations. Its main applications in the 4.0 industry are:

1. Quality, which continuously improves production quality.
2. Generative design through AI and automation algorithms.
3. OEE optimization through predictive repair and maintenance.
4. Robotics through robotic and collaborative machines that support the operators to free them from methodical and/or extremely precise tasks.

Manufacturers are using Industry 4.0 solutions across many industrial applications. Bell is using AI technologies to prepare an intelligent unmanned aircraft to identify landing zones and land autonomously. 3M uses AI in its smart factory, customizing the capabilities of the industrial internet of things (IOT) to reduce downtime to save money and effort. GE Aviation's Digital Group used AI capabilities to bring multiple sources of data together to build a flexible digital model of any aircraft and analyse its health, efficiency, and complete history. Microsoft uses autonomous smart building technology to work toward the goal of becoming carbon negative by 2030.

Limitations in AI

Despite the advances in AI, most current AI systems are 'narrow' applications. They are specifically designed to tackle a well-specified problem in one domain, such as a particular task. All current AI from self-driving cars to AlphaGo's defeat of Go champion breakthroughs are examples of Narrow AI. Such approaches cannot adapt to new or broader challenges without significant redesign. While it may be far superior to human performance in one domain, it is not superior in other domains. However, a long-held goal in the field has been the development of artificial intelligence that can learn and adapt to a very broad range of challenges - artificial general Intelligence (AGI).

Although AI applications are impressive, according to Lee (2019), there are many limitations. Firstly, although artificial neural networks (ANNs) can perfect the strength of their connections until they can complete the task with high accuracy, these machine learning systems are set up with narrow mathematical structures. Because each algorithm is tailored to the task at hand, relearning a new task often erases the established connections. This leads to catastrophic forgetting: when the AI learns the new task, it overwrites the previous one. Current AI cannot do continuous learning. Thirdly, current AI systems cannot have Embodied cognition. That is the ability to build knowledge from interacting with the world through sensory and motor experiences and creating abstract thought from there. Fourthly, it lacks imagination. Imagination and innovation rely on models we've already built about our world and extrapolating new scenarios from them.

According to Silva (2019), despite the name, AI has nothing much to do with the real human brain. He argues that successes of AI owe much to the arrival of more powerful processors and ever-growing quantities of training data. Silva argues that neuroscience, the study of the brain, offers us the solutions to address artificial general intelligence. The reason is that brain researchers have learned a huge amount about the physical connections in the brain and about how the nervous system routes information and processes it. But there is still a vast amount yet to be discovered. He believes that finding out more about how the brain processes information can help AI researchers translate the concepts of thinking biology into all-new forms of machine learning in the digital world.

He used an example to show why current AI is limited. For Silva (2019), "Machine learning is one part of technologies that are often labelled "artificial intelligence." Because it can perform better than humans at finding complex and subtle patterns in very large data sets, but the brain is not a machine. These systems are simply variations on a single statistical-based algorithm.

The most common mainstream approach to machine learning is Artificial neural networks. These Artificial neural networks are highly interconnected networks of digital processors that accept inputs, process measurements about those inputs and generate outputs. They need to learn what outputs should result from various inputs, until they develop the ability to respond to similar patterns in similar ways. Silva (2019) argues that this is not how the brain works. Instead, the brain takes in a very small amount of input data – like a photograph of a cow and a drawing of a cow. Very quickly, and after only a very small number of examples, a child will grasp the idea of what a cow looks like and be able to identify one in new images, from different angles and in different colours.

Today, AI systems can perform tasks and solve problems better than humans, achieving performance that rivals or even exceeds human capability. We have systems in AI that can play video games to out-perform the best StarCraft players; detecting breast cancer faster and better than doctors and Tesla's self-driving cars. Despite these impressive results, we are still years away from building artificial human intelligence. The reason is that these artificial intelligence systems differ from human intelligence in crucial ways. The authors concur with Jing (2020), that for AI to behave like a human, we need to be able:

1. To learn to acquire knowledge
2. To explain or understand problems
3. To generalise knowledge to new tasks and situations

Despite these recent achievements, AI still has some way to go before it coming close to truly imitating and even surpassing human intelligence. Current AI is still relatively narrow in its scope and has yet to embody the full range of cognitive abilities that humans use daily in solving a wide range of problems. (Mok, 2017). The aim of future AI is artificial general intelligence (AGI). That is an intelligence that is as successful in performing any intellectual task that a human being can.

Research in AI has always been about trying to build machines that think. According to Hawkins (2021), although Computers have transformed work and play, transportation and medicine, entertainment and sports, these machines still cannot perform simple tasks a child can do such as using a pencil. He argues that "We'll never have true AI without first understanding the brain". The answer said Hawkins (2021) lies in the intersection of two major pursuits: the reverse engineering of the brain and the burgeoning field of artificial intelligence.

The primary objective of AI research is to create new algorithms that go beyond deep learning to perform cognitive tasks in a way that is like how biological brains think According to Demis Hassabis, (Hassabis et al 2017), co-founder of AI startup DeepMind, it is important that we forge a stronger connection between neuroscience and AI. Doing this may help us to come a bit closer to solving the issue by first gaining a better understanding of how the human intelligence works. Hassabis and his co-authors pointed out that there are many advantages of translating lessons learned from studying biological intelligence - Neuroscience. These authors argue that "Neuroscience provides a rich source of inspiration for new types of algorithms and architectures, independent of and complementary to the mathematical and logic-based methods and ideas that have largely dominated traditional approaches to AI." They further pointed out that by studying how the brain's cognitive systems work, we can create new structures and algorithms for electronic intelligence. Also, lessons learned from building and testing cutting-edge AIs could help us better define what intelligence really is.

It is our belief that Researchers trying to imitate the remarkable functionality of our human brain will benefit by learning more about neuroscience, and the differences between Natural and Artificial Intelligence.

The objectives of this chapter are:

1. To briefly review AI, its benefits, and applications
2. To describe the current limitations of AI
3. To describe what is human intelligence
4. To discuss why we need neuroscience in AI
5. To describe how neuroscience inspires AI.
6. To discuss the Symbiotic Relationship between neuroscience and AI
7. To describe Brain's knowledge that are crucial to intelligence for AI
8. To discuss A thousand brains: a new theory of intelligence
9. To describe Neuroscience and AI applications

10. To describe examples of neuroscience Based AI
11. To suggest further research

BACKGROUND

According to Barr & Feigenbaum (1981). Artificial Intelligence (AI) is the part of computer science concerned with designing intelligent computer systems, that is, systems that exhibit characteristics we associate with intelligence in human behaviour – understanding language, learning, reasoning, solving problems, and so on.

Techniques for Artificial Intelligence

There are several techniques that come in the domain of artificial intelligence such as Natural Language Processing (NLP), Automation and Robotics, computer vision, expert system, and machine learning.

Natural Language Processing (NLP)

It is the interactions between computers and human language where the computers are programmed to process natural languages. It is a technique of computational processing of human languages. It enables a computer to read and understand data by mimicking human natural language. NLP is a method that deals in searching, analysing, understanding, and deriving information from the text form of data. In order to teach computers how to extract meaningful information from the text data, NLP libraries are used by programmers. NLP uses algorithms to recognize and abstract the rules of the natural languages where the unstructured data from the human languages can be converted to a format that is understood by the computer. A common example of NLP is spam detection, computer algorithms can check whether an email is a junk or not by looking at the subject line, or text of an email. Some of the NLP applications are text translation, sentiment analysis, and speech recognition. For example, Twitter uses NLP technique to filter terroristic language from various tweets, Amazon implements NLP for interpreting customer reviews and enhancing their experience.

Automation and Robotics

Automation is to get the monotonous and repetitive tasks done by machines which also improve productivity and receiving cost-effective and more efficient results. Many organizations use machine learning, neural networks, and graphs in automation. Such automation can prevent fraud issues while financial transactions online by using CAPTCHA technology. Robotic process automation is programmed to perform high volume repetitive tasks which can adapt to the change in different circumstances.

Robotics has emerged as a very popular field of artificial intelligence. An interesting field of research and development which mainly focuses on designing and constructing robots. It is an interdisciplinary field of science and engineering incorporated with mechanical engineering, electrical engineering, computer science, and many others. Robotics determines the designing, producing, operating, and usage of robots. It deals with computer systems for their control, intelligent outcomes, and information transformation. Robots are deployed often for conducting tasks that might be laborious for humans to perform.

Machine Vision

Machine vision technique enables computers and systems to derive meaningful information from digital images, videos, and other visual inputs, and based on those inputs, it can take action. This ability to provide recommendations distinguishes it from image recognition tasks. Machines can capture visual information and then analyse it. Cameras are used to capture the visual information, the analogue to digital conversion is used to convert the image to digital data, and digital signal processing is employed to process the data. Then the resulting data is fed to a computer. In machine vision, two vital aspects are sensitivity, which is the ability of the machine to perceive impulses that are weak and resolution, the range to which the machine can distinguish the objects. The usage of machine vision can be found in signature identification, pattern recognition, and medical image analysis, etc. Powered by convolutional neural networks, computer vision has applications within photo tagging in social media, radiology imaging in healthcare, and self-driving cars within the automotive industry.

Expert System (ES)

Expert system refers to a computer system that mimics the decision-making intelligence of a human expert. It achieves this by deriving knowledge from its knowledge base by implementing reasoning and insights rules in terms with the user queries. Expert system helps in decision making for complex problems using both facts and heuristics like a human expert. It is called expert system because it contains the expert knowledge of a specific domain and can solve complex problems of that particular domain. These systems are designed for a specific domain, such as medicine, science, etc. The performance of an expert system is based on the expert's knowledge stored in its knowledge base. The more knowledge stored in the KB, the more that system improves its performance. One of the common examples of an ES is a suggestion of spelling errors while typing in the Google search box. For example, the expert system provides suggestions for spelling and errors in the Google Search Engine.

Machine Learning

Machine learning (ML) is the subset of AI that can automatically learn from the data without explicitly being programmed or assisted by domain expertise.

Differences Between Artificial Intelligence and Machine Learning

Artificial intelligence and machine learning are two popular and often hyped terms these days. People often use them interchangeably to describe an intelligent software or system. Although both AI and ML are based on statistics and mathematics, they are not the same thing. Artificial intelligence, or AI, is the ability of a computer or machine to mimic or imitate human intelligent behaviour and perform human-like tasks. It performs tasks that require human intelligence such as thinking, reasoning, learning from experience, and making its own decisions. Artificial intelligence is a technology which enables a machine to simulate human behaviour. The goal of AI is to make a smart computer system like humans to solve complex problems. In AI, we make intelligent systems to perform any task like a human. AI is working to create an intelligent system which can perform various complex tasks. The main applications of AI are Siri, customer support using catboats, Expert System, Online game playing, intelligent humanoid robot, etc. Artificial Intelligence is the broader concept of machines being able to carry out tasks in a way that we would consider "smart". It includes learning, reasoning, and self-correction.

Learning in ML refers to a machine's ability to learn based on data and an ML algorithm's ability to train a model, evaluate its performance or accuracy, and then make predictions. (Dais 2021). The intention of ML is to enable machines to learn by themselves using data and finally make accurate predictions. The goal of ML is to allow machines to learn from data so that they can give accurate output. Machine learning is working to create machines that can perform only those specific tasks for which they are trained. For example, we can train a system with supervised machine learning algorithms such as Random Forest and Decision Trees. The main applications of machine learning are Online recommender systems, Google search algorithms, Facebook auto friend tagging suggestions, etc. Machine learning can also be divided into mainly three types that are Supervised learning, Unsupervised learning, and Reinforcement learning.

Supervised Learning

Supervised learning is one of the most basic types of machine learning. In this type, the machine learning algorithm is trained on labelled data. In supervised learning, the ML algorithm is given a small training dataset to work with. This training dataset is a smaller part of the bigger dataset and serves to give the algorithm a basic idea of the problem, solution, and data points to be dealt with. The training dataset is also very similar to the final dataset in its characteristics and provides the algorithm with the labelled parameters required for the problem. The algorithm then finds relationships between the parameters given, by establishing a cause-and-effect relationship between the variables in the dataset. At the end of the training, the algorithm has an idea of how the data works and the relationship between the input and the output. This solution is then deployed for use with the final dataset, which it learns from in the same way as the training dataset. This means that supervised machine learning algorithms will continue to improve even after being deployed, discovering new patterns and relationships as it trains itself on new data. There are two types of Supervised Learning techniques: Regression and Classification.

Unsupervised Learning

Unsupervised machine learning works with unlabelled data. Unsupervised techniques aim to uncover hidden structures, like find groups of photos with similar cars, but it's a bit difficult to implement and is not used as widely as supervised learning. Relationships between data points are perceived by the algorithm in an abstract manner, with no input required from human beings. Unsupervised techniques may be used as a preliminary step before applying supervised ones. The internal structure of the data may provide information on how to better reproduce outputs. The two types of unsupervised learning are: clustering and dimensionality reduction. Examples of Unsupervised Learning are: Apriori algorithm and K-means.

Reinforcement Learning (RL)

Reinforcement Learning (RL) is a machine learning technique that enables an agent to learn in an interactive environment by trial and error using feedback from its own actions and experiences. Both supervised and reinforcement learning use mapping between input and output. But unlike supervised learning where feedback provided to the agent is a correct set of actions for performing a task, reinforcement learning uses rewards and punishment as signals for positive and negative behaviour. Reinforcement learning is different in terms of goals when compared to unsupervised learning. While the goal in unsupervised learning is to find similarities and differences between data points, in reinforcement learning the goal is to find a suitable action model that would maximize the total cumulative reward of the agent. Because Reinforcement Learning requires a lot of data, it is most suitable in domains where simulated data is readily available like gameplay, robotics.

Deep Reinforcement Learning (RL)

It is possible for the decisions to become too complex for the reinforced learning approach. This is where deep reinforcement learning come in. Deep reinforcement learning has been used in programs that have beaten some of the best human competitors in such games as Chess and Go, and are also responsible for many of the advancements in robotics. Deep reinforcement learning combines artificial neural networks with a framework of reinforcement learning that helps software agents learn how to reach their goals. Reinforcement learning combines with neural networks can be used to create something astounding like Deepmind's AlphaGo, an algorithm that beat the world champions of the Go board game.

The difference between deep learning and reinforcement learning is that is that deep learning is learning from a training set and then applying that learning to a new data set, while reinforcement learning is dynamically learning by adjusting actions based on continuous feedback to maximize a reward. The main difference between them is that deep learning is learning from a training set and then applying that learning to a new data set, while reinforcement learning is dynamically learning by adjusting actions based in continuous feedback to maximize a reward. Another difference between Reinforcement learning and Deep learning is that the Deep learning algorithm is learning from some training data set and then applying the trained model to other test data, while Reinforcement learning interacts with the environment, seeking ways to maximize the reward by dynamically learning from feedback. In other words, Reinforcement learning may not require a data set for training, while Deep learning may require a large data set and considerable computation power.

Meta-Leaning

Although deep learning-based approaches specifically have seen great successes in a variety of fields, there are clear limitations. According to Hospedale et al (2020), successes have largely been in areas where vast quantities of data can be collected or simulated, and where huge computer resources are available. This excludes many applications where data is intrinsically rare or expensive or computer resources are unavailable. Meta-learning provides an alternative paradigm where a machine learning model gains experience over multiple learning episodes – often covering a distribution of related tasks – and uses this experience to improve its future learning performance.

Meta learning, also known as "learning to learn", is a subset of machine learning in computer science. It is used to improve the results and performance of a learning algorithm by changing some aspects of the learning algorithm based on experimental results. Meta learning helps researchers understand which algorithm(s) generate the best/better predictions from datasets. The performance of a learning model depends on its training dataset, the algorithm, and the parameters of the algorithm. Many applications required us to find the best performing algorithm and parameters of the algorithm. Meta learning helps to find these and optimize the number of experiments. This results in better predictions in shorter time. (Takimoglu, 2021).

The Difference Between Meta-Learning and Traditional Machine Learning

Traditional machine learning has a single learning task, and a model is trained based on the current task to solve the current task. Meta-learning is to allow the machine to have the ability to learn and faces multi-tasks. After training the machine for 100 different tasks, it will perform better when facing the 101st task. A good meta-learning model is capable of well adapting or generalizing to new tasks and new environments which have never been encountered during training time. The tasks can be any well-defined family of machine learning problems: supervised learning, reinforcement learning, etc. Meta-learning and transfer learning have many similarities. Both are helpful to the current task through the experience of past tasks. The difference is that meta-learning makes the machine face new tasks, parameters and models, while transfer learning always has only one model.

Artificial Intelligence Applications

According to Advani (2021), uses of Artificial Intelligence broadly come under the data processing category, which include the following:

1. Logic-chains for if-then reasoning, that can be applied to execute a string of commands based on parameters

   Searching within data, and optimising the search to give the most relevant results
   Applied probabilistic models for predicting future outcomes
   There are numerous, real-world applications of AI systems today. Below are some of the most common examples (IBM education 2020):

2. Speech Recognition:

   This uses natural language processing (NLP) to process human speech into a written format. Speech Recognition also known as computer speech recognition, or speech-to-text or automatic speech recognition (ASR).

3. Customer Service:

   Online chatbots are replacing human agents for customer service. They answer frequently asked questions (FAQs) around topics in shipping, or provide personalized advice, cross-selling products or suggesting sizes for users.

4. Computer Vision:

This enables computers and systems to derive meaningful information from digital images, videos, and other visual inputs. Based those inputs, the system can take action. This ability to provide recommendations distinguishes it from image recognition tasks.

5. Recommendation Engines:

AI algorithms using past consumption behaviour data can help to discover data trends that can be used to develop more effective cross-selling strategies. This is used to make relevant add-on recommendations to customers during the checkout process for online retailers.

6. Automated stock trading:

AI-driven high-frequency trading platforms make thousands or even millions of trades per day without human intervention.

7. Robotics:

This is an interdisciplinary field of science and engineering incorporated with mechanical engineering, electrical engineering, computer science, and many others. Robotics determines the designing, producing, operating, and usage of robots. It deals with computer systems for their control, intelligent outcomes, and information transformation. The majority of robotics tasks involved - assembly line for automobile manufacturing, for moving large objects in space by NASA.

Advantages of AI

AI has been used in such diverse realms of application as linguistics, law, engineering, economics, manufacturing, and medicine, as well as many modelling tasks. There are many advantages for using AI in applications (Chowdhury & Sadek 2012). Firstly, AI has already proven to be quite reliable in many different applications because of its ability to simulate human intelligence in a reasoning process. It reduces cost because it enables reduction on the need of personnel time using AI in decision making. Because decisions are often made under obvious uncertainties (i.e., with incomplete and uncertain knowledge), AI methods can be used when a direct mathematical relationship cannot be established between cause and effect.

Another benefit of AI is that AI methods are also capable of dealing with both qualitative as well as quantitative data, a feature that most strictly analytical methods lack. AI can support faster solutions to complex problems by automating the decision-making process. One main advantage of AI is its rigorous use on the Internet such as in search engines. AI can be used to overcome many risky limitations of humans by using robots to do the jobs such as diffusing bombs and mining oil.

TYPES OF ARTIFICIAL INTELLIGENCE (AI)

Escott (2017) grouped AI into three types: Artificial narrow intelligence (ANI), Artificial General Intelligence (AGI) and Artificial Superintelligence (ASI)

Artificial Narrow Intelligence (ANI)

Artificial narrow intelligence (ANI) is also known as weak AI or narrow AI. It is what we are currently able to achieve in AI. Narrow AI is designed to perform singular tasks such as facial recognition, speech recognition/voice assistants, driving a car, or searching the internet. The intelligence is to complete the specific task it is programmed to do. It is referred to as weak because it can only operate under a narrow set of constraints and limitations. Narrow AI only simulates human behaviour based on a narrow range of contexts and parameters. Examples include speech and language recognition of the Siri virtual assistant on iPhones, vision recognition of self-driving cars, and recommendation engines that suggest products you like based on your purchase history. These systems can only learn or be taught to complete in specific tasks.

Some examples of narrow AI listed by Escott (2017) are:

1. Image / facial recognition software
2. Entertainment or marketing content recommendations based on watch/listen/purchase behaviour
3. Self-driving cars
4. Disease mapping and prediction tools
5. Manufacturing and drone robots
6. Rankbrain by Google / Google Search
7. IBM's Watson
8. Siri by Apple, Alexa by Amazon, Cortana by Microsoft and other virtual assistants
9. Email spam filters / social media monitoring tools for dangerous content

Artificial General Intelligence (AGI) / Strong AI / Deep AI

Artificial general intelligence (AGI) is also known as strong AI or deep AI. It is the concept of a machine with general intelligence that mimics human intelligence and/or behaviours, with the ability to learn and apply its intelligence to solve any problem. In AGI, the machine will have the ability to think, understand, and act in like a human in any given situation. The machine not only be competent in solving logical problems, but also have emotion. We still have not yet achieved strong AI. The reason is that to achieve strong AI, we must make machines conscious by programming a full set of cognitive abilities.

Artificial Superintelligence (ASI)

Aims to surpass strong AI in human intelligence and ability. However, Super AI is still purely speculative because we still have not achieved Strong AI yet. It is imaginary AI that not only understands or mimics human intelligence and behaviour, but become self-aware and surpass the capacity of human intelligence and ability. Super AI is the one most people mean when they talk about robots taking over the world. super AI is purely speculative at this point. That is, it's not likely to exist for an exceedingly long time (if at all).

Existing AI Cannot be Human Intelligent

Husain (2017) defined Artificial intelligence (AI) as the study of techniques that allow computers to learn, reason, and act to achieve goals. According to Hole and others (2021), current AI research is focused on systems that are narrow AI that perform one well-defined task in a single domain, such as facial recognition, Internet search, driving a car, or playing a computer game. The aim of long-term AI is to design general AI with human-like cognitive capabilities that allows us to perform broad range of cognitive tasks.

Another criticism from Vincent (2017) regarding the limitation of current AI is, Despite the hype about AI, the creation of super-intelligent AI is just around the corner, according to Vincent (2017), this is unrealistic. The reason is that contemporary AI programs are extremely narrow in their abilities. Current AI does not possess the hard-to-define but easy-to-spot skills such as "common sense." They are not that intelligent.

According to Husain (2017), current narrow AI techniques alone are unlikely to bring about general AI because it is proactive. Current AI cannot learn continuously from data streams and make updated predictions like humans. Husain (2017) argues that more biologically plausible neuron models must replace the point neurons used in artificial neural networks to allow the networks to predict their future states. Another limitation of current narrow AI is the lack of sensorimotor integration providing the ability to learn by interacting with the environment.

According to Escott (2017), a theory of mind AI framework is needed to discern needs, emotions, beliefs and thought processes of other intelligent entities. It is concerned with training machines to truly understand humans. To do this, we must understand the human brain, that is the study of general intelligence. The lack of comprehensive knowledge on the functionality of the human brain has made it difficult for researchers to replicate basic functions of sight and movement. It is the authors' belief that until we know and understand about intelligence, we are not going to achieve this. However, today, we have neuroscience, the study of human brain that can pave the way to help us getting nearer to the goal of strong AI.

Traditional AI Design

Although the AlphaZero (Silver 2018), achieved superhuman performance and outperformed the expert, Hole and others (2020) argue that AlphaZero and all other narrow AI programs do not know what they do. They cannot transfer their performance to other domains without redesign and extensive practice. Although these shortcomings are all serious, but the main problem is that all narrow AI systems are allowed because they lack abstract reasoning abilities and possess no common sense about the world. Traditionally Researchers in AI have preferred mathematical and logical rather than biologically constrained approaches to creating intelligence (Russell & Norvig, 2020). Previously, classical, or symbolic AI applications such as game playing programs and expert systems used explicit rules to process high-level (human-readable) input symbols (Hole et al 2020). Recently, artificial neural networks are used to process vectors of numerical input symbols. However, unlike the brain's sensorimotor integration and embodied reasoning, current AI is almost independent of the environment. These AI programs run internally on the computer without much interaction with the world through sensors. Current narrow AI techniques cannot lead to general AI because these techniques lack necessary biological properties (Hawkins 2021).

What is the Solution?

Researchers trying to imitate the remarkable functionality of our human brain will benefit by learning more about neuroscience, and the differences between Natural and Artificial Intelligence (Potter 2007). According to Balland (2015), human intelligence is the brain's ability to learn a model of the world and use it to understand new situations, handle abstract concepts, and create novel behaviours, including manipulating the environment. Research in AI has always been about trying to build machines that think. According to Hawkins (2021), "We'll never have true AI without first understanding the brain". Hawkins (2021) argues that Although machine-learning techniques such as deep neural networks have recently made impressive gains, they are still a long way from being intelligent, from being able to understand and act in the world the way that humans do. He further argues that the only example of intelligence, of the ability to learn from the world, to plan and to execute, is the brain. Therefore, it is imperative that we must understand the principles underlying human intelligence and use them to guide us in the development of truly intelligent machines.

What is Neuroscience

Neuroscience is the study of the anatomy and physiology of the human brain, including structures, neurons, and molecules. It studies how the brain works in terms of mechanics, functions, and systems in order to create recognizable behaviours (Goswami 2020). It is the science of neurons which are the active component, or the component responsible for thinking, acting, and perceiving in our brains. Neuroscience is the science of the brain and the nervous system. There are many types of neuroscience. Neuroscientists study how brain cells signal to each other, for example which chemicals they use; they study how brain cells connect to each other, for example by sending small electrical pulses; and they study whole systems of brain cells at work, for example looking at connected activity in the visual areas of the brain, the auditory areas of the brain and the thinking areas of the brain. Neuroscientists also study how the brain evolved, how cells in the developing brain differentiate themselves into, say, visual versus auditory brain cells, and how brain cells know where in the brain to go to do their designated jobs.

According to Farnsworth (2021), there are many different branches of neuroscience – everything from computational, to pharmacological, to molecular neuroscience and well beyond. The branches that are concerned in AI are Cognitive neuroscience, Behavioural neuroscience, and Computational neuroscience. Cognitive neuroscience is concerned with the scientific study of biological substrates underlying cognition and mental processes and addresses questions such as how psychological/cognitive functions are reflected by neural activity in the brain. In contrast, behavioural neuroscience (also known as biopsychology), addresses the impact of the nervous system on attention, perception, motivation, performance, learning, and memory and their manifestations in human behaviour. Studies in behavioural neuroscience focus on the interaction of brain and behaviour in real or simulated environments.

Computational neuroscience is an attempt to take the complex and poorly understood behaviours of the human brain and associated nervous system and develop both mathematical and algorithmic models to try to understand their behaviour (Cappelli, 2019). According to Cappelli (2019), AI and computational neuroscience have many similarities. Computational neuroscience can be used to help us to overcome some of the limitations of current AI. One of the suggestions by Cappelli (2019) is that we should look at the architecture of the brain as a starting point to design an optimal architecture for the interaction of various AI algorithms.

Another suggestion is the role of robots. As industry becomes more and more interested in robotics (the application of AI to automation) there will be an increased focus on how intelligence and AI algorithms interact with physical world processes. So, as robotics moves from being theoretical to a genuine industrial endeavour, the models that have been built to understand how the brain interacts with the nervous system and the external world will play an increasing role in the advancement of AI.

Neuroscience Core Concepts

1. According to the Society for Neuroscience, the following "Neuroscience Core Concepts" are:
2. The brain is the body's most complex organ.
3. Neurons communicate using both electrical and chemical signals.
4. Genetically determined circuits are the foundation of the nervous system.
5. Life experiences change the nervous system.
6. Intelligence arises as the brain reasons, plans, and solves problems.
7. The brain makes it possible to communicate knowledge through language.
8. The human brain endows us with a natural curiosity to understand how the world works.
9. Fundamental discoveries promote healthy living and treatment of disease.

What is Intelligence?

It is difficult to define Intelligence. It is very notoriously elusive. In Legg and Hotter (2007) comprehensive survey of available definitions of intelligence, reviewed more than 70 different notions. They Extracted the most common features and defined intelligence as the measure of an agent's ability to achieve goals in a wide range of environments. According to Merriam-Webster, intelligence is defined as having the ability to understand or learn and able to deal with new and trying situations as well as the skill to reason. Intelligence is also having the ability to apply knowledge to manipulate one's environment or to think abstractly as measured by objective criteria (such as tests). It is a much sought-after characteristics of all Humans. Psychologist Robert Sternberg (1997) defined intelligence as "the mental abilities necessary for adaptation to, as well as shaping and selection of, any environmental context" (1997, p. 1). Sir Francis Galton was one of the first people to study intelligence in the late 1800s. He had an idea that intelligence is a general mental ability that is a product of biological evolution. Galton then set up a lab to measure reaction times and other physical characteristics to test his hypothesis. Regarded as one of the fathers of modern-day intelligence research, Galton pioneered psychometric and statistical methods. Given the technology of the day, he wasn't particularly successful at measuring biological parameters. But he did create testable hypotheses about intelligence that later researchers used.

Theories of Intelligence

There are many theories regarding intelligence. Many researchers argue that intelligence is a general ability. However, some argue that intelligence is comprised of specific skills and talents. In Psychology, some researchers believe that intelligence is genetic, or inherited, whereas others argue that it is mainly influenced by the surrounding environment. Because of this, there are several contrasting theories of intelligence and individual tests that try to measure it.

Spearman's General Intelligence (g)

General intelligence, also known as g factor, was developed by Charles Spearman, an English psychologist, in 1904 (Spearman, 1904). It refers to a general mental ability to underlie multiple specific skills, including verbal, spatial, numerical, and mechanical. Spearman used a technique known as factor analysis. Factor analysis is a procedure through which the correlation of related variables is evaluated to find an underlying factor that explains this correlation. Spearman argued that people who did well in one area of intelligence tests such as mathematics also did well in other areas (Ruhl 2020). According to Spearman (1904), there was a strong correlation between performing well in math and music. He attributed this relationship to a central factor, that of general intelligence (g). According to him, there are two main factors contributed to general intelligence known as the Spearman's two-factor theory. Firstly, the g-factor which represents an individual's general intelligence across multiple abilities, and that a second factor, s, refers to an individual's specific ability in one particular area (Thomson, 1947).

Thurstone's Primary Mental Abilities

Spearman's idea of general intelligence was challenged by Thurstone (1938). Thurstone (1938) did not reject Spearman's idea of general intelligence. Instead, he argued that intelligence consists of both general ability and several specific abilities. He analysed data from 56 different tests of mental abilities, and identified several primary mental abilities that comprise intelligence, as opposed to one general factor. Thurstone (1938) identified seven primary mental abilities: verbal comprehension, verbal fluency, number facility, spatial visualization, perceptual speed, memory, and inductive reasoning (Sternberg, 2003).

American psychologist Howard Gardner (1983) extended the idea of Thurstone (1938) arguing that that there is no single intelligence, but rather distinct, independent multiple intelligences exist, each representing unique skills and talents relevant to a certain category. Initially Gardner (1983) proposed seven multiple intelligences. These include linguistic, logical-mathematical, spatial, musical, bodily-kinesthetic, interpersonal, and intrapersonal, also naturalist intelligence. He argued that activity such as dancing involves several multiple intelligences such as spatial and bodily-kinesthetic intelligences, He further suggested that the multiple intelligences can also help us to understand concepts beyond intelligence, such as creativity and leadership. However, according to Sternberg (2003), the main criticism of this theory is that it does not account for other types of intelligence beyond the ones Gardner listed.

Triarchic Theory of Intelligence

To overcome the criticism, Robert Sternberg (1985) proposed a three-category theory of intelligence, integrating components that were lacking in Gardner's theory. Sternberg's (1985) theory is based on the definition of intelligence as the ability to achieve success based on one's personal standards and sociocultural context. According to Sternberg (1985), in the triarchic theory, there are three aspects to intelligence: analytical, creative, and practical.

Analytical intelligence is also known as componential intelligence. It refers to intelligence that is applied to analyse or evaluate problems and arrive at solutions. The traditional IQ test is used to measure the Analytical intelligence. Creative intelligence is the ability to go beyond what is given to create novel and interesting ideas. This type of intelligence involves imagination, innovation and problem-solving. Practical intelligence is having the ability to solve problems in daily life, when a person finds the best fit between themselves and the demands of the environment. Adapting to the demands the environment requires either utilizing knowledge gained from experience to purposefully change oneself to suit the environment (adaptation), changing the environment to suit oneself (shaping), or finding a new environment in which to work (selection).

Other Types of Intelligence

Besides the above types of intelligence, there are others such as Emotional Intelligence, Fluid intelligence, Crystallized intelligence. Salovey & Mayer (1990) defined Emotional Intelligence as the "ability to monitor one's own and other people's emotions, to discriminate between different emotions and label them appropriately, and to use emotional information to guide thinking and behaviour". According to Salovey and Mayer (1990), the four key components of emotional Intelligence are (i) self-awareness, (ii) self-management, (iii) social awareness, and (iv) relationship management. Raymond Cattell (1963) defined Fluid intelligence as the ability to problem solve in novel situations without referencing prior knowledge, but through the use of logic and abstract thinking. It can be applied to any novel problem because no specific prior knowledge is required (Cattell, 1963). Cattell (1963) argued that fluid increases with age and starts to decrease in the late 20s. According to Cattell (1963), Crystallized intelligence refers to the use of previously acquired knowledge, such as specific facts learned in school or specific motor skills or muscle memory. It increases as one grows older and accumulates knowledge.

Why We Need to Study the Brain to Build Intelligent Machines

Although machine-learning techniques such as deep neural networks have recently made impressive improvements, they are still not able to perform tasks that a baby can do. The brain is the only example of intelligence that can learn from the world, to plan and to execute. It is imperative that we understand the principles underlying human intelligence and use them to guide us in the development of truly intelligent machines. (Hawkins 2017).

Hawkins in an interview with Heaven (2021) argues that there are four minimum attributes of intelligence, a kind of baseline that is crucial to intelligence that AI needs to address. Firstly, learning by moving because we cannot sense everything around us at once. It is necessary that we build a mental model of things. Hawkins calls it embodiment. Secondly, the thousand brains idea. According to Hawkins, the sensory input is taken up by thousands of cortical columns, each with a partial picture of the world. The cortical columns compete and combine via a sort of voting system to build up an overall viewpoint. He further elaborates that in an AI system, this could involve a machine controlling different sensors—vision, touch, radar and so on—to get a more complete model of the world. Although, there will typically be many cortical columns for each sense, such as vision. Thirdly continuous learning, where we learn new things without forgetting previous stuff. Current AI systems cannot do this. Fourthly, we structure knowledge using reference frames, which means that our knowledge of the world is relative to our point of view. An example he used is that 'if I slide my finger up the edge of my coffee cup, I can predict that I'll feel its rim, because I know where my hand is in relation to the cup.'

Combining Neuroscience and Machine Learning

According to Silva (2017), although we can discover how the brain works, it is still unclear, which brain processes might work well as machine learning algorithms, or how to make that translation. The solution is to conduct research in both the brain (neuroscience) and AI together to improve both machine learning and identifying new areas of neuroscience.

Demis Hassabis, (Hassabis et al 2017) the founder of Google's AI powerhouse DeepMind, said that the answer lies in neuroscience. In a review published in the journal Neuron, Hassabis and three co-authors argue that the field of AI needs to reconnect to the world of neuroscience. It is by finding out more about natural intelligence that we can truly understand and create the artificial kind. The authors argue that reconnecting the two disciplines will create a "virtuous cycle," They further pointed out that AI researchers will be inspired by what they learn about natural intelligence, while the task of "distilling intelligence into an algorithmic construct [could] yield insights into some of the deepest and most enduring mysteries of the mind."

According to Hassabis (Hassabis et al 2017), there are two ways to do it. The first is use neuroscience as a source of inspiration for algorithmic and architectural ideas. The reason is that the human brain is the only source that we know to possess general intelligence. It is important to see if there are ideas we can transfer over into machine learning and AI. The second is that we need to understand what intelligence is— including natural intelligence, our own minds. Hassabis argued that there should be some flow back, from AI algorithms that do interesting things, that leads to ideas about how and what we should look for in the brain itself. Then we can use these AI systems as models for what's going on in the brain.

How Does Neuroscience Inspire AI?

A recent study by AI researchers at DeepMind shows connections between dopamine and reinforcement learning. Reinforcement learning is a hot area of AI research.

From neuroscience, we know that one of the basic mechanisms through which humans and animals learn is rewards and punishments. Positive outcomes encourage us to repeat certain actions while negative results detract us from repeating mistakes. Research from neuroscience shows that dopamine, a neurotransmitter chemical produced in the midbrain, plays a great role in regulating the reward functions of the brain. (Dicken 2020)

According to Russell & Nerving (2010), the aim of AI is to investigate theories and develop computer systems that can conduct tasks that require biological or human intelligence, with functions such as perception, recognition, decision-making, and control. According to Miller (2003), the goal of Neuroscience, on the other hand is to study the structures, functions, and operating mechanisms of biological brains, such as how the brain processes information, makes decisions, and interacts with the environment. Neuroscience can help AI build neural networks that mimic brain structure. It is feasible for us to borrow ideas from the structure of a human brain to design neural networks of today. The reason is that neurons in neural networks have similar characteristics to the biological neurons in the brain. Our human brain consists of billions of neurons. Each individual neuron is linked to other neurons. When one neuron gets activated, it generates a spike and sends signals to other neurons. Like the human brain, the machine learning neural network also consists of interconnected neurons. When a neuron receives inputs, it gets activated and it sends information to other neurons (Jing, 2020). The plasticity of our brain allows us to learn and improve our skills. Each time we learn new things, we are creating and strengthening the connections between neurons. This is the reason why when we practise a task, we become better at it. When we feed the neuron with lots of data, a neural network learns. Each connection on the neural network is associated with a weight that dictates the importance between neurons.

Researchers in AI around the world are increasingly using the knowledge, techniques, and programs developed from neuroscience - a new understanding of how our brains learn. They are trying to imitate the remarkable functionality of our human brain by learning more about neuroscience, and the differences between Natural and Artificial Intelligence (Potter 2007). Neuroscience has played a key role in artificial intelligence. Jing (2020) argues that there are two ways that neuroscience inspires the design of AI systems. Firstly, AI emulates human intelligence, and Secondly, AI builds neural networks that mimic brain structure. Thirdly, neuroscience can be used to improve the quality of algorithms in AI. Fourthly, neuroscience can be used for verifying and validating AI's current models and technologies. (Joshi 2021). Fifthly, Data generated from neuroscience is invaluable for AI's long-term development. Sixthly, vast sources of data from neuroscientific studies can provide an AI system with a basic understanding of how human intelligence works. Lastly, Neuroscience is producing new tools for exploring the brain's circuits with higher resolution and in greater detail than previously possible. (Chance et al 2020).

How AI Revolutionizes Neuroscience

AI helps us to understand how our brain works. Artificial intelligence is increasingly becoming an important tool in neuroscience research. It helps us to understand how the human brain works and to accelerate neuroscience development. (Fan 2019). Researchers in neuroscience have been studying how the human brain processes thoughts and how it moves our bodies. By knowing more about the brain, we are better equipped to diagnose mental diseases and help people with disabilities to improve movement capabilities. AI models can be used to accurately simulate the various neuron-to-neuron connections in the body. (Joshi 2021). Neural networks in AI act as "virtual brains" that capture the representation of our brain that can produce patterns of neural activities that resemble the patterns recorded from the brain. These patterns allow neuroscientists to test hypotheses and observe the results from simulations. AI is also helping neuroscientists to crack the so-called neural code—the activation patterns of individual groups of neurons that underlie a thought or behaviour. (Joshi 2021). Advanced computer vision can assist neurologists with recreating actual neural linkages to get accurate information about their working (from a genomic perspective). Neuroscientists can use AI tools to profile single neurons at their genetic level, or digitally reconstruct massive portions of neural connections. (Joshi 2021).

However, it is important to remember that because AI output resembles the brain, it does not mean that's how the brain works. The analogy between neuron in our brain and Neural networks is a rough one. Unlike machine intelligence, our brains are not machines, but the result of evolutionary pressure. Much of what we learned are interactions with our changing environment that AI models may not be able to capture because our brain is a very sophisticated biological organ that uses chemical and electrical activity making us different from machines. Instead, AI is more likely to offer one or more solutions that neuroscientists can experimentally confirm.

INTEGRATION OF NEUROSCIENCE AND ARTIFICIAL INTELLIGENCE

The steady development of AI is mostly attributed to studies and research in neuroscience. Future AI will be continually influence or be inspired by advances in neuroscience. At the same time, AI will contribute to neuroscience research. The reason is both AI and neuroscience are closely related. Firstly, AI has been heavily influenced by neuroscience especially the influence of the perceptron model, essentially a simple model of a biological neuron.

According to Joshi (2021), the goal of AI is to replicate the workings of the human brain to make machines and digital applications as intuitive and efficient as possible. Researchers in AI build neural networks (with intelligent algorithms) that mimic the structure and processes of the human nervous system to achieve this. Similarly, he argues that neuroscientists can benefit from deep learning and other AI components.

Although AI has made tremendous progress such as the emergence of automated man-machine dialogue and service systems, and Google Auto Driving. However, all such systems are only intelligent in certain perspective in a particular field and related theories. They are not able to be extended to other fields to solve other types of problems. Recently, Neuroscience research has resulted in breakthroughs in AI, such as deep learning. Despite the applications of AI surpassing expectations, an insurmountable gap remains between AI and human intelligence. To narrow this gap, it is important for us to establish a bridge between neuroscience and AI research by linking the two. It is important to set up a dynamic connection of the brain and to integrate neuroscience experiments with theory, models, and statistics because results from neuroscience reveal important issues related to the principles of intelligence (Fan et al 2020).

Neuroscience and AI: A Symbiotic Relationship

Human brain neuroscience has inspired the building of human-like artificial intelligence to build new algorithms. Conversely, artificial intelligence accelerates research in neuroscience by allowing Neuroscientists to learn from the behaviour of artificial agents to interpret our brains. There is synergy between neuroscience and AI. The design of today's AI systems that mimic the human nervous system was possible mainly due to neuroscientific research by using artificial neural networks that modelled on the network of nerves running throughout our bodies. Neuroscience has made the replication of AI possible. On the other hand, AI systems are helping us paint an increasingly accurate picture of the human brain and its functioning. Consequently, progress in each of these fields is not just critical for the other, but also valuable for other fields and industries that rely on them. It is obvious that these two subjects need each other, and we should continue to build on each other. We concur with Hassabis and others (2017) that leveraging insights gained from neuroscience research will expedite progress in AI research because the exchange of ideas between AI and neuroscience can create a 'virtuous circle' advancing the objectives of both fields.

A Thousand Brains: A New Theory of Intelligence (Hawkins 2021)

Hawkins (2021) has developed a framework called the Thousand Brains Theory of Intelligence that will be fundamental to advancing the state of artificial intelligence and machine learning. He argues that by applying this theory to existing deep learning systems, we are addressing today's bottlenecks while enabling tomorrow's applications. At Hawkins' company, Numenta, they study the neocortex, the brain's largest component and the one most responsible for intelligence. The brain is the most complex and important part of our human body. Figure 1 shows an anatomy of the human brain.

Figure 1. Anatomy of the brain (adapted from (Cuffari 2020)

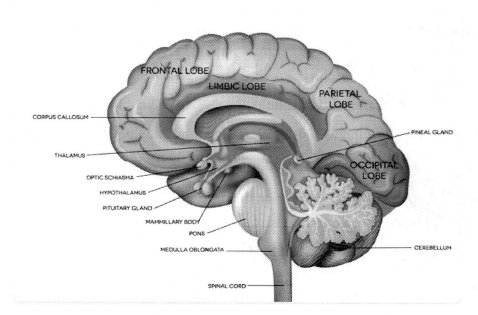

ANATOMY OF THE BRAIN

Functions of the Neocortex

The neocortex is the primary brain area associated with intelligence. (Hole et al 2021). The neocortex is comprised of 4 regions: frontal, parietal, occipital, and temporal lobes. (Bennett, 2019). It is based on the patterns of sulci (grooves) and gyri (ridges). The frontal lobes are responsible for the selection and coordination of goal directed behaviour. It is the human executive function managing the multiple complex processes such as decision-making, reinforcement learning and task switching etc. Disorders of the frontal lobe cause Parkinson's disease, frontotemporal dementia, and Alzheimer's disease. The Parietal Lobe is often referred to as the association cortex. It is responsible for the decision-making, numerical cognition, processing of sensory information, and spatial awareness. The occipital lobe is the bulge seen at the back of the brain. It is responsible for visual function and visual perception which is closely surrounded by the visual association area. The temporal lobe houses the hippocampus and the amygdala. The functions of temporal lobe are to process sensory information and derive language, emotions, and meaningful memories. It is also responsible for declarative memory, which is memory that can be spoken aloud (such as learned facts) and is further divided into two subgroups— semantic and episodic memory.

Hawkins (2021) describes the neocortex as a deeply folded sheet some 2 millimetres thick that, if laid out flat, would be about as big as a large dinner napkin. In humans, it takes up about 75 percent of the brain's volume. This is the part that makes us intelligent. According to Hawkins (2021), the neocortex knows almost nothing at birth. He argues that we learn through experiences. Everything we learn about the world is stored in the neocortex. The neocortex also generates motor commands, when we make a meal or write software it is the neocortex controlling these behaviours. Language, too, is created and understood by the neocortex.

The neocortex is made up of cells called neurons. It has about 30 billion of them. A typical neuron has a single tail-like axon and several treelike extensions called dendrites. The neuron is like a kind of signalling system. The axon is the transmitter, and the dendrites are the receivers. Along the branches of the dendrites lie some 5,000 to 10,000 synapses, each of which connects to counterparts on thousands of other neurons. There are more than 100 trillion synaptic connections. Figure 2 shows two neurons that are connected.

Figure 2. Illustrating two neurons that are connected (adapted from (Blanchette et al 2020)

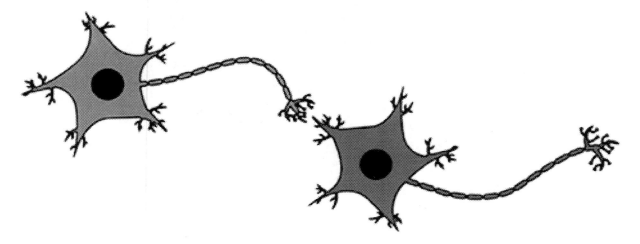

The neocortex has six horizontal layers as shown in Figure 3. The hippocampus has at most three cellular layers). Neurons in various layers connect vertically to form small microcircuits, called 'columns'. (Physiopedia 2021). The neocortex is the largest and most powerful area of the human brain. All of its important cognitive functions are made possible by the convergence of two distinct streams of information: a "bottom-up" stream, which represents signals from the environment, and a "top-down" stream, which transmits internally generated information about past experiences and current aims.

Neocortex

Figure 3. Cerebral cortex

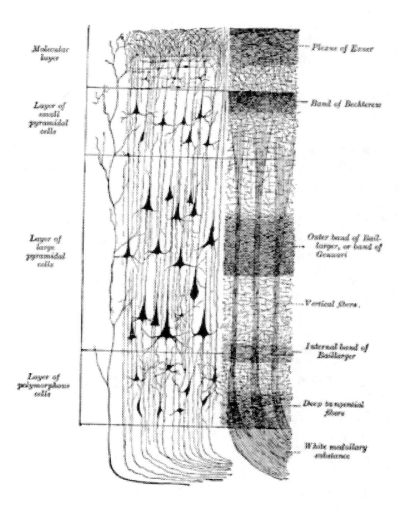

To the left, the groups of cells; to the right, the systems of fibres. Quite to the left of the figure a sensory nerve fibre is shown. Cell body layers are labelled on the left, and fibre layers are labelled on the right.

According to Hawkins (2021), our experience of the world around us such as recognizing a friend's face or holding a bar of soap in our hand is the result of input from our eyes, ears, and other sensory organs traveling to our neocortex and causing groups of neurons to fire causing an electrochemical spike to travel down the neuron's axon and crosses synapses to other neurons. If a receiving neuron gets enough input, it might fire in response and activate other neurons. Of the 30 billion neurons in the neocortex, 1 or 2 percent are firing at any given instant, which means that many millions of neurons will be active at any point in time. The set of active neurons changes as we move and interact with the world. Hawkins (2021) pointed out that our perception of the world, that is our conscious experience, is determined by the constantly changing pattern of active neurons.

The neocortex stores these patterns primarily by forming new synapses. This storage enables us to recognize faces and places when we see them again and recall them from our memory. An example Hawkins (2021) gives is when we think of our friend's face, a pattern of neural firing occurs in the neocortex that is similar to the one that occurs when we are actually seeing our friend's face.

Many different activities are going on inside different parts of the neocortex. What differentiates them is not their structure, but their connections. These connections are strengthened when we learn something. They are weakened when we forget something.

Cortical Columns

According to Hawkins (2021), the cortical columns are the basic units of the neocortex. Each column contains upwards of a hundred neurons, and there are between one and two million of them in the neocortex. Hawkins (2021) argues that what cortical columns do is to attach reference frames to objects in the world and to abstract concepts. There are "what" columns that attach frames to external objects, and "where" columns that attach frames to the body. New Theory of Intelligence by Hawkins (2021) argues that this is what enables our brain to understand where it is in the world, and to navigate it.

Hawkins further argues that, the neocortex "learns a model" of the world collectively and continuously updates it. According to Hawkins (2021) there is no central control room in our brains. Rather, our perception is a consensus that the columns reach by voting. Within the columns – indeed, within the neurons – predictions are made, and depending how successful their predictions are, the neurons will vote for their version of events. The model which emerges is the result of their aggregate strength of those predictions.

NEUROSCIENCE BASED AI APPLICATIONS

Silva (2019) describes an example of combining neuroscience and machine learning research at his lab. His team has developed a way to think about how individual neurons contribute to their overall network. He found out that for every neuron, no matter how broad the network, local interactions collectively influence the activity, He also found out that the mathematics that describe these layers of interaction are equally applicable to artificial neural networks and biological neural networks in real brains. As a result, he and the team are developing a fundamentally new form of machine learning that can learn on the fly without advance training that seems to be highly adaptable and efficient at learning. Silva (2019) and his team are currently using those ideas and mathematics to explore why the shapes of biological neurons are so twisted and convoluted. He found out that they may develop those shapes to maximize their efficiency at passing messages, following the same computational rules that this has used to build the artificial learning system.

Examples of Neuroscience Based AI Implementations

Replay

At DeepMind, Hassabis, and others (2017) are currently researching in neuroscience and AI to find a common language, allowing a free flow of knowledge that will allow continued progress on both fronts.

The group have developed deep-Q network (DQN), an algorithm that learnt to master a diverse range of Atari 2600 games to superhuman level with only the raw pixels and score as inputs. DQN mimics "experience replay", by storing a subset of training data that it reviews "offline", allowing it to learn anew from successes or failures that occurred in the past. The idea came from neuroscience: the discovery of offline experience "replay". Hassabis and others (2017) found that during sleep or quiet resting, biological brains "replay" temporal patterns of neuronal activity that were produced in an earlier active period. They observed that when rats run through a maze, "place" cells activate as the animal moves around. According to these authors, they saw that the same sequence of neuronal activity is observed during rest as if the rats were mentally reimagining their past movements and using them to optimise future behaviour. These authors suggested that interfering with replay impairs performance when they later perform the same tasks. This shows that neuroscience is an important source of ideas for AI and can helps to build better AI systems. Conversely, Hassabis (2017, cited by Fan 2019) argues that Distilling intelligence into algorithms and comparing it to the human brain "may yield insights into some of the deepest and most enduring mysteries of the mind,"

Transfer Learning

Transfer learning is another key challenge in contemporary AI research. Artificial agents on AI need the ability to build on existing knowledge to make sensible decisions. Humans are good at it, but not machines. Researchers in AI are now starting to tackle the problem. They are using a new class of network architecture known as a "progressive network" that can use knowledge learned in one video game to learn another. According to Hassabis and others (2017) the same architecture has also been shown to transfer knowledge from a simulated robotic arm to a real-world arm, massively reducing the training time. They found that networks bear some similarities to models of sequential task learning in humans. This example shows that there is great potential to link AI with neuroscience.

Deep Learning Networks using Sparse Techniques

In Numenta (Hawkins (2021), they have demonstrated a 100x Performance Acceleration in Deep Learning Networks using Sparse Techniques (Numenta whitepaper 2021). In May, -Numenta, Inc. announced it has achieved greater than 100x performance improvements on inference tasks in deep learning networks without any loss in accuracy by using sparse algorithms derived from its neuroscience research to achieve breakthrough performance in machine learning in a proof-of-concept demonstration. In their released paper, Numenta demonstrates that it is possible to construct sparse networks that deliver equivalent accuracy to their dense counterparts, by leveraging today's hardware, delivering over two orders of magnitude performance improvement. The Numenta's sparse networks rely on key aspects of brain sparsity: activation sparsity (number of active neurons) and weight sparsity (interconnectedness of neurons). The combination of the two yields multiplicative effects, enabling large efficiency improvements. (Numenta Whitepaper 2021)

This research is not only in one direction. Hassabis and others (2017) argued that Neuroscience can also benefit from AI research. An example is that of reinforcement learning in AI. Reinforcement learning from AI has help us understand neurophysiological phenomena, such as the firing properties of dopamine neurons in the mammalian basal ganglia. Hassabis and others (2017) suggested creating a virtuous circle whereby AI researchers use ideas from neuroscience to build new technology, and neuroscientists learn from the behaviour of artificial agents to better interpret biological brains is the way forward for both AI and neuroscience research.

Neuroscience Based Approach to Unsupervised Real-Time Anomaly Detection for Streaming Data

Neural networks mostly perform supervised learning but not unsupervised learning. An example of neuroscience-based learning system is the Unsupervised real-time anomaly detection for streaming data proposed by Ahmad and others (2017). Real-world streaming analytics calls for novel algorithms that run online, and corresponding tools for evaluation. The detection of anomalies in streaming data is becoming increasingly important especially for machine learning in IOT. It can give action-able information in critical scenarios, but currently there is no reliable solution for it. Ahmad and others (2017) have proposed a novel anomaly detection algorithm for such applications based on Hierarchical Temporal Memory (HTM) networks. Based on known properties of cortical neurons, Hierarchical Temporal Memory (HTM) is a theoretical framework for sequence learning in the cortex. Using HTM, the algorithm can detect spatial and temporal anomalies in predictable and noisy domains. According to these authors the algorithm meets the requirements of real-time, continuous, online detection without look ahead and supervision. Anomaly detection with Hierarchical Temporal Memory (HTM) is a state-of-the-art, online, unsupervised method.

Neuroscience Based Approach for Movement-Based Visual Object Recognition

According to Leadholm et al (2021), grid cells in the entorhinal cortex enable the brain to model the physical space of the world and navigate effectively via path integration, updating self-position using information from self-movement. Researchers argued that grid cell-like computations might be used to build object representations in diverse sensory modalities including vision. Whereas humans do naturally and effortlessly in object recognition given a sequence of sensory samples of an image, such as saccades, it is a challenging problem for machine vision.

Leadholm et al (2021), set out to address the problem by implementing a biologically plausible network, called GridCellNet, based on cortical columns and grid cell-like computations to integrate visual information and make predictions based on movements. The system uses rapid Hebbian-style learning to associate sensed features and their spatial location in the reference frame of an object, while dendritic segments enable the system to encode predictive states. Locations are encoded by activity in grid cell modules that are updated with self-movement. In addition to addressing the challenge of arbitrary sequence inputs, this system also includes the desirable properties of rapid learning (functioning with both few training examples and few weight updates), and predictive capabilities, enabling completion of an image given partial inputs. They found that GridCellNet can reliably perform classification, generalizing to both unseen examples and completely novel sequence trajectories.

Leadhom and others (2021) also show that inference is often successful after sampling a fraction of the input space, enabling the predictive GridCellNet to reconstruct the rest of the image given just a few movements. In addition, they argue that that dynamically moving agents with active sensors can use grid cell representations not only for navigation, but also for efficient recognition and feature prediction of seen objects. When compared to typical machine-learning approaches, the system outperforms other approaches. This example represents the first demonstration that grid cell-like computations that can be leveraged to enable generalization on a visual task to unseen examples of an object class.

Neuroscience Based Approach Language Modelling

Another example of using a neuroscience-based approach is to boost the performance of a Sparse Predictive Autoencoder in Sequence Modelling in language modelling. (Gordon et al 2020). According to Gordon and others (2020), in sequence learning tasks such as language modelling, Recurrent Neural Networks must learn relationships between input features separated by time. A variety of architectures have achieved excellent language modelling performance. State of the art models such as LSTM and Transformer are trained by backpropagation of losses into prior hidden states and inputs held in memory. This allows gradients to flow from present to past and effectively learn with perfect hindsight, but at a significant memory cost.

In their paper, Gordon, and others (2020) show that that it is possible to train high performance recurrent networks using information that is local in time, and thereby achieve a significantly reduced memory footprint using a predictive autoencoder called bRSM featuring recurrent connections, sparse activations, and a boosting rule for improved cell utilization. The architecture demonstrates near optimal performance on a non-deterministic (stochastic) partially observable sequence learning task consisting of high-Markov-order sequences of MNIST digits. The model also learns the sequences faster and more completely than an LSTM and offer several possible explanations why the LSTM architecture might struggle with the partially observable sequence structure in this task. The research shows that challenging tasks such as language modelling may be possible using less memory intensive, biologically plausible training regimes

Summary

The above examples show that AI researchers can use ideas from neuroscience to build new technology, and neuroscientists can learn from the behaviour of artificial agents to better interpret biological brains. This synergy will likely accelerate thanks to recent advances, such as optogenetics, that allow us to precisely measure and manipulate brain activity, yielding vast quantities of data that can be analysed with tools from machine learning.

As mentioned earlier, we are still years away from building artificial general intelligence, machines that can solve problems as efficiently as humans. It is our belief that the path to create General AI, the human brain is the best guide. We concur with Dicken (2020) that Advances in neuroscience, the study of nervous systems, provide important insights into how the brain works, a key component for developing better AI systems. Conversely, advance in AI will help to drive neuroscience forward and further unlock the secrets of the brain. convolutional neural networks (CNN), one of the key contributors to recent advances in artificial intelligence, are largely inspired by neuroscience research on the visual cortex. At the same time, neuroscientist leverage AI algorithms to study millions of signals from the brain and find patterns. The two should be studied together because they are closely related,

FUTURE RESEARCH

For future research, it is our belief that It is important to distil intelligence into algorithms and compare them to the human brain. This allows us to develop artificial general intelligence and also to better understand what's going on inside our own heads. By focusing on the principles and mathematics that AI and neuroscience share we can help to advance research into neuroscience and AI to achieve new levels of ability for AI and understanding of the natural brain. The need for both fields to come together is now more urgent than before.

However, there are still many things we still do not understand about human intelligence. It is our belief that we can start of taking the work of Hawkins (2021) at Numenta from his paper, 'What Intelligent Machines Need to Learn from the Neocortex,'.

Insights from Neuroscience for Future AI

Hawkins (2017) argues that machines won't become intelligent unless they incorporate certain features of the human brain. He argues that there are three aspects of biological intelligence that are essential, but missing from today's AI. These are: learning by rewiring, sparse representations, and embodiment, which refers to the use of movement to learn about the world.

Learning by Rewiring

According to Hawkins (2017), our brains exhibit some remarkable learning properties. We learn quickly. Fast, incremental, and continuous learning are essential ingredients that enable intelligent systems to adapt to a changing world. Hawkins (2017) suggested that the neuron is responsible for learning, and the complexities of real neurons are what make it a powerful learning machine. According to Hawkins (2017), most learning results from growing new synapses between cells—by "rewiring" the brain. Up to 40 percent of the synapses on a neuron are replaced with new ones every day. New synapses result in new patterns of connections among neurons, and therefore new memories. Because the branches of a dendrite are mostly independent, when a neuron learns to recognize a new pattern on one of its dendrites, it doesn't interfere with what the neuron has already learned on other dendrites. Although Intelligent machines don't have to model all the complexity of biological neurons, but the capabilities enabled by dendrites and learning by rewiring are essential.

Sparse Representations

Hawkins (2017) argues that brains and computers represent information quite differently. In a computer's memory, all combinations of 1s and 0s are potentially valid, so if you change one bit it will typically result in an entirely different meaning. Brains, on the other hand, use what's called sparse distributed representations, or SDRs. They're called sparse because relatively few neurons are fully active at any given time. According to Hawkins (2017), there are two properties in SDRs. The first is the overlap property, making it easy to see how two things are similar or different in meaning. The second is the union property, which allows the brain to represent multiple ideas simultaneously. The ability of neurons to constantly form unions of SDRs makes them very good at handling uncertainty. Hawkins (2017) argues that these two properties of SDRs are fundamental to understanding, thinking, and planning in the brain. We can't build intelligent machines without embracing SDRs.

Embodiment

The neocortex receives input from the sensory organs. Every time we move our eyes, limbs, or body, the sensory inputs change. This constantly changing input is the primary mechanism the brain uses to learn about the world. According to Hawkins (2017), Learning through movement is the brain's primary means for learning. It will be a central component of all truly intelligent systems. He made an important discovery in his lab at Numenta in 2016. He discovered that in the neocortex, sensory input is processed in a hierarchy of regions. He pointed out that as sensory input passes from one level of the hierarchy to another, more complex features are extracted, until at some point an object can be recognized. Deep-learning networks also use hierarchies, but they often require 100 levels of processing to recognize an image, whereas the neocortex achieves the same result with just four levels. Deep-learning networks also require millions of training patterns, while the neocortex can learn new objects with just a few movements and sensations. Hawkins (2017) suggested that sensorimotor integration occurs in every region of the neocortex. It is not a separate step but an integral part of all sensory processing. Sensorimotor integration is a key part of the "intelligence algorithm" of the neocortex. He claimed he has a theory at Numenta and a model of exactly how neurons do this, one that maps well onto the complex anatomy seen in every neocortical region. According to Hawkins (2017), Sensorimotor integration doesn't occur in a few places in the brain; it is a core principle of brain function, part of the intelligence algorithm. He argues that Intelligent machines also must work this way.

Hawkins and others (2017) believe and argue that the three fundamental attributes of the neocortex—learning by rewiring, sparse distributed representations, and sensorimotor integration—will be cornerstones of machine intelligence.

CONCLUSION

Recent progress in AI has been remarkable. Artificial systems now outperform expert humans at the ancient board game Go, and chess. They can also produce handwriting and translate between multiple languages and we now have driverless cars. Although AI systems are impressive, they are limited because each one is limited in the scope of what it can do. The goal of AI is to build general AI with the ability to think, reason and learn flexibly and rapidly. Doing this requires us to study the human brain. It is a good goal, but we are still a long way from having strong AI. Early AI development was inspired by the way humans seemed to think using decision-making processes and information storage systems. Today AI systems are loosely based on deep neural networks inspired by the way interconnected neurons fire in the brain.

Both neuroscience and AI solve the same central problem—intelligence from different angles, and at different levels of abstraction. In AI, we try to build intelligent systems using the language of machines. In neuroscience, we try to understand the brain and how intelligence works. It is therefore imperative that we should study the two to identify common language between the two fields. Doing so will enable us to create shared interests to accelerate shared theoretical insights and common empirical advances to build artificial general intelligence. Our desire is that by reading this paper, colleagues will be inspired to pursue research in both fields to understand our brains better and build human intelligence AI systems.

REFERENCES

Ahmad, S., Lavin, A., Purdy, S., & Agha, Z. (2017). Unsupervised real-time anomaly detection for streaming data. *Neurocomputing*, *262*, 134–147.

Chance, F. S., Aimone, J. B., & Musuvathy, S. S. (2020). Crossing the cleft: Communication challenges between neuroscience and artificial intelligence. *Frontiers in Computational Neuroscience*, *14*, 39.

Cuffari, B. (2020, December 20). *The Anatomy of the Human Brain*. News-Medical. Retrieved on August 14, 2021 from https://www.news-medical.net/health/The-Anatomy-of-the-Human-Brain.aspx

Dickson, B. (2020). *Neuroscience shows what's right and wrong with AI*. https://bdtechtalks. com/2020/01/20/neuroscience-artificial-intelligence-synergie/

Fan, J., Fang, L., & Wu, J. (2020). From brain science to artificial intelligence. *Engineering*, *6*(3), 248–252.

Fan, S. (2019). *Three Invaluable Ways AI and Neuroscience Are Driving Each Other Forward*. https://singularityhub.com/2019/08/08/three-invaluable-ways-ai-and-neuroscience-are-driving-each-other-forward/

Gordon, J., Rawlinson, D., & Ahmad, S. (2020). Long Distance Relationships Without Time Travel: Boosting the Performance of a Sparse Predictive Autoencoder in Sequence Modeling. In F. P. Schilling & T. Stadelmann (Eds.), Lecture Notes in Computer Science: Vol. 12294. Artificial Neural Networks in Pattern Recognition. ANNPR 2020. Springer. https://doi.org/10.1007/978-3-030-58309-5_4

Hassabis, D., Kumaran, D., Summerfield, C., & Botvinick, M. (2017). Neuroscience-Inspired Artificial Intelligence. *Neuron*, *95*(2), 245–258.

Hassabis, D., Summerfield, C., & Botvinick, M. (2017). *AI and Neuroscience: A virtuous circle*. https://deepmind.com/blog/article/ai-and-neuroscience-virtuous-circle

Hawkins, J. (2017). *What Intelligent Machines Need to Learn From the Neocortex*. https://spectrum. ieee.org/what-intelligent-machines-need-to-learn-from-the-neocortex

Hawkins, J. (2017). *What Intelligent Machines Need to Learn From the Neocortex*. https://spectrum. ieee.org/what-intelligent-machines-need-to-learn-from-the-neocortex

Hawkins, J. (2021). *A thousand brains: A new theory of intelligence* (1st ed.). Basic Books.

Hawkins & Maver. (2019). *Numenta, The Thousand Brains Theory of Intelligence*. https://numenta.com/ blog/2019/01/16/the-thousand-brains-theory-of-intelligence

Heaven. (2021). *We'll never have true AI without first understanding the brain*. https://www.technologyreview.com/2021/03/03/1020247/artificial-intelligence-brain-neuroscience-jeff-hawkins/

Hole, K. J., & Ahmad, S. (2021). *A thousand brains: toward biologically constrained AI*. doi:10.1007/ s42452-021-04715-0

Jing, H. (2020). *Fascinating Relationship between AI and Neuroscience: How they inspire & advance together to benefit each other.* https://towardsdatascience.com/the-fascinating-relationship-between-ai-and-neuroscience-89189218bb05

Jing, H. (2020). *Fascinating Relationship between AI and Neuroscience: How they inspire & advance together to benefit each other.* https://towardsdatascience.com/the-fascinating-relationship-between-ai-and-neuroscience-89189218bb05

Joshi, N. (2021). *Why Neuroscience and AI Need Each Other.* https://www.allerin.com/blog/why-neuroscience-and-ai-need-each-other

Joshi, N. (2021). *Why Neuroscience and AI Need Each Other.* https://www.allerin.com/blog/why-neuroscience-and-ai-need-each-other

Leadholm, Lewis, & Ahmad. (2021). *Grid Cell Path Integration For Movement-Based Visual Object Recognition.* arXiv preprint arXiv:2102.09076.

Lee. (2019). *How neuroscience enables better Artificial Intelligence design.* https://medium.com/swlh/how-neuroscience-enables-better-artificial-intelligence-design-5d254098470b

Legg & Hutter. (2007). A collection of definitions of intelligence. *Frontiers in Artificial Intelligence and Applications, 157,* 17.

Lungarella, M., Bongard, J., & Pfeifer, R. (Eds.). (2007). *What can Artificial Intelligence get from Neuroscience?* Springer-Verlag.

Miller, G. A. (2003). The cognitive revolution: A historical perspective. *Trends in Cognitive Sciences, 7*(3), 141–144. doi:10.1016/S1364-6613(03)00029-9 PMID:12639696

Mok. (2017). *Why Artificial Intelligence Needs Neuroscience for Inspiration.* Academic Press.

Peres, R. S., Jia, X., Lee, J., Sun, K., Colombo, A. W., & Barata, J. (2020). Industrial artificial intelligence in industry 4.0-systematic review, challenges and outlook. *IEEE Access: Practical Innovations, Open Solutions, 8,* 220121–220139. doi:10.1109/ACCESS.2020.3042874

Physiopedia. (2021). *Cerebral Cortex.* https://www.physio-pedia.com/Cerebral_Cortex

Russell, S., & Norvig, P. (2020). *Artificial intelligence: A modern approach* (4th ed.). Pearson.

Silva. (2019). *Neuroscience and artificial intelligence can help improve each other.* https://theconversation.com/neuroscience-and-artificial-intelligence-can-help-improve-each-other-110869

Chapter 10
Applications of the Bees Algorithm:
Nature–Inspired Optimisation of Manufacturing Processes

Marco Castellani
University of Birmingham, UK

Luca Baronti
University of Birmingham, UK

Yuanjun Laili
Beihang University, China

Duc Truong Pham
🆔 https://orcid.org/0000-0003-3148-2404
University of Birmingham, UK

ABSTRACT

The bees algorithm is a popular intelligent optimisation algorithm inspired by the foraging behaviour of honeybees. This chapter describes the application of two combinatorial variants of the bees algorithm to the optimisation of manufacturing processes. The first variant was created for minimisation of printed circuit board assembly times, whilst the second was devised for fast replanning of robotic disassembly of mechanical parts. In both cases, the bees-inspired paradigm proved effective in efficiently solving complex engineering optimisation problems. Compared to a number of state-of-the-art combinatorial optimisation algorithms, the bees algorithm excelled in terms of efficiency of the solutions.

DOI: 10.4018/978-1-7998-8686-0.ch010

INTRODUCTION

In today's highly competitive and globalised market, automation is a common solution to reduce labour costs and improve the efficiency and consistency of manufacturing processes (Frohm et al. 2006). A crucial step in the manufacturing of products is the assembly of the individual components and sub-components into the finished product. Assembly operations in today's manufacturing processes account for 20%-50% of the whole production time, and more than 40% of the whole production costs (Boothroyd, 1994). One of the main challenges in the automation of assembly operations is the optimisation of the sequence of placement of the components, in order to minimise the total manufacturing time. Efficient assembly operations contribute to increasing plant throughput and reducing machine hours.

Assembly sequence optimisation is typically an NP-complete combinatorial problem ((Rashid et al. 2012; Han et al. 2021), where the computational time-complexity using any known solver grows in non-polynomial fashion with the number of elements (i.e. components to assemble). For any non-trivial assembly problem, a brute force evaluation of all possible assembly sequences is not feasible, and heuristic search methods must be used.

Of even greater complexity is the problem of disassembling End-of-Life (EoL) products. Disassembly is a critical operation in closed-loop supply chain since it is a prerequisite for recycling, remanufacturing and reusing of EoL products and components (Guo et al. 2020). It is nowadays gaining increasing importance due to the need of making more efficient use of limited natural resources, and reduce environmental pollution. In many ways, disassembly is more challenging than assembly to automate, due to variability in the condition of the components (Vongbunyong et al. 2015). Unlike the assembly of new or remanufactured products, which is deterministic because the components to be assembled are of known geometries, dimensions and states, disassembly is stochastic as has to contend with used products of uncertain shapes, sizes and conditions. For example, components might be worn-out, corroded, or deformed, they might have been intentionally modified or replaced with equivalents of a different maker, or they might be altogether missing. Due to these uncertainties, the sequence of disassembly operations can not be pre-set and fixed as it is customary for assembly, and has to be adapted to the state of each individual product.

In this chapter, two case studies involving the assembly and disassembly of products will be examined, and tackled using the popular Bees Algorithm metaheuristics (Pham et al. 2006a; Pham and Castellani 2009). The Bees Algorithm takes inspiration from the collective problem-solving abilities of biological bees (*apis mellifera*) to provide solution to complex search problems. It mimics the foraging behaviour of bee colonies to scout the space of candidate solutions, and perform parallel local searches in the most promising regions. The Bees Algorithm has found application in several manufacturing fields involving the solution of NP-hard optimisation problems such as preliminary design (Pham et al. 2007a), job scheduling for a machine (Pham et al. 2007b), quality control (Pham et al. 2006b), control of robotic manipulators (Fahmy et al. 2012), manufacturing cell formation (Pham et al. 2007c), and assembly line balancing (Baykasoglu et al. 2009).

The first case study considered is Printed Circuit Board (PCB) assembly sequence optimisation. PCB manufacturing is a wide and continuously growing market, due to the widespread application of PCBs in consumer electronics devices and all electronics and electrical equipment. The task of PCB assembly consists of placing electronic components (resistors, capacitors, transistors) of various shapes and sizes at specific locations on the bare board. PCB assembly is customarily automated using various kinds of surface mount technology (SMT) placement machines. These machines are designed for fast placement of components, and are able of handling high and rapid production demands. Despite the speed of SMT placement machines, assembly is currently one of the most time consuming steps in the manufacturing of PCB components. For this task, the original formulation of the Bees Algorithm has been modified to deal with the specific requirements of PCB assembly sequence optimisation (Castellani et al. 2019).

The second case study considered is robotic disassembly re-planning. State-of-the-art techniques assume that the relationships between the components of a product are known and fixed, typically extracted from its original CAD model (Gungor and Gupta, 1998; Hui et al. 2008; Tao et al. 2018; Tseng et al. 2018). They follow a series of predetermined operations, and as such they have limited flexibility to cope with real life EoL conditions. A two-pointer detection strategy and a modified ('*super-fast*') Bees Algorithm were developed to identify detachable elements in a partially disassembled product, and adjust disassembly sequences and directions when components interlock (Laili et al. 2019).

The objective of this chapter is to present the above two modified versions **of the** Bees Algorithm **respectively for assembly and disassembly operations**, their application to the two selected manufacturing case studies, and test the performance of the proposed bees inspired methods against that of **various** state-of-the-art intelligent optimisation techniques.

BACKGROUND

In this section, the two manufacturing case studies of PCB assembly sequence optimisation and robotic disassembly re-planning are formalised, and the relevant literature is discussed.

Printed Circuit Board Assembly Sequence Optimisation – The Problem

In this study, the moving board with time delay (MBTD) assembly machine (Figure 1) is used for placing the through-hole and surface-mount components in sequence onto the PCB (Pham et at. 2007d). Henceforth, the number of components to be placed onto the board will be denoted as N. The MBTD machine comprises three moving parts:

- A carrier that moves an array of R feeders along one axis (y), and brings the feeder with the required component to the pre-set pick-up location for assembly.
- A fixed-axis multi-head rotating turret. The turret picks up the required component from the aligned feeder with one head, whilst concurrently placing another component onto the PCB board with one of the other head(s). It then rotates along the z axis to pick up and deploy new components.
- A moving table which holds the PCB. The table moves in the x–y plane to align the desired placement location on the PCB to the turret head that is releasing the component, according to the assembly sequence.

Component pick-up and placement take place at the same time as the feeder carrier and PCB have reached their designated positions, and the turret has completed indexing the appropriate pick-up and placement heads (Ayob et al. 2002). To place components of different kind on the board, the multiple feeders, the multi-head turret pick-and-place system, and the assembly table of the MBTD machine must be synchronised.

Before a pick-up and place operation can take place, all three moving parts of the MBTD machine (PCB, feeders, and turret) must have completed their movement. Therefore, the placement speed of the machine is given by the most time-consuming of the three movements. Whilst the turret indexing speed is fixed, the speed of the other two movements depends on the placement sequence of the components (table alignment speed) and the position of the various types of components on the feeders (feeder carrier alignment speed). That is, the following two combinatorial optimisation problems need to be solved concurrently (Ho and Ji, 2005):

- The placement sequence of the board components needs to be optimised
- The arrangement of the feeders with the various types of components on the carrier needs to be optimised

The first problem was shown to be akin to the travelling salesman problem, the second to the quadratic assignment problem (Khoo and Ng, 1998; Alkaya and Duman, 2015).

Figure 1. PCB assembly machine of the mbtd type with 2 rotary turret heads, 10 feeder slots and a moveable assembly table
Source: (Otri, 2016)

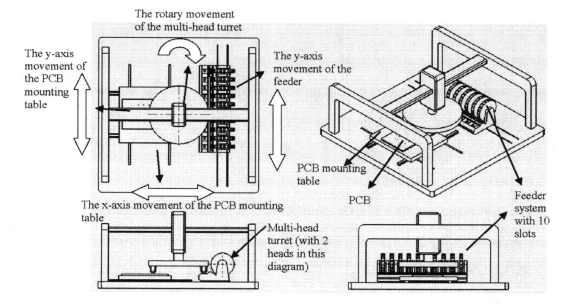

Placement sequence optimisation is essentially a component sequencing problem. Hereafter, the sequence in which the electronic components are placed on the board will be denoted as $C= \{c_1, c_2, \ldots, c_N\}$, where c_i is the ith component that is placed. Each c_i is instantiated to a different integer number (label) $p \in [1, N]$, representing the pth location on the board where the component has to be placed. For example, a very simple PCB has only four components ($N=4$): a placement sequence $C= \{3,2,4,1\}$ indicates that the first component to be placed is the one which needs to be assembled at position 3 on the PCB, the second is the one which needs to be assembled at position 2, and so forth. The goal of the optimisation effort is to minimise the movements of the table, and thus placement time.

An arrangement R feeders will be henceforth indicated as a vector $F = \{f_1, f_2, \ldots, f_R\}$, where f_j is the jth feeder in the sequence. Each feeder f_j is instantiated to a different integer number (label) $r \in [1,R]$, representing the rth type of component (each feeder contains components of only one type). For example, an arrangement of three feeders $F = \{3,2,1\}$ ($R=3$) indicates that the first feeder in the array contains components of type 3, the second feeder components of type 2, and the third feeder components of type 1,

The goal of the arrangement effort is to minimise the movements of the feeder carrier, and hence component pick-up time.

The total PCB assembly time T_{Total} is defined as follows (Ho and Ji, 2006):

$$T_{Total} = \sum_{i=1}^{N+\frac{h}{2}} T_i, \tag{1}$$

where N is the number of components to be placed onto the PCB, h is the number of assembly heads on the moving turret, and T_i is the time required to place component c_i. T_i depends on three terms, each one related to a different operation of the MBTD machine. The largest of the three terms determines T_i. That is:

$$T_i = max\left[t_1\left(c_{i-1}, c_i\right), t_2\left(f_{i+\frac{h}{2}-1}, f_{i+\frac{h}{2}} \right), t_3 \right]. \tag{2}$$

The first term $t_1\left(c_{i-1}, c_i\right)$ is the time needed to move the table from the location where component c_{i-1} is placed on the PCB, to the fixed location where component $c_i(x_i, y_i)$ is placed. This time is given by the Chebyshev metric (Ho and Ji, 2006):

$$t_1\left(c_{i-1}, c_i\right) = max\left(\frac{x_{i-1} - x_i}{v_x}, \frac{y_{i-1} - y_i}{v_y} \right), \tag{3}$$

where $v_f = (v_x, v_y)$ is the velocity of the table in the x–y plane. In essence, the Chebyshev metric considers the x and y movements of the table as independent, and the slowest determines the total movement time. This metric is accurate when the table is controlled by two motors, one for each axis. In this study, the starting position c_0 of the table is set at the origin (0,0) of the Cartesian frame of reference, and the maximum v_x and v_y velocities along the two axes are fixed to $60 \bullet 10^{-3} ms^{-1}$.

The second term $t_2\left(f_{i+\frac{h}{2}-1}, f_{i+\frac{h}{2}} \right)$ accounts for the time needed to move the feeder array from the slot where component $c_{i+\frac{h}{2}-1}$ is picked up, to the slot where component $c_{i+\frac{h}{2}}$ is **to be** picked up. The distance between feeders is calculated using the Euclidean metric (Ho and Ji, 2006).

$$t_2\left(f_i, f_j\right) = \frac{\sqrt{\left(x_i^f - x_j^f\right)^2 + \left(y_i^f - y_j^f\right)^2}}{v_f}, \tag{4}$$

where $\left(x_i^f, y_i^f\right)$ are the Cartesian coordinates of feeder f_i. In this study, the feeders are aligned in a straight line along the y axis (Figure 1) and separated by a distance of 15 mm. Consequently, there will be no displacement along the x axis, and Equation 4 can be simplified:

$$t_2\left(f_i, f_j\right) = \frac{\left|y_i^f - y_j^f\right|}{v_f}. \tag{5}$$

The third term t_3 is the turret assembly heads indexing time. Each step, the assembly heads are indexed by one position, always in the same direction, and the operation takes 0.25 seconds.

PCB assembly time optimisation requires the minimisation of a function g such as $T_{Total} = g(C,F)$. The function $g(C,F)$ expresses the dependence of the total assembly time (Equation 1) on the combinatorial arrangement of the elements of C and F. Formally, the problem can be expressed as the optimisation of a long vector of $N+R$ heterogeneous variables $V = \{C, F\} = \{c_1, c_2, \ldots, c_N, f_1, f_2, \ldots, f_R\}$, formed by concatenating the two sequences of component placements (C) and feeder positions (F). The constraints on the solutions are that both sequences C and F contain all the N components (all components need to be placed) and R feeders (all feeders need to be present), and only one instance of component (no component can be placed twice and there can not be two feeders with identical components).

Printed Circuit Board Assembly Sequence Optimisation – State-of-the-Art

Various intelligent optimisation methods have been applied to the PCB assembly time minimization problem, including evolutionary algorithms (Ong and Khoo, 1999; Ho and Ji, 2005), swarm optimisation (Hsu, 2016 and 2020), minimal spanning trees (Leipälä and Nevalainen, 1989), integer programming (Li and Yoon, 2017), and combinations of different optimisation algorithms (Alkaya and Duman, 2015; Luo et al. 2017; Han and Seo, 2017). A review of intelligent optimisation techniques for the general problem of assembly line planning was made by Rashid et al (2012).

Evolutionary algorithms (EAs, Fogel, 2006) have their strong points in their simple implementation and global outlook, which helps them to avoid local minima of fitness. Typically, they are customised to combinatorial optimisation via bespoke genetic operators of crossover and mutation, which respect the constraints of the problem (e.g. all components need to be placed, no component can be placed twice). This approach was followed by both Ong and Khoo (1999) and Ho and Ji (2005), who combined problem-specific crossover and mutation operators with the standard mutation inversion operator. Similarly to EAs, Swarm Intelligence (SI, Bonabeau et al. 1999) is characterised by a global search approach and ease of implementation. The first application of SI to the PCB assembly time minimization problem was Pham's et al's (2007a) implementation of the Bees Algorithm. Tested on a benchmark PCB assembly task, the Bees Algorithm obtained a significant reduction in assembly time compared to various EAs (Pham, et al. 2007d). Ang et al. (2009) reported good results on the same task from hybridisation of the Bees Algorithm with various operators created from Theory of Inventive Problem Solving (TRIZ) principles (Sheng and Kok-Soo, 2010). However, the TRIZ-enhanced Bees Algorithm used some form of population seeding, which brought the initial population already close to the optimum. Castellani et al. (2019) enhanced the standard formulation of the Bees Algorithm with five new bespoke search operators specific to the PCB assembly problem. Hsu proposed two alternative SI based PCB assembly optimisers respectively using Particle Swarm Optimisation (Hsu, 2016) and the Firefly Algorithm (Hsu, 2020). Alkaya and Duman (2015) used the SI Artificial Bee Colony optimisation (Karaboga 2007) algorithm for feeder layout optimisation, and a more traditional Simulated Annealing optimiser (Van Laarhoven and Aarts, 1987) for component placement search. Griffiths et al. (2021) hybridized a Genetic Algorithm (GA) and the Bat Algorithm to optimise feeder arrangement and placement sequence in PCB assembly operations. Likewise, Mumtaz et al. (2020) hybridised the Spider Monkey Optimisation algorithm with additional GA operators, and used this new algorithm for PCB component allocation and placement sequence optimisation.

In this study, the version of the Bees Algorithm proposed by Castellani et al. (2019) will be used for optimisation of both the feeder arrangement and component placement sequence.

Robotic Disassembly: The Problem

One of the main goals of the disassembly of End-of-Life (EoL) manufactured products is the retrieval of reusable parts and materials with the purpose of making a more efficient use of limited natural resources (Ilgin and Gupta 2010; Lambert 2003). In contrast with the case of assembly of new products, the disassembly of EoL components is characterised by a high level of uncertainty about the components condition (Riggs et al. 2015). Structure degradation, corrosion and missing parts are some of the factors that need to be considered in the design of the disassembly strategy. The disassembly literature usually focuses on three broad topics. The first topic is disassembly scheduling, that is the problem of determining the quantity and timing of the dismantling of components with respect to the demand for their parts. This is often the first stage of the process (Kim and Paul Xirouchakis 2010). The second topic is disassembly sequencing, that is the problem of identifying the optimal dismantling order of the parts (Kang and Xirouchakis 2006), giving priority to hazardous components (Ozceylan et al. 2019). The third topic is disassembly line balancing, that is the problem of finding the dismantling order which minimises the number of required workstations and their idle times. This study focuses on the sequencing problem for automatic disassembly.

A number of robotic systems able to automatically take apart EoL products have been proposed in Li's et al.'s (2018). For the sequencing problem, solutions have been devised to identify relationships such as disassembly interference and precedence between the components of products (De Mello and Sanderson 1990; Jin et al. 2013; Güngör and Gupta 2001), whilst several studies focused on the disassembly sequencing problem itself (Tao et al. 2018; Zhu et al. 2013; Tseng et al. 2018; Friedrich et al. 2017; Vongbunyong et al. 2015). These studies were based on the two assumptions that (i) the relationships between the parts are known and do not change, and (ii) the physical disassembly process can either be executed without interruptions or can recover from one. Unfortunately, given the variability in the conditions of EOL products, these conditions do not always apply, and adaptation (replanning) might be needed.

Despite some adaptive approaches have been proposed (ElSayed et al. 2012; Zussman and M. Zhou 1999; Tripathi et al. 2009), most adaptive techniques like Particle Swarm Optimisation (PSO) and GAs are not suitable for online applications, due to their computational overheads and iterative nature.

248

Within the context of disassembly sequencing, this work addresses the replanning problem with a focus on real-time operations.

Robotic Disassembly: State of the Art

A solution for an automatic disassembly problem generally includes a component removal sequence plan and a robot trajectory plan (Gonnuru et al. 2013). Since the latter plan depends on the former, this study will focus on disassembly sequencing.

The first step in finding a disassembly sequence is to establish a suitable representation for the product and its parts. A common solution to this problem is to use three matrices: an interference matrix, a contact matrix, and a connection matrix. This practice replicates the procedure used in many early-stage disassembly planning applications (Dini and Santochi 1992), such as the disassembly precedence description introduced by González and Adenso-Díaz (2006), Ong's et al.'s study on subassembly detection (Ong and Wong 1999), and Huang's et al.'s disassembly matrix (Y. M. Huang and C.-T. Huang 2002). Other authors instead devised different representation matrices which suited their disassembly representations. For example, Tao et al. (2018) used four matrices to describe constraints and feasible directions for fasteners and components. An adjacent matrix has been used by Afsharzadeh (2016) to direct the greedy search of a disassembly sequence. Finally, an expanded matrix was used by Behdad et al. (2012) to include disassembly tools and operational directions.

An alternative representation that doesn't use a matricial form involves the use of AND/OR graphs (Gungor and Gupta 1998). In this representation, the vertices are the components and the edges are the disassembly operations. This representation has the advantage of being more intuitive (Dong et al. 2007; B. Yu et al. 2017) and has been expanded (Koc et al. 2009) to integrate all possible disassembly paths in the graph.

In the literature, the inference matrix is most commonly used for disassembly sequencing tasks (Liu et al. 2018; Kheder et al. 2017) whilst graph representation is most commonly used for disassembly line balancing problems (Ren, D. Yu, et al. 2017; Mete et al. 2016).

There are three main categories of disassembly sequence planning problems. Complete disassembly is the task of disassembling all the parts of an object (Tang et al. 2002; Giri and Kanthababu 2015). In contrast, partial disassembly focuses on removing a subset of components, whilst selective disassembly is the task of safely and rapidly removing just a single valuable component (Tao et al. 2018; Z. Zhou et al. 2019). Different approaches can be found in literature (Ghandi and Masehian 2015) to generate effective disassembly sequences, for example graph-based and sampling-based methods. Variants of well-known adaptive metaheuristics have also been devised, like Hui's et al.'s (2008) Genetic Algorithm (GA) to generate a disassembly information graph. Alshibli et al. (2016) hybridised a GA with the Tabu search metaheuristic to solve a disassembly sequencing problem. Other metaheuristics used to solve the disassembly sequencing problem include Rickli's et al.'s (2013) multi-objective GA for partial disassembly, Ghandi's et al.'s (2017) Ant Colony algorithm, and Liu's et al.'s (2018) Bees Algorithm.

Regardless of the strategy used to devise it, even an optimal disassembly plan may not be executable in practice due to the highly variable and uncertain conditions of the product components. The problem of adjusting the plan (i.e. replanning) based on the contingent conditions of the components has been discussed by Gungor et al. (1998). Solutions to this problem include the use of a Petri-net based pre-sorted list of transitions to perform online adjustments of the disassembly sequence, and the use of an optical module to detect detachable components and a GA to determine the new disassembly order

(ElSayed et al. 2012). However, the above re-planning techniques were not designed for recovery from failed operations.

ASSEMBLY AND DISASSEMBLY PLANNING WITH THE bEES ALGORITHM

In this section, the solutions to the two manufacturing case studies of PCB assembly sequence optimisation and robotic disassembly re-planning are proposed. Both solutions are variants of the standard Bees Algorithm (Pham and Castellani 2009), which is briefly outlined in a dedicated subsection.

The Bees Algorithm

The Bees Algorithm (Pham and Castellani, 2009) mimics the behaviour of a colony of honeybees searching for and exploiting multiple food sources (solutions). At start, the algorithm uses a number of software agents (scout bees) to perform an initial random search of the solution space. That is, each scout visits (generates) a random feasible solution and evaluates it.

In the main cycle of the algorithm, each scout recruits a number of new agents (foragers) according to the quality (fitness) of the solution it visited, via a procedure inspired by the waggle dance of biological bees (Seeley, 2009). The role of the foragers is to conduct local exploitative search: that is, to search in the neighbourhood of the solution visited by the scout. Each neighbourhood in the solution space can be thought of as a flower patch in nature, where forager bees are directed by the scouts. If a forager finds a better solution than the scout, that forager will then substitute the scout and 'waggle dance' in the next iteration of the main procedure to recruit new foragers. If no forager landed on a better solution than the scout, the old scout is kept.

In essence, the Bees Algorithm performs a number of simultaneous local searches around the highest quality solutions found by the scouts, looking for solutions of even better quality. When the search in a neighbourhood stops yielding improvements in quality for a given number stlim of iterations, the area is considered exhausted (the local optimum has been found), and the scout is sent to search a new location (is randomly re-initialised). This procedure in Bees Algorithm terminology is called 'site abandonment', and prevents the Bees Algorithm from being trapped into sub-optimal peaks of performance. If the abandoned site contained the best-so-far solution, this solution is saved, and if not bettered by any other local search result, it will become the final result of the optimisation procedure.

The main cycle of the Bees Algorithm is repeated for a given number itr of times. After the last cycle, the best found solution is returned as the final result of the optimisation procedure.

The Printed Circuit Board Assembly Sequence Optimiser

As discussed in the previous section, each candidate solution to the PCB assembly problem comprises two concatenated arrays: one encoding the sequence of component placements and the second encoding the feeder arrangement. A valid feeder arrangement is any of the possible permutations of feeder labels, each label corresponding to a fixed feeder and component type. For example, label $r \in [1,R]$ might indicate that feeder r supplies 100KΩ resistors. The number of labels R in a valid feeder arrangement must be equal to the number of feeders in the assembly machine. A valid placement sequence is also a permutation of labels, each label $p \in [1,N]$ representing a placement position on the PCB. The total number of labels N must be equal to the number of placement positions. The objective of the Bees Algorithm is to optimise the sequence of component placement steps and feeders in order to minimise assembly time. That is, the Bees algorithm is used to solve a minimization problem where fitness= T_{Total}.

The proposed procedure adapts the standard Bees Algorithm described by Pham and Castellani (2009) to the PCB assembly problem. The flowchart of the algorithm is shown in Figure 2, and the individual steps are described below.

Figure 2. Flowchart of the bees algorithm. full details in Castellani et al. (2019)

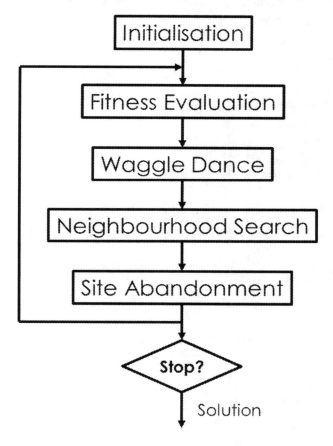

The Printed Circuit Board Assembly Sequence Optimisation Algorithm

At start, n scout bees are randomly distributed with uniform probability in the solution space. That is, n candidate solutions are randomly initialised. The algorithm enters then the main loop (Figure 2), and the assembly time is calculated according to Equation 1 for each candidate solution (feeder arrangement and placement sequence). The $ne \leq n$ scouts that found the solutions of highest fitness (shortest assembly time) are called 'elite bees'. Elite bees recruit the largest number of foragers (nre) for local search, whilst the remaining scouts recruit $nrb \leq nre$ foragers. The foragers 'visit' (generate) solutions similar to those visited by the scout. The solutions visited by the foragers are created using five custom-made operators:

Block Insertion, Single-Point Insertion, 2-Opt, Simple Swap, and Neighbour Swap. These operators are described in the following of the section, they modify the solution found by the scout via random permutations of the feeder arrangement and component placement sequence.

The five custom-made operators were designed to generate only valid instances of feeder arrangements and placement sequences. They are described below for the component placement sequence optimisation problem, and operate in the same way on the feeder sequences. The five operators are applied separately to the two arrays encoding respectively the feeder arrangement and component placement sequence. During one cycle of the main loop, local search is performed either on the feeder arrangement or the component placement sequence of the candidate solutions. That is, feeder arrangement and components placement are optimised in alternate steps. Preliminary tests (not included) indicated that the best results are obtained when one cycle of feeder arrangement optimisation is alternated to five cycles of component placement optimisation.

Figure 3. Block insertion and 2-opt operators (Castellani et al. 2019)

Original sequence :	$\{3, 2, 5, 1, 4, 6\}$
Sequence after removal of section $\{2, 5\}$:	$\{3, 1, 4, 6\}$
Sequence following shift of $\{2, 5\}$:	$\{3, 1, 4, 2, 5, 6\}$

a) Block Insertion operator

Original sequence :	$\{3, 2, 5, 1, 4, 6\}$
Broken-up sequence:	$\{3, 2\} \leftrightarrow \{5, 1, 4, 6\}$
Section 1:	$\{3, 2\}$
Section 2:	$\{5, 1, 4, 6\}$
Section 2 – inverted sub-sequence:	$\{6, 4, 1, 5\}$
New sequence (Section 1 + Section 2):	$\{3, 2, 6, 1, 4, 5\}$

b) 2-Opt Operator

The *Block Insertion* operator acts as follows. Given a placement sequence $\{c_1, c_2, c_3, c_4, c_5, c_6\} = \{3,2,5,1,4,6\}$, it picks two randomly chosen positions (c_1 and c_4), and removes the sequence ($\{c_2, c_3\} = \{2,5\}$) in between. The removed section is then inserted at a randomly selected location within the sequence, in the example of Figure 3 after c_5. The new sequence becomes: $\{c_1, c_2, c_3, c_4, c_5, c_6\} = \{3,1,4,2,5,6\}$. The effect is that a group of placement operations is moved earlier or later in the overall sequence (Castellani et al. 2019). The action of this operator is described in Figure 3.

The *Single-Point Insertion* operator acts like the block insertion operator, but is limited to one single placement operation instead of a sequence. Given the sequence $\{c_1,c_2,c_3,c_4,c_5,c_6\}= \{3,2,5,1,4,6\}$, the single-point insertion operator takes one random element (e.g. $c_3=5$) and moves it at a randomly selected new position (e.g. after $c_5=4$). The new sequence becomes $\{3,2,1,4,5,6\}$.

The 2-Opt operator randomly splits a solution into two sections. The component placement sequence in one of the sections is reversed, and the two sections are then rejoined. Given the placement sequence $\{c_1,c_2,c_3,c_4,c_5,c_6\}= \{3,2,5,1,4,6\}$ used in the previous examples, let's assume the 2-Opt operator breaks it into two sections: $\{3,2\}$ and $\{5,1,4,6\}$. The second section has its placement sub-sequence inverted ($\{6,4,1,5\}$), and is then re-joined to the first to form the new sequence ($\{3,2,6,1,4,5\}$). This operator effectively performs an edge exchange operation (Lin and Kernighan, 1973). Its action is described in Figure 3.

The *Simple Swap* operator takes two random components in the sequence, and swaps their position (Lin and Kernighan, 1973). For example, given the sequence $\{c_1,c_2,c_3,c_4,c_5,c_6\}= \{3,2,5,1,4,6\}$ and two randomly picked loci $c_3=5$ and $c_5=4$, the order of placement of components 5 and 4 is swapped. The new sequence becomes $\{3,2,4,1,5,6\}$.

Finally, the *Neighbour Swap* operator randomly selects two neighbouring elements in the placement sequence, and exchanges their position. For example, given the sequence $\{c_1,c_2,c_3,c_4,c_5,c_6\}= \{3,2,5,1,4,6\}$ and two randomly picked loci $c_3=5$ and $c_4=1$, the order of placement of components 5 and 1 is swapped. The new sequence becomes $\{3,2,1,5,4,6\}$. The action of this operator is similar to the Simple Swap operator, but is more localised.

The Robotic Disassembly System

Given a product to disassemble, the first step is to define a representation of its components and their relationships. In this work, it was decided to adopt the interference matrix, since it allows including information on how components block one another (i.e. the constraints of the problem). Each element I_{ij} of the matrix is a multi-dimensional binary vector, where each vector dimension I_{ijd} indicates whether component j constrains the movement of component i along a fixed direction d. If component j obstructs the movement of component i along direction d, $I_{ijd}=1$, otherwise $I_{ijd}=0$. In this context, both contact and geometrical obstructions qualify as interferences. Each element of the interference matrix represents the possible obstruction in one of the four $(x\text{-},x+,y\text{-},y+)$ directions for a 2D model, or six $(x\text{-},x+,y\text{-},y+,z\text{-},z+)$ directions for a 3D model. An example of an interference matrix (2D model) is shown in Figure 4.

Using the interference matrix, a plan including the sequence of components and their disassembly directions can be generated. A common planning approach involves the use of the OR operator to check whether a component is freely detachable along a given direction. In Fig 1, the last column shows for each component (row) the results of the OR operation for each direction. For example, component C1 is blocked in all four directions, since at least one other component blocks its movement in every direction. Component F1 instead can be moved in the third dimension (direction y-).

Once unobstructed components have been identified, they are removed and the interference matrix is updated. The process iterated until complete disassembly (Y. M. Huang and C.-T. Huang 2002; Liu et al. 2018). The main limitation of this approach is its inability to deal with interlocked components where only subassemblies are detachable. This problem can be overcome by replacing the OR operator with the SUM operator, which adds all the elements (vectors) of the interference matrix in a row. The SUM operator is used to identify interference loops via the two-pointer algorithm. These loops indicate the presence of a subassembly (Ong and Wong 1999). For more details on the two-pointer algorithm, the reader is referred to Laili's et al.'s (2019) formulation.

The Ternary Bees Algorithm for Disassembly Re-Planning

The goal of disassembly re-planning is to identify an alternative disassembly sequence for the yet assembled components, when the original sequence is not viable. Alternative disassembly plans are evaluated on their execution time, which includes all the physical activities involved in the actual disassembly of the components (e.g. robotic arm movement, fastener removal, extra lubrication, etc.). The Ternary Bees Algorithm (TBA) approach (Laili et al. 2019) involves the use of three individuals (bees).

Figure 4. Example of product to be disassembled and its interference matrix (Laili et al, 2019)

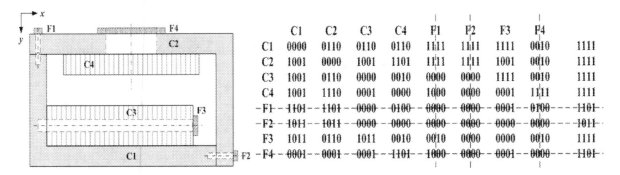

The solutions found by the three bees are modified by three different search operators: the local search operator, the evolutionary operator, and the global search operator. At every iteration of the procedure, each operator modifies one single solution. The local search operator performs a greedy search between parts that can be safely swappable in the sequence. The evolutionary operator is modelled on the recombination operator used in EAs, and performs directional changes in the solutions. This operator uses a modified version of Partially Matched Crossover (Gao et al. 2010), where one parent is the solution - among the three - of middle score, whilst the other is randomly selected among the best and worst solutions. Finally, a global operator is used to replace the worst solution with another solution randomly selected among the viable ones. Similarly to the standard Bees Algorithm a site abandonment procedure is used, and solutions that are not improved in the latest iterations are discarded and replaced with new random solutions.

SOLUTIONS AND RECOMMENDATIONS

In this section, the experimental results obtained using the two implementations of the Bees Algorithm are discussed.

Printed Circuit Board Assembly Sequence Optimisation – Experimental Results

The modified Bees Algorithm was tested on the moving board with time delay (MBTD) benchmark assembly problem described by Leu et al. (1993). The benchmark requires the placement at given positions on the PCB of 50 components. The components are to be picked up from 10 feeders, each feeder containing a different type of component. The coordinates of the component placement positions on the PCB and the specifications of the assembly machine (speed of movement of the table, assembly heads and indexing time of the turret) are described in Leu et al. (1993), and summarised in Table 1.

The parameters of the Bees Algorithm were optimised by trial and error and are given in Table 2. A total of 100 independent runs of the algorithm were executed, and the five-number summary of the results is presented in Table 3. The 100 alignment times are all within a very narrow window of about 2 seconds, showing the consistency of the proposed algorithm. The best solution (vectors F and C) is shown in Figure 5.

Figure 5. Optimal solution (23.46 s assembly time). c1→c50 is the component placement sequence, f1→f10 the feeder arrangement

$c1 \rightarrow c10$	6	1	2	8	3	9	16	21	26	33
$c11 \rightarrow c20$	38	25	30	46	45	44	29	37	43	36
$c21 \rightarrow c30$	41	42	35	28	23	14	7	12	18	13
$c31 \rightarrow c40$	19	24	20	15	4	10	5	11	22	27
$c41 \rightarrow c50$	34	40	50	49	48	47	39	32	31	17
$f1 \rightarrow f10$	10	4	1	6	5	2	3	9	8	7

Table 1. The parameters of the MBTD assembly machine (Leu et al. 1993)

Parameter	Value
Number of components	50
Number of feeders	10
Number of turret heads	2
Indexing time of turret	0.25s/index
Average PCB mounting table speed	60mm/s
Average feeder system speed	60mm/s
Distance between feeders	15mm

Table 2. The parameters of the bees algorithm for the MBTD problem

Bees Algorithm parameter	Symbol	Value
Total colony size	N	2000
Number of elite sites	ne	4
Number of recruited bees for elite sites	nre	300
Number of best (non elite) sites	$nb\text{-}ne$	8
Number of recruited bees for non elite sites	nrb	100
Stagnation limit	$stlim$	100
Number of iterations	itr	3000

Table 3. Optimisation results for the MBTD benchmark: five-number summary of 100 statistically independent trials. The statistics of the assembly times are given in seconds.

Statistics	Value (s)
Minimum	23.46
First quartile	24.71
Median (second quartile)	24.96
Third quartile	25.13
Maximum	25.63

To relate the results obtained by the Bees Algorithm with the state-of-the-art in the literature, the best solutions obtained in seven studies which used the same PCB assembly benchmark are shown in Table 4. They are compared with the best and average results obtained using the Bees Algorithm. The comparison includes various EAs (Fogel, 2006) such as genetic algorithms (GAs) and evolutionary programming (EP), different versions of the Bees Algorithm (BBA, cBA), and hybrid procedures such as an hybrid

GA (HGA) and BBA+TRIZ. Some of these algorithms used a seeding procedure which simplified the optimisation task. The comparison shows that the proposed version of the Bees Algorithm outperformed all the algorithms that did not use a seeding procedure, and was competitive with algorithms that used a seeding procedure. The overall best assembly time (23.46 s) was found by the proposed method.

Unfortunately, the information on the statistical analysis of the solutions is missing for most of the literature reported in Table 4. In particular, it is not known whether the figures reported in the table are the expected values of the distribution of results, or the best results of several optimisation trials (and hence potential outliers to said distribution). Also, the seeding procedure brought several algorithms (Ho and Ji, 2007, Pham et al. 2009, Ang et al. 2013) already near to the optimum before the start of the optimisation process (see third row of Table 4). In these cases, it is difficult to distinguish the merits of the optimisation technique from those of the seeding procedure.

Table 4. MBTD benchmark: comparison between the results obtained using the proposed customised Bees Algorithm (cBA) and the state-of-the-art in the literature. The statistics of the assembly times are given in seconds. Algorithms using the seeding procedure started the search from noticeably better (lower average assembly times) initial solutions.

Optimisation technique	GA	EP	GA	HGA	BBA	BBA + seeding	BBA + TRIZ	cBA
Source	Leu et al. 1993	Nelson & Wille, 1995	Ong & Tan, 2002	Ho & Ji, 2006	Pham et at. 2007d	Pham et at. 2007d	Ang et al. 2013	
Initial solution	70	n/a	60	28.83*	54.59	29*	35.5*	71.08
Best solution	51.5	36	26.9	25.5	25.92	24.08	23.58	23.46
Average solution	n/a	n/a	n/a	n/a	n/a	n/a	n/a	24.96
* A seeding procedure was used								

It is also difficult to compare the time complexity of the algorithms compared in Table 4. In general, the authors reported only the number of solutions sampled by the main routine, and not by the whole optimisation procedure (possibly including the seeding subroutine). The lack of details on the statistical distribution of the results makes it also impossible to know whether the reported sampling was a reliable estimate of the average, or the result of one lucky run of the algorithm. For these reasons, the number of fitness evaluations was not compared in Table 4.

For the proposed Bees Algorithm the total number of fitness evaluations executed in one full optimisation trial is equal to the bee colony size (n=2000, Table 2) times the duration of the algorithm (itr=3000 optimisation cycles, Table 2), namely $6 \cdot 10^6$ evaluations. The best solution obtained by Ang et al. (2013) corresponded to an assembly time of 23.58 s, slightly inferior to the best solution found by the proposed Bees Algorithm (23.46 s assembly time). However, Ang's et al's (2013) TRIZ-enhanced Bees Algorithm sampled nearly $12 \cdot 10^6$ candidate solutions during the optimisation process, plus an additional $11 \cdot 10^6$ solutions for the seeding procedure. Thus, it can be concluded that the proposed version of the Bees Algorithm is able to find top quality solutions at a modest computational cost.

Robotic Disassembly Re-Planning – Experimental Results

The two-pointer detection strategy and the TBA were evaluated on three products; the first is shown in Figure 4, the other two in Figure 6. Whilst the first two products are benchmark test cases, the latter is a real-life engine piston. Four disassembly directions were considered for the first product, whilst for the second (Kheder et al. 2017) and the third product six directions were considered.

Three different condition failures have been considered in the disassembly, which makes for nine different test cases. The two-pointer strategy and the TBA approach were tested, and their search time has been compared to those obtained using two GAs henceforth referred as GA(1) and GA(2), and two Greedy Strategies (GS) henceforth referred as GS(1) and GS(n). The two GSs evaluate alternative solutions starting from the leftmost position in search of the component of minimum cost. In the case of GS(1) only a single search is performed, whilst GS(n) performs several searches - up to 1000 function evaluations - returning the best solution found. Both the GAs are characterised by the same population size (10 candidate solutions) and use the same two genetic manipulation operators: precedence preserve crossover (PPX) (Ren, Zhang, et al. 2018) and a basic mutation operator. They differ by the kind of selection routines used, respectively tournament selection (GA(1)) and the roulette wheel selection procedure (GA(2)). All the tested algorithms use a stopping criterion of 1000 function evaluations.

The above five procedures evaluate the candidate solutions on the total disassembly time of the product. This time includes the basic disassembly time for each component/subassembly (between 10s and 30s depending on the element), the moving time between two gripping points (between 5s and 15 s), and the direction changing time (between 2s and 10s). As the five tested re-planning algorithms are non-deterministic, 20 independent runs are performed for each, and the results averaged.

Figure 6. Representation of two different products used in the tests (Laili et al. 2019)

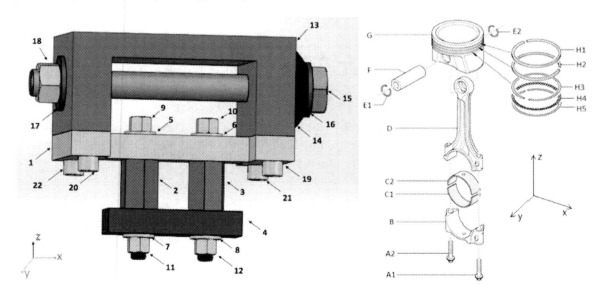

Table 5 reports the completion time of the two-pointer strategy for the nine cases, along with the components that are non-detachable. The sequences found with the two-pointer algorithms for the products B and C are used for testing the disassembly re-planning. The re-planning in the case of product A is trivial, so it is excluded from the tests. The Ternary Bees Algorithm has been tested with the standard colony size of 3 (TBA-3), as well as with modified colony sizes of 2 (TBA-2), 5 (TBA-5) and 10 (TBA-10). As TBA-2 contains only two individuals for three operators, the fittest solution in each iteration is updated by the local search operator, whilst the other solution is modified by one of the other two operators picked at random.

Figure 7 shows the fitness value of the best solution (disassembly time) found by the re-planning algorithms. A Wilcoxon test (Conover, 1999) reported in Table 6 shows that the TBA results are, in most cases, significantly dissimilar to those obtained using the two GS and two GA algorithms. That is, that TBA-3 outperforms the GA and GS algorithms in a statistically significant manner. Table 6 also shows that the differences in performance between TBA-3, and TBA-5 and TBA-10, are not statistically significant. This result indicates there is no improvement of performance when the colony size is increased from 3, to 5, or 10, and only 3 agents (bees) are sufficient to achieve top accuracy.

In summary, the results of the experimental tests indicate that the metaheuristics (GAs and TBAs) provided on average better performances than the greedy algorithms. The performance of TBA-2 is often characterised by a large spread of the results (disassembly times) which indicates a lack of consistency. The other three TBAs (3, 5, and 10) outperform TBA-2 and the two GAs.

The average running time of the TBA algorithm was within 1ms. This result is perfectly compatible with on-line use of the algorithm.

Figure 7. Fitness score (total disassembly time of the product in seconds) of the best solution found by the tested algorithms in re-planning the disassembly for the products in Fig. 4.

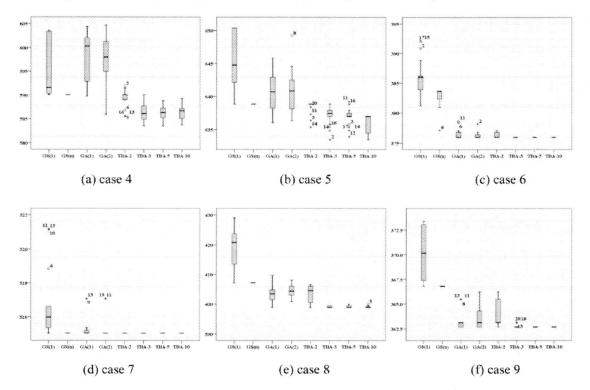

(a) case 4	(b) case 5	(c) case 6
(d) case 7	(e) case 8	(f) case 9

Table 5. Results of the two-pointer strategy for the nine cases on the three tested products.

Product	No.	Non-detachable components	Time (ms)
A	1	6	0.076
	2	8	0.088
	3	7, 8	0.080
B	4	15	0.314
	5	4	0.257
	6	12, 18	0.448
C	7	1	0.169
	8	1, 3	0.180
	9	4, 9	0.184

Table 6. Pair-wise Wicoxon test of differences between the results obtained by the TBA and the comparing algorithms. The p-values indicate the probability that the null hypothesis can be rejected, i.e. that the two distributions are different.

No. of case	TBA-3 vs	GS (1)	GS (n)	GA (1)	GA (2)	TBA-2	TBA-5	TBA-10
4	p	0.000	0.000	0.000	0.000	0.001	0.970	0.809
5	p	0.000	0.000	0.001	0.001	0.000	0.530	0.059
6	p	0.000	0.000	0.017	0.034	0.023	1.000	1.000
7	p	0.000	1.000	0.038	0.083	1.000	1.000	1.000
8	p	0.000	0.000	0.000	0.000	0.000	0.782	0.291
9	p	0.000	0.000	0.005	0.008	0.000	0.083	0.083

FUTURE RESEARCH DIRECTIONS

The role of automation in manufacturing has been constantly expanding in the last 60 years, thanks also to the dramatic increase in the availability and capabilities of machines and sensors. Automation has not only become widespread, but also complexified in terms of operations and processes. An increasing number of applications nowadays require the planning of long sequences of operations, whilst cut-throat global competition makes it essential to optimise these sequences in terms of efficiency and cost. Unfortunately, many sequence planning problems are NP-complete, and can not be solved via exhaustive sampling for non-trivial applications. When the problem is not strictly structured, uncertainties further complicate the planning task, and often require real-time adaptation of the solution.

In this paper, the popular Bees Algorithm metaheuristics was proven to be an effective solution for complex planning problems. Although originally designed to exploit the concurrent search of many artificial scout and forager bees, experimental evidence indicates that a much stripped down version of the algorithm could solve the disassembly replanning problem using only three individuals.

Rather than an exhaustive assessment of the application potential of the Bees Algorithm, this study is meant to be a proof of concept of its applicability. Further tests are necessary to benchmark the capabilities of the TBA against a wider range of replanning problems. For larger or more complex problems than those examined in this study, parallelisation and GPU programming of the Bees Algorithm can be used to obtain real-time performances using large colony sizes.

Both the versions of the Bees Algorithm tested in this study used ad-hoc operators. Further research on efficient search operators for combinatorial optimisation may increase the search capabilities of the Bees Algorithm.

CONCLUSION

This chapter presented two applications of the Bees Algorithm to the problem of planning the optimal sequence of manufacturing operations. In the first case, the Bees Algorithm was used to optimise the placing sequence of components on a PCB. This was a typical manufacturing application, where the problem is fully defined at start and there are no uncertainties. The second case concerned the replanning of the disassembly sequence in a remanufacturing application. It differed from the first for the significant uncertainties on the presence and integrity of the components which characterises remanufacturing applications. Another important difference between the two applications was that the first was an off-line one-off task, where the complexity and hence execution time of the algorithm was not a concern. The second application required a real-time output which constrained the allocation of computational resources. In this latter case, experimental tests showed the Bees Algorithm colony size could be reduced to only three individuals, whilst still obtaining high quality solutions.

ACKNOWLEDGMENT

This research was part of the Autonomous Remanufacturing (AutoReman) project, supported by the UK Engineering and Physical Sciences Research Council (EPSRC) [grant number EP/N018524/1].

REFERENCES

Afsharzadeh, A. (2016).*Automatic disassembly task sequence planning of aircrafts at their end-of-life* (Doctoral dissertation). Ecole Polytechnique, Montreal, Canada.

Alkaya, A. F., & Duman, E. (2015). Combining and solving sequence dependent traveling salesman and quadratic assignment problems in PCB assembly. *Discrete Applied Mathematics, 192*, 2–16. doi:10.1016/j.dam.2015.03.009

Alshibli, M., El Sayed, A., Kongar, E., Sobh, T. M., & Gupta, S. M. (2016). Disassembly sequencing using tabu search. *Journal of Intelligent & Robotic Systems, 82*(1), 69–79. doi:10.100710846-015-0289-9

Ang, M. C., Ng, K. W., Pham, D. T., & Soroka, A. (2013, November). Simulations of PCB assembly optimisation based on the Bees Algorithm with TRIZ-inspired operators. In *International Visual Informatics Conference* (pp. 335-346). Springer. 10.1007/978-3-319-02958-0_31

Ang, M. C., Pham, D. T., & Ng, K. W. (2009). Application of the Bees Algorithm with TRIZ-inspired operators for PCB assembly planning. In *Proceedings of 5th Virtual International Conference on Intelligent Production Machines and Systems (IPROMS2006)* (pp. 454-459). Academic Press.

Ayob, M., Cowling, P., & Kendall, G. (2002). Optimisation for surface mount placement machines. In *2002 IEEE International Conference on Industrial Technology, 2002. IEEE ICIT'02* (*Vol. 1*, pp. 498-503). IEEE Press.

Baykasoglu, A., Ozbakir, L., & Tapkan, P. (2009). The bees algorithm for workload balancing in examination job assignment. *European Journal of Industrial Engineering*, *3*(4), 424–435. doi:10.1504/EJIE.2009.027035

Behdad, S., & Thurston, D. (2012). Disassembly and reassembly sequence planning trade-offs under uncertainty for product maintenance. *ASME Journal Mechanical Design*, *134*(4), 041011. doi:10.1115/1.4006262

Bonabeau, E., Marco, D. D. R. D. F., Dorigo, M., Théraulaz, G., & Theraulaz, G. (1999). Swarm intelligence: from natural to artificial systems (No. 1). Oxford University Press.

Boothroyd, G. (1994). Product design for manufacture and assembly. *Computer Aided Design*, *26*(7), 505–520. doi:10.1016/0010-4485(94)90082-5

Castellani, M., Otri, S., & Pham, D. T. (2019). Printed circuit board assembly time minimisation using a novel Bees Algorithm. *Computers & Industrial Engineering*, *133*, 186–194. doi:10.1016/j.cie.2019.05.015

Conover, W. J. (1999). *Practical nonparametric statistics* (Vol. 350). john Wiley & Sons.

De Mello, L. H., & Sanderson, A. C. (1990). And/or graph representation of assembly plans. *IEEE Transactions on Robotics and Automation*, *6*(2), 188–199. doi:10.1109/70.54734

Dini, G., & Santochi, M. (1992). Automated sequencing and subassembly detection in assembly planning. *CIRP Annals*, *41*(1), 1–4. doi:10.1016/S0007-8506(07)61140-8

Dong, J., Gibson, P., & Arndt, G. (2007). Disassembly sequence generation in recycling based on parts accessibility and end-of-life strategy. *Proceedings of the Institution of Mechanical Engineers. Part B, Journal of Engineering Manufacture*, *221*(6), 1079–1085. doi:10.1243/09544054JEM697

ElSayed, A., Kongar, E., Gupta, S. M., & Sobh, T. (2012). A robotic-driven disassembly sequence generator for end-of-life electronic products. *Journal of Intelligent & Robotic Systems*, *68*(1), 43–52. doi:10.100710846-012-9667-8

Fahmy, A. A., Kalyoncu, M., & Castellani, M. (2012). Automatic design of control systems for robot manipulators using the bees algorithm. *Proceedings of the Institution of Mechanical Engineers. Part I, Journal of Systems and Control Engineering*, *226*(4), 497–508. doi:10.1177/0959651811425312

Fogel, D. B. (2006). *Evolutionary computation: toward a new philosophy of machine intelligence* (Vol. 1). John Wiley & Sons.

Friedrich, C., Csiszar, A., Lechler, A., & Verl, A. (2017). Efficient task and path planning for maintenance automation using a robot system. *IEEE Transactions on Automation Science and Engineering*, *15*(3), 1205–1215. doi:10.1109/TASE.2017.2759814

Frohm, J., Lindström, V., Winroth, M., & Stahre, J. (2006). The industry's view on automation in manufacturing. *IFAC Proceedings Volumes*, *39*(4), 453-458.

Gao, L., Qian, W., Li, X., & Wang, J. (2010). Application of memetic algorithm in assembly sequence planning. *International Journal of Advanced Manufacturing Technology*, *49*(9-12), 1175–1184. doi:10.100700170-009-2449-1

Ghandi, S., & Masehian, E. (2015). Review and taxonomies of assembly and disassembly path planning problems and approaches. *Computer Aided Design*, *67*, 58–86. doi:10.1016/j.cad.2015.05.001

Giri, R., & Kanthababu, M. (2015). Generating complete disassembly sequences by utilising two-dimensional views. *International Journal of Production Research*, *53*(17), 5118–5138. doi:10.1080/00207543.2015.1005249

Gonnuru, V. K. (2013). Disassembly planning and sequencing for end-of-life products with RFID enriched information. *Robotics and Computer-integrated Manufacturing*, *29*(3), 112–118. doi:10.1016/j.rcim.2012.05.001

Gonzalez, B., & Adenso-Diaz, B. (2006). A scatter search approach to the optimum disassembly sequence problem. *Computers & Operations Research*, *33*(6), 1776–1793. doi:10.1016/j.cor.2004.11.018

Griffiths, C. A., Giannetti, C., Andrzejewski, K., & Morgan, A. (2021). Comparison of a bat and genetic algorithm generated sequence against lead through programming when assembling a PCB using a 6 axis robot with multiple motions and speeds. *IEEE Transactions on Industrial Informatics*.

Gungor, A., & Gupta, S. M. (1998). Disassembly sequence planning for products with defective parts in product recovery. *Computers & Industrial Engineering*, *35*(1-2), 161–164. doi:10.1016/S0360-8352(98)00047-3

Gungor, A., & Gupta, S. M. (2001). Disassembly sequence plan generation using a branch-and-bound algorithm. *International Journal of Production Research*, *39*(3), 481–509. doi:10.1080/00207540010002838

Han, J., & Seo, Y. (2017). Mechanism to minimise the assembly time with feeder assignment for a multi-headed gantry and high-speed SMT machine. *International Journal of Production Research*, *55*(10), 2930–2949. doi:10.1080/00207543.2016.1229071

Han, Z., Wang, Y., & Tian, D. (2021). Ant colony optimization for assembly sequence planning based on parameters optimization. *Frontiers of Mechanical Engineering*, *16*(2), 393–409. doi:10.100711465-020-0613-3

Ho, W., & Ji, P. (2005). A genetic algorithm to optimise the component placement process in PCB assembly. *International Journal of Advanced Manufacturing Technology*, *26*(11), 1397–1401. doi:10.100700170-004-2132-5

Ho, W., & Ji, P. (2006). *Optimal production planning for PCB assembly*. Springer Science & Business Media.

Hsu, H. P. (2016). Solving feeder assignment and component sequencing problems for printed circuit board assembly using particle swarm optimization. *IEEE Transactions on Automation Science and Engineering*, *14*(2), 881–893. doi:10.1109/TASE.2016.2622253

Hsu, H. P. (2020). Printed Circuit Board Assembly Planning for Multi-Head Gantry SMT Machine Using Multi-Swarm and Discrete Firefly Algorithm. *IEEE Access: Practical Innovations, Open Solutions*, *9*, 1642–1654. doi:10.1109/ACCESS.2020.3046495

Huang, Y. M., & Huang, C. T. (2002). Disassembly matrix for disassembly processes of products. *International Journal of Production Research*, *40*(2), 255–273. doi:10.1080/00207540110079770

Hui, W., Dong, X., & Guanghong, D. (2008). A genetic algorithm for product disassembly sequence planning. *Neurocomputing*, *71*(13-15), 2720–2726. doi:10.1016/j.neucom.2007.11.042

Ilgin, M. A., & Gupta, S. M. (2010). Environmentally conscious manufacturing and product recovery (ECMPRO): A review of the state of the art. *Journal of Environmental Management*, *91*(3), 563–591.

Jin, G., Li, W., & Xia, K. (2013). Disassembly matrix for liquid crystal displays televisions. *Procedia CIRP*, *11*, 357–362. doi:10.1016/j.procir.2013.07.015

Kang, J. G., & Xirouchakis, P. (2006). Disassembly sequencing for maintenance: A survey. *Proceedings of the Institution of Mechanical Engineers. Part B, Journal of Engineering Manufacture*, *220*(10), 1697–1716. doi:10.1243/09544054JEM596

Karaboga, D., & Basturk, B. (2007). A powerful and efficient algorithm for numerical function optimization: Artificial bee colony (ABC) algorithm. *Journal of Global Optimization*, *39*(3), 459–471. doi:10.100710898-007-9149-x

Kheder, M., Trigui, M., & Aifaoui, N. (2017). Optimization of disassembly sequence planning for preventive maintenance. *International Journal of Advanced Manufacturing Technology*, *90*(5), 1337–1349. doi:10.100700170-016-9434-2

Khoo, L. P., & Ng, T. K. (1998). A genetic algorithm-based planning system for PCB component placement. *International Journal of Production Economics*, *54*(3), 321–332. doi:10.1016/S0925-5273(98)00010-3

Kim, H.-J., & Xirouchakis, P. (2010). Capacitated disassembly scheduling with random demand. *International Journal of Production Research*, *48*(23), 7177–7194. doi:10.1080/00207540903469035

Koc, A., Sabuncuoglu, I., & Erel, E. (2009). Two exact formulations for disassembly line balancing problems with task precedence diagram construction using an and/or graph. *IIE Transactions*, *41*(10), 866–881. doi:10.1080/07408170802510390

Laili, Y., Tao, F., Pham, D. T., Wang, Y., & Zhang, L. (2019). Robotic disassembly re-planning using a two-pointer detection strategy and a super-fast bees algorithm. *Robotics and Computer-integrated Manufacturing*, *59*, 130–142. doi:10.1016/j.rcim.2019.04.003

Lambert, A. J. (2003). Disassembly sequencing: A survey. *International Journal of Production Research*, *41*(16), 3721–3759. doi:10.1080/0020754031000120078

Leipälä, T., & Nevalainen, O. (1989). Optimization of the movements of a component placement machine. *European Journal of Operational Research*, *38*(2), 167–177. doi:10.1016/0377-2217(89)90101-X

Leu, M. C., Wong, H., & Ji, Z. (1993). Planning of component placement/insertion sequence and feeder setup in PCB assembly using genetic algorithm. *ASME. Journal of Electronic Packaging*, *115*(4), 424–432. doi:10.1115/1.2909352

Li, D., & Yoon, S. W. (2017). PCB assembly optimization in a single gantry high-speed rotary-head collect-and-place machine. *International Journal of Advanced Manufacturing Technology*, *88*(9-12), 2819–2834. doi:10.100700170-016-8942-4

Li, J., Barwood, M., & Rahimifard, S. (2018). Robotic disassembly for increased recovery of strategically important materials from electrical vehicles. *Robotics and Computer-integrated Manufacturing*, *50*, 203–212. doi:10.1016/j.rcim.2017.09.013

Lin, S., & Kernighan, B. W. (1973). An effective heuristic algorithm for the traveling-salesman problem. *Operations Research*, *21*(2), 498–516. doi:10.1287/opre.21.2.498

Liu, J., Zhou, Z., Pham, D. T., Xu, W., Ji, C., & Liu, Q. (2018). Robotic disassembly sequence planning using enhanced discrete bees algorithm in remanufacturing. *International Journal of Production Research*, *56*(9), 3134–3151. doi:10.1080/00207543.2017.1412527

Luo, J., Liu, J., & Hu, Y. (2017). An MILP model and a hybrid evolutionary algorithm for integrated operation optimisation of multi-head surface mounting machines in PCB assembly. *International Journal of Production Research*, *55*(1), 145–160. doi:10.1080/00207543.2016.1200154

Mete, S., Çil, Z. A., Ağpak, K., Özceylan, E., & Dolgui, A. (2016). A solution approach based on beam search algorithm for disassembly line balancing problem. *Journal of Manufacturing Systems*, *41*, 188–200. doi:10.1016/j.jmsy.2016.09.002

Mumtaz, J., Guan, Z., Yue, L., Zhang, L., & He, C. (2020). Hybrid spider monkey optimisation algorithm for multi-level planning and scheduling problems of assembly lines. *International Journal of Production Research*, *58*(20), 6252–6267. doi:10.1080/00207543.2019.1675917

Nelson, K. M., & Wille, L. T. (1995, March). Comparative study of heuristics for optimal printed circuit board assembly. *Proceedings of Southcon*, *95*, 322–327. doi:10.1109/SOUTHC.1995.516124

Ong, N., & Wong, Y. (1999). Automatic subassembly detection from a product model for disassembly sequence generation. *International Journal of Advanced Manufacturing Technology*, *15*(6), 425–431. doi:10.1007001700050086

Ong, N. S., & Khoo, L. P. (1999). Genetic algorithm approach in PCB assembly. *Integrated Manufacturing Systems*, *10*(5), 256–265. doi:10.1108/09576069910280648

Ong, N. S., & Tan, W. C. (2002). Sequence placement planning for high-speed PCB assembly machine. *Integrated Manufacturing Systems*, *13*(1), 35–46. doi:10.1108/09576060210411495

Otri, S. (2011). *Improving the bees algorithm for complex optimisation problems* (Doctoral dissertation). Cardiff University.

Ozceylan, E., Kalayci, C. B., Gungor, A., & Gupta, S. M. (2019). Disassembly line balancing problem: A review of the state of the art and future directions. *International Journal of Production Research, 57*(15-16), 4805–4827. doi:10.1080/00207543.2018.1428775

Pham, D. T., Afify, A., & Koc, E. (2007c). *Manufacturing cell formation using the Bees Algorithm*. In *Innovative Production Machines and Systems Virtual Conference*, Cardiff, UK.

Pham, D. T., & Castellani, M. (2009). The bees algorithm: Modelling foraging behaviour to solve continuous optimization problems. *Proceedings of the Institution of Mechanical Engineers. Part C, Journal of Mechanical Engineering Science, 223*(12), 2919–2938. doi:10.1243/09544062JMES1494

Pham, D. T., Castellani, M., & Ghanbarzadeh, A. (2007a). Preliminary design using the bees algorithm. In *Proceedings of eighth international conference on laser metrology, CMM and machine tool performance, LAMDAMAP* (pp. 420-429). Academic Press.

Pham, D. T., Ghanbarzadeh, A., Koç, E., Otri, S., Rahim, S., & Zaidi, M. (2006a). The bees algorithm—a novel tool for complex optimisation problems. In *Intelligent production machines and systems* (pp. 454–459). Elsevier Science Ltd. doi:10.1016/B978-008045157-2/50081-X

Pham, D. T., Koc, E., Lee, J. Y., & Phrueksanant, J. (2007b). Using the bees algorithm to schedule jobs for a machine. In *Proceedings Eighth International Conference on Laser Metrology, CMM and Machine Tool Performance, LAMDAMAP* (pp. 430-439). Academic Press.

Pham, D. T., Otri, S., & Darwish, A. H. (2007d). Application of the Bees Algorithm to PCB assembly optimisation. In *Proceedings of the 3rd virtual international conference on intelligent production machines and systems* (pp. 511-516). Academic Press.

Pham, D. T., Soroka, A. J., Ghanbarzadeh, A., Koc, E., Otri, S., & Packianather, M. (2006b). Optimising neural networks for identification of wood defects using the bees algorithm. In *2006 4th IEEE International Conference on Industrial Informatics* (pp. 1346-1351). IEEE. 10.1109/INDIN.2006.275855

Rashid, M. F. F., Hutabarat, W., & Tiwari, A. (2012). A review on assembly sequence planning and assembly line balancing optimisation using soft computing approaches. *International Journal of Advanced Manufacturing Technology, 59*(1), 335–349. doi:10.100700170-011-3499-8

Ren, Y., Yu, D., Zhang, C., Tian, G., Meng, L., & Zhou, X. (2017). An improved gravitational search algorithm for profit-oriented partial disassembly line balancing problem. *International Journal of Production Research, 55*(24), 7302–7316. doi:10.1080/00207543.2017.1341066

Ren, Y., Zhang, C., Zhao, F., Xiao, H., & Tian, G. (2018). An asynchronous parallel disassembly planning based on genetic algorithm. *European Journal of Operational Research, 269*(2), 647–660. doi:10.1016/j.ejor.2018.01.055

Rickli, J. L., & Camelio, J. A. (2013). Multi-objective partial disassembly optimization based on sequence feasibility. *Journal of Manufacturing Systems, 32*(1), 281–293. doi:10.1016/j.jmsy.2012.11.005

Riggs, R. J., Battaïa, O., & Hu, S. J. (2015). Disassembly line balancing under high variety of end of life states using a joint precedence graph approach. *Journal of Manufacturing Systems, 37*, 638–648. doi:10.1016/j.jmsy.2014.11.002

Seeley, T. D. (2009). *The wisdom of the hive: the social physiology of honey bee colonies*. Harvard University Press. doi:10.2307/j.ctv1kz4h15

Sheng, I. L., & Kok-Soo, T. (2010). Eco-efficient product design using theory of inventive problem solving (TRIZ) principles. *American Journal of Applied Sciences*, *7*(6), 852–858. doi:10.3844/ajassp.2010.852.858

Tang, Y., Zhou, M., Zussman, E., & Caudill, R. (2002). Disassembly modeling, planning, and application. *Journal of Manufacturing Systems*, *21*(3), 200–217. doi:10.1016/S0278-6125(02)80162-5

Tao, F., Bi, L., Zuo, Y., & Nee, A. Y. (2018). Partial/parallel disassembly sequence planning for complex products. *Journal of Manufacturing Science and Engineering*, *140*(1), 011016. doi:10.1115/1.4037608

Tripathi, M., Agrawal, S., Pandey, M. K., Shankar, R., & Tiwari, M. (2009). Real world disassembly modeling and sequencing problem: Optimization by algorithm of self-guided ants (ASGA). *Robotics and Computer-integrated Manufacturing*, *25*(3), 483–496. doi:10.1016/j.rcim.2008.02.004

Tseng, H. E., Chang, C. C., Lee, S. C., & Huang, Y. M. (2018). A block-based genetic algorithm for disassembly sequence planning. *Expert Systems with Applications*, *96*, 492–505. doi:10.1016/j.eswa.2017.11.004

Van Laarhoven, P. J., & Aarts, E. H. (1987). Simulated annealing. In *Simulated annealing: Theory and applications* (pp. 7–15). Springer. doi:10.1007/978-94-015-7744-1_2

Vongbunyong, S., Kara, S., & Pagnucco, M. (2015). Learning and revision in cognitive robotics disassembly automation. *Robotics and Computer-integrated Manufacturing*, *34*, 79–94. doi:10.1016/j.rcim.2014.11.003

Yu, B., Wu, E., Chen, C., Yang, Y., Yao, B., & Lin, Q. (2017). A general approach to optimize disassembly sequence planning based on disassembly network: A case study from automotive industry. *Advances in Production Engineering & Management*, *12*(4), 305–320. doi:10.14743/apem2017.4.260

Zhou, Z., Liu, J., Pham, D. T., Xu, W., Ramirez, F. J., Ji, C., & Liu, Q. (2019). Disassembly sequence planning: Recent developments and future trends. *Proceedings of the Institution of Mechanical Engineers. Part B, Journal of Engineering Manufacture*, *233*(5), 1450–1471. doi:10.1177/0954405418789975

Zhu, B., Sarigecili, M. I., & Roy, U. (2013). Disassembly information model incorporating dynamic capabilities for disassembly sequence generation. *Robotics and Computer-integrated Manufacturing*, *29*(5), 396–409. doi:10.1016/j.rcim.2013.03.003

Zussman, E., & Zhou, M. (1999). A methodology for modeling and adaptive planning of disassembly processes. *IEEE Transactions on Robotics and Automation*, *15*(1), 190–194. doi:10.1109/70.744614

ADDITIONAL READING

Baronti, L., Castellani, M., & Pham, D. T. (2020). An analysis of the search mechanisms of the bees algorithm. *Swarm and Evolutionary Computation*, *59*, 100746. doi:10.1016/j.swevo.2020.100746

Pham, D. T., Baronti, L., Zhang, B., & Castellani, M. (2018). Optimisation of Engineering Systems with the Bees Algorithm. *International Journal of Artificial Life Research*, 8(1), 1–15. doi:10.4018/IJALR.2018010101

Pham, D. T., & Castellani, M. (2014). Benchmarking and Comparison of Nature-Inspired Population-Based Continuous Optimisation Algorithms. *Soft Computing*, 18(5), 871–903. doi:10.100700500-013-1104-9

KEY TERMS AND DEFINITIONS

Assembly: Building a finished product from components and sub-components.

Bees Algorithm: A nature-inspired optimisation algorithm mimicking the foraging behaviour of honeybees.

Disassembly: The reverse process of assembly, separating end-of-life products into their individual parts.

Disassembly Sequencing: Generally divided in three categories, complete, partial, and selective disassembly, it is the problem of identifying a viable disassembly sequence.

Interference Matrix: Compact way to represent obstruction relations between components.

Re-Planning: The problem of finding alternative viable disassembly sequences when the original planning cannot be carried out on a specific product due to differences in its conditions.

Remanufacturing: Environmentally sustainable product end-of-life strategy which restores products at their end of service life to at least original performance via a combination of re-processing and substitution of used components.

Chapter 11
Model Optimisation Techniques for Convolutional Neural Networks

Sajid Nazir
Glasgow Caledonian University, UK

Shushma Patel
De Montfort University, UK

Dilip Patel
London South Bank University, UK

ABSTRACT

Deep neural networks provide good results for computer vision tasks. This has been possible due to a renewed interest in neural networks, availability of large-scale labelled training data, virtually unlimited processing and storage on cloud platforms and high-performance clusters. A convolutional neural network (CNN) is one such architecture better suited for image classification. An important factor for a better CNN performance, besides the data quality, is the choice of hyperparameters, which define the model itself. The model or hyperparameter optimisation involves selecting the best configuration of hyperparameters but is challenging because the set of hyperparameters are different for each type of machine learning algorithm. Thus, it requires a lot of computational time and resources to determine a better performing machine learning model. Therefore, the process has a lot of research interest, and currently a transition to a fully automated process is also underway. This chapter provides a survey of the CNN model optimisation techniques proposed in the literature.

DOI: 10.4018/978-1-7998-8686-0.ch011

INTRODUCTION

Artificial Intelligence (AI) is transforming the healthcare, financial, academic, entertainment and industrial domains and is the driving engine for the applications we use every day. The increased processing power of Graphical Processing Units (GPUs) and the availability of large image datasets has fostered a renewed interest in extracting semantic information from images. This in part is due to the large amounts of visual data available with the rise of big data and social media networks. This coupled with the advances in storage and processing technologies has made it possible to progress from image processing to interpreting images for extracting contextual information.

Machine learning is a sub-field of AI that makes it possible for the machine learning models to make predictions without explicitly being programmed (Neetesh, 2017). Machine learning for vision problems comprises techniques that can provide intelligent solutions to complex problems of interpreting and describing a scene, given sufficient data. Much progress has been made in this area although improvements are still needed. In a machine learning model, we have two types of parameters. Model parameters are initialised and get updated through the learning process, such as neuron weights in neural networks. The other type are the hyperparameters that have to be set before training a model, as these define the model architectures (Yang, 2020). The hyperparameter type could be continuous, categorical or an integer (Victoria & Maragatham, 2021).

A general sequence of steps to be followed for a machine learning application is shown in Figure 1. The quality and quantity of data together with an optimum set of hyperparameters governs the performance of any machine learning model. There are many traditional machine learning approaches such as Random Forest but the recent trend for image classification applications is the use of deep learning.

Figure 1. General sequence of steps for a machine learning application.

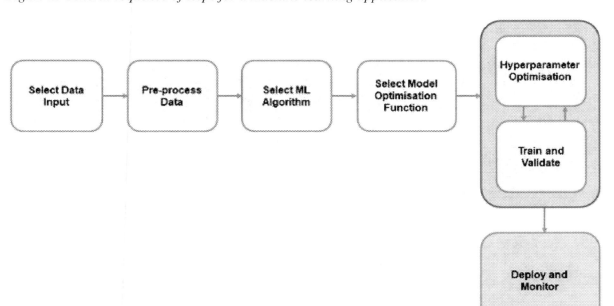

Deep learning is a branch of machine learning (Bhandare & Kaur, 2018) that derives its name from neural networks that comprise of many layers. Multiple layers are used to model high-level features from complex data, with each successive layer using the outputs from the preceding layer as an input (Benuwa, 2016). The increased research interest in neural networks is due to the promising results obtained for ImageNet competitions (Krizhevsky et al., 2012). A review of recent advances in deep learning is provided in Minar (2018) as well as taxonomy of deep learning techniques and applications. A review of deep supervised learning, unsupervised learning and reinforcement learning is provided in Schmidhuber (2015) covering developments since 1940. Benuwa (2016) reviewed deep learning techniques along with algorithm principles and architectures for deep learning.

The majority of deep learning applications are related to the field of computer vision (Shaziya, 2021). Computer vision applications such as object detection, object classification, image labelling and face recognition are very amenable to the deep learning architectures. Promising results for complex image categorization problems have been achieved using deep learning, with neural networks comprising of many layers. Computer vision technologies for object recognition have undergone rapid advances and better techniques with improved results have been proposed (Krizhevsky et al., 2012; Deng et al., 2009). The emergence of neural networks for computer vision applications can be attributed to Lecun et al., (1989) and Deng et al., (2009). Although different types of deep neural networks have been used for image-based applications, the most dominant use is of the Convolutional Neural Networks (CNNs) (Alzubaidi, 2021). An overview of deep learning techniques with a focus on CNNs and Deep Belief Networks (DBNs) is provided together with a discussion on sparsity and dimensionality reduction (Arel, 2010). CNNs have also been applied to combine image information for longer videos of up to two minutes (120 frames) to solve classification problems (Yue-Hei Ng et al., 2015). A dynamically trained CNN was proposed for object classification in video streams (Yaseen, Anjum, Rana, & Antonopoulos 2019). The image features from hidden layers of deep neural networks were extracted for image recognition in (Hayakawa, Oonuma, & Kobayashi 2017). These networks require a lot of time, processing power and data in order to be trained. After training, a neural network can be used to make predictions on unseen test data (Neetesh, 2017).

The aim of training neural networks is to find weightings that achieve better classification accuracy (Nguyen, 2018). Deep learning algorithms are complex to develop, train and evaluate. A neural net (Krizhevsky, Sutskever, & Hinton, 2012) with 60 million parameters and 650,000 neurons took a long time to train on ImageNet (Deng et al., 2009) to classify 1.2 million images. CNNs, the leading type of neural networks have been used for classifying large image datasets (Krizhevsky et al., 2012; Szegedy et al., 2015). The application of deep learning for different medical image modalities is provided in (Shen, Wu, & Suk 2017).

However, irrespective of the machine learning model, the model's performance has to be optimum (Agrawal, 2021a). The performance of a CNN architecture depends on the data quality and the model hyperparameters. This can be addressed by either working on improving the data, with techniques such as pre-processing, data augmentation, and model optimisation, and also by selecting an optimum configuration of the hyperparameters. Ensuring the data quality is also achievable through feature engineering which is quite a time-consuming process (Alzubaidi, 2021). Before a neural network can be trained, hyperparameter values must be determined.

An important aspect of the neural networks performance is the hyperparameters or the model parameters, and their impact on results (Yang, 2020). This aspect is critical to designing and developing efficient models. CNN architectures are dependent on hyperparameters and an incorrect choice can have a significant effect on performance (Albelwi & Mahmood, 2016). The number of hyperparameters increases with complex deep neural networks (Ozaki, Yano, & Onishi, 2017). These need to be carefully fine-tuned for a particular application to yield good results (Soon, 2018). Hyperparameter tuning requires a good understanding of the algorithm and the role of its hyperparameters relating to algorithm performance (Agrawal, 2021a). Deep neural networks are very sensitive to hyperparameter values (Domhan, Springenberg, & Hutter, 2015) and may fail to train slightly non-optimal values (Ozaki et al., 2017). Therefore, the success of a neural network, to a large extent, is governed by the correct values of its hyperparameters (Soon, 2018). Hyperparameter optimisation is the process of optimising a loss function over a configuration space (Bergstra, Bardenet, Bengio, & Kégl, 2011). Optimising hyperparameters for a suitable CNN architecture is an iterative and lengthy process (Hinz, Navarro-Guerrero, Magg, & Wermter 2018).

The recent focus in model optimisation is to make the process easier, reproducible and efficient. The automated machine learning (AutoML) approach makes it easier for developers with less experience of machine learning to create an efficient model. A survey of the AutoML techniques for feature engineering, neural architecture search (NAS), and hyperparameter optimisation (He, Zhao & Chu, 2021). Also, there is research effort to make the CNN explainable so that an understanding and appreciation of the model's decision process helps to build users' trust and confidence in the model's outcomes. An interactive tool, CNN Explainer is proposed by Wang (2020) for visualising CNN architectures. A visual analytics tool named VisEvol was proposed for hyperparameter exploration using evolutionary algorithms (Chatzimparmpas, 2021).

The objective function for a hyperparameter optimisation problem is not known hence the traditional approaches such as gradient descent will not work (Wu et al., 2019). A survey of evolutionary neural network architectures is provided by Liu et al., (2021); Yu & Zhu (2020) reviewed algorithms for hyperparameter optimisation; and Yang (2020) surveyed hyperparameter optimisations covering machine learning techniques including CNN. In contrast, our study is different because we focus on CNN architectures and cover a wide range of techniques including AutoML, and other recent approaches.
The contributions of this chapter are:

- The importance of data and model in relation to the model performance and a comprehensive categorisation and coverage of model's hyperparameter optimisation techniques
- The challenges, issues and future research directions for hyperparameter optimisation of CNN models

This chapter reviews the techniques for determining the optimal hyperparameters for convolutional neural networks. The background section, provides the necessary context for Machine Learning models and their parameters. The section on CNN and Hyperparameters describes the CNN model and the important hyperparameters. Hyperparameter optimisation methods cover the major optimisation techniques. A comparison of the various optimisation techniques is provided. The research directions section covers the developments taking place in deep learning research that will shape future research for building better architectures.

BACKGROUND

The machine learning approaches can be broadly classified as traditional and deep learning-based models. However, for each of these types of models, it is important to understand the role played by the hyperparameter configuration in determining the model performance. This section covers the introductory information on model optimisation, machine learning models and deep learning.

Model Parameters and Hyperparameters

A model for machine learning is created by going through the data inputs to learn the weights which help to classify an unseen sample. A machine learning algorithm has two types of variables: (i) training parameters, that are learnt from the data during training phase, and (ii) hyperparameters that have to be specified before the model training or learning starts, these would be different for different algorithms and data (Agrawal, 2021a; Andonie, 2020).

The model parameters and also the hyperparameters affect the performance of a trained model. That is, some parameters can be considered to be inside the model whereas the others, hyperparameters are outside the model. It is very important to set the hyperparameters with appropriate values for a given model and data, otherwise the model performance will not be optimum. An example of hyperparameters in a neural network could be the learning rate to train the neural network, or the optimiser to minimise the loss function (Yang, 2020). The relationship between the model's inner and outer parameters is shown in Figure 2.

Figure 2. The relationship between the model parameters that are learned during the model training phase and the hyperparameters that need to be set.

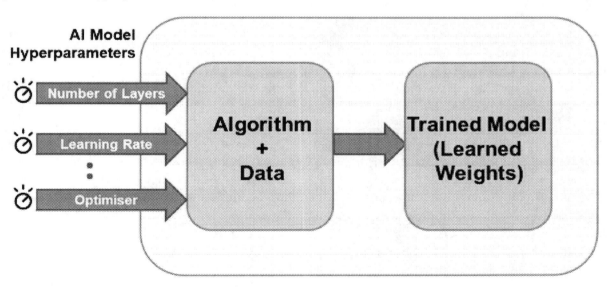

Model Optimisation

Optimisation is the process of finding the best alternative from the possible choices to minimise or maximise the objective function (Yang, 2020). A machine learning model is built by solving an optimisation problem. For a neural network the weight parameters are optimised using an optimisation method to achieve maximum value for the model accuracy or objective function reaches a minimum value (Yang, 2020).

Hyperparameter optimisation or tuning is a process applied to tune the model by tweaking the parameters for the best results. The optimisation can be represented as (Victoria & Maragatham, 2021):

$$y^* = \text{argmin } f(y)$$

where y is the set of hyperparameters and belongs to the domain space, and f(y) represents the objective score.

The model may be susceptible to degradation by small changes to its parameters. Thus, a lot of mutual interdependencies might exist amongst the identified optimum hyperparameters (Chatzimparmpas, 2021). The number of training parameters to be considered for a deep network is large and the required time and computational resources make it infeasible to sweep through the entire parameter space (Benuwa, 2016). Hyperparameters can have a range and domain of the values to be searched in the search space, with numeric, categorical or conditional values (Yang, 2020).

Simpler models can have very few hyperparameters and it may be possible to employ more traditional approaches to tune the hyperparameters. However, for a more complex machine learning model it is of utmost importance to use the more advanced methods for hyperparameter tuning.

Traditional Machine Learning Models

The major difference between machine learning and deep learning models, is that in traditional machine learning applications the features had to be extracted. However, deep learning models can autonomously extract the features required to train the model. Deep learning results have surpassed the results achievable by traditional machine learning techniques in domains such as robotics, control, cybersecurity and natural language processing (Alzubaidi, 2021).

For K-Nearest Neighbour (KNN) algorithm, K is the number of neighbours nearest points that the algorithm should find and consider in the close proximity of a sample to be predicted, and increasing it can produce more smoother separation boundaries (Agrawal, 2021a). The distance metric and the value of K are the model's hyperparameters and need to be specified by the user (Agrawal, 2021a). Changing K would also affect the algorithm running time and thus requires the knowledge and role of different hyperparameters before assigning values to these.

Random Forest, Support Vector Machines (SVMs) and eXtreme Gradient Boosting (XGBoost) algorithms are important machine learning algorithms (Bartz, 2021). SVMs are based on statistical techniques (Gambella, Ghaddar, & Naoum-Sawaya, 2021).

A decision tree can be used for classification and regression tasks (Gambella, Ghaddar, & Naoum-Sawaya, 2021) and predictions are based on a top-down search with each class represented as a leaf (Matache, 2019). The model accuracy of a single decision tree can be improved by using a combination of several trees, using random forests, bagging and boosting (Gambella, Ghaddar, & Naoum-Sawaya,

2021). Random forest is an ensemble of trees used for classification and regression (Wu et al., 2019). After the decision trees have been built, the votes by the decision trees determines the classification result (Wu et al., 2019). Random Forest hyperparameters such as node size, number of trees, splitting rule, and hyperparameter tuning strategies are described by Probst, Wright, and Boulesteix (2019).

Traditional machine learning models cannot capture complex relationships between the inputs and the class to be predicted. In such cases, deep learning models can be used for the classification tasks (Gambella, Ghaddar, & Naoum-Sawaya, 2021).

Deep Learning Models

Deep learning or the Artificial Neural Networks (ANNs) are modelled on the human nervous system (Kienzler, 2017) and need computational power and large volumes of data to be trained before they can be used. Although biological vision systems and processes are not fully understood, the current method of ANNs yields promising results.

ANNs can learn from any mathematical relation between the input and output (Kienzler, 2017). A large number of labelled true and false examples are required in supervised learning to train the ANN before good results can be obtained. Deep learning, a sub-field of machine learning has provided promising results in pattern recognition (Benuwa, 2016).

The ImageNet Large Scale Recognition Challenge (ILSVRC) has been running since 2009 and provides a common platform for comparing computer vision algorithms for object detection and classification (Russakovsky et al., 2015).

Deep learning is a driver for many applications in AI (Tibbetts, 2018). Handcrafted features have been replaced by deep learning through use of feature learning algorithms (Benuwa, 2016). A deep neural network is comprised of many layers with the number of layers determining the depth of a network. The layers between the input and output layers are termed hidden layers (Fig 3).

Figure 3. Artificial Neural Network (ANN) with the number of hidden layers defining the depth of network. Each layer transforms its inputs through trainable parameters, that is, weights. A shallow network has fewer hidden layers compared to a deep network

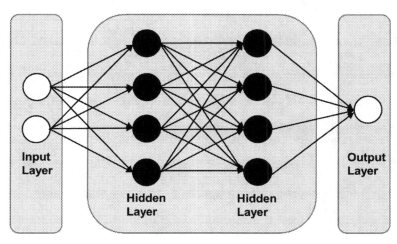

A neural network with more layers and features in the hidden layers is termed a Deep Neural Network (DNN). Hyperparameter optimisation has become more important with DNNs for better accuracy (Yu & Zhu, 2020). Of particular interest are CNNs that can process spatial data and take a fixed size input and generate fixed size outputs. The hyperparameter choice for a CNN affects the training accuracy and network structure (Yu & Zhu, 2020).

CNN MODEL AND HYPERPARAMETERS

The initial layers in deep learning networks extract the low-level features such as lines, edges whereas the later layers extract the high-level features. The depth increases interconnections and complexity of nodes. The initial layers work on low-level features, lines, circles etc., whereas the deeper layers work on higher or complex features, until the whole image is recognized (Kienzler, 2017). Such systems can perform at the same or better levels than humans (Alzubaidi, 2021; Kienzler, 2017). Deep learning models are able to recognize more complex features accurately, and in less time, compared to a human (Tibbetts, 2018).

CNNs, due to their inherent nature, are more applicable for object recognition problems exploiting the spatial dimensions of height and width. Generally Deep Neural Networks (DNNs) are considered difficult to train compared to CNNs. Better generalization is possible by CNN architecture for vision tasks (Bengio, 2009) because CNNs are designed to work on two-dimensional data (Arel, 2010). CNNs generally perform better at extracting important features from images making them better suited for image analysis (Arel, 2010).

Convolutional Neural Networks Architecture

Figure 4. Convolutional neural networks can have varying combinations of convolutional and pooling layers, together with a fully connected layer.

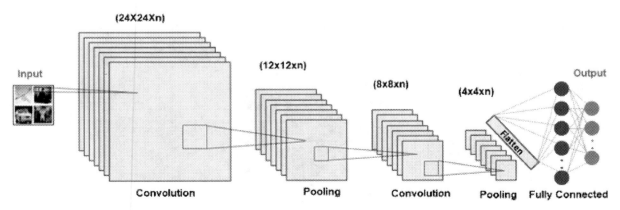

The architecture of a CNN model (Figure 4) comprises of many layers but has the following three main types of layers:

- **Convolutional Layer**

The convolution layer performs a filtering operation. The filters are normally of odd sizes and are used to convolve the image. The output of the filter or kernel is used to replace the selected overlap position, usually middle in the convolved image data. The weights of the kernel determine the type of the intended operation on the image, for example, detecting vertical edges. The output of the first convolution layer is given as (Su et al., 2020):

$$a^l = f\left(z^l\right) = f\left(\sum_{k=1}^{K} a_k^{l-1} * W_k^l + b^l\right)$$

where f is the activation function, K is the number of feature maps, W is the convolution kernel, and b is the bias.

- **Pooling Layer**

The pooling layer reduces the resolution of the image (down sampling) by selecting one value from a 2x2 grid. Thus, for an image size of 8x8, a 2x2 pooling layer will yield an image size of 2x2. The process ensures that the most important features are retained and also results in a computational speedup.

- **Fully Connected Layer**

The purpose of the fully connected layer is to be able to classify the given image to one of the classes. The fully connected layer occurs as the last layer.

The other important aspects of CNN architecture are activation functions and regularisation. The regularisation comprises of many techniques that can be used to avoid overfitting.

CNN Model Hyperparameters

It is important to understand that there is an interplay and interdependence of hyperparameters. Saari (2018) found that the two chosen hyperparameters, depth of CNN and a regularization technique (Dataset Augmentation) affected the results and it was concluded that instead of applying both, only one could be used for optimal results. In addition, the selection of the hyperparameters for tuning also affects the results as all hyperparameters do not have the same significance for the training or test accuracy of the model. A brief summary of the important hyperparameters is provided below:

Architecture Type and Number of Hidden Layers

The number of hidden layers defines the depth of the network. The depth of the proposed architectures has been consistently increasing and in general was shown to yield better results (Agrawal, 2021a). However, alternate architectures with less depth have also been proposed. These less deeper architectures are useful for embedded systems with less processing power and demonstrated that networks with less depth can perform competitively to deeper and therefore complex networks (Hasanpour, Rouhani, Fayyaz, & Sabokrou, 2016).

Number of Nodes

The number of nodes can vary in the different layers but are equal to the number of features in the first hidden layer and are equal to the number of classes in the last hidden layers. In the hidden layers, by convention the number of nodes is in powers of 2, to aid implementation, but as such has no proof for being the best choice (Agrawal, 2021a). Having fewer or more nodes than required in the hidden layer can lead to underfitting and overfitting respectively (Yu & Zhu, 2020).

Optimisers

There are many optimisers reported in the literature but Stochastic Gradient Descent (SGD) is mostly used and also its significant variants include RMSProp, Stochastic Gradient Descent (SGD) and Adam (Yu & Zhu, 2020). SGD provides good results with a batch size of 32 to 512 but larger batch sizes for deep learning applications have also been studied (Keskar et al., 2017). An important and common parameter in all these optimisers is the learning rate that determines the convergence speed (Yu & Zhu, 2020). The value of the learning rate is chosen to be between 0 and 1. In general, the optimiser and learning rate are to be considered together (Yu & Zhu, 2020).

Activation Function

Activation functions introduce a non-linearity (Agrawal, 2021a). Koutsoukas, Monaghan, Li and Huan (2017) compared the activation functions and found that ReLU provided the best results overall. More complex variants of ReLU have been proposed recently, that is, LeakyReLU signifying improvement in results with rectifier non-linearities as compared to sigmoidal ones (Maas, Hannam, & Ng, 2013) and PReLU (He, Zhang, Ren, & Sun, 2015). The implementations are available in Keras (Keras) as "Advanced Activations".

Loss Function

Loss function measures the difference between the output of the model and the expected value (Matache, 2019). In general, the longer the model is run, the more accurate it is expected to be (Matache, 2019). The loss function would be chosen based on the type of required task, that is, regression, binary or multiclass classification. The choice of loss function can affect the algorithm learning rate and therefore needs knowledge of its use (Agrawal, 2021a). One could, for instance, use Mean Squared Error (MSE) for regression problems.

Dropout Regularization

A trained model should perform well on unseen data during testing (Deep Learning tutorial, 2015). However, a complex model can learn the training data perfectly and then fail to generalize to unseen examples, a phenomenon termed as overfitting. Overfitting can be avoided by regularization techniques, such as Dropout (Srivastava et al., 2014). Data Augmentation is another mechanism to augment the existing data by generating new images through simple operations such as flip and rotation on existing data.

Convolution Layer

A convolution layer comprises of many parameters. The important ones are the number of kernels applied to each layer, the height and width of each convolutional kernel, zero padding and stride (Bacanin et al., 2020). Without zero padding the size of the convolved image will reduce. Stride defines the amount of movement of the kernel after calculating a value. If it is more than one then the convolved image will again reduce in size.

Dimensions of Pooling Matrices in Pooling Layers

The pooling layer selects the important image information and, in the process, reduces the image size, thereby reducing the computational complexity (Su et al., 2020). Generally, a 2x2 size for the pooling is used for down sampling the image into half. A larger pooling matrix size would reduce the image size further than half.

Number of Epochs and Batch Size

An epoch consists of one pass of the entire data through the network. The data is passed through the network by dividing it into batches or sets. A batch is a subset of data to conserve memory and to calculate gradient and weight updating (Agrawal, 2021a). Thus, many iterations would be required to process all the data through the network. In general, a higher value for epoch will provide better results.

CNN HYPERPARAMETER OPTIMISATION

Many different hyperparameter methods have been reported in the literature. The choice of a particular method depends on the chosen architecture, number of selected hyperparameters to be tuned, availability of time and processing power. The parameter search space can be pruned to reduce the time for the hyperparameter optimisation (Truong, 2019).

After considering the various strategies, we categorized these into conventional, Bayesian, meta-heuristics algorithms, reinforcement learning, hyperparameter selection and speedup, multi-fidelity and automated machine learning (AutoML) optimisation approahes. This categorization helps to show an evolution from earlier conventional to recent methods that are focussed on automated optimisations, reduction of hyperparameters, and speedup. We survey and provide state-of-the art techniques for hyperparameter optimisations from the research literature.

Conventional Optimisation Methods

Conventional methods either try out all the selected hyperparameters exhaustively or restrict the search to a chosen subset based on its significance or selection. These methods represent a class of simple optimisation methods, which were good for simple networks, but have limited performance for complex networks having a large number of hyperparameters.

Manual Search

The manual search method can have promising results in terms of time and selected hyperparameters because unlike the grid search, a human can rule out sub-optimum hyperparameters easily. A manual search for DNNs is described in Koutsoukas et al. (2017) by considering hyperparameters such as activation functions, learning rate, number of neurons per layer, number of hidden layers and dropout regularisation.

In earlier work (Nazir, et al., 2018), a simple architecture was used to investigate the effect of parameter change on improving image classification results with CIFAR-10 dataset (Krizhevsky et al., 2012; He et al., 2015). The focus was on investigating a large selection of important hyperparameters for learning rates, activation layer, momentum and batch size.

A manual process for investigating all but one fixed hyperparameter to obtain a set of hyperparameters is reported by Nguyen (2018), aimed at achieving hyperparameters with high classification accuracies and to shorten the training time. Manual optimisation is not hindered by any technical overhead (Bergstra & Bengio, 2012) but could be inefficient for many problems, due to large search space or complex models (Yang, 2020).

Grid Search

Grid search is a common method for hyperparameter optimisation (Bergstra & Bengio, 2012) and has been a standard for decades (Hutter, Lucke and Schmidt-Thieme, 2015). It is an exhaustive search for all the selected values of the hyperparameters. This is available in many software packages and can be easily specified by listing the values for the selected hyperparameters to be investigated. Under software control, it will step through all the possible combinations to determine the combination that yields the best results. For example, optimising a set of 6 parameters where each has 10 different values to be considered will require 10^6 evaluations (Victoria & Maragatham, 2021).

Grid search-based methods worked well in earlier machine learning models with limited parameters. It is argued in (Bergstra & Bengio, 2012) that grid search may be a poor choice as it also considers hyperparameters that might not be important for a given dataset. It tries all possible combinations thus having an exponential growth with an increase in the number of hyperparameters (Hinz et al., 2018). However, for a large search space, it is computationally inefficient and expensive (He, Zhao & Chu, 2021).

Random Search

Bergstra and Bengio (2012) showed that random search can be used to search for hyperparameter values yielding better results compared to Grid search in higher hyperparameter spaces. Random search also requires less computational power. It was revealed that many datasets have only a few hyperparameters that are really important and that for different datasets, different hyperparameter configurations may be required. It works by drawing a random value from each parameter of interest based on given distribution (Hinz et al., 2018). Random search doesn't guarantee an optimum value (He, Zhao & Chu, 2021) and can be parallelised (Ozaki et al., 2017).

Random search can act as a baseline against which other optimisation methods can be evaluated. Weighted Random Search was proposed by Andonie (2020) combining Random Search and greedy heuristic (Andonie, 2020).

Bayesian Optimisations

Bayesian optimisation is rooted in Bayes theorem and can work well for non-convex functions and hard to calculate derivatives (Greenhill et al., 2020; Wu et al., 2019). The equation for the model Z is as given below (Victoria & Maragatham, 2021):

$$P(Z|Y) = (P(Y|Z)P(Z) / P(Z)$$

where $P(Y|Z)$ is the conditional probability or the likelihood, and $P(Z|Y)$ is the posterior probability.

Bayesian Optimisation uses probabilistic Gaussian processes for approximating and minimizing the error function for hyperparameter values. To avoid trapping in a local minima it uses exploitation, to find best decision based on current information, and exploration, to gather more information (Yu & Zhu, 2020). However, this requires estimates of many statistics of the error function that can make these methods inefficient for evaluating deep neural network hyperparameters (Ilievski, Akhtar, Feng, & Shoemaker, 2017).

Unlike Grid and Random Search, many evaluations are avoided because it finds the next set of hyperparameters based on the previously tested hyperparameters (Yang, 2020; Yu & Zhu, 2020). This helps to find the optimum hyperparameters in less iterations compared to grid or random search (Andonie, 2020; Yang, 2020).

Bayesian Optimisation comprises of a Bayesian surrogate model for modelling the objective function and an acquisition function for determining the next sampling point (Yu and Zhu, 2020). Gaussian Process (GP) is the most widely used surrogate function (Yu & Zhu, 2020).

Many other models can be used as a surrogate function to model the objective function, such as Gaussian Process (GP), Random Forest (RF) and Tree-structured Parzen Estimator (TPE) method (Yang, 2020). Bergstra et al. (2011) have considered the Bayesian optimisation with a Gaussian Process based method, Sequential Model-Based Optimisation (SMBO), and Tree-structured Parzen Estimator method (TPE).

A tutorial on Bayesian optimisations is provided by Brochu et al. (2010). Bayesian optimisations use Bayesian techniques to get a posterior function. Two techniques, active user modelling and hierarchical reinforcement learning are also described therein. The limitations of Bayesian Optimisations such as feature selection and time-varying models are also described.

Bayesian optimisations with standard parameters were used by Borgli (2018) to optimise the hyperparameters of CNN to transfer learning for two publicly available image gastroenterology datasets. It was shown that automatic hyperparameter optimisation provided 10% better results than the baseline in transfer learning compared to manual methods.

Some studies have attempted to improve the Bayesian Optimisation. A Bayesian Multi-Objective hyperparameter optimisation network accelerator is proposed by Parsa (2020). The proposed system was shown to predict hyperparameters with less evaluations required for hierarchical Bayesian optimisation and agent-based modelling (Hierarchical-PABO) (Parsa, 2020).

A deterministic algorithm based on Radial Basis Function (RBF) is proposed that requires lesser function evaluations compared to Bayesian Optimisation (Ilievski et al., 2017). The evaluations on MNIST and CIFAR datasets were shown to be better, that is about 6 times faster for obtaining the best set of 19 hyperparameters, compared to Bayesian Optimisations such as GP, Sequential Model-based Algorithm Configuration (SMAC) and TPE.

An improved algorithms N-RReliefF was proposed to overcome the limitations of Bayesian Optimisation to select hyperparameters, by evaluating importance weights between hyperparameters and the hyperparameter importance (Sun, Gong & Zhang, 2019). The algorithm was tested for determining hyperparameter importance in Random Forest and SVM to determine the effectiveness of the proposed algorithm (Sun, Gong & Zhang, 2019).

Metaheuristic Algorithms

These algorithms are motivated by biological evolution (He, Zhao & Chu, 2021) to solve non-convex, large search space optimisation problems (Yang, 2020). In comparison with an exhaustive search, these are global methods which are widely used (He, Zhao & Chu, 2021).

Evolutionary Algorithms

An evolutionary algorithm will typically have the four steps of Selection, Crossover, Mutation and Update (He, Zhao & Chu, 2021). Genetic algorithms pass the best performing hyperparameters from one generation to the next, in order to find the best performing hyperparameter (Yang, 2020). Genetic algorithms were used to automatically learn the CNN architecture. The network structures are represented using a fixed-length binary string and each generation used standard methods of selection, mutation, and crossover (Xie & Yuille, 2017). The genetic algorithms were used for MNIST and CIFAR-10, and it was shown that the automatically generated structures performed better than the manual ones. The structures were then used for a larger dataset, ILSVRC2012.

A genetic algorithm was proposed in (Bhandare & Kaur, 2018) for hyperparameter optimisation on MNIST dataset. A number of hyperparameters were selected for optimisations. It was reported that the accuracy was over 90% but the best run had an accuracy of 99.2%. The simulation results for the genetic algorithm-based method were better than manual search methods (Loussaief & Abdelkrim, 2018). A genetic algorithm fast-CNN was proposed by Bakhshi (2019) for CNN architectures for hyperparameter optimisation and suitable architectures. Visual analytics were proposed for genetic algorithm by Chatzimparmpas (2021).

An Enhanced Elite CNN Model Propagation method is proposed by Loussaief & Abdelkrim (2018) that can automatically learn an optimised structure of CNN using a genetic algorithm. The classification accuracy was found to be better than public CNNs using transfer learning.

An evolutionary algorithm-based framework is proposed for automatic optimisations of CNN hyperparameters (Bochinski, Senst, & Sikora, 2017). This framework was then extended for joint optimisation of CNNs to provide significant improvement over state-of-the-art algorithms on MNIST dataset. Other techniques using committees of multiple CNNs are outlined by Bochinski, Senst, & Sikora (2017).

Evolutionary algorithms were proposed for automatic discovery of image classifier networks (Real, et al., 2017). Simple evolutionary algorithms were used to discover models for CIFAR-10 and CIFAR-100 datasets achieving an accuracy of 94.6%, although the computation costs were significant.

An evolutionary algorithm for hyperparameter optimisation with surrogate assistance is proposed by Zhang (2021). The author used a non-stationary kernel for measuring the difference between hyperparameter points, as opposed to surrogate models using stationary covariance functions. The proposed method was shown to perform better compared to Tree-structured Parzen Estimator (TPE), Gaussian processes (GP) besides others (Zhang, 2021).

The control of evolutionary hyperparameter optimisation with a visual analytics tool was proposed that supported interactive exploration and intervention for hyperparameters. The proposed tool is helpful to explore the hyperparameter search space and evolve to an optimum set (Chatzimparmpas, 2021).

Differential Evolution

A large search hyperparameter space search for continuous hyperparameters can be complex. Differential Evolution was proposed for complex hyperparameter spaces for deep learning models which reduced the overfitting and variation in the models (Han, Gondro, Reid & Steibel, 2021). Differential Evolution included four steps of initialisation, mutation, crossover and selection (Han, Gondro, Reid & Steibel, 2021). It was concluded that the technique was more important in working with smaller datasets (Han, Gondro, Reid & Steibel, 2021).

Swarm Intelligence Algorithms

These mimic self-organised population-based systems in nature representing collective intelligence of a bird flock, ant colony etc. In Particle Swarm optimisation, each particle communicates with all the other particles in each iteration to determine global optimum for the final and best performing optimum value (Yang, 2020). Particle swarm optimisation was used to automatically select the architecture and CNN hyperparameters with an aim to reduce the user variability in training (Soon, 2018). With optimised hyperparameters, CNN architecture was trained for better convergence and classification. The proposed methods were applied to vehicle log images, producing better results compared to other state-of-the art methods and obtaining 99.1% accuracy. A distributed Particle Swarm Optimisation approach was proposed to automatically determine the hyperparameters and a globally efficient hyperparameter combination in significantly reduced time. (Guo, 2020). A multi-level Particle Swarm optimised hyperparameter is proposed by Singh (2021).

An enhanced version of tree growth and firefly algorithm was proposed and used for hyperparameter optimisation (Bacanin et al., 2020). The proposed algorithms were also used for the network design and provided better performance compared to other approaches on MNIST dataset in terms of computational resources and classification accuracy (Bacanin et al., 2020).

Harmony Search

A metaheuristic optimisation method, parameter-setting-free harmony search (PSF-HS) is proposed (Lee, 2018) to adjust the hyperparameters. Hyperparameter tuning was proposed for CNN in the feature extraction step. The hyperparameter to be adjusted was set as a harmony; harmony memory was updated based on CNN loss by generating the harmony memory after the harmony. Simulations were performed using CNN architectures for LeNet-5, MNIST, CifarNet and CIFAR-10 datasets. The simulation results show improved performance compared to other techniques through hyperparameter tuning.

Reinforcement Learning

In Reinforcement machine learning the algorithm or the agent learns from its environment and its performance gets better with rewards for correct actions that take it towards its goal (Agrawal, 2021a).

A reinforcement learning based meta-modelling algorithm that can generate better CNN architectures automatically is proposed by Baker, Gupta, Naik, & Raskar (2017). CNN layers are chosen using Q-learning with greedy exploration strategy to train the learning agent. The agent selects higher performing CNN models through random exploration.

Q-Learning

Q-learning with a greedy exploration strategy was used by Zhong, Yan, Wei, Shao, & Liu (2018) with a learning agent to choose component layers. They used a block-wise generation that provided better results compared to hand-crafted networks and decreased the search space. An early stopping strategy was also used for fast block search.

An algorithm is proposed in (Mortazi, 2018) for an automatic search of optimal hyperparameters for neural architecture design for medical image segmentation. The proposed method was based on policy gradient reinforcement learning and was computationally efficient, compared to other medical image segmentation methods. The proposed hyperparameter search algorithm was applied to a proposed architecture with dense connected encoder-decoder CNN. The results with better accuracy were obtained for cine cardiac Magnetic Resonance Images (MRI) from Automated Cardiac Diagnosis Challenge (ACDC) MICCAI 2017, without any trial-and error or close supervision of hyperparameter changes as in other methods.

Multiagent System

A Multi-Agent Reinforcement Learning (MARL) is proposed by Iranfar (2021). Q-learning was adopted with the design space split into multiple sub-spaces with a learning agent for each layer and each agent optimising the hyperparameter for its assigned layer based on reward. A communication mechanism for the agents was provided through a proposed Q-table with new update rule (Iranfar, 2021). The approach provided 83 times, 52% and 54% reduction to model size, training time and inference time (Iranfar, 2021).

In general, the reinforcement learning techniques limit optimisation to architectural hyperparameters and manually choose other hyperparameters like learning rate and regularization parameters (Hinz et al., 2018).

An exploration into the reinforcement learning algorithms' variation in performance training runs, with various random seeds, is reported by Hertel (2020). Successive Halving, Bayesian Optimisation, and Random Search were considered and it was shown that for reinforcement learning tasks, Bayesian Optimisation was the best choice (Hertel, 2020).

Hyperparameter Selection and Speedup Approaches

The methods in this category are aimed at reducing the time taken, for example, by using techniques to exploit the CNN architecture. This section describes various speedup approaches.

Quantum CNN Optimisation

A quantum bit, qubit, represents binary information using probability. A convolutional CNN architecture is proposed by Lu (2020) for determining the number of convolutional layers in a network. With optimisation, the model test accuracy was improved with the number of network parameters reduced to a half of those without optimisation (Lu, 2020). Using quantum CNN architecture with qubit encoding, the network architecture was simplified and accuracy improved (Lu, 2020).

Optimisation of Selected Hyperparameter

Hyperparameter optimisations have generally low effective dimensionality. Although there are a large number of hyperparameters, only few have a significant impact on performance (Hinz et al., 2018). The selected hyperparameter optimisation algorithms were applied to CNN hyperparameters for images with increasing resolutions. It was found that the same hyperparameters were relevant, independent of the image resolution. This was used to speed up the hyperparameter optimisation. The result was that it took less time to find significant hyperparameters and the method can also be applied to data other than images, if its dimensions can be reduced.

Multi-Objective Optimisation

A fast converging multi-objective optimisation algorithm, MODE-CNN was proposed by İnik et al., (2021) based on a multi-objective differential evaluation (MODE) algorithm. İnik et al., (2021) also provide comparison with four other multi-objective optimisation algorithms. The proposed algorithm requires setting of the general stride, neighbour distance and patch accuracy (İnik et al., 2021).

Parameter Reduction

Hyperparameter reduction for CNN for field devices with low resources is proposed by Atanbori (2018) for segmentation of plant phenotyping. The results show trade-off between number of hyperparameters and accuracy were obtained using four baseline neural networks by increasing the network depth and reducing the number of hyperparameters, termed "Lite" CNNs.

Complexity Reduction

Reduction in computation by factorization of the convolutional layer was proposed by Wang (2017). The operations in convolution layer were treated separately as spatial convolution in each channel while maintaining the accuracy and reducing the computations. The model's performance was evaluated on ImageNet LSVRC 2012 dataset. The proposed model achieved many times less computations with similar performance for VGG-16, ResNet-34, ResNet-50 and ResNet-101.

Flattened convolutional neural networks are presented by Jin (2014) that were trained to obtain similar performance to conventional CNNs. For similar performance in accuracy as 3D filters, speed-up of about two times compared to baseline was obtained during the feedforward pass. After the model has been trained there is no requirement for manual tuning or post processing.

A small CNN architecture, termed SqueezeNet, requiring 50 times less parameters but achieving AlexNet level of accuracy (ImageNet 80.3% top-5 accuracy with 4.8MB SqueezeNet model) was proposed by Iandola (2016).

Early Stopping

A probabilistic model was used for early termination of bad runs (He, Zhao & Chu, 2021) and it was shown that the method provided a twofold increase compared to human experts for selected optimisation methods. This follows the strategy used by human experts for early termination of a bad run to save time. Learning curve extrapolation was used to devise an early termination criterion. The method that was used to investigate small and larger neural networks was independent of hyperparameter optimiser (Domhan et al., 2015).

Transfer Learning

By utilising the selected CNN primitives and transfer learning, the optimisation time was significantly reduced from hours to seconds (Mulder, 2020). This was achieved by replacing the expensive profiling stage with performance modelling based on machine learning (Mulder, 2020). The proposed improvement helped a CNN model to achieve a high performance on the chosen hardware platform (Mulder, 2020). A transfer neural AutoML was proposed that accelerated network design by using knowledge from prior tasks (He, Zhao & Chu, 2021).

Massively Parallel Hyperparameter Tuning

A large scale parallel hyperparameter tuning is proposed by Li et al. (2018) to evaluate many hyperparameter configurations in parallel to reduce the training time significantly. They also used early stopping in conjunction with parallelism to further reduce time. The proposed algorithm can find optimal hyperparameters much faster than random search. Separate GPUs were used to train each model but the speedup did not increase linearly due to communications cost.

POP Scheduling

A scheduling algorithm is proposed by Rasley, He, & Yan (2017), called POP that quickly identifies the promising, opportunistic, and poor hyperparameter configurations. An infrastructure was also proposed that could work across different scheduling algorithms. A speedup of about 6.7 times was reported compared to random/grid search and 2.1 compared to state-of-the-art methods.

Multi-Fidelity Optimisation

Multi-fidelity optimisation algorithms are designed to overcome the limited resources for training a machine learning model (Yang, 2020). A Bandit-based approach for hyperparameter optimisation, termed Hyperband was proposed that used early stopping and adaptive resource allocation for speedup of random search. The results showed that hyperband method provided a speedup over different deep learning problems (Li, 2017). The proposed method extended the Successive Halving by calling it as a subroutine (Li, 2017). The Hyperband algorithm was also shown to be parallelised which can provide significant speedup (Li, 2017). Hyperband explores as many configurations possible by utilising the limited resources to determine the final result (Su et al., 2020).

Using a multi-armed bandit network, a progressive multi-fidelity technique was combined with successive halving; it was shown that the proposed method achieved better performance compared to state-of-the-art optimisation methods (Zhu, 2020). The method also provided the speedup of hyperparameter optimisation (Zhu, 2020).

Bayesian Optimisation and Hyperband (BOHB) for hyperparameter optimisation was proposed to combine the benefits of both methods to obtain a fast convergence and better performance (Falkner, Klein, & Hutter, 2018). A multi-fidelity optimisation, Auto-Pytorch is proposed by Zimmer (2021) which combined BOHB (Bayesian Optimisation and Hyperband) with portfolios of hyperparameters and architectures using ensembling to obtain a superior performance. The author showed that a better configuration space for a joint architecture and hyperparameter search can determine efficient models, and that a combination of multi-fidelity optimisation and Bayesian optimisation can lead to efficient search of the configuration space.

Automated Machine Learning (AutoML)

Machine learning models are quite complex and demanding. The main idea is to use intelligent optimisation algorithms to streamline the hyperparameter and model selection without the dependence on expert humans (Su et al., 2020). The AutoML approach makes using machine learning model building easier for non-experts and builds a complete pipeline (Agrawal, 2021b). AutoML makes it possible to boost the productivity of data scientists and non-experts alike by automating many tasks in the machine learning pipelines (Truong, 2019). The support for deep learning has become available and popular on AutoML (Zimmer, 2021).

AutoML methods cover hyperparameter optimisation, as well as data preparation, feature engineering, and neural architecture search (NAS) (He, Zhao & Chu, 2021; Truong, 2019). The recent increase is in NAS to find the best architecture, and hyperparameter optimisation, with AutoDL systems optimising both jointly (Zimmer, 2021).

Libraries

There are libraries for hyperparameter optimisation such as Hyperopt and Optuna (Agrawal, 2021b). Some of the other libraries for AutoML are Auto-WEKA, Auto-Skllearn, H2O AutoML, AutoKeras, TPOT, and Auto-Keras (Agrawal, 2021b; He, Zhao & Chu, 2021; Truong, 2019).

Scikit-optimise library implements different optimisations. The impact of hyperparameters was studied using scikit-optimise library for MNIST dataset classification (Shaziya, 2021). Different sets of numbers of nodes, layers, learning rates and number of dense layers were used with three functions based on decision trees, gradient boosted and Gaussian process (Shaziya, 2021).

Frameworks

There are many AutoML tools and frameworks such as Tree-based Pipeline Optimisation Tool (TPOT) which use genetic programming for optimisation (Agrawal, 2021b). TPOT handles the complex tasks of feature engineering and determines the best model with the optimum set of hyperparameters (Agrawal, 2021b).

Cloud Based Solutions

The CSPs have also made available AutoML features. Google Cloud Platform (GCP) AutoML has features for natural language, tables, translation, video intelligence and vision. AutoML Vision deals with object detection and image classification (Google AutoML). Microsoft Azure also provides AutoML services (Microsoft AutoML). Amazon Web Services (AWS) provides Forecast (Amazon Forecast AutoML). AutoML can be activated using the Amazon Forecast console or Software Development Kit (SDK) and can be used for hyperparameter optimisation (Amazon Forecast). The AutoML features for Microsoft Azure are shown in Figure 5. As shown in the figure, the data, optimisation metric e.g., accuracy and the constraints have to be specified based on the model that can be generated automatically with the best hyperparameter configuration.

Google Vizier is a service based on black-box optimisation and is easy to use. The users can obtain a hyperparameter set by submitting a configuration file and indicating the search algorithm (Yu &Zhu, 2020). Neural Network Intelligence (NNI) is released by Microsoft and can be used for AutoML and hyperparameter optimisation (Yu & Zhu, 2020).

The comparison of various AutoML tools by Truong (2019) reported there is not yet a perfect tool that can perform better on all selected tasks. However, most tools performed reasonably well across many datasets. An ensemble of AutoML systems is proposed by Yoo (2020) that ensembles the output of open-source AutoML models. The proposed system ensembled AutoML systems such as, Auto-Sklearn, AutoGluon, CMU AutoML and H2O AutoML, and were found to outperform any of the constituent ensembled systems (Yoo, 2020).

Figure 5. AutoML on the Microsoft Azure [Microsoft AutoML].

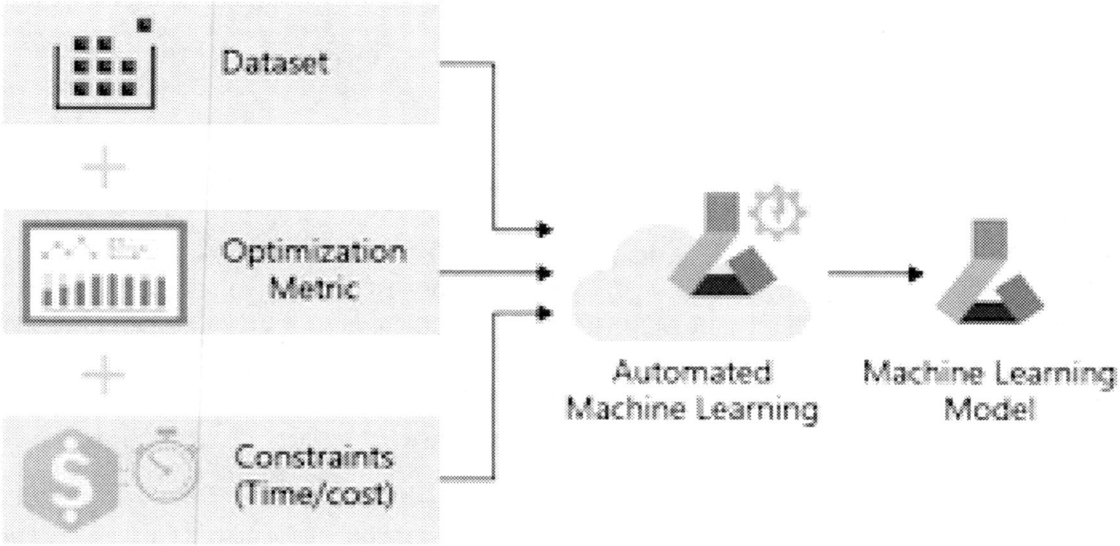

COMPARISON OF OPTIMISATION TECHNIQUES

Manual Search requires an insight and understanding of the relative importance of the hyperparameters for the given model (Yang, 2020). The expert could detect failures and terminate training at an early stage (Ozaki et al., 2017). In Grid search an exhaustive search is carried out for optimum values. This is one of the most popular method for hyperparameter optimisation (Albelwi & Mahmood, 2016) and can find better values than a purely manual search given that sufficient computing resources are available (Bergstra & Bengio, 2012). However, it can perform reliably for one and two-dimensional hyperparameter spaces (Bergstra & Bengio, 2012) and can be effective if the number of hyperparameters is small (Bacanin et al., 2020). Random Search can also be used to investigate the effect of one hyperparameter, similar to a manual search (Bergstra & Bengio, 2012) and can handle integer and categorical hyperparameters (Ozaki et al., 2017).

All of these traditional methods, that is, manual, grid and random search require domain knowledge and time (Bacanin et al., 2020). The limitation of conventional manual or exhaustive search methods is that they require lot of computation and time, and may require expert insights for optimal hyperparameter selection. The traditional hyperparameter optimisation techniques are no longer used on their own due to their exhaustive search nature and the complexity of the models has increased.

Genetic Algorithms are useful for applications in large search spaces. These could perform better than Bayesian Optimisation in some cases, however, they require more computational resources and prolonged running time (Matache, 2019). Similarly, although reinforcement learning has somewhat relaxed constraints on exploration and exploitation compared to Bayesian methods, it also requires lot of computational resources which might not be accessible to the users (Matache, 2019).

Hyperband can be parallelised and therefore scales better (Matache, 2019) and can be between 5 to 30 times faster than Bayesian Optimisation for deep learning problems (Matache, 2019). An advantage of Bayesian Optimisation is that it can be applied irrespective of the objective function being convex, non-convex, stochastic or discrete (Yu & Zhu, 2020). GP is a non-parametric model but as surrogate for Bayesian Optimisation, it can be difficult to understand and for high dimensional or large data could have poor scalability (Yu & Zhu, 2020). Bayesian optimisation with TPE provides good results with discrete and high dimensional optimisations, whereas Bayesian Optimisation with GP is better suited for numerical problems (Hutter, Lucke & Schmidt-Thieme, 2015). Although Bayesian Optimisation is useful in cases where the function is a black box and is not easily differentiable, a limitation is that the search space is set early by the activation function resulting in the model missing an important feature (Victoria & Maragatham, 2021). Bayesian optimisation techniques are still important and relevant as these are being used by many of the toolkits such as HyperOpt and HpBandSter, and automated frameworks such as Google Vizier and AWS Sagemaker (Yu & Zhu, 2020).

Multi-armed bandit algorithms are computationally efficient and therefore useful for deep learning (Yu & Zhu, 2020). Bayesian Optimisation and Hyperband (BOHB) could be the first choice for most neural networks, due to its accuracy and efficiency (Yu & Zhu, 2020).

In all hyperparameter optimisation methods, it is important to determine the relative importance of the hyperparameters. Techniques such as N-RReliefF algorithm (Sun, Gong & Zhang, 2019) can make it easier to determine the importance and contribution of the hyperparameters. In future, more emphasis will be on the automation of hyperparameter optimisation for reproducibility of the results. Increasing focus will be on data centric techniques as explainability is becoming more and more important. On the other hand, automated hyperparameter optimisations can be used by non-experts.

FUTURE RESEARCH DIRECTIONS

Despite substantial progress in the learning algorithms, many challenges still remain. The models need to be reproducible so that further advancements and improvements are facilitated. The need for reproducible and optimum CNN models will move towards automated machine learning. The AutoML methods were introduced covering data preparation, feature engineering, hyperparameter optimisation, and neural architecture search (NAS) (He, Zhao & Chu 2021). NAS (Neural Architecture Search) is also a recent trend in AutoML. (Zimmer, 2021). Although AutoML can provide optimum configuration settings, there is little evidence as to why the selected settings perform better (He, Zhao & Chu, 2021). More work is required to explain the ability of the model, and how AutoML algorithms can be generalised to different problems, which can adjust to new data and also utilise old data (He, Zhao & Chu2021). AutoML is now being supported by the machine learning frameworks and also cloud service providers (CSPs) have started to provide these services. In future, the CSPs will be leading research efforts for AutoML and hyperparameter optimisations.

Another emerging trend, related to machine learning models in general, is to make the models explainable. The corresponding research area is responsible, interpretable and explainable AI, that aims to provide insights into the decisions made by a machine learning model.

Quantum computers promise many orders of magnitude and speedup in processing time. Unlike conventional computers with a bit representing, one of the two states, quantum computation is based on qubits. Quantum computing is still in experimental stages and it will take time for quantum computers to become available. In view of the achievable speedup, it can be surmised that Quantum computing would be very helpful to speed up the process of hyperparameter optimisation.

Hyperparameter optimisation is also helped by the ensembles, that is, if there are many models then it makes sense to improve the performance by ensembling the models (Zimmer, 2021). This would become more important and a useful concept for hyperparameter optimisation. The advantages of two or more metaheuristic algorithms, termed as hybridisation of metaheuristic algorithms provides better accuracy and a faster convergence (Bacanin et al., 2020).

Hybrid Optimisation methods can be used for combining the advantages of two or more methods. For example, although Evolutionary Algorithms has a high robustness, it required lot of computational resources, thus combining it with Reinforcement Learning, or SMBO can result in improvement (He, Zhao & Chu, 2021). A hybrid optimisation method combined TPE and Hyperband, and the results were validated by comparing against each Hyperband and TPE (Matache, 2019).

There is an overlap between the methods used for hyperparameter optimisation and architecture optimisation in neural networks. With research into the problem of a joint optimisation of both the hyperparameters and the architectures, it becomes possible to jointly optimise (He, Zhao & Chu, 2021).

CONCLUSION

There have been many advances in the application of convolutional neural networks to image classification with promising results, similar or better than a human. The tuning of model architectures could be driven by intuition and experimentation, resulting in the optimal values of the hyperparameters. This method of experimental tuning to determine the values does not scale well with the number of hyperparameters, which increase exponentially with the number of network layers.

The search for an optimal configuration of hyperparameters for CNNs requires computational power, time, and associated cost. With large numbers of hyperparameters, it is critical to quickly converge to an optimal set from the search space.

The initial models were manually optimised by the researchers that enabled image classification results comparable to humans but required good model understanding. With the rise in the number of hyperparameters, research efforts were focussed on using traditional methods, such as grid search, wherein different sets or configurations were tried out sequentially. The need for early termination was initially met by a manual process and some automated processes could also terminate non-performing hyperparameter selection.

The choice of a particular hyperparameter optimisation strategy depends on the chosen architecture, number of selected hyperparameters to be tuned, availability of time and processing power. We have provided an overview of the hyperparameter optimisation techniques signifying the contribution of each method. A natural progression in the research methods is from simple methods to state-of-the-art techniques. Better hyperparameter optimisations would be aided by shallow neural networks (with results comparable to deep networks), parallel execution of hyperparameter configurations, and optimisation frameworks that might take care of all the intricate optimisation details for researchers in the future. The state-of-the-art methods have automated the process for hyperparameter optimisations, as well as employed parallel processing to exploit the CNN architecture in order to save time.

Current research is focussed on automated optimisations, for which we provide state-of-the art techniques from the research literature. The term automated machine learning (AutoML) refers to an automated process for model creation, including hyperparameter optimisation, and this reduces the complexity and time for the machine learning practitioners, and also for non-experts. This recent development is now provided by Cloud Service Providers (CSPs), and machine learning frameworks. The future is promising for automated hyperparameter optimisation, where the operation would not only be fully automated but would help to generate results that are reproducible and explainable.

This research received no specific grant from any funding agency in the public, commercial, or not-for-profit sectors.

REFERENCES

Agrawal, T. (2021a). Introduction to Hyperparameters. In *Hyperparameter Optimization in Machine Learning* (pp. 1–30). Apress. doi:10.1007/978-1-4842-6579-6_1

Agrawal, T. (2021b). Optuna and AutoML. In *Hyperparameter Optimization in Machine Learning* (pp. 109–129). Apress. doi:10.1007/978-1-4842-6579-6_5

Albelwi, S., & Mahmood, A. (2016, December). Automated optimal architecture of deep convolutional neural networks for image recognition. In *2016 15th IEEE International conference on machine learning and applications (ICMLA)* (pp. 53-60). IEEE. 10.1109/ICMLA.2016.0018

Alzubaidi, L., Zhang, J., Humaidi, A. J., Al-Dujaili, A., Duan, Y., Al-Shamma, O., Santamaría, J., Fadhel, M. A., Al-Amidie, M., & Farhan, L. (2021). Review of deep learning: Concepts, CNN architectures, challenges, applications, future directions. *Journal of Big Data*, 8(1), 53. doi:10.118640537-021-00444-8 PMID:33816053

Amazon Forecast AutoM. L. (n.d.). https://docs.aws.amazon.com/forecast/latest/dg/automl.html

Andonie, R., & Florea, A. C. (2020). *Weighted random search for CNN hyperparameter optimization.* arXiv preprint arXiv:2003.13300.

Arel, I., Rose, D. C., & Karnowski, T. P. (2010). Deep machine learning-a new frontier in artificial intelligence research. *IEEE Computational Intelligence Magazine*, *5*(4), 13–18. doi:10.1109/MCI.2010.938364

Atanbori, J., Chen, F., French, A. P., & Pridmore, T. (2018). Towards low-cost image-based plant phenotyping using reduced-parameter CNN. In *CVPPP 2018: Workshop on Computer Vision Problems in Plant Phenotyping*, Newcastle upon Tyne, UK.

Bacanin, N., Bezdan, T., Tuba, E., Strumberger, I., & Tuba, M. (2020). Optimizing Convolutional Neural Network Hyperparameters by Enhanced Swarm Intelligence Metaheuristics. *Algorithms*, *13*(3), 67. doi:10.3390/a13030067

Baker, B., Gupta, O., Naik, N., & Raskar, R. (2017). Designing neural network architectures using reinforcement learning. *Proceedings of Int. Conf. Learning Representations.*

Bakhshi, A., Noman, N., Chen, Z., Zamani, M., & Chalup, S. (2019, June). Fast automatic optimisation of CNN architectures for image classification using genetic algorithm. In *2019 IEEE Congress on Evolutionary Computation (CEC)* (pp. 1283-1290). IEEE. 10.1109/CEC.2019.8790197

Bartz, E., Zaefferer, M., Mersmann, O., & Bartz-Beielstein, T. (2021). *Experimental investigation and evaluation of model-based hyperparameter optimisation.* arXiv:2107.08761v1 [cs.LG].

Bengio, Y. (2009). Learning Deep Architectures for AI. *Foundations and Trends in Machine Learning*, *2*(1), 1–127. doi:10.1561/2200000006

Benuwa, B. B., Zhan, Y. Z., Ghansah, B., Wornyo, D. K., & Banaseka Kataka, F. (2016). A review of deep machine learning. *International Journal of Engineering Research in Africa*, *24*, 124–136. doi:10.4028/www.scientific.net/JERA.24.124

Bergstra, J., Bardenet, R., Bengio, Y., & Kégl, B. (2011). Algorithms for hyper-parameter optimization. Adv Neural Inf Process Syst (NIPS), 24, 2546-2554.

Bergstra, J., & Bengio, Y. (2012). Random search for hyper-parameter optimization. *Journal of Machine Learning Research*, *13*(2).

Bhandare, A., & Kaur, D. (2018). Designing convolutional neural network architecture using genetic algorithms. In *Proceedings on the International Conference on Artificial Intelligence (ICAI)* (pp. 150-156). The Steering Committee of The World Congress in Computer Science, Computer Engineering and Applied Computing (WorldComp).

Bochinski, E., Senst, T., & Sikora, T. (2017, September). Hyper-parameter optimization for convolutional neural network committees based on evolutionary algorithms. In 2017 IEEE international conference on image processing (ICIP) (pp. 3924-3928). IEEE. doi:10.1109/ICIP.2017.8297018

Borgli, R. J. (2018). *Hyperparameter optimization using Bayesian optimization on transfer learning for medical image classification* [Master thesis]. University of Oslo.

Brochu, E., Cora, V. M., & De Freitas, N. (2010). *A tutorial on Bayesian optimization of expensive cost functions, with application to active user modeling and hierarchical reinforcement learning.* arXiv preprint arXiv:1012.2599.

Chatzimparmpas, A., Martins, R. M., Kucher, K., & Kerren, A. (2021, June). VisEvol: Visual analytics to support hyperparameter search through evolutionary optimization. *Computer Graphics Forum, 40*(3), 201–214. doi:10.1111/cgf.14300

Deng, J., Dong, W., Socher, R., Li, L. J., Li, K., & Fei-Fei, L. (2009, June). Imagenet: A large-scale hierarchical image database. In 2009 IEEE conference on computer vision and pattern recognition (pp. 248-255). IEEE. doi:10.1109/CVPR.2009.5206848

Domhan, T., Springenberg, J. T., & Hutter, F. (2015, June). Speeding up automatic hyperparameter optimization of deep neural networks by extrapolation of learning curves. *Twenty-fourth international joint conference on artificial intelligence.*

Falkner, S., Klein, A., & Hutter, F. (2018). *BOHB: Robust and efficient hyperparameter optimization at scale.* arXiv:1807.01774v1 [cs.LG].

Gambella, C., Ghaddar, B., & Naoum-Sawaya, J. (2021). Optimization problems for machine learning: A survey. *European Journal of Operational Research, 290*(3), 807–828. doi:10.1016/j.ejor.2020.08.045

Google AutoM. L. (n.d.). https://cloud.google.com/automl/

Greenhill, S., Rana, S., Gupta, S., Vellanki, P., & Venkatesh, S. (2019). Bayesian Optimization for Adaptive Experimental Design: A Review. *IEEE Access: Practical Innovations, Open Solutions, 8*, 2020.

Guo, Y., Li, J. Y., & Zhan, Z. H. (2020). Efficient hyperparameter optimization for convolution neural networks in deep learning: A distributed particle swarm optimization approach. *Cybernetics and Systems, 52*(1), 36–57. doi:10.1080/01969722.2020.1827797

Han, J., Gondro, C., Reid, K., & Steibel, J. P. (2021). Heuristic hyperparameter optimization of deep learning models for genomic prediction. *G3 (Bethesda, Md.), 11*(7), jkab032. doi:10.1093/g3journal/jkab032 PMID:33993261

Hasanpour, S. H., Rouhani, M., Fayyaz, M., & Sabokrou, M. (2016). *Lets keep it simple, using simple architectures to outperform deeper and more complex architectures.* arXiv preprint arXiv:1608.06037.

Hayakawa, Y., Oonuma, T., Kobayashi, H., Takahashi, A., Chiba, S., & Fujiki, N. M. (2017). Feature Extraction of Video Using Artificial Neural Network. *International Journal of Cognitive Informatics and Natural Intelligence, 11*(2), 25–40. doi:10.4018/IJCINI.2017040102

He, K., Zhang, X., Ren, S., & Sun, J. (2015). Delving deep into rectifiers: Surpassing human-level performance on imagenet classification. In *Proceedings of the IEEE international conference on computer vision* (pp. 1026-1034). IEEE. 10.1109/ICCV.2015.123

He, X., Zhao, K., & Chu, X. (2021). AutoML: A Survey of the State-of-the-Art. *Knowledge-Based Systems, 212*, 106622. doi:10.1016/j.knosys.2020.106622

Hertel, L., Baldi, P., & Gillen, D. L. (2020). *Quantity vs. Quality: On Hyperparameter Optimization for Deep Reinforcement Learning.* arXiv preprint arXiv:2007.14604.

Hinz, T., Navarro-Guerrero, N., Magg, S., & Wermter, S. (2018). Speeding up the Hyperparameter Optimization of Deep Convolutional Neural Networks. *International Journal of Computational Intelligence and Applications, 17*(2), 1850008. doi:10.1142/S1469026818500086

Hutter, F., Lucke, J., & Schmidt-Thieme, L. (2015). Beyond Manual Tuning of Hyperparameters. *Kunstl Intell, 29*(4), 329–337. doi:10.100713218-015-0381-0

Iandola, F. N., Han, S., Moskewicz, M. W., Ashraf, K., Dally, W. J., & Keutzer, K. (2016). *SqueezeNet: AlexNet-level accuracy with 50x fewer parameters and< 0.5 MB model size.* arXiv preprint arXiv:1602.07360.

Ilievski, I., Akhtar, T., Feng, J., & Shoemaker, C. (2017, February). Efficient hyperparameter optimization for deep learning algorithms using deterministic rbf surrogates. *Proceedings of the AAAI Conference on Artificial Intelligence, 31*(1).

İnik, Ö., Altiok, M., Ülker, E., & Koçer, B. (2021). MODE-CNN: A fast converging multi-objective optimization algorithm for CNN-based models. *Applied Soft Computing, 109*, 107582. doi:10.1016/j.asoc.2021.107582

Iranfar, A., Zapater, M., & Atienza, D. (2021). Multi-Agent Reinforcement Learning for Hyperparameter Optimization of Convolutional Neural Networks. *IEEE Transactions on Computer-Aided Design of Integrated Circuits and Systems*, 1. doi:10.1109/TCAD.2021.3077193

Jin, J., Dundar, A., & Culurciello, E. (2014). *Flattened convolutional neural networks for feedforward acceleration.* arXiv preprint arXiv:1412.5474.

Keskar, N. S., Mudigere, D., Nocedal, J., Smelyanskiy, M., & Tang, P. T. P. (2017). On Large-batch Training for Deep Learning: Generalization Gap and Sharp Minima. *ICLR 2017.*

Kienzler, R. (2017). *IBM Report, Developing cognitive IoT solutions for anomaly detection by using deep learning, Part 1: Introducing deep learning and long-short term memory networks: Detecting anomalies in IoT time-series data by using deep learning.* IBM.

Koutsoukas, A., Monaghan, K. J., Li, X., & Huan, J. (2017). Deep-learning: Investigating deep neural networks hyper-parameters and comparison of performance to shallow methods for modeling bioactivity data. *Journal of Cheminformatics, 9*(1), 1–13. doi:10.118613321-017-0226-y PMID:29086090

Krizhevsky, A., Sutskever, I., & Hinton, G. E. (2012). Imagenet classification with deep convolutional neural networks. *Advances in Neural Information Processing Systems, 25*, 1097–1105.

LeCun, Y., Boser, B., Denker, J. S., Henderson, D., Howard, R. E., Hubbard, W., & Jackel, L. D. (1989). Backpropagation applied to handwritten zip code recognition. *Neural Computation, 1*(4), 541–551. doi:10.1162/neco.1989.1.4.541

Lee, W. Y., Park, S. M., & Sim, K. B. (2018). Optimal hyperparameter tuning of convolutional neural networks based on the parameter-setting-free harmony search algorithm. *Optik (Stuttgart), 172*, 359–367. doi:10.1016/j.ijleo.2018.07.044

Li, L., Jamieson, K., DeSalvo, G., Rostamizadeh, A., & Talwalkar, A. (2017). Hyperband: A novel bandit-based approach to hyperparameter optimization. *Journal of Machine Learning Research*, *18*(1), 6765–6816.

Li, L., Jamieson, K., Rostamizadeh, A., Gonina, E., & Talwalkar, A. (2018). *Massively Parallel Hyperparameter Tuning.* arXiv:1810.05934.

Liu, Y., Sun, Y., Xue, B., Zhang, M., Yen, G. G., & Tan, K. C. (2021). A Survey on Evolutionary Neural Architecture Search. *IEEE Transactions on Neural Networks and Learning Systems*, 1–21. doi:10.1109/TNNLS.2021.3100554 PMID:34357870

Loussaief, S., & Abdelkrim, A. (2018). Convolutional neural network hyper-parameters optimization based on genetic algorithms. *International Journal of Advanced Computer Science and Applications*, *9*(10), 252–266. doi:10.14569/IJACSA.2018.091031

Lu, T. C. (2020). CNN Convolutional layer optimisation based on quantum evolutionary algorithm. *Connection Science*, 1–13.

Maas, A. L., Hannun, A. Y., & Ng, A. Y. (2013, June). Rectifier nonlinearities improve neural network acoustic models. In Proc. ICML (Vol. 30, No. 1, p. 3). Academic Press.

Matache, C. (2019). *Efficient Design of Machine Learning Hyperparameter Optimizers.* MEng Individual Project. Imperial College London. https://docs.microsoft.com/en-us/azure/machine-learning/concept-automated-ml

Minar, M. R., & Naher, J. (2018). *Recent advances in deep learning: An overview.* arXiv preprint arXiv:1807.08169.

Mortazi, A., & Bagci, U. (2018, September). Automatically designing CNN architectures for medical image segmentation. In *International Workshop on Machine Learning in Medical Imaging* (pp. 98-106). Springer. 10.1007/978-3-030-00919-9_12

Mulder, R., Radu, V., & Dubach, C. (2020). *Optimising the Performance of Convolutional Neural Networks across Computing Systems using Transfer Learning.* arXiv preprint arXiv:2010.10621

Nazir, S., Patel, S., & Patel, D. (2018, July). Hyper parameters selection for image classification in convolutional neural networks. In *2018 IEEE 17th International Conference on Cognitive Informatics & Cognitive Computing (ICCI* CC)* (pp. 401-407). IEEE. 10.1109/ICCI-CC.2018.8482081

Neetesh, M. (2017). The Connect between Deep Learning and AI. *Open Source for You.*

Nguyen, H. N., & Lee, C. (2018). Effects of Hyper-parameters and Dataset on CNN Training. *Journal of IKEEE*, *22*(1), 14–20.

Ozaki, Y., Yano, M., & Onishi, M. (2017). Effective hyperparameter optimization using Nelder-Mead method in deep learning. *IPSJ Transactions on Computer Vision and Applications*, *9*(1), 1–12. doi:10.118641074-017-0030-7

Parsa, M., Mitchell, J. P., Schuman, C. D., Patton, R. M., Potok, T. E., & Roy, K. (2020). Bayesian multi-objective hyperparameter optimization for accurate, fast, and efficient neural network accelerator design. *Frontiers in Neuroscience*, *14*, 667. doi:10.3389/fnins.2020.00667 PMID:32848531

Probst, P., Wright, M. N., & Boulesteix, A-L. (2019). Hyperparameters and tuning strategies for random forest. *2019 WIREs Data Mining Knowl Discov.*

Rasley, J., He, Y., Yan, F., Ruwase, O., & Fonseca, R. (2017, December). Hyperdrive: Exploring hyper-parameters with pop scheduling. In *Proceedings of the 18th ACM/IFIP/USENIX Middleware Conference* (pp. 1-13). ACM.

Real, E., Moore, S., Selle, A., Saxena, S., Suematsu, Y. L., Tan, J., Le, Q. V., & Kurakin, A. (2017). Large-scale evolution of image classifiers. In *Proceedings of Int. Conf. Machine Learning*. ACM.

Russakovsky, O., Deng, J., Su, H., Krause, J., Satheesh, S., Ma, S., Huang, Z., Karpathy, A., Khosla, A., Bernstein, M., Berg, A. C., & Fei-Fei, L. (2015). ImageNet Large Scale Visual Recognition Challenge. *International Journal of Computer Vision*, *115*(3), 211–252. doi:10.100711263-015-0816-y

Saari, M. (2018). *The effect of two hyper parameters in the learning performance of the convolutional neural networks* (Bachelor thesis). Tampere University of Technology.

Schmidhuber, J. (2015). Deep learning in neural networks: An overview. *Neural Networks*, *61*, 85–117. doi:10.1016/j.neunet.2014.09.003 PMID:25462637

Shaziya, H., & Zaheer, R. (2021). Impact of Hyperparameters on Model Development in Deep Learning. In *Proceedings of International Conference on Computational Intelligence and Data Engineering* (pp. 57-67). Springer. 10.1007/978-981-15-8767-2_5

Shen, D., Wu, G., & Suk, H. I. (2017). Deep learning in medical image analysis. *Annual Review of Biomedical Engineering*, *19*(1), 221–248. doi:10.1146/annurev-bioeng-071516-044442 PMID:28301734

Singh, P., Chaudhury, S., & Panigrahi, B. K. (2021). Hybrid MPSO-CNN: Multi-level Particle Swarm optimized hyperparameters of Convolutional Neural Network. *Swarm and Evolutionary Computation*, *63*, 100863. doi:10.1016/j.swevo.2021.100863

Soon, F. C., Khaw, H. Y., Chuah, J. H., & Kanesan, J. (2018). Hyper-parameters optimisation of deep CNN architecture for vehicle logo recognition. *IET Intelligent Transport Systems*, *12*(8), 939–946. doi:10.1049/iet-its.2018.5127

Srivastava, N., Hinton, G., Krizhevsky, A., Sutskever, I., & Salakhutdinov, R. (2014). Dropout: A simple way to prevent neural networks from overfitting. *Journal of Machine Learning Research*, *15*(1), 1929–1958.

Su, M., Liang, B., Ma, S., Xiang, C., Zhang, C., & Wang, J. (2020). Automatic machine learning method for hyper-parameter Search. *Journal of Physics: Conference Series*, 1802.

Sun, Y., Gong, H., Li, Y., & Zhang, D. (2019). Hyperparameter importance analysis based on N-RReliefF algorithm. *International Journal of Computers, Communications & Control*, *14*(4), 557–573. doi:10.15837/ijccc.2019.4.3593

Szegedy, C., Liu, W., Jia, Y., Sermanet, P., Reed, S., Anguelov, D., Erhan, D., Vanhoucke, V., & Rabinovich, A. (2015). Going deeper with convolutions. In *Proceedings of Conference on Computer Vision and Pattern Recognition* (CVPR). IEEE.

Tibbetts, J. H. (2018). The Frontiers of Artificial Intelligence. *Bioscience*, *68*(1), 5–10. doi:10.1093/biosci/bix136

Truong, A., Walters, A., Goodsitt, J., Hines, K., Bruss, C. B., & Farivar, R. (2019, November). Towards automated machine learning: Evaluation and comparison of AutoML approaches and tools. In *2019 IEEE 31st international conference on tools with artificial intelligence (ICTAI)* (pp. 1471-1479). IEEE.

Tutorial, D. L. (2015). *Release 0.1, LISA Lab*. University of Montreal. http://deeplearning.net/tutorial/deeplearning.pdf

Victoria, A. H., & Maragatham, G. (2021). Automatic tuning of hyperparameters using Bayesian Optimization. *Evolving Systems*, *2021*(12), 217–223. doi:10.100712530-020-09345-2

Wang, M., Liu, B., & Foroosh, H. (2017). Factorized convolutional neural networks. In *Proceedings of the IEEE International Conference on Computer Vision Workshops* (pp. 545-553). IEEE.

Wang, Z. J., Turko, R., Shaikh, O., Park, H., Das, N., Hohman, F., Kahng, M., & Chau, D. H. P. (2020). CNN explainer: Learning convolutional neural networks with interactive visualization. *IEEE Transactions on Visualization and Computer Graphics*, *27*(2), 1396–1406. doi:10.1109/TVCG.2020.3030418 PMID:33048723

Wu, Chen, Zhang, Xiong, Lei, & Deng. (2019). Hyperparameter optimization for machine learning models based on Bayesian Optimization. *Journal of Electronic Science and Technology*, *17*(1).

Xie, L., & Yuille, A. (2017). Genetic cnn. In *Proceedings of the IEEE international conference on computer vision* (pp. 1379-1388). IEEE.

Yang, L., & Shami, A. (2020). On hyperparameter optimization of machine learning algorithms: Theory and practice. *Neurocomputing*, *415*, 295–316. doi:10.1016/j.neucom.2020.07.061

Yaseen, M. U., Anjum, A., Rana, O., & Antonopoulos, N. (2019). Deep learning hyper-parameter optimization for video analytics in clouds. *IEEE Transactions on Systems, Man, and Cybernetics. Systems*, *49*(1), 253–264. doi:10.1109/TSMC.2018.2840341

Yoo, J., Joseph, T., Yung, D., Nasseri, S. A., & Wood, F. (2020). *Ensemble squared: A meta automl system.* arXiv preprint arXiv:2012.05390.

Yu, T., & Zhu, H. (2020). *Hyper-Parameter Optimization: A Review of Algorithms and Applications.* arXiv:2003.05689v1 [cs.LG].

Yue-Hei Ng, J., Hausknecht, M., Vijayanarasimhan, S., Vinyals, O., Monga, R., & Toderici, G. (2015). Beyond short snippets: Deep networks for video classification. In *Proceedings of the IEEE conference on computer vision and pattern recognition* (pp. 4694-4702). 10.1109/CVPR.2015.7299101

Zhang, M., Li, H., Pan, S., Lyu, J., Ling, S., & Su, S. (2021). Convolutional neural networks based lung nodule classification: A surrogate-assisted evolutionary algorithm for hyperparameter optimization. *IEEE Transactions on Evolutionary Computation*, *25*(5), 869–882. doi:10.1109/TEVC.2021.3060833

Zhong, Z., Yan, J., Wu, W., Shao, J., & Liu, C. L. (2018). Practical block-wise neural network architecture generation. In *Proceedings of the IEEE conference on computer vision and pattern recognition* (pp. 2423-2432). IEEE.

Zhu, G., & Zhu, R. (2020). Accelerating Hyperparameter Optimization of Deep Neural Network via Progressive Multi-Fidelity Evaluation. *Advances in Knowledge Discovery and Data Mining*, *12084*, 752–763. doi:10.1007/978-3-030-47426-3_58

Zimmer, L., Lindauer, M., & Hutter, F. (2021). Auto-Pytorch: Multi-Fidelity MetaLearning for Efficient and Robust AutoDL. *IEEE Transactions on Pattern Analysis and Machine Intelligence*, *43*(9), 3079–3090. doi:10.1109/TPAMI.2021.3067763 PMID:33750687

KEY TERMS AND DEFINITIONS

Automated Machine Learning: Automated machine learning automates the complex and time-consuming process of model development and is thus very useful for machine learning specialists. It also makes it possible for non-experts in the machine learning domain to create machine learning models that provide optimum results.

Convolutional Neural Networks: It is the most common deep learning architecture and is based on the convolution process. These models are mainly applied to the computer vision applications.

Deep Learning: A recent branch of machine learning based on neural network architectures that are modelled after the human brain. Deep learning provides excellent results for computer vision, natural language processing, etc.

Ensemble: A technique to combine the outputs of two or more models to form a better prediction result than that provided by either of the models.

Explainable Artificial Intelligence (AI): A form of AI in which the process and the model helps a human, usually a non-expert, in understanding why a particular model outcome was generated. This increases the degree of trust in the outcomes, and the accompanying confidence to act on the outcomes of an AI based system.

Hyperparameter: These are the parameters that define the model itself and have to be set before a model can be trained. These are different from the parameters that the model learns during training such as node weights.

Hyperparameter Optimisation: A process through which a configuration of hyperparameters is selected from the available range of the hyperparameter values so as to achieve an optimum model performance. The model performance to a large extent is governed by the choice of its hyperparameters.

Chapter 12
Formalizing Model–Based Multi–Objective Reinforcement Learning With a Reward Occurrence Probability Vector

Tomohiro Yamaguchi

Nara College, National Institute of Technology (KOSEN), Japan

Yuto Kawabuchi

Nara College, National Institute of Technology (KOSEN), Japan

Shota Takahashi

Nara College, National Institute of Technology (KOSEN), Japan

Yoshihiro Ichikawa

Nara College, National Institute of Technology (KOSEN), Japan

Keiki Takadama

The University of Electro-Communications, Tokyo, Japan

ABSTRACT

The mission of this chapter is to formalize multi-objective reinforcement learning (MORL) problems where there are multiple conflicting objectives with unknown weights. The objective is to collect all Pareto optimal policies in order to adapt them for use in a learner's situation. However, it takes huge learning costs in previous methods, so this chapter proposes the novel model-based MORL method by reward occurrence probability (ROP) with unknown weights. There are three main features. First one is that average reward of a policy is defined by inner product of the ROP vector and a weight vector. Second feature is that it learns the ROP vector in each policy instead of Q-values. Third feature is that Pareto optimal deterministic policies directly form the vertices of a convex hull in the ROP vector space. Therefore, Pareto optimal policies are calculated independently with weights and just one time by Quickhull algorithm. This chapter reports the authors' current work under the stochastic learning environment with up to 12 states, three actions, and three and four reward rules.

DOI: 10.4018/978-1-7998-8686-0.ch012

INTRODUCTION

This chapter describes solving multi-objective reinforcement learning problems where there are multiple conflicting objectives with unknown weights. Reinforcement learning (RL) is the popular algorithm for automatically solving sequential decision problems. It is commonly modeled as Markov decision processes (MDPs). There are many reinforcement learning methods, most of them are focused on single-objective settings where the goal of an agent is to decide a single solution by the optimality criterion. These reinforcement learning methods are classified according to the learning algorithms and the optimality criteria. The former, there are two kinds of learning algorithms whether directly estimating the parameters of MDP model or not, one is the *model-based* approach such as Dyna architecture (Sutton, 1990, 1991), real-time dynamic programming (RTDP) (Barto et al., 1995) and H-Learning (Tadepalli and Ok 1998) which takes a small time complexity but a large space complexity, and another one is the *model-free* approach (Yang et al., 2016) such as Q-learning which takes a large time complexity but a small space complexity.

The *model-based* approach starts with directly estimating the MDP model statistically. When s is a state, a is an action, and (s, a) is a state action pair which is called a *rule*, it calculates V(s) which is the value of each state or Q(s, a) which is the quality of each *rule* using the estimated MDP. The goal is to search the optimal solution that maximizes V(s) of each state. In contrast, the *model-free* approach which directly learning V(s) or Q(s, a) without estimating the MDP model. According to Plaat et al. (2020), in Deep Reinforcement Learning (DRL) research field, above model-based approaches are called classic (non-deep) model-based methods since model-based DRLs treat high-dimensional problems. An overview of the model-based RL including deep RL is described in the next section.

The latter, there are two kinds of optimality criteria whether using a discount factor or not, one is maximizing the sum of the *discounted rewards*, and another one is maximizing the *average reward* without any discount factor (Mahadevan 1996; Tadepalli and Ok 1998; Gao 2006; Yang et al., 2016). Most previous RL methods are model-free approaches with a discount factor since the model-based approach takes the large space complexity. Note that the role of a discount factor is to control the range of sum of the expected rewards, in other words, it considers the risk of achieving future rewards. The demerit is to take the large time complexity until every V(s) or Q(s, a) in which the discount sum of rewards is converged.

A multi-objective MDP (MOMDP) is an MDP in which the reward function describes a vector of n rewards (reward vector), one for each objective. To decide a single solution, a scalarization function with a vector of n weights (weight vector), one for each objective is commonly used. The simple scalarization function is linear scalarization such as weighted sum. This chapter mainly targets the weighted sum function for the scalarization function, however this method can be applied other scalarization function such as Tchebycheff norm method.

There are several multi-objective reinforcement learning methods (Roijers et al., 2013; Roijers et al., 2015; Liu et al., 2016; Pinder 2016), they are two main approaches which are scalar combination and pareto optimization (Herrmann 2015). In the former case, scalar combination is to find a single policy that optimizes a combination of the rewards. MOMDP and known weights are input to the learning algorithm, then it output a single solution. In the latter case, Pareto optimization is to find multiple policies that cover the Pareto front, which requires collective search for sampling the Pareto set (Natarajan and Tadepalli 2005). MOMDP is input to the learning algorithm, then it outputs a solution set. Note that there are two ways to select a single solution in the set, one is the scalarization with known weight, and another way is a user selection.

The objective of multi-objective reinforcement learning (MORL) is to collect all Pareto optimal policies in order to adapt them for use in a learner's situation. However, it takes huge learning costs in previous MORL methods. Most state-of-the-art MORL methods are model-free value-based reinforcement learning algorithms (Hiraoka et al., 2009; Moffaert and Nowe 2014; Lizotte et al., 2012; Roijers et al., 2013). Firstly, they need a sufficient number of executions for each state-action pair (*rule*) to collect all Pareto optimal policies since they are model-free methods. Secondly, Pareto optimal set is calculated for each $V(s)$ or $Q(s, a)$ since these methods are value-based. Thirdly, when updating $V(s)$ or $Q(s, a)$, Pareto candidates of them are added or updated as $V(s)$ or $Q(s, a)$ vector, it must keep a large number of candidates until each Pareto optimal set is converged. Therefore, previous MORL methods take large number of calculations to collect Pareto optimal set for each V/Q-value vector. In contrast, model-based MORL can reduce such a calculation cost (Wiering et al., 2014) than model-free MORLs. However, second and third problems as described above are still remained, and this method is for only deterministic environments (Wiering et al., 2014). So it is hard to learn high dimensional Pareto optimal policies by previous methods.

To solve these problems, this chapter proposes the novel model-based MORL method by reward occurrence probability (ROP) with unknown weights. This approach (Yamaguchi et al., 2020) is based on the average reward model-based reinforcement learning (Mahadevan 1996) and is based on not *V/Q*-values but the *reward occurrence probability* (ROP) for each reward rule. The essential point is that it learns *reward occurrence probabilities* in each policy instead of *V/Q*-values for each state. A *reward occurrence probability* (ROP) of a reward is the probability to acquire the reward per step when executing specific policy constantly. For example, when a reward is acquired once for each five steps, the ROP is 0.2 Note that each ROP only depends on the occurrences of each reward, does not depend on the value of each reward. When an environment has multiple rewards, a *ROP vector* is introduced in which each element of the ROP vector corresponds to the ROP of each reward. After the MDP model is identified, all reward acquisition policies are collected by tree search, then *the ROP vector* for each reward acquisition policy is calculated to decide Pareto optimal deterministic policies in the ROP vector space. *A ROP vector space* is the n-dimensional space, in which the dimension is the number of rewards, and each axis is the ROP of each reward. Each ROP vector is located as a point in the ROP vector space. Note that a ROP vector is an index of a policy, so several policies may have the same ROP vector.

Thus, there are three main features. First one is that average reward of a policy is defined by inner product of the ROP vector and a weight vector. Second feature is that it learns the ROP vector in each policy instead of V/Q-values. Third feature is that Pareto optimal deterministic policies directly form the vertices of a convex hull in the ROP vector space. Therefore, Pareto optimal policies are calculated independently with weights and just one time by Quickhull algorithm.

The key points of this chapter are as follows;

1.   The proposed model-based reinforcement learning method under *average reward optimality* reduces the learning cost since it collects all reward acquisition cycles of policies by *parallel tree search*. Note that every reward acquisition *deterministic* policy consists of *a reward acquisition cycle* and *temporally paths* that converge on the cycle.

2. Multi-objective is defined by the fixed reward rule set called the *reward vector* and an unknown *weight vector* (Hiraoka et al., 2009). Each element of a weight vector represents the importance of an associated objective.

3. A reward occurrence probability (ROP) vector of a reward acquisition cycle which is a representative of the involved policies is introduced to treat Pareto optimal policies independently from a weight vector.

4. Each policy is assigned the *ROP vector* where nth value is the occurrence probability of nth reward rule of the policy. Then average reward of a policy is defined by the inner product of the ROP vector of the policy and a weight vector.

5. Pareto optimal policies in *the ROP vector space* is calculated as *the vertex of convex hull*. In the ROP vector space, any stationary policy is mapped as a point which coordinate is indicated by its ROP vector. Pareto optimal deterministic policies form *the vertex of convex hull* in the ROP vector space.

6. The reduced learning costs of the proposed method is evaluated by experimental results. The average number of different ROP vectors is about 1/46 times that of the average number of reward acquisition policies under fifty different stochastic MDP environments with twelve states, three actions and three rewards.

7. Partial computation is discussed which can postpone searching *temporally paths* of each policy since *average reward optimality* narrows the search for the optimal policy to *reward acquisition cycles*.

MODEL-BASED REINFORCEMENT LEARNING

This section describes the overview of the Model-based Reinforcement Learning (MBRL).

Classical and Theoretical Approach: MDP Model-Based RLs

Since 1990's, several (classical) model-based RL methods have been researched (Kaelbling et al, 1996) (Sutton & Barto 1998). Theoretically, a dynamic model for a learning environment is often assumed as the MDP model (Puterman 1994). Some comparisons have shown that model-based RL methods which are Dyna architecture (Sutton, 1990, 1991) and realtime DP (Barto et al., 1995) learn more effective than model-free learning such as Q-learning. Given an experience tuple $<s, a, s', r>$, model-based RL behaves as follows:

Update the model, incrementing statistics for the state transition from s to s' on action a and for receiving reward r for taking action a in state s. The updated models are T and R.

Note that updating the model is unsupervised learning in which $<s, a, s', r>$ are input data and there is no output data for learning. The model T estimates each $P(s' | s, a)$ which is the probability of the transition from s to s' on action a, and the model R estimates the received average reward when execute rule (s, a). Model T estimates the probability of next state, the quality of it depends on the number of samples by Law of Large Numbers.

It is important to learn independently between the *exploration* method to collect samples from the environment to update the model and the *exploitation* method to optimize policy by the learned model. If they are not independent, the *learning bias* problem may occur. When observed samples are biased by some executed policies, the number of samples of particular rules is low on. It causes to converge one of the local maximum policies. In other words, the current learned policy will justify itself. To keep the better quality of whole model T, large enough number of samples on each rule (s, a) are needed. To guarantee this, Miyazaki et al. (1997) proposed the k-Certainty Exploration Method for identifying an environment. In that, a rule is k-certainty if and only if it has been executed k times or more, and a model T is k-certainty if and only if every rule in the model is k-certainty or more.

After the Beginning of Deep Reinforcement Learning (DRL)

According to Plaat et al. (2020), first model-based Deep Reinforcement Learning (DRL) is PILCO (Deisenroth and Rasmussen 2011), the learning task is to control a real Cart-Pole Swing-up system. A transition model is a Gaussian Process $T_a(s, s')$ as a probabilistic function which can accurately learn simple processes with good sample efficiency. However, Gaussian Processes do not scale to high dimensional environments such as image input, and the method is limited to smaller applications.

In 2013, image based DRL research (Mnih et al, 2013, 2015) has been published with the NN based model-free learning method called Deep Q-Network (DQN). As the benchmark tasks, 49 classic video games of Atari 2600 (from 1977 to 1980's) are tested to demonstrate DQN's general learning ability. To keep (simple) Markov property approximately, DQN's input state is defined as the image consists of the series of last four frames of the video game. There are several independent improvements to the DQN algorithm, Rainbow (Hessel et al, 2018) combines these improvements in DQN.

According to Daaboul (2020), "Model-free algorithms tend to achieve optimal performance, are easy to implement, and are generally applicable. However, this can only be done if there is a lot of data available." "In contrast, MBRL methods can learn with notably fewer samples by using a learned dynamics model of the environment." In this reason, model-based DRL is one of the hot research topics recently.

Issues of Model-Based DRLs

This subsection summarizes the major issues of model-based DRL. To apply model-based approach into a high dimensional state action space, the model T does not estimates $P(s'| s, a)$ but estimates a next state s' and the function $s' = f(s, a)$ approximately by supervised learning method. Daaboul (2020) discusses the five kinds of issues on model-based RL (MBRL) as follows;

1. Overfitting (Model Bias)
2. Computing time of MBRL algorithms (not real-time)
3. High dimensional input space
4. Limited to short horizon
5. Objective mismatch between policy optimization and model learning

In authors' opinion, the basic issue of model-based DRL is third issue which prevents MBRL from complete model identification of classical approach. Since the model-based DRLs apply high-dimensional input spaces like pixel spaces (images), the transition model is estimated approximately using deep NN, and collecting sampling data for supervised learning in the input spaces may be not global.

First issue is the two kinds of *overfitting* on supervised learning called "*model bias*" (Clavera et al. 2018) described in first subsection as "*learning bias*". First *overfitting* can happen when training the dynamics model with sample data collected from the environment. Second *overfitting* may occur if policies are optimized within the learned dynamics model. In other words, the policy optimized in the model tends to collect the sampling data for justifying the policy itself.

Second issue is that the calculation of MBRL algorithms takes much time compared to model-free variants. Fourth issue is that the approximate model cannot accurately predict many time steps into the future since the error in each step is summed, then it would be massive after a few steps. Fifth issue is the trade-off between exploration and exploitation. When the model identification is completed, optimizing the policy in the identified model is global optimal. If not, it would be local optimal.

From Local to World Model, From Continuous to Discrete Model

This subsection summarizes the research directions on current model-based DRLs, then introduces several good survey papers on model-based DRL for additional readings.

As the research directions on model learning toward identification, global and abstract model. There are two kinds of issues which are a *world model* and a *discrete model*. First issue is from a local model for an optimal policy to a world model. In early model-based DRLs, training models tends to maximize the reward in optimizing the policy than to identify the transition probabilities of the whole environment (Daaboul 2020). The former is called the *local model*, the latter is called the *world model*. To solve the first issue, the goal of model-based DRLs shifts from local and single to an ensemble toward the world model to improve the learning performance.

Clavera et al (2018) discuss the *model bias* problem then they propose Model-Based Meta-Policy-Optimization (MB-MPO) under an ensemble of learned dynamic models, in which "MB-MPO meta-learns a policy that can quickly adapt to any model in the ensemble with one policy gradient step". Kaiser, et al. (2020) propose Simulated Policy Learning (SimPLe), a model-based deep RL algorithm based on video prediction models which go for learning the game rule as a *world model*. Their experiments evaluate SimPLe on 26 Atari games of 100k, 200k, 500k and 1M learning steps. The ratios of Atari games in which SimPLe outperforms Rainbow (Hessel et al, 2018) as the model-free algorithm are 20/26, 16/26, 1/26 and 1/26. It suggests that in fewer steps of learning, SimPLe learns efficiently with fewer samples. However, according to the increase of learning steps, Rainbow learns better performance than SimPLe.

Second issue is from a continuous NN model to the abstract discrete model. Hafner et al, (2021) present DreamerV2, it is the first *Discrete World Model* that treats Atari video games as the high dimensional tasks. DreamerV2 constitutes the first agent that achieves human-level performance on the Atari benchmark of 55 tasks by learning behaviors inside a separately trained *world model*. With the same computational budget and 200M learning steps (frames), Dreamer V2 surpasses the final performance of the top single-GPU agents IQN, Rainbow (Hessel et al, 2018), and SimPle (Kaiser, et al. 2020).

Next, several good survey papers on model-based DRL are introduced for additional readings. Wang, et al. (2019) gather a wide collection of benchmark 11 model-based RL algorithms and 4 model-free RL algorithms across 18 environments based on the standard OpenAI Gym from low dimensional simple tasks to high dimensional complex tasks (Brockman et al, 2016). Daaboul (2020) summarizes five kinds of problems in model-based RL as described before. Plaat et al. (2020) survey recent researches on model-based DRL (from 2011 to 2020, except for TD-Gammon in 1995) in detail.

Plaat et al. (2020) propose three approaches of model-based DRL as follows;

1. Explicit planning on given transitions. In game play such as Go and chess, the model is given by clear transition rules, so the game play is learned by self-play using heuristic search algorithms such as MCTS.
2. Explicit planning on a learned transition model. When the learning environment has no clear rules exist, the transition model must be learned from sampling the environment. The learned model is used by classical, explicit, planning algorithms.
3. End-to-end learning of both planning and transitions. This means that the neural network represents both the transition model and executes the planning steps with it.

Note that this section mainly describes second approach. First approach considers the environment itself as the (world) model it is effective when a simulator environment. The main issue of third approach will be the independence between *exploration* and *exploitation* described in the first subsection.

According to Plaat et al. (2020), relevant important issue is "*latent models* which replace the single transition model with separate, smaller, specialized, representation models, for the different functions in a reinforcement learning algorithm".

MODEL-BASED REINFORCEMENT LEARNING UNDER AVERAGE REWARD

This section describes the our framework of model-based RL methods (Barto, 1995)(Wiering 2014) that estimate a model of the environment while interacting with it and that search for the best policy of its current estimated model under average reward optimality criterion. Figure 1 shows an overview of the model-based reinforcement learning system. A learning agent is a decision maker who is in the environment. The environment with some goals is modeled as a MDP model with a reward function.

At each time step, the agent as a decision maker is in some state which can be observed as s, and the agent may choose any action a that is available in the state s. At the next time step, the environment responds by partially randomly moving into a new state s', sometimes giving the agent a corresponding reward $r(s, a)$.

Next, the agent as a learner is described. In Figure 1, the learning agent consists of three blocks which are the model identification block, the optimality criterion block and the policy search block. The details of these blocks are described in following subsections. The novelty of the proposed method lies in policy search block which collects all *reward acquisition cycles* associated with *reward acquisition policies* by partial computation. The detail of this block is described in next section.

Figure 1. It is an overview of the model-based reinforcement learning system

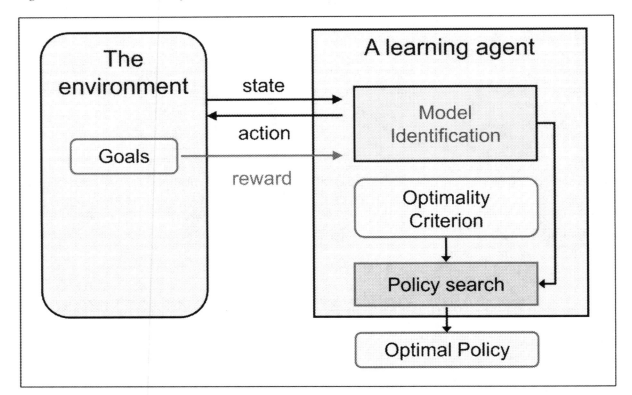

MDP Model and Markov Chains

A Markov decision process (MDP) (Puterman 1994) in this chapter is a stochastic control process with a discrete time and a discrete state space. It provides a mathematical framework for modeling decision making in situations where outcomes are partly random and partly under the control of a decision maker. Note that for a decision maker, actions are the allowing choice, and rewards are giving motivations. A MDP model is defined by of following four elements:

1. Set of states: $S = \{s_0, s_1, s_2,, s_n\}$
2. Set of actions: $A = \{a_0, a_1, a_2,, a_m\}$
3. State transition probabilities $P(s'|\,s, a)$: A probability of an occurring state s' when an action a is executed at a state s.
4. Reward function $R(s, a)$: It returns a scalar value as an acquired reward when an action a is executed at a state s.

$R(s, a)$ means that a reward is assigned to a rule(s, a) which is called a *reward rule* when $R(s, a)$ is not zero. $P(s'|\,s, a)$ means that the probability that a process moves into a new state s' is influenced by a chosen rule(s, a). Thus, the next state s' depends on the current state s and the decision maker's action a, and is independent of all previous executed rules which is called *simple Markov property*. A *stochastic policy* π is a probability distribution over actions for every possible state. A *deterministic policy* is defined by a function that selects an action for every possible state. This chapter mainly deals with *deterministic policies*.

A *Markov chain* is a stochastic model describing a sequence of possible states in which the probability of each state depends only on a previous state. It's an intension of Markov decision processes, the difference is that there is no actions in a *Markov chain*. This chapter focuses on the property that a *policy* of a MDP forms a *Markov chain*, it is described later in next section.

The authors assume a MDP model is *ergodic* where the model satisfies these conditions as follows:

1. *Irreducible*: All states can be reached from all others.
2. *Aperiodic*: Each state is visited without any systematic period.
3. *Finite States*: The number of states is finite.

Model Identification

The objective of the model identification is to know the learning environment. Each observation which consists of a state transition, an executed action, and a received reward is traced to update the MDP model which consists of the state transition probabilities $P(s'| s, a)$ and the reward function $R(s, a)$. One of the most important issues in modern RL problems is to find goals awaked by receiving rewards in a learning environment since model-free RL methods do not start to learn before receiving a reward. Therefore, explorations to find rewards in a learning environment are important. In contrast to them, the major merit of model-based RL methods is that the observations for exploration to find rewards are stored in the models, then they can be reused to search an optimal policy which acquires rewards.

In the model identification block, the state transition probabilities $P(s'| s, a)$ and the reward function $R(s, a)$ are estimated incrementally by observing a sequence of (s, a, r). This estimated model is generally assumed to be MDP model of an environment by non-supervised learning. It makes use of counters that are used in a Maximum-Likelihood Estimation (MLE) to compute approximate transition probabilities and average rewards. A transition model is described as the state transition probability matrix in each action. Figure 2 shows an illustrated example of the identified model. Figure 2 (a) is an example of the identified MDP model with two actions in each state. Note that each transition between states is described as an arrow and is distinguished by action. A transition may stochastically branch such as the transition from state 2 toward state 0 or state 1. Figure 2 (b) and (c) are the state transition probability matrices in each action and each of them is described as the Markov chain.

Figure 2. It is an illustrated example of the identified model. (a) is a MDP model which consists of four states {0, 1, 2, 3}, two actions {a_1, a_2} in each state, and two kinds of rewards {r_1, r_2}. One of the transitions from state 2 branches stochastically toward state 0 or state 1. (b) is a state transition probability matrix under action a_1 called $\mathbf{P}a_1$ (upper) and the Markov chain of $\mathbf{P}a_1$ (downer). (c) is a state transition probability matrix under action a_2 called $\mathbf{P}a_2$ (upper) and the Markov chain of $\mathbf{P}a_2$ (downer).

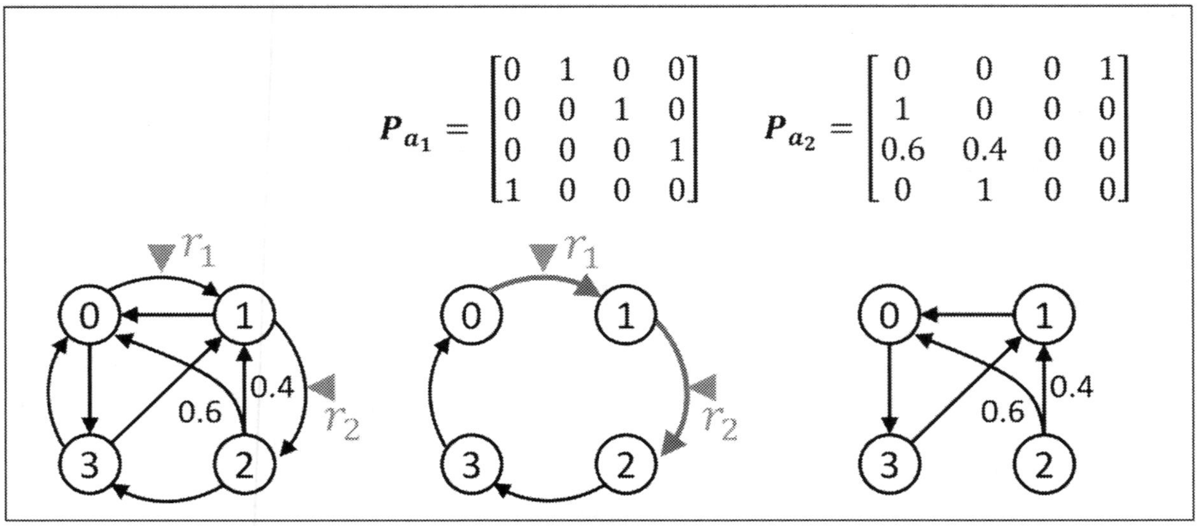

$$P_{a_1} = \begin{bmatrix} 0 & 1 & 0 & 0 \\ 0 & 0 & 1 & 0 \\ 0 & 0 & 0 & 1 \\ 1 & 0 & 0 & 0 \end{bmatrix} \quad P_{a_2} = \begin{bmatrix} 0 & 0 & 0 & 1 \\ 1 & 0 & 0 & 0 \\ 0.6 & 0.4 & 0 & 0 \\ 0 & 1 & 0 & 0 \end{bmatrix}$$

(a)   (b)   (c)

Next, model identification process is described. Eq.(1) shows the definitions of $P(s'|s, a)$ and $R(s, a)$. Firstly, $C(s, a, s')$ is the number of state transitions from s to s' under action a. $C(s, a)$ is the number of executed *rule(s, a)*. Then $P(s'|s, a)$ is the occurrence based probability of state s' under *rule(s, a)*. Note that the MLE probability is same as the occurrence based probability. When the agent executes *rule(s, a)* then makes a transition to state s', the counter values $C(s, a)$ and $C(s, a, s')$ are increased by one.

Secondly, $R_{sum}(s, a)$ is the incremental sum of all rewards obtained by executing *rule(s, a)*. Then, $R(s, a)$ is the incremental average reward of *rule(s, a)*. Then for each rule, acquired incremental average reward is computed independently. Finally, the estimated model of the MDP is computed as Eq. (1). Note that the proposed method guarantees that the number of sampling of each rule $C(s, a)$ in Eq.(1) is not lower than $k = 100$ times by k-certainty exploration method (Miyazaki et al, 1997).

$$P(s'|s, a) = C(s, a, s') / C(s, a) \text{ and } R(s, a) = R_{sum}(s, a) / C(s, a) \tag{1}$$

Average Reward Optimality Criterion

The optimality criterion block defines the optimality criterion of the learned policy. In this research, a policy which maximizes average reward is defined as an optimal policy. An *Average reward* is the expected received rewards per step when an agent performs state transitions routinely according to a policy. A *step* is a time cost to execute an action. Note that every reward acquisition *deterministic* policy consists of *a reward acquisition cycle* and *temporally paths* that converge on the cycle. Figure 3 shows an illustrated example of the reward acquisition cycle and two kinds of associated policies. Figure 3 (a) shows the common reward acquisition cycle of two kinds of associated policies (b) and (c). Figure 3 (b) is the reward acquisition policy consists of a temporally path with reward r_1, Figure 3 (c) is the reward acquisition policy consists of a temporally path without reward.

There are two kinds of optimality criteria on average reward RL, one is *gain-optimal* which considers acquired rewards only in a stationary cycle, the other is *bias-optimal* which considers acquired rewards both on a temporally path and the stationary cycle (Mahadevan 1996). This research is based on gain-optimal average reward. Eq. (2) shows the definition of gain optimal average reward.

$$g^{\pi}(s) \equiv \lim_{N \to \infty} E\left(\frac{1}{N} \sum_{t=0}^{N-1} r_t^{\pi}(s) \right) \tag{2}$$

where N is the number of step, $\Gamma_t^{\pi}(s)$ is the expected value of reward that an agent acquired at step t where policy is π and initial state is s and $E()$ denotes the expected value.

There are two kinds of advantages of *gain-optimal* average reward over bias-optimal average reward. Firstly, gain-optimal average reward only depends on a cycle in a policy. Figure 3 shows an illustrated example of the reward acquisition cycle and associated policies of the MDP model as shown in figure 2. In figure 3, (a) is an example of the reward acquisition cycle. Then, gain-optimal average reward can be calculated easily by dividing the expected sum of rewards on the cycle by the expected length of the cycle.

Secondly, a reward acquisition cycle is a representative for the reward acquisition policies which have same reward acquisition cycle. In Figure 3, (b) and (c) are the reward acquisition policies which have same reward acquisition cycle (a). In Figure 3 (b), reward r_1 has no effect on gain-optimal average reward since it is on the temporally path from state 0 to state 1.

Figure 3. It is an illustrated example of the reward acquisition cycle and associated policies. (a) is one of the reward acquisition cycles of the MDP model as shown in Figure 2 (a). (b) and (c) show two kinds of reward acquisition policies including the reward acquisition cycle (a). (b) is the reward acquisition policy which consists of the temporally path with reward r_1. (c) is the reward acquisition policy which consists of the temporally path without reward.

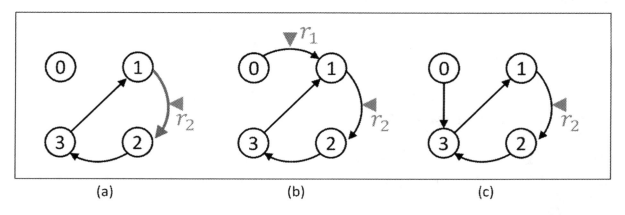

LC-Learning

This subsection summarizes *LC-Learning* (Konda 2002)(Satoh 2006) which is the basic search method for *deterministic* policies in this chapter. *LC-Learning* is one of the average reward model-based reinforcement learning methods. Note that *LC* means *Length of Cycle* in a policy. It collects all reward acquisition *deterministic* policies, each of them has single reward acquisition cycle.

The features of *LC-Learning* are as follows;

1.   Collecting all reward acquisition policies by breadth search started by each *reward rule*.
2.   Calculating gain-optimal average reward using reward acquisition cycle of each policy.

Next section, ROP based *LC-learning* is described.

MODEL-BASED MORL BY REWARD OCCURRENCE PROBABILITY VECTOR

This section starts with describing the definition of a weighted reward vector to apply reinforcement learning to multiple objectives. Then, a *reward occurrence probability (ROP) vector* is introduced to define average reward with a weighted vector.

Weighted Reward Vector

To represent multi-objective, a reward is divided into d reward types one for each objective, and a weight which represents the importance or preference of that reward is associated with each reward type (Natarajan 2005) (Hiraoka 2009). In this chapter, the reward function is defined by a vector of d rewards (reward vector) $\vec{r} = (r_1, r_2, \ldots, r_d)$ where each r_i represents a position of reward rule i and the weight vector $\vec{w} = (w_1, w_2, \ldots, w_d)$ which represents a trade-off among multi objective. A scalarization function with a weight vector is called a *weighted sum of rewards*. Eq. (3) shows a weighted sum of rewards defined by the inner product of a reward vector $\vec{r} = (r_1, r_2, \ldots, r_d)$ and a weight vector $\vec{w} = (w_1, w_2, \ldots, w_d)$. Note that $|\vec{w}| = 1$.

$$r(\vec{w}) = \sum_{i=1}^{d} w_i r_i = \vec{w} \cdot \vec{r} \tag{3}$$

Average Reward by Reward Occurrence Probability

Under a policy π and reward vector $\vec{r} = (r_1, r_2, \ldots, r_d)$,

Eq. (4) shows the definition of a *Reward Occurrence Probability* (ROP) vector $\vec{P}_A$.

In that, P_i is the expected occurrence probability per step for the reward r_i.

$$\vec{P}_{\hat{A}} \equiv \left(P_1, P_2, \ldots, P_d \right) \tag{4}$$

Eq. (5) shows the definition of an *Average reward* ρ_π under both a policy π and a weight vector $\vec{w}$. It is defined by the inner product of $\vec{w}$ and a ROP vector $\vec{P}_{\hat{A}}$. Note that $|\vec{w}|=1$.

$$\rho_\pi\left(\vec{w}\right) = \sum_{i=1}^{d} w_i P_i = \vec{w} \cdot \vec{P}_\pi \tag{5}$$

Figure 4 shows the geometrical meaning of Eq. (5) under d = 2. It is the two dimensional ROP vector space $P_1 \times P_2$ in which P_i is the occurrence probability of reward *i*. An ROP vector $\vec{P}_\pi = (p_1, p_2)$ is located in the ROP vector space. Note that θ is the angle between $\vec{P}_\pi$ and $\vec{w}$. The average reward of the inner product for the ROP vector $\vec{P}_{\hat{A}}$ is $|\vec{P}_{\hat{A}}| \cos \theta$ since $|\vec{w}|=1$. It is equal to the distance between (0, 0) and the foot of a perpendicular on the $\vec{w}$ from the point (p_1, p_2). This research assumes that $\vec{P}_{\hat{A}0}$ is zero vector where π_0 is any policy without reward.

Figure 4. It shows the geometrical meaning of an average reward by the inner product of a weight vector $\vec{w}$ and a ROP vector $\vec{P}_{\hat{A}}$

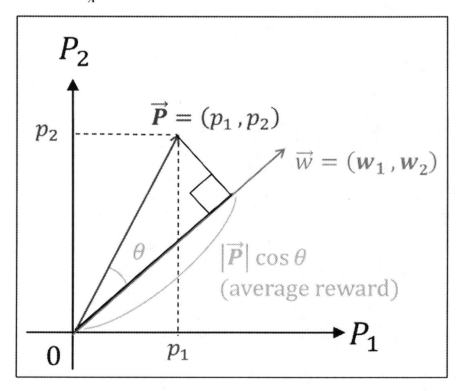

The Flow of the Parallel Policy Search with Preprocess

Figure 5 shows the flow of the policy search block as shown in Figure 1. There are two kinds of Main features of this block in this chapter version. Firstly, intermediate learning results are ROP vectors which are calculated from *reward acquisition cycles*. Secondly, *policy search is parallelized by multi-processing and preprocess* to delete redundant ROP vectors is added for reducing the computation costs.

Figure 5. It is the flow of the ROP vector based policy search. Parallel policy search and two kinds of preprocesses are added for reducing the computation cost.

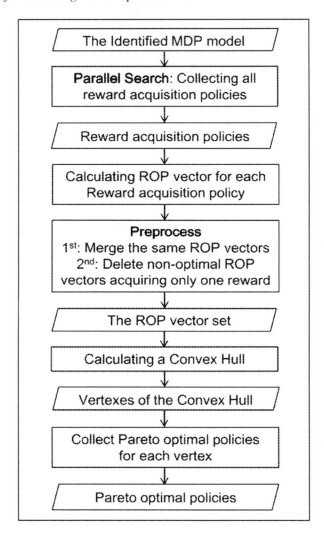

Next, an overview of the flow is described. After the learning environment is identified as the MDP model, it is copied into several MDP models for parallel policy search. Reward acquisition cycles are searched in parallel with respect to each reward acquisition rules as a *root rule* of each search tree. It is described in next subsection. After all reward acquisition cycles (and their policies) are collected, the *ROP vector* for each cycle is calculated by a *balance equation* of each cycle as a *Markov chain* with transition matrix. The *balance equation* describes the stationary distribution of probabilities of all states in the cycle. Next, *preprocess* to delete redundant ROP vectors are performed by multiple sort. There are two kinds of preprocesses, one is to merge the same ROP vectors. Another one is to delete non-optimal ROP vectors which acquires only one reward. The preprocessed ROP vectors form a ROP vector set.

Then, each element of the ROP vector set is mapped in the ROP vector space, Pareto optimal ROP vectors are decided by calculating a convex hull from the ROP vector set by Quickhull algorithm. Since the Pareto optimal ROP vector for each vertex of the convex hull is associated with the cycle and the associated policies, all Pareto optimal policies are collected.

Collecting All Reward Acquisition Cycles by Parallel Search

The parallel search method for reward acquisition policies is based on *LC-learning* as the authors described before. These deterministic policies which acquire some rewards are searched from an identified MDP model into the tree structures where each rule of reward acquisition rules is a *root rule* of each search tree. For parallel search, the identified MDP model is copied into several MDP models. Note that the number of copies including original is the same as the number of reward rules. To avoid duplicate search for reward acquisition cycles, there are some orders of copied MDP models for parallel search. Firstly, a *root rule* with reward of the search in each MDP model is different. Secondly, a *root rule* is excluded in subsequent MDP models. For example, when an original MDP model has three reward rules as $\{r_1, r_2, r_3\}$, r_1 is a root rule of the tree search in the first MDP model. In the second MDP model, rule r_1 is excluded and a root rule of the tree search is r_2. In the third MDP model, rules r_1 and r_2 are excluded and a root rule of the tree search is r_3. Therefore, parallel number of this search is same as the number of rewards. This search is implemented by multi-processing of CPU core parallelization. Note that the parallel number is limited by the number of CPU threads.

Figure 6. It is an illustrated example of prepared MDP models for parallel search. (a) is the original identified MDP model with two reward rules $\{r_1, r_2\}$ in which a root rule is r_1. (b) is the second MDP model in which rule r_1 is excluded and a root rule is r_2.

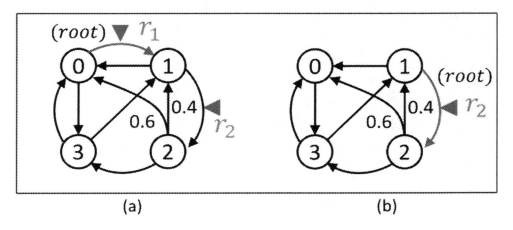

Figure 6 shows an illustrated example of prepared MDP models for parallel search. Figure 6 (a) shows an example of the identified MDP model which consists of four states, two actions in each state, eight (state transition) rules and two reward rules $\{r_1, r_2\}$. It is a stochastic environment, one of the transition rules from state 2 is branching stochastically toward state 0 or 1. It is also the first MDP model in which a root rule is r_1. Figure 6 (b) shows the second MDP model in which rule r_1 is excluded then a root rule is r_2.

Figure 7 shows an illustrated example of parallel search trees of collecting all reward acquisition cycles from prepared MDP models as shown in Figure 6. In each search tree, reward acquisition cycles including the root rule with a reward are collected. Figure 7 (a) is the first search tree in which the root rule is r_1 as shown in figure 6 (a). In Figure 7 (a), three reward acquisition cycles {cycle 1-1, cycle 12-1, cycle 12-2} are collected. Note that the root node of the search tree is state 0. Any branch of the tree is closed with success (it finds a reward acquisition cycle) when the expanded node is the same as the root node such as cycle 1-1 and cycle 12-2. If the case of stochastically branches such as cycle 12-1, the expanded nodes including the root node make good. The branch is closed with failure if the expanded node is the same as the already expanded nodes in the path toward the root node, since it is a cycle without a root rule such as 1-> 2-> 3-> 1. Figure 7 (b) is the second search tree in which the root rule is r_2 as shown in figure 6 (b). In Figure 7 (b), two reward acquisition cycles {cycle 2-1, cycle 2-2} are collected.

Note that any multi-chain policy which has isolated cycles is not searched since a cycle without the root node is not reachable. In this example, total seven paths are searched and five reward acquisition cycles are collected so that the success rate to search reward acquisition cycles is 5/7. Owing to the search which starts from a reward rule, it is efficient to collect all reward acquisition cycles. Theoretically, the number of deterministic policies is $|A|$ to the power of $|S|$ where $|S|$ is the number of states and $|A|$ is the number of actions. In figure 6, the number of deterministic policies is $2^4 = 16$.

Figure 7. It is an illustrated example of parallel search trees of collecting all reward acquisition cycles from prepared MDP models as shown in Figure 6. (a) is the first search tree in which the root rule is r_1. (b) is the second search tree in which the root rule is r_2.

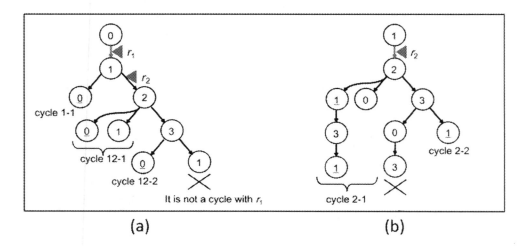

(a)   (b)

Calculating ROP Vector for Each Reward Acquisition Cycles by Balance Equation

After collecting all reward acquiring cycles, the state transition probability matrix P_c of each cycle c is prepared as a *Markov chain* as the authors described in previous section. Figure 8 shows illustrated examples of the ROP vector $\vec{P}_c$ from the reward acquisition cycles using the property of a *Markov chain*.

In case of the reward acquisition cycles are as shown in Figure 7, Figure 8 (a) shows examples of two kinds of *Markov chains* for reward acquisition cycles {cycle1-1, cycle 12-2} with rewards r_1 and/or r_2. Figure 8 (b) is the two kinds of state transition probability matrices { $\vec{P}_{C1-1}$, $\vec{P}_{C12-2}$ } of each cycle. Note that any element p_{ij} in the matrix is the state transition probability from state *i* to state *j*. Figure 8 (c) is described later.

Figure 8. It is an illustrated example of the ROP vector $\vec{P}_C$ from the reward acquisition cycle. (a) is two kinds of Markov chains for each reward acquisition cycle. (b) is two kinds of state transition probability matrices of each cycle. (c) is the two pairs of the probability vectors of cycle states $\vec{\alpha}_C$ and the corresponding ROP vectors $\vec{P}_C$.

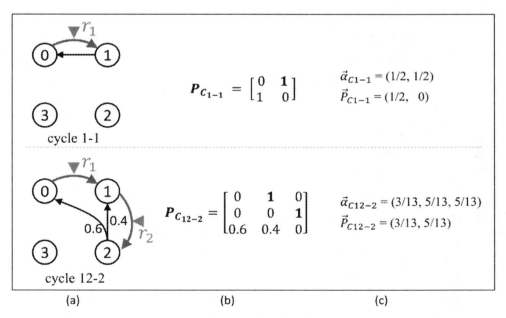

The ROP vector for each cycle is calculated by a *balance equation* of each cycle as a *Markov chain* with a transition matrix. The *balance equation* describes the stationary distribution of probabilities of all states $\vec{\alpha}_C$ in a *Markov chain* c under the transition matrix P_C. Eq. (6) is the definition of $\vec{\alpha}_C$ which is an occurrence probability vector for all states in cycle c. αi is an occurrence probability of state i in a reward acquisition cycle. Note that in Eq. (6), the sum of all αi ,s 1.

$$\vec{\alpha}_C \equiv \left(\alpha_1, \alpha_2, \ldots, \alpha_{|S|} \right) \tag{6}$$

Eq. (7) is the *balance equation* on a *Markov chain* with a transition matrix $\boldsymbol{P}_C$. $\vec{\alpha}_C$ is the solution of the *balance equation*.

$$\vec{\alpha}_C \boldsymbol{P}_C = \vec{\alpha}_C \tag{7}$$

Next, the method to calculate a ROP vector of a reward acquisition cycle from the balance equation is described. Calculating method of each ROP vector $\vec{P}_C$ for each reward acquisition cycle c associated with $\boldsymbol{P}_C$ is as follows:

Step 1: Set up simultaneous linear equations for each $\boldsymbol{P}_C$.
Under a cycle c, the occurrence probability vector for all states $\vec{\alpha}_C$ is defined as Eq. (6). Simultaneous linear equations between $\boldsymbol{P}_C$ and $\vec{\alpha}_C$ is the balance equation as shown in Eq. (7).
Step 2: For each $\boldsymbol{P}_C$, solve Eq. (7) by *Gaussian elimination*. Note that $\vec{\alpha}_C$ is the solution of the *balance equation* of Eq. (7).
Step 3: For each $\vec{\alpha}_C$ derived at step 2, forms a ROP vector $\vec{P}_C$ by picking up the occurrence probabilities of the states associated with each reward rule in the cycle. If a reward rule is not in the cycle, the occurrence probability of it is zero.
Step 4: If all $\vec{\alpha}_C$ of the reward acquisition cycles are calculated as $\vec{P}_C$, output all $\vec{P}_C$ as the ROP vectors.

Finally, **Step 4**: the method to decide a ROP vector by solving the balance equation is described. The ROP vector $\vec{P}_C$ for the reward acquisition cycle c in a policy π is equal to ROP vector $\vec{P}_A$ as shown in Eq. (4). Note that the occurrence probability of the reward rule (i, a) in the cycle c is equivalent to αi. Figure 8 (c) is the examples of two pairs of $\vec{\alpha}_C$ and the corresponding ROP vector $\vec{P}_C$. The upper side of Figure 8 (c), each element of $\vec{\alpha}_{C1-1}$ is the occurrence probabilities of state 0 and 1, $\vec{P}_{C1-1}$ which is the ROP vector of cycle 1-1 is the vector of the occurrence probabilities of reward rules $\{r_1, r_2\}$. Since the reward rule r_2 is not in the cycle 1-1, the occurrence probability of reward rule r_2 is zero. The downer side of Figure 8 (c), each element of $\vec{\alpha}_{C12-1}$ is the occurrence probabilities of state 0, 1 and 2, $\vec{P}_{C12-1}$ which is the ROP vector of cycle 12-1 is the vector of the occurrence probabilities of reward rules $\{r_1, r_2\}$. Note that when a transition between states is deterministic, the occurrence probabilities of these states are the same, it is the reason why the occurrence probabilities of cycle 12-2 between state 1 and 2 is the same.

Preprocess to Delete Redundant ROP Vectors

Next, *preprocess* to delete redundant ROP vectors is performed by multiple sort. This is one of the bottleneck process of time complexity of our previous method. There are two kinds of *preprocesses*, one is to merge the same ROP vectors. The time complexity of the previous method is $O(n^2)$ since it compares the ROP vectors sequentially. Compare to it, the proposed method uses the multiple sort technique, Therefore, the time complexity is reduced to $O(\text{n log n})$.

Another one is to delete non-optimal ROP vectors which acquires only one reward to reduce the computation space costs which was not previously implemented. Note that ROP vectors on each axis are the cycles which acquire only single reward, then for each axis, these are selected either maximum or minimum element of the ROP vector by multiple sort. Figure 9 shows an image of the *preprocess* deleting non-optimal ROP vectors in each axis. Figure 9 (a) shows the distribution of the non-Pareto optimal ROP vectors. Figure 9 (b) shows the *preprocess* deleting non-optimal ROP vectors in each axis. Note that in this example, the ROP vectors which element is either maximum or minimum element in each axis still remain as Pareto optimal or minimum but not zero ROP vector.

Figure 9. It is an image of the preprocess deleting non-optimal ROP vectors in each axis. (a) is the example of two dimensional ROP vectors mapped in the 2D ROP vector space. It shows the density distributed ROP vectors on the axes. (b) is the image of the preprocess deleting non-optimal ROP vectors on each axis. It also shows the two kinds of non Pareto-optimal ROP vector subset.

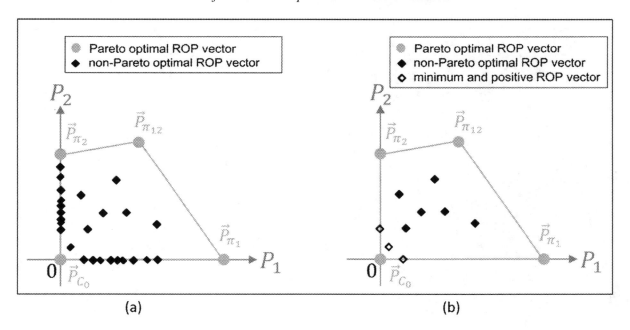

(a)   (b)

Calculating a Convex Hull from a ROP Vector Set

After collecting all ROP vectors as a set, each ROP vector is located at a point in the reward occurrence probability (ROP) vector space. Figure 10 shows an illustrated example of the six ROP vectors including $\vec{P}_{C0}$ of the identified MDP model as shown in Figure 6 and Figure 7 located in two dimensional ROP vector space. In Figure 10, there are two axis, where the horizontal axis is P_1, and the vertical axis is P_2.

Figure 11 is an illustrated example of the convex hull in two dimensional ROP vector space of Figure 10. Figure 11 (a) shows the covex hull of six ROP vectors in the $P_1 \times P_2$ ROP vector space. In the ROP vector space, there are five kinds of different ROP vectors { $\vec{P}_{C1-1}$, $\vec{P}_{C12-1}$, $\vec{P}_{C12-2}$, $\vec{P}_{C2-1}$, $\vec{P}_{C2-2}$ } each of them is related to {cycle 1-1, cycle 12-1, cycle 12-2, cycle 2-1, cycle 2-2} and one zero vector $\vec{P}_{C0}$. Among them, four ROP vectors { $\vec{P}_{C1-1}$, $\vec{P}_{C12-2}$, $\vec{P}_{C2-2}$, $\vec{P}_{C0}$ } are Pareto optimal which are the vertices of the convex hull, and rest two ROP vectors are non-Pareto optimal which are inside of the convex hull, Note that the authors use n dimensional Quick Hull algorithm (Barber 1996) of Python library.

Figure 10. It is an illustrated example of the six ROP vectors including $\vec{P}_{C0}$ of the identified MDP model as shown in Figure 6 and Figure 7 located in two dimensional P_1 x P_2 ROP vector space

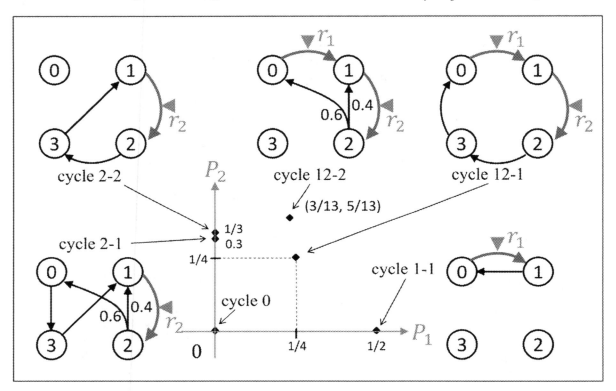

Figure 11. It is an illustrated example of the convex hull in two dimensional ROP vector space of Figure 10. (a) is the covex hull of six ROP vectors in the $P_1 \times P_2$ ROP vector space. (b) is four divisions of weight vectors among four vertices of the convex hull as Pareto optimal policies.

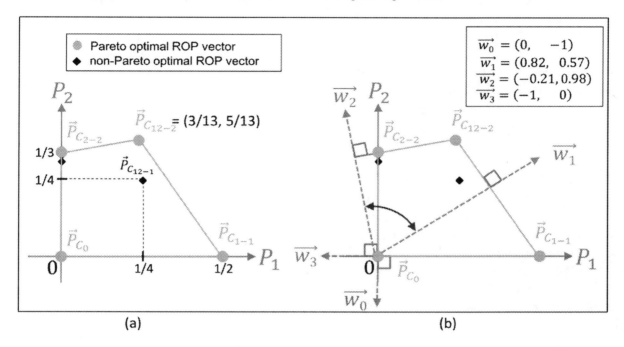

(a)   (b)

Figure 11 (b) shows four divisions of weight vectors among four vertices of the convex hull as Pareto optimal cycles. Each vertex of the ROP vector { $\vec{P}_{C1-1}$, $\vec{P}_{C12-2}$, $\vec{P}_{C2-2}$, $\vec{P}_{C0}$ } has the optimal zone of weighted vectors. The dotted arrows are the limits of optimal zones of weighted vectors. In Figure 11 (b), there are four limits on weighted vectors, $\vec{w}_0$, $\vec{w}_1$, $\vec{w}_2$ and $\vec{w}_3$. For example, $\vec{w}_1$ is the limit weight vector between $\vec{P}_{C1-1}$ and $\vec{P}_{C12-2}$ where the average reward of them is the same under $\vec{w}_1$. The optimal zone for each ROP vector is as follows;

1. $\vec{P}_{C1-1}$ is from $\vec{w}_0$ to $\vec{w}_1$
2. $\vec{P}_{C12-2}$ is from $\vec{w}_1$ to $\vec{w}_2$
3. $\vec{P}_{C2-2}$ is from $\vec{w}_2$ to $\vec{w}_3$
4. $\vec{P}_{C0}$ is from $\vec{w}_3$ to $\vec{w}_0$

Experiments

This section shows the authors' previous and current experimental results collecting all Pareto optimal deterministic policies with three or four rewards under stochastic learning environments. Major differences between the previous and current methods are whether the parallel policy search and preprocess are implemented or not.

Preliminary Experiment

This subsection shows the preliminary experiment of the authors' previous method to compare the computation space and time cost of it with the current method in this chapter. Experimental conditions on learning environments which are generated as the different stochastic and models are as follows;

- The number of states is from 4 to 10 states.
- The number of actions is three.
- The number of rewards is four.
- The transition probability of each rule is setup randomly under the condition that the number of branches of transitions is randomly setup between 1, 2 or 3.

Experimental results are averaged one hundred experiments with different learning environments.

Figure 12 shows the preliminary experimental results of the authors' previous method to evaluate the computation space and time cost of it. Firstly, the computation space costs of the previous method is described. Figure 12 (a) shows the experimental results comparing the number of reward acquisition cycles with the number of reward acquisition policies. According to an increase of the number of states which is the horizontal axis, the increase rate of the number of reward acquisition cycles is much smaller than that of the number of reward acquisition policies. The reason is that a cycle which consists of the small number of states derives the large number of policies.

Figure 12. It is the preliminary experimental results of the authors' previous method to evaluate the computation space and time cost of it. (a) is the experimental results of the computation space costs comparing the number of reward acquisition policies with the number of reward acquisition cycles. (b) is the experimental results of the computation time costs according to the number of states.

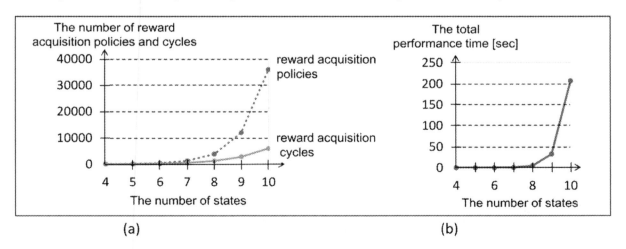

(a)   (b)

Secondly, the computation time costs of the previous method is described. Figure 12 (b) shows the previous experimental results of the averaged total performance time according to an increase of the number of states. The previous method takes over 200 seconds to collect all Pareto optimal policies of stochastic MDP environment with 10 states. To examine the breakdown of the total performance time, most of total time is from calculating ROP vectors to forming the ROP vector set which time is average 207 seconds. Contrast to it, the most of the remaining time is the search process for collecting all reward acquisition policies, it takes only average 2.8 seconds. The time of calculating a convex hull from a ROP vector set is only 6.1 milli-seconds. Note that in case of 12 states with four rewards, the total performance time becomes 1590 seconds.

Therefore, the bottleneck of the previous method is the process of from calculating ROP vectors to forming the ROP vector set. To solve them, next subsection reports the experimental results by authors' current method which is implemented the parallel policy search and preprocess.

Experimental Setup of the Authors' Current Method

The authors have conduct the learning experiment under the stochastic environments to analyze the bottle neck of the proposed method. The PC with Intel Core i7-7700, 3.60 GHz (max 4.20GHz), 4 cores and 8 threads, RAM 16.00 GB is used, and programming language is Python 3.5.2 with Python libraries such as scipy 1.2.0 and numpy 1.15.4.

Experimental conditions on the learning environments which are generated as the stochastic MDP model are as follows;

- The number of states is from 5 to 12 states.
- The number of actions is three.
- The number of rewards is three and four.
- The transition probability of each rule is setup randomly under the condition that the number of branches of transitions is randomly setup between 1, 2 or 3.

Experimental results are averaged fifty experiments in which different stochastic MDP models are generated under the experimental conditions described above. Measurement items are the calculation time and the number of collected policies or ROP vectors for each process as follows;

1. The time cost of model identification [sec]
2. The time cost of parallel search process for collecting all reward acquisition policies [sec]
3. The time cost of calculating ROP vectors [sec]
4. The time cost of calculating a convex hull from a ROP vector set [msec]
5. total performance time [sec]
6. the number of reward acquisition policies by parallel search
7. the number of different ROP vectors
8. the number of vertexes of convex hull in the ROP vector space
9. the number of Pareto optimal policies

Experimental Results

The authors have conducted the learning experiment for one hundred times and each measurement item is averaged. In stochastic environments up to 12 states, the proposed method successfully collects all reward acquisition deterministic policies including all Pareto optimal policies under unknown weights.

Firstly, the computation time costs of the authors' current method is described. Figure 13 shows the experimental results of the measurement items (3) and (5) under three and four rewards. Figure 13 (a) is the total performance time under four rewards. In case of 12 states with four rewards, the total performance time is reduced from 1590 seconds (previous method) to 19 seconds (current method). The decrease rate is about 1/80. Figure 13 (b) is the total performance time under three rewards. Comparing (a) with (b), large number of rewards case takes large time costs. Figure 13 (c) and (d) are the time cost of calculating ROP vectors under four and three rewards. Note that these graphs (a) (b) (c) (d) have similar increase curve.

Figure 13. It is the experimental results of the time costs by the authors' current method according to the number of states. (a) is the total performance time under four rewards. (b) is the total performance time under three rewards. (c) is the time cost of calculating ROP vectors under four rewards. (d) is the time cost of calculating ROP vectors under three rewards.

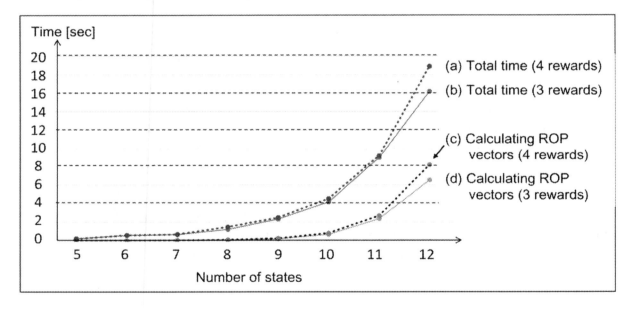

Next, analyzing the bottleneck processes of the current method, measurement items of the calculation time from (1) to (5) are compared. Figure 14 shows the experimental results of the measurement items (1) to (5) under three rewards. According to an increase of the number of states which is the horizontal axis, the measurement items (1) (2) (3) and (5) except for item (4) is exponential increase. Note that (4) the time cost of calculating a convex hull is about 1 milli-seconds under 12 states. Look at the increase rate from 11 states to 12 states, (3) the time cost of calculating ROP vectors becomes the maximum increase rate. Therefore, it is important to reduce the number of calculating ROP vectors in order to reduce the total computation costs.

Figure 14. It is the experimental results of the authors' current method. The measurement items (1) to (5) are compared according to the number of states from 5 to 12.

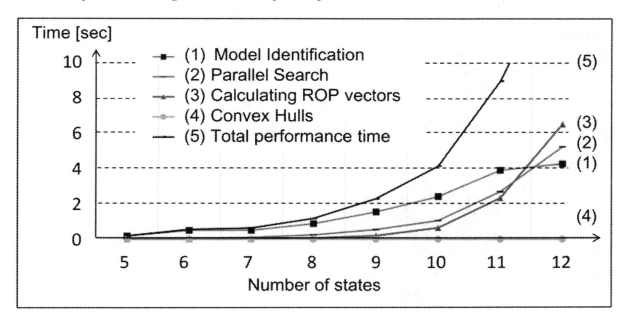

Table 1. It is the experimental results of the authors' current method. The measurement items (6) to (9) are compared according to the number of acquired rewards from 0 to 2 under 12 states, 3 actions and 3 rewards.

Number of acquired rewards	(6) Number of reward acquisition policies			(7) Number of different ROP vectors						(8) Number of Vertexes of convex hull			(9) Number of Pareto optimal policies		
				1st preprocess: merge the same ROP vectors			2nd preprocess: for acquiring only one reward								
	Avg	±	S.D.	Avg	±	S.D.	Avg	±	S.D.	Avg	±	S.D.	Avg	±	S.D.
0	48400	±	33300	1.00	±	0.00				1.00	±	0.00	48400	±	33300
1	148000	±	53000	**10400**	±	7670	**6.00**	±	0.00	3.00	±	0.00	15100	±	30000
2	50000	±	21500	4670	±	4320				9.02	±	4.21	2070	±	3100
3	6520	±	3950	760	±	888				6.14	±	6.05	359	±	544
Total	**253000**	±	82800	**15800**	±	12600	**5430**	±	5130	**19.2**	±	9.47	65900	±	46600

Secondly, the computation space costs of the authors' current method is described. Table 1 shows the results of the measurement items (6) to (9) under three rewards. Looking at the largest number of reward acquisition policies in (6), it is the policies with single reward. The reason is described before subsection. Next, focusing on the measurement item (7), first preprocess reduce the computation space cost in which total 253000 reward acquisition policies are merged to 15800 different ROP vectors by multiple sort. Owing to the second preprocess which is the vectors with single reward, the number of the ROP vectors reduced from 148000 to 6, then total 253000 reward acquisition policies are merged to 5430 different ROP vectors, the reduction rate is about 46.6. Then, looking at the measurement item (8), the averaged total number of the Pareto optimal ROP vectors is only 19.2. Finally, focusing on the measurement item (9), the number of Pareto optimal policies is 65900. However, almost of them are either policies without reward or policies with single reward. It suggests that focusing on the Pareto optimal ROP vectors related to the Pareto optimal cycles facilitates the Pareto optimal policies.

SOLUSIONS AND RECOMMENDATIONS

This section firstly discusses the effect on the two kinds of speed up improvements. The proposed method, policy search is parallelized by multi-processing and preprocess to delete redundant ROP vectors is added. At the parallel policy search, since the decrease rate depends on the number of rewards d, best decrease rate is less than $1/d$. The preprocess to merge the same ROP vectors, owing to the multiple sort, the time complexity is reduced to $O(n \log n)$. Note that the time complexity of previous method is $O(n^2)$ since it compares the ROP vectors sequentially. Owing to the preprocess, the redundant ROP vectors are reduced, then total 253000 reward acquisition policies are merged to 5430 different ROP vectors, the decrease rate is about $1/46.6$. Then the total performance time is reduced from 1590 seconds (previous method) to 19 seconds (current method) in case of 12 states with four rewards. The decrease rate is about $1/80$.

Secondly, the way to reduce the total learning time is discussed. It is important to reduce the search cost before calculating ROP vectors by partial computation. Described as the previous section, a ROP vector depends on only the reward acquisition cycle in each policy, do not depend on the temporally paths. Therefore, the *partial computation* to collect Pareto optimal Policies will be effective. *Partial computation* consists of two processes. In the first *partial computation* process, all reward acquisition cycles are collected instead of searching all reward acquisition policies. This reduces the computation space cost. After all Pareto optimal ROP vectors which are the vertex of the convex hull are decided, second *partial computation* for collecting reward acquisition policies is started again from searching *temporally paths* of each Pareto optimal cycle. Therefore, all Pareto optimal policies are collected with low computation time since the number of Pareto optimal ROP vectors is much smaller than the total number of ROP vectors, i.e. reward acquisition cycles. There are two kinds of roles of *partial computation* for collecting Pareto optimal policies. Firstly, *gain-optimal average reward* narrows the search for the optimal policy to *reward acquisition cycles*. Secondly, it postpones searching *temporally paths* of each policy after selecting Pareto optimal ROP vectors.

FUTURE RESEARCH DIRECTIONS

This section discusses the possibilities of this research. Firstly, the significance of the proposed method is discussed. Since the proposed method is one of the classical model-based MORL, it can play the abstract discrete model role in model-based DRL to extend it toward multi-objective. To design the abstract state space model, one of the promising approaches is to define states as subgoals in a high dimensional state space. A local policy $lp(sg_i, sg_j)$ between a subgoal pair (sg_i, sg_j) in the high dimensional state space is defined as an abstract action. A transition cost from sg_i to sg_j under $lp(sg_i, sg_j)$ is defined as the transition probability p, note that 1-p is the transition probability from sg_i to sg_j. Therefore, identifying the abstract model for multi-objective is to learn all local policies and their transition costs among all subgoal pairs.

Secondly, focusing on the aspect of a distribution of a ROP vector set in a convex hull is discussed. How non Pareto-optimal ROP vectors work is discussed. Figure 9 (b) shows the two kinds of non Pareto-optimal ROP vector subset. One is the minimum and positive ROP vector set, the other is non-Pareto optimal ROP vectors inside of the convex hull without minimum and positive ROP vectors. Now the meaning of Pareto optimal ROP vectors in the proposed method is described. In this research, each Pareto optimal policy has a shorter length of cycle than non-Pareto optimal ones since the Reward occurrence probability per step is larger. As figure 7 shows the policy search process by breadth search, reward acquisition cycles with short length are found at first. This suggests that the mastery task of human or robot behavior learning, the length of the reward acquisition cycle means the complexity of the learned output. Therefore, considering the ROP vector space as the mastery space as shown in Figure 9 (b), the minimum and positive ROP vector set suggests the mastery goals, and ROP vectors in the convex hull are sub-goals toward the mastery goals.

CONCLUSION

This chapter proposed a novel model-based MORL method by a reward occurrence probability vector with unknown weights. The proposed method under *gain-optimal average reward* reduces the learning cost since it collects all ROP vectors of reward acquisition policies. To speed up them, policy search to collect all reward acquisition policies is parallelized according to the number of rewards by multi-processing, then preprocess to delete redundant ROP vectors by multiple sort is added for reducing the computation costs. In the experimental results, the proposed method is evaluated, then the total performance time is reduced from 1590 seconds (previous method) to 19 seconds (current method) in case of 12 states with four rewards. The decrease rate is about 1/80.

Future work is to apply the proposed method to cart-pole swing-up task in OpenAI Gym (Brockman et al, 2016) which is one of the low dimensional continuous state space, and to study how to utilize two kinds of non Pareto-optimal ROP vectors.

ACKNOWLEDGMENT

The authors would like to thank Prof. Habib for offering a good opportunity to present this research. The authors also thank reviewers for useful comments. This work was supported by JSPS KAKENHI(Grant-in-Aid for Scientific Research ©) [Grant Number 20K11946].

REFERENCES

Barber, C. B., David, P., Dobkin, D. P., & Huhdanpaa, H. (1996). The Quickhull Algorithm for Convex Hulls. *ACM Transactions on Mathematical Software*, 22(4), 469–483. doi:10.1145/235815.235821

Barrett, L., & Narayanan, S. (2008). Learning All Optimal Policies with Multiple Criteria. In *Proceedings of the 25th International Conference on Machine Learning (ICML-2008)*. ACM. 10.1145/1390156.1390162

Barto, A. G., Steven, J., Bradtke, S. J., & Singh, S. P. (1995). Learning to Act Using Real-Time Dynamic Programming. *Artificial Intelligence*, *72*(1-2), 81–138. doi:10.1016/0004-3702(94)00011-O

BrockmanG.CheungV.PetterssonL.SchneiderJ.SchulmanJ.TangJ.ZarembaW. (2016). *Openai gym*. Retrieved from https://arxiv.org/pdf/1606.01540.pdf

Clavera, I., Rothfuss, J., Schulman, J., Fujita, Y., Asfour, T., & Abbeel, P. (2018). Model-based reinforcement learning via meta-policy optimization. *Proceedings of 2nd Conference on Robot Learning*, 617-629. Retrieved from https://arxiv.org/pdf/1809.05214.pdf

Daaboul, K. (2020). Towards Further Practical Model-Based Reinforcement Learning. *Becoming Human: Artificial Intelligence Magazine*. Retrieved from https://becominghuman.ai/towards-further-practical-model-based-reinforcement-learning-b671dd862e57

Deisenroth, M., & Rasmussen, C. (2011). Pilco: A model-based and dataefficient approach to policy search. *Proceedings of the 28th International Conference on Machine Learning (ICML-2011)*, 465–472.

Gao, Y. (2006). *Research on Average Reward Reinforcement Learning Algorithms*. National Laboratory for Novel Software Technology, Nanjing University. Retrieved from https://pdfs.semanticscholar.org/a428/b91e4f13edd8e69ec9cc932f1d084b8a2e5d.pdf

Hafner, D., Lillicrap, T., Norouzi, M., & Ba, J. (2021). *Mastering Atari with Discrete World Models*. In *Proceedings of The International Conference on Learning Representations (ICLR-2021), Poster*. Retrieved from https://iclr.cc/virtual/2021/poster/2742, https://openreview.net/pdf?id=0oabwyZbOu

Handa, H. (2009). Solving Multi-objective Reinforcement Learning Problems by EDA-RL -, Acquisition of Various Strategies. *Proceedings of the Ninth International Conference on Intelligent Systems Design and Applications*, 426-431. 10.1109/ISDA.2009.92

Herrmann, M. (2015). *RL 16: Model-based RL and Multi-Objective Reinforcement Learning*. University of Edinburgh, School of Informatics. Retrieved from http://www.inf.ed.ac.uk/teaching/courses/rl/slides15/rl16.pdf

Hessel, M., Modayil, J., van Hasselt, H., Schaul, T., Ostrovski, G., Dabney, W., Horgan, D., Piot, B., Azar, M., & Silver, D. (2018). Rainbow: Combining Improvements in Deep Reinforcement Learning. *Proceedings of the AAAI Conference on Artificial Intelligence*, *32*(1). Retrieved from https://ojs.aaai.org/index.php/AAAI/article/view/11796

Hiraoka, K., Yoshida, M., & Mishima, T. (2009). Parallel reinforcement learning for weighted multi-criteria model with adaptive margin. *Cognitive Neurodynamics*, *3*(1), 17–24. doi:10.100711571-008-9066-9 PMID:19003453

Kaelbling, L. P., Littman, M. L., & Moore, A. W. (1996). Reinforcement Learning: A Survey. *Journal of Artificial Intelligence Research*, *4*, 237–285. doi:10.1613/jair.301

Kaiser, L., Babaeizadeh, M., Milos, P., Osinski, B., Campbell, R. H., Czechowski, K., Erhan, D., Finn, C., Kozakowski, P., Levine, S., Mohiuddin, A., Sepassi, R., Tucker, G., & Henryk Michalewski, H. (2020). Model-Based Reinforcement Learning for Atari. In *Proceedings of 2020 International Conference on Learning Representations (ICLR2020)*. Error! Hyperlink reference not valid.Retrieved from https://openreview.net/pdf?id=S1xCPJHtDB

Konda, T., Tensyo, S., & Yamaguchi, T. (2002). LC-Learning: Phased Method for Average Reward Reinforcement Learning - Preliminary Results. In *Proceedings of 7th Pacific Rim International Conference on Artificial Intelligence (PRICAI2002)*. Springer. 10.1007/3-540-45683-X_24

Liu, C., Xu, X., & Hu, D. (2015). Multiobjective Reinforcement Learning: A Comprehensive Overview. *IEEE Transactions on Systems, Man, and Cybernetics. Systems*, *45*(3), 385–398. doi:10.1109/TSMC.2014.2358639

Lizotte, D. J., Bowling, M., & Murphy, S. A. (2012). Linear Fitted-Q Iteration with Multiple Eeward Functions. *Journal of Machine Learning Research*, *13*, 3253–3295. PMID:23741197

Mahadevan, S. (1996). Average Reward Reinforcement learning: Foundations, Algorithms, and Empirical Results. *Machine Learning*, *22*(1-3), 159–196. doi:10.1007/BF00114727

Miyazaki, K., Yamamura, M., & Kobayashi, S. (1997). *k*-Certainty Exploration Method: An action selector to identify the environment in reinforcement learning. *Artificial Intelligence*, *91*(1), 155–171. doi:10.1016/S0004-3702(96)00062-8

Mnih, V., Kavukcuoglu, K., Silver, D., Graves, A., Antonoglou, I., Wierstra, D., & Riedmiller, M. (2013). Playing Atari with Deep Reinforcement Learning. In *NIPS Deep Learning Workshop 2013*. Retrieved from https://arxiv.org/pdf/1312.5602.pdf

Mnih, V., Kavukcuoglu, K., Silver, D., Rusu, A. A., Veness, J., Bellemare, M. G., & Petersen, S. (2015). Human-level control through deep reinforcement learning. *Nature*, *518*(7540), 529–533. doi:10.1038/nature14236 PMID:25719670

Moffaert, K. V., & Nowe, A. (2014). Multi-Objective Reinforcement Learning using Sets of Pareto Dominating Policies. *Journal of Machine Learning Research*, *15*, 3663–3692.

Natarajan, S., & Tadepalli, P. (2005). Dynamic Preferences in Multi-Criteria Reinforcement Learning. *Proceedings of the 22nd international conference on machine learning (ICML-2005)*, 601-60. 10.1145/1102351.1102427

Pinder, J. M. (2016). *Multi-Objective Reinforcement Learning Framework for Unknown Stochastic & Uncertain Environments* (Unpublished doctoral dissertation). Retrieved from http://usir.salford.ac.uk/id/eprint/39978/2/John%20Pinder%20PhD%20Thesis%20Complete.pdf

Plaat, A., Kosters, W., & Preuss, M. (2020). *Deep Model-based Reinforcement Learning for High-Dimensional Problems, a Survey*. Retrieved from https://arxiv.org/pdf/2008.05598.pdf

Puterman, M. L. (1994). *Markov Decision Processes: Discrete Stochastic Dynamic Programming*. John Wiley & Sons, Inc. doi:10.1002/9780470316887

Roijers, D. M., Vamplew, P., Whiteson, S., & Dazeley, R. (2013). A Survey of Multi-Objective Sequential Decision-Making. *Journal of Artificial Intelligence Research, 48*, 67–113. doi:10.1613/jair.3987

Roijers, D. M., Whiteson, S., Vamplew, P., & Dazeley, R. (2015). Why Multi-objective Reinforcement Learning? *Proceedings of the 12th European Workshop on Reinforcement Learning (EWRL 2015)*, 1-2.

Satoh, K., & Yamaguchi, T. (2006). *Preparing various policies for interactive reinforcement learning.* Paper presented at the meeting of SICE-ICASE International Joint Conference 2006.

Sutton, R., & Barto, A. (1998). *Reinforcement Learning: An Introduction.* MIT Press.

Sutton, R. S. (1990). Integrated Architectures for Learning, Planning, and Reacting Based on Approximating Dynamic Programming. *Proceedings of the Seventh International Conference on Machine Learning (ICML-1990)*, 216-224. 10.1016/B978-1-55860-141-3.50030-4

Sutton, R. S. (1991). Planning by Incremental Dynamic Programming. In *Proceedings Ninth Conference on Machine Learning (ICML-1991)*. Morgan-Kaufmann. doi:10.1016/B978-1-55860-200-7.50073-8

Tadepalli, P., & Ok, D. (1998). Model-based Average Reward Reinforcement Learning. *Artificial Intelligence, 100*(1-2), 177–224. doi:10.1016/S0004-3702(98)00002-2

Tajmajer, T. (2017). *Multi-Objective Deep Q-learning with Subsumption Architecture.* Retrieved from https://arxiv.org/pdf/1704.06676v1.pdf

Tsitsiklis, J. N. (2007). NP-Hardness of checking the unichain condition in average cost MDPs. *Operations Research Letters, 35*(3), 319–323. doi:10.1016/j.orl.2006.06.005

Wang, T., Bao, X., Clavera, I., Hoang, J., Wen, Y., Langlois, E., Zhang, S., Zhang, G., Abbeel, P., & Ba, J. (2019). *Benchmarking model-based reinforcement learning.* Retrieved from https://arxiv.org/abs/1907.02057

Wiering, M. A., Withagen, M., & Drugan, M. M. (2014). Model-Based Multi-Objective Reinforcement Learning. *Proceedings of the IEEE Symposium on Adaptive Dynamic Programming and Reinforcement Learning*, 1-6.

Yamaguchi, T., Nagahama, S., Ichikawa, Y., Honma, Y., & Takadama, K. (2020). Model-based Multi-Objective Reinforcement Learning by a Reward Occurrence Probability Vector. *Advanced Robotics and Intelligent Automation in Manufacturing*, 269-296.

Yang, S., Gao, Y., Bo, A., Wang, H., & Chen, X. (2016). Efficient Average Reward Reinforcement Learning Using Constant Shifting Values. *Proceedings of the Thirtieth AAAI Conference on Artificial Intelligence (AAAI-16)*, 2258-2264.

ADDITIONAL READING

Drugan, M., Wiering, M., Vamplew, P., & Chetty, M. (2017). Special Issue on Multiobjective Reinforcement Learning. *Neurocomputing, 263*(8), 1–2. doi:10.1016/j.neucom.2017.06.020

Drugan, M., Wiering, M., Vamplew, P., & Chetty, M. (2017). Multiobjective Reinforcement Learning: Theory and Applications. *Neurocomputing*, *263*(8), 1–86. doi:10.1016/j.neucom.2017.06.020

Gábor, Z., Kalmár, Z., & Szepesvári, C. (1998). Multi-criteria Reinforcement Learning. In *Proceedings of the Fifteenth International Conference on Machine Learning*, 197-205. Morgan Kaufmann Publishers Inc.

Moffaert, K. V., Drugan, M., & Nowe, A. (2013). Scalarized Multi-Objective Reinforcement Learning: Novel Design Techniques. In *Proceedings of IEEE Symposium on Adaptive Dynamic Programming and Reinforcement Learning (ADPRL)*, IEEE. 10.1109/ADPRL.2013.6615007

Mossalam, H., Assael, Y. M., Roijers, D. M., & Whiteson, S. (2016). Multi-Objective Deep Reinforcement Learning. arXiv preprint arXiv:1610.02707. Retrieved from https://arxiv.org/pdf/1610.02707.pdf

Nguyen, T. T. (2018). A Multi-Objective Deep Reinforcement Learning Framework. Retrieved from http:// arxiv.org/ftp/arxiv/papers/1803/1803.02965.pdf

Tanner, B., & White, A. (2009). RL-Glue: Language-Independent Software for Reinforcement Learning Experiments. *Journal of Machine Learning Research*, *10*(Sep), 2133–2136.

Uchibe, E., & Doya, K. (2008). Finding intrinsic rewards by embodied evolution and constrained reinforcement learning. *Neural Networks*, *21*(10), 1447–1455. doi:10.1016/j.neunet.2008.09.013 PMID:19013054

Vamplew, P., Dazeley, R., Berry, A., Issabekov, R., & Dekker, E. (2011). Empirical evaluation methods for multiobjective reinforcement learning algorithms. *Machine Learning*, *84*(1-2), 51–80. doi:10.100710994-010-5232-5

Vamplew, P., Webb, D., Zintgraf, L. M., Roijers, D. M., Dazeley, R., Issabekov, R., & Dekker, E. (2017). MORL-Glue: A Benchmark Suite for Multi-Objective Reinforcement Learning. In *Proceedings of the 29th Benelux Conference on Artificial Intelligence (BNAIC 2017)*, 389. Groningen, The Netherlands. Retrieved from http://roijers.info/pub/morl-glueBnaic17.pdf

Vamplew, P., Yearwood, J., Dazeley, R., & Berry, A. (2008). On the Limitations of Scalarisation for Multi-Objective Reinforcement Learning of Pareto Fronts. In *Proceedings of Australasian Joint Conference on Artificial Intelligence*, 372-378. Springer, Berlin, Heidelberg. 10.1007/978-3-540-89378-3_37

KEY TERMS AND DEFINITIONS

Average Reward: The expected received rewards per step when an agent performs state transitions routinely according to a policy. In this research, an average reward of a policy is defined by the inner product of a ROP vector of the policy and a weight vector.

Deterministic Policy: It is defined by a function that selects an action for every possible state.

LC-Learning: One of the average reward model-based reinforcement learning methods. It collects all reward acquisition deterministic policies under the unichain condition.

Markov Chain: A stochastic model describing a sequence of possible states in which the probability of each state depends only on the previous state. It is an intension of Markov decision processes; the difference is the subtraction of actions and rewards.

Markov Decision Process (MDP): It is a discrete time and a discrete state space stochastic control process. It provides a mathematical framework for modeling decision making in situations where outcomes are partly random and partly under the control of a decision maker.

Model-Based Approach: The reinforcement learning algorithm which starts with directly estimating the MDP model statistically, then calculates the value of each state as $V(s)$ or the quality of each state action pair $Q(s, a)$ using the estimated MDP to search the optimal solution that maximizes $V(s)$ of each state.

Multi-Objective MDP (MOMDP): A MDP in which the reward function describes a vector of n rewards (reward vector), one for each objective, instead of a scalar.

Pareto Optimization: It is to find multiple policies that cover the Pareto front, which requires collective search for sampling the Pareto set.

Reinforcement Learning: The popular learning algorithm for automatically solving sequential decision problems. It is commonly modeled as Markov decision processes (MDPs).

Reward Occurrence Probability (ROP): The expected occurrence probability per step for the reward.

Reward Occurrence Probability (ROP) Vector: A vector where n^{th} value is the occurrence probability of nth reward rule of a policy.

Reward Occurrence Probability (ROP) Vector Space: It is one of the rectangular coordinate system in which any ROP vector associated with a stationary policy is mapped to a point where coordinates are indicated by its ROP vector.

Reward Rule: It is a state action pair (s, a) assigned a non-zero reward in a MDP model.

Rule: It is a state action pair (s, a) in a MDP model.

Simple Markov Property: A property that the next state s' depends on the executed rule(s, a), that is the current state s and the decision maker's action a, and is independent of all previous executed rules.

Weight Vector: A trade-off among multi objective, and each element of the vector represents a weight of each objective.

Chapter 13
Entropy, Chaos, and Language

Daniela Lopez De Luise
https://orcid.org/0000-0003-3130-873X
CI2S Labs, Argentina

ABSTRACT

Natural language is a rich source of information, with a complex structure and a kaleidoscope of contents. This arises from the flexibility that living languages exhibit in order to reflect the speaker's intention, and also due to communication needs. From computational linguistics, multiple strategies have been developed that allow detecting and interpreting textual contents, but there is an uncovered margin, an interpretive range that remains outside the scope of automatic processing, and that requires rethinking the scope and perspectives of these tools. This chapter aims to show this gap and its implications, exploring dialectical and technical reasons. It also proposes a new perspective of interpretation and scope of textual processing, a sort of thermodynamics of productions that involve the communication of certain types. As part of the scope, there is a bibliographic analysis and a statistical and heuristic exploration of the proposal applied to 20Q game.

INTRODUCTION

Language distinguishes humans from the rest of the species. It can be considered a code associated with a grammar, which is a set of rules that allow people to communicate. It is relevant during childhood to a proper cognitive evolution and for emotional and social maturity (Sala Torrent, 2020).

Logic reasoning follows premises in which the rules accepted as valid are applied, link by link, until the conclusions are produced, which is known as the logical consequence. The natural deduction system shows an intimate relationship between symbolic language and the logic of Natural Language (Kemel, 2020). Both languages, from their scopes, are coupled by rules of inference, validity, argumentation, deduction, and proof. According to Kemel the only possible explanation for the link that relates both languages is a "natural" isomorphism between them. There is a surprisingly close relationship with human thought in a way that is still not fully explained. Natural Language manages to represent, figure, interpret, compose and symbolize real objects and virtual objects in the mind, in order to produce logical reasoning processes. This is precisely the subject that occupies the work of Kemel: explaining and

DOI: 10.4018/978-1-7998-8686-0.ch013

using the capacity that Natural Language has to make abstract constructions from concrete instances. The current work of this chapter also seeks to study the process of linguistic reasoning but starting from scratch (sentences and words without rules of grammar) to assign certain meaning to them, and exposing the processes behind it.

There are many reasons to consider Natural Language as a system working under the laws of chaos (Sala Torrent, 2020). This complex production of the human brain, presents logarithmic and fractal behaviors like many other productions of nature. There are dialectic, biological, practical, and technical background that partially supports the idea of an inborn strategy that underlies the brain mechanism of spoken and written text production. Although there are practical statistical explanations that work pretty well in general, and a Zipf-Mandelbrot fractal law that approximates with some error the word distribution in texts, the core of the linguistic mechanism is still under study. This chapter starts with a review of many of the ideas and concepts from different perspectives. These fundamentals help builds an approximation of the essence and implications of productions in Natural Language.

The main focus of this work is the determination of basic rules that govern words selection when the goal is to communicate an idea, in the context of a dialog between two individuals speaking in their native language. In order to perform a careful analysis, the study performed is reduced to a simple game named 20Q, whose target is to guess a word initially thought by another player. The play consists of asking him a series of questions. These can only be answered by yes or no. The words and questions studied in this chapter are in Spanish. A curious thing here is the fact that there is a high probability to get the right word even though that there are about 93000 words, according to RAE (Spain Royal Academy) in its Spanish Dictionary Edition of 2014 (Real Academia Española, 2021). Tests performed here use an AI system available for free on the web. This system is a Neural Network trained when visitors play with it. The fact that such a system is able to guess the correct word is very impressive. This strange phenomenon could be explained considering the language has many but very precise rules, some of them some used unconsciously. The findings shown here are part of a much larger work of extensive analysis to reveal the rules that govern language dynamics.

Background

Chaos is a very well-known work in the normative universe of systems theory. Many interdisciplinary works emerge in this context and much of the effort can be applied also to language production systems. Yet in 1936, the biologist Ludwig von Bertalanffy considered the general systems theory involves natural and social sciences (Von Bertalanffy, 1984). According to him, systemic thinking should not only consider things and objects but also relationships, interactions, and processes. According to Rodríguez Duch (2016), understanding chaos derives involves two main concepts: chaos has an inner order and order can turn to chaos. From this perspective, chaos is not a lack of order but a very complex one. Entities and individuals are inserted in an environment of this type. Therefore it becomes very hard to understand the dynamics of interchanges as a picture, but rather as a movie. As a consequence, the notion of equilibrium is lost when a large combination of variables is influencing at every instant.

Chaos is a common property of many systems and works well to infer future status in many cases. But the equilibrium as a goal changes to a status of transient concept that gives way to chaos theory, the science of processing, of changes and dynamics. What is not transient, the immutable is not the main source of interest: the random, complex and unexpected are the focus now. There is a need for new heuristics and a proper combination with preexistent approaches to complement them.

Predictable facts with static and absolute rules are then replaced by a more open conception of instability, and possibility. Mario Bunge (1969) explains this as a coexistence of random and causation.

In *Follow up for a Complexity Theory*, Fravegat (2008) presents how many sciences out of traditional physics are incorporating categories and codes of that field. Thus, thermodynamics and entropy (usually represented as H), chaos and uncertainty, random and predictions, among others, are concepts used to explain (with a proper metaphor) complex events in these alternate fields. The cultural complexity is one of the beneficiaries, and at the same time one of the basements of language production. Fravegat extends thermodynamics defining the energy of a cultural source, and a statement similar to the first law. He agrees with Rodríguez Duch in the existence of a system confined to a context or environment dominated by a cultural reality that could be expressed by thermodynamics.

From the biological perspective there is evidence of our brain as a complex system processing information in a very precise way. Culture performs a high change in its nature. It has been proven that between 6 and 8 years old, patterns of estimates progressed from consistently natural logarithmic (ln) to a mixture of logarithmic and linear to a primary linear pattern (Siegler & Booth, 2004). Siegler et col, show several tests and previous findings to explain that psychological distance in children is logarithmic. According to Karen Wynn (1992) the human brain can just distinguish between numbers 1, 2 and many. Ancient numerations describe numbers between 1 and 3 following a pattern and from 4 in a different way. This also is imprinted in the language since singular works with just one element and plural with more elements.

The logarithmic bias of the brain has been detected also in other fields like music (Rodriguez Santos, 2011). The increase of frequencies among musical notes is logarithmic (see Figure 1).

Figure 1. Logarithmic distribution of musical notes

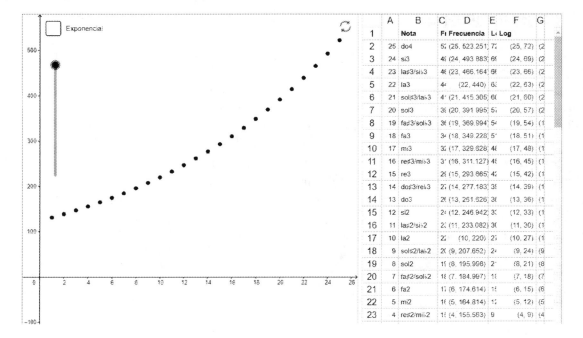

Regarding the practical reasons to consider fractals, many disciplines like biology, geography, medicine, astronomy, architecture among others, take advantage of its powerful geometric administration (Sulbarán Sandoval, 2016).

From the technical perspective, Natural Language Processing (NLP) is the field of sciences that takes the linguistic baggage and develops models to computationally manage human texts, dialogs, and oral expressions. Many scientists have proposed models using Genetic Algorithms, Neural Networks, Hidden Markov Models, and other advanced algorithms for processing the different expressions of individual's verbal behaviors: gestures (Kaluri & Reddy, 2018) (Kaluri & Pradeep, 2017), detect anomalous interactions (Bhattacharya et col., 2020), etc. Entropy has also been used in many proposals were the complexity arises. In fact these type of models have become very popular in applications related to Speech recognition Kuo, 2004), to process n-gram models (instead of conventional linear interpolation method to integrate the restricted semantic information) (Chueh et col., 2004), to extract keywords from cross-language documents (Zhang et col., 2019), to enhance segmentation in statistical machine translation (Xiong, 2011), etc.

According to a study performed by Ai21 Labs, the high level of difficulty of NLP requires expensive architectures (Sharir, O.; Peleg, B. & Shoham, 2020). Currently, large systems using a combination of Neural Networks (NN) and filters try to cover the big data challenge, which involves much of the language processing difficulties. But researchers do not think that large NN as models operating on massive corpora. The increasing complexity could also contribute to expanding the size of the artificial networks in order to reflect the external knowledge in the embedding space. Indeed, authors see several factors that may help tame this explosion and prevent things from getting out of hand. Despite current status, the uncontrolled growth of textual information in Natural Language indicates that scientists must explore alternative approaches and technologies to understand and manage linguistic productions.

Fractals and Language

Fractals have many applications, most are based on analysis from geometric and image processing studies. They present specific arrangements that can be studied analytically or by simulations. When something presents fractal behavior, its patterns provide information about the system behind it. Widyarto et. al. (2019) also present simulations and recommend them for prospective purposes and applications. According to authors: "*The prospective application may help in predictive patterns of many fields. The predictive pattern will lead to pattern control and pattern disruptions*". Technically speaking, fractals have been formally studied for many years in relation to language production, since the Polish mathematician Benoit Mandelbrot defined them (Spinadel, 2008). They have many properties but the main principle is the invariance despite scale changes. Fractals determine a specific type of geometry denoted as fractal geometry, that differs from the traditional Euclidean geometry. The first one is more close to nature processes behavior and the latter one is best suited for describing artificial artifacts created by humans. One element of fractal geometry that is being used in this chapter is the fractal dimension given by the relation:

$$N = \frac{1}{L^D} \tag{1}$$

with
D: dimension,
N: number of identical parts of the fractal,
L: total length of the subject of the fractal.

George Kingsley Zipf was the first researcher that suggested the existence of a certain distribution for a given text corpus. The distribution of words ranked by their frequency approximate a distribution known as Zipf's law (Zipf, 1932). It is a power-law distribution, with its exponent close to one:

$$f_n \sim \frac{1}{N^a} \tag{2}$$

with

f_n: frequency of the nth word (sorted from the most frequent one),
$a \in \mathbb{R}$, *usually over 1.1.*

This means that the second word appears 1/2 times respecting the most frequent. Third is 1/3 frequency and so on. But it is considered as an empiric approximation, not very precise.

Later on, in 1965, Benoit Mandelbrot improves its precision and generalizes the equation with the known Zipf–Mandelbrot distribution that derives from the work of Claude Shannon and converges for $a > 1$.

This new version changes the original Zipf's law via a discrete probability distribution (Mandelbrot, 1965). Also known as the Pareto–Zipf law, it is a power-law distribution on ranked data. The probability mass function is given by:

$$f\left(k;N,q,s\right) = \frac{\left(\dfrac{1}{\left(k+q\right)^s}\right)}{H_{N,q,s}} \tag{3}$$

with

$$H_{N,q,s} = \sum_{i=1}^{N} \frac{1}{\left(i+q\right)^s},$$

k: rank of data,
q, s: parameters of the distribution.

When $N \to \yen$ then $f \to \zeta(s,q)$, being ζ the Hurwitz Zeta function [Apostol, 1976], a member of the family of the known zeta functions. It is formally defined by arguments $s \in \mathbb{C}$ and $q \in \mathbb{R}$ as follows:

$$\zeta\left(\text{s,q}\right)=\sum\nolimits_{k=0}^{\infty}\left(\text{k+q}\right)^{-s} \tag{4}$$

This series converges for q > 0 and Re(s) > 1. When $q \in \mathbb{Z} < 0$ the terms in the series with null denominator are discarded. In general $0 < q \leq 1$. Note that q could be a complex number (then Re(q) > 0 is natural, but not a restriction). The original Zipf's law is obtained when N = q = 0:

$$f\left(k;N,q,s\right)=f_{\zeta}\left(h,q,s\right), N = q = 0 \tag{5}$$

Fractals self-replication is a sort of recursive behavior that can also be represented as a system of iterated functions (**SIF**) (Yi Lee & Prieto, 2010), which are a useful mathematical tool for modeling Euclidean geometry as well. But fractals relate to a geometry that better explains the figures and behavior in nature. As Mandelbrot stated: *"the beauty of the everyday escapes the models of Euclidean Geometry [...] since clouds are not spherical, nor the mountains are conical, nor the circular coasts"*(Spinadel, 2003). In general natural forms are irregular and fragmented. The complexity in nature is higher and at a completely different level: the number of scales that natural forms present are, for all practical purposes, infinite. Mandelbrot notices this in 1982 with his book *The Fractal Geometry of Nature*. There, he defines the concept of fractal dimension, one that is higher than its topological counterpart. This is one of the concepts used in this chapter to evaluate the process of communication from the fractal perspective.

As explained earlier, fractals can be thought of as geometric figures that are characterized by their self-similarity. They are useful in areas such as architecture, astronomy, biology, medicine, botany, economics, image design, video games, and in the analysis of a great diversity of phenomena such as turbulence, stock market, smoke dispersion, and percolation.

In 1990, Kenneth Falconer, published *Fractal Geometry: Mathematical Foundations and Applications*, which introduces not a definition but a set of main features and properties:

1. **Detail:** It has details at all scales of observation.
2. **Complexity**: It is not possible to describe it with Euclidean geometry, both locally and globally.
3. **Self-similarity:** It has some kind of self-similarity, possibly statistical.
4. **High dimension:** Its fractal dimension is greater than its topological dimension.
5. **Simplicity:** The algorithm used to describe it is very simple, and possibly recursive in nature.

From the second property, a fractal changed to classical geometry loses chaos and self-similarity. Therefore Euclidean geometry needs to be replaced with a new one, that is fractal geometry.

Fractal dimension (D) is a mathematical index that quantifies the characteristics of any object and phenomena in this fractal geometry. It assesses some kind of subjective perception of the density of a figure in its space. This fuzziness explanation is similar to the use of fuzzy sets for explaining possibility instead of factual membership of an element to a set.

There are several definitions of D. The one given by Hausdorff is probably the most relevant, but it is very complex to implement and some other alternates are taken instead. A workaround gets **SIF** as fractals, considering it as a contractive function. Intuitively, a contractive application is a function in $\mathbb{R}^{n}$ that zooms in on the points of a figure and contracts the shape. This contractive application is a composition of isometries (translations, rotations, and symmetries) and a contractive homothecy (Yi Lee & Prieto, 2010).

SIF are a finite family $\{f_i\}_{i=1}^{N}$ of contractive applications $f_i : \mathbb{R}^n \rightarrow \mathbb{R}^n$ that exhibit a contractivity ratio r= $\max\{r_1,r_2,\ldots,f_N\}$ with $0 \leqslant r_i < 1$ being the contractivity of f$_i$. The mathematical theory demonstrates that the family converges to an image called "System Attractor" that is the image of the fractal. These has been used in a previous work to evaluate the fractal behavior of dialogs in Spanish (López De Luise & Azor, 2015).

Thermodynamics, Chaos, Nature and Human Activity

Probabilities constitute the mathematical modeling of random effects and their laws. Complexity also requires mathematical concepts by means of entropy (commonly denoted as H). The concept of entropy was introduced by Clausius during the 19th century. It corresponds to a measure of the "disorder" presented by the molecules of a gas and has made it possible to account for thermodynamic equilibrium (Rebolledo, 2018). Many relevant mathematicians have studied it and founded the mathematical theory of chaos. Researchers like Hilbert, Poincaré, Kolmogorov, Shannon, Kullback, among others evaluated how Nature, probability and chaos are related. New theories derived from that work, among others the Information Theory (Shannon, 1948) and Ergodic Theory (Billingsley, 1965). The first is the scientific study of the quantification, storage, and communication of digital information. The other is a branch of mathematics that studies the statistical properties of deterministic dynamical systems. According to Rebolledo, both of them were used by Chomsky and Eco to explain phenomena in linguistics and semiotics. Eco stated that the coding process reduces the entropy of the communication system because it reduces the possibility of a chaotic understanding of a message. This concept underlies this chapter to evaluate sentences in a dialog: the interpretation of a message analyzing its complexity measured by its degree of chaos.

From the perspective of the human sciences, it is a general rule that the amount of entropy or chaos in a set of transformations of reality assesses the event or phenomena complexity. It is also related to the Knowledge Theory as it depends on those changes (Rebolledo, 2018). Entropy is the tool to introduce a mathematical model of cognitive processes characterized by events denoted as demarcations and breakthrough of knowledge (Costa dos Santos & Ascher, 2017). These events manifest as polarizations known as reversibility/ irreversibility, and equilibrium/imbalance. This is inspired by thermodynamics, the branch of physics that focuses on energy and its transformations for systems (Callen, 1985). It considers the following elements:

Q: heat
W: work
E: energy
V: volume
m: mass

Energy was not originally related to the ability to share certain information but defined as the capacity to perform work or to take chances (i.e. kinetic, potential, heat, etc). A system is not a sender and a receiver of a message: it is any part of the universe that is being isolated to the aim of the study. Status is the condition of a system, denoted by its properties. It is one of the possible combinations of its properties. But from the extended perspective in Computational Linguistics, it is represented by the level of entropy that the model has been able to extract from the system.

The main focus of traditional thermodynamics is the equilibrium state and its characteristics: a balanced system with no changes in its properties unless it has interactions with its environment. But for the linguistics perspective it lacks any sense to get into the equilibrium. It concerns is no entropy to be drained. Therefore no new information is available for the model, since it is supposed to have perfect knowledge.

In thermodynamics an irreversible process occurs when the system becomes chaotic and its entropy scales to infinite. Then, it is supposed that the system reaches its permanent balance. It is like a butterfly in nature, a more complex system than a larva. From this point of view, there has been an increase of entropy, a breakthrough, so that the new larva-butterfly system extends the larva original system. This change has a quantum of energy that reaches its highest value. This qualitative change implies a global entropy change as well. The emerging butterfly will have at this time a local entropy that will evolve and determine the duration of this new status (Rebolledo, 2018).

A process in classical thermodynamics is described as the change from one equilibrium state to another, but from the communication theory it involves the fact that some messaging is under its way.

In any case, to describe a status it is necessary to describe the local entropy and the global entropy of the type of phenomena to be explained. Every representation of a state relates to a degree of complexity expressed in its local entropy. It is dialectically conditioned by the global entropy, that describes the complexity of every possible state.

From the linguistic perspective, local entropy analyzes the complexity evolution of certain phenomena. It is associated with the dialectical mutation from order to chaos and from that chaos to a new level of organization, an improved one. This change generates a new type of relationship between the object under study and new wider types of phenomena. According to Rebolledo (2018), global entropy grows as a consequence of this set of new relationships with human observers. In the context of a dialog, the global entropy reflects more features aggregated to the original information shared.

As mentioned previously, language is also a fractal process. Therefore, this evolution of the linguistic system, is also a fractal evolution producing some change in the fractal dimension D. This chapter evaluates the changes in D due to the changes produced in the communication system between two ends of a dialog.

From the epistemological perspective, the irregular changes in the entropy evolution during some knowledge interchange can be explained as a breakthrough process and a set up of a new upgraded evolution level in the interchange. As a dialectical fact, this change determines the entropy as a category consisting of two poles (local and global entropy) and their mutual relationship.

In the tests performed as part of this chapter, it will become clear those breakthrough in the interchange, as big peaks and valleys in the entropy evolution of a dialog.

The entropy of the knowledge development was explained in *Complexity and Chance (Rebolledo, 2018)* as a process with breakthroughs that might correspond with the *epistemological breakthrough* defined by Fichant–Pecheux [8], also known as point of no return in theory or emergency. In the other extreme, there are certain jumps in the local entropy that denote *epistemological demarcation* points that might correspond to an established status of knowledge. Those conditions will be studied in section Test of Dimension and Rhythm.

Characteristics of a Thermodynamic System

A system is denoted by its characteristics. Every science may assign a meaning to entropy and relate it with specific concepts in its own field. In classical thermodynamics, properties are classified as intensive (independent of the mass) or extensive (depend on the mass measured). In computational linguistics, information depends on the number and type of words, the structure of sentences, etc.

(P)reassure, (V)olume, and (T)emperature, are the building blocks for equations that explain different manifestations of the energy as heat (Q), (W)ork, and many others. Sometimes they are partially isolated (for instance in adiabatic processes $Q = 0$) or represent some production coming out of the system (one case is when $W > 0$). These thermodynamic elements, could be related to other system features, and the global entropy could have different meanings. The properties get a specific meaning depending on the field to which it is being extrapolated.

In the context of the testings performed in the following sections, for example, it can be considered an adiabatic process since dialogs do not get any information from other sources than the direct interaction through those questions and answers. Local entropy relies on global entropy to explain and cover the evolution of a system. The system in the dialogs tested is composed of a person (a volunteer), an Artificial Intelligent system (AI) based on Neural Networks (NN), a communication channel (text interchanged through an internet site), and (S)entences with words that can be (N)ouns, (V)erbs and (A) collection of words for describing (adjectives, adverbs, etc.). Here, as in Information Theory, information is the most important element.

Laws of thermodynamic in gases are simple and universal, but the entropy dynamics in natural systems and, specifically in language, go a step further. In the case of gases they explain the following facts:

- **LAW 0**: if system A is in equilibrium with B, and B with C => A is in equilibrium with C.
- **LAW 1**: energy is preserved and $Q = \square U + W$, being U the internal and potential energy in the system, W= work.
- **LAW 2**: S increases or keeps identical upon any thermodynamic process, with S the universe entropy.
- **LAW 3**: it is not possible to get a system to $0°F$ in a finite number of physical processes.

In physics, it is possible to determine the state of a system and to agree about its properties. The epistemological performance has no drawbacks. It could be due to its historical origin as it has been long studied as a natural event. The subject under study isn't a mere logical-formal definition as in the case of language pragmatics (Rebolledo, 2018). For language productions, laws become cumbersome and need to be determined in a practical way. The concept of equilibrium needs to be extended to imply the complete understanding of certain communication between two (or more) persons. Energy, work, and heat now get another dressing as will be presented in the rest of this work.

ABOUT THE PROPOSAL

Following the concept introduced in sections I and II, language is a natural production of the human brain and a way to communicate information of any kind. It is encoded in grammars based on numbers and letters, symbols that properly organized represent some energy related to the meaning of the message.

Symbols and symbolic systems can express in very different ways the same content. A receiver able to understand a coded message by a sender will receive it with the same meaning. The brain decodes the message and certain inner ordering and assimilation are produced. This way language leads human faculties from perception, guiding the creation of relationships, equivalence categories, resemblance and reasoning. An example of the entire process is music harmonics vibrating at different levels: the human mind detects that those different notes are related only using some kind of inner classification. The result is more than a collection of notes: it is harmony.

But representations of ontologies could make distant something close and vice-versa, due to the effect that it evokes in resonating and feelings. According to the famous writer Jorge Luis Borges, symbols are a unique and secret algebra and in its vague field one thing may become many. Spoken words move in an atmosphere in which the "collective personality" prevails, while in societies where writing dominates, individualism is increasingly imposed as a determining attitude of human behavior and relationship.

This chapter analyzes an intermediate step among spoken and written texts, in order to get the dynamics of communication between two ends of a dialog expressed as a text. The main reason is that the information must be more precise in order to get the counterpart aligned with the goal of the dialog. Most of the spoken interchange in Natural Language is complemented with the collective personality and a number of other visual and sound symbols whose analysis makes the study very complex. Linguists like Skinner (1957) performed a large study of it.

In order to restrict even more this study, the dialogs are simple sentences from a game named 20Q, performed by an Artificial Intelligence (AI) system based on a Neural Networks (NN), and the responses by a human. The AI system has to guess the word previously thought by the human with no other information but its questions. The reason to use an AI is to hold the vocabulary limited to a standard and the syntax as simple as a Wh-question. Answers are also limited to three possibilities. The first consequence is that the entire dialog is simple and short (less than 30 questions) to let the machine win the game.

Even in this limited context presented for the tests, the results are that the machine is able to guess almost all of the target words or get close to them. Considering that the human player can select any word, a question arises: How is it possible that a NN with a reduced vocabulary can get the correct word with a few questions?

Test

This section describes the steps performed to build a corpus, and the approaches to evaluate how the entropy changes with the evolution of short dialogs with a specific goal: to guess a word. It is intended to evaluate communication dynamics.

The Corpus

The aim of this chapter is to evaluate dialogs in Natural Language and not in separate sentences. To do that, the corpus was built with sentences from a set of plays of a game known as 20 questions (in the following referred to as *20Q*). The reasons are diverse:

- The game's goal is to guess a word referring to something never mentioned in the context.
- The interaction must provide a maximum of information at every couple of question-answer.
- The language is not limited but to common words.

- The interaction is guided by the player asking the questions not by the respondent.
- Cultural context is the one providing the clues to the gamers.

The following subsections describe 20Q, the steps to build the corpus and its main characteristics.

The Game 20Q

20Q is a game recommended for individuals over 7 years old (20Q, 2021) since it focuses on the insight of the player to interrogate its opponent. The rules are quite simple:

1. The first player starts the game thinking a word. It can be a prominent person, a place and object, or any other simple word. The word is kept in secret.
2. One at a time, the remaining players ask Yes/No questions trying to guess the word.
3. There can be 20 questions before ending the game.
4. At any time, any player in its turn or not, can try and anticipate which word could be the right one
5. The winner is the gamer that can guess the secret word.
6. When no one addresses the word the first player wins.

From Data to the Corpus

In order to focus the study on the behavior of just one of the participants of the dialog, the 20Q corpus registered the games of an online application that belongs to the Technological observatory (Ministery of Education of Spain, 2021) of the Education, culture and sports Ministry of Spain State. Under the title *20Q funny Artificial Intelligence*, there is an Artificial Intelligence implementation of the game, ready to guess any word. It is important to note that all the tests here are valid just for Spanish productions.

Although the original version just allows 20 questions to be performed prior to the end of the game, this implementation admits a top of 30, if it couldn't guess the target then it closes the game with several candidate words.

Other changes are that the user can select extra answers besides *yes* and *no*. But these extra options are not being used in the tests here. Some questions made by the AI can have small grammatical errors, but the semantics is always very clear for a human (that is, the user).

20 volunteers from 14 to 60 years old played the game. The complete sequence of questions and answers were logged as well as the target word of every game. A total of 432 questions are in the data set under study. About 85% of the games end with a right guessing or a semantically close word. The next section explains how it works. The sequence of questions and answers involves a total of 3530 words and 1042 sentences distributed as shown in Table 1.

Table 1. Content of the Corpus

TestID	Questions	Target word
ID1	30	WEB (WEB)
ID2	30	Stomias (estomias)
ID3	30	Cake (torta)
ID4	30	Sewing machne (máquina de coser)
ID5	30	Pen (bolígrafo)
ID6	17	Flag (bandera)
ID7	29	Computer (computadora)
ID8	20	Dog (perro)
ID9	30	Friend (amigo)
ID10	29	Salt (sal)
ID11	19	Rose (rosa)
ID12	27	Lamp (lámpara de escritorio)
ID13	23	Sparrow (gorrión)
ID14	30	Onix (ónix)
ID15	20	Church (iglesia)
ID16	29	Physician (médico)
ID17	30	Chair (silla)
ID18	26	Egg (huevo)
ID19	17	Tree (árbol)
ID20	25	Keys (llaves)

The corpus was pre-processed to get an appropriate format to be analyzed:

1. Text data was imported in Open Office Calc as Data Sheet.
2. Conversion of sentence ID to a number.
3. Reversion of the sequence of sentences from the original sort, letting the first question as the first row.
4. Deletion of the last sentence (the one that guesses the word) .
5. Addition of Yes/No at the end of the first question. Originally it presents an option between: an object, a plant or an animal. The interaction is changed to Yes / no question.
6. Export as csv the sampled data renaming from dxx to txx to distinguish the processed from the original version.
7. Change "." by ",".
8. Delete the sentence number.
9. Change the file extension to ".txt".

A third version of every test was created and named txx_<target>, with "*<target>*" being the target word. This version has CSV format and every row is as follows: *idQuestion*, question and Answer. This way every test is in its original textual version (dxx), a sorted version from first to last but without sentence number (txx) and a last CSV version also sorted.

For the information analysis, entropy will be calculated. According to Spinadel (2003), it is as in the following equation:

$$H(V) = -\sum_{i=1}^{k} p_i \log_2(p_i) \tag{6}$$

Hardware and Software

Hardware

All the processing is performed in two notebooks:

-A Processor Intel→ Core™ i7-7600U CPU @ 2.80GHz × 4, with 7,4 GiB RAM and 256,1 GB Hard disk, operating system Linux Ubuntu 20.04.2 LTS of 64 bits.
-A Processor Intel→ Dual Core™ i7-7600U CPU @ 2.80GHz × 2, with 8 GiB RAM and 256 GB Hard disk, operating system Linux Ubuntu 20.04.2 LTS of 64 bits.

Software

Every process was performed with *Python*, using the *NLP* library for Spanish, and some other processes in *Octave (c)* for more simplicity.

The IDE used is Atom version 1.57 (ATOM, 2021). Also *WEKA (c)* for data analysis with data science approaches and *Open Office Calc (c)* and *PSPP (c)* for more traditional statistics. All the platforms and tools are open, multi-platform and for free.

NLTK as NLP Library

The Stanford library for NLTK was installed (NLP, 2021) to perform a language processing of texts, tagging and basic statistics. After a careful evaluation of the tagging and lemmatization using NLTK and NLP (trained with corpus *cess*), the results were unsatisfactory, with a bad performance (about 10,9% of precision using standard linguistics labels). For that reason and due to the small size of the corpus to be processed, a handmade tokenization was performed. The tokens are determined by a specialist and reviewed by a second person in order to guarantee a precision of 100%. Thereafter the tools in NLTK were just used to simplify certain routine processing. Most of the processing is performed by specially developed modules in Python and Octave, including linguistic processing that are required for some of the steps in the following testing.

RESULTS AND ANALYSIS

This section describes the results of processing the logs recorded from 20Q plays. Some global numbers as distributions were performed with NLTK library of Python, and NLP from Stanford. As mentioned before, the kit trained with corpus 'cess_esp' for its TAGGER did not get good results. Several modules in Python and Octave were used for more advanced processing. In order to evaluate the parameters presented in previous sections in the context of current data-sets platform WEKA, and PSPP were used.

Study of Main Behavior

The game 20Q is ideal to make explicit rules of information interchange since it is the simplest way to identify certain global dynamic parameters. This section considers a communication C between the gamer and the AI counterpart (that is, the NN with the knowledge from previous plays). Every interchange is in Spanish.

Let $C = \{+t_1 +t_2 +t_3 \dots +t_n\}$ a sequence of **n** questions performed by the user in order to infer some target word w that represents an ontological concept E.

Statement 1 to be tested:

Whenever communication C succeeds in covering a complete interchange of entropy by sentence communications t_i*, then E will be guessed by the receiver of the knowledge. It is considered then that the entropy is completely transferred from the human user to the AI.*

From the perspective of E, it is like being transferred from a sender to a receiver. The AI wins if the full information is successfully moved, and loses at any other circumstance. There are certain occasions when the AI can guess a word that is very close in meaning to the target. Then the information is not fully but mostly moved.

To evaluate statement 1 using the game 20Q is a good choice since it requires a player to guess something with no previous clues. The only restriction is to be one of the 93000 words in the Spanish dictionary, a word that is supposed to be in the cultural background of both players (in this case the AI and the user).

Furthermore, the game approach makes it evident when the communication reinforces or not certain concept (yes/no questions) related to the target word.

In the current version the user can opt between several extra options like *"a veces"* (*sometimes*), *"tal vez"* (*might be*) and *"lo dudo"* (*I guess no*), among others. The game is also different at the first round because it starts querying the type of word between three options: *"animal"*, *"vegetal"* or *"otra cosa"* (*animal, plant* and *anything else* respectively). This first step is changed in the logs to a similar question as the rest of the rounds. Answers are also restricted to *"Si"*, *"No"*, *"A veces"* (*yes, no, sometimes* respectively).

Probably the extra options were added to let the NN behind the game, learn more quickly about words.

Table 2 presents a complete set of rounds for the third game (ID 3). The target word in this play is $w = $ *"torta"* (*cake*).

Table 2. Sequence of questions for test ID 3, w=torta

Qid	Question	Answer
1	Se clasifica como Otra cosa *(it is classified as anything else)*	Sí *(yes)*
2	Tiene algo escrito *(it has something written on it)*	A veces *(sometimes)*
3	Es pequeño *(it is small)*	No *(No)*
4	Es duro *(it is hard)*	A veces *(sometimes)*
5	Se utiliza en público *(it is used in public)*	A veces *(sometimes)*
6	Es de sangre fría *(it is cold blooded)*	No *(No)*
7	Hacen falta conocimientos especiales para usarlo *(it requires specific knowledge to use it)*	No *(No)*
8	Es pesado *(it is heavy)*	No *(No)*
9	Puede encontrarse en una clase *(it can be found in a classroom)*	No *(No)*
10	Está hecho por el hombre *(it is man made)*	Sí *(yes)*
11	Es útil *(it is useful)*	A veces *(sometimes)*
12	Lo pueden usar personas de todas las edades *(people of any age can use it)*	Sí *(yes)*
13	Se utiliza en los viajes *(it is used in travels)*	No *(No)*
14	Está hecho de madera *(it is made of wood)*	No *(No)*
15	Está hecho de plástico *(it is made of plastic)*	No *(No)*
16	Se puede lavar *(it can be washed)*	No *(No)*
17	Se puede pedir en un restaurante *(you can ask it at a restaurant)*	Sí *(yes)*
18	Está frío *(it is cold)*	A veces *(sometimes)*
19	Es crujiente *(it is crispy)*	A veces *(sometimes)*
20	Conjeturo que es un trozo de pizza *(I guess it is a portion of pizza)*	No *(No)*
21	Es suave *(it is soft)*	A veces *(sometimes)*
22	Es multicolor *(it is multicolored)*	A veces *(sometimes)*
23	Es marrón *(it is brown)*	A veces *(sometimes)*

Continued on following page

Table 2. Continued

Qid	Question	Answer
24	Es un color concreto *(it is a specific color)*	A veces *(sometimes)*
25	Se mete dentro de otra cosa *(it can get inside another thing)*	A veces *(sometimes)*
26	Provoca adicción *(causes addiction)*	A veces *(sometimes)*
27	Es suave *(it is soft)*	A veces *(sometimes)*
28	Conjeturo que es una tarta de chocolate *(I guess it is a chocolate cake)*	No *(No)*
29	Conjeturo que es tarta de queso *(I guess it is a cheese cake)*	No *(No)*
30	Estoy sospecho que es mayonesa *(I guess it is mayonnaise)*	No *(No)*

It is interesting to observe in sample 3 (the one in Table 2), even playing an automatic system (with limited experience) it is able to approximate the concept pretty well. The selected case is guessing right about it is a food, since round 20, and keeps on this way in rounds 28, 29 and 30, discarding any other option.

The evaluation with statistical platform **PSPP** and a module in Python, is shown in **Table 3**. The tagging process was performed manually but following certain guidelines:

- **Use tag &V** if there is an action (verbal phrase of any type).
- **Use tag &N** if there is any type of nominal reference (noun phrase or short noun sentences).
- **Use tag &A** if there is any type of qualification, description, properties or characteristic (adjectives, adverbs, etc.).

The AI system provides some sentences that are grammarly incorrect: "ESTOY SOSPECHOSO" (I am "a" suspicious), instead of a sentence that a native speaker could say for example "SOSPECHO" (I guess). These mistakes are not considered. It is the only error detected in the sentences.

Taking the advantage of hand-made tagging, the sentences that represent a single object or action is collapsed with just one tag, even though there could be many words involved. The only exception is the presence of any other taxonomic category present.

Table 3. Summary of games performed

Play	Success	Approximation	Classification	Target word	# words	# sentences	# nouns	# verbs
ID1	N	N	no	WEB	204	60	11	35
ID2	N	Y	Aquatic animal	stomias	208	60	21	36
ID3	N	Y	Food	cake	222	60	20	36
ID4	N	Y	Machine for domestic use	Sewing machine	220	60	18	37
ID5	Y	Y	Pen	Pen	232	60	21	39
ID6	Y	Y	Flag	Flag	117	34	14	18
ID7	Y	Y	Computer	Computer	226	58	19	33
ID8	Y	Y	Dog	Dog	140	40	8	25
ID9	N	Y	Soul mate	Friend	223	60	23	36
ID10	Y	Y	Salt	Salt	203	58	16	33
ID11	N	Y	Rosebush	Rose	134	38	14	20
ID12	Y	Y	Desk lamp	Desk lamp	185	54	10	30
ID13	Y	Y	Sparrow	Sparrow	154	46	16	25
ID14	N	N	Milk	Onyx	235	60	17	37
ID15	N	Y	Cathedral	Church	148	40	11	25
ID16	N	N	Pirate	Physician	208	58	20	40
ID17	N	N	Cane	Chair	220	60	16	36
ID18	Y	Y	Egg	Egg	167	52	15	29
ID19	Y	Y	Tree	Tree	138	34	13	19
ID20	Y	Y	Keys	Keys	178	50	15	31

Figure 2. Cumulative distribution of verbs for a game

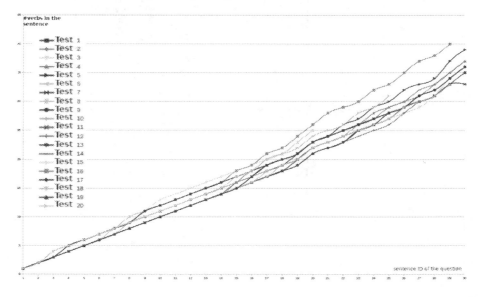

347

Figure 3. Cumulative distribution of nouns a game

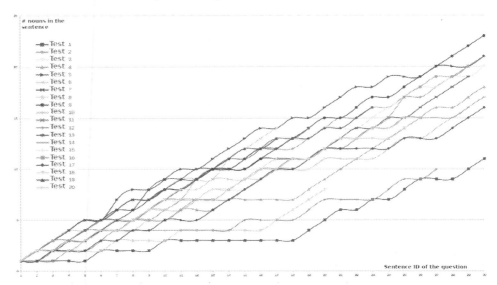

The accumulative number of nouns and verbs in the successive questions of a typical game are in Figures 2 and 3 respectively. It can be seen how different is the curve for verbs and nouns. The evolution along the plays is somewhat stepped for nouns and with higher dispersion in the slope.

Table 4. EM for question sentences in 20Q games

Cluster ID	#questions	Cluster colour
0	181 (35%)	
1	69 (13%)	
2	28 (5%)	
3	243 (47%)	
4	5 (1%)	

The trend of the accumulated curves shows a larger dispersion for nouns than for verbs. This is evidence of the diverse use of verbs. This can also be observed in the two last columns of Table 3: # nouns (number of nouns), and # verbs (number of verbs) for every sentence in the games played. Also # nouns < # verbs in all the cases.

From Data Mining perspective, data behavior can also be modeled by observing the sentence's main characteristics. By Expectation Maximization (EM) natural similarities arise as 5 clusters, that can be seen in Table 4.

The maximum value of Log likelihood is 5.65331 when the number of nouns and verbs are considered during the model training, while game (ID) and sentence number (QID) are ignored.

Figure 4 is the cluster distribution for the test set (x-axe is QID, and y-axe is the game identified as TEST ID in the image). As cluster 4 has very few instances, the plot in WEKA doesn't show it. Note that clusters 2 and 3 are the last questions of every game.

Figure 4. Question clusters (QID) in every game (TESTID)

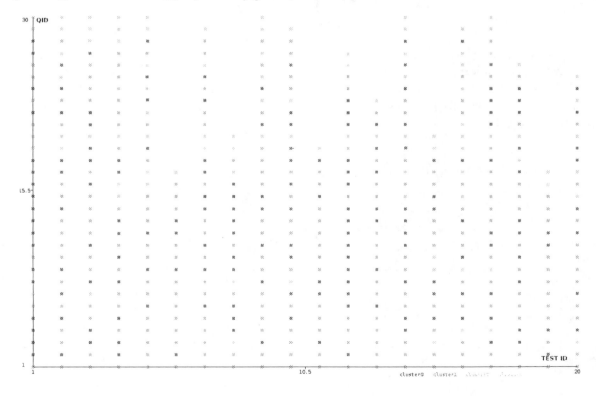

Games have a combination of clusters 1, 2, and 4. Games 2, 6, 9, 11, 13, and 18 don't have cluster 3. These cases correspond to games that get close to the goal (same type of object) but just half of them (50%) correspond to a successful game (that is the inferred word is exactly the target). Figure 5 shows better this distribution as percentages at every test.

Figure 5. Percentage of clusters in every game (Test 1 to 20)

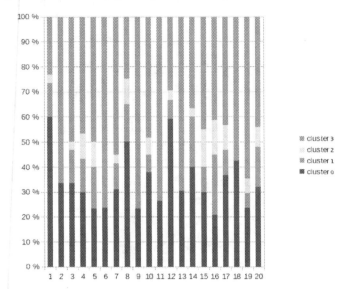

Regarding the cluster composition, there are more verbs in clusters 2 and 3 (see Table 5), but clusters 1 and 2 have more nouns. Cluster 0 has more nouns than cluster 1. Cluster 2 has more variation in the number of verbs than Cluster 3. Cluster 4 has a tiny part of the questions with no common patterns, but probably to be outliers.

Table 5. Clusters characteristics

	Cluster				
	0	**1**	**2**	**3**	**4**
Attribute	(0.46)	(0.35)	(0.13)	(0.06)	(0.01)
cantV					
mean	1	1	2.0293	2	1
std. dev.	0.0016	0.0001	0.1769	0.4024	0
cantN					
mean	0.9805	0.0503	0.9608	0.2041	1.6602
std. dev.	0.2316	0.2185	0.194	0.403	0.4847

These results and descriptive statistics (see Figure 6) confirm that even though there is certain dispersion in values, there is a trend to questions with just one verb and up to one noun.

Figure 6. Global characteristics (without clusters)

	# V	# N
N Valid	521	521
Lost	0	0
Media	1,19	,61
Std dev	,40	,51
Min	1	0
Max	3	2

 # V

		Freequency	Percentage	Valid %	Accumulated %
Valid	1	424	81,4%	81,4%	81,4%
	2	95	18,2%	18,2%	99,6%
	3	2	,4%	,4%	100,0%
Total		521	100,0%		

 # N

		Freequency	Percentage	Valid %	Accumulated %
Valid	0	209	40,1%	40,1%	40,1%
	1	306	58,7%	58,7%	98,8%
	2	6	1,2%	1,2%	100,0%
Total		521	100,0%		

Figures 7 and 8 show cluster noun and verb distributions as histograms, making it more evident the trend mentioned before.

Figure 7. Verbs in every cluster

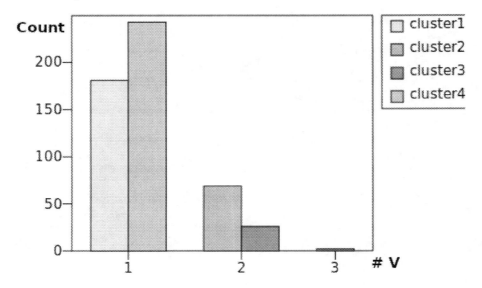

Figure 8. Nouns in every cluster

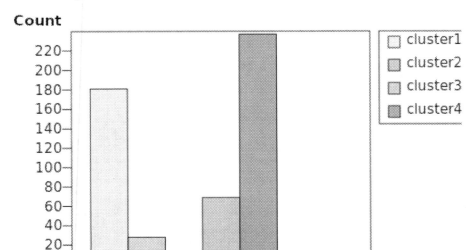

Results indicate that games are with questions in one of four styles, that differ mainly in the way to combine nouns and verbs in the questions. To visualize this finding, an induction tree J48 is performed, since its classifications are based on *Information gain* due to entropy obtained by nodes in the model. Figure 9 is the model as a tree graph.

Figure 9. J48 tree graph

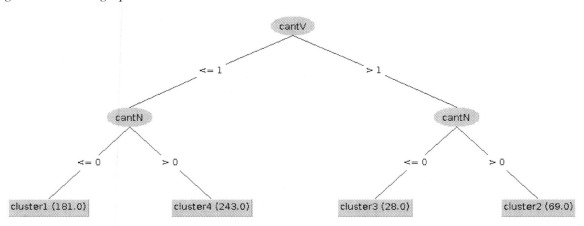

The confusion matrix (see Table 6) denotes a classification of 100% (and Kappa statistics 1), which is a perfect *description* of the data. This is another version of the EM clustering decisions. Note that EM has considered (as well J48) that the maximum entropy has taken when the number of verbs considered is >= 1. Then, when the number of nouns is chosen between zero (in the figure <=0) or more. J48 selects two variables: cantV (or #V) and cantN (or #N) as relevant in the same sequence even when the data set has other values like ET, ET(V), ET(N), and ET(A).

Table 6. Confusion matrix for J48

Confusion J48				
a	*b*	*c*	*d*	*<-- classified as*
243	0	0	0	*a = cluster4*
0	181	0	0	*b = cluster1*
0	0	28	0	*c = cluster3*
0	0	0	69	*d = cluster2*

Test of Dimension and Rhythm

Words and Entropy

The information drifted from every sentence in a game can be measured by its entropy (H_S). The amount of H_G remaining (more precisely $\sim H_G$) is considered in this context as the information required to solve successfully the game (to find out the target word). This section is to evaluate the amount of $H = H_S + H_G$ as a process with an associated dimension, and its changes following a cycle and rhythm.

From the first findings in *Sound Model for Dialog Profiling* (López De Luise & Azor, 2015), there is a fractal relationship between entropy and sentence sequences in dialogs. The work explains the relevance of sound processing to evaluate linguistics performance, and fractal point of view for written text and how Verbal Behavior may be connected. It also introduces some motivations to analyze and model speech and sounds and evaluates fractal behavior for energy distribution, according to the Dragon curve.

This work continues those findings in the context of written dialogs, with the analysis centered on nouns (S) and verbs (V), and how they change the amount of H_S when the dialog needs to be an efficient use of entropy to get a target word (the goal of the 20Q game).
Statement 2 to be tested:

There is a complement between V and N, though not perfect they balance each other as H and ~H does. The behavior has a certain rhythm and cycle.

In this context, *rhythm* is considered as its original sense: *A regular movement or pattern of movements, and a regular pattern of change* (Cambridge dictionary, 2021). The pattern of change will be evaluated in this sub-section as the flow of entropy (H_S) respecting the presence of V, A, and N. A *cycle* is *A group of events that happen in a particular order, one following the other, and are often repeated* (Cambridge dictionary, 2021): from a fractal perspective, there is a cycle at every scaling of the original pattern. Sections V.B.1, V.B.2, and V.B.3 study how entropy evolves when fractal dimension (D) is considered.

The Rhythm

Table 7 presents H (column *ET*) for every game (that is every test ID), H_S in black, and how it behaves for V and N (*ET(V)* and *ET(N)*). The graphs have a third curve for attributes and descriptors (globally denoted as *ET(A)*).

Table 7. Entropy evolution for tests ID 1 to 20

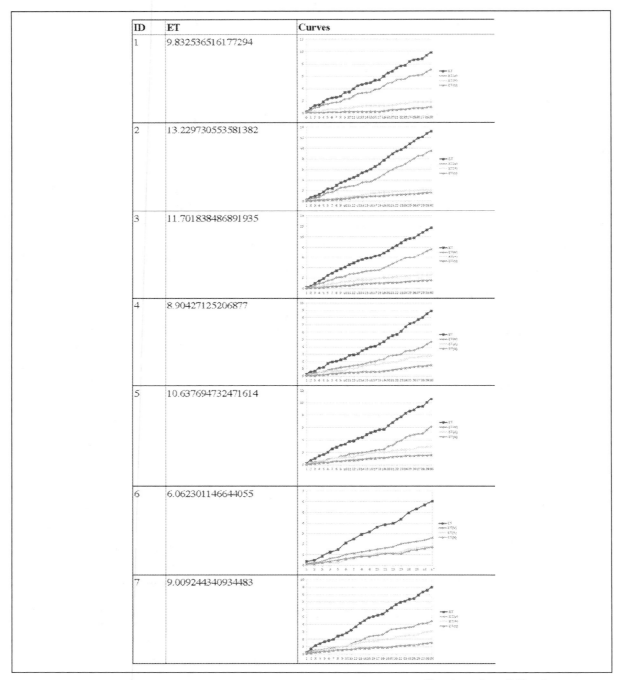

ID	ET	Curves
1	9.832536516177294	
2	13.229730553581382	
3	11.701838486891935	
4	8.904271252066877	
5	10.637694732471614	
6	6.062301146644055	
7	9.009244340934483	

Continued on following page

Table 7. Continued

ID	ET	Curves
8	6.798612751961287	
9	8.998432864112107	
10	8.790222947263285	
11	6.77136782637394	
12	7.493834497432596	
13	8.341462466542284	
14	10.43031484076085	

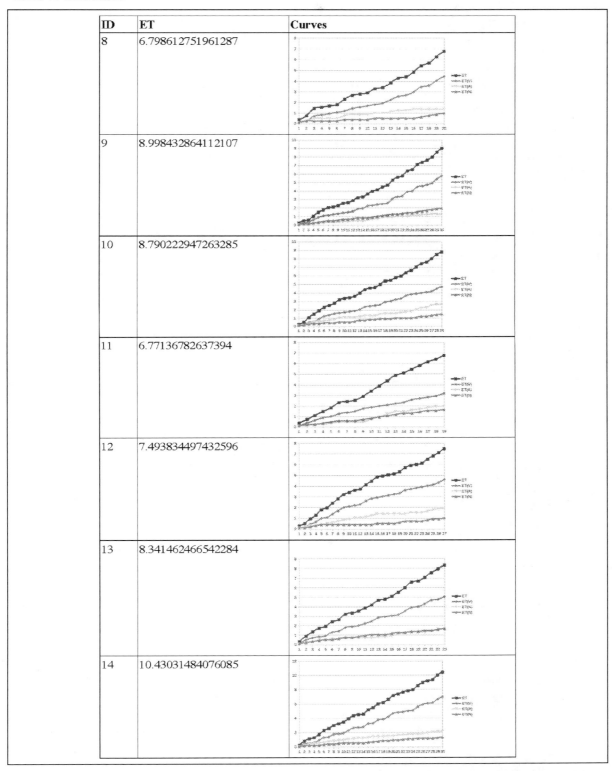

Continued on following page

Table 7. Continued

ID	ET	Curves
15	6.81171271756928	
16	10.772917798947017	
17	10.182639279099895	
18	9.666639965703993	
19	6.732769532076325	
20	8.821279889907554	

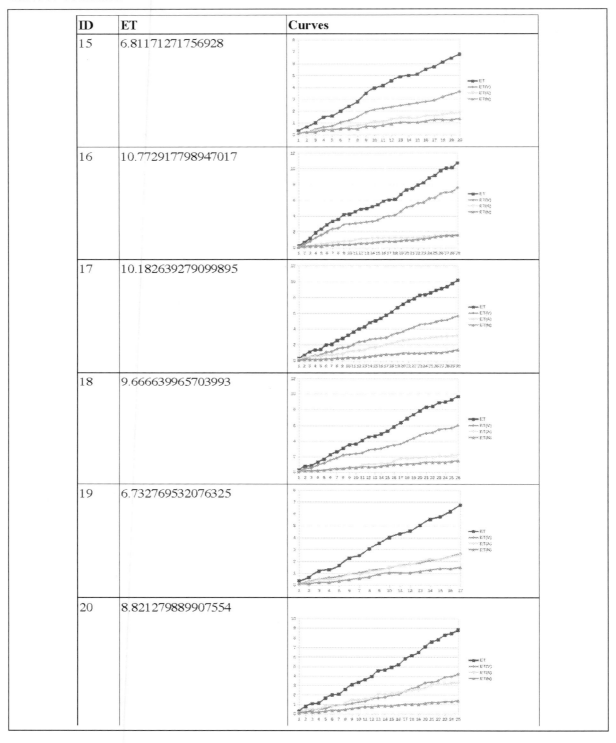

A common behavior in all tests is that ET(V), the variation of ET due to Verbs, are higher than ET(N) and ET(A), variations for Nouns and descriptors respectively.

Curve ET(N) is typically the lower one. Another interesting finding is that ET values explain most of the success of the game: values in [6.06 – 9.66] are for games that never lose. Values in [9.83 – 10.77] are for values that always lose. Values higher than 11.7 are for games that may infer the class but not the word (approximate the target word). Game 5 is the only exception and could be due to the fact that the counterpart of the user is a neural network that could have learned certain extra biases during training. In any case, these results are initial and need to be confirmed with more testings.

Note that there is a cyclical alternation of games successful and lost along the values of ET values, a certain rhythm (see Figure 10).

Figure 10. Hit and fail according to ET values

Out of the region with NO hits (values between 9.83 and 10.77), there is an alternation between hit and approximation. The rhythm and trends need to be confirmed with more testings.

Entropy and Sentences

The sequence of sentences in a dialog can be thought of as a flow of entropy between two ends: the sender of the message and the receiver. In the current context questions are from 20Q system and the receiver is the player (a human).

The dynamics are evaluated by H_S (*ET(IDQ)*): it reflects how much entropy is conveyed through question sentences by using just nouns, verbs and descriptors (adjectives, adverbs, etc). The equation is as follows:

$$ET\left(\text{IDQ}\right) = -p\left(s\right).\log_2\left(p\left(s\right)\right) \text{ and } p\left(s\right) = \frac{s}{T} \tag{7}$$

With
s: number of verbs (V), nouns (N) or descriptive word (A).
T:total number of words.

Considering the dialog dynamics as an entropy interchange, the sequence of questions and answers along a 20Q game is an interaction that aims to get enough information about certain secret word. Note that the target is a common noun of any type (it is not allowed slang or very special words that are known just by one of the players). As there is a limit in the number of interactions, imposed by the rules of the game, the interchange needs to have a rhythm that enables the systematic acquisition of enough entropy by the participant that has to find out the target word. He has to select just one word in its entire vocabulary (remember there are currently about 93000 words in the Spanish dictionary). In the universe of concepts just one is the winner.

The rhythmic evolution of ET (H) can be expressed as some type of fractal (López De Luise & Azor, 2015). Even in the case there is no visual self-similarity, H_S can be analyzed as a different fractal instance with a fractal dimension and certain characteristics, some of them explained in previous sections. As in any other fractal, there is a rate for H evolution and change between a stage H_S and the next (H_{S+1}).

Let set H_S the entropy of 20Q sentences in a game, the rhythm is the amount of H sent in a question or, from the receiver perspective, the quantity of H acquired (also proportional to the ~H remaining at each time). It is possible to assess the entropy following the fractal dimension D (Spinadel, 2003) as:

$$D = \frac{\log_x N}{\log_x (1/r)} \tag{8}$$

With
N: number of partitions.
r: change rate.

The rest of sub-sections explore different considerations for N and r, to show how is the cycle in H, and to explain a *second statement*:

There is a rhythmic evolution of H (or ET) mainly due to N and V. In this context ET due to N is a counterpart of ET due to V. Though they do not perfectly compensate each other they act mainly symmetrically.

First Dimension Analysis

D parameter values are considered to evaluate the change rate in ET as the number of partitions (N) and ET value in a question of the game (H_S) as the change rate. As entropy, the logarithm is 2. Then:

x=2
$N = \Delta ET = ET_q - ET_{q-1}$ (the change in ET between two questions or sentences)
$r = ET_q$ (ET value in question or sentence q)

Table 8 has the summary of the plots. It is interesting to observe the behavior of ET, where most of the question sequences present a pulse (a peak in H_S).

Table 8. Tests with N=ΔET, r=ET

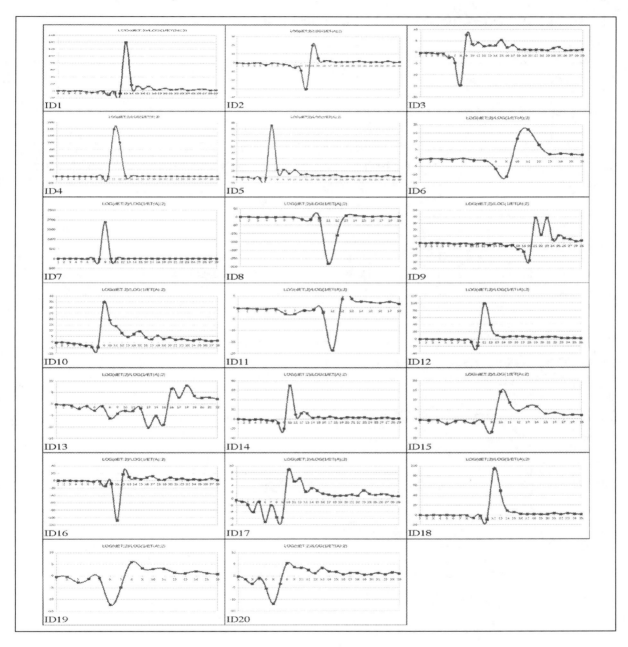

Graphics are smooth curves with just one maximum and one minimum. The only exception is case ID 9. The minimum represents a status when there is an exploration of complement characteristics of the concept represented by the target. Note that soon after there is a fast increase of the entropy, that fits the class determination and a decrease when the specificity increases. This is like a strategy for the game: the best way to get success is to find the class and then the specific word.

Case ID 9 has two top peaks corresponding to a difference in entropy between questions 24 – 23, and 22 – 21. To understand the problem here it is important to analyze the sentence sequence:

24. Is it used regularly? (Answer: no)
23. I guess it is a compositor (Answer: sometimes)
22. Can it be resized? (Answer: No)
21.Is it spontaneous? (Answer: Sometimes)

In other cases, the classification was correct from the beginning, but in this case, the NN behind 20Q had to change the class after a first approach. It is probably due to the current knowledge of the system (it depends on the concepts learned in past games).

Second Dimension Analysis

The second test focuses on how different is the ET variation due to V (*ET(v)* or $H_{s,v}$) when ET has a certain value due to N. It intends to evaluate how N impacts the ET level given by the current set of V during the game.

Values are now:

$x=2$
$N=\Delta ET(V)=ET(V)_q - ET(V)_{q-1}$ (the change in ET due to V between two questions)
$r=ET(N)_q$ (ET value due to N in question q)

Table 9 has the curves for each game considering these parameters.

Table 9. Tests with N=ΔET(V), r=ET(N)

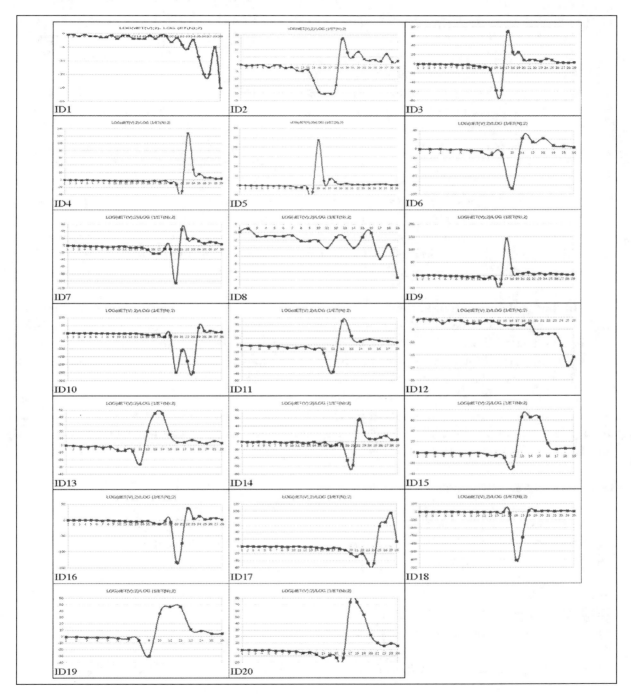

Note that soft curves in the table present four main behaviors:

1. **Drop to negative values**: The oscillation trend to the negative axis and never gets back to the x-axis. Cases ID 1, 8 and 14. Corresponds to cases in which the NN makes conjectures about concepts that are dissimilar to each other, which have certain ambiguous properties in common. This strategy of trying very different things at random worked in one of the 3 plays in which it was used. In the other two, it failed to hit or even approximate the result.

2. **A higher peak in negative values**: The curve rises to a positive value, but is always less marked than its negative counterpart. Cases ID 6, 7, 10, 16, and 18. This approach succeed in 4 of the 5 cases and failed in one. Correspond to an initial classification strategy by discarding typical actions and qualities. Case ID 16, the one unsuccessful has as target the word "physician". According to the explanation after the game, the NN did not know the concept previously, therefore it was a special case of lack of domain in the knowledge.

3. **A higher peak in positive values**: this is the most numerous class. Presents a negative peak but is much less marked than the positive one. Cases ID 4, 5, 9, 13, 15, 17, 19, and 20. This strategy fails in one case (ID 17, chair) but succeeds in 4 games. It approximates very well the target concept in the rest of the plays. It is based on discarding fundamental properties at the beginning and classifying quickly. Then try to progressively specify the concept considering associations with other concepts.

4. **Similar peaks in both directions**: this is the less numerous class together with class 1. Cases ID 2, 11, and 12. It has the most diverse results (it fails one game, approximates another, and succeeds in a third one). Here the classification by discard is performed by associations with concepts. After a very fast group determination, it attempts to specify the concept using actions and attributes of things. It is possible that its poor results are due ti a very fast classification.

Test show that strategies to model entropy using N have better performance when it is used to classify by process of elimination, but it must rely on actions and characteristics of known objects to infer quickly the target word upon classification.

Third Dimension Analysis

The last test evaluates for each question the rate ET due to V ($H_{s,v}$) when ET has a certain value by N. It intends to evaluate how N relates to ET level given by N and V along with the game.
Values are now:

x=2
N=ET(V)$_q$ (ET value due to V in question q)
r=ET(N)$_q$ (ET value due to N in question q)

Table 10 has the complete set of curves for each game with these values.

Table 10. Tests with N=ET(V), r=ET(N)

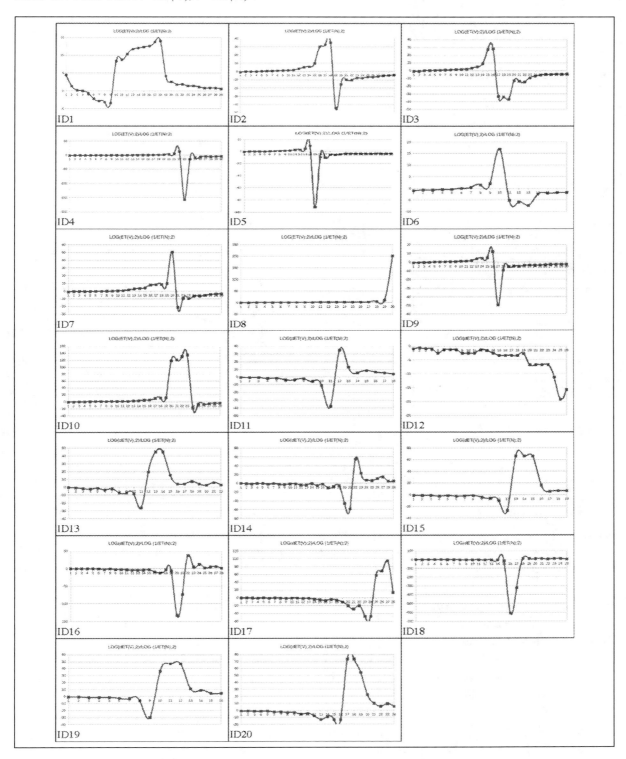

In general, there is a positive peak and then a negative slope. This is almost a kind of symmetric behavior respecting the ones in the previous section. Figure 11 is a composition of both tests in the same graph for game ID 2.

Figure 11. Composite graph for ID 2

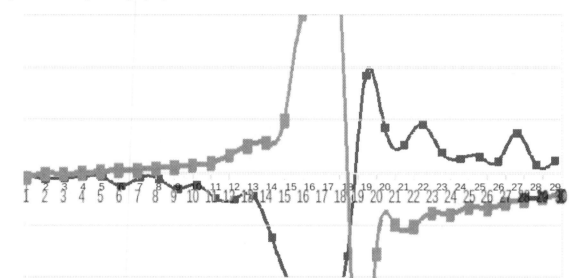

This explains that ET due to V complements ET due to N: for case ID 2, the classification is fast and based on association with concepts. This way N provides more information than V (see curve below zero). Then the specific word is searched using a combination of actions and characteristics, where V takes more relevance. The curve remains below zero since part of the process uses also A words.

There are cases like ID 1 that diverge in one graph but not in both. Figure 12 shows this case.

In this case ET was spent making conjectures about concepts that are dissimilar to each other, which have certain ambiguous properties in common. From the perspective of V, it plays an important role in the second part of the strategy (after the main classification), but after a lot of interchange of entropy (many sentences trying different verbs), it changes to sentences with more N, trying to get the specific word. This way the curve is going down while the lighter curve does not change so much because it has the contribution of N (and A).

Since curves are approximately symmetric to the ones obtained in the previous analysis, there are again four main types of behaviors, but cases are not all in the opposite type. This is so because there are influences of A words in the sentences, that sometimes help in the resolution of the game and sometimes not.

1. **Diverging values**: There is a trend to infinite negative/positive axis and never gets back to the x-axis. Cases ID 8 and 12. Note that in this case the divergence can be of any sign.

2. **A higher peak in negative values**: The main rise of the curve is not in the positive value, but in its negative counterpart. Cases ID 1, 2, 3, 4, 5, 9, 13, 15, 17, 19 and 20. Note that cases 1, 2, and 17 are new in this group, because of A words.

3. **A higher peak in positive values**: Presents a negative peak but much less marked than the positive one. Cases ID 6, 7, 10, 15, 16, and 18. In this group cases ID 14 and 15 are new.

4. **Similar peaks in both directions**: Here cases are ID 2, 3, 11, and 14.

Figure 12. Composite graph for ID 1

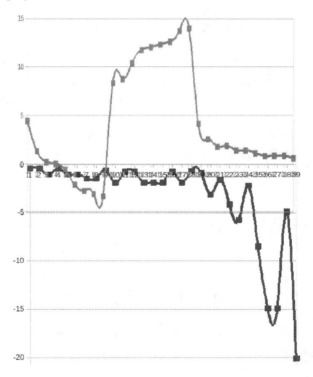

From this analysis N and V can be seen as competing in the process of drifting entropy. The more it can be obtained in the classification and specification processes, the higher possibility to infer the correct word. When ET is based on V, N holds with the rest of the information required for finding out the specific concept.

CONCLUSION

This chapter evaluates the dynamics between two ends of Spanish dialogs: a sender and a receiver, in the context of a game named 20Q consisting of querying sentences that can be answered by YES/NO and SOMETIMES. The goal is to infer a target word making no more than 20 questions.

The information is interchanged through a set of words structured according to grammar in sentences and can be evaluated by its entropy (H_S) dynamics.

The chapter proposes two statements to be tested. The first is:

Whenever communication C succeeds in covering a complete interchange of entropy by sentence communications $\mathbf{t}_i$*, then E will be guessed by the receiver of the knowledge. It is considered then that the entropy is completely transferred from the human user to the AI.*

From the 20 games performed, EM shows a specific behavior that agrees with the previous statement (as well J48). The tree J48 performs its classifications based on *Information gain*, the entropy obtained by nodes in the model. It could be considered a tree graph version of the EM clustering decisions. Both models (EM and J48) explain that the maximum entropy is taken when the number of verbs is 1 or more. Then, when the number of nouns is zero (in the figure <=0) or more.

Tests show a specific distribution of sentences during the game. Results indicate that games are with questions in one of four styles, that differ mainly in the way to combine nouns and verbs within the questions. Lasts questions have more verbs than others. Every game has a combination of specific types of sentences (clusters 1, 2 and 4 of Figure 4). Good games don't need many verbs but a balance with nouns (cluster 3).

The dimensional analysis also confirms that entropy needs to be properly gained in order to succeed in the game (get the target word), which is in this context the same as gathering all the required entropy from the other player.

A second statement tested is:

There is a rhythmic evolution of H (or ET) mainly due to N and V. In this context ET due to N is a counterpart of ET due to V. Though they do not perfectly compensate each other they act mainly symmetrically.

From the global analysis of the games ET(V), that is variation of ET due to Verbs, is higher than ET(N) and ET(A), the variations for Nouns and descriptors respectively. Another interesting finding is that ET values explain most of the success of the game: values in [6.06 – 9.66] are for games that never lose. Values in [9.83 – 10.77] are for values that always lose. Values higher than 11.7 are for games that may infer the class but not the word (approximate the target word). The behavior of ET in a game presents a pulse (a peak in H).

Out of the region with no hits, there is an alternation between hit and approximation. This rhythm and trends need to be confirmed with more testings.

Three analyses were performed, considering as a fractal dimension ET and its changes from one sentence to another. The following are the results:

- *First Dimension Analysis*: Graphics are smooth curves with just one maximum and one minimum. The minimum represents a status when there is an exploration of complement characteristics of the concept represented by the target. Note that soon after there is a fast increase of the entropy, that fits the class determination and a decrease when the specificity increases. This is coherent with a strategy for the game: the best way to get success is to find the class and then the specific word. Curves present also four main behaviors: Drop to negative values, higher peak in negative values, higher peak in positive values and similar peaks in both directions

- ***Second Dimension Analysis***: This part of the test shows that strategies to model entropy using N have better performance when it is used to classify by process of elimination, but it must rely on actions and characteristics of known objects to infer quickly the target word upon classification.
- ***Third Dimension Analysis***: In general, there is a positive peak and then a negative slope. This is almost a kind of symmetric behavior respecting the ones in the second dimension analysis. Since curves are approximately symmetric, there are four main types of behaviors, but cases are not all in the opposite type. This is so because there are influences of A words in the sentences, that sometimes help in the resolution of the game and sometimes not.

From this analysis N and V can be seen as competing in the process of extracting entropy. The more it can be obtained in the classification and specification processes, the higher possibility to infer the correct word. When ET is based on V, N holds the rest of information required for finding out the specific concept. Then both H and ~H hold a cycle that is different, but they finally compensate each other.

There are certain breakthroughs in the interchange, emerged as big peaks and valleys in the entropy evolution of the interchange.

This alternate generation of H has a pending ~H, whenever it is produced a sentence. The dialogs, considered as having a fractal dimension (D) hold a macro rhythm along the complete domain of time (the duration of the game). This D allows interpreting the approach taken to infer the target goal, which is confirmed with the global study performed at the beginning. D can be considered as a change rate r of the cycle taken by the entropy during the process of fractal instantiation, that is, the message movement.

FUTURE RESEARCH DIRECTIONS

Natural Language is a complex field. From the fractal perspective of entropy there are many pendings. This chapter is a part of an extensive work covering several rules, hypotheses and statements that aim to explain the complete dynamics of language production. There are 7 rules and more than a dozen of statements under study. This chapter shows a tiny study of one of the rules and some part of a second rule. In future publications the remaining of the work will be presented with proper tests and statistical analysis.

Also, the tests presented in this chapter need to be further testing with other types of dialogs, and texts. The rhythm and trends shown here will be more deeply discussed, analyzed and tested.

It is expected that a complete set of language rules and statements will allow scientists to develop better chat-bots, will give a better understanding of how works linguistic reasoning in humans, how it could be affected, and how people with certain language deficiencies could be helped.

REFERENCES

2021). http://www.20q.net/

Apostol, T. M. (1976). *Introduction to Analytic Number Theory*. Springer Verlang.

ATOM. (2021). https://atom.io

Bhattacharya, S., Somayaji, S., Reddy, P. K., Kaluri, R., Gadekallu, T., Alazab, M., & Tariq, U. (2020). A novel PCA-firefly based XGBoost classification model for intrusion detection in networks using GPU. *Electronics (Basel)*, *9*(2), 219. doi:10.3390/electronics9020219

Billingsley, P. (1965). *Ergodic theory and information*. Wiley.

Bunge, M. (1969). Probability and law [Probabilidad y ley]. *Magazine Diánoia.*, *15*(15), 141–160. doi:10.22201/iifs.18704913e.1969.15.1118

Callen, H. B. (1985). *Thermodynamics and an Introduction to Thermostatistics* (2nd ed.). John Wiley & Sons.

Cambridge Dictionary. (2021). https://dictionary.cambridge.org

Chueh, C. H., Chien, J. T., & Wang, H. M. (2004). A maximum entropy approach for integrating semantic information in statistical language models. *International Symposium on Chinese Spoken Language Processing*, 309-312. 10.1109/CHINSL.2004.1409648

Costa dos Santos, R. & Ascher, D. (2017). Popper epistemology and management as an applied social science: A theoretical essay. *Espacios, 38*(16), 20.

Esteva Fabregat, C. (2008). Follow-Up for a Complexity Theory [Acompañamientos a una teoría de la complejidad]. *Desacatos*, *12*(28).

Kaluri, R., & Pradeep, C. H. (2017). An enhanced framework for sign gesture recognition using hidden Markov model and adaptive histogram technique. *Int J Intell Eng Syst*, *10*(3), 11–19. doi:10.22266/ijies2017.0630.02

Kaluri, R., & Reddy, C. H. P. (2018). Optimized Feature Extraction for Precise Sign Gesture Recognition Using Self-improved Genetic Algorithm. *IACSIT International Journal of Engineering and Technology*, *8*(1), 25–37.

Kemel, G. (2020) *The logical reasoning in symbolic language and natural language* [El razonamiento lógico en el lenguaje simbólico y en el lenguaje natural]. UNIMAGDALENA.

Kuo, H. (2004) Maximum entropy modeling for speech recognition. *International Symposium on Chinese Spoken Language Processing*, T-2. 10.1109/CHINSL.2004.1409569

Yi Lee, M. & Prieto, F. R. (2010) Generation of fractals with akin transformations [Generación de fractales a partir de transformaciones afines]. *Trans. III REPEM*.

López De Luise, D. & Azor, R. (2015). *Sound Model for Dialog Profiling*. Inderscience Publishers Ltd.

Mandelbrot, B. (1965). *Information Theory and Psycholinguistics* (B. B. Wolman & E. Nagel, Eds.). Scientific Psychology.

Ministery of Education of Spain. (2021). *Ministerio de educación de España*. https://www.educacionyfp.gob.es/

NLP. (2021). https://nlp.stanford.edu/software/tagger

Real Academia Española. (2021). https://www.rae.es/

Rebolledo, R. (2018). Complexity and Chance [Complejidad y azar]. *Humanities Journal of Valparaiso*. doi:10.22370/rhv.2018.12.1322

Rodríguez Duch, M. F. (2016). Chaos, entropy and public health: Legal analysis from a multidimensional perspective [Caos, entropía y salud pública: Análisis desde una perspectiva jurídica multidimensional]. *Argentina Association of Administrative Law Magazine*.

Rodriguez Santos, A. (2011) *Epswiclas*. I.E.S. San Cristóbal de los Ángeles de Madrid.

Sala Torrent, M. (2020). Trastornos del desarrollo del lenguaje oral y escrito. Congreso de actualización en Pediatría, 251 – 263.

Shannon, C.E. (1948). A Mathematical Theory of Communication. *Bell System Technical Journal, 3*(27), 379–423 & 623–656.

Sharir, O., Peleg, B., & Shoham, Y. (2020). *The cost of training NLP Models*. Available at: https://arxiv.org/pdf/2004.08900.pdf

Siegler, R. S. & Booth, J. L. (2004). Development of numerical estimation in Young Children. *Child Development, 2*(75), 428 – 444.

Spinadel, V. M. (2008) Fractals [Fractales]. *Segundo Congreso Internacional de Matemáticas en la Ingeniería y la Arquitectura*, 113 - 123.

Spinadel, V. W. (2003). Fractal geometry and Euclidean thermodynamics [Geometría fractal y geometría euclidiana]. *Magazine Education and Pedagogy, 15*(1), 85-91.

Sulbarán Sandoval, J. A. (2016). Fractal as architectural paradigm: deconstruction vs vivid patterns language [El fractal como paradigma arquitectónico: deconstrucción vs lenguaje de patrones viviente]. *Procesos Urbanos*, (3), 79–88. doi:10.21892/2422085X.268

Von Bertalanffy, L. (1984). *General System Theory; Foundations, Development, Applications* [Teoría general de los sistemas; fundamentos, aplicaciones]. Fondo de Cultura Económica.

Widyarto, S., Syafrullah, M., Sharif, M. W., & Budaya, G. A. (2019). Fractals Study and Its Application. *6th International Conference on Electrical Engineering, Computer Science and Informatics (EECSI)*, 200-204. 10.23919/EECSI48112.2019.8977124

Wynn, K. (1992). Addition and Subtraction by human infants. *Letters to Nature, 358*(6389), 749–750. doi:10.1038/358749a0

Xiong, D., Zhang, M., & Li, H. (2011, November). A Maximum-Entropy Segmentation Model for Statistical Machine Translation. *IEEE Transactions on Audio, Speech, and Language Processing, 19*(8), 2494–2505. doi:10.1109/TASL.2011.2144971

Zhang, X., Wang, Y., & Wu, L. (2019). Research on Cross Language Text Keyword Extraction Based on Information Entropy and TextRank. *2019 IEEE 3rd Information Technology, Networking, Electronic and Automation Control Conference (ITNEC)*, 16-19. 10.1109/ITNEC.2019.8728993

Zipf, G. K. (1932). *Selected Studies of the Principle of Relative Frequency in Language*. Harvard Univ. Press. doi:10.4159/harvard.9780674434929

ADDITIONAL READING

Corral, A., & Serra, I. (2019). *The Brevity Law as a Scaling Law, and a Possible Origin of Zipf's Law for Word Frequencies*. MDPI Communication.

López De Luise, D., Márquez, M. E., Párraga, C., Cayla, I., Quel, J. L., Morelli, J., Aguero, M., Del, O., Azor, R., Aparicio, R., & Ocanto, V. (2016). *Epistemological Metrics based on linguistics and fractals* (Métricas Epistemológicas para modelos basados en fractales lingüísticos). *ARGENCON, 2016*, 1–7. Advance online publication. doi:10.1109/ARGENCON.2016.7585257

Luque, J., Lacasa, L., & Luque, B. (2014). *Speech earthquakes: scaling and universality in human voice*. Computer Science, Physics.

Skinner, B. (1957). *Verbal Behavior*. ProQuest. doi:10.1037/11256-000

Słomczyński, W. (2000). *Entropy computing via integration over fractal measures*. Chaos: An Interdisciplinary Journal of Nonlinear Science. *Chaos (Woodbury, N.Y.), 10*(180).

Zmeskal, O., Dzik, P., & Vesely, M. (2016). Entropy of fractal systems. *Computers & Mathematics with Applications (Oxford, England), 66*(2), 135–146. doi:10.1016/j.camwa.2013.01.017

KEY TERMS AND DEFINITIONS

Corpus: A specific compilation of textual data following certain criteria and usually with added meta data with linguistic value.

Entropy: In general, it is the lack of order or predictability. In communications a measure of information that can be transmitted through certain channel.

Fractal: Curves or shapes that has the property of self-similarity (chosen part is similar in shape to a given larger or smaller part when magnified or reduced to the same size).

Fractal Dimension: Ratio providing a statistical index of complexity comparing how detail in a pattern (strictly speaking, a fractal pattern) changes with the scale at which it is measured.

Lematization: Process of grouping together the inflected forms of a word so they can be analyzed as a single item.

Linguistic Reasoning: It a reasoning and its components articulated in order to understand and produce using certain language regulated by a grammar. It aims at evaluating ability to think constructively, rather than at simple fluency or vocabulary recognition.

Natural Isomorphism: Isomorphism between Symbolic Language and Natural Language.

Natural Language: Language that emerged naturally as an interchange between humans, in contrast to artificial languages.

Symbolic Language: Language that employs symbols and has been artificially constructed for the purpose of precise formulations (as in symbolic logic, mathematics, or chemistry).

Tagging: In linguistics it is the action of attaching a label to some part of a text, usually to denote something of interest.

Thermodynamics: Branch of physical science that deals with the relations between heat and other forms of energy (such as mechanical, electrical, or chemical energy), and, by extension, of the relationships between all forms of energy.

Zeta Function: Function formed by a sum of infinite functions raised to powers and convergent.

Chapter 14
Improve Imbalanced Multiclass Classification Based on Modified SMOTE and Feature Selection for Student Grade Prediction

Siti Dianah
https://orcid.org/0000-0003-3306-3246
Universiti Teknologi Malaysia, Malaysia

Ali Selamat
https://orcid.org/0000-0001-9746-8459
Universiti Teknologi Malaysia, Malaysia

Ondrej Krejcar
https://orcid.org/0000-0002-5992-2574
Hradec Kralove University, Czech Republic

ABSTRACT

In higher education institutions (HEI), the ability to predict student grades as an early warning system is one of the important areas that gained attention to improve educational outcomes. Over the years, machine learning techniques have facilitated and successfully addressed student grade prediction for identifying the potentially weak students in a particular course. However, dealing with an imbalanced multiclass classification dataset is challenging due to biased results towards predicting the minority class. Therefore, this chapter proposes a method that can increase the classification performance by using a modified synthetic minority oversampling technique and feature selection (MSMOTE-FS). The experiments tested the proposed method's effectiveness by utilizing four oversampling techniques and six standard classification algorithms. This finding indicated that the proposed method gives promising results to improve the accuracy in multiclass classification of student grade prediction.

DOI: 10.4018/978-1-7998-8686-0.ch014

INTRODUCTION

In higher education institutions (HEI), tracking and monitoring students' academic performance is essential in improving student success. This is driven by many factors, such as improving the institution's curriculum, producing quality students, and the ranking purpose. Based on previous studies (Alyahyan & Düştegör, 2020), there are many definitions of student success by considering student academic achievement, student demographics, e-learning activity, psychological attributes, and environments. The widely defined student success has caused a complex measure for determining the desired outcome (York & York, 2015). Student grade prediction is one of the most popular and valuable applications to measure student success (Zhang, Yupei, Yue Yun, Huan Dai, 2020). The aim is to predict the final score or grade of courses enrolled by the students to ensure they have achieved the minimum level for eligibility to the next academic semester. The output of student grade prediction can provide the early reference to the students and the lecturers and institution for self-planning in preparing decision making for personalized learning and teaching materials for suitable courses based on the student's ability and achievement. However, the application of student grade prediction is not as popular as in other developing countries that used it tremendously to improve student success (Liz-Domínguez et al., 2019).

The student grades could be divided into binary or multiple classes based on student results, leading to an imbalanced multi-class classification problem. Multi classification is one of the significant research problems that related to imbalanced dataset. Previously, many researchers have presented their solutions with differences on predictive to improve classification performance, but the related works on the educational field are scarce to be gathered (Hassan et al., 2020). With such vast practices of machine learning used on different datasets and samples, it can be challenging to identify the suitable prediction model that can perform high accuracy of prediction, especially when involving the minority class samples.

Due to this, our study aims to address the imbalanced classification by integrating the modified synthetic minority oversampling technique and feature selection method. This study focuses on multi-class classification by improving the minority class performance over two imbalanced multi-class student grade datasets.

The remainder of the paper is organized as follows. Section 2 discusses related works and clarifies the weaknesses of the proposed predictive model done by the previous research. Section 3 presents the proposed method for developing a predictive model of multi-class classification in student grade prediction. Section 4, the experimental results, and discussion of the whole findings are presented in detail. Finally, the future directions are present in Section 5, and the study's conclusion is summarized in Section 6.

RELATED STUDIES

Developing prediction models using machine learning for student grade prediction has been increased to determine student success. Previous researchers have given the contribution in predicting student grade prediction in many areas of the case study. Zhang et al. (X. Zhang et al., 2018) introduced Synthetic Minority over-sampling Technique (SMOTE) and feature selection to reduce the overfitting for student grade prediction using 538 of student data. They compared the performance using four traditional classifiers, including Naïve Bayes (NB), Decision Tree (DT), Multilayer Perceptron (MLP), and Support Vector Machine (SVM). The results showed that MLP was found the most effective with an accuracy of 65.90% and 64.02% for training and testing, respectively.

Bithari et al. show the use of SMOTE and feature selection can improve the imbalanced minority classes. They compared traditional classifiers Decision Tree, SVM, and Linear Regression with ensemble voting to predict 2445 records of engineering students based on four categories (Excellent, Good, Medium, Satisfactory). The results indicated that voting obtains promising results of 82% accuracy compared to a traditional single classifier (Bithari et al., 2020). Another study demonstrates the effect of using SMOTE by increasing the value of k neighbors varied from 2, 4, 6, and 8 to handle an imbalanced dataset with a Random Forest (RF) classifier. The RF with SMOTE provides the best accuracy results of 93.4% that be an effective method to handle the imbalanced classification. However, RF often occurs long processing time that could be better for applying feature selection method in the future (Utari et al., 2020).

A study conducted by (Almasri et al., 2019) found that the proposed methods using an ensemble meta-based tree model (EMT) classifier obtained high accuracy performance of 98.5% for predicting the student performance. To improve the quality of the dataset, only 13 features and 400 student records were selected to be conducted using 47 classifiers in different types of algorithms. The results indicated that the J48 classifier was outperformed with consistent results when applied to the boosting method (Adaboost_J48) compared to other classification models. Kumari et al. show the importance of students' behavioral features gave potential results to improve the prediction accuracy for multi-classification of students' academic performance using an ensemble methods model. They performed comparative analysis on 480 records of students after applied feature selection between traditional classifiers (ID3, NB, K-Nearest Neighbor (KNN), SVM) and ensemble methods (Bagging, Boosting, Voting). The results indicated that NB and SVM performed well using ensemble boosting compared to bagging and voting. However, from the overall classifiers, voting obtains consistent results with an accuracy of 89.0%, which gave better results compared to others (Kumari et al., 2018).

Another research has combined DT, KNN, and NB to predict student dropout and optimize the result using ensemble methods. They used 13856 data with 11 variables after the cleaning process and applied the SMOTE due to the imbalance of the two classes used in the dataset. The results showed that ensemble stacking using Gradient Boosting as a meta-classifier performed the highest accuracy with 98.82% compared to other single classification methods (Hutagaol, 2019). Another work in (Yan & Liu, 2020) has also built an ensemble model using 2-layer stacking consisting of Random Forest, SVM, and Adaboost as base-learners and LR as the meta-learner to predict and analyze student performance in academic competition. The results revealed that the proposed model could boost the predictive accuracy of 87.1% with an Area under Curve (AUC) value of 0.9138. However, the present model is only reliable for binary classification, which is the same approach proposed by (Hutagaol, 2019) regardless of handling the multi-classification problems for future results.

Imbalanced Classification

Imbalanced classification is a common problem in machine learning, where the distribution of each class does not have an equal balance ratio over the data space. This poses a difficulty for the training algorithms as they tend to be biased towards the majority class. This problem occurs when the models usually tend to be influenced by the majority class. Therefore, the minority class is generally misclassified, leading to poor performance and low accuracy. The minority examples are considered outliers of the majority class for the worst-case scenario, which leads to being ignored in the learning process (Soni, 2018; Haya, 2019). Moreover, the problems of having an imbalanced class can lead to biased machine learning algorithms or measurement errors that can affect the overall accuracy performance. There are two scenarios of imbalanced classification problems that need to be considered: the traditional binary and multi-class classification. However, the impact of the multi-class imbalanced is more risk due to the complexity level, and the relationship between classes does not reflect the entire problems. In practice, there are two methods to address the class imbalanced problems consist of data level and algorithm level (Ali et al., 2015; Krawczyk, 2016). Mainly at the data level, researchers used data sampling techniques and feature selection methods, whereas, at the algorithm level, they used cost-sensitive and hybrid approaches to resolve the imbalanced class problem (Leevy et al., 2018)

Data Level Approach

Data level solutions employ a pre-processing step to rebalance the class distributions. It used oversampling and under-sampling methods to reduce the imbalance ratio in the training dataset (Mohammed et al., 2020). Oversampling techniques are instances from the minority class that are duplicated to the given dataset by producing new instances or via repetition. On the other hand, under-sampling techniques can be performed by decreasing the amount of the majority class by removing the instances from the given sample dataset. There are two types of oversampling techniques included informative sampling and random sampling. Many researchers applied Synthetic Minority Oversampling Technique (SMOTE) as a benchmark in learning from imbalanced datasets to combat the imbalanced class problem in the educational field of areas (Barros et al., 2019; Jishan et al., 2015). This is because SMOTE used synthetic instances to oversample the minority class where each minority class sample is taken for improving the model performance.

The very simple undersampling algorithm is random undersampling (RUS) and it is fast as compared to SMOTE. It is known as non-heuristic algorithm which try to balance target distributions over eliminating randomly from majority class instances. However, the limitation of RUS is that it can removes possibly important data in the majority class which can be essential for classifier models (Kaur & Gosain, 2018). On the other hand, undersampling techniques can be performed by decreasing the amount of the majority class by removing the instances from the given sample dataset. The concept of both methods is shown in Figure 1.

Figure 1. Under-sampling and oversampling method

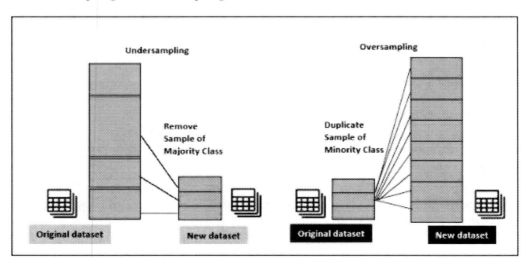

In this study, the oversampling method was preferred due to the ability to continuously retain all samples in the original dataset (Polat & Alhudhaif, 2021). Several existing approaches of oversampling used as the benchmark were described as follows (De & Do, 2020):

- SMOTE, known as Synthetic Minority Oversampling Technique, is an oversampling approach that most commonly uses synthetic instances to oversample the minority class where each minority class sample is taken to improve the model performance (Chawla et al., 2002). The algorithm is based on the distance from the k nearest neighbor samples in the minority sample set. However, SMOTE has a problem when generating synthetic samples that can lead to overlapping classes, especially in multi-class cases.
- SVMSMOTE is a variant of SMOTE that uses the SVM algorithm to detect samples and generate new synthetic samples. It employs SVM to assist in creating class boundaries by creating new minority class instances around the borderlines.
- ADASYN known as Adaptive Synthetic is considered an extension of SMOTE that uses density distribution as a criterion to automatically decide the number of synthetic samples that need to be generated for each minority data. It will adaptively generate synthetic data samples for the minority class to reduce the bias introduced by the imbalanced data distribution (He et al., 2008).
- BSMOTE known as Borderline-SMOTE is a method where only the borderline examples of the minority class are oversampled. First, these borderline examples should be accurately identified, and then synthetic entries are generated from them and added to the original training set. Even though this technique performs better in two-class examples, it still suffers from the same original techniques' problems when dealing with multi-class due to the augmented risk of overlap and overgeneralization (Han et al., 2005).

Algorithm Level Approach

Algorithm-level solutions can be categorized as dedicated algorithms that directly learn the imbalanced distribution from different datasets by using cost-sensitive methods and hybrid or ensemble methods. The aim is to reduce misclassification costs when conducting a learning process. Numerous classification methods have been proven to perform well to fit the requirement to learn directly from the imbalanced class datasets. Ensemble methods are an approach that can be used as cost-sensitive methods, where the classification outcome is some combination of multiple classifiers built on the dataset. Two common types of ensemble learners are Bagging and Boosting (Singhal et al., 2018). Bagging minimizes the predictive variance by producing several training sets from the given dataset. A classifier is generated for each training set, and then their models are combined for the final classification. Boosting also uses several training sets from the given dataset. After iteratively assigning different weights to each classifier based on their misclassifications, a weighted approach combining the individual classifier's results yields the final classification.

MATERIALS AND METHODS

The experiment used the open-source tool Waikato Environment for Knowledge (WEKA) version 3.8.3 developed at the University of Waikato, New Zealand (https://www.cs.waikato.ac.nz/ml/Weka/) (S.

Hussain et al., 2018) and Python Scikit-Learn programming. In the remaining part of the section, we described the datasets and the method used in the experiments as well as the performance evaluation metrics used for evaluation.

Dataset Preparation

In this section, the performance of the proposed method is evaluated using two real standard student datasets collected from the Department of Information and Communication Technology at one of the Malaysian Polytechnic repositories. The suggested method results are compared with four state-of-the-art oversampling approaches: SMOTE, ADASYN, BSMOTE, and SVMSMOTE. Meanwhile, six widely used standard classifiers were used to evaluate the prediction performance accuracy of oversampling and the proposed method. The six standard classification algorithms include Logistic Regression (LR), Random Forest (RF), k-Nearest neighbor (kNN), Decision Tree (DT), Support Vector Machine (SVM), and Naïve Bayes (NB). Table 1 summarizes the student grade multi-class datasets by showing the number of classes, number of instances, number of features, and data distribution belonging to each class.

Table 1. Summary of the characteristics of the imbalanced multi-class dataset used in the experimental study

Dataset	#Classes	#Features	#Instances	Data Distribution
SG1	5	18	3904	1571/843/511/102/96
SG2	5	10	1282	508/303/149/52/13

The study used two student grade datasets containing 3904 and 1282 records for SG1 and SG2, respectively. Each dataset contains demographic, course information, and student academic performance. The class label has multi-class based on student grade category defined as 'Fail', 'Pass', 'Good', 'Excellent' and 'Exceptional'. Figure 2 contains the number of records per class label for both datasets.

Figure 2. Number of students' records per grade category as a class label in datasets SG1 and SG2

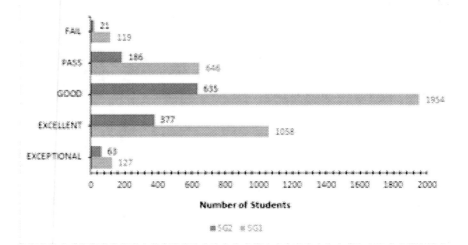

Figure 3. Features correlation heatmap for student grade in dataset SG1

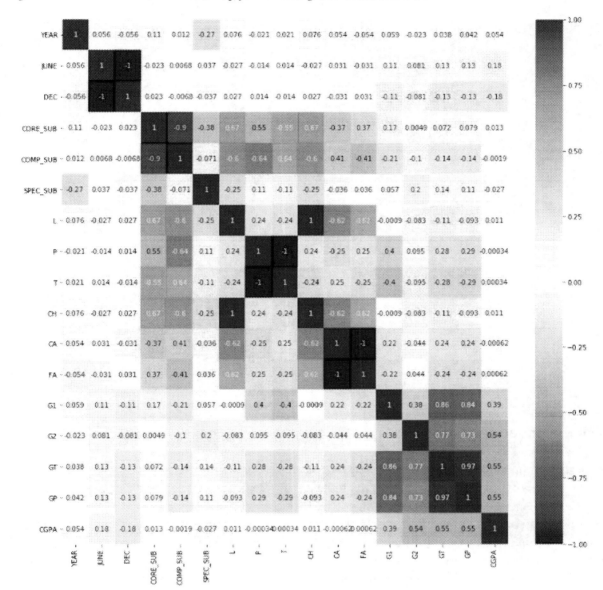

Figure 3 and Figure 4 show the correlation among the features for both datasets. The academic grades Grade 1(G1), Grade 2 (G2), Last Grade (GT), and Student Pointer Grade (GP) have a high correlation when compared with other features for the SG1 dataset. Meanwhile, Student Grade Pointer (GPA1) and Student Final Mark (TM1) is the most significant feature for the SG2 dataset.

Figure 4. Features correlation heatmap for student grade in dataset SG2

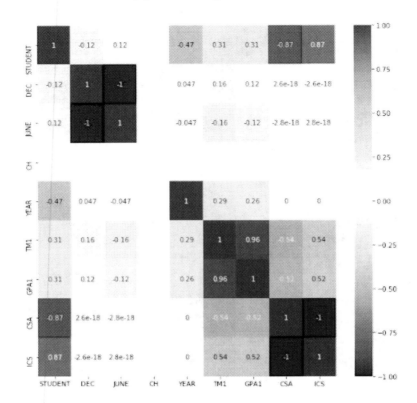

The Proposed Method: MSMOTE-FS

This study proposes a combination approach of SMOTE and feature selection approaches known as MSMOTE-FS by balancing the data spread ratio with the relevant selected features in the pre-processing for the imbalanced multi-class dataset. Most classification decisions are often biased against minority classes due to data distribution, which leads to the misclassification of the majority class instances. The idea behind the SMOTE is to generate the synthetic samples of minority classes from the nearest neighbors (k) that are randomly selected to create a more balanced distribution (Blagus & Lusa, 2013; Chawla et al., 2002). The default parameter of k defined the element of sample SG represent the minority class, select N samples randomly and described them as SG_i. The new sample of SG_{new} is defined by the following formula:

$$SG_{new} = SG_{origin} + rand \times \left(SG_i - SG_{origin} \right), i = 1, 2, 3, ..n \tag{1}$$

where *rand* is a seed used of random sampling and index class 0 with the ratio of generating new samples approximates 100%. Meanwhile, selecting effective features can improve the model's performance and help understand the complex data's appropriate characteristics and underlying patterns (Ma & Fan, 2017). The proposed solution enhances the SMOTE based on the modification of selection parameters constituted of three-phase. The overall architecture of the proposed MSMOTE-FS method is shown in Figure 5.

Phase 1: The Sampling Technique

Predicting student grades is part of the critical element to determine student success in the future. Since our datasets suffer from data imbalanced problems, we need to balance before training the model to improve the prediction results. In the proposed method, SMOTE is used as the balancing algorithm to solve student grade prediction's multi-class classification. First, we randomly selected 80% of the imbalanced multi-class dataset to be the training set for sampling. We set the parameter of index class value 0 to auto-detect the non-empty minority class. Then, the number of the nearest neighbor is set to be $k = 10$, where this method detects ten neighbors of a random sample with the percentage of instances 100% and default random state $= 42$. This method will balance the minority class to majority class sampling ratio by synthesizing new synthetic samples into the new training set. To improve the prediction model's performance for student grade prediction, we compare the performance with the other four approaches of oversampling on the imbalanced multi-class dataset used in this study.

Figure 5. Proposed architecture of MSMOTE-FS

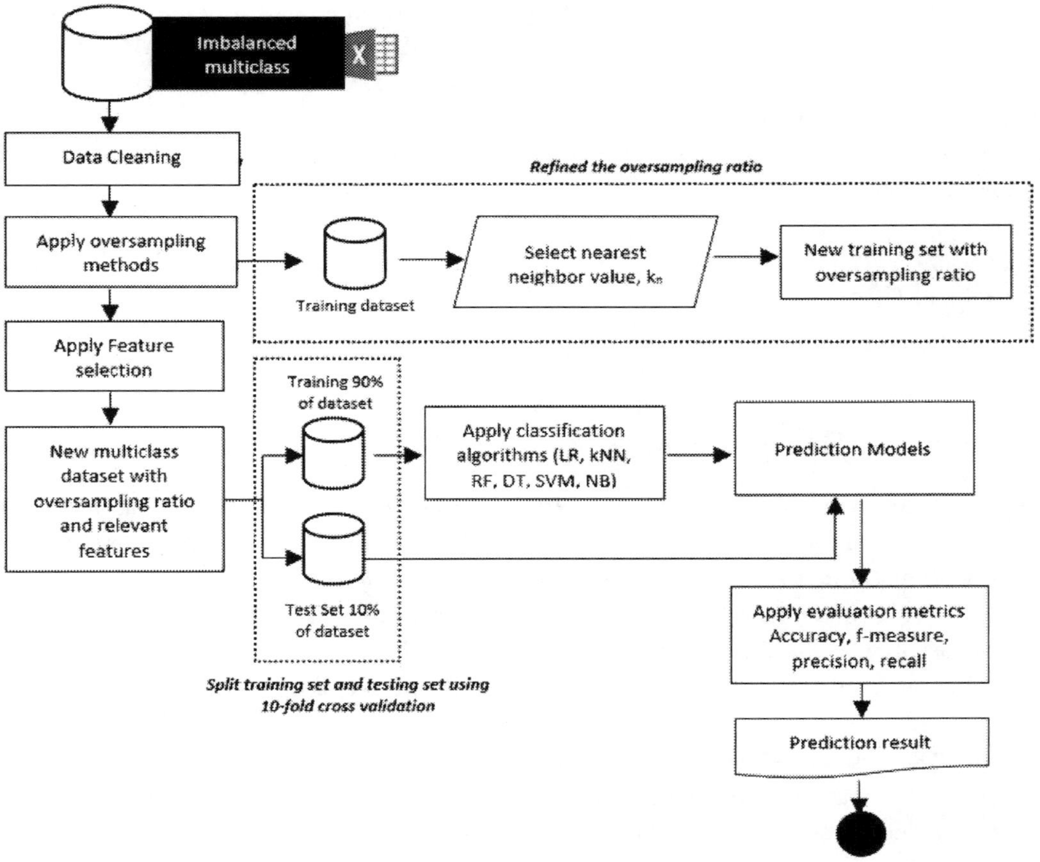

Phase 2: Feature Selection

Feature selection is the process of selecting a subset of relevant features from a large dataset which can be improved the quality of the prediction models. Many feature selection techniques help reduce the redundancy of features by selecting the most relevant features (Jalota & Agrawal, 2021). We used the wrapper-based method with the best first search for optimal feature subset based on the J48 algorithm for selecting the best combination of relevant features to improve the prediction model.

Phase 3: Classification using Machine Learning Algorithms

In this study, we apply 10-fold cross-validation techniques to split the dataset. Six different classification algorithms were used to evaluate the prediction model performance of oversampling using the proposed MSMOTE-FS. A brief description of each classification algorithms is as follows:

- Logistic Regression (LR) is a cost function that uses the logistic function to represent mathematical modeling to solve classification problems. The model performs great contextual analysis for categorical data to understand the relationship between variables (M. Hussain et al., 2018).
- Naïve Bayes (NB) is a probabilistic model based on the Bayesian theorem that is widely used due to its simplicity and ability to make fast predictions. It is easy to implement and suitable for small datasets that combine complexity with a flexible probabilistic model. (Predić et al., 2018). According to Bayes' theorem, the variable y represent the class variable that suitable to the given parameters or features of x.

$$P(y|x) = \frac{P(x|y)P(y)}{P(x)} \tag{2}$$

where $x = (x_1, x_2, x_3, \ldots, x_n)$ (3)

- Decision Tree (J48) is widely used in several multi-class classifications that can handle missing values with high dimensional data. It has been implemented effectively to give optimum accuracy results with a minimum number of features (Srivastava et al., 2019).
- Support Vector Machine (SVM) is based on decision planes that state decision boundaries that handle classification problems successfully (Brodic et al., 2018). It takes a sorted dataset and predicts two conceivable classes that include the information, making the SVM a non-probabilistic binary linear classifier.
- K-Nearest Neighbor (kNN) is a non-parametric algorithm that classifies and calculates the difference between instances in the dataset. It uses a distance function to suitability performs in small features of the dataset to predict the label of a test data point by selecting the nearest vectors k value (S. Zhang et al., 2017).
- Random Forest (RF) is a classifier based on ensemble learning that uses the number of decision trees on various subsets to find the best features for high accuracy and prevents overfitting. It is relatively robust to outliers and noise that operates effectively in classification (Breiman, 2001).

Performance Evaluation Metrics

The classification model for the imbalanced dataset will cause to bias results. Therefore, using only an accuracy performance matrix cannot reflect reliable prediction, especially for the minority class. To increase the reliability of our model, the performance of the classification model was based on standards formulas of accuracy, precision, recall, and f-measure curve in four labels of features; True Positive (TP), True Negative (TN), False Positive (FP) and False Negative (FN). TP means the fundamental data is correctly predicted positive values when the actual and predicted class value is yes. TN means the real data correctly predicts negative values when the actual and predicted class value is no. For the FP and FN, the values occur when the actual class contradicts the predicted class. Data will be classified as FP when the actual class is no, but the predicted class is yes. Data is classified as FN when the actual class is yes, but the predicted class is no. Based on the standard formulas, the formulas for computing the performance of the prediction model are derived as follows:

$$Accuracy = \frac{TP + TN}{TP + TN + FP + FN} \tag{4}$$

$$Precision = \frac{TP}{FP + TP} \tag{5}$$

$$Recall = \frac{TP}{FN + TP} \tag{6}$$

$$F - Measure = \frac{2x(Precision \ x \ Recall)}{Precision + Recall} \tag{7}$$

RESULT AND DISCUSSION

This section present and discuss the results obtained for the experiment conducted. Initially, the proposed method was compared based on the performance evaluation metrics. Six standard classifiers using four oversampling techniques and the proposed method are used in the experiment. Among the classifier trained, all results show improvement after balancing the multi-class labels. Table 2 shows the result of accuracy performance on two datasets, SG1 and SG2.

Table 2. Comparison of the MSMOTE-FS accuracy performance against other standard oversampling methods

Dataset	Sampling Technique	LR	RF	KNN	DT	NB	SVM
SG1	None	0.913	0.992	0.956	0.997	0.862	0.954
	SMOTE	0.939	0.995	0.963	0.989	0.841	0.968
	SVMSMOTE	0.919	0.991	0.956	0.992	0.829	0.967
	ADASYN	0.898	0.994	0.958	0.995	0.826	0.964
	BSMOTE	0.911	0.993	0.969	0.995	0.874	0.965
	MSMOTE-FS	0.931	0.992	**0.979**	0.994	**0.908**	**0.983**
SG2	None	0.961	0.973	0.798	0.984	0.898	0.802
	SMOTE	0.949	0.984	0.844	0.984	0.856	0.864
	SVMSMOTE	0.926	0.981	0.837	0.981	0.852	0.848
	ADASYN	0.949	0.984	0.852	0.984	0.891	0.859
	BSMOTE	0.946	0.911	0.800	0.991	0.905	0.793
	MSMOTE-FS	0.927	**0.988**	**0.913**	**0.988**	**0.918**	**0.872**

Figure 6. Classification performance of oversampling methods for dataset SG1 in terms of accuracy

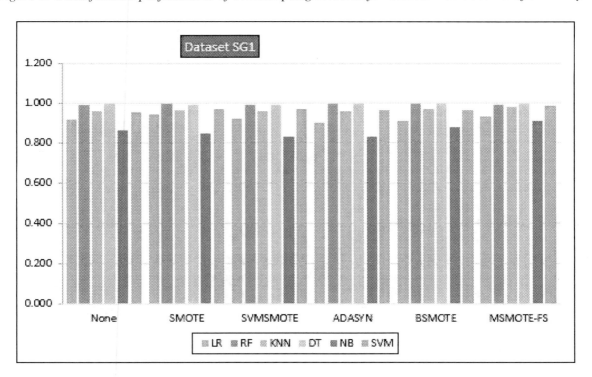

The table shows that MSMOTE-FS achieves the best accuracy over KNN, NB, and SVM for dataset SG1 with a score value of 0.979, 0.908, and 0.983, respectively. Whereas for dataset SG2, the results outperformed where most of the classifiers gained a high score of the accuracy better than other standard oversampling methods. We believe that in this context of the situation, the results obtain are relevant. It is well known that SMOTE efficiently reduces the imbalanced class problem with selected features settings (Aslam et al., 2021; Blagus & Lusa, 2013). However, the benefit is more significant when feature selection is performed after using more neighbor k in SMOTE. Other than that, from the observation, we found that the proposed model results do not show a significant impact for LR even in the selected features setting for both datasets. Here, we considered that the LR classifier does not become beneficial from MSMOTE-FS due to the parameter setting of k weight for the imbalanced distribution (Fithria Siti Hanifah et al., 2015). Figure 6 and Figure 7 show the classification performance of oversampling methods for datasets SG1 and SG2, respectively.

Figure 7. Classification performance of oversampling methods for dataset SG2 of accuracy

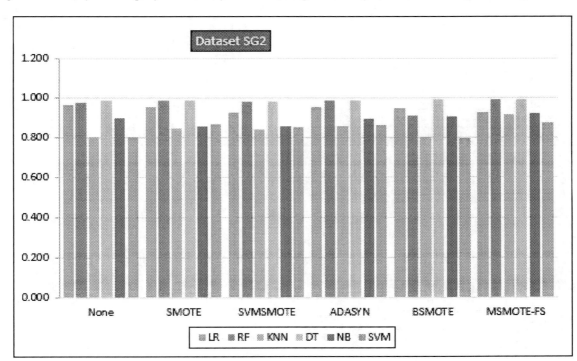

Then, we compare the precision, recall, and f-measure result of MSMOTE-FS and without applied oversampling methods. Considering the results obtained, our models outperformed four other oversampling methods: SMOTE, SVMSMOTE, ADASYN, and BSMOTE for two datasets. When we examined the metrics belonging to minority class (Fail), it is shown that the performance of these classes is consistently performed higher after MSMOTE-FS being applied. Furthermore, the results show RF and DT have the highest performance accuracy in predicting the minority class in both datasets. This is because RF and DT can produce lower errors, and reducing the overfitting due to bias makes it generalize good results in classification (Utari et al., 2020). Therefore, this indicated that MSMOTE-FS improves the precision, recall, and f-measure of the minority class in multi-class classification in predicting student grades.

Table 3. Performance metrics of the MSMOTE-FS for dataset SG1 when k=10

Without Oversampling Method					MSMOTE-FS				
Classifier	**Class**	**Precision**	**Recall**	**F-Measure**	**Classifier**	**Class**	**Precision**	**Recall**	**F-Measure**
LR	Excellent	0.89	0.94	0.92	LR	Excellent	0.89	0.87	0.88
	Exceptional	0.50	0.24	0.32		Exceptional	0.98	1.00	0.99
	Good	0.95	0.97	0.96		Good	0.94	0.90	0.92
	Pass	0.90	0.87	0.89		Pass	0.88	0.87	0.87
	Fail	0.81	0.74	0.77		Fail	0.93	0.96	**0.94**
RF	Excellent	1.00	1.00	1.00	RF	Excellent	1.00	1.00	1.00
	Exceptional	1.00	1.00	1.00		Exceptional	1.00	1.00	1.00
	Good	1.00	1.00	1.00		Good	1.00	1.00	1.00
	Pass	0.97	1.00	0.99		Pass	0.99	0.96	0.98
	Fail	1.00	0.78	0.88		Fail	0.97	0.99	**0.98**
KNN	Excellent	0.97	0.97	0.97	KNN	Excellent	0.97	0.99	0.98
	Exceptional	0.91	0.8	0.85		Exceptional	1.00	1.00	1.00
	Good	0.98	0.98	0.98		Good	1.00	0.97	0.98
	Pass	0.92	0.95	0.93		Pass	0.97	0.92	0.95
	Fail	0.65	0.57	0.60		Fail	0.95	1.00	**0.97**
DT	Excellent	1.00	1.00	1.00	DT	Excellent	1.00	1.00	1.00
	Exceptional	1.00	1.00	1.00		Exceptional	1.00	1.00	1.00
	Good	1.00	1.00	1.00		Good	1.00	1.00	1.00
	Pass	0.99	1.00	1.00		Pass	0.98	0.98	0.98
	Fail	1.00	0.91	0.95		Fail	0.99	0.99	**0.99**
NB	Excellent	1.00	0.94	0.97	NB	Excellent	1.00	0.94	0.97
	Exceptional	0.68	1.00	0.81		Exceptional	0.97	1.00	0.99
	Good	0.99	0.81	0.89		Good	0.93	0.97	0.95
	Pass	0.60	0.92	0.72		Pass	0.75	0.88	0.81
	Fail	0.56	0.43	0.49		Fail	0.89	0.74	**0.81**
SVM	Excellent	0.97	0.98	0.97	SVM	Excellent	0.98	0.99	0.99
	Exceptional	1.00	0.8	0.89		Exceptional	1.00	1.00	1.00
	Good	0.96	0.98	0.97		Good	0.98	0.98	0.98
	Pass	0.93	0.96	0.95		Pass	0.99	0.94	0.96
	Fail	0.65	0.48	0.55		Fail	0.96	0.99	**0.98**

However, despite the outperformed performance of the proposed model, our research has limitations due to the limited dataset and classifiers used in the experiment. The effectiveness of the proposed model can be better results when compared with other benchmarks of the imbalanced dataset by using hybrid or ensemble classifiers rather than standard supervised learning methods alone.

Table 4. Performance metrics of the MSMOTE-FS for dataset SG2 when k=10

Without Oversampling Method					MSMOTE-FS				
Classifier	Class	Precision	Recall	F-Measure	Classifier	Class	Precision	Recall	F-Measure
LR	Excellent	0.97	1.00	0.99	LR	Excellent	1.00	1.00	1.00
	Exceptional	1.00	0.91	0.95		Exceptional	1.00	1.00	1.00
	Good	0.99	0.99	0.99		Good	0.98	0.98	0.98
	Pass	0.84	1.00	0.91		Pass	0.89	0.85	0.87
	Fail	0.00	0.00	0.00		Fail	0.83	0.87	**0.85**
RF	Excellent	1.00	1.00	1.00	RF	Excellent	1.00	1.00	1.00
	Exceptional	1.00	1.00	1.00		Exceptional	1.00	1.00	1.00
	Good	0.99	1.00	1.00		Good	0.98	1.00	0.99
	Pass	0.86	1.00	0.92		Pass	0.99	0.97	**0.98**
	Fail	1.00	0.12	0.22		Fail	0.97	0.98	0.97
KNN	Excellent	0.83	0.81	0.82	KNN	Excellent	0.86	0.81	0.84
	Exceptional	0.90	0.82	0.86		Exceptional	0.97	0.93	0.95
	Good	0.81	0.85	0.83		Good	0.86	0.83	0.84
	Pass	0.67	0.76	0.71		Pass	0.90	0.97	0.93
	Fail	0.00	0.00	0.00		Fail	0.97	0.97	**0.97**
DT	Excellent	1.00	1.00	1.00	DT	Excellent	1.00	1.00	1.00
	Exceptional	1.00	1.00	1.00		Exceptional	1.00	1.00	1.00
	Good	1.00	1.00	1.00		Good	0.98	1.00	0.99
	Pass	0.90	1.00	0.95		Pass	0.99	0.97	0.98
	Fail	1.00	0.51	0.67		Fail	0.97	0.98	**0.97**
NB	Excellent	0.97	0.99	0.98	NB	Excellent	0.97	1.00	0.99
	Exceptional	0.90	0.82	0.86		Exceptional	1.00	0.98	0.99
	Good	0.99	0.87	0.92		Good	0.98	0.92	0.95
	Pass	0.63	1.00	0.77		Pass	0.84	0.89	0.86
	Fail	1.00	0.25	0.40		Fail	0.86	0.86	**0.86**
SVM	Excellent	0.92	0.8	0.86	SVM	Excellent	0.98	0.55	0.70
	Exceptional	1.00	0.64	0.78		Exceptional	1.00	0.90	0.95
	Good	0.75	0.94	0.84		Good	0.63	0.98	0.77
	Pass	0.77	0.54	0.63		Pass	0.99	0.89	0.93
	Fail	0.00	0.00	0.00		Fail	0.98	0.89	**0.93**

Another limitation of this study is the problem of determining the performance measure using other performance evaluation metrics. In the experiment, it was decided by standard accuracy, precision, recall, and f-measure. Still, it is necessary to study how another performance measure such as Receiver Operating Characteristics (ROC), Area Under the Curve (AUC), Kappa, and other standard statistical methods.

FUTURE RESEARCH DIRECTIONS

Future research needs to be done to address the limitations mentioned in the previous section. Some of the issues discussed were the problem of data set limitations and the use of limited performance evaluation to produce adequate results for the proposed model. Therefore, for further improvement, the model can be further validated by using an imbalanced multi-class dataset with many sizes and features in the future by using other performance evaluation metrics to see better results.

CONCLUSION

Dealing with an imbalanced multi-class classification is difficult, although many studies have been done in most fields. This study proposed a model to address the imbalanced classification focus on multi-class datasets to improve minority class performance in student class prediction. We suggest MSMOTE-FS to reduce the risk of bias by changing the parameters and weights of SMOTE k neigbors to obtain different balanced ratios by considering the relevant characteristics. Notably, for imbalanced multi-class problems, the proposed model shows better performance when compared to other benchmark oversampling methods using the same dataset. Furthermore, this study also found the important features contribute significantly to predicting student grades that can improve student success in the future.

ACKNOWLEDGMENT

The authors wish to thank Universiti Teknologi Malaysia (UTM) for its support under Research University Grant Vot-20H04, Malaysia Research University Network (MRUN) Vot 4L876, and the Fundamental Research Grant Scheme (FRGS) Vot (FRGS/1/2018/ICT04/UTM/01/1) supported by the Ministry of Higher Education Malaysia.

REFERENCES

Ali, A., Shamsuddin, S. M., & Ralescu, A. L. (2015). Classification with class imbalance problem: A Review. *Int. J. Advance Soft Compu. App*, *7*(3).

Almasri, A., Celebi, E., & Alkhawaldeh, R. S. (2019). *EMT : Ensemble Meta-Based Tree Model for Predicting Student Performance*. Academic Press.

Alyahyan, E., & Düştegör, D. (2020). Predicting academic success in higher education: Literature review and best practices. *International Journal of Educational Technology in Higher Education*, *17*(1), 3. Advance online publication. doi:10.118641239-020-0177-7

Aslam, N., Khan, I. U., Alamri, L. H., & Almuslim, R. S. (2021). An Improved Early Student's Performance Prediction Using Deep Learning. *International Journal of Emerging Technologies in Learning*, *16*(12), 108–122. doi:10.3991/ijet.v16i12.20699

Barros, T. M., Guedes, L. A., & Silva, I. (2019). *Education Sciences Predictive Models for Imbalanced Data : A School Dropout Perspective.* doi:10.3390/educsci9040275

Bithari, T. B., Thapa, S., & Hari, K. C. (2020). Predicting Academic Performance of Engineering Students using Ensemble Method. *A Peer Reviwed Technical Journal Nepal Engineers' Association Gandaki Province, 2*(1), 89–98.

Blagus, R., & Lusa, L. (2013). *Open Access SMOTE for high-dimensional class-imbalanced data.* Academic Press.

Breiman, L. E. O. (2001). *Random Forests.* Academic Press.

Brodic, D., Amelio, A., & Jankovic, R. (2018). Comparison of different classification techniques in predicting a university course final grade. *2018 41st International Convention on Information and Communication Technology, Electronics and Microelectronics, MIPRO 2018 - Proceedings*, 1382–1387. 10.23919/MIPRO.2018.8400249

Chawla, N. V., Bowyer, K. W., Hall, L. O., & Kegelmeyer, W. P. (2002). SMOTE: Synthetic minority over-sampling technique. *Journal of Artificial Intelligence Research, 16*(June), 321–357. doi:10.1613/jair.953

De, A., & Do, N. (2020). *Techniques to deal with imbalanced data in multi-class problems : A review of existing methods.* Mestrado Integrado Em Engenharia Informática e Computação.

Han, H., Wang, W., & Mao, B. (2005). Borderline-SMOTE : A New Over-Sampling. *Methods*, 878–887.

Hanifah, F. S., Wijayanto, H., & Kurnia, A. (2015). SMOTE bagging algorithm for imbalanced dataset in logistic regression analysis (case: Credit of bank X). *Applied Mathematical Sciences, 9*(137–140), 6857–6865. doi:10.12988/ams.2015.58562

Hassan, H., Ahmad, N. B., & Anuar, S. (2020). *Improved students ' performance prediction for multi-class imbalanced problems using hybrid and ensemble approach in educational data mining.* doi:10.1088/1742-6596/1529/5/052041

Haya, A. (2019). *Handling Class Imbalance Using Swarm Intelligence Techniques, Hybrid Data and Algorithmic Level Solutions.* Academic Press.

He, H., Bai, Y., Garcia, E. A., & Li, S. (2008). ADASYN. *Adaptive Synthetic Sampling Approach for Imbalanced Learning., 3*, 1322–1328.

Hussain, M., Zhu, W., Zhang, W., Abidi, S. M. R., & Ali, S. (2018). Using machine learning to predict student difficulties from learning session data. *Artificial Intelligence Review, 52*(1), 381–407. doi:10.100710462-018-9620-8

Hussain, S., Dahan, N. A., Ba-Alwib, F. M., & Ribata, N. (2018). Educational data mining and analysis of students' academic performance using WEKA. *Indonesian Journal of Electrical Engineering and Computer Science, 9*(2), 447–459. doi:10.11591/ijeecs.v9.i2.pp447-459

Hutagaol, N. (2019).. . *Predictive Modelling of Student Dropout Using Ensemble Classifier Method in Higher Education., 4*(4), 206–211.

Jalota, C., & Agrawal, R. (2021). Feature Selection Algorithms and Student Academic Performance: A Study. In Advances in Intelligent Systems and Computing (Vol. 1165). Springer Singapore. doi:10.1007/978-981-15-5113-0_23

Jishan, S. T., Rashu, R. I., Haque, N., & Rahman, R. M. (2015). *Improving accuracy of students' final grade prediction model using optimal equal width binning and synthetic minority over-sampling technique.* 1–25 doi:10.1186/s40165-014-0010-2

Kaur, P., & Gosain, A. (2018). ICT Based Innovations. Advance online publication. doi:10.1007/978-981-10-6602-3

Krawczyk, B. (2016). Learning from imbalanced data: Open challenges and future directions. *Progress in Artificial Intelligence*, *5*(4), 221–232. doi:10.100713748-016-0094-0

Kumari, P., Jain, P. K., & Pamula, R. (2018). *An Efficient use of Ensemble Methods to Predict Students Academic Performance.* Academic Press.

Leevy, J. L., Khoshgoftaar, T. M., Bauder, R. A., & Seliya, N. (2018). A survey on addressing high - class imbalance in big data. *Journal of Big Data*, *5*(1), 42. Advance online publication. doi:10.118640537-018-0151-6

Liz-Domínguez, M., Caeiro-Rodríguez, M., Llamas-Nistal, M., & Mikic-Fonte, F. A. (2019). Systematic literature review of predictive analysis tools in higher education. *Applied Sciences (Switzerland)*, *9*(24), 5569. Advance online publication. doi:10.3390/app9245569

Ma, L., & Fan, S. (2017). CURE-SMOTE algorithm and hybrid algorithm for feature selection and parameter optimization based on random forests. *BMC Bioinformatics*, *18*(1), 1–18. doi:10.118612859-017-1578-z PMID:28292263

Mohammed, R., Rawashdeh, J., & Abdullah, M. (2020). Machine Learning with Oversampling and Undersampling Techniques. *Overview Study and Experimental Results.*, (April), 243–248. Advance online publication. doi:10.1109/ICICS49469.2020.239556

Polat, K., & Alhudhaif, A. (2021). *Classification of imbalanced hyperspectral images using SMOTE-based deep learning methods.* doi:10.1016/j.eswa.2021.114986

Predić, B., Dimić, G., Rančić, D., Štrbac, P., Maček, N., & Spalević, P. (2018). Improving final grade prediction accuracy in blended learning environment using voting ensembles. *Computer Applications in Engineering Education*, *26*(6), 2294–2306. doi:10.1002/cae.22042

Singhal, Y., Jain, A., Batra, S., Varshney, Y., & Rathi, M. (2018). Review of Bagging and Boosting Classification Performance on Unbalanced Binary Classification. *2018 IEEE 8th International Advance Computing Conference (IACC)*. 10.1109/IADCC.2018.8692138

Srivastava, A. K., Singh, D., Pandey, A. S., & Maini, T. (2019). A Novel Feature Selection and Short-Term Price. *Energies*, 1–18.

Utari, M., Warsito, B., & Kusumaningrum, R. (2020). Implementation of Data Mining for Drop-Out Prediction using Random Forest Method. *2020 8th International Conference on Information and Communication Technology, ICoICT 2020*. 10.1109/ICoICT49345.2020.9166276

Yan, L., & Liu, Y. (2020). An Ensemble Prediction Model for Potential Student Recommendation using Machine Learning. *Symmetry*, *12*(728), 1–17. doi:10.3390ym12050728

York, T. T., & York, T. T. (2015). *Defining and Measuring Academic Success.* Academic Press.

Zhang, S., Li, X., Zong, M., Zhu, X., & Cheng, D. (2017). Learning k for kNN Classification. *ACM Transactions on Intelligent Systems and Technology*, *8*(3), 1–19. Advance online publication. doi:10.1145/2990508

Zhang, X., Xue, R., Liu, B., Lu, W., & Zhang, Y. (2018). Grade Prediction of Student Academic Performance with Multiple Classification Models. *2018 14th International Conference on Natural Computation, Fuzzy Systems and Knowledge Discovery (ICNC-FSKD)*, 1086–1090.

Zhang, Y., Yun, Y., Dai, H., Cui, J., & Shang, X. (1755). Graphs Regularized Robust Matrix Factorization and Its Application on Student Grade Prediction. *Applied Sciences (Basel, Switzerland)*, *10*(5), 1–19. doi:10.3390/app10051755

Chapter 15

Contextualising Computational Thinking Disposition Framework From an Affective Perspective

Kamisah Osman
Universiti Kebangsaan Malaysia, Malaysia

ABSTRACT

Recent studies have revealed that the existing measurement methods related to computational thinking (CT) pivot on gauging thinking skills, recommending an extended understanding of CT as disposition. Disposition reflects inclination towards learning CT and indicates the interest to think intelligently about issues confronting them. Hence, the aim of this chapter is to assess students' affection towards learning CT as problem solving tool that can transform knowledge more productively. In the context of the affective domain, attitudes and beliefs can be regarded of as generic responses to something, the core quality of an emotion, feeling, mood, or temperament, and hence as affective mental activities. The framework of the CT disposition proposed in this chapter was developed based on tripartite classification of mental activities known as of trilogy of mind: cognitive, affective, and conative. The basic tenet of this chapter is aligned with the theoretical underpinnings of thinking dispositions which is expected to suit different contexts and needs.

INTRODUCTION

Individuals' interests in society have been swept up by technological breakthroughs. A computer or a computer science application today pervades every aspect of human life. People are now inquiring about three factors: science, technology, and society (Wing, 2006). Children of the Millennial generation are exposed to computers from an early age. Education in the twenty-first century must try to enhance young people's abilities to be skilled and confident when confronted with a variety of challenging situations. Furthermore, these kids aren't hesitant to experiment with technology and play with it. Researchers and

DOI: 10.4018/978-1-7998-8686-0.ch015

educators required a technique to explicitly capture this skill. According to Bundy (2007), anyone attempting to comprehend the fast-paced twenty-first century must first comprehend Computational Thinking (CT). CT is a way of thinking that is widely viewed as a necessary talent for 21st-century students to develop in order to handle real-world problems effectively and efficiently.

The necessity of addressing computer science fundamentals in K-12 education is currently being emphasized (Barr & Stephenson, 2011; Wing, 2006; Yadav, Mayfield, Zhou, Hambrusch, & Korb, 2014). While there is a surge of attention in establishing CT among school students and a lot of money invested in CT projects, there are many challenges and constraints to overcome. Consequently, the education sector faces rising pressure to utilize computing technology to boost computational thinking in everyday lives. In a similar vein, urge for students to learn at least complementary skills of CT to become reflective participants as it is one of the contributing factors before entering the industry has risen worldwide. Students who learn CT may begin to discover correlations between academic disciplines and life outside of the classroom. However, an adaptation of CT concepts in everyday life are not going to be easy and require thorough study (Sondakh, Osman & Zainudin, 2020a). The last decade's focus on integrating CT has been on skill integration in students with only little prominence about their perception, feeling or attitude towards the application of CT in problem solving across various discipline or specifically in daily life (Sondakh, Osman & Zainudin., 2020b). Thus, development of an instrument to measure students' disposition towards CT critically required.

While it is crucial to provide students with interesting and worthwhile topics, this "content curriculum" should be complemented by attention to attitudes, values and learning habits that are built (or diminished) as a result of the process. They are ready, willing, and able to engage in profitable learning, as we have characterized them. These attributes, in whole or part, have been variously called dispositions (Katz, 1993; Perkins et al., 1993) orientations (Dweck, 1999), habits of mind (Costa & Kallick, 2009) and participation repertoires (Carr, 2001; Comber, 2000). Recent research has demonstrated that conventional CT measurement methods are based on assessing thinking skills, advocating a more comprehensive understanding of CT as a disposition.

Background

Early studies in computer-assisted educational methods (Papert 1980; Pea & Kurland, 1984) and widespread perceptions of computer scientists' approach on issues using computational thinking idea (Denning, 2009). Seymour Papert coined the phrase "computational thinking" in his work about children and computers in the 1980s (Tendre & Denning, 2016). As a result, when Papert taught LOGO programming to children to develop their procedural thinking (Grover & Pea, 2013), the term 'computational thinking' became popular. However, it provides constructive programming environments where children can reflect on their thinking procedures and build concrete understandings from abstract concepts such as mathematics (Clements & Battista, 1989). In the context of K-12 education, his groundbreaking work, which combined a heuristic approach to the conceptual strength of theoretical notions linked with computation, received broad appeal. Thus, the design of Scratch, an interactive programming tool for kids, was influenced by LOGO programming (Resnick et al., 2009). Moreover, Wing's 2006 book "Computational Thinking" introduced CT to a wider audience. She sparked a conversation about computational thinking and raised funds to bring it to K–12 schools" (Denning, 2017).

Wing (2006) contends that all students should be taught CT, which she defines as a problem-solving, system design, and a variety of mental techniques linked to programme design. Her research concluded that CT is a key talent that pupils learn and that students should receive training in this area beginning in elementary school. This ability will aid pupils in organizing their thoughts into a procedure and solving difficult tasks. Since 2006, numerous improvements in K-12 education have happened as a result of the increased understanding of the value of CT and computing education (Wing, 2017). CT has now been taught and implemented in schools K-12, focusing on computational skills and student engagement (Kafai & Burke, 2017; Weintrop et al., 2016). There is currently no agreed-upon definition of computational thinking. Some definitions of CT focus on the process dimension, while others use computers to describe abilities and problems. Researchers have agreed, however, that computational thinking is a mental process that encompasses critical thinking, generalization, abstraction, algorithmic reasoning, and mistake detection and correction. On the other side, the International Society for Technology in Education (ISTE) describes computational thinking as a blend of creativity, algorithmic thinking, critical thinking, problem solving, cooperative thinking, and communication skills (ISTE, 2015). According to another study, CT is a problem-solving talent that aids in first understanding the problem and then formulating solutions (Curzon, 2015). Meanwhile, CT, according to Moschella (2019), is described as the mental capacities to solve issues, abstract, use algorithms, restructure processes, reformulate difficulties, and execute solutions. To comprehend computability, intelligence, the mind, and human behavior, CT uses an analytical method. Analysis, demonstration, and modelling are also included (Kormaz, Cakir, & Ozden, 2017). Many conceptualizations of CT include at their heart the idea of creating and solving problems using computational power (Aho, 2012; Barr & Stephenson, 2011; Cuny, Snyder, & Wing, 2010; ISTE, 2016: Rambally, 2017). Some definitions of CT have additionally incorporated CT-specific abilities, talents, and tenets. Barr and Stephenson (2011), for example, identified issue such as deconstruction, abstraction, and automation as well as affective components such as confidence in coping with complexity and persistence with tough challenges as abilities associated in CT.

Nearly a decade later, the practice of imparting CT abilities to students has infiltrated all levels of elementary and secondary schools. This integration is taking place through the development of new curriculum in computer science education programmes as well as other subject areas like mathematics and science (Weintrop et al., 2016). In other words, CT acts as a link between technology and the physical world. Code to create computer programmes to enable the development of increasingly powerful next-generation computers and the implementation of ever more determined computer science ideas. These initiatives are intended to facilitate people's productive interactions with computers and to make the notion of CT more approachable. CT has grown in popularity as a means of channeling students' talents and expertise toward computer-assisted learning. Furthermore, according to Tim Bell, CT is more about humans than computers (Bell & Roberts, 2016). Consequently, CT become a useful toolbox in the problem-solving process rather than a product, and it can be applied to a wide range of circumstances, not all of which require the use of a computer. As a result, delving deeper into the meaning of CT will aid in resolving ambiguities. CT tries to solve problems by using computers to access various data and resources, and teachers encourage pupils to "think computationally" by providing technology-based projects. CT tries to solve problems by combining the human intellect with the computer's capabilities. Students should think about how to build tools and information rather than just using them. Hence, CT differs from programming in that it is students' thinking skills that allow them to understand an issue and come up with a solution before they code.

DISPOSITION

Thurstone used the term 'disposition' in a 1928 article to refer to attitude and how to assess them (Diez & Raths, 2007). However, the term disposition has a complicated history, since it was frequently used interchangeably with other terms describing a person's thinking, such as attitude, beliefs, habits, and values. The term "disposition" has become contentious in the field of education due to the variety of definitions used in the classroom. Then, in 1985, Katz and Raths defined disposition as a behaviour rather than an attitude; an attitude was a predisposition to act, but dispositions were a compilation of observable acts (Diez & Raths, 2007). Cook defined an attitude in 1992 as an individual's good or negative feelings about a subject, implying that how individual acts are closely tied to their attitudes (Diez & Raths, 2007). Unlike Katz and Raths (1985), attitudes were directly related to behaviours or dispositions rather than influencing how an individual performed. Cook saw attitudes as reflecting action, whereas Katz and Raths saw attitudes as influencing but not necessarily resulting in specific behaviours.

As a result, social psychologists frequently refer to disposition as "an attitude tendency" (Facione, 2000; Sands, Yadav, & Good, 2018). A cognitive disposition is a collection of attitudes, intellectual qualities, and mental habits (Facione, Facione, & Sanchez, 1995). They are internal drives to 'act in habitual, albeit pliable, ways toward or in response to others, events, or circumstances' (Facione, 2000). Desire to act or respond in predictable yet flexible ways toward other people, events, or circumstances is also a disposition (Computer Science Teacher Association [CSTA], 2017). Furthermore, disposition is viewed as a "collection" of preferences, attitudes, and intentions, in addition to a number of capabilities (Salomon, 1994). Perkins et al. (2013) extended further, stating that a cognitive disposition is a "triadic construct" comprised of sensitivity, proclivity, and capacity. McCune and Entwistle (2011) proposed that thinking dispositions have characteristics such as capability, willingness (similar to attitude), awareness of the process, and context sensitivity, all of which indicate situational preparedness that can induce the inclination and capacities to solve problems via CT (McCune & Entwistle, 2011).

Though the term 'disposition' is inherently vague, it is extremely useful in referring to a subset of human characteristics that are obviously distinct from 'knowledge, skill, and understanding. "Dispositions form a different kind of learning from skills and knowledge," argues Katz (1988). They might be thought as mental habits, or propensities to react in specific situations. The attitudes that students develop toward certain subject matter disciplines should be included in content conceptions. We describe a disposition as a student's views, values, and approaches to a discipline as they mature in a class and go on to the next (Wenger, 1998). Our focus is on both the classroom discipline and the students' connection to it. A person's real interests are defined by what they accomplish in carrying out a style of action with which they have connected themselves (1913,1975). Because of this, a student's progress in a discipline is intrinsically tied to their involvement in that discipline (Greeno & MMAP, 1998; Lampert, 1990, 2001; Lave & Wenger, 1991).

Despite this, dispositions are frequently defined as a "mental cast or habit" or "frame of mind" required for critical thinking (Beyer, 1995). Dispositions are neither deliberative or judgmental statements, but rather emotive states. They include attitudes toward critical thinking and a knowledge of a person's psychological predisposition to be critical. They are comparable to what Passmore referred to first as a 'critical spirit' (Passmore, 1967). While dispositions have long been acknowledged as a psychological phenomenon, the definition of mental dispositions remains mostly ambiguous due to divergent interpretations. Likewise, it is critical to establish terminologies, identify conceptual aspects, and construct a validated assessment framework before examining students' learning outcomes via the lens of dispositions. Consequently, while disposition is characterised in this context as "an attitude tendency" (Facione, 2000; Sands et al., 2018), it is also a collection of attitudes, intellectual virtues, mental habits, and internal drives (Facione et al., 1995, 2000; Salomon, 1994; Beyer, 1995).

Attitudes

In reality, the term "attitude" is frequently used to refer to a collection of notions that include preferences, sentiments, emotions, beliefs, expectations, judgments, evaluations, values, principles, opinions, and intentions (Bagozzi, 1992). Allport (1954) argues for the importance of attitude in human activity and calls it the foundation stone of social psychology. A person's fundamental behavioral beliefs describe the behavior's perceived results or qualities, according to Conner and Armitage (1998). Thus, an attitude is not static; it influences behavior. Allport (1935) defined an attitude as a mental or neurological state of readiness that is shaped by experience and has a direct or dynamic influence on an individual's conduct towards all things and circumstances. It's a tendency to respond to something. However, according to Agarwal and Malhotra (2005), an attitude is a quick assessment of anything. Emotions directed toward or away from a psychological object (Thurstone, 1931). Moreover, attitude relates to the object or phenomena that a person categorizes or remembers. (Bohner & Wanke, 2002).

In the subject of attitude research, there is a substantial controversy over the definition of attitude. As defined by Krech, Crutchfield, and Ballackey (1962), attitude consists of three independent components: affective, behavioral (conative), and cognitive. In contrast, Fishbein and Ajzen (1975) suggest that attitude assessment should only focus on the emotional domain, omitting the behavioral (conative) and cognitive components. Nonetheless, as Koballa (1989) points out, regardless of which of the age-old trilogies or monologies of attitude one accepts, what matters is that attitudes are acquired either actively or vicariously and hence can be taught.

According to Gibson, Ivancevich, and Donnelly, attitude is defined as "a good or negative emotion or mental state of readiness that is learnt and organized via experience and exerts a specific influence on a person's response to other people, objects, and situations" (Gibson, Ivancevich, & Donnelly, 1991). Rosenberg defines attitude more precisely as "the way an individual feels about and is disposed toward a "thing" (Rosenberg et al., 1960). Thus, Triandis (1971) argued that attitude is composed of affective, cognitive, and behavioral components, adhering to the Krech et al. (1962) school of thinking. The affective component of attitude is the emotional or "feeling" component, which includes statements about one's preferences or disapproval of particular items. As such, a statement such as "I enjoy thinking computationally" or "I despise the procedures used in CT" is a measure of the emotive component of attitude in the context of CT. The cognitive component of attitude consists of assertions of beliefs. For instance, an individual may believe that CT has the potential to dramatically improve the quality of his or her problem-solving method. The behavioral component of attitude refers to what an individual does or intends to do. Thus, a statement such as "I will use this new way of thinking to solve difficulties" is an intended behavior statement. Thus, attitude encompasses how individuals feel (affective), what they believe (cognitive), and what they want to do (behavioral).

Additionally, Spooncer's (1992) model of attitude, dubbed the Tripartite Model, proposed three components of attitude: feelings, beliefs, and behavior. The first component is an individual's emotion, which is expressed verbally, the second component is an individual's cognitive response, which is expressed verbally, and the third component is an individual's overt action, which is expressed verbally as intended behavior in response to environmental stimuli. Similarly, Schiffman, Kanuk and Hansen (2012) propose that attitudes are composed of three components: cognitive (beliefs), affective (feelings), and conative (perceptions) (behavior).

Gagne and Medsker (1996) asserted that these three components of attitude are inextricably linked and that each can be beneficially handled during attitude formation. After analyzing numerous definitions and models, it is now widely acknowledged that attitude refers to a person's or place's favorable or negative mental and neurological preparedness toward a person, place, thing, or event. It is composed of three components: an emotional (Feeling/Emotion) component, a behavioral (Response/Action) component, and a cognitive component (Belief/Evaluation). The proposed theoretical model sheds light on attitudes by examining the influence of feelings, responses, and beliefs.

Cognitive Component

The cognitive components are the ideas and beliefs that the holder of the attitude has about the object, according to the Encyclopedia of Educational Research (1992). Attitudes vary in their degree of dependence on knowledge and beliefs. Certain viewpoints are highly intellectualized. Others are founded on a large body of incorrect information and erroneous beliefs. Attitudes may have a cognitive basis in misinformation. A person may have an attitude toward something while having no strong feelings about it; the affective component may be minor. On the other hand, his attitudes may be highly intellectualized while also containing a significant affective component. While the intellectual and affective components work in tandem, they remain distinct. Attitude's intellectual component is occasionally referred to as its cognitive (knowing) component. Thus, the cognitive component of an attitude is that aspect that is founded on or derived from knowledge (Travers, 1977). Knowledgeable, thoughtful, and reflective make up the cognitive component. Through the development of the CT idea and application, this construct represents a cognitive process that necessitates a profound understanding of learning and knowledge. Furthermore, cognition reflect how the mind acts during learning; how thoughts, feelings, and actions interact with one another is described by the concept of interdependence. Enhancing learning, building confidence and helping learners understand new knowledge better are some of cognitive benefits. It can also help learners learn new things faster and perceive and interpret information in a way that could enhance creativity and lead to inventions.

Affective Component

Travers (1977) defined affective components as those that have a positive or negative effect (feelings). Attitudes vary in their degree of involvement with such emotive components. Certain attitudes are completely illogical and consist solely of this emotive component. The person who prefers one set of ideas and despises another but cannot explain why exhibits an attitude that is heavily emotional, but lacking in other dimensions. Numerous attitudes are of this type, and common observation indicates that they are relatively easily learnt; the majority of people exhibit numerous attitudes of this type. According to the Encyclopedia of Educational Research (1992), The affective component refers to a person's sentiments towards an object.

Eventually, people who are confident and feel good about themselves are said to possess the affective construct or emotional talent. In order to attain personal identity, one must rethink one's self-concept, incorporating prior identifications, current strengths and abilities, and future aspirations. Everyone has a natural desire to recognize, experience, accept and express a spiritual component of life. As early as

1950, Erik Erikson proposed the psychosocial theory, which focuses on lifelong patterns of development in self-understanding, identity formation, and social connections (Erikson, 1968). Most teenagers try on several different selves along the road to determine which one fits best; they explore numerous roles and concepts, create objectives, and strive to uncover their "adult" selves along the route. They have a strong sense of self-identity and can hold fast to their beliefs despite hurdles or opposing viewpoints.

Secondly, Peter Salovey and John Mayer established Emotional Intelligence as a psychological theory. Emotional intelligence is the ability to sense, access, and produce emotions to help with thinking, comprehend emotions and emotional knowledge, and reflect on emotions to help with emotional and intellectual growth (Mayer & Salovey, 1997 Researchers established four levels of emotional intelligence: emotional perception, emotional reasoning, emotional understanding, and emotional management (Mayer & Salovey, 1990). Perceiving emotions accurately are the first step towards comprehending emotions. In many situations, interpreting nonverbal cues like body language and facial emotions is necessary. Argumentation based on emotions is the use of emotions to stimulate cognitive activity and thinking. When we pay attention to and react to something, our emotions play a role in helping us prioritize.

Conative Component

The conative or behavioral component is made up of an individual's actions and proclivities toward an object (The Encyclopedia of Educational Research, 1992). Travers (1977) asserts that many articulated attitudes bear little resemblance to conduct. The fact that the action component can exist independently of the other components is critical when it comes to educational planning. Much of attitude education is concerned with the development of attitudes' affective and cognitive components, which may never be carried over into action systems. As a result, the conative component includes the characteristics of inquirers and principles. Theories of goal orientation and achievement goals presume that people have different ways of defining success and judging perceived ability. Goals are "a set of behavioral intentions that govern how students approach and engage in learning activities" (Meece, Blumenfeld, & Hoyle, 1988, p. 514). According to student characteristics and performance, the collection of learner qualities associated with goal orientation was generally deemed positive. Although students placed high emphasis on learning, they also tended to adopt deep information processing strategies such as constructing multiple examples of concepts (Butler, 1987; Covington, 1999). When faced with a task failure, they were likely to use strategies to manage themselves, such as self-monitoring or organizational procedures. As a result of this, people began to devote a lot of time to certain tasks (Schunk, 1996).

Aside from the personal motivation for success, the traits of strong communication and a collaborative network also contributed to an individual action. Each individual can respect appreciation for cultural variety and differences of opinion. The social learning approach addresses mental processes and their role in deciding whether or not to copy an action. The social learning theory of Albert Bandura stresses observing, modelling, and copying others' behaviors, attitudes, and emotional reactions. The Cultural Dimensions Theory, established by Geert Hofstede, is a framework used to comprehend cultural differences and collaborate. In other words, the framework distinguishes across cultures and promotes student collaboration.

Psychomotor

Additionally, the psychomotor domain encompasses physical movement, coordination, and motor-skill application. Simpson's psychomotor domain is particularly beneficial for the growth of children and adolescents, as well as for the development of abilities in adults that require them to step outside their comfort zones (Simpson, 1972). For example, perception (awareness) is the capacity to guide motor activity using sensory signals. This includes everything from sensory stimulation to cue selection and translation. Additionally, a person's preparedness to act, which encompasses mental, physical, and emotional capacities, predetermines how they respond to certain situations (sometimes called mindsets). The pupil demonstrates a drive to master a new skill (motivation). This Psychomotor subdivision is closely tied to the Affective domain's "Responding to phenomena" subdivision.

Mental Model

Researchers have underlined the necessity of examining thinking from the standpoint of both talents and dispositions by employing the term "disposition" and/or similar phrases such as Dewey's (1930) concept of good habits of mind or Siegel's (1988) critical spirit. Dispositions are roughly defined as behavioral tendencies- the proclivity to cheat or play it straight, the proclivity to be brave or cautious, the proclivity to give thought time, to explore broader viewpoints, to fiercely seek proof, and so on. Dispositions might be cognitive in nature (as the last three described are) or non-cognitive in nature. We present a theory of thought in this chapter, highlighting the significance of dispositions. As with other dispositional viewpoints, this notion runs counter to conventional ability-based theories. In contrast to previous dispositional viewpoints, this theory recasts the concept of dispositions as "triadic dispositions." In our meaning, a disposition is a psychological component comprised of three components: cognitive, affective, and conative. Historically, psychology has defined and examined three distinct components of mind: cognition, affect, and conation (Hilgard, 1980; Huitt, 1996; Tallon, 1997).

Cognition is the process by which we acquire knowledge and understanding; by which we encode, perceive, store, process, and retrieve information. It is frequently used in conjunction with the inquiry "what" (e.g., what happened, what is going on now, what is the meaning of that information.) Affective is used to describe the emotional interpretation of senses, data, or knowledge. It is typically associated with one's connection (good or negative) to people, items, ideas, and the like, and is related to the inquiry "How do I feel about this knowledge or information?" Conation is a term that alludes to the relationship between knowledge and emotion and behavior, and is related with the question "why." It is the proactive (as opposed to reactive or habitual) component of behavior (Baumeister, Bratslavsky, Muraven, & Tice, 1998; Emmons, 1986). Atman (1987) defined conation as "personal energy with direction and magnitude." Motivation, agency, self-direction and self-regulation are synonyms (Kane, 1985; Mischel, 1996). Both Bagozzi (1992) and Miller (1991) suggest that omitting the notion of conation is a major factor in the inability to properly predict behavior.

Modes of Mental Functioning

Three modes of mental functioning have been used to classify mental processes: cognition, affect (also known as affection), and conation (also known as volition) (Snow, Corno, & Jackson III, 1996). A cognitive mental function is considered dispositional for the purposes of this discussion, i.e., a dispositional cognitive function with respect to CT if an individual has a tendency or inclination to engage (or not engage) in a particular cognitive mental process associated with perceiving, recognizing, conceiving, judging, reasoning, and the like in CT. Affective mental functions are defined as "a collective term consisting of sensation, emotion, mood, and temperament." an individual emotional reaction to a specific object or concept...the collective reaction to anything loved or disliked...the dynamic or basic element of emotion; the emotion's energy" (English & English, 1958, p. 15). If a person has a proclivity to have or experience certain attitudes, beliefs, feelings, emotions, moods, or temperaments with regard to CT, the affective mental function is said to be dispositional, i.e., a dispositional affective function with regard to CT. Conative mental functions, on the other hand, are characterized as "that component of mental activity that tends to convert into something else; an innate disturbance within the organism...almost the polar opposite of homeostasis." [An impulse to act], a deliberate attempt... It is today rarely used to describe a specific conduct, but rather a universal quality. Instinct, desire, volition, and goal-directed striving" (English & English, 1958, p. 104). A dispositional mental function is the tendency to strive, exert diligence, effort, or perseverance in the face of computational task. To the extent that conative functions are dispositional, students who are given difficult CT tasks may show varying degrees of tenacity or effort.

CT DISPOSITION FRAMEWORK

The cognitive, emotional, and conative and attitude models were used to construct the framework for the CT disposition. Individuals' mental states or attitudes during CT development are referred to as "CT dispositions", for instance "confidence in coping with complexity" and "persistently working through hurdles" (Lee et al., 2011; Woolard, 2016; Weintrop et al., 2016). The cultivation of CT dispositions requires sustained involvement in computational practices with an emphasis on the CT process and abundant learning opportunities in a stimulating context (Brennen & Resnick, 2012). According to Wing, attitude is also a key component of CT (2006). However, just a few researches have been undertaken in recent years to study the attitude aspect of cognitive therapy (CT). Almost all of the research has been focused on technical skills and knowledge. When it comes to attitudes required for CT, even Wing (2006), in her first and subsequent studies, didn't go into great depth.

Consequently, Barr et al. (2011) categorized the results as CT ideas (skill) and what are known as dispositions or attitudes (or both). CT attitudes include confidence in dealing with complexity, persistence in working through challenging issues, tolerance for ambiguity, endurance for open-ended challenges, and flexibility for putting aside differences to collaborate with others (Barr et al., 2011). Socializing allows for group collaboration and brainstorming. Coordination and collaboration are covered in teamwork abilities (Baker & Salas, 1992).

In addition to technical capabilities, the ACM/IEEE computer science curriculum specifies non-technical, or soft skills and personal traits, as skills that will help workers use technological knowledge more holistically (ACM and IEEE Computer Society 2013). Moreover, to the soft skills of working in a team and communicating verbally and in writing as well as managing time and solving problems, there are also personal attributes such as tolerance for risk and a sense of collegiality as well as work ethic, opportunity identification, and social responsibility. As a result of CSTA & ISTE's perceptions of CT, this study investigated problem-solving, teamwork, and communication abilities. Problem-solving skills include the capacity to deal with ambiguity and open-ended situations with confidence and tenacity. Teamwork is the process of solving problems in a cooperative manner. This skill includes the capacity to recognize one's own strengths and flaws when dealing with others, as well as the ability to appreciate variety and put differences aside. Written and vocal communication skills are both required. In a seminal paper, she argues that CT was presented by Wing (2006) as a set of universally relevant attitudes and skills. A CT's attitude can be operationally defined by Barr and Stephenson (2011) using the term disposition. Soft skills are personal specialized skills, which include character qualities, attitudes, and behaviors, according to Robles (2012). Thus, dispositions refer to the soft skills and attitude required for CT issue resolution.

A learner's computational thinking abilities are also determined by their cognitive habits. Complexity and open-ended problems are viewed as key computational views in the meantime (Atmatzidou & Demetriadis, 2016). For students to be able to deal with complicated real-world problems by drawing upon their CT, they must have the disposition to do so. How well an individual can reframe problems inside a computational framework and apply their knowledge of computer science to solve difficulties is considered to be flexible. In addition, disposition is an indication of a person's enthusiasm in learning CT, as well as their ability to think critically about the difficulties they face. To cultivate students' CT dispositions, it is therefore necessary to cultivate their confidence and perseverance when tackling hard tasks.

Figure 1 Theoretical framework (Adaptation from Hawkins & Mothersbaugh, 2010)

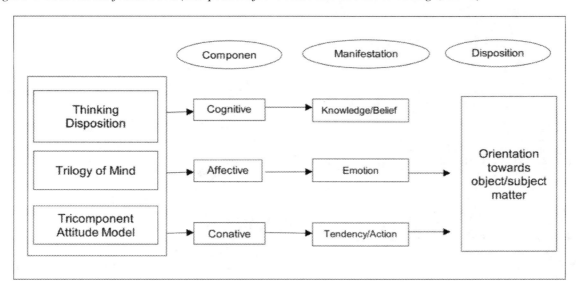

According to the research study, learners' disposition and attitude toward learning CT are equally important in assessing their CT growth. In knowing oneself, learners' motivational ideas, particularly worth and expectation (Wigfield & Eccles, 2000). Here, value refers to internal reasons such as a desire to study programming or CT. Self-efficacy and self-concept are two components of expectation. Researchers generally agree that evaluating learners' attitudes should be included. Since, dispositions have been recognized as a psychological construct, social psychologists classify disposition as "an attitudinal tendency" (Facione, 2000; Sands et al., 2018). Despite this, dispositions are often been defined as a "cast or habit of the mind" or "frame of mind" which is necessary for exercising critical thinking (Beyer, 1995).

In addition, theorists argue that thinking requires something more fundamental than knowledge or skill i.e., a set of dispositions (Beyer, 1988; Norris & Ennis, 1989). Therefore, in this study, disposition is defined as internal motivation and a combination of attitudes, values and beliefs which comprises, dispositional thinking theory (Beyer, 1995), Tripartite Classification of Mind (Hilgard, 1980) and Tricomponent Attitude Model (Schiffman et al., 2012) to form a theoretical framework for this study. Figure 1 describes the integration of cognitive, affective and conative components which accomplish neither the three modes of mental functioning nor modes of attitudes to distinguish the disposition construct towards CT.

In addition, Wing (2006) defined attitudes as part of CT in her initial work, but did not comment on the attitudes that go along with the set of skills in CT. Undergraduates in computer science must possess soft skills and personal traits, according to the Computer Science Curricula of 2013. Table 1.0 shows that, based on a literature assessment, there were relatively few researchers who took attitudes into account.

Table 1. Description of CT attitude or dispositions

Reference	Attitude / Disposition
Hambrusch et al., 2009	§ Teamwork
Barr et al., 2011	§ Confidence in dealing with complexity § Persistence in working with difficult problems § Ability to handle ambiguity § Ability to deal with open-ended problems § Setting aside differences to work with others to achieve a common goal § Knowing one's strengths and weaknesses when working with others
CSTA & ISTE, 2011	§ Confidence in dealing with complexity. § Persistence in working with difficult problems. § Tolerance for ambiguity. § The ability to deal with open-ended problems. § The ability to communicate and work with others to achieve a common goal or solution
Kazimoglu, Kiernan, Bacon, & MacKinnon, 2012	§ Socializing: Coordination, Cooperation, Competition
ACM and IEEE Computer Society, 2013	§ Teamwork § Verbal and written communication § Time management § Problem-solving § Flexibility § Ability to tolerate ambiguity § Work well with others from different backgrounds and disciplines § Personal attributes: risk tolerance, collegiality, patience, work ethic, identification of opportunity, sense of social responsibility, appreciation of diversity
Perez, 2018	§ Tolerance for ambiguity § Persistence on difficult problems § Collaboration with others to achieve a common goal

In accordance with that, the author relied on two main journal databases: Scopus and Web of Science (WoS) as the primary source in the search process of studies related to the attitude/disposition to computational thinking which have been published over the last 5 years (2016 – 2020). A total of 35 studies from all 17 countries were identified. This systematic review or specifically thematic analysis has highlighted the types of attitudes/dispositions that influence practices of CT among school students on global. Based on the systematic reviews performed, authors have identified three attitudes/dispositions patterns namely cognitive component, affective component and conative(behavioral) component which then extended into sub-themes as stated in Figure 2. The author referring to Barr and Stephenson (2011) definition of dispositions as the basis for defining and identifying the expected CT disposition/ attitudes. Cognitive and behavioral components were the most frequently studied factors, followed by affective component of the total four subthemes.

Figure 2. Category of attitude/disposition that influence student computational thinking

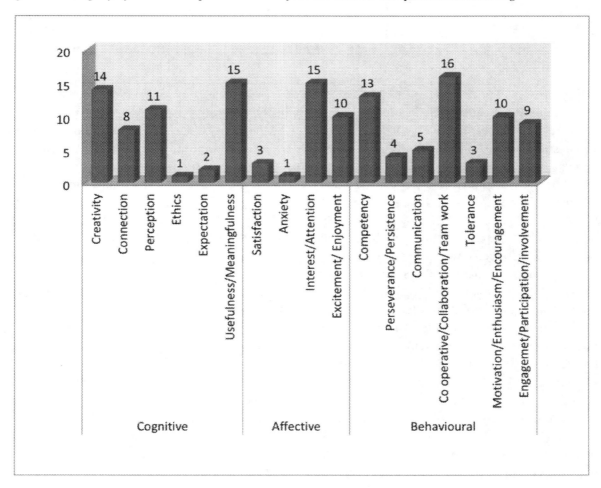

These attitudes and dispositions are presented as theoretical constructs in the present study. It is expected that various situations and requirements will require different types of thinking dispositions, as indicated by the study's findings. Student's CT tendencies will be assessed, and they will be empowered to use CT for problem solving accordingly. Figure 3 represents the CT Disposition framework which has been recommended based on theoretical grounds.

Figure 3. CT Disposition framework

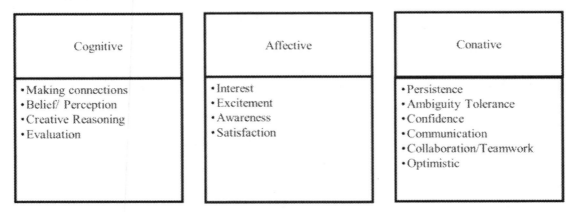

Cognitive is defined as a tendency to draw connections, evaluate the accuracy of statements based on belief, reason creatively, and support ethical statements involving CT procedures and processes. A cognitive dispositional function, it would seem, would be the ability to form CT connections, given that certain students may not be inclined to do so and that such connections might serve as a foundation for the acquisition of new CT knowledge. To deal effectively with complexity, good thinkers tend to be adept at coming up with innovative solutions that can be applied to various settings. Finding computationally acceptable answers, whether through the use of heuristics or by treating each situation as a unique comparison, is undoubtedly a mental activity that develops new knowledge consciousness in the individual. Subcategory of dispositional functioning defined as the tendency to feel that CT can help you satisfy current or future needs, whether at school, in your work, etc.

Based on the thematic analysis, cognitive components needed as a feasible and essential mindset to engage in CT. Conceptually, Computational thinking intersects with 21st century skills such as creativity, critical thinking and problem solving (Lye & Koh, 2014). Thus, most of the researchers believe that CT is intertwined creative thinking (Romero et al., 2017). Creativity promotes out-of-the-box thinking and innovative approaches to problem solving; and as a means of creative expression, it seeks to promote the development of computational artefacts. Creative reasoning could provide learners with a better understanding of CT practices (Romero et al., 2017). It has been suggested that CT can foster creativity, one of the 21st century's critical abilities, by helping students to become not simply technology consumers, but also creators of sources with a substantial influence on society (Mishra & Yadav, 2013). It entails cultivating modes of thought that enable students to make innovative use of computational tools within their fields. The primary rationale for include creativity in this category is because computers not only increase conventional modes of human expression, but also promotes the generation of new modes of expression (The College Board, 2012). Therefore, creativity is a fundamental attitude that learners can develop and to embed a certain amount of ambiguity and complexity in CT which allows students to incorporate ideas yet to understand the CT concepts well.

Secondly, in dealing with difficult real-world problems, students' emotions and feelings are measured to see whether they like, practice, and enhance their CT thinking skills. Students' attitudes, such as their enthusiasm in programming, are considered by most studies to be part of this dimension (Kong, Chiu & Lai, 2019). Asking learners whether they like or dislike CT is insufficient for understanding their intrinsic values. People who are genuinely driven, according to Deci and Ryan (1985), experience curiosity and delight, as well as a feeling of competence and self-determination. Along with attitudes, self-actualization/satisfaction determines if learners feel competent after practicing CT in problem-solving tasks. This can be determined by assessing the learners' sense of attachment and their sense of belongingness to CT. Besides that, learners' sense of affiliation can also indicate whether they have a feeling of belongingness regarding their interest. Moreover, an individual's ability to create and design solutions using CT approaches might be termed as CT empowerment. In addition to meaning, empowerment highlights a person's perceived worth. Empowerment emphasizes meaningfulness, and can be defined as a person's experiences creating and designing strategies to enable them tackle problems using CT. In addition, a learner's problem-solving ability increases as he or she becomes more aware of their learning processes. They are better able to create a multi-perspective thinking awareness to address complex situations. Numerous sub-topics within the area of affective, such as enjoyment and interest, have also prompted academics to do more research. When we focus on K-12 education, we discover a current wave of studies demonstrating how new visual programming languages like as Scratch, Phyton, and video games such as 'Blockly' are increasing primary and secondary students' interest, motivation, and self-efficacy in programming tasks (Kong et al., 2018; Carlborg et al., 2019; Zhao & Shute, 2019).

Contrary to popular belief, the growth of the thinking process is heavily dependent on conation. "Problem solving" is defined by Heppner and Petersen (1982) as "the process of generating solutions to issues that require a set of cognitive, affective and behavioral skills." Affective and behavioral skills, i.e., attitudes, are essential in CT. Following Beaver (1994) and Zakaria, Haron and Daud (2004), attitudes required of problem solvers include: curiosity in the problem, a desire to find a solution, confidence in one's ability to solve the problem, and willingness to do so. They are the ability to deal with ambiguity and open-ended challenges, as well as the confidence to deal with complex problems (Barr & Stephenson, 2011). Solving difficulties takes patience, perseverance, persistence, and a willingness to take chances, according to O'Connell (1999), referenced by Mohd and Mahmood (2011). An engagement in CT activities, a sense of affiliation, and career orientation can all be used to gauge a learner's level of interest in CT. When learners are more interested in CT activities, their participation in activities is organically deeper. Thus, self-training by engagement is a vital component that can directly represent your enthusiasm and delight in CT learning. Soft-skills in the Computer Science 2013 curriculum and CSTA/ISTE attitudes about CT are used in this study to examine CTE's perspectives. Defined as confidence and tenacity in dealing with complicated and challenging situations, as well as the ability to handle ambiguity and open-ended difficulties, these attitudes are examined in this study. Due to the fact that collaboration and communication tendencies are included in this component since conation is also considered a behavioral skill. According to Barr et al. (2011) and Hambrusch et al. (2009), collaboration or cooperation is a part of CT attitudes. It is important to collaborate with others, work efficiently and professionally with various teams, and be flexible and prepared to make necessary concessions to accomplish a shared objective, according to Fadel and Trilling (2009) as cited by the OECD in 2017. Communication, cooperation, and response are required to achieve this (Hesse, Care, Buder, Sassenberg, & Griffin, 2015). In addition, collaboration in CT also described as the attitude and capacity to understand the work of others, where students need to be able to decipher and interpret (Korkmaz et al., 2017; Perez, 2018). In general, students who value teamwork are more inclined to consider common goals and benefits. These kids may work harder with others, develop stronger collaboration abilities, and tackle tough issues more creatively (Kong et al., 2018; Sharma et al., 2016).

In a nutshell, technical abilities are important in problem solving yet insufficient as there is also a complementary psychological side of CT required as an essential component to complement technical skills in the mental process used to formulate issues into solutions or opportunities.

CONCLUSION

Reframing teaching and learning entails rearranging classroom processes to incorporate an emphasis on students' attitudes toward a subject area. Attending to the way in which the discipline is really carried out in the classroom, as well as how it impacts students' formation of a sense of attachment with it, is required when teaching with the mindset of cultivating disposition in pupils (Boaler & Greeno, 2000). The effort required to implement these improvements will not be without rewards, but it will involve a considerable amount of work. In order to close the well-documented achievement gap that exists in classrooms, we must begin to recognize how dispositions are formed and work to enhance the development of more positive and productive attitudes toward learning in a subject-matter area. One of the main requirements for the growth of CT practices is to put in place well-developed CT dispositions.

Teachers and researchers should better grasp the CT attitudes and disposition of learners. Teachers with little or no CT expertise and understanding could also need clear explanations of previous studies to assist their practice. As a result, the summary will inform teachers on the lessons' content. Therefore, it is critical to carry out this systematic investigation in order to assist with CT training curriculum creation and assessment. This research findings can also help to guide the learners on how to create the attitude for CT to have a positive influence in day-to-day activities.

Developing students as problem-solvers who are able to solve problems in the digital environment, as well as providing them with CT (or computer technology) skills and knowledge may not be adequate. The CT approach is about employing coding to solve problems; however, it doesn't take into consideration whether or not the skills have been used to help make progress in other aspects of one's life. Moreover, the scope of CT measurement methods must be broadened in order to represent the growing range of applications. Thus, according to these researchers, the need for ongoing dedication to difficult, real-world problems necessitates having CT dispositions as a source of motivation. For the purpose of this explanation, the terms "computational problem-solving" and "computational thinking" will be used interchangeably. The results of previous research reveal that distinct thinking skills are associated with an internal drive to think and form thinking dispositions.

We strive to raise young learners to see how the digital technologies of today may assist in solving tomorrow's issues. They must be able to think intelligently about creating and developing new technology, rather than only consuming and utilizing it. To summarize, even while basic problem-solving competencies are intertwined with CT, there is a complementing non-skill side. The CT curriculum is designed to foster creative problem solvers who can engage in all aspects of life. The students' disposition in the computational context must therefore be evaluated. With suitable evaluation components and methodologies, schools are regarded to be better able to foster young learners in the digitalized environment to become innovative problem formulators.

ACKNOWLEDGMENT

The authors thankful to Ministry of Education, experts, teachers and students who helped in data collection and instrument validation. The authors would also like to honor and give high appreciation to the Faculty of Education, Universiti Kebangsaan Malaysia (UKM).

FUNDING STATEMENT

The authors would like to express special words of thanks and their acknowledgement to the Ministry of Higher Education and Universiti Kebangsaan Malaysia (TRGS/1/2018/UKM/01/6/1).

CONFLICTS OF INTEREST

The authors declare that they have no conflicts of interest to report regarding the present study.

REFERENCES

ACM/IEEE-CS Joint Task Force on Computing Curricula. (2013). *Computer Science Curricula 2013*. ACM Press and IEEE Computer Society Press., doi:10.1145/2534860

Agarwal, J., & Naresh, K. M. (2005). An integrated model of attitude and affect: Theoretical foundation and empirical investigation. *Journal of Business Research*, *58*(4), 483–493. doi:10.1016/S0148-2963(03)00138-3

Aho, A. V. (2012). Computation and computational thinking. *The Computer Journal*, *55*(7), 833–835. doi:10.1093/comjnl/bxs074

Allport, G. W. (1935). *Attitudes. In Handbook of social psychology*. Clark University Press.

Allport, G. W. (1954). *The nature of prejudice*. Addison-Wesley.

Atman, K. (1987). The role of conation (striving) in the distance learning enterprise. *American Journal of Distance Education*, *1*(1), 14–28. doi:10.1080/08923648709526568

Bagozzi, R. P. (1992). The self-regulation of attitudes, intentions, and behaviour. *Social Psychology Quarterly*, *55*(2), 178. doi:10.2307/2786945

Baker, D. P., & Salas, E. (1992). Principles for measuring teamwork skills. *Human Factors*, *34*(4), 469–475. doi:10.1177/001872089203400408

Bandura, A. (1977). *Social learning theory*. Prentice Hall.

Bandura, A. (1986). *Social foundations of thought and action: A social cognitive theory*. Prentice-Hall, Inc.

Bandura, A., Freeman, W. H., & Lightsey, R. (1999). Self-efficacy: The exercise of control. *Journal of Cognitive Psychotherapy*, *13*(2), 158–166. doi:10.1891/0889-8391.13.2.158

Barr, D., Harrison, J., & Conery, L. (2011). Computational thinking: A digital age skill for everyone. *Learning and Leading with Technology, 38*(6), 20–23.

Barr, V., & Stephenson, C. (2011). Bringing computational thinking to K–12: What is involved and what is the role of the computer science education community? *ACM Inroads, 2*(1), 48–54. doi:10.1145/1929887.1929905

Baumeister, R. E. F., Bratslavsky, E., Muraven, M., & Tice, D. M. (1998). Ego Depletion: Is the active self a limited resource. *Journal of Personality and Social Psychology, 74*(5), 1252–1265. doi:10.1037/0022-3514.74.5.1252 PMID:9599441

Beaver, J. R. (1994). *Problem solving across the curriculum.* International Society for Technology in Education.

Bell, T., & Roberts, J. (2016). Computational thinking is more about humans than computers. set. *Research Information for Teachers, 1*(1), 3–7. doi:10.18296et.0030

Beyer, B. K. (1988). *Developing A Thinking Skills Programme.* Allyn and Bacon Inc.

Beyer, B. K. (1995). *Critical Thinking.* Phi Delta Kappa Educational Foundations.

Boaler, J., & Greeno, J. G. (2000). Identity, agency, and knowing in mathematics worlds. In J. Boaler (Ed.), *Multiple perspectives on mathematics teaching and learning* (pp. 171–200). Ablex.

Bohner, G., & Wanke, M. (2002). *Attitudes and Attitude Change.* Psychology Press.

Brennan, K., & Resnick, M. (2012). *New frameworks for studying and assessing the development of computational thinking.* Retrieved from http://web.media.mit.edu/~kbrennan/files/Brennan_ Resnick_AERA2012_CT.pdf

Bronfenbrenner, U. (1979). *The Ecology of Human Development.* Harvard University Press.

Bruner, J. (1996). *The Culture of Education.* Harvard University Press.

Bundy, A. (2007). Computational thinking is pervasive. *Journal of Scientific and Practical Computing, 1*(2), 67–69.

Butler, J. (1993). *Thinking skills in human development: At school and at work.* Paper Presented at the *International Convention on Excellence in Thinking*, Universiti Kebangsaan Malaysia, Malaysia.

Butler, K. A. (1987). *Learning & teaching style: In theory & practice.* Learner's Dimension.

Carlborg, N., Tyrén, M., Heath, C., & Eriksson, E. (2019). The scope of autonomy when teaching computational thinking in primary school. *International Journal of Child-Computer Interaction, 21*, 130–139. doi:10.1016/j.ijcci.2019.06.005

Carr, M. (2001). *Assessment in early childhood settings: Learning stories.* Paul Chapman.

Chapman, D. W., & Carter, J. F. (1979). Translation procedures for the cross-cultural use of measurement instruments. *Educational Evaluation and Policy Analysis, 3*(3), 71–76. doi:10.3102/01623737001003071

Clements, D. H., & Battista, M. T. (1989). Learning of geometric concepts in a Logo environment. *Journal for Research in Mathematics Education, 20*(5), 450–467. doi:10.2307/749420

Comber, B. (2000). What really counts in early literacy lessons? *Language Arts, 78*(1), 39–49.

Computer Science Teachers Association. (2017). *CSTA K–12 Computer Science Standards.* Revised 2017. Retrieved from https://www.csteachers.org/standards

Conner, M., & Armitage, C. J. (1998). Extending the theory of planned behaviour: A review and avenues for further research. *Journal of Applied Social Psychology, 28*(15), 1429–1464. doi:10.1111/j.1559-1816.1998.tb01685.x

Costa, A. L. (2000). Describing the habits of mind. In A. L. Costa & B. Kallick (Eds.), *Habits of mind: Discovering and Exploring* (pp. 21–40). Association for Supervision and Curriculum Development.

Covington, M. V. (2000). Intrinsic Versus Extrinsic Motivation in Schools: A Reconciliation. *Current Directions in Psychological Science, 9*(1), 22–25. doi:10.1111/1467-8721.00052

Curzon, P. (2015). *Computational thinking: Searching to speak.* Available at: https://teachinglondon-computing.org/free-workshops/computational-thinkingsearching-to-speak/

Denning, P. J. (2007). Computing is a natural science. *Communications of the ACM, 50*(7), 13–18. doi:10.1145/1272516.1272529

Denning, P. J. (2017). Remaining trouble spots with computational thinking. *Communications of the ACM, 60*(6), 33–39. doi:10.1145/2998438

Dewey, J. (1975). *Interest and effort in education.* Southern Illinois University Press.

Diez, M., & Raths, J. (2007). *Dispositions in teacher education.* Information Age Publishing, Inc.

Dweck, C. S. (1999). *Self-theories: Their role in motivation, personality, and development.* Psychology Press.

Emmons, R. (1986). Personal strivings: An approach to personality and subjective well-being. *Journal of Personality and Social Psychology, 51*(5), 1058–1068. doi:10.1037/0022-3514.51.5.1058

English, H. B., & English, A. C. (1958). *A Comprehensive Dictionary of Psychological and Psycho-analytical Terms.* Longmans Green.

Erikson, E. (1968). *Identity, Youth and Crisis.* Norton.

Facione, P. A. (2000). The Disposition Toward Critical Thinking: Its Character, Measurement, and Relationship to Critical Thinking Skill. *Informal Logic, 20*(1), 61–84. doi:10.22329/il.v20i1.2254

Facione, P. A., Facione, N. C., & Sanchez, C. A. (1995). *Test Manual for the CCTDI* (2nd ed.). The California Academic Press.

Fishbein, M., & Azjen, I. (1975). *Belief, attitude, intention and behaviour: An introduction to theory and research.* Addison and Wesley Pub.

Gagne, R. M., & Medsker, K. L. (1996). *The conditions of learning: Training applications.* Harcourt Brace.

Gibson, J. L., Ivancevich, J. M., & Donnelly, J. H. (1991). *Organizations: Behavior, structure, processes* (7th ed.). Irwin.

Greeno, J. G. (1998). The stativity of knowing, learning and research. *The American Psychologist, 53*(1), 5–26. doi:10.1037/0003-066X.53.1.5

Grover, S., & Pea, R. (2013). Computational thinking in K–12: A review of the state of the field. *Educational Researcher, 42*(1), 38–43. doi:10.3102/0013189X12463051

Guilford, J. P. (1970). Creativity: Retrospect and prospect. *The Journal of Creative Behavior, 4*(3), 149–168. doi:.1970.tb00856.x doi:10.1002/j.2162-6057

Hambrusch, S., Hoffmann, C., Korb, J., Haugan, M., & Hosking, A. (2009). A multidisciplinary approach towards computational thinking for science majors. *ACM SIGCSE Bulletin, 41*(1), 183–187. doi:10.1145/1539024.1508931

Hawkins, D. I., & Mothersbaugh, D. L. (2010). *Consumer behavior: Building marketing strategy* (11th ed.). McGraw-Hill Irwin.

Heppner, P. P., & Petersen, C. H. (1982). The development and implications of a personal problem-solving inventory. *Journal of Counseling Psychology, 29*(1), 66–75. doi:10.1037/0022-0167.29.1.66

Hesse, F., Care, E., Buder, J., Sassenberg, K., & Griffin, P. (2015). A framework for teachable collaborative problem-solving skills. In P. Griffin & E. Care (Eds.), *Assessment and teaching of 21st century skills: Methods and approach* (pp. 37–56). Springer.

Hilgard, E. R. (1980). The Trilogy of Mind Cognition, Affection and Conation. *Journal of the History of the Behavioral Sciences, 6*(2), 107–117. doi:10.1002/1520-6696(198004)16:2<107::AID-JHBS2300160202>3.0.CO;2-Y PMID:11608381

Hofstede, G. H. (1991). *Cultures and Organizations: Software of the Mind.* McGraw Hill.

Huitt, W., & Cain, S. (2005). An Overview of the Conative Domain. In *Educational Psychology Interactive* (pp. 1–20). Valdosta State University.

International Society for Technology in Education (ISTE). (2016). *ISTE standards for students.* Retrieved from: http://www.iste.org/docs/Standards-Resources/iste-standards_students-2016_onesheet_final.pdf

ISTE. (2015). *CT leadership toolkit.* Available at: http://www.iste.org/docs/ct-documents/ct-leadershipt-toolkit.pdf?sfvrsn=4

Kafai, Y., & Burke, Q. (2013). The social turn in K-12 programming: Moving from computational thinking to computational participation. *Proceedings of the 44th ACM Technical Symposium on Computer Science Education, SIGCSE 2013,* 6–9. 10.1145/2445196.2445373

Kane, R. (1985). *Free will and values.* State University of New York Press.

Katz, L. G. (1988). What Should Young Children Be Doing? *American Educator: The Professional Journal of the American Federation of Teachers, 12*(2), 28-33, 44-45.

Katz, L. G. (1993). *Dispositions: Definitions and implications for early childhood practices* (Perspectives from ERIC/EECE Monograph No. 4). ERIC Clearinghouse on Elementary and Early Childhood Education.

Kazimoglu, C., Kiernan, M., Bacon, L., & MacKinnon, L. (2012). Learning programming at the computational thinking level via digital game-play. *Procedia Computer Science*, *9*, 522–531. doi:10.1016/j.procs.2012.04.056

Koballa, T. R. (1989). *Changing and measuring attitudes in the science classroom, Research Matters to the Science Teacher*. National Association for Research in Science Teaching.

Kong, S.-C., Abelson, H., & Lai, M. (2019). Introduction to computational thinking education. In S.-C. Kong & H. Abelson (Eds.), *Computational thinking education* (pp. 1–10). Springer. doi:10.1007/978-981-13-6528-7_1

Kong, S. C., Chiu, M. M., & Lai, M. (2018). A study of primary school students' interest, collaboration attitude, and programming empowerment in computational thinking education. *Computers & Education*, *127*, 178–189. doi:10.1016/j.compedu.2018.08.026

Korkmaz, Ö., Cakir, R., & Ozden, M. Y. (2017). A validity and reliability study of the computational thinking scales (CTS). *Computers in Human Behavior*, *72*, 558–569. doi:10.1016/j.chb.2017.01.005

Krech, D., Crutchfield, R. S., & Ballackey, E. L. (1962). *Individual in Society*. McGraw Hill.

Lampert, M. (1990). Connecting inventions with conventions: The teachers' role in classroom communication about mathematics. In L. Steffe & T. Wood (Eds.), *Transforming Early Childhood Mathematics Education* (pp. 253–265). Erlbaum.

Lampert, M. (2001). *Teaching problems and the problems in teaching*. Yale University Press.

Lave, J., & Wenger, E. (1991). *Situated learning: Legitimate peripheral participation*. Cambridge University Press., doi:10.1017/CBO9780511815355

Lee, I., Martin, F., Denner, J., Coulter, B., Allan, W., Erickson, J., Malyn-Smith, J., & Werner, L. (2011). Computational thinking for youth in practice. *ACM Inroads*, *2*(1), 32–37. doi:10.1145/1929887.1929902

Lye, S. Y., & Koh, J. H. L. (2014). Review on teaching and learning of computational thinking through programming: What is next for K-12? *Computers in Human Behavior*, *41*, 51–61. doi:10.1016/j.chb.2014.09.012

Mayer, R. E. (1983). *Thinking, problem solving and cognition*. W. H. Freeman and Co.

McCune, V., & Entwistle, N. (2011). Cultivating the disposition to understand in 21st century university education. *Learning and Individual Differences*, *21*(3), 303–310. doi:10.1016/j.lindif.2010.11.017

Meece, J. L., Blumenfeld, P. C., & Hoyle, R. H. (1988). Students' goal orientations and cognitive engagement in classroom activities. *Journal of Educational Psychology*, *80*(4), 514–523. doi:10.1037/0022-0663.80.4.514

Michael, J. (1991). A behavioural perspective on college teaching. *The Behavior Analyst*, *14*(2), 229–239. doi:10.1007/BF03392578 PMID:22478107

Miller, A. (1991). Personality types, learning styles and educational goals. *Educational Psychology*, *11*(3-4), 217–238. doi:10.1080/0144341910110302

Mischel, W. (1996). From good intentions to willpower. In P. Gollwitzer & J. Bargh (Eds.), The psychology of action. *Guilford Press*.

Mishra, P., & Yadav, A. (2013). Of art and algorithms: Rethinking technology & creativity in the 21st century. *TechTrends*, *57*(3), 11.

Mohd, N., & Mahmood, T. F. P. T. (2011). The effects of attitude towards problem solving in mathematics achievements. *Australian Journal of Basic and Applied Sciences*, *5*(12), 1857–1862.

Moschella, M. (2019). Observable computational thinking skills in primary school children: How and when teachers can discern abstraction, decomposition and use of algorithms. *INTED2019 Proceedings*, *1*(March), 6259–6267. 10.21125/inted.2019.1523

Norris, S. P., & Ennis, R. H. (1989). *Evaluating critical thinking*. Midwest Publications.

OECD. (2017). Collaborative problem-solving framework. *PISA 2015*.

Papert, S. (1980). *Mindstorms: Children, computers, and powerful ideas*. Basic Books.

Passmore, J. (1967). Logical Positivism. In P. Edwards (Ed.), The Encyclopedia of Philosophy. Macmillan.

Pea, R. D., & Kurland, D. M. (1984). On the cognitive effects of learning computer programming. *New Ideas in Psychology*, *2*(2), 137–168. doi:10.1016/0732-118X(84)90018-7

Perez, A. (2018). A Framework for Computational Thinking Dispositions in Mathematics Education. *Journal for Research in Mathematics Education*, *49*(4), 424–461. doi:10.5951/jresematheduc.49.4.0424

Perkins, D. (2008). Beyond understanding. In *Threshold Concepts within the Disciplines*. Sense Publishers.

Perkins, D. N. (1993). Person-plus: a distributed view of thinking and learning. In G. Salomon (Ed.), *Distributed cognitions: psychological and educational considerations*. Cambridge University Press.

Perkins, D. N., Jay, E., & Tishman, S. (1993). Beyond Abilities: A dispositional theory of thinking. *Merrill-Palmer Quarterly*, *39*(1), 1–21.

Piaget, J. (1936). *Origins of intelligence in the child*. Routledge & Kegan Paul.

Piaget, J. (1971). The Stages of Intellectual Development of the Child. Readings in Child Development, 55(2), 178-204.

Rambally, G. (2017). Integrating Computational Thinking in Discrete Structures. In P. Rich & C. Hodges (Eds.), *Emerging Research, Practice, and Policy on Computational Thinking. In Educational Communications and Technology: Issues and Innovations*. Springer. doi:10.1007/978-3-319-52691-1_7

Resnick, M., Maloney, J., Monroy-Hernández, A., Rusk, N., Eastmond, E., Brennan, K., Millner, A., Rosenbaum, E., Silver, J., Silverman, B., & Kafai, Y. (2009). Scratch. *Communications of the ACM*, *52*(11), 60–67. doi:10.1145/1592761.1592779

Robles, M. M. (2012). Executive perceptions of the top 10 soft skills needed in today's workplace. *Business Communication Quarterly*, *75*(4), 453–465. doi:10.1177/1080569912460400

Román-gonzález, M., Perez-Gonzelez, J. C., & Jimenez-Fernandez, C. (2016). Which cognitive abilities underlie computational thinking? Criterion validity of the Computational Thinking Test. *Computers in Human Behavior*, *72*, 678–691. doi:10.1016/j.chb.2016.08.047

Romero, M., Lepage, A., & Lille, B. (2017). Computational thinking development through creative programming in higher education. *Int J Educ Technol High Educ*, *14*(1), 42. doi:10.118641239-017-0080-z

Rosenberg, M. J., Hovland, C. I., McGuire, W. J., Abelson, R. P., & Brehm, J. W. (1960). *Attitude organization and change: An analysis of consistency among attitude components*. Yale University Press.

Ryan, R., & Deci, E. (2000). Self-Determination theory and the facilitation of intrinsic motivation, *social development, and well-being. The American Psychologist*, *55*(1), 68–78. doi:10.1037/0003-066X.55.1.68 PMID:11392867

Salomon, G. (Ed.). (1993). *Distributed cognitions: psychological and educational considerations*. Cambridge University Press.

Salomon, G. (1994). *Interaction of media, cognition, and learning*. Erlbaum.

Salovey, P., & Mayer, J. D. (1990). Emotional intelligence. *Imagination, Cognition and Personality*, *9*(3), 185–211. doi:10.2190/DUGG-P24E-52WK-6CDG

Sands, P., Yadav, A., & Good, J. (2018). Computational think: In-service Teacher Perceptions of Computational Thinking. In *Computational thinking in the STEM disciplines*. Springer.

Schiffman, L. G., Kanuk, L., & Hansen, H. (2012). *Consumer Behaviour: A European Outlook* (2nd ed.). Pearson Education Limited.

Schunk, D., & Zimmerman, B. (2008). *Motivation and self-regulated learning: Theory, research, and applications*. Routledge.

Sharma, K., Papavlasopoulou, S., & Giannakos, M. (2019). Coding games and robots to enhance computational thinking: How collaboration and engagement moderate children's attitudes? *International Journal of Child-Computer Interaction*, *21*, 65–76. doi:10.1016/j.ijcci.2019.04.004

Shute, V., Sun, C., & Asbell-Clarke, J. (2017). Demystifying computational thinking. *Educational Research Review*, *22*.

Siegel, H. (1988). *Educating for reason: Rationality, critical thinking, and education*. Routledge.

Simpson, E. J. (1972). *The classification of educational objectives in the psychomotor domain: The psychomotor domain*. Gryphon House.

Snow, R. E., Corno, L., & Jackson, D. III. (1996). Individual differences in affective and conative functions. In D. C. Berliner & R. C. Calfee (Eds.), *Handbook of educational psychology* (pp. 243–310). Macmillan Library: Prentice Hall International.

Sondakh, D. E., Osman, K., & Zainudin, S. (2020). A Proposal for holistic assessment of computational thinking for undergraduate: Content validity. *European Journal of Educational Research*, *9*(1), 33–50. doi:10.12973/eu-jer.9.1.33

Sondakh, D. E., Osman, K., & Zainudin, S. (2020). A pilot study of an instrument to assess undergraduates' computational thinking proficiency. *International Journal of Advanced Computer Science and Applications*, *11*(11). Advance online publication. doi:10.14569/IJACSA.2020.0111134

Spooncer, F. (1992). *Behavioural studies for marketing and business*. Stanley Thornes, Leckhampton.

Tallon, A. (1997). *Head and heart: Affection, cognition, volition as triune consciousness*. Fordham University.

Tedre, M., & Denning, P. J. (2016). The long quest for computational thinking. In *ACM International Conference Proceeding Series* (pp. 120–129). Association for Computing Machinery. 10.1145/2999541.2999542

The College Board. (2012). *Computational thinking practices and big ideas, key concepts, and supporting concepts*. http://www.csprinciples.org/home/about-the-project

Thurstone, L. L. (1931). The measurement of social attitudes. *Journal of Abnormal and Social Psychology*, *26*(3), 249–269. doi:10.1037/h0070363

Travers, R. M. W. (1977). *Essentials of learning* (4th ed.). Macmillan.

Triandis, H. C. (1971). *Attitude and Attitude Change (Foundations of Social Psychology)*. John Wileys & Sons Inc.

Trilling, B., & Fadel, C. (2009). *21st century skills: Learning for life in our times*. Jossey-Bass/Wiley.

Weintrop, D., Beheshti, E., Horn, M., Orton, K., Jona, K., Trouille, L., & Wilensky, U. (2016). Defining computational thinking for mathematics and science classrooms. *Journal of Science Education and Technology*, *25*(1), 127–147. doi:10.100710956-015-9581-5

Wenger, E. (1998). *Communities of Practice: learning, meaning and identity*. Cambridge University Press. doi:10.1017/CBO9780511803932

Wing, J. M. (2006). Computational thinking. *Communications of the ACM*, *49*(3), 33–35. doi:10.1145/1118178.1118215

Wing, J. M. (2017). Computational thinking's influence on research and education for all. *Italian Journal of Educational Technology*, *25*(2), 7–14.

Woollard, J. (2016). CT driving computing curriculum in England. *CSTA Voice*, *12*, 4–5.

Yadav, A., Mayfield, C., Zhou, N., Hambrusch, S., & Korb, J. T. (2014). Computational thinking in elementary and secondary teacher education. *ACM Transactions on Computing Education*, *14*(1), 1–16. doi:10.1145/2576872

Zakaria, E., Haron, Z., & Daud, M. (2004). The reliability and construct validity of scores on the attitudes toward problem solving scale. *Journal of Science and Mathematics Education in South East Asia*, *27*(2), 81–91.

Zhao, W., & Shute, V. J. (2019). Can playing a video game foster computational thinking skill? *Computers & Education*, *141*, 103653. doi:10.1016/j.compedu.2019.103633

Chapter 16
Advanced Portfolio Management in Big Data Environments With Machine Learning and Advanced Analytical Techniques

Goran Klepac
Hrvatski Telekom d.d., Croatia & Algebra University College, Croatia

Leo Mršić
ⓘ https://orcid.org/0000-0002-5093-3453
Algebra University College, Croatia

Robert Kopal
Algebra University College, Croatia

ABSTRACT

The chapter will propose a novel approach that combines the traditional machine learning approach in churn management and customer satisfaction evaluation, which unite traditional machine learning approach and expert-based approach, which leans on event-based management. The core of the proposed framework is hybrid fuzzy expert system, which can contain a variety of data mining predictive models responsible for some specific areas as additions to traditional rule blocks. It can also include social network analysis metrics based on linguistic variables and incorporated within rule blocks. The chapter will introduce how revealed patterns can be applied for continual portfolio management improvement. The proposed solution unites advanced analytical techniques with the decision-making process within a holistic self-learning framework.

DOI: 10.4018/978-1-7998-8686-0.ch016

INTRODUCTION

Big data environment gives new opportunities in analytics. From one hand it demands new way of thinking in combination of unstructured data sources. Decision support system which could unite most important factors and find sensitiveness between recognized factors could be useful decision support tool for portfolio management. Tool which can predict, with certain level of probability potential values of observed outputs, regarding recognized inputs, or simulated inputs can be valuable tool for decision.

Unstructured data sources bring new approaches and opportunities in better understanding business areas like early warning systems. Main advantage challenge even we are talking about big data environment to recognize rare events in such environment which statistically does not have a major influence on target attributes, but when it happened, they have huge impact on target attribute like churn.

Example for that can be complaints on service delivery. In general, we do not expect statistically huge number of complaints in regular business, except in extreme situation. Among other information, share of complaints within data as cases are rare. Traditional machine learning algorithms potentially during machine learning process will not recognize it as important regarding low occurrence ratio. Generally speaking, such events can be very important for detection situations like churn. Here we can talk about paradox in big data environment where significant attributes and values in big data environment cannot be adequately incorporated into machine learning models because of rare value occurrence.

Value of the existing data, dislocated within different transactional systems could be increased by integration into data lake. It still does not mean that company does not have limited information about some problem space. Other problem in relation with traditional analytical approach is often avoidance of unstructured data source usage for business modeling purposes, even unstructured data exists within systems like call centers data or similar sources.

Modern decade fights with problem how to interact and efficiently use large available data collections.

Also in our case we are talking about adequate recognition and usage of important, but rare events.

Such conditions demands combination industry and expert knowledge but are easy to use. Described as Early Warning Systems (EWS) those models are packed with state-of-the-art knowledge and KPI's which helps business people to deal with numerous influences, large data sets and market trends. Early Warning Systems are also in close connection with risk assessment and modeling. Risk management methods often precede development phase and are used as starting point for early warning systems development.

By dealing with knowledge, term intelligence and, furthermore, business intelligence needs to be introduced first. Intelligence concerns the awareness and knowledge of the external business environment. The definition that is used here is that business intelligence is a systematized and continuous approach to focus, collect, analyze, communicate, and use information about customers, competitors, distributors, technology, political issues, macroeconomic issues, and political issues in order to increase the competitiveness of the organization (Hedin, Kovero 2006).

Ability to capture business rules starts with trading company's way back in the past. In modern management, intelligence was implicitly referred to as environmental scanning in the early writings of strategy in the 1960s. A decade later, intelligence was often included as a subset of market analysis while in 1980s, industry analysis researches argued that there is a "need for some form of formalized competitor intelligence system" since the informal approach is not rigorous enough to navigate today's turbulent and complex business environment. End if 20th Century brings analysis tools for understanding the competitive forces of an industry, which gave industry analysts, intelligence professionals, and managers a framework for understanding the external business environment (Hedin, Kovero 2006). While looking for company's understanding of the environment, intelligence systems and early warning systems start to be more and more formalized. Many organizations state that they rely mostly on informal mechanisms to support this external knowledge. This disproportionate reliance on informal mechanisms is a vestige of management thinking from the previous century. No well-managed modern business corporation should rely on an informal sales system, R&D process, or any other process that is of paramount importance to the success of their business model (Hedin, Kovero 2006). While developing early warning systems and models, several approaches are usually applied, like probit/logit approach and signaling approach (Chang, 2009). The former is often applied on a multivariate model, which allows testing of statistical significance of explanatory variables. This type of models requires large samples and can only accommodate a limited number of explanatory variables to avoid multicolinearity. On the other hand, the signaling approach is frequently applied in univariate models, which involve monitoring a set of high-frequency leading indicators. It is noted that those selected indicators would behave differently prior to some extraordinary event (why early warning systems are developed in first place). In period of crisis they reach their individual threshold values which are historically associated with the onset of a crisis. Univariate models work better with small samples and impose no restriction on the number of explanatory variables (Xing, 2014).

Big data analytics integrates variety disciplines from traditional data mining techniques along with social network analysis and text mining (Scott, 2012), (Watts, 1998) (Klepac, 2014), (Klepac, 2013).

In a world increasingly seen as a globalized, it has become more difficult to ignore different influences and effects even though in some cases they are unfolding thousands of kilometers away (Lavoix, 2008).

Traditional data mining approach, which is commonly used, offers well known methods usually used on internal data sources.

Chapter will show methodology of fuzzy expert system development with integration of AI methods as linguistic variables in service of early warning system development. In that direction elements of Social Network Analytics will be integrated within expert models, as well as methodology of integration of other AI developed models.

BACKGROUND

Analytical process from perspective of needed steps for achieving aims is not much different in big data environment, or in situation where company leans on traditional data sources.

Main difference is in strategic analytical thinking, which demands conscious about possible directions and integration of external data sources as well as techniques, which can be applied on such data integrated with internal data sources.

Regarding that, in situation where company considers external data sources, and other disposable data sources like unstructured data which we can declare as big data, analytical process are much more complex and holistic.

As it was previously mentioned additional challenges are in events which are rare but significantly contribute to some actions like churn.

In such cases early warning systems are good approach for solution.

Early warning system, or specifically a functional early warning system, is a chain of information communication systems comprising sensor, detection, decision, and broker subsystems, in the given order, working in conjunction, forecasting, and signaling disturbances adversely affecting the stability of the physical world, and giving sufficient time for the response system to prepare resources and response actions to minimize the impact on the stability of the physical world. Company during information system planning does not have in mind future analytical needs. Most important thing during planning of information system design is operative process coverage, as well as regulatory requirements. In this stage, company puts focus on operative processes like item, or raw materials ordering, warehousing processes, selling processes, and their adequate monitoring. Even in case when companies develop its own solution regarding transactional system, and they have an influence on data model design, they rarely think about future needs for data in fraud detection area, early warning, churn modeling. Partially, the reason for that is fact that at the moment of information system development company does not have need for this kind of systems, or it is not aware which one of them or couple of them it will need in the future period. Other reason for that is fact that everyone in the project team is concentrated on operative business, and problems like churn or fraud is not so evident or recognized as potential problem within company, and during information system planning data readiness and data requirements for that purposes is out of scope. Most of the companies buys core systems from software producers, and they mostly do not have an opportunity to collect additional data within those system which could be valuable for churn detection purposes or fraud detection purposes, new product planning purposes etc. On the other hand, analytical problems like churn detection, fraud detection early warning system development are very complex and it is very hard to design data model and data collection system, which will be sufficient for analysis and model development. Companies often decide to start with projects like churn detection, fraud detection, early warning system development, segmentation, when some negative market trend became evident, or competitors became much more aggressive and became threat for the company in way that it could lose market position or market share.

Developing sophisticated analytical system, or model for churn detection purposes, or fraud mitigation purposes in given conditions starts with detecting of disposable data within existing core systems or/and data warehouse as well on additional transactional systems within company. That approach is logical and it in most cases as an output gives plausible solutions. Problem lies in fact that produced solution leans on data sources, which primarily is not designed for those specific purposes. In that conditions project teams uses disposable data and attributes, as well as derived variables from existed internal data sources. Main issue we can illustrate with fact when we are trying, for example to develop efficient churn detection system, which should give us the answer why buyers stop to buy in our shops. Company on disposition has only transactional data, collected for transactional purposes. Predictive models use history data (like behavioral, transactional, socio demographics). There is no guarantee that disposable data set is sufficient data set from which valuable patterns, trends or conclusions could be extracted, because disposable data set are mainly transactional or process oriented. Other evident fact is that buyer after committing churn does not give us any feedback about reasons for committing churn. Sometimes/often from disposable transactional databases/data warehouse analyst could dig interesting patterns like most frequent age group of churners, or fact that churners before hard churn committed soft churn, which means that soft churn increases probability of hard churn. With such revealed knowledge analyst could construct plausible profiling, and it could be base for churn stopping criteria. Let assume that customers which committed churn in previous period had intensive contacts via call center. During predictive modeling those fact could be used in attribute relevance analysis and analysis will show relation within churn and intensive calls into call center. Calls into call center could be register via call center and customer comments could be saved within memo fields as a textual data. Traditional predictive modeling often neglected power of textual data, because there is no common methodology for usage of this kind of data sources for predictive modeling, like churn. This leads us to conclusion that maybe some valuable pattern could stay unrevealed. Same customer, or bunch of customers can start topic on forums regarding their potential dissatisfaction with company or their product/services or sales representatives. It could be the same with blog contents and followers within those blogs, or social network users. Expressing attitudes in such way is valuable source of information. Value of those data became much more evident for early warning system construction.

Traditional approach for early warning system development, which is based on key performance indicators and their monitoring, are limited on assumed area of potential risk. Data source for key performance indicators lies on internal database sources. Periodical monitoring of those indicators gives company justified, but potentially limited scope on potential risks. Experts in each field knows which indicators are crucial in relation with risk for specific area, but most dangerous situation is bad events which we, as a company could not predict, or company is not aware of them. For example, dissatisfaction with quality of service could become evident within unstructured external data like blogs, forums, and social networks. From the other hand, if we are talking about telecommunication company and their subscribers with calculated low probability of churn in recent period, with great influence (high influencer on other subscribers) like members of social network, as telecom users they can disintegrate whole network. If company is not aware about existence of such nodes, with high influence on other nodes (subscribers), it could be dangerous from perspective of potential business risks. Another example is fraud detection modeling and finding patterns. Local models are concentrated on local data, and could show potentially usable patterns like profiles, and conditions where fraud was committed. Information that some object (company, organization, lawyer etc.) was involved in fraudulent activities with another company in past, can stay unrevealed, unless company as an integral part of fraud model /analysis does not include sources like newspaper articles or similar sources. It also could be trigger for making additional analysis based on revealed fact like social network analysis. There is no guaranty that those extended data sets will provide optimal information for building much more predictive or reliable models. The basic idea is to use such unstructured /structured data sets for analytical purposes, and to confirm or reject some hypothesis. In that way, company uses resources of disposable data sources, which before big data era were not recognized as relevant, and it could take it in account during defining analytical strategy for future business challenges. Optimal situation would be that company from the start, define adequate data model and dependent transactional system, which would collect as many as possible relevant data for churn model developing needs, fraud model developing needs, segmentation model developing needs, etc. Expectation for that is little bit unrealistic, because companies start to develop such kind of models after they evaluate business need for them, caused by market conditions. However, existing data within local databases could be usable for analytical modeling with satisfying results, but it has limitations, which are previously described. Big data concept offers new solution, which has direct impact on modeling quality, but it also demands change in strategic way of analytical thinking. Considering unstructured data from external sources, their integration, modeling and analyzing along with internal data sources, demands changes in traditional analytical methodology as well as strategic thinking about infrastructure and solutions which should be base for decision making processes.

By looking at this definition we can find that one of the problems in the field of early warning systems is the existence of a variety of different notions of what defines and constitutes an early warning system. Although one of general definitions explains early warning systems as provision of timely and effective information, through identifying institutions, that allow individuals exposed to hazard to act to avoid or reduce their risk and prepare for effective response (UN/ISDR, 2006), the views and the understanding of early warning are often considerably different and depend on the domain of a user or developer. This is partly due to fact of wide appliance of early warning systems in different industries and areas. Early warning systems are created in order to identify risks and uncertainties and to minimize them by continuously monitoring events that might lead to a threatening situation. By providing an early enough warning that a potentially harmful sequence of events has been evolving, it should be possible to take actions in a proactive manner and thus avoid the threat (GIA, 2006). These definitions identify two main perspectives involved in the process. Although aim of this paper is to explain business appliance of early warning systems, those can be easily explained on environment case. In the first perspective, environmental changes are primarily perceived as a risk or a source of a potential crisis responsible for behavior conflicting with the organization's objectives. In the second, changes in the environment are considered to be business opportunities. Neither perspective is mutually exclusive, nor should both perspectives be included in a competitive early warning system that looks at both risks and opportunities. The way an organization deals with environmental changes and actors often decides the end result, a threat can become an opportunity if known well in advance and dealt with properly. Some systems do not highlight both because they are unbalanced and do not search for risks as well as opportunities while opportunities are seen as more positive than risks, because they provide a better and more desirable basis for executive rewards (Comai, 2007).

After business aim definition, which includes strategy based on big data paradigm, disposable data and their potential has strong influence on solution design, and solution building. It can consolidate traditional model development along with analytical solutions, based on big data paradigm.

It is important to stress that in that situation, knowledge extraction demands much more human expert involvement. Especially in situation where results and knowledge from different kind of models exists, and it demands expert judgment and evaluation. It means that during business decision process, expert explanation and conclusions plays crucial role in understanding and interpretation of given results.

One of the reasons lies in fact, that results given from different data sources, which provides different perspective of problem explanation, needs expert for their explanation.

Two types of early warning systems can also be observed. Proactive implies a two-step approach. First seek and make choices about issues that are relevant for the organization's future, and then introduce those issues into the system for continuous monitoring. The company makes the deliberate effort to identify relevant issues as much in advance of their impact as possible. On the other hand, reactive managers take a radar view of monitoring the environment, looking for unexpected changes that could generate a surprise. Once the surprise has been detected, it introduces a new element into the competitive early warning system. The ability to anticipate potential environmental changes is key factor to a good intelligence unit's operation. Different studies show that companies do not invest sufficient resources in predictive analysis models. If an organization is to be an "eagle," it should have the "ability to recognize significant industry shifts and assess their impact." Anticipating events that could have an immediate or potential impact on the organization is the essence of the entire process. The time span between becoming aware of a potential threat and the event itself is frequently described in military intelligence warning terminology. The "warning lead time" is the period between the issuing of the strategic warning and the beginning of hostilities - where possible action can be taken. This period may include strategic warning pre-decision and post-decision time.

After a warning is received by or from the market, the time before a decision is (or is not) made is the pre-decision time. Once the decision has been made, the time before the event happens is the post-decision time. In both time spans, the decision is made on the assumption that the event will occur, and it is always made from a future-oriented perspective. In a hypothetical situation, this definition assumes that: the intelligence function does not fail to detect early signals, these signals are well understood and there is no misperception of them, the analysis and the decision is made on time.

Early Warning and Early Response

Thanks to the evolution of communication infrastructure that ensures information flow, businesses are faced with constant change, today more rapidly than ever before. Business model adoption programs have become popular because the rate at which business models change has accelerated due to the pervasive free communication network. Early warning systems are needs to identify when business conditions fail to fit into the status quo used to devise business models. From the perspective of an organization that has to determine its root causes, impacts, action plans and systemic changes to business models that require alterations. With a disruptive technology that either benefits consumers through new capabilities or services that radically alter the cost structure used to price goods or services, the speed at which these disruptions can be dispensed with are likely to greatly impact organizational health (Albala, 2013).

Common methodology used for analytical purposes leaned mostly on internally disposable data sources, which cause usage of methods, which are mostly focused on structured databases. Projects, which are oriented on unstructured data sources like text or web, are mostly independent conceptually, and methodologically from project like predictive fraud detection models, predictive churn detection models or segmentation models etc. For methodological synergies prerequisite is data synergism, and for achieving those aims clear strategy and knowledge on management level (strategic, operative and organizational part responsible for analytic solution development) should exists. The big data phenomena should not be observed from perspective of huge data amounts only, and to be concentrated only on methodology and infrastructure for effective processing huge data sets. Variety data sources, often unconnected with unique relational keys, which are expected for traditional analysis purposes, are not the case if companies would like to use benefits from data sources, which could be classified in "big data area". It could produce confusion especially in way when companies would like to use standard analytical approach. Regarding that it is evident that "big data analytic" are mostly concentrated on external data sources (Cointet, 2009), (Raine, 2012), (Reips, 2012), (Snijders, 2012) mostly without clear concept how to connect internal transactional data, with external data sources mostly unstructured and unconnected. Other fact is that known analytical methodology is mostly oriented on structured data sources, and in situation when unstructured data sources are used for e.g. text mining purposes, other type of analytical techniques should be used. Sometimes relatively lower data sets also could be declared as complex, because of their combinatory complexity. From the perspective of the companies it is very important thing to combine external and internal data sources, because knowledge about some global trends or attitudes about some subject or behavior, should be analyzed from the perspective of the company's portfolio. Comparison between global and local trends could give holistic picture sufficient for decision-making. Problem lies in fact that there is no common methodology how to develop efficient model, which would consolidate both data sources for developing efficient models as a base for business decision.

Basic idea of early warning system as a system which are capable for recognising negative trends in early stage is in collision with methodology of traditional predictive modelling, because of mentioned problems.

It does not mean that predictive models should not be used for modelling early warning systems; it only means that predictive models should not be only element or base for early warning system.

Early warning systems should not depend on attribute significance on aim variable, because early attribute insignificance in the light of early warning systems does not mean that it will not became significant in some near future. Sometimes some trends can remain unrevealed because it is insignificant on whole portfolio level, but it can have great influence on some part of portfolio and can generate high costs or other negative trends.

Another important topic is aim variable construction in case when we are developing early warning system as a predictive model.

Better solution for early warning system development is using expert systems as a base. Expert systems are based on expert knowledge and it can recognise potential bad event on single case level. It does not demand statistical significance as a condition for recognition of deviant, or potential problematic case or event. Also it also can contain predictive models as a part of the rules and in that case we are talking about hybrid expert systems. In that case it has power based on predictive models, but also it contains expert rules which does not depend on frequencies within data and which can recognise suspicious trends and events.

Base for it is expert knowledge, and important thing is adequate knowledge elicitation and key indicator recognition as a first step in expert system development.

Knowledge, which should be important in early warning system development, should recognise situations, which are not expectable or specific. For this purpose it is important to extract knowledge from the experts and to challenge it in way to assume different kind of situations, which could generate potential problems to company.

As it was already stated analytical process from perspective of needed steps for achieving aims is not much different in big data environment, or in situation where company leans on traditional data sources.

Main difference is in strategic analytical thinking, and integration of business needs within analytical pipelines and solution which will contribute to final solution. It is very important to find appropriate combination of different analytical methods which will fits into holistic solution.

When we're talking about portfolio management in big data environment It is important to make strategic plan which will fits into analytical needs. That means that analytics are following business strategic. It is not enough to change different methods and expect some magical solution. Key factor to be successful is common business understanding es on business site as well on analytical side.

A company during information system planning does not have in mind future analytical needs. Most important thing during planning of information system design is operative process coverage as well as regulatory requirements. In this stage company puts focus on operative processes like item or raw materials ordering, warehousing processes, selling processes, and their adequate monitoring. Even in case when companies develops its own solution regarding transactional system and they have an influence on data model design they rarely think about future needs for data in fraud detection area, early warning, churn modeling.

Partially, the reason for that is fact that at the moment of information system development company does not have need for this kind of systems or it is not aware which one of them or couple of them it will need in the future period.

Other reason for that is fact that everyone in the project team is concentrated on operative business, and problems like churn or fraud is not so evident or recognized as potential problem within company and during information system planning data readiness and data requirements for that purposes is out of scope.

Most of the companies buys core systems from software producers, and they mostly does not have an opportunity to collect additional data within those system which could be valuable for churn detection purposes or fraud detection purposes, new product planning purposes etc.

On the other hand analytical problems like churn detection, fraud detection early warning system development are very complex and it is very hard to design data model and data collection system, which will be sufficient for analysis and model development.

Companies often decide to start with projects like churn detection, fraud detection, early warning system development, segmentation when some negative market trend became evident, or competitors became much more aggressive and became threat for the company in way that it could lose market position or market share.

Appliance of Structured Analytic Techniques in EWS

As mentioned, main task of EWS is to alert company on time that changes are coming in order to prepare organization to avoid unwanted consequences. Because of this large usability of EWS, many companies and industries are looking for implementation different kind of EWS. For example, in telco industry companies are interested to evaluate growing trends and churn management. Insurance companies are looking for better understanding of customer needs and how to attract customers with their products. Finance industry is looking for payment delays, identification of lazy payers and methods how to manage and change negative trends. EWS are becoming more and more important in crisis periods when negative trends are coming from almost every direction but it is not clear which industry or segment will be affected the most or when disruption will take place. We can say that in period of global crisis, EWS are essential tool for monitoring in order for companies to became proactive in such competitive environment.

Best way to manage negative trends is to prevent it from happening in the first place. EWS can help management of the company to have insight in every event that can affect company's performance. By implementing structured process of capturing, storing data, evaluating risk and risk management business can be secured for major threats.

Appliance of SNA Concepts and Metrics in EWS

Recent work in the area EWS shown that using SNA tools and analyzing customer's interactions by "assessing the social vicinity of recent churners" can improve the accuracy of churn prediction as mentioned one of the main targets for EWS in telco. Richter et al. (2010) proposed "a novel framework, termed Group-First Churn Prediction, which eliminates the *a priori* requirement of knowing who recently churned". Their approach "exploits the structure of customer interactions to predict which groups of subscribers are most prone to churn, before even a single member in the group has churned". Method they used to identify closely-knit groups of subscribers was second-order social metrics. They kept only the strongest connections, and divided the network into a collection of small disjoint clusters, each representing a dense social group. Then they analyzed the social interactions within each cluster and established the relative social status of each of its members. The most important step was to identify social leaders. Based on Key Performance Indicators derived from these groups, they proposed a novel statistical model to predict the churn of the groups and their members. They provide empirical evidence that their method "captures social phenomena in a highly significant manner". They further suggest: "A good churn prediction system should not only pinpoint potential churners successfully, but further provide a sufficiently long horizon forecast in its predictions. Once a potential churner is identified, the retention department usually makes contact and, if the customer is established to be a churn risk, takes appropriate measures to preserve her business. Thus, a long forecast horizon is an obvious advantage since the further away the customer is from actually making the churn decision, the easier it is to prevent that decision at a significantly lower cost."

Therefore, it is highly recommended to integrate SNA concepts into EWS combining methods into hybrid systems as base for fuzzy logic.

Generally speaking, a social network is a social structure made up of actors (individuals or organizations) called "nodes", which are tied (connected) by one or more specific types of interdependency, such as friendship, kinship, common interest, financial exchange, dislike, or relationships of beliefs, knowledge or prestige. In other words, social network analysis views social relationships in terms of network theory consisting of nodes and ties (also called edges, links, or connections). Nodes are the individual actors within the networks, and ties are the relationships between the actors.

In SNA, graphs and matrices are typically used to represent social network data. In the network structure modeled as a graph, vertices represent actors, and edges represent ties, which show the existence of a relation between two actors. Apart from indicating the links between vertices, the data also provide us with additional information on directionality and link weights (de Nooy et al., 2008). The network can also be used to measure social capital – the value that an individual gets from the social network.

Social network analysis has now become a scientific field, with its own theoretical statements, methods, software, and researchers. Analysts reason from whole to part; from structure to relation to individual; from behavior to attitude. They typically either study whole or complete networks, meaning all of the ties containing specified relations in a defined population, or personal or egocentric networks, meaning the ties that specified people have, such as their "personal communities" (Wellman and Berkowitz, 1998). A group of individuals with connections to other social worlds is likely to have access to a wider range of information. It is better for individual success to have connections to a variety of networks rather than many connections within a single network. Similarly, individuals can exercise thier influence or act as brokers within their social networks by bridging two networks that are not directly linked. The latter concept is called "filling structural holes" (Scott, 1991).

Network thinking and methodology help the analyst deal with multiple levels of analysis simultaneously. Differences among actors arise from their attributes and the nature of their relations, and these relations depend on how they are embedded in the network. On the other hand, the structure and behavior of the network depends on local interactions among actors. This dichotomy of the individual and structure is the first major emphasis of social network analysis. Another emphasis is to see how individual choices lead to patterns which in turn give rise to more holistic patterns (Hanneman and Riddle, 2005).

SNA combines organizational theories with mathematical models to help understand the dynamics of groups and organizations in which we are interested. The structure of a network can determine:

- The performance of the network as a whole and its ability to achieve its key goals.
- Characteristics of the network that are not immediately obvious, such as the existence of a smaller sub-network operating within the network.

- The relationships between prominent actors of interest whose position may provide the greatest influence over the rest of the network.
- How directly and quickly information flows between actors in different parts of the network (IBM, 2012).

SNA is equally used in mathematical sociology and quantitative analysis. Major difference in approach is the fact that statistical analysis methods need probabilistic approach to calculate probability distributions of relationship strengths. Mathematical approaches to the analysis of networks use structural descriptive (deterministic) methods, assuming that the measured relationships and their strengths represent the real or final status of the network. Crucial advantage of statistic models according to Wasserman and Faust is that they "can cope easily with some lack-of-fit of a model to data", while descriptive or deterministic models "cannot be relaxed in this way". "Deterministic models usually force the aspect of social structure of interest (such as reciprocity, or complete transitivity or structural equivalence) to be present in the model, while statistical models assume these aspects to be absent" (Wasserman and Faust, 1994)

Analysis of social network data can be focused on five separate levels, depending on the aim and purpose of the analysis (Wasserman and Faust, 1994):

- *Individual actor level*: centrality, prestige and roles (isolates, liaisons, bridges, etc.);
- *Dyadic level* (two actors and their ties): distance and reachability, structural and other notions of equivalence, and tendencies toward reciprocity;
- *Triadic level* (three actors and their ties): balance and transitivity;
- *Subgroup or subset level*: cliques, cohesive subgroups, components, and
- *Global or network level*: connectedness, diameter, centralization, density, prestige.

Each of these levels requires different analytical approach, and the use of different tools correspondingly. Social network analysts have developed a number of tools and metrics that help conceptualize and calculate variations in relations within the structures they analyze. Most of the time people interact with a small number of others, and in most cases they know one another. In other cases, people are connected through some shared attributes or memberships in "categorical social units" or "sub-populations" (Hanneman and Riddle, 2005). There are different patterns specific for different populations, and many different approaches to defining the form and extent of embedddedness of actors in their populations.

Different models can be developed and implemented for analyzing customer behavior and predicting various business events. These models can include traditional tools and techniques based on artificial neural networks used for predictive modeling, or they can combine several methodologies aimed at prediction and retention of valuable customers. Pinheiro (2011), for example, proposes a two-dimensional model, combining traditional models based on artificial neural networks to predict business events acquisition, and social network analysis to "realize the magnitude of impact and influence of particular customers over others". He suggests that this combination of models can help companies establish effective processes for determining customer loyalty and bundle adoption. Some other techniques can also be used to develop predictive models, such as decision trees and regressions. All of the mentioned models have proved to achieve good results, and their use depends solely on the type and format of the collected data. Regarding the type of data, SNA also differs from other analytical models in that it requires data about observations, as well as data that describe the relationship among these observations. In other words, analyzing data about connections among the nodes in the network helps us learn not only about customer's behavior but also about customers' relationship behaviors (Pinheiro, 2011). It is these sorts of data that differentiate network data from the other models' data: data about links reveal important attributes about the network and the data about the nodes tell us a lot about the importance of the nodes in the networks and as such provide overall analysis of customers. The major difference between conventional and network data is that "conventional data focus on observations and attributes, whereas network data focus on observations and relations" (Pinheiro, 2011). However, as mentioned earlier, business events like churn and bundle acquisition are chain processes, and should be approached from a chain perspective to be able to assess the impact and the correlation among those business events inside the database. In such cases a specific model should be used and adjusted to specific needs of the event analysis. Social network analysis is the best approach to the perspective of a chain process, although combining SNA with traditional models should give optimal results in predictive modeling and analyzing customer behavior. "Also, some simple approaches, such as average billing or type of products and plans," Pinheiro (2011) suggests "can be used to categorize customers into distinct segments. The prediction score assigned to the client's segment can be a good way to define and perform distinct actions for customer retention, thereby decreasing the costs related to loyalty campaigns." To sum it up, Pinheiro proposes a different sort of statistical approach based on data mining techniques to be applied for analyzing various patterns of behavior for a particular social network. If we use temporal analysis that observes networks over time, predictive techniques such as regression, decision tree, and artificial neural networks can be implemented for defining possible scenarios of evolution for the social network. According to Pinheiro there are several ways to establish customer value - based on average billing, revenue, usage, or even behavior. He, thus, proposes that this type of customer value be determined by clustering models or even by simple statistical processes.

For example, we calculate client influence by using SNA methodology, client probability by predictive data mining models and score (value of client) by fuzzy expert systems. As mentioned in previous chapters, fuzzy expert systems are used in knowledge discovery processes for classification, segmentation and scoring purposes with main focus on expert knowledge which is implemented into models. Results which are provided from those models are mostly first step for more complex analysis and for usage in combination with other knowledge discovery techniques. Very often the profitability of client (in advanced systems observed as score) and client probability of churn have been taken as key parameters of the imperative of targeting clients in preventing and controlling churn. However, by introducing the third axis shown in the figure (client influence) it becomes quite clear that some clients will have to be kept although they have low score values (i.e. they are not profitable). These are the clients who have a large influence measure. On the other hand, we are well aware of the fact that marketing campaigns have restricted resources, but also aim at maximum efficiency. It means that they need to be as accurate in their campaigns as possible. Now, who are we going to target in a specific subset of clients if all of them have an equal scoring value (e.g. highly profitable), and we do not have enough resources to target all of them equally? We shall target leaders, i.e. clients with the largest influence. Or, what if the leader churns and there is a real danger that he will drag his followers along? We have to target those followers and prevent them from churning, but as we have already said, we do not have enough money to keep them all. Nevertheless, we would like to keep our customers and hopefully halt the diffusion of the "bad vibe" caused, for example, by an unsatisfied customer (leader) who has just churned.

Figure 1. Graphical abstract/flowchart for early warning system framework based on structured analytical techniques, SNA and fuzzy expert system

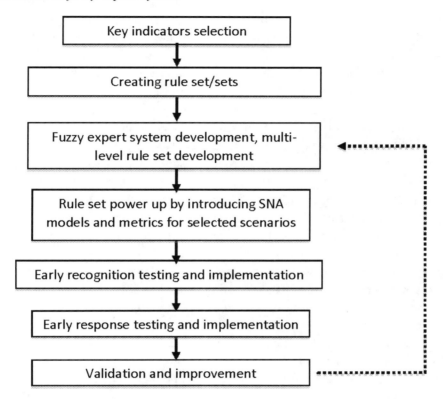

In line with this, the basic question is: Whom of his followers shall we primarily try to keep? The answer is: The gatekeeper entity, i.e., the client with the highest betweenness score. If we manage to keep this person and make him/her happy, we shall be able to prevent the diffusion of the "bad vibe", and hopefully stimulate the diffusion of the "good vibe". Additionally, integrated data mining and SNA approach should be observed as a two-way model. It means that, for example, SNA metrics of each node (calculated by SNA methodology) could and should be used as an intensifier of predictive data mining models. On the other hand, results of classification and segmentation of data mining models, for example, can be used as additional attributes on the node or edge levels in SNA methodology.

This sort of approach can lead companies to significant changes in terms of marketing and sales. It can certainly achieve a synergy effect as its overall result will be significantly better than any other individual result.

EARLY WARNING SYSTEM FRAMEWORK PROPOSAL FOR PORTFOLIO MANAGEMENT WITH ELEMENTS OF AI

Main purpose of the early warning systems is early recognition of deviant trends. Traditional approach, which leans on predictive models as a base for early warning system, could be insufficient. Main reason for that lays in fact that predictive model contains few most predictive attributes as integral part of predictive models. Reasons why they make predictive model imply fact that those attributes show highest impact on aim variable. That impact by traditional methodology is measured using attribute relevance analysis.

Recognition of most important factors with low occurrence and high impact on target attribute is something which can contribute to prevention of bad trends within portfolio.

Even it is not recognised as frequent valuable for machine learning integration, that events bring a lot of potential.

Criteria for highest impact on aim variable is statistical significance, and those fact hides pitfall, because if some trend became so obvious that it has statistical significance it is doubtful is it appropriate for early warning sign. That means that some deviant trend has happened during longest period of time and it makes statistically significant data pattern recognisable thought attribute relevance analysis. If some trend or event happens longer period of time, main question is it valuable subject for early warning systems. For predictive modelling those methodology is good enough, but for early warning system it is not sufficient. Basic idea of early warning system as a system which is capable for recognising negative trends in early stage is in collision with methodology of traditional predictive modelling, because of mentioned problems. It does not mean that predictive models should not be used for modelling early warning systems; it only means that predictive models should not be only element or base for early warning system. Early warning systems should not depend on attribute significance on aim variable, because early attribute insignificance in the light of early warning systems does not mean that it will not became significant in some near future. Sometimes some trends can remain unrevealed because it is insignificant on whole portfolio level, but it can have great influence on some part of portfolio and can generate high costs or other negative trends. Another important topic is aim variable construction in case when we are developing early warning system as a predictive model.

Solution is aimed on hybrid approach where elements of AI are incorporated as linguistic variables into fuzzy expert system. That means inclusion of previously trained models into final solution. On that way potential of fuzzy logic which are mainly focused on disruptive events will be extended with probability calculation which include long term experience incorporation into such models.

Adoption of AI are relatively slow in portfolio management because changes in portfolio management are not immediately visible in AI models in short periods of time. Reason for that is AI methodology usage where long observation periods should be used for model training. That approach is problematic in situation of disruptive events in portfolio. To be more efficient, hybrid approach which unite integration of AI methods into expert system are much suitable.

Key Indicators Selection and Model Development

Successful interviewing of users is one of the crucial factors, which leads us to solution. Interviews could be done on classical way or by usage of structured analytical techniques. Based on the interviews, we obtain a clearer picture of the users' perception of a problem we want to solve, i.e. in this case to model it using the fuzzy expert systems (Klepac, 2010). The primary goal of the structural analytic techniques usage was to define key indicators and basic categories as structural elements of a fuzzy expert system. The categories consist of more abstract notions defined using the key indicators. For example, key indicators are sales revenue, campaign costs, duration of business relationship. Based on these key indicators, a category of profitability is defined and limited with a set of rules (Klepac, 2014). For example, client riskiness, client loyalty, client outlook should be defined using key indicators, developed on the grounds of available databases. These indicators are input parameters for a fuzzy expert system model. Indicators should be firstly recognised through structural analytic techniques, and after their recognition ETL process from databases should be developed.

When we are talking about portfolio management it is important to recognise factors which are in strong correlation with observed event like churn and which are potentially rare and unrecognizable for classical attribute relevance analysis.

Also, auxiliary attributes like derived indexes (stability index, satisfaction index) can contribute in better understanding of customer sate within portfolio.

Illustrative definition of two key indicators for early warning systems in domain of churn detection is sown in following table.

Table 1. Key indicators definition

User outlook
Frequency of purchasing within the last six months (number of visits)
Response to campaigns aimed at loyalty card holders within last six months
Number of points on the loyalty card
Loyalty
Purchasing trends within the last two quarters
Tendency of purchasing new brands in the store within the last year
Cross selling trends within the last two quarters
Shift in habits
Stability index for monthly shop visit
Stability index for monthly purchase

In most cases, it is necessary to deduce the defined key indicators serving as an entrance to the fuzzy expert system model on the basis of the available data, because they do not exist in the transactional database in a form defined as entry into a fuzzy expert system. Recognised key indicators became base for ETL algorithm definition. It should be clearly defined and understandable to ETL developers. Key indicators could contain results from predictive models like logistic regression, neural network, and decision trees incorporated into linguistic variable. Social analysis network metrics could also be expressed through linguistic variables. On that way, early warning system relays not only on pure expert knowledge, but also on calculated values from databases. Integration of indexes contribute to overall evaluation of customer behaviour habits and shows direction of portfolio movement. Also, it can be used like input variables for segmentation principle to recognise segments with high intention for changes and to recognise reason for such trends. Most important thing is that those values give insight into new dimension. It means that for example, by social network metrics and combination of predictive model within fuzzy rule block we could measure information about probability for committing car accident in combination with connected person in process of damage appraisal. Rules within fuzzy expert system could show that there are connected persons related to insurance company business, which are involved in suspicious activities.

After defining the key indicators and the categories and subcategories using structured analytical techniques, the basis of a fuzzy scoring model was defined. The key indicators in the model comprise the input variables for rule blocks. Each rules block estimates the output value of a category based on the defined rules. Output category values enter the block of rules for final early warning status, where the final scoring is estimated on the basis of a defined set of rules. The expert team defined a number of fuzzy classes for each key indicator, as well as their titles and ranges. The key indicators should be defined in such a manner as were the ranges of output variables in the model and became the basic elements for forming the rules. One common error present during the implementation of the scoring system using fuzzy expert systems is neglecting the role of the number of indicators describing a category and number of fuzzy classes defined by the expert team. The same happened during the development of such a system in the mentioned company. During the early phases of system development, in the interviewing process, the expert team often emphasized the importance of a large number of indicators for describing a certain category. The consultant played a key role here, since he had to limit the expert team to define a maximum of four or five key indicators best describing a category. Otherwise, a combinatory explosion of a number of rules may occur. The following formula is used for the prediction of total number of rules in a system (Klepac, 2010):

$$p_j = \prod_{i=1}^{n} r_i \quad , \text{n} > 1$$

where p_j denotes a number of rules in block j, and is calculated as a product of a number of fuzzy categories of each i-th key indicator r. Based on that, the total number of rules in a system is calculated using the following formula:

$$P = \sum_{j=1}^{m} p_j$$

where P denotes a total number of rules in a system, calculated as a sum of number of rules in all rules blocks of the system. The following table illustrates the relation of number of rules in a block, with four key indicators and different number of fuzzy categories defined within the key indicators.

Table 2. Rule number growth example

Number of fuzzy categories of the first key indicator	Number of fuzzy categories of the second key indicator	Number of fuzzy categories of the third key indicator	Number of fuzzy categories of the fourth key indicator	Number of rules in a block
3	3	3	3	81
3	4	4	4	192
4	4	4	4	256

Table 3. Global portfolio view based on early warning system (based on hypothetic retailer data)

Highest abstraction level	Abstraction level 1 signals/key indicators	Abstraction level 2 signals/key indicators	Abstraction level 3 signals/key indicators	Abstraction level 4 signals/key indicators
Portfolio level Red 2% Yellow 4% Green 94%	**Riskiness** High-3% Medium -5% High- 92%	**Soft churn** High 12% Medium 2% Low 88%	**Customer activity** Bad 10% Moderate 20% Good 70%	**Buying trend in last 3 months vs. previous 3 months (in $)** Lower 10% Equal 60% Higher 30%
				Buying trend in last 3 months vs. previous 3 months Lower 10% Equal 60% Higher 30%
				Stability index on campaign acceptance in last 3 months Low 35% Medium 45% High 20%
			....	...
				...
				...
			...	...
				...
				...
		Estimated hard churn (in retail) Certain 1% Possible 2% No 97%	...	...
				...
				...
			...	...
				...
				...
		Net promoter score High 18% Medium 2% Low 80%	...	...
				...
				...
			...	...
				...
				...
			...	...
				...
				...
	...	... ...	...	...
				...
				...
		... ...	...	...
				...
				...
		... ...	...	...
				...
				...

In the table, we can observe a tendency towards growth in the number of rules in rule blocks with the increase in number of fuzzy categories. In addition to that, we can observe that the increase in number of rules is also influenced by the increase in number of key indicators. The control of the total number of rules in a fuzzy expert system may be exercised through reduction of the number of key indicators or reduction of the number of fuzzy categories within key indicators.

Main task of developed early warning system is not only to diagnose specific subject which has potentially risky characteristic based on gathered knowledge. Early warning systems have wider scope. Except targeting individual observed subject, early warning systems also should be portfolio management tool. It means that it can provide a view on global level.

As it is evident, consolidated results on portfolio level, after fuzzy expert system usage gives insight into portfolio current state from perspective of potential problems. Key indicators are structured within one table which could be representation of whole early warning system with real figures extracted by fuzzy expert system. In this hypothetic example it is evident that presented hypothetic company does not have in general serious problems from perspective of portfolio state. Problems became more obvious if we decompose category riskiness, where is obvious that customer dissatisfaction is not something which company should neglect. Customer dissatisfaction signal – rare one with high impact could be constructed for example from signals like: ratio between claims and all calls into call center, number of complaints about service/product /legal aspect of product service usage etc.

Example shows situation where we unite traditional key performance indicators along with index movement on specific features for getting complete picture about portfolio /user state.

Even, looking from portfolio perspective there is no problems, taking in consider other key indicators/signals it should be investigated, because it can be trigger for future problems. Another important feature of such constructed early warning systems is possibility to observe trends during period of time on whole portfolio level, as well as on key indicator/signal level. It gives new functionality and power to decision makers, because this approach has two mayor functions. First function is diagnostic trend tool on each signal level, which means that we can measure did for example loyalty has falling trend in portfolio in last 6 months, and what is more important, which is key driven factor that loyalty has falling trend in portfolio in last 6 months. Is it decreasing trend of shopping behavior, or low interest in previous campaigns or something else. Knowledge about that leads us to solution, because if it is low interest in previous campaigns, we can make hypothesis about inadequate campaigns for existing customer segments. Second function is monitoring on effect caused by decision making. Taking in consider previously described hypothetical situation, where company realize that it has inadequate campaigns for existing customer segments, business decision could be aimed on campaign adoption to adequate customer segments. Previously hypothesis about inadequate campaigns for existing customer segments should be proved. With additional analytics campaigns could be adopted to specific customer segments, and through developed system company could monitor effect of that business decision. In case that hypothesis and problem solution has been right, loyalty indicator should show rising or at least unchanged trend in portfolio in further months, as a reflection of highest interest on current campaigns. It is also possible that loyalty indicator shows falling trend. In that case that means that company made wrong hypothesis, or it is caused by other indicator which was not problematic in previous time. Precise answer on question did we make good decision is monitoring of key indicator interest in campaigns. From this perspective, early warning systems based on fuzzy expert systems could be used as toll for portfolio management and strategic planning. That leads us to the fact that early warning systems based on fuzzy expert systems became proactive tool, and it is not only passive system for recognition of problematic cases. Key factor for success is adequate key indicator selection, as well as good definition of the rules within fuzzy rule blocks.

FUTURE RESEARCH

Fuzzy expert system as a base for early warning systems has potential to recognize early warning sign much earlier than predictive models because it makes conclusion through expert rules integrated within system. Next step in research would be applying oversampling techniques for low occurrence events to integrate such machine learning model into fuzzy models to give more impact on rare events which contribute to prediction. It does not mean that it will replace approach where fuzzy models brings main solution, it will contribute to better accuracy. Also, data mining predictive models are also incorporated within it for detection and evaluation probabilities of e.g. fraud, churn and payment deviancy. As a single probability evaluation, it provides information based on collected significant data sample and most frequent profiles for each profile company has general picture e.g. who are typical churner based on model development and patterns based on model development. Those models are inappropriate for usage as an early warning system because it is torpid. In combination with fuzzy expert systems it is possible to recognize negative signals in very early stage. Social network analysis metrics gives opportunity to see potential negative trends even earlier. For example, if we are observing churn, predictive models give an evaluation of probability that somebody will commit churn in next six months, based on learning experience (patterns) on last six or twelve months. It does not have power to recognize some appearances like decrease in buying budget in comparison with last three-month average, or less frequent usage of service than in previous three/six months. Those influences could remain uncovered if ones do not have significant statistical impact on churn flag. On the other hand, mentioned appearances could have strong impact on future churn in long term period and on individual level. It maybe could not be recognized as statistically significant but experts are aware that it could have influence in long term period. This fact leads us to conclusion that early warning systems based on fuzzy expert systems gives useful and efficient spyglass to company. Synergy of expert rules and probability evaluation gives new dimension and quality to early warning systems. Let assume that potential churner in telecommunication company is great influencer and that lead us to conclusion that if he or she will commit churn most of his/her follower will do the same. With social network analysis incorporated within such early warning systems those systems give much stronger tool, using which is possible to see who would commit churn in future. It is possible to recognize those subjects, because if early warning system recognizes stagnation in product usage without committing churn yet, with survival analysis we can e.g. evaluate that those users could commit churn for seven months, or even earlier if churn probability is high. Regarding that fact that observed user are influencer will cause fact that it will have influence on his follower and survival analysis can show average time for committing churn of for months. Further research should be concentrated on integration of more variety methods and their impact on early warning systems, because fuzzy expert systems as a base have potentials to be central role of early warning system. Incorporation of additional techniques and their results within fuzzy expert systems as linguistic variable should improve their power and reliability.

CONCLUSION

Portfolio management is very complex task especially in complex business environment. Early warning systems contributes on early recognition of deviant and potentially dangerous trends related to specific industry/company business. There are numerous ways how to set up early warning system within industry. Often those solutions relay on single data mining method and it does not provide holistic and qualitative approach in environment of market uncertainty.

Proposed design has several advantages:

1. It takes in consideration rare events and attributes which mostly contribute to common business understanding which is in line with customer characteristics
2. It is robust and takes in consideration derived metrices like indexes which shows trends in customer behavior change which important when we are talking about fast reaction and portfolio defend against competition. That open us new horizons in better customer understanding.
3. Social network analysis metrics incorporated within described system gives new opportunities in analytical process if it is combined with the expert knowledge and output from the data mining models.
4. Proposed framework could be observed as an essential foundation for developing portfolio management system which contains early warning models for different industries like retail, telecommunications, finance, insurance and other.
5. Proposed system has role of periodically portfolio monitoring (monthly, quarterly, etc.). This can be foundation for decision support system and better observing performance of decision making

Once used, combination of different advanced analytic methods, provide robust and flexible way for creating and improving rule blocks. It is not only about classical machine learning approach, it is about holistic approach which equally observe frequent and not frequent events which have great impact on final output of events like churn fraud etc.

REFERENCES

I2 Group. (2010). *The Power of Social Network Analysis*. www.i2group.com

I2 Group. (2012). *i2 White Paper, Revealing Links*. IBM Software White Paper, i2 Analyst's Notebook.

Aguilar, F. J. (1967). *Scanning the Business Environment*. The Macmillian Company.

Al-Osaimy, M. H., & Bamakhramah, A. S. (2010). An Early Warning System for Islamic Banks. *J. KAU: Islamic Econ., 17*(1), 3-14.

Albala M. (2013). Triggering Business Model Innovation Programs Through Early Warning Systems. *Cognizant 20-20 Insight*.

Anacapa Sciences. (2003). *Criminal Intelligence Analysis: Development of Inferences" (1982-2003)*. Anacapa Sciences, Inc.

Ansoff, H. I. (1975). Managing Strategic Surprise by Response to Weak Signals. *California Management Review*, *18*(2), 21–33. doi:10.2307/41164635

Bernal, E., Castillo, O., Soria, J., & Valdez, F. (2017). Imperialist competitive algorithm with dynamic parameter adaptation using fuzzy logic applied to the optimization of mathematical functions. *Algorithms*, *10*(1), 18.

Bernhardt, D. (1999). Consumer versus producer: Overcoming the disconnect between management and competitive intelligence. *Competitive Intelligence Review*, *10*(1).

Caradonna, G., Lionetti, S., Tarantino, E., & Verdoscia, C. (2018). A comparison of low-poly algorithms for sharing 3D models on the web. In *New Advanced GNSS and 3D Spatial Techniques. LNGC* (pp. 237–244). Springer. doi:10.1007/978-3-319-56218-6_19

Cargata, P. J. (1999). *Business Early Warning Systems – A guide for managers, executives & investors*. Butterworths.

Cheang, N. (2009). *Early Warning System for Financial Crises, Research and Statistics Department*. Monetary Authority of Macao.

Comai A (2007). *Early warning systems for competitive your landscape*. ESADE Business School, SCIP 2007, University of Pompeu Fabra.

Daveis, J. L., & Gurr, T. R. (2010). *Preventive Measures: Building Risk Assessment*. Academic Press.

EUROPOL. (2002). *Strategic Intelligence Analysis Course*. Reading Material File No: 2520-47 Rev 1.

EWC. (2006). Developing Early Warning Systems: A Checklist. *EWC III Third International Conference on Early Warning, From concept to action*, Bonn, Germany.

Fazel Zarandi, M. H., & Abdolkarimzadeh, M. (2018). Fuzzy rule based expert system to diagnose chronic kidney disease. *AISC, 648*, 323–328. doi:10.1007/978-3-319-67137-6_37

Fleisher, C. S., & Bensoussan, B. E. (2003). *Why is analysis performed so poorly and what can be done about it?* Academic Press.

Fleisher, C. S., & Bensoussan, B. E. (2007). *Business and Competitive Analysis: Effective Application of New and Classic Methods*. Pearson Education, Inc.

Fleisher, C. S., & Blenkhorn, D. L. (Eds.), *(n.d.)*. *Controversies in Competitive Intelligence: The Enduring Issues*. Praeger Publishers.

Gilad, B. (2000). Industry Risk management: CI's next step. Competitive Intelligence Magazine, 4(3).

Gilad, B. (2003). Early Warning: Using Competitive Intelligence to Anticipate Market Shifts, Control Risk, and Create Powerful Strategies. AMACOM.

Gilad, B. (2004). *Early Warning*. AMACOM.

Gilbert, X. (2000). *From information to knowledge – How managers learn in Competing with Information*. Wiley.

Gilovich, T. (1991). *How We Know What Isn't So: The Fallibility of Human Reason in Everyday Life*. The Free Press.

Hanneman, R. A., & Riddle, M. (2005). *Introduction to Social Network Methods*. University of California.

Hedin, H., & Kovero, J. (2006). *Does Your Business Radar Work?* Early Warning / Opportunity Systems for Intelligence, GIA White Paper 1/2006.

Heuer, J. R. (1999). *The Psychology of Intelligence Analysis*. Center for the Study of Intelligence.

Heuer, R. J., & Pherson, R. H. (2010). *Structured Analytic Techniques for Intelligence Analysis*. Washington DC CW Press College.

Hunt, M. (1982). *The Universe Within*. Simon & Schuster.

Johnston, R. (2005). *Analytic Culture in the U. S. Intelligence Community*. The Center for the Study of Intelligence.

Jones, M. D. (1998). The Thinker's Toolkit: Fourteen Powerful Techniques for Problem Solving. Three Rivers Press.

Khalsa, S. (2004). *Forecasting Terrorism: Indicators and Proven Analytic Techniques*. Scarecrow Press, Inc.

Klepac, G. (2010). Preparing for New Competition in the Retail Industry. In A. Syvajarvi & J. Stenvall (Eds.), Data Mining in Public and Private Sectors: Organizational and Government Applications (pp. 245-266). Hershey, PA: Information Science Reference. doi:10.4018/978-1-60566-906-9.ch013

Klepac, G. (2013). Risk Evaluation in the Insurance Company Using REFII Model. In S. Dehuri, M. Patra, B. Misra, & A. Jagadev (Eds.), *Intelligent Techniques in Recommendation Systems: Contextual Advancements and New Methods* (pp. 84–104). Information Science Reference. doi:10.4018/978-1-4666-2542-6.ch005

Klepac, G. (2014). Data Mining Models as a Tool for Churn Reduction and Custom Product Development in Telecommunication Industries. In P. Vasant (Ed.), *Handbook of Research on Novel Soft Computing Intelligent Algorithms: Theory and Practical Applications* (pp. 511–537). Information Science Reference. doi:10.4018/978-1-4666-4450-2.ch017

Klepac, G. (2014). Data Mining Models as a Tool for Churn Reduction and Custom Product Development in Telecommunication Industries. In P. Vasant (Ed.), Handbook of Research on Novel Soft Computing Intelligent Algorithms: Theory and Practical Applications (pp. 511-537). Hershey, PA: Information Science Reference. doi:10.4018/978-1-4666-4450-2.ch017

Kopal, R., Korkut, D., & Knežević, H. (2009). *Primjena analitičkih tehnika u poslovnim istraživanjima*. Zbornik Visoke poslovne škole Libertas, Zagreb, godina II.

Kopal, R. & Korkut, D. (2011) *Kompetitivna analiza 2 – strukturirane i kreativne analitičke tehnike.* Zagreb: Comminus d.o.o. & Visoko učilište Effectus.

Kouchaksaraei, H. R., & Karl, H. (2018). Joint orchestration of cloud-based microservices and virtual network functions. *Future Generation Computer Systems*, *78*, 1–2.

Lavoix, H. (2008). *Developing an early warning system for crises*. Academic Press.

Li, L., & Goodchild, M. F. (2010). The Role of Social Networks in Emergency Management: A Research Agenda. *International Journal of Information Systems for Crisis Response and Management, 2*(4), 48–58. doi:10.4018/jiscrm.2010100104

Lombardo, R. (2011). Data Mining and Explorative Multivariate Data Analysis for Customer Satisfaction Study. In A. Koyuncugil & N. Ozgulbas (Eds.), *Surveillance Technologies and Early Warning Systems: Data Mining Applications for Risk Detection* (pp. 243–266). Information Science Reference. doi:10.4018/978-1-61692-865-0.ch013

Meissen, U., & Voisard, A. (2010). *Current State and Solutions for Future Challenges in Early Warning Systems and Alerting Technologies,* published. In E. Asimakopoulou & N. Bessis (Eds.), *Advanced ICTs for Disaster Management and Threat Detection: Collaborative and Distributed Frameworks* (pp. 108–130). Information Science Reference. doi:10.4018/978-1-61520-987-3.ch008

Miller, G. A. (1959). The Magical Number Seven - Plus or Minus Two: Some Limits on Our Capacity for Processing Information. *Psychological Review, 63*(2), 81–97. doi:10.1037/h0043158 PMID:13310704

Mršić, L. (2014). Widely Applicable Multi-Variate Decision Support Model for Market Trend Analysis and Prediction with Case Study in Retail. In P. Vasant (Ed.), Handbook of Research on Novel Soft Computing Intelligent Algorithms: Theory and Practical Applications (pp. 989-1018). Hershey, PA: Information Science Reference. doi:10.4018/978-1-4666-4450-2.ch032

Nooy de, W., Mrvar, A., & Batagalj, V. (2008). Exploratory Social Network Analysis with Pajek. Cambridge University Press.

Osmanagić Bedenik, N. (2003). *Kriza kao šansa: kroz poslovnu krizu do poslovnog uspjeha*. Zagreb: Školska knjiga d.d.

Page, A. M. (1996). Providing effective early warning: Business Intelligence as a strategic control system. In The Art & Science of Business Intelligence Analysis. JAI Press.

Page, A. M. (1996). The Art & Science of Collection Management. In The Art & Science of Business Intelligence Analysis. JAI Press.

Pinheiro, C. A. R. (2011). *Social Network Analysis in Telecommunications*. John Wiley and Sons, Inc.

Porter, M. (1980). *Competitive Strategy*. Amacom.

Richter, Y., Yom-Tov, E., & Slonim, N. (2010). Predicting customer churn in mobile networks through analysis of social groups. *Proceedings of the SIAM International Conference on Data Mining*, 732-741.

Sawka, K. (2006). *Intelligence Ostriches and Eagles: Why Some Companies Soar at Competitive Intelligence and Why Others Just Don't Get It*. Paper presented at the International SCIP Conference, Orlando, FL.

Scott, J. (1991). *Social Network Analysis*. Sage.

Self, K. (2003). *Why do so many firms fail at competitive intelligence?* Academic Press.

Simon, H. A. (1957). *Models of Man: Social and Rational*. John Wiley and Sons, Inc.

Simon, T. (1967). *Administrative Behaviour*. Free Press.

Valdez, F., Melin, P., & Castillo, O. (2017). Comparative study of the use of fuzzy logic in improving particle swarm optimization variants for mathematical functions using co-evolution. *Appl. Soft Comput. J.*, *52*, 1070–1083.

Waidyanatha, N. (2010). Towards a typology of integrated functional early warning systems. *International Journal of Critical Infrastructures*, *6*(1), 31–51. Retrieved August 3, 2012, from. doi:10.1504/IJCIS.2010.029575

Wasserman, S., & Faust, K. (1994). *Social Network Analysis: Methods and Applications*. Cambridge University Press. doi:10.1017/CBO9780511815478

Wellman, B., & Berkowitz, S. D. (Eds.). (1988). *Social Structures: A Network Approach*. Cambridge University Press.

Wheaton, K. J. (2001). *The Warning Solution – Intelligent analysis in the age of information overload*. AFCEA.

Wilensky, H. (1969). *Organizational Intelligence*. Basic Books.

Xing, B., & Gao, W. (2014). Post-Disassembly Part-Machine Clustering Using Artificial Neural Networks and Ant Colony Systems. In *Computational Intelligence in Remanufacturing* (pp. 135–150). Information Science Reference., doi:10.4018/978-1-4666-4908-8.ch008

ADDITIONAL READING

Cebi, S., Kahraman, C., & Kaya, I. (2012). Soft Computing and Computational Intelligent Techniques in the Evaluation of Emerging Energy Technologies. In P. Vasant, N. Barsoum, & J. Webb (Eds.), *Innovation in Power, Control, and Optimization: Emerging Energy Technologies* (pp. 164–197). Engineering Science Reference. doi:10.4018/978-1-61350-138-2.ch005

Dieu, V. N., & Ongsakul, W. (2012). Hopfield Lagrange Network for Economic Load Dispatch. In P. Vasant, N. Barsoum, & J. Webb (Eds.), *Innovation in Power, Control, and Optimization: Emerging Energy Technologies* (pp. 57–94). Engineering Science Reference. doi:10.4018/978-1-61350-138-2.ch002

Dostál, P. (2013). The Use of Soft Computing for Optimization in Business, Economics, and Finance. In P. Vasant (Ed.), *Meta-Heuristics Optimization Algorithms in Engineering, Business, Economics, and Finance* (pp. 41–86). Information Science Reference. doi:10.4018/978-1-4666-2086-5.ch002

Klepac, G. (2013). Risk Evaluation in the Insurance Company Using REFII Model. In S. Dehuri, M. Patra, B. Misra, & A. Jagadev (Eds.), *Intelligent Techniques in Recommendation Systems: Contextual Advancements and New Methods* (pp. 84–104). Information Science Reference. doi:10.4018/978-1-4666-2542-6.ch005

Klepac, G. (2014). Data Mining Models as a Tool for Churn Reduction and Custom Product Development in Telecommunication Industries. In P. Vasant (Ed.), *Handbook of Research on Novel Soft Computing Intelligent Algorithms: Theory and Practical Applications* (pp. 511–537). Information Science Reference. doi:10.4018/978-1-4666-4450-2.ch017

Purnomo, H. D., & Wee, H. (2013). Soccer Game Optimization: An Innovative Integration of Evolutionary Algorithm and Swarm Intelligence Algorithm. In P. Vasant (Ed.), *Meta-Heuristics Optimization Algorithms in Engineering, Business, Economics, and Finance* (pp. 386–420). Information Science Reference. doi:10.4018/978-1-4666-2086-5.ch013

Scott, J. (2012). *Social Network Analysis*. SAGE Publications.

Vasant, P. (2010). Innovative Hybrid Genetic Algorithms and Line Search Method for Industrial Production Management. In M. Chis (Ed.), *Evolutionary Computation and Optimization Algorithms in Software Engineering: Applications and Techniques* (pp. 142–160). Information Science Reference. doi:10.4018/978-1-61520-809-8.ch008

Vasant, P. (2013). *Meta-Heuristics Optimization Algorithms in Engineering*. Business, Economics, and Finance. doi:10.4018/978-1-4666-2086-5

Vo, D. N., & Schegner, P. (2013). An Improved Particle Swarm Optimization for Optimal Power Flow. In P. Vasant (Ed.), *Meta-Heuristics Optimization Algorithms in Engineering, Business, Economics, and Finance* (pp. 1–40). Information Science Reference. doi:10.4018/978-1-4666-2086-5.ch001

KEY TERMS AND DEFINITIONS

Betweenness Centrality: Measure of a node's centrality in a network; it is equal to the number of shortest paths from all vertices to all others that pass through that node.

Data Mining: Discovering hidden useful knowledge in large amount of data (databases).

EWS: Early Warning Systems.

Fuzzy Expert System: Expert system based on fuzzy logic.

Fuzzy Logic: Logic which presumes possible membership to more than one category with degree of membership, and which is opposite to (exact) crisp logic.

SNA: Social network analysis.

Social Network Bridge: Individual, whose weak ties fill a structural hole, providing the only link between two individuals or clusters.

Social Network Centrality: Refers to a group of metrics that aim to quantify the "importance" or "influence" (in a variety of senses) of a particular node (or group) within a network.

Chapter 17
Hyperspectral/Multispectral Imaging Methods for Quality Control

Dhanushka Chamara Liyanage

(iD) https://orcid.org/0000-0003-4526-0837

Tallinn University of Technology, Estonia

Mart Tamre

Tallinn University of Technology, Estonia

Robert Hudjakov

Tallinn University of Technology, Estonia

ABSTRACT

Product quality assurance is a vital component in any manufacturing process. With the advancement of machine vision, the product quality inspection has been vastly improved. This couldn't be achieved with human inspection otherwise when it comes to consistency, accuracy, and the speed. The advance sensor technologies and image processing algorithms are ensuring the product and process quality in various industries including pharmaceutical manufacturing, food production, agriculture, and waste sorting. In contrast to the RGB imaging technology, multispectral and hyperspectral imaging technologies carry more information about the objects under inspection. With the help of both spectral and spatial information, it is possible to discriminate the quality indices of various products with higher accuracy than RGB imaging methods. This chapter discusses the state-of-the-art product quality inspection applications using hyperspectral imaging and multispectral imaging using modern machine learning and other statistical algorithms.

DOI: 10.4018/978-1-7998-8686-0.ch017

INTRODUCTION

According to Crosby, the quality of a product is defined as its conformity to the specification (Crosby, 1979). There are various processes employed in production environments to assure product compliance to its specifications. Visual product inspection is one of such methods used in production environments to assure the absence of defects in products. Mostly, the product quality inspection is done by human operators visually on factory floors. However, human inspection is unreliable as there are various factors affecting product quality determination. Different human operators may have different judgements in their product quality inspection due to work experience, conditions at the work environment, level of understanding of the product, psychological factors, fatigue, biological factors of the worker. Products with more than one type of defect take a longer time for visual inspection. When the acceptance criterion of defects changes, it complicates visual inspection. The human inspection has more downfalls with qualitative measurements as results for the qualitative measurements are varying and difficult to compare. Moreover, human perception can easily accept false positives (Kerkeni et al., 2016). As a result, human inspection is inconsistent, subjective, and slow.

FurthermoreMoreover, the visual inspection is incapable of determining physicochemical characteristics of the product, such as moisture content, presence of various microorganisms, texture, etc. The physicochemical characteristics estimations are vital to ensure the quality of different products such as pharmaceuticals, food, and beverages. There are various analytical methods used in production floors to estimate those physicochemical parameters of products.

The process control methods can be distinguished into four categories: in-line, on-line, at-line, and off-line methods. In-line methods are directly immersed into the process flow, while on-line methods use a bypass channel from the main process flow. The at-line methods analyse the samples next to the process flow by sample extraction and off-line methods process analysis separately from the process flow by withdrawing some samples (Boldrini et al., 2012). Even though some manufacturing processes can employ off-line quality evaluation methods by taking random samples, they are not suitable for quality critical production processes. The food and beverages manufacturing, pharmaceuticals manufacturing industries require a complete quality inspection prior to human consumption, requiring in-line quality checks. Again, in some cases, random sample testing is not suitable as it may destroy the product. In such cases, non-destructive in-line process control is a vital requirement in ensuring product quality.

Therefore, it is proved that the industry needs consistent, accurate, fast, cost-effective and in-line automated inspection methods to increase the effectiveness of visual inspection. With the recent developments in imaging and computer technology, machine vision solves most quality inspection and control needs in production environments.

Machine Vision for Quality Inspection and Control

A machine vision system combines image acquisition cameras, illumination sources, processing computers and analysing algorithms to produce accurate decisions to assure various visible characteristics of the products (Du & Sun, 2006). These systems are used to detect product defects, make visual measurements and check various product markings as part of the quality control process in various industries. Detection of scratches on the visible area of aerosol metal-can production, dimension check of mechanical parts in the automobile industry, identifying the electronic components' location and orientation, identifying the types of the components in electronics assembly lines are a few examples of machine vision-based quality inspection using RGB (Red, Green, Blue) and monochrome imaging cameras.

Even though machine vision based on RGB sensors solves a significant part of visual quality inspection problems, it has some drawbacks too. The RGB and monochrome vision systems can only detect the objects' colour and shape properties. It does not help industrial problems where product quality cannot be assured using colour, shape, detecting specific patterns or checking dimensions, i.e. meat freshness, quantitative determination of various chemical presence in fruits and vegetables. Moreover, the products like fruits and vegetables of the same kind and variety do not have the same shape and colour in all the items, making it more complex to analyse using RGB imaging methods. In order to cover those needs, there should be a method that can acquire more information than RGB sensors can do. Spectral imaging is an advanced imaging technology that captures spectral and spatial information of the product under inspection.

Spectral Imaging

Spectroscopy gives light absorption or reflectance characteristics of a point on the object under inspection (Wallace et al., 2009). The imaging spectroscopy or spectral imaging method combines spectroscopy and imaging, first introduced in the 1970s for remote sensing applications with the Landsat program (Wulder et al., 2019). The technology has evolved into other application domains such as agriculture, food, pharmaceuticals, etc. Over recent decades, steady development in spectral imaging technologies has been happening in image acquisition hardware, software, and analysis methods.

The computer vision-based inspection systems have advanced with the introduction of imaging sensors capable of seeing beyond the visible light range, which is 400 – 700 nm wavelength range in the electromagnetic spectrum. Now they can take advantage of ultraviolet (UV) and infrared (IR) regions of the electromagnetic spectrum for machine vision applications.

Unlike monochrome or RGB colour imaging methods, spectral imaging or imaging spectroscopy is a technology that acquires tens or hundreds of images in various contiguous wavelengths in the electromagnetic spectrum. In the monochrome imaging method, the image contains a single grayscale colour channel. In contrast, RGB colour images contain Red, Green and Blue as three separate channels within the visible light spectrum. Spectral imaging is classified into two categories according to the number of images bands contained in a spectral image cube. Multispectral Imaging (MSI) and Hyperspectral Imaging (HSI) are the two main branches. The difference between those two branches is that the multispectral image consists of tens of spectral bands, where the hyperspectral image contains hundreds of spectral bands. Below, Figure 1 illustrates the differences between each imaging technology.

Figure 1. Different imaging methods and their characteristics

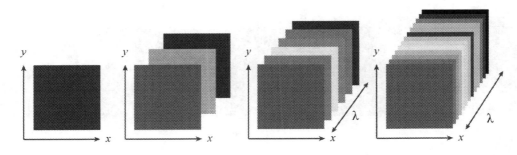

Imaging Method	Monochrome	RGB	Multispectral	Hyperspectral
Color Channels	1	3	3 - ~10	~10 - ~100
Information Depth	Spatial	Spatial	Spatial + spectral	Spatial + spectral

Due to their unique design in sensor construction, spectral imaging technology uses various image acquisition techniques to capture image data. These methods are whisk-broom, push-broom and tunable filter techniques, where each method is used in point-scanning, line-scanning and area-scanning, respectively (Iqbal et al., 2014). The point scan method, which is the whisk broom technique, can acquire spectral data of one pixel at a time. Hence, the whisk broom method scans the object in lateral (X) and longitude (Y) directions. With line scanning, the imaging sensor can acquire a wider strip of pixels. Therefore, it is needed to sweep the sensor across the object under inspection to record a complete image. Most hyperspectral imaging sensors are line scan sensors, as it is technically challenging to embed hundreds of light filters on top of neighbouring pixels to create an area scanning sensor. Area scan captures the image in either one wavelength or a few wavelengths simultaneously. Therefore the area-scan method is standard with multispectral sensors. In multispectral imaging, either a few light bandpass filters are deposited on top of the sensor or external filters use to capture the images in several wavelength bands. More about the construction of spectral imaging sensors and other relevant hardware is discussed in "Hyperspectral and multispectral imaging for evaluating safety and quality" journal article (Qin et al., 2013).

Together with different image acquisition methods, spectral imaging uses different electromagnetic wavelength ranges for machine vision applications. They are mainly Visible Near Infrared (VNIR), Short-Wave Infrared (SWIR), Medium-Wave InfraRed (MWIR) and Long-Wave Infrared (LWIR). The VNIR is in the 400 – 1000 nm wavelength range, SWIR spans 1000 – 2500 nm, MWIR spans 3 – 5 μm and LWIR spans 8 – 12 μm (Edmund Optics Inc, n.d.). Figure 2 illustrates the electromagnetic wavelength spectrum with all the above wavelength range classifications.

Figure 2. Electromagnetic spectrum

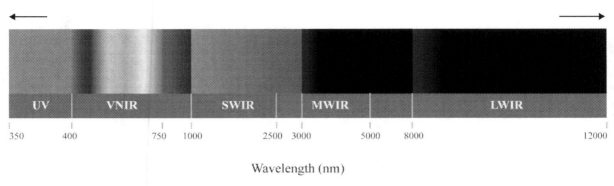

Wavelength (nm)

A Hyperspectral or multispectral image is a series of images captured at different wavelength bands in a continuous spectrum that forms an image data cube (Amigo, 2020). These datacubes are also called hypercubes. Spectral signatures of the subjects are the essential characteristics to extract from the hypercube. Every material, substance, or compound has unique spectral reflectance, transmittance characteristics which is the spectral signature of the same. Below Figure 3 shows an example of spectral reflectance characteristics or spectral signature of a plant leaf. With the help of hyperspectral signature, it has been possible to detect various infections, diseases to crops (Yuan et al., 2019), (ElMasry et al., 2012), and defects in vegetables and fruits (ElMasry et al., 2007), (ElMasry et al., 2008), (Xing et al., 2005). There has also been a considerable number of researches on the use of HSI for meat production industry for meat quality analysis (Qiao et al., 2007), (Elmasry, Barbin, et al., 2012), (Kamruzzaman et al., 2012). Waste sorting and recycling is also one of the research areas where HSI is used (Serranti et al., 2015).

Figure 3. The reflectance spectrum of one pixel is the spectral signature of the object in the pixel. X and Y are spatial dimensions, while lambda is the wavelength

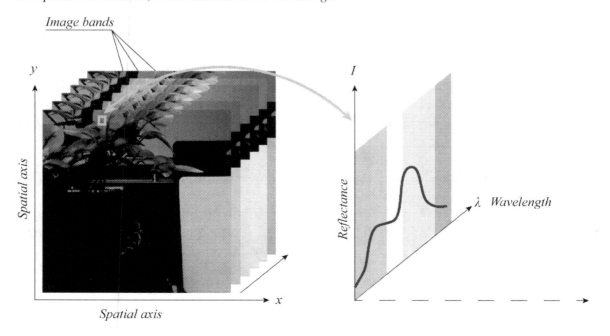

Hyperspectral Image Acquisition Hardware Set-Up

Typical hyperspectral imaging camera imaging acquisition follows push-broom technique as those cameras are mostly line scan cameras. Thus, it uses a linear or rotary motion mechanism for scanning the object under inspection. These systems use special lighting to illuminate the object depending on the wavelength range of the camera. The most suitable lighting option in the visible light (VNIR) range is incandescent lights (Zahavi et al., 2019). In HSI, the image acquisition control, storing and analysing are done by a computer in the same set-up. A typical set-up for hyperspectral imaging is shown in Figure 4. Unlike hyperspectral cameras, the simultaneous spatial and spectral data acquisition ability eliminates the need for a moving table. Therefore, multispectral cameras can grab images faster than hyperspectral counterparts.

Figure 4. A typical hyperspectral imaging system

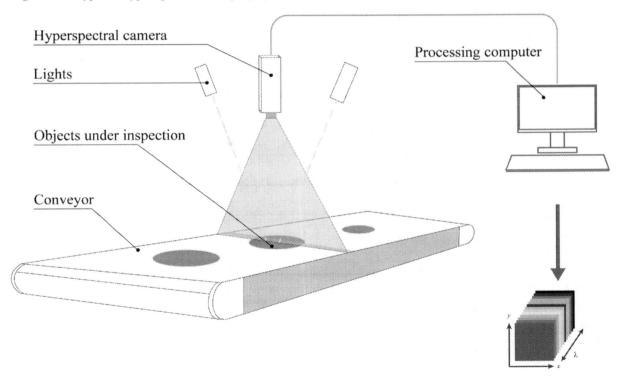

This chapter surveys product quality assessment methods based on HSI/MSI technologies in various industrial sectors. The article covers the research literature published in recent years related to quality assurance. Moreover, various image processing, analysis methods are presented as well.

INDUSTRIAL APPLICATIONS OF HYPERSPECTRAL / MULTISPECTRAL IMAGING METHODS FOR QUALITY EVALUATION

Hyperspectral and multispectral imaging methods have a wide range of applications in the food, agriculture, pharmaceuticals, material inspection and waste recycling industries. However, product quality inspection in the food and agriculture industry is the most dominant application area compared to other industrial sectors. In this section, the applications and analytical methods are discussed according to those industrial sectors.

Textile Industry

The textile industry finds various applications for hyperspectral imaging as it is possible to discriminate various textile materials and chemical coatings based on their spectral characteristics. Evaluations of several textile quality indices have been published by Mirschel et al., related to the application of various chemicals on textiles. One of their studies proposed a method to monitor the thickness and homogeneity of hot melt adhesive layers in the laminates made of black polyester textiles. The authors have used partial least squares regression (PLSR) for thickness estimation of the adhesive layer in the near-infrared (NIR) spectral range. The importance of this study is that the laminate adhesive layer covered by the top black textile layer and NIR wavelength range penetrates to a sufficient depth until the adhesive layer. This research revealed that it could estimate the thickness and homogeneity of the adhesive layer with sufficient precision to carry out process control. The proposed method showed the Root Mean Square Error of Prediction (RMSEP) 6 gm^{-2} (Mirschel et al., 2019). The same authors proposed a method to quantitatively estimate the application weight and homogeneity of finishing chemicals in textiles. In this study, the researchers have used the NIR wavelength range (1320 – 1900 nm). The chemical agents used in this research were colourless, which cannot be detected with machine vision methods in the visible light wavelength range. PLS model has been employed to determine the application weight, which yielded results with predicted precision of the chemical for a flame retardant RSMEP 2 gm^{-1} and stiffening agent with RMSEP 1,6 gm^{-1} (Mirschel et al., 2018) (Mirschel et al., 2017).

Another crucial task in the textile industry is Fibre fabric identification, which demands a fast, non-destructive method to identify the fibres. The classification of eight different such woven fabric fibres was achieved in the SWIR wavelength range. The k-nearest neighbour (kNN) method yielded 80% or more accuracy in classification for cotton, polyester, polyethene, wool, PVC, nylon and linen fabrics where Locally Preserving Projection (LPP) method used for band reduction (Li et al., 2019). Jin and others also proposed a method to discriminate synthetic fibres in textile production using NIR spectral range. This study covers six types of synthetic fibres such as polyethene, para-aramid, polypropylene, polyester, polyamide, acrylic fibres. The hyperspectral images were pre-processed before performing classification by averaging spectra pixels and applying the Savitzky-Golay filtering method. Pre-processed images of fabric samples were analysed using Principal Component Analysis – Linear Discriminant Analysis (PCA-LDA) model with discrimination accuracy of 100% (Jin et al., 2017). In contrast to the first research on fibre identification which uses a mix of natural and synthetic fibres, the second research was entirely based on synthetic fibres. Another remark is that the PCA-LDA method can achieve better classification accuracy over kNN for synthetic fibres.

Detection of foreign objects in products or contamination is an essential part of the manufacturing sector. In cotton production, there are possibilities to contaminate the cotton lint from various sources.

During the ginning process of cotton, the cotton seeds and other foreign objects filtered out. However, there can be some foreign matter that remains with the lint affecting the cotton quality. Detection of foreign matter in cotton using fluorescence hyperspectral imaging has been explored by Mustafic et al. They were using UV lights of 365 nm at the peak intensity, and the chosen wavelength range was 425 – 700 nm in visible light range. The authors have used 19 spectral bands for the classification, where the dimensionality reduction has been done with PCA. A 90% average classification rate has been achieved using linear discriminant analysis, and they claim that the method is suitable to detect foreign matter with a higher amount of fluorophores (Mustafic et al., 2016).

In waste sorting applications, the objective is to classify various materials into separate groups for recycling. For textile waste sorting, E. Herrala et al. researched the possibilities of using NIR hyperspectral imaging methods for various natural and synthetic textile materials sorting. The research showed successful classification of cotton, polyester, linen, wool materials. However, the mixed fabric materials with tiny amounts of natural or synthetic material content were difficult to classify (Herrala & Oy, 2020). Similarly, Makela and others proposed a method to determine the polyester content of man-made and natural cellulose and polyester blends. They have used Principal Component Analysis (PCA) for the identification of characteristic wavelengths, and the estimation of polyester content was achieved by using the PLSR method with a prediction error of 4.5% within a range of 0 -100% polyester (Mäkelä et al., 2020).

Below Table 1 summarises hyperspectral imaging-based quality indices evaluation methods in the textile industry.

Table 1. Textile quality parameters evaluation using hyperspectral imaging methods

Application	Spectral range	Methods	Reference
Polyester content estimation in natural and man-made cellulose and polyester blends	NIR	PCA, PLSR	(Mäkelä et al., 2020)
Fibre discrimination in woven fabrics		SWIR LPP, kNN	(Li et al., 2019)
Synthetic fibres discrimination	SWIR (900 – 2500 nm)	PCA-LDA	(Jin et al., 2017)
Adhesive layer thickness and homogeneity estimation of textile laminates	NIR	PLSR	(Mirschel et al., 2019)
Quantitative analysis of application weight s of chemical additives in textile production. (Flame retardants and stiffening agents)	NIR (1320 – 1900 nm)	PLS, PCA	(Mirschel et al., 2018), (Mirschel et al., 2017)
Detection of foreign matter in cotton	VIS (425 – 700 nm)	LDA	(Mustafic et al., 2016)

Impact of HSI in Food Production Quality Assurance

Most of the HSI and MSI based quality inspection efforts have been made into food and agriculture-related areas. In food quality assurance, it is essential to use non-destructive methods that need a thorough quality inspection for the entire production. However, the non-destructive tests are not that important for batch quality checking scenarios as it is only required to test a small sample randomly taken from a batch. In agriculture, in-situ monitoring of the plants is essential to minimise the risk of poor harvest caused by the poor nutrient in plants. Timely estimation of plant nutrients can significantly enhance the yield. Therefore, it is obvious the necessity of optical methods for quality assurance over any other methods.

Agriculture Industry

As most of the applications for spectral imaging can be found in the agricultural sector, a detailed description of the vital quality indices evaluation for each crop can provide a greater understanding of the uses of the technology.

Strawberry serves as one of the main ingredients for various food products, including cakes, jams, flavoured juices, milk products, etc. The internal quality attributes of strawberries which are moisture content (MC), total soluble solids (TSS), acidity estimation of strawberries, have been done using HSI methods. Visible Near Infrared (VNIR) wavelength range has been used for capturing the hyperspectral data cubes. The data cubes were pre-processed using mean centring and automatic baseline correction before using the Partial Least Squares (PLS) method for the analysis. The optimal wavelength bands have been selected using the highest absolute values of regression coefficients - β from the PLS model (ElMasry et al., 2007). Visual detection of bruises on Mcintosh apples is a difficult task for colour imaging methods. Mainly due to different background colours where imaging takes place and different ages of bruises. However, using the HSI method, the early detection (< 12 h) of apple bruises has been achieved using spectral imaging in the VNIR wavelength range. Three spectral bands in NIR region 750, 820, and 960 nm have been identified as the most influential spectral bands based on stepwise discrimination analysis along with VIP scores from the PLS method. With a limited number of spectral bands, it is possible to implement a multispectral imaging system to in-line monitoring of apple bruises on the field. The multilevel adaptive thresholding method proved that the apple bruises could be detected, from as new as 1hour to as old as 3days (ElMasry et al., 2008). Like those strawberry internal quality parameters evaluation, mango fruit internal quality parameters prediction has been experimented with using HSI. The selected quality parameters were firmness, total soluble solids, and titrable acidity. Even though the PLSR prediction model has been developed for VNIR spectral range imaging, excessive prediction errors in the PLSR model restricted its use only for early screening. As a result, the authors claim that titrable acidity and total soluble solids estimation need further improvements (Rungpichayapichet et al., 2017). An on-line quality assessment method for pomegranate fruits using the MSI system has been proposed by Khodabakhshian et al. to predict pH, total soluble solids, and titrable acidity. In this application, four significant wavelength bands were selected as 700, 800, 900, 1000 nm, and multiple linear regression models have been used to estimate the internal quality parameters (Khodabakhshian et al., 2017). Bruise detection or mechanical damage detection method for pickling cucumber has been proposed using HSI. In this research, the hyperspectral images were acquired within NIR / SWIR spectral range. The research suggests that the best wavelength range for mechanical damage detection lies within 950 - 1350 nm. Band ratio and band differences in selected wavelength bands were used as classification methods where 988, 1085 nm was used for the band ratio, and 1346 and 1425 nm were used for the band difference method. The results show that both methods achieved more than 80% classification accuracy (Ariana et al., 2006).

Crop growth status is an essential factor in industrial agriculture to reduce the risk of poor harvest. In rice cultivation, the nitrogen content estimation of the rice plant during the panicle initiation stage helps to calculate optimum nitrogen fertiliser requirement. Using VNIR hyperspectral imaging, Onoyama and others estimated the nitrogen content of rice plants in their panicle initiation stage. The reflectance intensities have been extracted using the difference of GreenNDVI-NDVI with three selected spectral bands in near-infrared, green and red bands at 845 nm, 564 nm and 668 nm, respectively. The nitrogen estimation models have been developed using the partial least squares regression method with 0.95 gm-2 of RMSE (Onoyama et al., 2013).

Food quality can deteriorate during its storage under different climate conditions. Freeze damages during storage of white button mushrooms before they are visually evident could be identified using HSI. Their research suggests that ice formation causes structural damage in mushrooms, which results in reflectance characteristics change. The research has been conducted within the 400 – 1000 nm wavelength range and was analysed using PCA and LDA methods. According to the authors, Gowen et al., the classification results yielded 97.9% accuracy of freeze damage detection (Aoife A. Gowen et al., 2009).

HSI has been used to detect mycotoxins and mycotoxigenic fungi in cereal grain sorting such as wheat, maise and barley. One such application is Deoxynivalenol (DON) detection in cereals. Since prolonged DON exposure can cause health hazards to humans and farm animals, it is vital to identify such mycotoxins. The most significant wavelength bands for this task were found in 750 – 1650 nm, the near-infrared wavelength range. Various studies have been conducted about DON detection using different analytical / classification methods such as PLSR, PLS-DA, SVM to determine the concentration. A comprehensive review of fungi assessment on cereals has been published by Femenias et al. (Femenias et al., 2020).

Dried vegetable quality inspection is possible with multispectral imaging, according to numerous studies. Primarily it has a large number of use cases in moisture content prediction. The real-time quality inspection is possible due to the limited number of wavelength bands used from multispectral imaging in the range of 675-975 nm with 25 bands. Prediction of moisture content and shrinkage ratio has been achieved using PLSR and LS-SVM in dried carrot slices with a coefficient of determination for the shrinkage ratio as 0.942 while 0.953 for the moisture content (Yu et al., 2020).

Tomato paste is a highly consumed vegetable product globally. The viscosity of tomato paste can vary according to Sucrose content, affecting the taste and negatively impacting the industry. An MSI based method for sucrose adulteration detection in tomato paste has been proposed by Liu et al. The research suggests PLSR, LS-SVM, BPNN models for quantitative and qualitative assessments within the wavelength range of 405 – 970 nm. Their study reveals LS-SVM model has achieved a 1% accuracy level in the quantitative estimation of adulterated sucrose content (Liu et al., 2017).

HSI and MSI have numerous applications in the agricultural sector for product quality assurance as it provides a non-destructive solution to the industry. Agriculture crops related quality parameters evaluation and the used methods are summarised in Table 2.

Table 2. Summary of agriculture crops/products quality parameters prediction using HSI

Product	Quality Indices	Wavelength Range	Analysis Methods	Reference
Strawberry	MC, TSS, Acidity	VNIR (400 – 1000 nm)	PLS	(ElMasry et al., 2007)
Rice	Nitrogen	VNIR (400 – 1000 nm)	PLSR	(Onoyama et al., 2013)
Apple	Bruise detection	VNIR (400 – 1000 nm)	Multilevel adaptive thresholding of selected bands	(ElMasry et al., 2008)
White button Mushrooms	Freeze damage detection	VNIR (400 – 1000 nm)	PCA, LDA	(Aoife A. Gowen et al., 2009)
Cereals (Wheat, Maise, Barley)	Mycotoxins detection	NIR		(Femenias et al., 2020)
Pickling cucumber	Bruise detection	NIR (900 – 1700 nm)	PCA, Band ratio, Band difference	(Ariana et al., 2006)
Dried carrot		VNIR (675-975 nm) Multispectral – 25 bands	PLSR and LS-SVM	(Yu et al., 2020)
Mango	Firmness, Total Soluble Solids (TSS), Titrable Acidity (TA)	VNIR (450-998 nm)	PLSR	(Rungpichayapichet et al., 2017)
Pomegranate fruits	Total Soluble Solids (TSS), Titrable Acidity (TA), pH	VNIR (400-1100 nm)	MLR	(Khodabakhshian et al., 2017)

Seafood Production

The quality evaluation in fish and other seafood is primarily about the consistency of the meat, visual aspects, and odour. An instrumental method for fish quality estimation is freshness based on chemical spoilage assessment caused by microbiological bacteria presence (Menesatti et al., 2010).

The moisture content is one of the quality parameters which determines prawns' taste, shelf life and price. Prawns are dehydrated to extend the shelf life. However, it is essential to maintain a certain amount of moisture within prawns as too high moisture can cause microorganism growth while too low moisture can destroy nutrition content. Dehydrated prawns' moisture content and distribution were determined in the spectral range of 380 – 1100 nm by Di Wu et al. The research suggests the Successive Projections Algorithm (SPA) as hyperspectral band selection algorithm, which selected 12 spectral bands for moisture determinations in the VNIR range (428 – 999 nm). The proposed MLR algorithm yielded a coefficient of determination of 0.962, proving the suitability of the method for moisture estimation (Wu et al., 2012).

The freshness and safety of fish are determined by quality parameters such as Thiobarbituric Acid Reactive Substances (TBARS), Total Volatile Basic Nitrogen (TVB_N) and total viable counts (TVC). These parameters prediction for rainbow trout fillets have been developed using multispectral imaging in the spectral range of 430- 1010 nm. The most significant six wavelength bands have been identified to predict the above quality indices. The prediction models have been developed using the PLSR method, and the best prediction results were achieved for TVC while TBARS prediction was poor (Khoshnoudi-Nia & Moosavi-Nasab, 2019a). The same authors have extended the research to optimise the method to conduct a quality evaluation using multispectral imaging for the additional parameters such as Psychrotrophic Plate Count (PPC) and sensory score. The authors have identified nine optimal spectral bands using a genetic algorithm for their proposed method (Khoshnoudi-Nia & Moosavi-Nasab, 2019b).

Fish product freshness assessment was conducted to find the possibilities to assess the freshness as storage of days for fresh and frozen-thawed cod fillets using HSI. The authors claim that their proposed VNIR hyperspectral imaging method can determine the storage duration of cod fillets on ice. They achieved a prediction accuracy of 1.6 days as the product storage duration on ice. Also, this method can be used as an on-line quality inspection technique as it can process one fillet per second (Sivertsen et al., 2011).

Meat Production

The quality of fresh meat largely depends on its water holding capacity. For beef water holding capacity, estimation has been investigated by using NIR hyperspectral imaging. In this research, six wavelengths were identified as crucial wavelengths for the PLS model, and they were 940, 997, 1144, 1214, 1342, and 1443 nm. The authors, ElMastry et al., have used PCA and PLS methods to quantify the water holding capacity, producing prediction accuracy with 0.87 as the coefficient of determination (ElMasry et al., 2011). Tenderness prediction of cooked beef has been proposed using VNIR (400 – 1000 nm) hyperspectral imaging method by Govindarajan et al. The proposed model predicts tenderness of cooked beef in three tenderness categories with 96.4% accuracy (Naganathan et al., 2008). The fresh beef quality indices prediction ElMasry, G et al. have proposed a PLSR model to predict colour, pH and tenderness in a separate study. This method has been done in the NIR wavelength range of 900 – 1700 nm (Elmasry, Sun, et al., 2012).

Pork quality evaluation in terms of colour, texture (firmness), and exudation (drip loss) characteristics have been carried out by Qiao. J et al. in the spectral range of 430 – 1000 nm. In the proposed method, they have used PCA for dimensionality reduction. Artificial Neural Networks (ANN) based classifier has been able to classify the samples by 85% with 10 PCs (Qiao et al., 2007). Water holding capacity estimation and tenderness sensing method of pork has been proposed using three wavebands using NIR multispectral imaging. The three wavebands used to estimate those parameters were 1280, 1440 and 1660 nm, where a backpropagation neural network has been used as an analytical model (Huang et al., 2015). Likewise, lamb meat quality evaluation for four different sheep breeds has been investigated by Kamruzzaman et al. using a NIR spectral imaging-based method. They have developed a prediction model for quality indices evaluations. Their approach aimed to estimate the lamb meat's pH, colour and drip loss (Kamruzzaman et al., 2012).

The bacterias such as Listeria monocytogenes growing in ready-to-eat meat and fish can be a severe health threat, especially for pregnant women, newborns, and adults with weak immune systems (Centre for Disease Prevention & Food Safety Authority, 2019). Some studies have used VNIR HSI methods for the rapid identification of bacteria. Several bacteria strains of Cronobacter, Salmonella, Escherichia Coli, Staphylococcus, and Listeria monocytogenes, have been analysed using PCA and K- Nearest Neighbor (k-NN) classification method. The Listeria was detected with 100% accuracy (Michael et al., 2019). A detailed review of microorganisms on food until 2017 was published by Wang et al. (K. Wang et al., 2018). Agglutination detection in fried minced meat during initial frying is important for ready-to-eat fast food production, and this has been investigated in minced beef and diced turkey. The proposed classification method is canonical discriminant analysis or Fisher's discriminant analysis. Also, the most informative spectral bands have been identified as 470, 700, 850 and 970nm for the classification (Daugaard et al., 2010).

The Aerobic Plate Count (APC) is considered a microbiological indicator for porks' sanitary quality and food safety. The APC count of cooked pork sausages has been investigated in VNIR spectral range using a multispectral camera with 19 bands. The primary wavelengths which are significant for APC detection have been identified within 570 – 850 nm. A PLSR model has been proposed to detect APC with a coefficient of determination of 0.89 (Ma et al., 2014). Multispectral imaging system for industrial-scale poultry quality assessment has been suggested for the microbial level, which can be used to obtain Total Viable Counts (TVC) and Pseudomonas spp. Chicken breast fillets, thigh fillets, marinated souvlaki and burgers were used in the experiments (Spyrelli et al., 2020).

Below Table 3 summarises the quality indices estimation and prediction methods proposed by various researchers on meat quality.

Table 3. Summary of meat quality parameters prediction using HSI

Product	Quality Indices	Wavelength Range	Analysis Methods	Reference
Fresh beef	pH, Tenderness, Color	NIR (900–1700 nm)	PLSR	(Elmasry, Sun, et al., 2012)
Cooked beef	Tenderness	VNIR (400–1000 nm)		(Naganathan et al., 2008)
Pork	Colour, Texture, Exudation	VNIR (430–1000 nm)		(Qiao et al., 2007)
Pork	Water holding capacity, Tenderness	1280 nm, 1440 nm and 1660 nm MSI	BPNN	(Huang et al., 2015)
Lamb	pH, Tenderness, Color	NIR (900 – 1700 nm)	PLSR	(Kamruzzaman et al., 2012)
Read-to-eat meat and fish	Listeria bacteria	VNIR (400 – 1000 nm)	k-NN	(Michael et al., 2019),
Ready-to-eat meat	Agglutination on minced meat frying	VNIR (430-970 nm) multispectral – 18 bands	FDA	(Daugaard et al., 2010)
Cooked pork sausages	Aerobic Plate Count	VNIR (400-970 nm) Multispectral – 19 bands		(Ma et al., 2014)
Poultry products	Total Viable Counts, Pseudomonas spp (microbial level assessment)	VNIR 18 bands (405 – 970 nm)	PLSR	(Spyrelli et al., 2020)

Beverage Production Industry

Hyperspectral imaging has been in use for foliar disease detection in tea plants which is known as anthracnose. The researchers have identified three spectral bands which are instrumental in detecting afore mentioned foliar disease as 542, 686 and 754 nm in the visible light wavelength range. Their classification method was based on unsupervised learning and adaptive two-dimensional thresholding. The results of the proposed method proved that they could detect the disease with 98% accuracy (Yuan et al., 2019). Mishra et al. suggest that near-infrared hyperspectral imaging could be used for green teas classification according to the country of origin. The study has been conducted wavelength range is 950 – 1760 nm. Even though there are some misclassifications, the authors suggest that the HSI and machine learning could achieve successful results for tea quality assessment (Mishra & Nordon, 2020). The amount of Free Amino Acids (FAA) indicates the freshness, taste and aroma of yellow tea. Yang et al. have used spectral image pre-processing and band selection to identify the most significant wavelength bands for FAA content detection in yellow tea. The pre-processing method was Savitzky-Golay filtering, while band selection was done using SPA. The authors have proposed a Genetic Algorithm-Support Vector Regression (GA_SVR) algorithm for predicting FAA with the selected five characteristic wavelength bands in the NIR region of the electromagnetic spectrum(Yang et al., 2019).

In dairy production, melamine is used to boost protein content which causes health problems. Therefore, a research group has investigated the detection of melamine concentration using HSI in milk powders using different approaches. One of their research methods used NIR spectral range HSI of 990 – 1700 nm. Their PLSR model was successfully used to evaluate melamine-milk samples of concentration 0.02% - 1% (Lim et al., 2016). For the other approach, they have employed spectral similarity analysis (Fu et al., 2014).

Pharmaceutical Industry

The pharmaceutical production process requires an in-line monitoring method for Active Pharmaceutical Ingredients (API) in micro tablets for quality assessment. The API could monitor within VNIR and SWIR wavelengths regions of the electromagnetic spectrum. The prediction model developed using the PLSR achieved a coefficient of determination of more than 0.90, suggesting that the proposed HSI-based rapid in-line quality inspection method is suitable for pharmaceutical production (Kandpal et al., 2016). In earlier research, Franch-Lage et al. have proposed a Multivariate Curve Resolution (MCR) technique for Lorazepam surface homogeneity assessment (Franch-Lage et al., 2011). Franch-Lage et al. suggested that the VNIR spectral range is sufficient for the pharmaceutical surface homogeneity inspection. Moreover, some researchers suggest that UV multispectral imaging could be used for pharmaceutical tablet coating defect identification (Klukkert et al., 2016).

Other Application Areas

Apart from the above applications, there are a few other areas where hyperspectral imaging is used for quality assurance. Confectionaries, food ingredients, various chemical coatings, and coated materials production are some of those applications.

The quality assessment of butter cookies based on surface browning and water content has been proposed by Andresen et al. using multispectral imaging. In this study, the authors found that surface browning can be detected within the visible light wavelength range while water content can be determined in the near-infrared spectrum. The authors have identified two wavelengths to determine the browning score of cookies as 395 and 525 nm. Moreover, the authors suggest that the NIR region is suitable for water content determination and evaluated using a PLSR model (Andresen et al., 2013).

The HSI could use of as a replacement for analytical methods to classify flavoured and unflavored olive oil. According to Romaniello et al.'s findings, the 400 – 570 nm and 695 nm spectral bands gives characteristic signatures for oils (Romaniello & Baiano, 2018).

Assessment of heavy metal contamination of water sources is usually done in laboratories. However, Rostom et al. suggest an HSI based method for heavy metal concentration estimation in water bodies such as Mn, Co, Cu, Cd, Pb, Ni, Cr, Fe, and Zn using a portable spectroradiometer. They have conducted their experiments in Mariut Lake in Egypt. Moreover, the authors have used Chlorophyll absorption wavelengths which are 450 nm and 675 nm, for the detection of algae. For heavy metal detection, they have proposed spectral bands ranging from 350 nm to 1200 nm. The authors have used Linear Regression Analysis for developing the heavy metal estimation model (Rostom et al., 2017). Wang et al. have used an airborne panchromatic-multispectral imaging system to detect pollutants on large water bodies. The work was focused on detecting aquatic vegetation, algae and other pollutants such as garbage, sewage, etc. (Z. Wang et al., 2019).

Photographic papers are coated with a light-sensitive chemical layer. A nine-band LED multispectral imaging method presented by Lalonde et al. suggests density measurements of colourants in photographic paper manufacturing is feasible (Lalonde et al., 2015). However, the authors claim their current results are inferior for certain photographic paper products, which could be improved by fine-tuning the inspection apparatus.

A coefficient independent scattering model could be used for coating thickness determination applications using VIS-NIR HSI. Dingemans et al.'s novel approach could measure coating of 250 μm with 11 μm accuracy according to the published results. In this study, the coating material was a semitransparent film-forming low-gloss wood lacquer for outdoor usage (Dingemans et al., 2017). Thickness estimation of thin aluminium oxide (Al2O3) layers on stainless steel foil was an example presented by Gruber et al. for HSI thin film imaging. The research has been conducted in VIS-NIR spectral range, where principal component regression (PCR) with a PLSR method has been used for layer thickness prediction. The alumina coating process is a part of single-wall carbon nanotubes (SW-CNT) production for battery applications (Gruber et al., 2016).

Polymer packaging materials hinder the quality inspection of food and pharmaceuticals. Even though they are transparent, the quality inspection can only be possible before packaging or after removing the packaging. The feasibility of HSI for packaged goods inspection and the influences of PVC and PET packaging for hyperspectral imaging have been published by Gowen et al. Their research confirms that combined with image and spectral processing of HSI data, it is possible to inspect packaged products (A. A. Gowen et al., 2010).

DISCUSSION

The literature survey was conducted by referring to the widely popular and high impact scientific research journals. The survey covered significant research publications during the past 15 years. However, this may not contain all the research articles published during the period. It is a prohibitively tedious task to cover all the articles published, and there are restrictions to access all the journals published worldwide. Figure 5 shows the distribution of the articles in this survey from each industrial sector from 2006 to 2020. The majority of the HSI based quality assessment has happened in food production during the above mentioned period.

Figure 5. Selected article from 2006 to2020 according to the industry

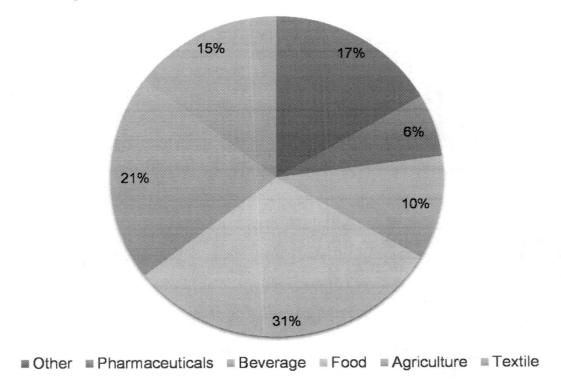

Quality assessment related publications from 2006 - 2020

■ Other ■ Pharmaceuticals ■ Beverage ■ Food ■ Agriculture ■ Textile

The number of publications is growing in hyperspectral imaging methods for quality assessment for the surveyed period. Even though early research literature related to the agriculture sector, the other industrial sectors find spectral imaging methods provide feasible solutions for quality evaluations. According to Figure 6, the food industry has a broader spread of research with spectral imaging. All the quality evaluation methods were conducted in VNIR, NIR or SWIR wavelength regions.

Figure 6. Number of publications per each year throughout the survey

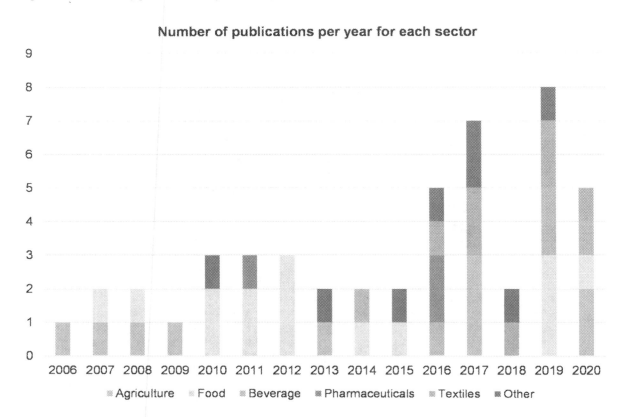

Number of publications per year for each sector

CONCLUSION

The objective of the chapter was to present an in-depth overview of the current developments in hyperspectral and multispectral imaging for product quality assessments. Spectral imaging is still an emerging technology, where novel processing methods, hardware and applications rapidly developing.

The article presented numerous examples of hyperspectral imaging use cases in agriculture, pharmaceutical production, the textile industry, etc. Some studies suggest that the product quality inspection could be feasible using hyperspectral imaging, even the goods are packaged using polymer materials. At the same time, research evidence shows that hyperspectral remote sensing technology is a suitable method to determine the water quality on large water bodies. Such examples prove that spectral imaging could perform machine inspection, which could not do otherwise.

The survey revealed that most spectral imaging inspection methods are conducted within visible and near-infrared wavelength regions.

As a non-destructive, fast, in-situ quality inspection method, spectral imaging could benefit many industries.

REFERENCES

Amigo, J. M. (2020). Hyperspectral and multispectral imaging: Setting the scene. *Data Handling in Science and Technology, 32,* 3–16. doi:10.1016/B978-0-444-63977-6.00001-8

Andresen, M. S., Dissing, B. S., & Løje, H. (2013). Quality assessment of butter cookies applying multispectral imaging. *Food Science & Nutrition, 1*(4), 315–323. doi:10.1002/fsn3.46 PMID:24804036

Araújo, M. C. U., Saldanha, T. C. B., Galvão, R. K. H., Yoneyama, T., Chame, H. C., & Visani, V. (2001). The successive projections algorithm for variable selection in spectroscopic multicomponent analysis. *Chemometrics and Intelligent Laboratory Systems, 57*(2), 65–73. doi:10.1016/S0169-7439(01)00119-8

Ariana, D. P., Lu, R., & Guyer, D. E. (2006). Near-infrared hyperspectral reflectance imaging for detection of bruises on pickling cucumbers. *Computers and Electronics in Agriculture, 53*(1), 60–70. doi:10.1016/j.compag.2006.04.001

Boldrini, B., Kessler, W., Rebner, K., & Kessler, R. (2012). Hyperspectral imaging: A review of best practice, performance and pitfalls for in-line and on-line applications. *Journal of Near Infrared Spectroscopy, 20*(5), 438. doi:10.1255/jnirs.1003

Centre for Disease Prevention & Food Safety Authority. (2019). Multi-country outbreak of Listeria monocytogenes sequence type 6 infections linked to ready-to-eatmeat products – November 25 2019. *EFSA Supporting Publications, 16*(12). doi:10.2903/sp.efsa.2019.EN-1745

Cheng, J. H., & Sun, D. W. (2014). Hyperspectral imaging as an effective tool for quality analysis and control of fish and other seafoods: Current research and potential applications. *Trends in Food Science & Technology, 37*(2), 78–91. doi:10.1016/j.tifs.2014.03.006

Crosby, P. (1979). *Quality Is Free: The Art of Making Quality Certain.* McGraw-Hill.

Daugaard, S. B., Adler-Nissen, J., & Carstensen, J. M. (2010). New vision technology for multidimensional quality monitoring of continuous frying of meat. *Food Control, 21*(5), 626–632. doi:10.1016/j.foodcont.2009.09.007

Dingemans, L. M., Papadakis, V. M., Liu, P., Adam, A. J. L., & Groves, R. M. (2017). Quantitative coating thickness determination using a coefficient-independent hyperspectral scattering model. *Journal of the European Optical Society. Rapid Publications, 13*(1), 40. Advance online publication. doi:10.118641476-017-0068-2

Du, C. J., & Sun, D. W. (2006). Learning techniques used in computer vision for food quality evaluation: A review. *Journal of Food Engineering, 72*(1), 39–55. doi:10.1016/j.jfoodeng.2004.11.017

Edmund Optics Inc. (n.d.). *What is SWIR?* Retrieved November 30, 2019, from https://www.edmundoptics.com/knowledge-center/application-notes/imaging/what-is-swir/

Elmasry, G., Barbin, D. F., Sun, D. W., & Allen, P. (2012). Meat Quality Evaluation by Hyperspectral Imaging Technique: An Overview. *Critical Reviews in Food Science and Nutrition, 52*(8), 689–711. doi:10.1080/10408398.2010.507908 PMID:22591341

ElMasry, G., Kamruzzaman, M., Sun, D. W., & Allen, P. (2012). Principles and Applications of Hyperspectral Imaging in Quality Evaluation of Agro-Food Products: A Review. *Critical Reviews in Food Science and Nutrition*, *52*(11), 999–1023. doi:10.1080/10408398.2010.543495 PMID:22823348

ElMasry, G., Sun, D. W., & Allen, P. (2011). Non-destructive determination of water-holding capacity in fresh beef by using NIR hyperspectral imaging. *Food Research International*, *44*(9), 2624–2633. doi:10.1016/j.foodres.2011.05.001

Elmasry, G., Sun, D. W., & Allen, P. (2012). Near-infrared hyperspectral imaging for predicting colour, pH and tenderness of fresh beef. *Journal of Food Engineering*, *110*(1), 127–140. doi:10.1016/j.jfoodeng.2011.11.028

ElMasry, G., Wang, N., ElSayed, A., & Ngadi, M. (2007). Hyperspectral imaging for non-destructive determination of some quality attributes for strawberry. *Journal of Food Engineering*, *81*(1), 98–107. doi:10.1016/j.jfoodeng.2006.10.016

ElMasry, G., Wang, N., Vigneault, C., Qiao, J., & ElSayed, A. (2008). Early detection of apple bruises on different background colors using hyperspectral imaging. *Lebensmittel-Wissenschaft + Technologie*, *41*(2), 337–345. doi:10.1016/j.lwt.2007.02.022

Femenias, A., Gatius, F., Ramos, A. J., Sanchis, V., & Marín, S. (2020). Use of hyperspectral imaging as a tool for Fusarium and deoxynivalenol risk management in cereals: A review. *Food Control*, *108*, 106819. doi:10.1016/j.foodcont.2019.106819

Franch-Lage, F., Amigo, J. M., Skibsted, E., Maspoch, S., & Coello, J. (2011). Fast assessment of the surface distribution of API and excipients in tablets using NIR-hyperspectral imaging. *International Journal of Pharmaceutics*, *411*(1–2), 27–35. doi:10.1016/j.ijpharm.2011.03.012 PMID:21419207

Gowen, A. A., O'Donnell, C. P., Esquerre, C., & Downey, G. (2010). Influence of polymer packaging films on hyperspectral imaging data in the visible-near-infrared (450-950 nm) wavelength range. *Applied Spectroscopy*, *64*(3), 304–312. doi:10.1366/000370210790918337 PMID:20223066

Gowen, A. A., Taghizadeh, M., & O'Donnell, C. P. (2009). Identification of mushrooms subjected to freeze damage using hyperspectral imaging. *Journal of Food Engineering*, *93*(1), 7–12. doi:10.1016/j.jfoodeng.2008.12.021

Gruber, F., Wollmann, P., Schumm, B., Grählert, W., & Kaskel, S. (2016). Quality control of slot-die coated aluminum oxide layers for battery applications using hyperspectral imaging. *Journal of Imaging*, *2*(2), 12. Advance online publication. doi:10.3390/jimaging2020012

Herrala, E., & Oy, S. I. (2020). *Textile identification and sorting using hyperspectral imaging*. Academic Press.

Huang, Q., Li, H., Zhao, J., Huang, G., & Chen, Q. (2015). Non-destructively sensing pork quality using near infrared multispectral imaging technique. *RSC Advances*, *5*(116), 95903–95910. doi:10.1039/C5RA18872E

Iqbal, A., Sun, D. W., & Allen, P. (2014). An overview on principle, techniques and application of hyperspectral imaging with special reference to ham quality evaluation and control. *Food Control, 46,* 242–254. Advance online publication. doi:10.1016/j.foodcont.2014.05.024

Jin, X., Memon, H., Tian, W., Yin, Q., Zhan, X., & Zhu, C. (2017). Spectral characterisation and discrimination of synthetic fibers with near-infrared hyperspectral imaging system. *Applied Optics, 56*(12), 3570. doi:10.1364/AO.56.003570 PMID:28430236

Kammies, T. L., Manley, M., Gouws, P. A., & Williams, P. J. (2016). Differentiation of foodborne bacteria using NIR hyperspectral imaging and multivariate data analysis. *Applied Microbiology and Biotechnology, 100*(21), 9305–9320. doi:10.100700253-016-7801-4 PMID:27624097

Kamruzzaman, M., ElMasry, G., Sun, D. W., & Allen, P. (2012). Prediction of some quality attributes of lamb meat using near-infrared hyperspectral imaging and multivariate analysis. *Analytica Chimica Acta, 714,* 57–67. doi:10.1016/j.aca.2011.11.037 PMID:22244137

Kandpal, L. M., Tewari, J., Gopinathan, N., Boulas, P., & Cho, B. K. (2016). In-process control assay of pharmaceutical microtablets using hyperspectral imaging coupled with multivariate analysis. *Analytical Chemistry, 88*(22), 11055–11061. doi:10.1021/acs.analchem.6b02969 PMID:27731983

Kerkeni, L., Ruano, P., Delgado, L. L., Picco, S., Villegas, L., Tonelli, F., . . . Masuelli, M. (2016). Understanding Color Image Processing by Machine Vision for Biological Materials. *Intech, 13.* Retrieved from https://www.intechopen.com/books/advanced-biometric-technologies/liveness-detection-in-biometrics

Khodabakhshian, R., Emadi, B., Khojastehpour, M., Golzarian, M. R., & Sazgarnia, A. (2017). Development of a multispectral imaging system for on-line quality assessment of pomegranate fruit. *International Journal of Food Properties, 20*(1), 107–118. doi:10.1080/10942912.2016.1144200

Khoshnoudi-Nia, S., & Moosavi-Nasab, M. (2019a). Non-destructive Determination of Microbial, Biochemical, and Chemical Changes in Rainbow Trout (Oncorhynchus mykiss) During Refrigerated Storage Using Hyperspectral Imaging Technique. *Food Analytical Methods, 12*(7), 1635–1647. doi:10.100712161-019-01494-8

Khoshnoudi-Nia, S., & Moosavi-Nasab, M. (2019b). Prediction of various freshness indicators in fish fillets by one multispectral imaging system. *Scientific Reports, 9*(1), 1–11. doi:10.103841598-019-51264-z PMID:31605023

Lalonde, M., Chapdelaine, C., Foucher, S., Team, I., Ave, O., & Qc, M. (2015). *Multispectral imaging: An application to density measurement in photographic paper manufacturing process control.* doi:10.1117/12.000000

Li, J., Meng, X., Wang, W., & Xin, B. (2019). A novel hyperspectral imaging and modeling method for the component identification of woven fabrics. *Textile Research Journal, 89*(18), 3752–3767. doi:10.1177/0040517518821907

Li, Q., He, X., Wang, Y., Liu, H., Xu, D., & Guo, F. (2013). Review of spectral imaging technology in biomedical engineering: Achievements and challenges. *Journal of Biomedical Optics, 18*(10), 100901. doi:10.1117/1.JBO.18.10.100901 PMID:24114019

Liang, F., Liu, H., Wang, X., & Liu, Y. (2018). Hyperspectral image recognition based on artificial neural network. *NeuroQuantology: An Interdisciplinary Journal of Neuroscience and Quantum Physics*, *16*(5), 699–705. doi:10.14704/nq.2018.16.5.1244

Lim, J., Kim, G., Mo, C., Kim, M. S., Chao, K., Qin, J., Fu, X., Baek, I., & Cho, B. K. (2016). Detection of melamine in milk powders using near-infrared hyperspectral imaging combined with regression coefficient of partial least square regression model. *Talanta*, *151*, 183–191. doi:10.1016/j.talanta.2016.01.035 PMID:26946026

Liu, C., Hao, G., Su, M., Chen, Y., & Zheng, L. (2017). Potential of multispectral imaging combined with chemometric methods for rapid detection of sucrose adulteration in tomato paste. *Journal of Food Engineering*, *215*, 78–83. doi:10.1016/j.jfoodeng.2017.07.026

Ma, F., Yao, J., Xie, T., Liu, C., Chen, W., Chen, C., & Zheng, L. (2014). Multispectral imaging for rapid and non-destructive determination of aerobic plate count (APC) in cooked pork sausages. *Food Research International*, *62*, 902–908. doi:10.1016/j.foodres.2014.05.010

Mair, P. (2018). *Principal Component Analysis and Extensions*. doi:10.1007/978-3-319-93177-7_6

Mäkelä, M., Rissanen, M., & Sixta, H. (2020). Machine vision estimates the polyester content in recyclable waste textiles. *Resources, Conservation and Recycling*, *161*(June), 105007. doi:10.1016/j.resconrec.2020.105007

Menesatti, P., Costa, C., & Aguzzi, J. (2010). Quality Evaluation of Fish by Hyperspectral Imaging. *Hyperspectral Imaging for Food Quality Analysis and Control*, 273–294. doi:10.1016/B978-0-12-374753-2.10008-5

Michael, M., Phebus, R. K., & Amamcharla, J. (2019). Hyperspectral imaging of common foodborne pathogens for rapid identification and differentiation. *Food Science & Nutrition*, *7*(8), 2716–2725. doi:10.1002/fsn3.1131 PMID:31428359

Mirschel, G., Daikos, O., & Scherzer, T. (2019). In-line monitoring of the thickness distribution of adhesive layers in black textile laminates by hyperspectral imaging. *Computers & Chemical Engineering*, *124*, 317–325. doi:10.1016/j.compchemeng.2019.01.015

Mirschel, G., Daikos, O., Scherzer, T., & Steckert, C. (2017). Near-infrared hyperspectral imaging of lamination and finishing processes in textile technology. *NIR News*, *28*(1), 20–25. doi:10.1177/0960336016687949

Mirschel, G., Daikos, O., Scherzer, T., & Steckert, C. (2018). Near-infrared chemical imaging used for in-line analysis of functional finishes on textiles. *Talanta*, *188*(February), 91–98. doi:10.1016/j.talanta.2018.05.050 PMID:30029452

Mishra, P., Asaari, M. S. M., Herrero-Langreo, A., Lohumi, S., Diezma, B., & Scheunders, P. (2017). Close range hyperspectral imaging of plants: A review. *Biosystems Engineering*, *164*, 49–67. doi:10.1016/j.biosystemseng.2017.09.009

Mishra, P., & Nordon, A. (2020). Classifying green teas with near infrared hyperspectral imaging. *NIR News*, *31*(1–2), 20–23. doi:10.1177/0960336019889321

Mustafic, A., Jiang, Y., & Li, C. (2016). Cotton contamination detection and classification using hyperspectral fluorescence imaging. *Textile Research Journal, 86*(15), 1574–1584. doi:10.1177/0040517515590416

Naganathan, G. K., Grimes, L. M., Subbiah, J., Calkins, C. R., Samal, A., & Meyer, G. E. (2008). Visible/near-infrared hyperspectral imaging for beef tenderness prediction. *Computers and Electronics in Agriculture, 64*(2), 225–233. doi:10.1016/j.compag.2008.05.020

Neath, R. C., & Johnson, M. S. (2010). Discrimination and classification. International Encyclopedia of Education, 135–141. doi:10.1016/B978-0-08-044894-7.01312-9

Onoyama, H., Ryu, C., Suguri, M., & Iida, M. (2013). Potential of hyperspectral imaging for constructing a year-invariant model to estimate the nitrogen content of rice plants at the panicle initiation stage. In *IFAC Proceedings Volumes (IFAC-PapersOnline)* (Vol. 4). 10.3182/20130828-2-SF-3019.00054

Pirouz, D. M. (2012). An Overview of Partial Least Squares. SSRN *Electronic Journal.* doi:10.2139/ssrn.1631359

Qiao, J., Ngadi, M. O., Wang, N., Gariépy, C., & Prasher, S. O. (2007). Pork quality and marbling level assessment using a hyperspectral imaging system. *Journal of Food Engineering, 83*(1), 10–16. doi:10.1016/j.jfoodeng.2007.02.038

Qin, J., Chao, K., Kim, M. S., Lu, R., & Burks, T. F. (2013). Hyperspectral and multispectral imaging for evaluating food safety and quality. *Journal of Food Engineering, 118*(2), 157–171. doi:10.1016/j.jfoodeng.2013.04.001

Romaniello, R., & Baiano, A. (2018, July). Discrimination of flavoured olive oil based on hyperspectral imaging. *Journal of Food Science and Technology, 55*(7), 2429–2435. Advance online publication. doi:10.100713197-018-3160-8 PMID:30042558

Rostom, N. G., Shalaby, A. A., Issa, Y. M., & Afifi, A. A. (2017). Evaluation of Mariut Lake water quality using Hyperspectral Remote Sensing and laboratory works. *The Egyptian Journal of Remote Sensing and Space Sciences, 20*, S39–S48. Advance online publication. doi:10.1016/j.ejrs.2016.11.002

Rungpichayapichet, P., Nagle, M., Yuwanbun, P., Khuwijitjaru, P., Mahayothee, B., & Müller, J. (2017). Prediction mapping of physicochemical properties in mango by hyperspectral imaging. *Biosystems Engineering, 159*(2011), 109–120. doi:10.1016/j.biosystemseng.2017.04.006

Seidl, T. (2009). Nearest Neighbor Classification. Encyclopedia of Database Systems, 1, 1885–1890. doi:10.1007/978-0-387-39940-9_561

Serranti, S., Palmieri, R., & Bonifazi, G. (2015). Hyperspectral imaging applied to demolition waste recycling: Innovative approach for product quality control. *Journal of Electronic Imaging, 24*(4), 043003. doi:10.1117/1.JEI.24.4.043003

Setser, A. L., & Waddell Smith, R. (2018). Comparison of variable selection methods prior to linear discriminant analysis classification of synthetic phenethylamines and tryptamines. *Forensic Chemistry (Amsterdam, Netherlands), 11*(October), 77–86. doi:10.1016/j.forc.2018.10.002

Sivertsen, A. H., Kimiya, T., & Heia, K. (2011). Automatic freshness assessment of cod (Gadus morhua) fillets by Vis/Nir spectroscopy. *Journal of Food Engineering*, *103*(3), 317–323. doi:10.1016/j.jfoodeng.2010.10.030

Spyrelli, E. D., Doulgeraki, A. I., Argyri, A. A., Tassou, C. C., Panagou, E. Z., & George-John, E. N. (2020). Implementation of multispectral imaging (MSI) for microbiological quality assessment of poultry products. *Microorganisms*, *8*(4), 1–14. doi:10.3390/microorganisms8040552 PMID:32290382

System Overview — Benchtop Assembly for Spectronon Version 3.1.1. (n.d.). Retrieved November 25, 2020, from http://docs.resonon.com/spectronon/BenchtopAssemblyGuide/html/SystemOverview_include.html

Vidal, M., & Amigo, J. M. (2012). Pre-processing of hyperspectral images. Essential steps before image analysis. *Chemometrics and Intelligent Laboratory Systems*, *117*, 138–148. doi:10.1016/j.chemolab.2012.05.009

Wallace, M. B., Wax, A., Roberts, D. N., & Graf, R. N. (2009). Reflectance Spectroscopy. *Gastrointestinal Endoscopy Clinics of North America*, *19*(2), 233–242. doi:10.1016/j.giec.2009.02.008 PMID:19423021

Wang, K., Pu, H., & Sun, D. W. (2018). Emerging Spectroscopic and Spectral Imaging Techniques for the Rapid Detection of Microorganisms: An Overview. *Comprehensive Reviews in Food Science and Food Safety*, *17*(2), 256–273. doi:10.1111/1541-4337.12323 PMID:33350086

Wu, D., Shi, H., Wang, S., He, Y., Bao, Y., & Liu, K. (2012). Rapid prediction of moisture content of dehydrated prawns using on-line hyperspectral imaging system. *Analytica Chimica Acta*, *726*, 57–66. doi:10.1016/j.aca.2012.03.038 PMID:22541014

Wulder, M. A., Loveland, T. R., Roy, D. P., Crawford, C. J., Masek, J. G., Woodcock, C. E., Allen, R. G., Anderson, M. C., Belward, A. S., Cohen, W. B., Dwyer, J., Erb, A., Gao, F., Griffiths, P., Helder, D., Hermosilla, T., Hipple, J. D., Hostert, P., Hughes, M. J., ... Zhu, Z. (2019). Current status of Landsat program, science, and applications. *Remote Sensing of Environment*, *225*, 127–147. doi:10.1016/j.rse.2019.02.015

Xing, J., Bravo, C., Jancsók, P. T., Ramon, H., & De Baerdemaeker, J. (2005). Detecting bruises on "Golden Delicious" apples using hyperspectral imaging with multiple wavebands. *Biosystems Engineering*, *90*(1), 27–36. doi:10.1016/j.biosystemseng.2004.08.002

Yang, B., Gao, Y., Li, H., Ye, S., He, H., & Xie, S. (2019). Rapid prediction of yellow tea free amino acids with hyperspectral images. *PLoS One*, *14*(2), 1–17. doi:10.1371/journal.pone.0210084 PMID:30785888

Yu, P., Huang, M., Zhang, M., Zhu, Q., & Qin, J. (2020). Rapid detection of moisture content and shrinkage ratio of dried carrot slices by using a multispectral imaging system. *Infrared Physics & Technology*, *108*(May), 103361. doi:10.1016/j.infrared.2020.103361

Yuan, L., Yan, P., Han, W., Huang, Y., Wang, B., Zhang, J., Zhang, H., & Bao, Z. (2019). Detection of anthracnose in tea plants based on hyperspectral imaging. *Computers and Electronics in Agriculture*, *167*(June), 105039. doi:10.1016/j.compag.2019.105039

Zahavi, A., Palshin, A., Liyanage, D. C., & Tamre, M. (2019). Influence of Illumination Sources on Hyperspectral Imaging. *2019 20th International Conference on Research and Education in Mechatronics (REM), 5*, 1–5. 10.1109/REM.2019.8744086

ADDITIONAL READING

Liyanage, D. C. (2021). *Smart terrain perception using hyperspectral imaging* [Unpublished doctoral dissertation]. Tallinn University of Technology, Tallinn, Estonia.

Martens, H., & Martens, M. (2001). *Multivariate Analysis of Quality: An Introduction.* Wiley & Sons, Inc.

Vinzi, V. E., Chin, W. W., Henseler, J., & Wang, H. (Eds.). (2010). *Handbook of Partial Least Squares.* Springer. doi:10.1007/978-3-540-32827-8

KEY TERMS AND DEFINITIONS

At-Line: The measurement task is carried out near the production process. However, they are physically separate processes.

In-Line: The measurement process is directly integrated into the main production process.

In-Situ: The necessary measurements or analysis of the process are conducted on-site and directly integrated into the main production flow.

Off-Line: The measurement samples are taken from the process and further analyses separately.

On-Line: Same as in-situ. The measurement or analysis is done in the exact location where the process occurs.

Chapter 18
Inspection of Power Line Insulators:
State of the Art, Challenges, and Open Issues

Rogério Sales Gonçalves
Federal University of Uberlândia, Brazil

Guilherme Salomão Agostini
Federal University of Uberlândia, Brazil

Reinaldo A. C. Bianchi
Centro Universitario FEI, Brazil

Rafael Zimmermann Homma

CELESC, Brazil

Daniel Edgardo Tio Sudbrack
CELESC, Brazil

Paulo Victor Trautmann
CELESC, Brazil

Bruno Cordeiro Clasen
CELESC, Brazil

ABSTRACT

Insulators are power transmission line components responsible for two key tasks: the first one is to support the mechanical stress originated by the weight of the cables and devices, and the second one is to avoid electrical dissipation from the cables to the tower structure. Even though the shape and material of the insulator is made in such a way as to avoid the conduction of electrical current on its surface, if some types of dirty accumulates excessively, the insulator can still conduct an electric arc to the tower, causing damage to the power grid. This chapter first presents the state-of-the-art power line insulator cleaning methods and the techniques used to identify insulators that require cleaning. Then, this chapter describes an algorithm that makes use of machine learning, deep learning, and computer vision technics, which can be used embedded in an unmanned aerial vehicle, to support the energy company in the assessment of the levels of dirt on the insulators. Finally, experimental results are presented showing the challenges and the open problems.

DOI: 10.4018/978-1-7998-8686-0.ch018

INTRODUCTION

Insulators are important components in power transmission lines as they maintain the cables away from the body of the tower, which is connected to the ground referential. The insulator has a repetitive geometric structure with stacked caps (discs), and the quantity of discs depends on the voltage level. Due the predominant outdoor working environment, insulators are exposed to the weather and vandalism that can result in its malfunction. The common insulators faults are missing caps and surface fault (Liu et al., 2020). Nevertheless, as the insulators are in open environment, they end up accumulating dirty. In normal circumstances, dirty has insulating properties; however, due to capacitive forces, they can form a conductive surface, creating a high potential electric arc from the tower body to the conductor over the insulator, a fault that is called flashover and damages the insulator (Siderakis et al., 2011). It is even worse in coastal regions in which salt is deposited. In case insulators lose their insulating capacity, then it may lead to unexpected outages and damages to equipment of power system, bringing economic and social problems (Hadipour and Shiran, 2017). For this main motive, it is essential for Power Distribution Companies to schedule assessments and cleaning routines (Siderakis et al., 2011; Gonçalves and Carvalho, 2013; Gonçalves and Carvalho, 2015; Gonçalves et al., 2021), which is done by energy sector worker, climbing the tower, or by helicopter.

This chapter aims improve the assessments capability using an unmanned aerial vehicle - a drone - controlled by a professional from the company. As these workers will end up assessing a high volume of insulators a day, it may lead to errors caused by fatigue. To mitigate that issue, an algorithm is being researched and developed: the same images, or video, shown to these professionals will also be used by our algorithm to provide a second opinion about the cleanliness status of the insulators.

This work is organized as follows: first we present the state-of art of cleaning power lines insulators and methods used to identify the insulator and its condition. Then, we describe an algorithm, with experimental results, that makes use of machine learning, deep learning, and computer vision technics, which can be used embedded in an unmanned aerial vehicle, to support the energy company in the assessment of insulators, looking for the ones with dangerous levels of dirty. Finally, a discussion about the challenges and open issues is made to point futures directions in the identification and necessity of clean power lines insulators.

BACKGROUND

In this section the state-of-art in power lines insulators maintenance and the ways to identify an insulator and its condition related to the dirty it accumulates are presented.

Cleaning Power Lines Insulator Chains

To accomplish the high voltage power lines isolation from the towers, devices known as insulators are required. The insulators must have, in addition to good dielectric characteristics, excellent mechanical characteristics, in view of the severe nature work that will be performed. The insulator must withstand high compression stresses, must be hard and have a highly polished surface.

The insulators are manufactured with dielectric materials, that is, they do not allow the free circulation of electrical charges and can be divided into three basic types of materials: ceramic, glass and polymeric/composite insulators.

Porcelain insulators are glazed to minimize pores and air bubbles, improving the dielectric strength of the insulators (Fig. 1-a), being the most used ones. The main advantages of these insulators are their long history of use and easy interchangeability (Sanyal et al., 2019). The main limitations are its weight, possibility of hidden defects and susceptible to vandalism.

Tempered glass insulators have the advantages of using glass in their manufacture, a long history of use and easy interchangeability (Fig. 1-b). Defects are more easily visible, and they have a lower expansion coefficient than porcelain insulators and, consequently, less deformation due to temperature changes (because it is transparent it absorbs less heat from the sun when compared to ceramics). The acquisition cost of glass insulators is lower than porcelain ones. The main limitations are its weight and vandalism.

Polymeric insulators (also called composites) are made of two insulating parts. The first is a fiberglass stick acting as a core and skirts made of polymeric material such as Teflon, epoxy resin, silicone rubber, etc. (Fig. 1-c). The advantages of polymeric insulators can be cited as their good performance in polluted environments, with low weight that makes installation easy and cost-effective. They are more difficult to be damaged by vandalism. As limitations of its use, one can mention the fragility of the core, early aging, less interchangeability, possibility of hidden defects and the material is hygroscopic (it tends to absorb water) which can lead to its deterioration.

Figure 1. Insulator types. (a) Ceramic Insulator disc; (b) Glass Insulator disc (Puchale, 2019); (c) polymeric insulator (Mantovani et al., 2013).

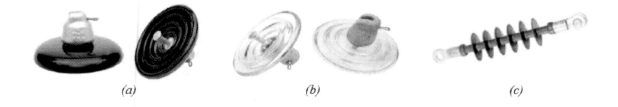

(a)   *(b)*   *(c)*

The insulators are subject to surface dirt deposits to some degree in all operating areas and the most commonly contaminants have little effect on insulators function when its surface is dry. But fog, mist or light rain can create conditions that will produce a conducting film on the dirty insulator surface, if the contaminants in its surface are not periodically removed. The contaminants are impurities related to the local agriculture, industrial and geographic conditions (Hadipour and Shiran, 2017).

The insulators become dirty due to birds, dust, salt (Hussain et al., 2015; Meyer et al., 2013) and chemicals from various smokes (Fig. 2-b), (Hadipour and Shiran, 2017). Near coastal areas most of the insulator contamination is due to airborne sea salt particles (Fig. 2-c), (Hussain et al., 2015). These dirt deposits form a conductive layer on the insulator's surface and can cause the flashover phenomenon. Most flashovers (Fig. 2-a), are unpredictable, leading to the need for maintenance operations that take hours to complete.

Figure 2. (a) Flashover (Sousa, 2010); (b) ash contamination (Wightman and Bodger, 2011); (c) salt contamination (Sousa, 2010).

(a)   *(b)*   *(c)*

The standard guide for cleaning contaminated electrical insulators, of all types, using varied equipment and techniques is the IEEE Std 957-2005.

Table 1. Contaminant types and washing types (IEEE Std 957-2005).

Contaminant	Water washing		Compressed air-dry cleaning		Wiping	
	Low pressure	High pressure	Corncob w/ nut shell	CO2 pellets	Hot wiping	Hand wiping
Salt	X	X	-	-	-	X
Cement/lime	-	-	X	X	X	X
Earth dust	X	X	X	X	X	X
Fertilizer dust	X	X	X	X	X	X
Metallic dust	-	-	X	X	X	X
Coal dust	X	X	X	X	X	X
Volcanic ash	X	X	X	X	X	X
Bird excrement	X	X	X	X	X	X
Chemical	X	-	X	X	-	X
Smog (vehicular)	X	X	X	X	X	X
Cooling tower effluent	X	X	X	X	-	-
Smoke/coal soot	X	X	X	X	X	X
Organic	X	X	X	X	X	X
Ice/Snow	-	X	X	-	-	X
Petroleum/grease	-	-	X	X	X	X

Cleaning porcelain or glass insulators must not deteriorate or damage the surfaces to be cleaned. The main way to clean these elements is using water with high pressure (400 psi to 1000 psi); medium pressure (300 psi to 400 psi) or low pressure (200 psi). The water used must be demineralized. Polymeric insulators cannot be cleaned with water. Table 1 show the main contaminant types and washing types presented in IEEE Std 957-2005.

In methods or equipment that adopt higher pressures, water is released in the form of droplets, on its surface. When this happens, due to the dielectric characteristic of the water that is pressurized and released in the form of droplets, the electric current is not conducted through the jet to the device, that is, to the nozzle of the injection gun that is releasing it.

Traditional cleaning of insulator chains is usually carried out by operators on the live line (called "hot line washing"), or when it is disconnected. This cleaning can be performed by technicians using tissues (Fig. 3-a), high pressure washers positioned in the towers (Fig. 3-b), or carried by technicians (Fig. 3-c), (Wang et al, 2016). Hand wiping using wet cloth and dry wiping rags is the most used cleaning method in some countries like China (Wang et al, 2016). Despite this method be effective and practical is very time-consuming, tedious, dangerous and expensive in terms of outage time and cost.

Figure 3. (a) Cleaning the insulator chain with cloths (Wang et al., 2016); (b-c) Insulator chain cleaning with high pressure washers (Sousa et al., 2009).

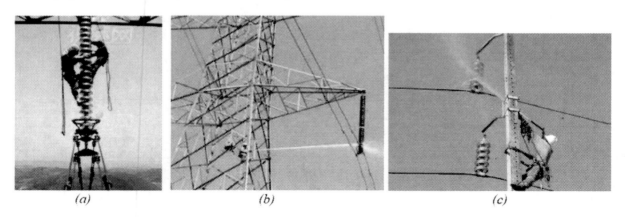

(a)   (b)   (c)

The cleaning of insulators presents several risks to the electricians: falling risks, personal injury or allergies, electric shock, cuts by damaged insulator, injury by crushing limbs and equipment collision with the structure and/or accessories and personal injury due to tools falling. The average time to perform this task is 1.5 hours per structure (COPEL, 2015).

The insulator cleaning process can be extremely dangerous, due to the high voltage passing through the transmission lines and any accident type can be fatal. To reduce the accident risk with live line operators, several solutions have been proposed, such as the use of trucks, robots, and drones.

Cleaning using trucks associated with platforms or with robotic devices (Fig. 4-a-b), have been used in the case of low voltages in applications within cities.

In the case of high voltage power lines in the transmission system, helicopters have also been used (Fig. 4-c). The insulators cleaning method with a high-pressure washer using a helicopter was first described in 1984 (Kurtgis, 1984).

Figure 4. (a) Cleaning of insulators with a tank truck; (b) detail of the robotic arm (Simas et al., 2010). (c) Cleaning of insulators by helicopter

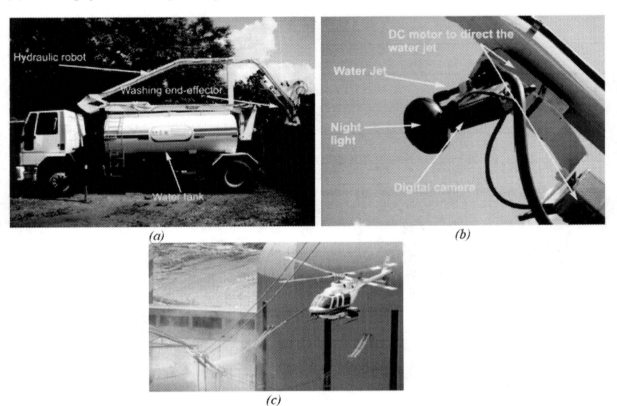

Compared to hand wiping and high-pressure water machines, the use of robots and drones to clean insulators is advantageous as it increases workers safety and cleaning efficiency.

Various researchers have been working on insulator inspection or/and cleaning robots (Wang et al., 2016; Park et al., 2012).

The inspection methods for insulators can be divided in methods based on non-electric quantities and methods based on electric quantities (Li and Huang, 2011). The methods based on non-electric quantities includes direct observing method, ultraviolet radiation or infrared image method or ultrasonic detecting method. Methods based on electric quantities include the measurement insulation resistance, electric field, leakage current and impulsive current. The most common inspection method is the manual inspection using an insulator tester (Wang et al., 2016). One way to automatize the process is using robots: a survey on insulator inspection robots for power transmission lines was presented by Wang et al. (2016).

The cleaning of insulators with the use of robots follows the same format, using complex devices that move along or around the insulators discs to perform their mechanical cleaning. One example is a robot for cleaning insulators based on the inchworm movement as the locomotion principle along the insulators chain using three rotating brushes (Fig. 5-a), (Wang et al., 2015).

Park et al. (2012) presented a robot for insulators inspection, with the robot being able to move along the insulator chain using a wheel-leg moving mechanism. The robot measures the distribution voltage of an insulator together with its insulation resistance (Fig. 5-b). In Park et al. (2009) a cleaning robot system for live-line suspension insulator strings was presented adopting a dry-cleaning method without water (Fig. 5-c). Among the operations performed, one is the cleaning of the insulator chain disks with brushes.

Figure 5. Robots applied to insulators. (a) Wang et al. (2015). (b) Adapted from Park et al., 2012. (d) Park et al., 2009.

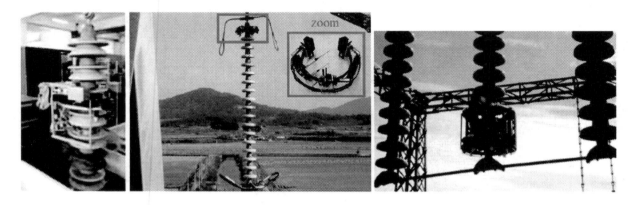

The main difficulty in using these robots concerns the maintenance of complex prototypes and the need to place them on the insulators by technicians, which ends up being risky in the same way, as technicians have to climb to place the robots, suffering with ergonomic problems due to the robots' high mass.

There are some applications of UAVs for insulators cleaning. In (Tengfei, 2015) a UAV with three nozzles for cleaning insulators is presented. One spout is responsible for the cleaning product, another for clean water and the third with a high-pressure spray. The cleaning process is monitored by a camera with images sent to a station on the ground, where the operator determines whether the cleaning has been carried out completely.

Aerones Enterprise has developed a UAV that can be applied to insulators cleaning (Fig. 6-a). French energy company Engie is developing UAVs to be used to clean insulators. The use of a moss cleaning solution (the same product used for cleaning roofs) is being tested. The UAV sprays the product on the insulators and after a few days, it dries out from the discs. In Brazil the company CELESC is working on a solution for cleaning insulator chains also using UAVs (Fig. 6-b).

Figure 6. (a) Drone developed by Aerones applied to insulator cleaning. (b) Scheme of drone-robot solution for washing insulator chain. (c) Detail of washing procedure with drone (Gonçalves et al. 2021).

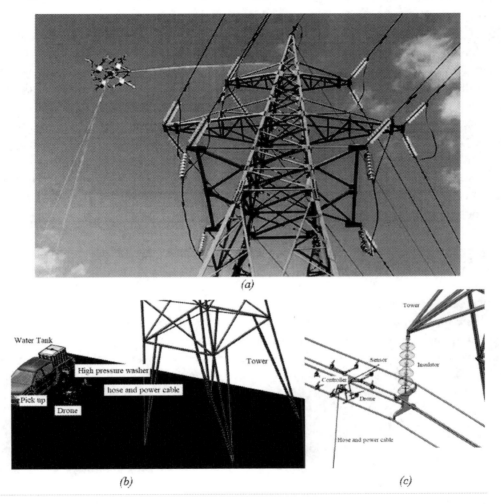

Identification of Insulator and Assessment of Their Cleaning Condition

Monitoring electricity distribution systems is one of the most significant tasks for energy companies, since knowledge of cables and components estimated lifetime could prevent the concessionaire's revenue compromise of millions of dollars. The efforts spent on monitoring the distribution system status are justified by the reduction of the failures occurrence due to the electricity supply interruption, equipment damage and repair costs (Gonçalves et al., 2021).

There are countless tasks for power lines maintenance/inspection such as cables detailed inspection, the physical and mechanical integrity visualization regarding defects and atmospheric discharges, proving the need for emergency or scheduled maintenance; visual inspection of the conductor cables; spacers; porcelain, glass or polymeric insulators; towers; installation or removal of aircraft warning spheres; cable splice services; cleaning; repairs and installations of new lines, vegetation management, identifying objects that may put the line integrity at risk, soil erosion, among others.

Due to climatic factors exposure, such as sun, rain, wind, and snow; natural aging; vandalism or human beings' improper activities can make the components used in the energy transmission system lose their electrical properties over time, requiring maintenance to correct possible failures in such components before they can compromise the energy distribution. In addition to the natural aging factors, most of the components used in distribution networks are not subjected to strict quality controls during their manufacturing process, allowing imperfections in them.

The focus of this chapter is the inspection of insulators. The inspection of these components and other presents in power lines transmission system is performed by operators who visually inspect the components. Thus, in addition to economic motivation, the reduction in human risks associated with inspection and maintenance operations on high voltage cables (such as exposure to intense electromagnetic fields) is also a problem.

The commonly used inspection methods (Gonçalves et al., 2021) are:

- In a helicopter operators perform a visual inspection. One of them makes a visual inspection with a binocular, observing the cables' physical structure, checking the towers, the conductors' connection and the insulators chain. The other operator uses a thermal imager and other sensors to check for overheating in the objects.
- In a helicopter, an operator, dressed in an insulating suit, is suspended on a platform. As the helicopter approaches the line, the operator uses a stick to equalize the platform potential with the transmission line potential. With the equalized potential, the operator places the safety equipment and the necessary inspection/maintenance devices hanging from the line. Then he passes to the line, sitting or crouching over it. The helicopter moves away, and the operator performs the inspection by dragging on the line.
- Another way is to suspend the operator on a platform with the aid of a vehicle. The platform is electrically isolated from the vehicle so that there is no risk of short circuit. To perform any activity on the line, the operator equalizes the platform potential with the transmission line potential. In this case, the operator remains on the platform while carrying out the inspection/maintenance and the vehicle moves towards the line. There are also platforms that are placed on the cables themselves and the technicians carry out its movement.
- Inspection of high voltage cables by UAVs (Unmanned Aerial Vehicles). These have cameras with high zoom capacity, thermal camera, and other sensors to identify the problem points in the power lines and objects.

New approaches are being studied worldwide to automate the inspection process on power transmission lines. Main advances include the identification and mapping through GPS (Global Positioning System) equipment of places where there may be cable failures; use of sophisticated cameras to identify possible problems; use of sensors; data acquisition equipment and computers (used for processing data obtained from sensors and images to identify problem locations); the application of mobile robots that act on the lines in inspection and/or maintenance activities and Unmanned Aerial Vehicles (UAVs) for inspection (Rubin, 2000; Gonçalves and Carvalho, 2013).

As advantages, the use of UAVs to inspect transmission lines present a significant reduction in the time spent on inspection operations and a considerable increase in their efficiency, in addition to decreasing risks with employees (Zhu et al., 2018; Li et al., 2016). When compared to the use of suspended mobile robots, the use of UAVs provides much faster inspection (Li, 2015).

It is possible to list several advantages related to the use of UAVs for inspection application, which are (Li, 2015):

- Wide overcoming of terrain restrictions.
- The same UAV can inspect transmission lines of different voltage levels.
- Fast inspection, with quick automated defect detection.
- Low cost of use and maintenance compared to the usage of helicopters.
- Can identify a variety of transmission lines defects.
- Greater approximation of lines and towers when compared to the use of helicopters.

Among the problems of using UAVs, we can highlight:

- Low autonomy when compared to the use of helicopters.
- Flight limitations due to bad weather, rain and strong winds.
- Regulatory problems in several countries that prevent UAVs from operating outside of human sight.
- Problems with electromagnetic interference that can affect the behavior of UAVs.

Literature Review of Identification of Insulators and Faults Using Images

Currently, the high voltage cables inspection can be made with the use of UAVs that can carry high-resolution cameras with great zoom capability, infrared cameras, and sensors to identify the corona effect. Corona discharges are ultraviolet emissions in ionized air caused by increasing in electrical fields, these generally triggered by defective components (Pagnano et al., 2013). Current research has focused on the development of software to optimize the acquired data analysis to identify the components and possible problems in these.

To inspection of power lines insulators is necessary first the component detection one key prerequisite for further analysis. The research about component detection can be divided into five groups in function of the image features used: color, shape, texture, fusion and deep learning (Liu et al., 2020). After the component identification is necessary proceed with the fault diagnosis that are summarized from the types of insulators faults that includes surface fault (dirty insulators, flashovers) and missing cap (discs).

The number of research articles about insulators identification and other components presents in the power lines distribution system are increased in the last decade. The insulator detection procedure can be divided in three steps: image acquisition, feature extraction and features classification. Image acquisition is discussed in the section of dataset construction. The features were extracted from images and then input to the classifier for identifying if belong to the component. The third step is the classification using IA/learning-based algorithms as the feature classifier (Fig. 7). In the case of insulator its shape has a repetitive circle geometric structure with multiple discs that can be detected by procedures of searching ellipsoid shapes in the acquired image.

Figure 7. Usual procedure to insulator detection.

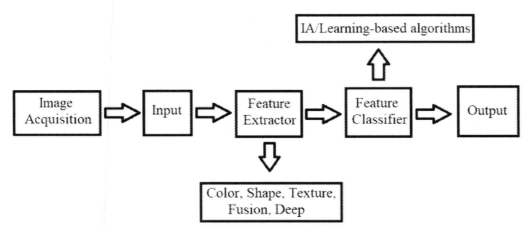

The color feature is related to the insulator color. The acquired images are converted to a specific color space that makes it easier to detect the insulator; most studies concentrated on using the HSI (Hue, Saturation, Intensity) color space (Zhang et al., 2010; Yao et al., 2012).

The shape feature when compared with color feature can show better representation (Liu et al., 2020). In the shape feature generally the contours or edges were extracted for classification. Li et al. (2012) used a profile projection method to locate the potential area of insulators using a SVM (Support Vector Machine).

Compared with the color feature extraction, the texture feature is more efficient as it characterizes the local feature that was appropriate for the detection of insulators that have repetitive geometric structure. Wu et al. (2012) used a texture segmentation algorithm. The texture feature was extracted by Gray Level Co-occurrence Matrix (GLCM) and classified into two classes by K-means and, after the insulators were recognized by means of the Global Minimization Active Contour Model (GMACM). Jabid et al. (2018) used Local Directional Pattern (LDP) method for insulators texture feature extraction. The evaluation set used images with 722 labeled insulators and this method achieved 95.74% recall.

In the case of Deep Feature, which is based on deep learning, the research extracted deep feature from aerial images for insulators detection and most of them obtain better performance than the other features. The disadvantages in deep learning approaches are the data quantity, that generally is increased applying data augmentation, to solve data insufficiency and build the dataset. Another common process used is the resizing of the image in function of some images have high resolution and smaller size can save the computation effort (Liu et al., 2020).

Within this perspective, recent works can be mentioned. Bhola et al. (2018) developed a method for detecting power lines in images captured by a UAV. The image processing approach is based on spectral-spatial methods.

Nguyen et al. (2019) present an automatic vision system linked to an inspection UAV, based on a deep learning algorithm. This algorithm is capable of automatically detecting and classifying components present in the lines, in addition to detecting significant failures that require maintenance, through the images captured by the UAV during inspection operations. Takaya et al. (2019) also present an inspection system that can be widely adapted to commercial UAV models.

Due to their location on the components of high-voltage power lines, their imaging can be cumbersome and time-consuming, especially under varying lighting conditions, Fig. 8. Images of insulators taken by aerial methods can also have different backgrounds like vegetation, rivers, sky, different power towers, buildings, etc. (Liu et al., 2021).

Insulator diagnostics with the use of visual methods may require localizing insulators in the scene. Studies focused on insulator localization in the scene apply a number of methods, including texture analysis, MRF (Markov Random Field), Gabor filters or GLCM (Gray Level Co-Occurrence Matrix) (Jingjing et al., 2012; Hyunho et al., 2013). Some methods, e.g., those which localize insulators based on color analysis (Zhai et al., 2017), rely on object and scene illumination, which is why the images from the data set are taken under varying lighting conditions (Tomaszewski et al., 2018).

Figure 8. Insulator string (Red color), insulator fault (Blue color) background interference (Yellow color) in the aerial image (Han et al., 2019).

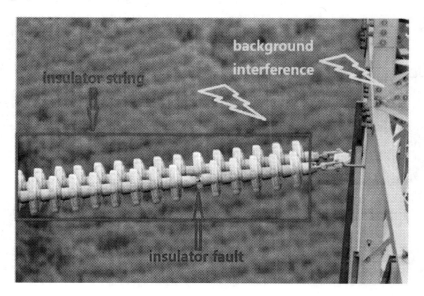

In Liu et al. (2021) was proposed a deep learning method based on the You Only Look Once (YOLO) Artificial Neural Network, capable of detecting insulators from aerial images with complex backgrounds. The average precision was 94.47% in detecting different size insulators in diverse backgrounds interference and can be applied for UAV- based real-time identification (8ms) of insulators.

In Pernebayeva et al. (2019) the problem of detection the insulator surface condition in the winter is analyzed. Authors used two different approaches to compare, one based on artificial neural networks (CNN, InceptionV3, MobileNet, VGG16 and ResNet50) and the other based on traditional machine learning classifiers (Bayes Networks, Decision Trees, Lazy Learning, Rules and Meta classifiers). The different technics are used to classify the insulator surface like clean, with snow, ice or wet. The experimental results showed that traditional machine learning methods with proper selection of features can obtain high classification accuracy.

In Tao et al. (2018) was proposed a Deep Convolutional Neural Network (CNN) cascading architecture to accurately localizing and defect detection of insulators appearing in input images captured from real inspection environments. The defect detection precision and recall of the proposed method are 0.91 and 0.96 using the standard insulator dataset.

In Siddiqui et al. (2018) an automatic electrical equipment that detects and inspect system was proposed, detecting problems in polymer insulators using Convolutional Neural Networks framework. The proposed system uses two cameras, one of low-resolution images that detects the insulators in the image from long-shot images, and one high-resolution camera which capture close-shot images with high-resolution to effective defect analysis. The defect analysis system achieves up to 98% accuracy and the insulators detection reach 93% recall with 92% precision.

Han et al. 2019 presented a convolutional network to obtain accurate insulator string positions and multi-fault in the UAV-based aerial image.

Gao et al. (2019) implement a modified conditional generative adversarial pixel-level insulator segmentation network. The proposed method has better computational efficiency than Pixe2pix and SegNet networks.

Tiantian et al. (2017) presented an insulator detection method for aerial inspection based on feature-fusion. The fusion feature is then combined by the HOG feature and LBP feature after PCA dimension reduction separately. The SVM classification algorithm is adopted to get the training model. Experimental results indicate that the proposed method can locate insulators under complex backgrounds.

It is important to note that the images available could be affected by uncertainty and/or inaccuracies. To enhancement image contrast in Versaci et al. (2017) and Versaci et al. (2015) was proposed a fuzzy geometrical preprocessing approach.

Fault Insulators Diagnosis

The fault diagnosis of insulators can be made using visible inspection images (Fig. 9). The usual procedure for fault diagnosis was made by the detect region of interest, cropped in order to filter out the background for after the fault identification method can be applied (Liu et al., 2020). In many cases the region of interest, that is the insulator, has already been identified and isolated as per the previous section.

Figure 9. The common procedure of fault diagnosis (Liu et al., 2020).

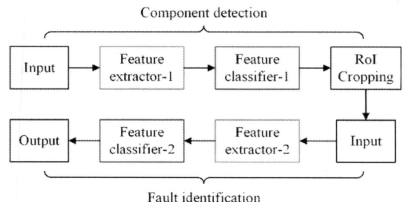

The studies about surface fault have the objective of identify different types of dirty on a single or multiples insulator surface. Pernebayeva et al. (2019) studied the classification of glass insulator from aerial images take outdoor, with the insulator chain fix in a simulate support, with a drone and camera with 20-megapixel CMOS sensor. The objective was classifying the glass insulator as clean, with water, with snow and with ice. Yang et al. (2017) presented a classification method of ice types (free of ice, glaze ice, heavy rime, medium rime, slight rime, partial rime and snow) on insulators based on the texture feature descriptor. An improved uniform LBP (IULBP) was proposed for feature extraction. Then, the extracted feature was compared with the predetermined template of the ice type. The method was evaluated with few images cropped to focus on the icing part.

Zhai et al. (2018) applied Faster Pixel-wise Image Saliency Aggregating (FPISA) to detect insulators and after used extracted based on the color determination in Lab color space to identify flashover area. The method was evaluated by using 100 insulator images with flashover fault and achieved 92.7% detection rate.

Some researchers worked with the fault diagnosis scheme to determine multiple surface faults of insulators using the procedure of detected the insulator first, then divided the insulator region into several parts and finally calculated the similarity between each part. Zhao et al. (2016) presented a deep-learning-based method for the classification of the insulator status including normal, damaged, dust contamination and missing caps. The insulator was detected by utilizing OAD-BSPK. After insulator detection, the insulator region was divided into several parts and used in one CNN framework to feature extracting. The feature vector obtained was classified using a trained SVM.

The other common insulator fault is the missing cap (disc), that which is not the focus of this chapter. Further details on this type of identification can be found at (Liu et al., 2020).

Works to identify the types of dirt in insulators from automated images and verify the need for cleaning were not found in the literature and is one objective of this chapter.

CONVOLUTIONAL ARTIFICIAL NEURAL NETWORKS

Artificial Neural Networks are bio-inspired mathematical tools used to obtain the relationship between an input array and an output array (Fig. 10). It is composed of processing units called artificial neurons, that works as a linear function approximator. These units are usually modelled as proposed by Rosenblatt (1958) and are called Perceptrons.

One Perceptron takes the values of an input vector and first makes a weighted sum of the individual values. The weights used in this sum are the parameters of the Perceptron, that can be leaned using a simple algorithm. After the weighted sum is computed, the result is feed into an activation function: it is a function that takes the sum and generates the output of the perceptron. Usual activation functions are the step function, the linear function, and the sigmoid function.

A very simple neural network consists of one layer of neurons, which is able to learn from examples the linear correlation between the input and the desired output of a system. Each neuron receives all the values in the input example and computes its output. More complex networks may have more layers, i.e., Perceptrons that are connected sequentially in a feedforward manner (Fig. 10).

To learn the parameters (i.e., the weights of the sum) of an Artificial Neural Network several algorithms can be used: a simple, one layer network can learn using the Delta Rule (Rosenblatt, 1958), which corrects the weighs proportionally to the error between the desired output and the output obtained by the neuron. A more complex network usually learns using the Backpropagation algorithm (Rumelhart et al, 1986), which performs descent gradient optimization on the squared output error.

Figure 10. Example of neural network schematic.

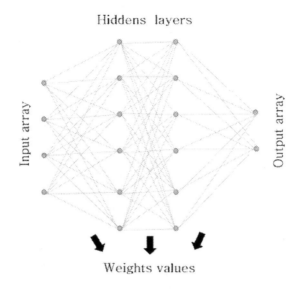

To use a neural network with images, is necessary flatten the image matrix into an array, and so, all the weights and bias would try to map the input with the expected output. For vision tasks this process may be inefficient since an image can change in so many different ways, making the weights values fluctuate (Andrade, 2019) and consequently not being able to learn the relation between input and desired output or leading to an overfitting, that happens when the model learns patterns for recognizing the train dataset but cannot recognize or classify images that were not used during its training, as shown by figure 2.

Figure 11. Comparison between neural network and convolutional neural network for vision task (Andrade, 2019).

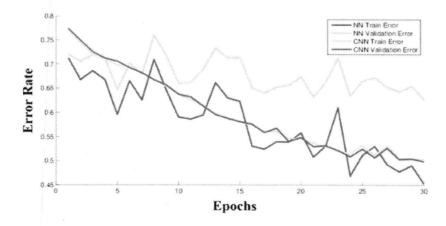

One of the techniques used to solve this problem is the so called Convolutional Neural Network, which instead of performing a weighted sum with the input vector, applies a convolution over the data. A convolution is a mathematical operation by which a matrix of weights, called kernel of the convolution, is multiplied over the input image in strides, creating an output matrix that was filtered by the convolution. This technique is able to extract patterns and create the feature maps, which can later, be used as input for a neural network, Fig. 12.

Figure 12. Example of a convolutional neural network architecture (Alon et al. 2019).

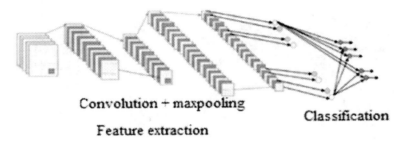

The Convolutional Neural Network (CNN) is the main methodology used nowadays for computer vision and object detection and recognition, and therefore it was chosen as the technique to be used in this work. However, the CNN can have many formats, with a different number of layers and neurons in each layer, which creates an architecture for the network. To be able to use a CNN to identify the insulators, we still have to determine the architecture, or in other words, the format of the CNN.

Architectures

The format on which convolutional neural network works is a very hot topical of study nowadays, as different ways on building a network can greatly change the number of parameters, its performance and accuracy (François, 2017; Bianco et al., 2018), as shown at Table 2 and Figure 13.

Table 2. Comparison between four modern CNN architectures: VGG-16, ResNet-152, Inception V3 and Xception architecture for ImageNet dataset (François, 2017).

	Top-1 accuracy	Top-5 accuracy
VGG-16	0.715	0.901
ResNet-152	0.770	0.933
Inception V3	0.782	0.941
Xception	**0.790**	**0.945**

Figure 13. Comparison between architectures used in the ImageNet dataset, mapping accuracy, number of parameters and Giga Float Operations (G-FLOPs) (Bianco et al., 2018).

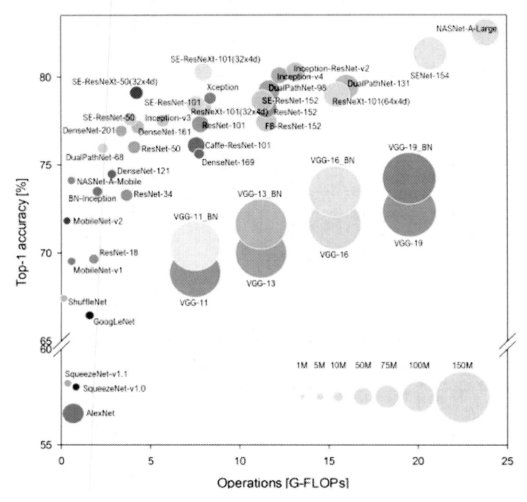

In this work we seek tradeoff between a small number of trainable parameters, low computing requirements and high accuracy: reducing the requirements of the processing hardware on our project. Consequently, it was chosen for this project an architecture based on Xception, with some modifications to decrease the number of trainable parameters, and also including in every layer Dropout operation, that reduces overfitting.

Dataset

One of the open problems for identifying dirty insulator chains by image analysis is having a representative database that the Artificial Neural Network can learn from. Most of the research in this area ends up using databases obtained manually and with few images. If researchers have different insulators dataset available, the impact of the identification, accuracy and speed can be increased. The dataset may also be used to compare the effectiveness of different methods of localizing insulators in images. Tomaszewski et al. (2018) presented a dataset with high-resolution images depicting a ceramic long rod electrical insulator under varying lighting conditions and against different backgrounds such as crops, forest and grass. The dataset contains images with visible laser and images without such spots (which yielded the total of 2630 images), as well as additional data concerning the illumination level and insulator position in the scene, the number of registered laser spots, and their coordinates in the image. The problem with this set of images is the format in which they were acquired, outside their natural environment in the high voltage towers (Fig. 14).

Figure 14. Apparatus to obtain insulators imagens of dataset presented in Tomaszewski et al. (2018).

In Gao et al. (2019) the insulator datasets were acquired in two ways: the UAV data acquisition system and the Internet images. The number of samples were enhanced by random rotation, mirroring, color perturbation, and blurring and resized to $256 \times 256 \times 3$ before training. The datasets consist of 6000 images with more than 6 insulator types, and each image contains 1 to 10 insulators, with an average of 4 insulators per image, adding up to a total of 24,000 insulators.

Figure 15. Dataset built by Gao et al. (2019).

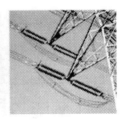

Pernebayeva et al. (2019) studied the classification of glass insulator from aerial images taken outdoor, with the insulator chain fixed in a simulated support, with a drone and camera with 20-megapixel camera. The objective was to classify the glass insulator as clean, with water, snow, and ice (Fig. 16). The image data set is further enhanced with 4000 aerial images, including four classes with 800 original images and 3200 pre-processed data using different types of noises such as Gaussian, Salt and Pepper, Poisson, and Speckle. The noises are applied to augment the database and consider possible environmental effects during data acquisition. Each class consists of 1000 original and filtered images, all with a resolution of 254×103 pixels.

Figure 16. Glass insulator images. (a) Clean, (b) Water, (c) Snow, (d) Ice.

Han et al. (2019) constructed a dataset to allow the identification of insulators faults from UAV aerial images. The dataset consists of 4031 images that contain different surroundings, and the acquisition distances and angles are varied in every image. The images in the dataset are normalized to the same size of 416 x 416 pixels. To verify the proposed insulator fault detection method, it was necessary to construct an insulator faults dataset too. However, although insulator faults detection is an important task in high-voltage transmission line inspection, it is well known that the main factor for limiting the development of insulator fault detection methods is that there are few insulator faults aerial images which can be collected (Han et al., 2019). The research obtained 42 images with one fault or multi-fault and a data augmentation method was used in this work. Photoshop software was used to erase the normal insulator regions and replace them with their nearby pixels to obtain a dataset containing 120 insulator fault images and there was a total of 228 insulator faults.

Tao et al. (2018) used a dataset with 1956 high resolution images, captured using an UAV with a M200 camera with resolution of 4608x3456 pixels, which include 900 images free of defect and 1056 defective insulator images (as shown in Fig. 17). For the defective image, 60 were images captured using a real UAV and 996 synthetic samples created by data augmentation, containing one or more defective insulators (Fig. 17).

Figure 17. Image segmentation using the U-Net. (a) Original image to be segmented. (b) Insulator segmentation results. (c) Detail of the segmentation result (Tao et al., 2018).

 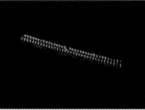 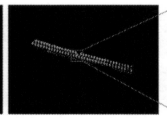 

A public insulator dataset built by Chinese Power Line Insulator Dataset (CPLID) is available online at: https://github.com/InsulatorData/InsulatorDataSet (accessed on 04 July 2021). The dataset contains 600 normal images insulators capture by UAVs and 248 defective image insulators obtained by data augmentation methods. This public dataset was used in Liu et al. (2021), who added 1400 aerial images of composite insulators. To increase the experimental dataset and avoid overfitting during training, data augmentation techniques were applied using Gaussian noise, blurring, and rotation were employed, transforming the original images into 5000 total aerial images with a resolution of 416x416 pixels. Liu et al. (2021) used a deep learning method based on the You Only Look Once (YOLO) CNN, capable of detecting insulators from aerial images with different complex backgrounds.

In Yan et al. (2017) a dataset was built with 500 images extracted from three videos, 400 of them contain insulators, others with absolute backgrounds. There are 430 insulators in total because of some images containing more than one insulator.

In Siddiqui et al. (2018) a dataset of long-shot low resolution, 667 images, and 5533 close-shot high-resolution images of equipment was built. The 6200 images were used to identify defective insulators.

As presented in this section, in recent years, object detection has benefited from the increasing availability of image data. However, exist lacks in function of specific tasks inspections of different type of insulator. Ji et al. (2019) proposed the use of virtual data, e. g., the virtual construction of devices with different virtual backgrounds using CAD tools and games engines like Unity 3D. The authors used the virtual data to build a dataset of vibration dampers. Virtual data can be easily acquired and automatically annotated and can serve as perfect training datasets for machine learning to identify insulators and after the possible defects.

ALGORITHM TO IDENTIFY THE CLEANING CONDITION OF INSULATORS

A state of art technique with the highest accuracy alongside with least computational power available was used in this application: the convolutional neural network and its preprocessing. It is composed of two steps: first, the background image is subtracted from the whole image and then, a Convolutional Network is used to classify the clean situation of the insulator. The first step allows the algorithm to identify the isolator and the second part classifies the image.

The CNN used to classify the images was the Xception (Chollet, 2017), a convolutional neural network architecture that relies solely on depth wise separable convolution layers, a modified type of convolution that makes the processing fates, without losing precision.

The proposed algorithm was implemented using Keras framework (2021), that already have the Xception CNN implemented, together with a high variety of pre-implemented functions.

The Adam optimizer at pattern learning rate, 0.001 was used. The L2 regularizer, at rate of 0.001, was used on the last dense layer.

Other parameters used are: five images in a batch and an epoch iterate a total of all the raw images. Our tests were performed using images with 800x800 pixel resolution, that were rescaled using OpenCV functions.

Creation of Our Dataset Insulators

It is essential for any machine learning project to have a large volume of quality images, on which the problem that the algorithm must learn is clearly defined. To solve the problem proposed in this chapter, the dataset should show insulators on different periods of the day, different types of insulators, types of dirty, weather, angle, and distance.

However, it is difficult to take photos from electric power facilities, on which security permission needs to be granted. With that topic in mind, the first tests were made using images produced by high-resolution camera (8 megapixels) in a laboratory, as shown by Figures 18.

Figure 18. (a) Sample of a dirty insulator; (b) Sample of a clean insulator.

A hundred twenty photos were taken, and due to the lack of images, data augmentation was implemented: rotating in full range, horizontal flipping, vertical flipping and zooming in a range of 0.5. The Keras ImageGenerator function was used to implement the data augmentation. The functions work randomizing the value, contained in the range, implementing it in the raw image at the same time as it runs.

All the images were hard labelled as dirty or clean: binary classification. The augmented image uses the same label as the original image.

For running the proposed algorithm, the raw dataset was shuffled and split into 80:20 for training and validation respectively.

TESTS AND RESULTS

A test using the dataset and our U-Net Convolutional Neural network, without background removal, was executed to define the possibility of detecting dirty using the augmented dataset, has shown in Figures 19(a) and 19(b).

The conclusion of this test is that it was not possible for the model to detect features to classify the training dataset into dirty or clean, as shown in validation error rate and the rapid overfitting, occurred as it started to train. We supposed that the main problem was the lack of dataset which leaded the neural network to learn background patterns instead of the dirty in the isolators.

To minimize this problem, another test was conducted subtracting the background of the images and then, training our model on these same 120 images. Results shown in Figures 19(c) and 19(d).

When the background of the images is removed, the proposed algorithm model can learn to classify the cleanliness of the insulator, or in other words, it is possible to reduce the effect of having a small dataset.

Figure 19. (a) Test 1 and its accuracy over 50 epochs; (b) Test 1 and its error over 50 epochs; (c) Test 2 and its accuracy over 100 epochs; (d) Test 2 and its error over 100 epochs.

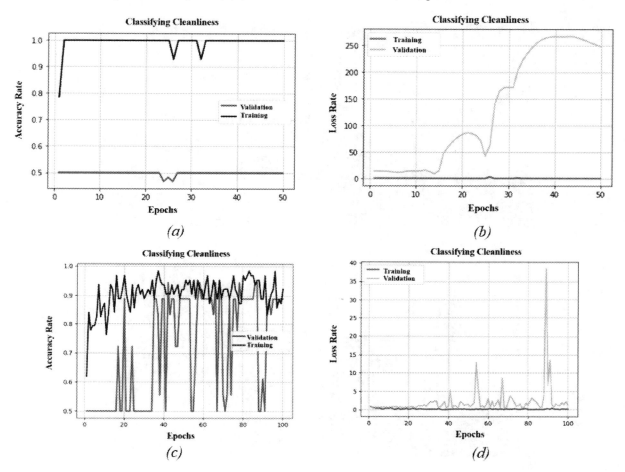

In order to remove the background another technique was tested: the U-Net (Ronneberg et al, 2015). The U-Net is "a network and training strategy that consists of a contracting path to capture context and a symmetric expanding path that enables precise localization of objects." (Ronneberg et al, 2015). This network has won several biomedical competitions and is very fast, being able to detect objects in 512 x 512 images in less than one second.

Therefore, using a U-Net network, and pixel labelling the 120 images, another model was trained for detecting the pixels that belongs to the insulators, as shown in Fig. 20(a-b).

The proposed model can learn to segment our task, shown by Fig. 20(a-b), however, with our current volume of images, even with regularization, the semantic segmentation model cannot learn all features correctly, shown by Fig. 20(c-d).

As the U-Nets could not segment the insulators from all images, and the method relies on high memory and processing power, it was temporarily disqualified for background extraction task.

Figure 20. Results with background removal using U-Net. (a) Original photo, belonging to training dataset; (b) Results; (c) Original photo belonging to validation dataset; (d) Results.

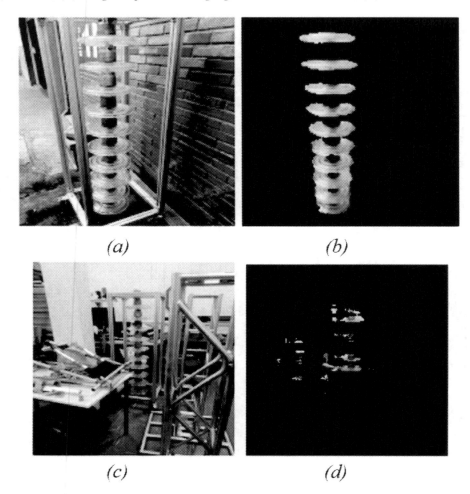

(a)   *(b)*

(c)   *(d)*

FUTURE RESEARCH DIRECTIONS

The insulators detection is a consolidate research area with different point of views and developed algorithms, but improvements in the use of deep learning networks are possible in function of the specific specialize task, e. g., identify dirty insulators with salt contaminant.

The insulators faults are an emergency field with few works developed to specific case, main to identify broken discs insulators. The research treats the fault diagnosis generally as object detection task and is limited to a specific fault rarely analyses of multiple faults is found and the multiples faults are the same feature like broken discs insulators. The other problem is the dataset with insulator faults be very small and built-in laboratory and not in real application.

The information/data like data size, image resolution, data collection approach, samples, etc., need be more complete to permits other researchers replied the works, with access to the dataset used and the programing codes.

The images can be pre-treated using fuzzy techniques to enhancement contrast or other techniques can be used to enhancement specific characteristic of the image.

Other open problem to compare the different adopted strategies is the definition a gold standard metric. Different metrics have been applied/developed to "sell" that the developed method is better. But the metrics, usually, are made with private dataset without opportunity to reproduce the work.

Traditional image processing methods often rely on a specific feature. The applicability of the different developed algorithms needs to be improved if the image segmentations is insufficient. Machine learning is more complicate and difficult to implement when compared with deep learning.

The methods developed to insulator detection and fault classification generally are test with part of the image of the dataset, e. g., the images are separated in training set and testing set but they have the same or near distribution, but in practical application with others backgrounds, lights etc., probably the training net will fail.

Other problem to practical application is the computational cost. The acquired images are with high pixel resolution and is necessary the use of computers with high processing capacity (i9 processors), high available memory (32 GB or more) and dedicated video cards. These computers are not readily available to much of the scientific community. With the advent of cloud computing with the availability of low-cost or free-to-use virtual machines, this barrier must be overcome in the coming years.

About the challenges and open research issues, despite the state-of-art promising results, the detection of faults in insulators is still in its infancy. One open issue is the dataset. Although the application of drones/UAVs has increased the capacity of build dataset is necessary the integration of the existents data set and created a public place to researches reach the images. High quality images dataset will permit better implementation/results when using machine learning algorithms.

With the access of a dataset image other problem is the high labor-cost to labeling the data, make, generally with manual annotations. The development of software's that can automatized the label process will decrease the time to obtain results.

In the last decade the object detection has benefited from the increasing availability of image data. But generally, the dataset is built to the researchers and not disponible, there are few public insulator datasets. The characteristics of the databases may also depend on the research objective. In the case of researches to identify the shape of objects, such as insulators, images taken from a great distance can be convenient for classification and identification of different types of objects. But for specific purposes such as determining possible problems such as broken disks the same database for identifying elements may not be enough. Another problem, directly addressed in this book chapter, is the presence of dirt in the insulators and the need for cleaning. In this case, the construction of a database from real images ends up being inconvenient for the different types of contaminants. One alternative is using the idea of construct virtual data like proposed by Ji et al. (2019). In this case the researchers can construct the virtual dataset as needed with the advantages of be easily changed and automatically annotated serving as perfect training datasets for machine learning.

CONCLUSION

A state of art technique with the highest accuracy alongside with least computational power available was used in this research: the convolutional neural network and its preprocessing. This chapter describe in detail the topics which leaded to the decision about the computational tools used, the convolutional neural networks model, the background subtraction and problems originated by the lack of a representative dataset.

Cleanliness classification can be performed using Convolutional Neural Network, shown in Figure 19; however, it is only possible, in small datasets, when the background is extracted.

To accomplish the background extraction, semantic segmentation was tested, which concluded that without enough data, its output does not have the awaited and needed quality, shown by figure 20.

The next steps for this project are to explore tools for background extraction. Other topics that can be improved is to build a realistic scenario, using the unmanned aerial vehicle and the high-resolution camera for data acquisition, increasing our dataset volume, testing it on others models and possibly applying a model distillation, targeting on reducing even more the trainable parameters.

ACKNOWLEDGMENT

The authors thank Universidade Federal de Uberlândia (UFU), Centrais Elétricas de Santa Catarina (CELESC P&D Program) and Agência Nacional de Energia Elétrica (ANEEL) for the financial support to this work.

REFERENCES

Alom, Taha, Yakopcic, Westberg, Sidike, Nasrin, Hasan, Van Essen, Awwal, & Asari. (2019). *A State-of-the-Art Survey on Deep Learning Theory and Architectures*. Academic Press.

Andrade. (2019). *Best Practices for Convolutional Neural Networks Applied to Object Recognition in Images*. Academic Press.

Bhola, R., Krishna, N. H., Ramesh, K. N., Senthilnath, J., & Anand, G. (2018). Detection of the Power Lines in UAV Remote Sensed Images Using Spectral-Spatial Methods. *Journal of Environmental Management, 206*, 1233–1242. doi:10.1016/j.jenvman.2017.09.036 PMID:28931461

Bianco, S. (2018). *Remi Cadene, Luigi Celona, Paolo Napoletano*. Benchmark Analysis of Representative Deep Neural Network Architectures.

Chollet. (2017). *Xception: Deep Learning with Depthwise Separable Convolutions*. Google Inc.

Chollet, F. (2017), *Xception: Deep Learning with Depthwise Separable Convolutions*. ArXiv:1610.02357.

COPEL. (2015). *Maintenance on high voltage distribution lines with dead line*. Author.

Gao, Z., & Yang, G. (2019). Insulator Segmentation for Power Line Inspection Based on Modified Conditional Generative Adversarial Network. Academic Press.

Gao, Z., Yang, G., Li, E., Shen, T., Wang, Z., Tian, Y., Wang, H., & Liang, Z. (2019). Insulator Segmentation for Power Line Inspection Based on Modified Conditional Generative Adversarial Network. *Journal of Sensors*.

Gonçalves, R. S., & Carvalho, J. C. M. (2013). Review and Latest Trends in Mobile Robots Applied in Power Transmission Lines. *International Journal of Advanced Robotic Systems.*

Gonçalves, R. S., & Carvalho, J. C. M. (2015). A Mobile Robot to be Applied in High Voltage Power Lines. *Journal of the Brazilian Society of Mechanical Sciences and Engineering, 37*(1), 349–359. doi:10.100740430-014-0152-0

Gonçalves, R. S., Souza, F. C, Homma, R. Z., Sudbrack, D. E. T., Trautmann, P. V., & Clasen, B. C. (2021). *Robots for Inspection and Maintenance of power transmission lines.* Academic Press.

Hadipour, M., & Shiran, M. A. (2017). Various Pollutions of Power Line Insulators. *Majlesi Journal of Electrical Engineering, 6*(1).

Han, Yang, Zhang, Chen, Li, Lai, Xu, Xu, Wang, & Chen. (2019). *A Method of Insulator Faults Detection in Aerial Images for High-Voltage Transmission Lines Inspection.* Março.

Han, J., Yang, Z., Zhang, Q., Chen, C., Li, H., Lai, S., Hu, G., Xu, C., Xu, H., Wang, D., & Chen, R. (2019). A Method of Insulator Faults Detection in Aerial Imagens for High-Voltage Transmission Lines Inspection. *Applied Sciences (Basel, Switzerland), 9.*

Hussain, M. M., Farokhi, S., McMeekin, S. G., & Farzaneh, M. (2015). The Effects of Salt Contamination Deposition on HV Insulators Under Environmental Stress. *IEEE 11th International Conference on the Properties and Applications of Dielectric Materials.*

Hyunho, L., Changhwan, K., Sunggi, P., Seok, L., Jaehun, K., & Kim Sun, J. (2013). *Vision Based Automatic Real Time Inspection of Power Transmission Line Inspection Metric.* Power Transmission Line.

IEEE Guide for Cleaning Insulators. (2005). IEEE Power Engineering Society, Transmission and Distribution Committee.

Jabid, T., & Ahsan, T. (2018). Insulator detection and defect classification using rotation invariant local directional pattern. *International Journal of Advanced Computer Science and Applications, 9*(2), 265–272. doi:10.14569/IJACSA.2018.090237

Ji, Z., Liao, Y., Zheng, L., Wu, L., Yu, M., & Feng, Y. (2019). An Assembled Detector Based on Geometrical Constraint for Power Component Recognition. *Sensors (Basel), 19*(16), 3517. doi:10.339019163517 PMID:31405244

Jingjing, Z., Xingtong, L., Jixiang, S., & Lin, L. (2012), Detecting insulators in the image of overhead transmission lines. Lecture Notes in Computer Science.

Keras A. P. I. Applications. (n.d.). https://keras.io/api/applications/

Kurtgis, M. P. (1984). *Method for washing voltage transmission line insulators.* US4477289.

Li, Su, & Liu. (2020). *Insulator Defect Recognition Based on Global Detection and Local Segmentation.* Academic Press.

Li, B., & Huang, Y. (2011). Study on the on-line monitoring method of insulator in the world. *Electrical Engineering,* (9), 1–5.

Li, B., Wu, D., Cong, Y., Xia, Y., & Tang, Y. (2012), A method of insulator detection from video sequence. *International Symposium on Information Science and Engineering*, 386–389.

Li, L. (2015). The UAV Intelligent Inspection of Transmission Lines. Atlantis Press. doi:10.2991/ameii-15.2015.285

Li, Z. (2016). *Transmission line intelligent inspection central control and mass data processing system and application based on UAV*. IEEE.

Ling, Qiu, Jin, Zhang, He, Liu, & Lei. (2018). *An Accurate and Real-time Self-blast Glass Insulator Location Method Based on Faster R-CNN and U-net with Aerial Images*. Janeiro.

Liu, C., Wu, Y., Liu, J., & Sun, Z. (2021). Improved YOLOv3 Network for Insulator Detection in Aerial Images with Diverse Background Interference. *Electronics (Basel)*, *10*(7), 771. doi:10.3390/electronics10070771

Liu, X., Miao, X., Jiang, H., & Chen, J. (2020), *Review of data analysis in vision inspection of power lines with an in-depth discussion of deep learning technology*. arXiv:2003.09802.

Mantovani, V. A., Franco, C. S., Mancini, S. D., Haseagawa, H. L., Gianelli, G. F., Batista, V. X., & Rodrigues, L. L. (2013). Comparison of polymers and ceramics in new and discarded electrical insulators: Reuse and recycling possibilities. *Revista Matéria*, *18*(04), 1549–1562. doi:10.1590/S1517-70762013000400015

Maraaba, L., Al-Hamouz, Z., & Al-Duwaish, H. (2014). Estimation of High voltage Insulator Contamination Using a Combined Image Processing and Artificial Neural Networks. *IEEE 8th International Power Engineering and Optimization Conference*.

Meyer, L. H., Beyer, W. W., & Molina, F. H. (2013). Salt fog testing of glass insulators with different surface conditions. *2013 3rd International Conference on Electric Power and Energy Conversion Systems*, 1-4. 10.1109/EPECS.2013.6713083

Nguyen, V. N., Jenssen, R., & Roverso, D. (2019). Intelligent Monitoring and Inspection of Power Line Components Powered by UAVs and Deep Learning. *IEEE Power and Energy Technology Systems Journal*, *6*(1), 11–21. doi:10.1109/JPETS.2018.2881429

Pagnano, A., Höpf, M., & Teti, R. (2013). A Roadmap for Automated Power Line Inspection. *Maintenance And Repair. Procedia Cirp*, *12*, 234–239. doi:10.1016/j.procir.2013.09.041

Park, J.-Y., Cho, B.-H., Byun, S.-H., & Lee, J.-K. (2009). Development of Cleaning Robot System for Live-line Suspension Insulator Strings. *International Journal of Control, Automation, and Systems*, *7*(2), 211–220. doi:10.100712555-009-0207-7

Park, J.-Y., Lee, J.-K., Cho, B.-H., & Oh, K.-Y. (2012). An Inspection Robot for Live-Line Suspension Insulator Strings in 345-kV Power Lines. *IEEE Transactions on Power Delivery*, *27*(2), 632–639. doi:10.1109/TPWRD.2011.2182620

Pernebayeva, D., Irmanova, A., Sadykova, D., Bagheri, M., & James, A. (2019). High voltage outdoor insulator surface condition evaluation using aerial insulator images. *High Volt.*, *4*(3), 178–185. doi:10.1049/hve.2019.0079

Puchale, L. H. B. (2019), *Metodologia para mitigação de desligamento intempestivos em linhas de transmissão correlacionados a umidade elevada* (Dissertation). Unisinos.

Ronneberger, O., Fischer, P., & Brox, T. (2015). *U-Net: Convolutional Networks for Biomedical Image Segmentation*. MICCAI.

Rosenblatt, F. (1958). The perceptron: A probabilistic model for information storage and organization in the brain. *Psychological Review*, *65*(6), 386–408. doi:10.1037/h0042519 PMID:13602029

Rubin, L. (2000). *The Future of Power Line Inspection*. Electrical World T&D.

Rumelhart, D., Hinton, G., & Williams, R. (1986). Learning representations by back-propagating errors. *Nature*, *323*(6088), 533–536. doi:10.1038/323533a0

Sanyal, S., Aslam, F., Kim, T., Jeon, S., Lee, Y-J., Yi, J., Choi, I-H., Son, J-A., & Koo, J-B. (2019). Deterioration of Porcelain Insulators Utilized in Overhead Transmission Lines: A Review. *Transactions on Electrical and Electronic Materials*.

Siddiqui, Z. A., Park, U., Lee, S.-W., Jung, N.-J., Choi, M., Lim, C., & Seo, J.-H. (2018). Robust Power-line Equipment Inspection System Based on a Convolutional Neural Network. *Sensors (Basel)*, *18*(11), 3837. doi:10.339018113837 PMID:30413123

Siderakis, Pylarinos, Thalassinakis, Vitellas, & Pyrgioti. (2011). *Pollution Maintenance Techniques in Coastal High Voltage Installations*. Academic Press.

Simas. (2010), Kinematic Conception of a Hydraulic Robot Applied to Power Line Insulators Maintenance. *ABCM Symposium Series in Mechatronics*, 4, 739-748.

Sousa, R. O. (2010). *A New Technique of Washing of Insulators of the Electric Distribution Grid*. Universidade Federal do Ceará – UFC.

Sousa, R. O, Pontes, R. S. T., Aguiar, V. P. B, Luna, A. M., Andrade, C. T. C. (2009), Technique of dry washing of the insulators of the electrical nets of distribution. *11° Conferência Espanhola-Lusa de Engenharia Elétrica*.

Takaya, K. (2019). Development of UAV System for Autonomous Power Line Inspection. *2019 23rd International Conference on System Theory, Control and Computing, Icstcc 2019 - Proceedings*, 762–767.

Tao, X., Zhang, D., Wang, Z., Liu, X., & Zhang, H., & Xu, D. (2018). Detection of Power Line Insulator Defects Using Aerial Images Analyzed with Convolutional Neural Networks. *IEEE Transactions on Systems, Man, and Cybernetics. Systems*.

Tengfei, S., Ronghai, L., Xin, Z., Zhangqin, W., Xinliang, G., Yingchun, Y., & Hongwei, X. (2015). *Electrified insulator cleaning method based on unmanned aerial vehicle*. CN105170523A.

Tiantian, Y., Guodong, Y., & Junzhi, Y. (2017). Feature fusion-based insulator detection for aerial inspection. *2017 36th Chinese Control Conference (CCC)*, 10972-10977. 10.23919/ChiCC.2017.8029108

Tomaszewski, M., Ruszczak, B., & Michalski, P. (2018). The collection of images of an insulator taken outdoors in varying lighting conditions with additional laser spots. *Data in Brief*, *18*, 765–768. doi:10.1016/j.dib.2018.03.063 PMID:29900234

Transmission and Distribution Committee. (2005). *IEEE Guide for Cleaning Insulators.* IEEE Std 957™.

Versaci, M., Calcagno, S., & Morabito, F. C. (2015)Fuzzy Geometrical Approach Base on Unit Hyper-Cubes for Image Contrast Enhancement. *IEEE International Conference on Signal and Image Processing Applications.* 10.1109/ICSIPA.2015.7412240

Versaci, M., Morabito, F. C., & Angiulli, G. (2017). Adaptive Image Contrast Enhancement by Computing Distances into a 4-Dimensional Fuzzy Unit Hypercube. *IEEE Access: Practical Innovations, Open Solutions, 5,* 26922–26931. Advance online publication. doi:10.1109/ACCESS.2017.2776349

Wang, L., & Wang, H. (2016). A survey on insulator inspection robots for power transmission lines. *4th International Conference on Applied Robotics for the Power Industry.* 10.1109/CARPI.2016.7745639

Wang, L., Wang, H., & Chang, Y., (2015) Mechanism Design of an Insulator Cleaning Robot for Suspension Insulator Strings. *Proceedings of the 2015 IEEE Conference on Robotics and Biomometics.* 10.1109/ROBIO.2015.7419103

Wang, L., Wang, H-G., & Song, Y-F. (2016), Development of a Bio-Inspired Live-Line Cleaning Robot for Suspension Insulator Strings. *International Journal of Simulation: Systems, 17*(48), 24.1-24.9.

Wightman, A., & Bodger, P. (2011). Volcanic Ash Contamination of High Voltage Insulators. *EEA Conference & Exhibition.*

Wu, Q., An, J., & Lin, B. (2012). A texture segmentation algorithm based on PCA and global minimization active contour model for aerial insulator images. *IEEE Journal of Selected Topics in Applied Earth Observations and Remote Sensing, 5*(5), 1509–1518. doi:10.1109/JSTARS.2012.2197672

Yang, L., Jiang, X., Hao, Y., Li, L., Li, H., Li, R., & Luo, B. (2017). Recognition of natural ice types on in-service glass insulators based on texture feature descriptor. *IEEE Transactions on Dielectrics and Electrical Insulation, 24*(1), 535–542. doi:10.1109/TDEI.2016.006049

Yao, C., Jin, L., & Yan, S. (2012). Recognition of insulator string in power grid patrol images. *Xitong Fangzhen Xuebao, 24*(9), 1818–1822.

Zhai, Y., Cheng, H., Rui, C., Qiang, Y., & Li, X. (2018). Multi-saliency aggregation-based approach for insulator flashover fault detection using aerial images. *Energies, 11*(2), 340. doi:10.3390/en11020340

Zhai, Y., Wang, D., Zhang, M., Wang, J., & Guo, F. (2017). Fault Detection of Insulator Based on Saliency and Adaptive Morphology. *Multimedia Tools and Applications, 76*(9), 12051–12064. doi:10.100711042-016-3981-2

Zhang, X., An, J., & Chen, F. (2010). A simple method of tempered glass insulator recognition from airborne image. *2010 International Conference on Optoelectronics and Image Processing, 1,* 127–130.

Zhao, Z., Xu, G., Qi, Y., Liu, N., & Zhang, T. (2016), Multi-patch deep features for power line insulator status classification from aerial images. *2016 International Joint Conference on Neural Networks,* 3187–3194.

Zhu, X., Li, X., & Yan, F. (2018). Design and implementation for integrated UAV multi-spectral inspection system. *IOP Conference Series. Earth and Environmental Science*, *133*(1), 012006. doi:10.1088/1755-1315/133/1/012006

KEY TERMS AND DEFINITIONS

Cleaning: The action of making something clean, in the case of this chapter making clean the insulators chain.

Deep Learning: Is part of machine learning methods based on artificial neural networks with representation learning.

Inspection: The act of inspecting or viewing, in the case of this chapter inspecting carefully the insulators.

Insulator: A string of discs used in power transmission lines to support and separate electrical conductors (lines) without allowing current to flow through the tower to ground.

Mobile Robots: Is a type of robot capable of moving in the case of this chapter in the cable power lines or along the insulator to inspection or clean.

Power Lines: Is a cable, above the ground, supported by pylons, poles or towers along which electrical power is carrying to an area to other.

UAV: Unmanned Aerial Vehicle, commonly denominate as a drone, is an aircraft piloted by remote control or onboard fly controls computers.

Compilation of References

2021). http://www.20q.net/

Abdaoui, A., Al-Ali, A., Riahi, A., Mohamed, A., Du, X., & Guizani, M. (2020). Secure medical treatment with deep learning on embedded board. In *Energy Efficiency of Medical Devices and Healthcare Applications* (pp. 131–151). Elsevier. doi:10.1016/B978-0-12-819045-6.00007-8

ACM/IEEE-CS Joint Task Force on Computing Curricula. (2013). *Computer Science Curricula 2013*. ACM Press and IEEE Computer Society Press., doi:10.1145/2534860

Afsharzadeh, A. (2016).*Automatic disassembly task sequence planning of aircrafts at their end-of-life* (Doctoral dissertation). Ecole Polytechnique, Montreal, Canada.

Agarwal, J., & Naresh, K. M. (2005). An integrated model of attitude and affect: Theoretical foundation and empirical investigation. *Journal of Business Research*, *58*(4), 483–493. doi:10.1016/S0148-2963(03)00138-3

Aggrey, P., Salimon, A., & Korsunsky, A. (2020). Diatomite inspired nanostructured quartz as a piezoelectric material. *Limnology and Freshwater Biology*, (4), 828–829. doi:10.31951/2658-3518-2020-A-4-828

Agrawal, T. (2021a). Introduction to Hyperparameters. In *Hyperparameter Optimization in Machine Learning* (pp. 1–30). Apress. doi:10.1007/978-1-4842-6579-6_1

Agrawal, T. (2021b). Optuna and AutoML. In *Hyperparameter Optimization in Machine Learning* (pp. 109–129). Apress. doi:10.1007/978-1-4842-6579-6_5

Aguilar, F. J. (1967). *Scanning the Business Environment*. The Macmillian Company.

Aguilar, W., Santamaría-Bonfil, G., Froese, T., & Gershenson, C. (2014). The past, present, and future of artificial life. *Frontiers in Robotics and AI*, *1*(8), 1–15. doi:10.3389/frobt.2014.00008

Ahad, A., Tahir, M., & Yau, K. A. (2019). 5G-Based Smart Healthcare Network: Architecture, Taxonomy, Challenges and Future Research Directions. *IEEE Access: Practical Innovations, Open Solutions*, *7*, 100747–100762. doi:10.1109/ACCESS.2019.2930628

Ahmadpour Khanghashlaghi, M., Yue, W. L., & Mohammadzaheri, M. (2009). *Neuro-fuzzy modelling of workders trip production* The 32nd Austalasian Transport Research Forum, Auckland, New Zealand.

Ahmad, S., Lavin, A., Purdy, S., & Agha, Z. (2017). Unsupervised real-time anomaly detection for streaming data. *Neurocomputing*, *262*, 134–147.

Aho, A. V. (2012). Computation and computational thinking. *The Computer Journal*, *55*(7), 833–835. doi:10.1093/comjnl/bxs074

Akshoomoff, N., Newman, E., Thompson, W. K., McCabe, C., Bloss, C. S., Chang, L., Amaral, D. G., Casey, B. J., Ernst, T. M., Frazier, J. A., Gruen, J. R., Kaufmann, W. E., Kenet, T., Kennedy, D. N., Libiger, O., Mostofsky, S., Murray, S. S., Sowell, E. R., Schork, N., ... Jernigan, T. L. (2014). The NIH toolbox cognition battery: Results from a large normative developmental sample (PING). *Neuropsychology, 28*(1), 1–10. doi:10.1037/neu0000001

Albala M. (2013). Triggering Business Model Innovation Programs Through Early Warning Systems. *Cognizant 20-20 Insight.*

Albayrak, İ., Aşan, N., & Yorulmaz, T. (2008). The natural history of the Egyptian fruit bat, Rousettus aegyptiacus, in Turkey (Mammalia: Chiroptera). *Turkish Journal of Zoology, 32*(1), 11–18.

Albelwi, S., & Mahmood, A. (2016, December). Automated optimal architecture of deep convolutional neural networks for image recognition. In *2016 15th IEEE International conference on machine learning and applications (ICMLA)* (pp. 53-60). IEEE. 10.1109/ICMLA.2016.0018

Albuquerque, M. P., Esquef, I., & Gesualdi Mello, A. R. (2004). Image Thresholding Using Tsallis Entropy. *Pattern Recognition Letters, 25*(9), 1059–1065. doi:10.1016/j.patrec.2004.03.003

Ali, A., Shamsuddin, S. M., & Ralescu, A. L. (2015). Classification with class imbalance problem: A Review. *Int. J. Advance Soft Compu. App, 7*(3).

Alkaya, A. F., & Duman, E. (2015). Combining and solving sequence dependent traveling salesman and quadratic assignment problems in PCB assembly. *Discrete Applied Mathematics, 192*, 2–16. doi:10.1016/j.dam.2015.03.009

Allen, R., & Mazumder, M. (2020). Toward an Autonomous Aerial Survey and Planning System for Humanitarian Aid and Disaster Response. *2020 IEEE Aerospace Conference*, 1-11. 10.1109/AERO47225.2020.9172766

Allport, G. W. (1935). *Attitudes. In Handbook of social psychology.* Clark University Press.

Allport, G. W. (1954). *The nature of prejudice.* Addison-Wesley.

Almasri, A., Celebi, E., & Alkhawaldeh, R. S. (2019). *EMT : Ensemble Meta-Based Tree Model for Predicting Student Performance.* Academic Press.

Alom, Taha, Yakopcic, Westberg, Sidike, Nasrin, Hasan, Van Essen, Awwal, & Asari. (2019). *A State-of-the-Art Survey on Deep Learning Theory and Architectures.* Academic Press.

Al-Osaimy, M. H., & Bamakhramah, A. S. (2010). An Early Warning System for Islamic Banks. *J. KAU: Islamic Econ., 17*(1), 3-14.

Alrashdi, I., Alqazzaz, A., Alharthi, R., Aloufi, E., Zohdy, M. A., & Ming, H. (2019). *FBAD: Fog-based attack detection for IoT healthcare in smart cities. 2019 IEEE 10th Annual Ubiquitous Computing, Electronics & Mobile Communication Conference.* UEMCON.

Alshibli, M., El Sayed, A., Kongar, E., Sobh, T. M., & Gupta, S. M. (2016). Disassembly sequencing using tabu search. *Journal of Intelligent & Robotic Systems, 82*(1), 69–79. doi:10.100710846-015-0289-9

Alyahyan, E., & Düştegör, D. (2020). Predicting academic success in higher education: Literature review and best practices. *International Journal of Educational Technology in Higher Education, 17*(1), 3. Advance online publication. doi:10.118641239-020-0177-7

Alzubaidi, L., Zhang, J., Humaidi, A. J., Al-Dujaili, A., Duan, Y., Al-Shamma, O., Santamaría, J., Fadhel, M. A., Al-Amidie, M., & Farhan, L. (2021). Review of deep learning: Concepts, CNN architectures, challenges, applications, future directions. *Journal of Big Data, 8*(1), 53. doi:10.118640537-021-00444-8 PMID:33816053

Amazon Forecast AutoM. L. (n.d.). https://docs.aws.amazon.com/forecast/latest/dg/automl.html

Amigo, J. M. (2020). Hyperspectral and multispectral imaging: Setting the scene. *Data Handling in Science and Technology*, *32*, 3–16. doi:10.1016/B978-0-444-63977-6.00001-8

Anacapa Sciences. (2003). *Criminal Intelligence Analysis: Development of Inferences" (1982-2003)*. Anacapa Sciences, Inc.

Andonie, R., & Florea, A. C. (2020). *Weighted random search for CNN hyperparameter optimization*. arXiv preprint arXiv:2003.13300.

Andrade. (2019). *Best Practices for Convolutional Neural Networks Applied to Object Recognition in Images*. Academic Press.

Andresen, M. S., Dissing, B. S., & Løje, H. (2013). Quality assessment of butter cookies applying multispectral imaging. *Food Science & Nutrition*, *1*(4), 315–323. doi:10.1002/fsn3.46 PMID:24804036

Ang, M. C., Pham, D. T., & Ng, K. W. (2009). Application of the Bees Algorithm with TRIZ-inspired operators for PCB assembly planning. In *Proceedings of 5th Virtual International Conference on Intelligent Production Machines and Systems (IPROMS2006)* (pp. 454-459). Academic Press.

Angiulli, G., Jannelli, A., Morabito, F. C., & Versaci, M. (2018). Reconstructing the membrane detection of a 1 D electrostatic-driven MEMS device by the shooting method: Convergence analysis and ghost solutions identification. *Computational & Applied Mathematics*, *37*(4), 4484–4498. doi:10.100740314-017-0564-4

Angiulli, G., & Versaci, M. (2002). A Neuro-Fuzzy Network for the design of circular and triangular equilateral microstrip antennas. *International Journal of Infrared and Millimeter Waves*, *23*(10), 1513–1520. doi:10.1023/A:1020333704205

Ang, M. C., Ng, K. W., Pham, D. T., & Soroka, A. (2013, November). Simulations of PCB assembly optimisation based on the Bees Algorithm with TRIZ-inspired operators. In *International Visual Informatics Conference* (pp. 335-346). Springer. 10.1007/978-3-319-02958-0_31

Ansoff, H. I. (1975). Managing Strategic Surprise by Response to Weak Signals. *California Management Review*, *18*(2), 21–33. doi:10.2307/41164635

Apostol, T. M. (1976). *Introduction to Analytic Number Theory*. Springer Verlang.

Araújo, M. C. U., Saldanha, T. C. B., Galvão, R. K. H., Yoneyama, T., Chame, H. C., & Visani, V. (2001). The successive projections algorithm for variable selection in spectroscopic multicomponent analysis. *Chemometrics and Intelligent Laboratory Systems*, *57*(2), 65–73. doi:10.1016/S0169-7439(01)00119-8

Arel, I., Rose, D. C., & Karnowski, T. P. (2010). Deep machine learning-a new frontier in artificial intelligence research. *IEEE Computational Intelligence Magazine*, *5*(4), 13–18. doi:10.1109/MCI.2010.938364

Ariana, D. P., Lu, R., & Guyer, D. E. (2006). Near-infrared hyperspectral reflectance imaging for detection of bruises on pickling cucumbers. *Computers and Electronics in Agriculture*, *53*(1), 60–70. doi:10.1016/j.compag.2006.04.001

Armitage, D. W., & Ober, H. K. (2010). A comparison of supervised learning techniques in the classification of bat echolocation calls. *Ecological Informatics*, *5*(6), 465–473. doi:10.1016/j.ecoinf.2010.08.001

Arshavsky, Y. I., Deliagina, T. G., & Orlovsky, G. N. (2016). Central pattern generators: Mechanisms of operations and their role in controlling automatic movements. *Neuroscience and Behavioral Physiology*, *46*(6), 696–718. doi:10.100711055-016-0299-5

Arthur, J. V., & Boahen, K. A. (2010). Silicon-neuron design: A dynamical systems approach. *IEEE Transactions on Circuits and Systems. I, Regular Papers*, *58*(5), 1034–1043. doi:10.1109/TCSI.2010.2089556 PMID:21617741

Aslam, N., Khan, I. U., Alamri, L. H., & Almuslim, R. S. (2021). An Improved Early Student's Performance Prediction Using Deep Learning. *International Journal of Emerging Technologies in Learning, 16*(12), 108–122. doi:10.3991/ijet.v16i12.20699

Atanbori, J., Chen, F., French, A. P., & Pridmore, T. (2018). Towards low-cost image-based plant phenotyping using reduced-parameter CNN. In *CVPPP 2018: Workshop on Computer Vision Problems in Plant Phenotyping*, Newcastle upon Tyne, UK.

Atman, K. (1987). The role of conation (striving) in the distance learning enterprise. *American Journal of Distance Education, 1*(1), 14–28. doi:10.1080/08923648709526568

ATOM. (2021). https://atom.io

Ayob, M., Cowling, P., & Kendall, G. (2002). Optimisation for surface mount placement machines. In *2002 IEEE International Conference on Industrial Technology, 2002. IEEE ICIT'02* (Vol. 1, pp. 498-503). IEEE Press.

Azimi-Pour, M., Eskandari-Naddaf, H., & Pakzad, A. (2020). Linear and non-linear SVM prediction for fresh properties and compressive strength of high volume fly ash self-compacting concrete. *Construction & Building Materials, 230*, 117021. doi:10.1016/j.conbuildmat.2019.117021

Bacanin, N., Bezdan, T., Tuba, E., Strumberger, I., & Tuba, M. (2020). Optimizing Convolutional Neural Network Hyperparameters by Enhanced Swarm Intelligence Metaheuristics. *Algorithms, 13*(3), 67. doi:10.3390/a13030067

Bagozzi, R. P. (1992). The self-regulation of attitudes, intentions, and behaviour. *Social Psychology Quarterly, 55*(2), 178. doi:10.2307/2786945

Baker, B., Gupta, O., Naik, N., & Raskar, R. (2017). Designing neural network architectures using reinforcement learning. *Proceedings of Int. Conf. Learning Representations.*

Baker, D. P., & Salas, E. (1992). Principles for measuring teamwork skills. *Human Factors, 34*(4), 469–475. doi:10.1177/001872089203400408

Bakhshi, A., Noman, N., Chen, Z., Zamani, M., & Chalup, S. (2019, June). Fast automatic optimisation of CNN architectures for image classification using genetic algorithm. In *2019 IEEE Congress on Evolutionary Computation (CEC)* (pp. 1283-1290). IEEE. 10.1109/CEC.2019.8790197

Bandura, A. (1977). *Social learning theory.* Prentice Hall.

Bandura, A. (1986). *Social foundations of thought and action: A social cognitive theory.* Prentice-Hall, Inc.

Bandura, A., Freeman, W. H., & Lightsey, R. (1999). Self-efficacy: The exercise of control. *Journal of Cognitive Psychotherapy, 13*(2), 158–166. doi:10.1891/0889-8391.13.2.158

Barber, C. B., David, P., Dobkin, D. P., & Huhdanpaa, H. (1996). The Quickhull Algorithm for Convex Hulls. *ACM Transactions on Mathematical Software, 22*(4), 469–483. doi:10.1145/235815.235821

Barr, D., Harrison, J., & Conery, L. (2011). Computational thinking: A digital age skill for everyone. *Learning and Leading with Technology, 38*(6), 20–23.

Barrett, L., & Narayanan, S. (2008). Learning All Optimal Policies with Multiple Criteria. In *Proceedings of the 25th International Conference on Machine Learning (ICML-2008).* ACM. 10.1145/1390156.1390162

Barros, T. M., Guedes, L. A., & Silva, I. (2019). *Education Sciences Predictive Models for Imbalanced Data : A School Dropout Perspective.* doi:10.3390/educsci9040275

Barr, V., & Stephenson, C. (2011). Bringing computational thinking to K–12: What is involved and what is the role of the computer science education community? *ACM Inroads*, *2*(1), 48–54. doi:10.1145/1929887.1929905

Barto, A. G., Steven, J., Bradtke, S. J., & Singh, S. P. (1995). Learning to Act Using Real-Time Dynamic Programming. *Artificial Intelligence*, *72*(1-2), 81–138. doi:10.1016/0004-3702(94)00011-O

Bartz, E., Zaefferer, M., Mersmann, O., & Bartz-Beielstein, T. (2021). *Experimental investigation and evaluation of model-based hyperparameter optimisation*. arXiv:2107.08761v1 [cs.LG].

Bastas, S., Majid, M. W., Mirzaei, G., Ross, J., Jamali, M. M., Gorsevski, P. V., ... Bingman, V. P. (2012, May). A novel feature extraction algorithm for classification of bird flight calls. In *2012 IEEE International Symposium on Circuits and Systems (ISCAS)* (pp. 1676-1679). IEEE. 10.1109/ISCAS.2012.6271580

Baumeister, R. E. F., Bratslavsky, E., Muraven, M., & Tice, D. M. (1998). Ego Depletion: Is the active self a limited resource. *Journal of Personality and Social Psychology*, *74*(5), 1252–1265. doi:10.1037/0022-3514.74.5.1252 PMID:9599441

Bausys, R., Karakeviciute-Januskeviciene, G., Cavallaro, F., & Usovaite, A. (2020). Algorithm Selection for Edge Detection in Satellite Images by Neutrosophic WASPAS Method. *Sustainability*, *12*(548), 1–12. doi:10.3390u12020548

Bay, H., Ess, A., Tuytelaars, T., & Gool, L. V. (2008). SURF: Speeded Up Robust Features. *Computer Vision and Image Understanding*, *110*(3), 346–359. doi:10.1016/j.cviu.2007.09.014

Baykasoglu, A., Ozbakir, L., & Tapkan, P. (2009). The bees algorithm for workload balancing in examination job assignment. *European Journal of Industrial Engineering*, *3*(4), 424–435. doi:10.1504/EJIE.2009.027035

Bazghaleh, M., Grainger, S., Cazzolato, B., & Lu, T.-f. (2010, December). *An innovative digital charge amplifier to reduce hysteresis in piezoelectric actuators*. Australian Robotics and Automation Association (ACRA), Brisbane, Australia.

Bazghaleh, M., Grainger, S., & Mohammadzaheri, M. J. J. I. M. S. (2018). A review of charge methods for driving piezoelectric actuators. *Journal of Intelligent Material Systems and Structures*, *29*(10), 2096–2104. doi:10.1177/1045389X17733330

Bazghaleh, M., Grainger, S., Mohammadzaheri, M., Cazzolato, B., & Lu, T. (2013). A digital charge amplifier for hysteresis elimination in piezoelectric actuators. *Smart Materials and Structures*, *22*(7), 075016. doi:10.1088/0964-1726/22/7/075016

Bazghaleh, M., Grainger, S., Mohammadzaheri, M., Cazzolato, B., & Lu, T.-F. (2013). A novel digital charge-based displacement estimator for sensorless control of a grounded-load piezoelectric tube actuator. *Sensors and Actuators. A, Physical*, *198*, 91–98. doi:10.1016/j.sna.2013.04.021

Bazghaleh, M., Mohammadzaheri, M., Grainger, S., Cazzolato, B., & Lu, T. F. (2013). A new hybrid method for sensorless control of piezoelectric actuators. *Sensors and Actuators. A, Physical*, *194*, 25–30. doi:10.1016/j.sna.2013.01.043

Beauvois, M., Dierckx, L., Bonaventure, O., & Nijssen, S. (2021). *Automated detection of bat species in Belgium*. http://hdl.handle.net/2078.1/thesis:30594

Beaver, J. R. (1994). *Problem solving across the curriculum*. International Society for Technology in Education.

Behdad, S., & Thurston, D. (2012). Disassembly and reassembly sequence planning trade-offs under uncertainty for product maintenance. *ASME Journal Mechanical Design*, *134*(4), 041011. doi:10.1115/1.4006262

Bejar, H. H., Ferzoli Guimaraes, S. J., & Miranda, P. A. V. (2020). Efficient hierarchical graph partitioning for imaage segmentation by optimum oriented cuts. *Pattern Recognition Letters*, *131*, 185–192. doi:10.1016/j.patrec.2020.01.008

Bellardita, C., & Kiehn, O. (2015). Phenotypic characterization of speed-associated gait changes in mice reveals modular organization of locomotor networks. *Current Biology*, *25*(11), 1426–1436. doi:10.1016/j.cub.2015.04.005 PMID:25959968

Bell, T., & Roberts, J. (2016). Computational thinking is more about humans than computers. set. *Research Information for Teachers*, *1*(1), 3–7. doi:10.18296et.0030

Ben Amor, L., Lahyani, I., & Jmaiel, M. (2020). AUDIT: AnomaloUs data Detection and Isolation approach for mobile healThcare systems. *Expert Systems: International Journal of Knowledge Engineering and Neural Networks*, *37*(1), e12390.

Benda, P., Vallo, P., Hulva, P., & Horáček, I. (2012). The Egyptian fruit bat Rousettus aegyptiacus (Chiroptera: Pteropodidae) in the Palaearctic: Geographical variation and taxonomic status. *Biologia*, *67*(6), 1230–1244. doi:10.247811756-012-0105-y

Bengio, Y. (2009). Learning Deep Architectures for AI. *Foundations and Trends in Machine Learning*, *2*(1), 1–127. doi:10.1561/2200000006

Benuwa, B. B., Zhan, Y. Z., Ghansah, B., Wornyo, D. K., & Banaseka Kataka, F. (2016). A review of deep machine learning. *International Journal of Engineering Research in Africa*, *24*, 124–136. doi:10.4028/www.scientific.net/JERA.24.124

Bergstra, J., Bardenet, R., Bengio, Y., & Kégl, B. (2011). Algorithms for hyper-parameter optimization. Adv Neural Inf Process Syst (NIPS), 24, 2546-2554.

Bergstra, J., & Bengio, Y. (2012). Random search for hyper-parameter optimization. *Journal of Machine Learning Research*, *13*(2).

Bernal, E., Castillo, O., Soria, J., & Valdez, F. (2017). Imperialist competitive algorithm with dynamic parameter adaptation using fuzzy logic applied to the optimization of mathematical functions. *Algorithms*, *10*(1), 18.

Bernhardt, D. (1999). Consumer versus producer: Overcoming the disconnect between management and competitive intelligence. *Competitive Intelligence Review*, *10*(1).

Beyer, B. K. (1988). *Developing A Thinking Skills Programme*. Allyn and Bacon Inc.

Beyer, B. K. (1995). *Critical Thinking*. Phi Delta Kappa Educational Foundations.

Bhandare, A., & Kaur, D. (2018). Designing convolutional neural network architecture using genetic algorithms. In *Proceedings on the International Conference on Artificial Intelligence (ICAI)* (pp. 150-156). The Steering Committee of The World Congress in Computer Science, Computer Engineering and Applied Computing (WorldComp).

Bhatia, N. (2010). *Survey of nearest neighbor techniques*. arXiv preprint arXiv:1007.0085.

Bhattacharya, S., Somayaji, S., Reddy, P. K., Kaluri, R., Gadekallu, T., Alazab, M., & Tariq, U. (2020). A novel PCA-firefly based XGBoost classification model for intrusion detection in networks using GPU. *Electronics (Basel)*, *9*(2), 219. doi:10.3390/electronics9020219

Bhatti, Z., Waqas, A., Mahesar, A. W., & Karbasi, M. (2017). Gait analysis and biomechanics of quadruped motion for procedural animation and robotic simulation. *Bahria University Journal of Information & Communication Technologies*, *10*(2), 1–7.

Bhola, R., Krishna, N. H., Ramesh, K. N., Senthilnath, J., & Anand, G. (2018). Detection of the Power Lines in UAV Remote Sensed Images Using Spectral-Spatial Methods. *Journal of Environmental Management*, *206*, 1233–1242. doi:10.1016/j.jenvman.2017.09.036 PMID:28931461

Bianco, S. (2018). *Remi Cadene, Luigi Celona, Paolo Napoletano*. Benchmark Analysis of Representative Deep Neural Network Architectures.

Billingsley, P. (1965). *Ergodic theory and information*. Wiley.

Bishop, J. C., Falzon, G., Trotter, M., Kwan, P., & Meek, P. D. (2019). Livestock vocalisation classification in farm soundscapes. *Computers and Electronics in Agriculture, 162*, 531–542. doi:10.1016/j.compag.2019.04.020

Biswal, P., & Mohanty, P. K. (2021). Development of quadruped walking robots: A review. *Ain Shams Engineering Journal, 12*(2), 2017–2031. doi:10.1016/j.asej.2020.11.005

Bithari, T. B., Thapa, S., & Hari, K. C. (2020). Predicting Academic Performance of Engineering Students using Ensemble Method. *A Peer Reviwed Technical Journal Nepal Engineers' Association Gandaki Province, 2*(1), 89–98.

Blagus, R., & Lusa, L. (2013). *Open Access SMOTE for high-dimensional class-imbalanced data*. Academic Press.

Blumstein, D. T., Mennill, D. J., Clemins, P., Girod, L., Yao, K., Patricelli, G., Deppe, J. L., Krakauer, A. H., Clark, C., Cortopassi, K. A., Hanser, S. F., McCowan, B., Ali, A. M., & Kirschel, A. N. (2011). Acoustic monitoring in terrestrial environments using microphone arrays: Applications, technological considerations and prospectus. *Journal of Applied Ecology, 48*(3), 758–767. doi:10.1111/j.1365-2664.2011.01993.x

Boaler, J., & Greeno, J. G. (2000). Identity, agency, and knowing in mathematics worlds. In J. Boaler (Ed.), *Multiple perspectives on mathematics teaching and learning* (pp. 171–200). Ablex.

Bochinski, E., Senst, T., & Sikora, T. (2017, September). Hyper-parameter optimization for convolutional neural network committees based on evolutionary algorithms. In 2017 IEEE international conference on image processing (ICIP) (pp. 3924-3928). IEEE. doi:10.1109/ICIP.2017.8297018

Bohner, G., & Wanke, M. (2002). *Attitudes and Attitude Change*. Psychology Press.

Bold, N., Zhang, C., & Akashi, T. (2019, October). Bird Species Classification with Audio-Visual Data using CNN and Multiple Kernel Learning. In *2019 International Conference on Cyberworlds (CW)* (pp. 85-88). IEEE. 10.1109/CW.2019.00022

Boldrini, B., Kessler, W., Rebner, K., & Kessler, R. (2012). Hyperspectral imaging: A review of best practice, performance and pitfalls for in-line and on-line applications. *Journal of Near Infrared Spectroscopy, 20*(5), 438. doi:10.1255/jnirs.1003

Bonabeau, E., Marco, D. D. R. D. F., Dorigo, M., Théraulaz, G., & Theraulaz, G. (1999). Swarm intelligence: from natural to artificial systems (No. 1). Oxford University Press.

Boothroyd, G. (1994). Product design for manufacture and assembly. *Computer Aided Design, 26*(7), 505–520. doi:10.1016/0010-4485(94)90082-5

Borgli, R. J. (2018). *Hyperparameter optimization using Bayesian optimization on transfer learning for medical image classification* [Master thesis]. University of Oslo.

Bostami, B., Ahmed, M., & Choudhury, S. (2019). False Data Injection Attacks in Internet of Things. In *Performability in Internet of Things* (pp. 47–58). Springer. doi:10.1007/978-3-319-93557-7_4

Breiman, L. E. O. (2001). *Random Forests*. Academic Press.

Brennan, K., & Resnick, M. (2012). *New frameworks for studying and assessing the development of computational thinking*. Retrieved from http://web.media.mit.edu/~kbrennan/files/Brennan_ Resnick_AERA2012_CT.pdf

Brochu, E., Cora, V. M., & De Freitas, N. (2010). *A tutorial on Bayesian optimization of expensive cost functions, with application to active user modeling and hierarchical reinforcement learning*. arXiv preprint arXiv:1012.2599.

BrockmanG.CheungV.PetterssonL.SchneiderJ.SchulmanJ.TangJ.ZarembaW. (2016). *Openai gym*. Retrieved from https://arxiv.org/pdf/1606.01540.pdf

Brodic, D., Amelio, A., & Jankovic, R. (2018). Comparison of different classification techniques in predicting a university course final grade. *2018 41st International Convention on Information and Communication Technology, Electronics and Microelectronics, MIPRO 2018 - Proceedings*, 1382–1387. 10.23919/MIPRO.2018.8400249

Bronfenbrenner, U. (1979). *The Ecology of Human Development*. Harvard University Press.

Brown, J. C., & Smaragdis, P. (2009). Hidden Markov and Gaussian mixture models for automatic call classification. *The Journal of the Acoustical Society of America*, *125*(6), EL221–EL224. doi:10.1121/1.3124659 PMID:19507925

Bruner, J. (1996). *The Culture of Education*. Harvard University Press.

Bruno, P., Melnyk, V., & Völckner, F. (2017). Temperature and emotions: Effects of physical temperature on responses to emotional advertising. *International Journal of Research in Marketing*, *34*(1), 302–320. doi:10.1016/j.ijresmar.2016.08.005

Bulagang, A. F., Mountstephens, J., & Wi, J. T. T. (2020). Tuning support vector machines for improving four-class emotion classification in virtual reality (VR) using heart rate features. *Journal of Physics: Conference Series*, *1529*, 052069.

Bundy, A. (2007). Computational thinking is pervasive. *Journal of Scientific and Practical Computing*, *1*(2), 67–69.

Bunge, M. (1969). Probability and law [Probabilidad y ley]. *Magazine Diánoia.*, *15*(15), 141–160. doi:10.22201/iifs.18704913e.1969.15.1118

Butler, J. (1993). *Thinking skills in human development: At school and at work*. Paper Presented at the *International Convention on Excellence in Thinking*, Universiti Kebangsaan Malaysia, Malaysia.

Butler, K. A. (1987). *Learning & teaching style: In theory & practice*. Learner's Dimension.

Callen, H. B. (1985). *Thermodynamics and an Introduction to Thermostatistics* (2nd ed.). John Wiley & Sons.

Cambridge Dictionary. (2021). https://dictionary.cambridge.org

Can, Y. S., Chalabianloo, N., Ekiz, D., & Ersoy, C. (2019). Continuous stress detection using wearable sensors in real life: Algorithmic programming contest case study. *Sensors (Basel)*, *19*(8), 1849. doi:10.3390/s19081849

Cao, J., Chen, L., Wang, M., & Tian, Y. (2018). Implementating a Parallel Image Edge Detection Algorithm Based on the Otsu-Canny Operator on the Hadoop Platform. *Computational Intelligence and Neuroscience*, *2018*, 1–12. doi:10.1155/2018/3598284 PMID:29861711

Cao, Z., Chen, X., Yu, Y., Yu, J., Liu, X., Zhou, C., & Tan, M. (2020). Image Dynamics-Based Visual Servoing for Quadrotors Tracking a Target with a Nonlinear Trajectory Observer. *IEEE Transactions on Systems, Man, and Cybernetics. Systems*, *50*(1), 376–384. doi:10.1109/TSMC.2017.2720173

Caradonna, G., Lionetti, S., Tarantino, E., & Verdoscia, C. (2018). A comparison of low-poly algorithms for sharing 3D models on the web. In *New Advanced GNSS and 3D Spatial Techniques*. LNGC (pp. 237–244). Springer. doi:10.1007/978-3-319-56218-6_19

Cargata, P. J. (1999). *Business Early Warning Systems – A guide for managers, executives & investors*. Butterworths.

Carlborg, N., Tyrén, M., Heath, C., & Eriksson, E. (2019). The scope of autonomy when teaching computational thinking in primary school. *International Journal of Child-Computer Interaction*, *21*, 130–139. doi:10.1016/j.ijcci.2019.06.005

Carr, M. (2001). *Assessment in early childhood settings: Learning stories*. Paul Chapman.

Castellani, M., Otri, S., & Pham, D. T. (2019). Printed circuit board assembly time minimisation using a novel Bees Algorithm. *Computers & Industrial Engineering*, *133*, 186–194. doi:10.1016/j.cie.2019.05.015

Cawley, G. C., & Talbot, N. L. (2010). On over-fitting in model selection and subsequent selection bias in performance evaluation. *Journal of Machine Learning Research*, *11*(Jul), 2079–2107.

Cazalets, J. R., Borde, M., & Clarac, F. (1995). Localization and organization of the central pattern generator for hindlimb locomotion in newborn rat. *The Journal of Neuroscience: The Official Journal of the Society for Neuroscience*, *15*(7), 4943–4951. doi:10.1523/JNEUROSCI.15-07-04943.1995 PMID:7623124

Centre for Disease Prevention & Food Safety Authority. (2019). Multi-country outbreak of Listeria monocytogenes sequence type 6 infections linked to ready-to-eatmeat products – November 25 2019. *EFSA Supporting Publications*, *16*(12). doi:10.2903/sp.efsa.2019.EN-1745

Chaira, T. (2015). *Medical Image Processing, Advanced Fuzzy Set Theoretic Techniques*. CRC Press. doi:10.1201/b18019

Chaira, T., & Ray, A. K. (2010). *Fuzzy Image Processing and Application with MatLab*. CRC Press.

Chance, F. S., Aimone, J. B., & Musuvathy, S. S. (2020). Crossing the cleft: Communication challenges between neuroscience and artificial intelligence. *Frontiers in Computational Neuroscience*, *14*, 39.

Chandu, B., Munikoti, A., Murthy, K. S., Murthy, G., & Nagaraj, C. (2020, January). Automated Bird Species Identification using Audio Signal Processing and Neural Networks. In *2020 International Conference on Artificial Intelligence and Signal Processing (AISP)* (pp. 1-5). IEEE. 10.1109/AISP48273.2020.9073584

Chapman, D. W., & Carter, J. F. (1979). Translation procedures for the cross-cultural use of measurement instruments. *Educational Evaluation and Policy Analysis*, *3*(3), 71–76. doi:10.3102/01623737001003071

Chatzimparmpas, A., Martins, R. M., Kucher, K., & Kerren, A. (2021, June). VisEvol: Visual analytics to support hyperparameter search through evolutionary optimization. *Computer Graphics Forum*, *40*(3), 201–214. doi:10.1111/cgf.14300

Chawla, N. V., Bowyer, K. W., Hall, L. O., & Kegelmeyer, W. P. (2002). SMOTE: Synthetic minority over-sampling technique. *Journal of Artificial Intelligence Research*, *16*(June), 321–357. doi:10.1613/jair.953

Cheang, N. (2009). *Early Warning System for Financial Crises, Research and Statistics Department*. Monetary Authority of Macao.

Cheein, F. A. A., & Carelli, R. (2013). Agricultural robotics: Unmanned robotic service units in agricultural tasks. *IEEE Industrial Electronics Magazine*, *7*(3), 48–58. doi:10.1109/MIE.2013.2252957

Chen, T. P., & Chen, H. (1995). Approximation capability to functions of several variables, nonlinear functionals, and operators by radial basis function neural networks. *IEEE Transactions on Neural Networks*, *6*(4), 904-910.

Cheng, J. H., & Sun, D. W. (2014). Hyperspectral imaging as an effective tool for quality analysis and control of fish and other seafoods: Current research and potential applications. *Trends in Food Science & Technology*, *37*(2), 78–91. doi:10.1016/j.tifs.2014.03.006

Chen, S. C., & Chen Chiu, C. C. (2019). Texture Construction Edge Detection Algorithm. *Applied Sciences (Basel, Switzerland)*, *9*, 1–25.

Chen, X., Zhao, J., Chen, Y. H., Zhou, W., & Hughes, A. C. (2020). Automatic standardized processing and identification of tropical bat calls using deep learning approaches. *Biological Conservation*, *241*, 108269.

Choi, J. S., Bang, J. W., Heo, H., & Park, K. R. (2015). Evaluation of fear using nonintrusive measurement of multimodal sensors. *Sensors (Basel)*, *15*(7), 17507–17533. doi:10.3390/s150717507

Choi, Y., Jeon, Y. M., Wang, L., & Kim, K. (2017). A biological signal-based stress monitoring framework for children using wearable devices. *Sensors (Basel)*, *17*(9), 1936. doi:10.3390/s17091936

Chollet, F. (2017), *Xception: Deep Learning with Depthwise Separable Convolutions.* ArXiv:1610.02357.

Chollet. (2017). *Xception: Deep Learning with Depthwise Separable Convolutions.* Google Inc.

Chopra, I. (2002). Review of state of art of smart structures and integrated systems. *AIAA Journal, 40*(11), 2145–2187. doi:10.2514/2.1561

Chueh, C. H., Chien, J. T., & Wang, H. M. (2004). A maximum entropy approach for integrating semantic information in statistical language models. *International Symposium on Chinese Spoken Language Processing*, 309-312. 10.1109/CHINSL.2004.1409648

Cinar Satekin, M., Polat, Z., Çögen, T., Yılar, S., & Cangökçe Yaşar, Ö. (2021). Preliminary Results of the Adaptation of Developmental Test of Auditory Perception (DTAP) to Turkish with Normal Hearing Children and Adolescents. *Archives of Health Science and Research, 8*(1), 3–9. doi:10.5152/ArcHealthSciRes.2021.20112

Cisco, C. (2015). *Fog computing and the Internet of Things: extend the cloud to where the things are.* https://www. cisco.com/c/dam/en_us/solutions/trends/iot/docs/computing-overview. pdf

Clavera, I., Rothfuss, J., Schulman, J., Fujita, Y., Asfour, T., & Abbeel, P. (2018). Model-based reinforcement learning via meta-policy optimization. *Proceedings of 2nd Conference on Robot Learning*, 617-629. Retrieved from https://arxiv.org/pdf/1809.05214.pdf

Clements, D. H., & Battista, M. T. (1989). Learning of geometric concepts in a Logo environment. *Journal for Research in Mathematics Education, 20*(5), 450–467. doi:10.2307/749420

Clerici, F., Ferro, N., Marconi, S., Micheletti, S., Negrello, E., & Perotto, S. (2020). Anisotropic adapted meshes for image segmentation: Application to three-dimensional medical data. *SIAM Journal on Imaging Sciences, 13*(4), 2189–2212. doi:10.1137/20M1348303

Cole, E. B., & Flexer, C. (2007). *Children with Hearing Loss: Developing Listening and Talking Birth to Six* (1st ed.). Plural Publishing Inc.

Comai A (2007). *Early warning systems for competitive your landscape.* ESADE Business School, SCIP 2007, University of Pompeu Fabra.

Comber, B. (2000). What really counts in early literacy lessons? *Language Arts, 78*(1), 39–49.

Combettes, P. L., & Pesquet, J. C. (2011). Proximal Splitting Methods in Signal Processing. *Fixed-Point Algorithms for Inverse Problems in Science and Engineering*, 185-212.

Computer Science Teachers Association. (2017). *CSTA K–12 Computer Science Standards.* Revised 2017. Retrieved from https://www.csteachers.org/standards

Conner, M., & Armitage, C. J. (1998). Extending the theory of planned behaviour: A review and avenues for further research. *Journal of Applied Social Psychology, 28*(15), 1429–1464. doi:10.1111/j.1559-1816.1998.tb01685.x

Conover, W. J. (1999). *Practical nonparametric statistics* (Vol. 350). john Wiley & Sons.

COPEL. (2015). *Maintenance on high voltage distribution lines with dead line.* Author.

Costa dos Santos, R. & Ascher, D. (2017). Popper epistemology and management as an applied social science: A theoretical essay. *Espacios, 38*(16), 20.

Costa, A. L. (2000). Describing the habits of mind. In A. L. Costa & B. Kallick (Eds.), *Habits of mind: Discovering and Exploring* (pp. 21–40). Association for Supervision and Curriculum Development.

Covington, M. V. (2000). Intrinsic Versus Extrinsic Motivation in Schools: A Reconciliation. *Current Directions in Psychological Science*, *9*(1), 22–25. doi:10.1111/1467-8721.00052

Cramer, J., Lostanlen, V., Farnsworth, A., Salamon, J., & Bello, J. P. (2020, May). Chirping up the right tree: Incorporating biological taxonomies into deep bioacoustic classifiers. In *ICASSP 2020-2020 IEEE International Conference on Acoustics, Speech and Signal Processing (ICASSP)* (pp. 901-905). IEEE.

Cramer, J., Wu, H. H., Salamon, J., & Bello, J. P. (2019, May). Look, listen, and learn more: Design choices for deep audio embeddings. In *ICASSP 2019-2019 IEEE International Conference on Acoustics, Speech and Signal Processing (ICASSP)* (pp. 3852-3856). IEEE.

Crespi, A., Badertscher, A., Guignard, A., & Ijspeert, A. J. (2005). AmphiBot I: An amphibious snake-like robot. *Robotics and Autonomous Systems*, *50*(4), 163–175. doi:10.1016/j.robot.2004.09.015

Crosby, P. (1979). *Quality Is Free: The Art of Making Quality Certain*. McGraw-Hill.

Cuffari, B. (2020, December 20). *The Anatomy of the Human Brain*. News-Medical. Retrieved on August 14, 2021 from https://www.news-medical.net/health/The-Anatomy-of-the-Human-Brain.aspx

Cui, D. (2021). Meta-Heuristic Techniques for Solving Computational Engineering Problems: Challenges and New Research Directions. *Journal of Intelligent & Fuzzy Systems*, *40*(4), 5945–5952. doi:10.3233/JIFS-189434

Curzon, P. (2015). *Computational thinking: Searching to speak*. Available at: https://teachinglondoncomputing.org/free-workshops/computational-thinkingsearching-to-speak/

Daaboul, K. (2020). Towards Further Practical Model-Based Reinforcement Learning. *Becoming Human: Artificial Intelligence Magazine*. Retrieved from https://becominghuman.ai/towards-further-practical-model-based-reinforcement-learning-b671dd862e57

Dang, L. M., Piran, M., Han, D., Min, K., & Moon, H. (2019). A survey on internet of things and cloud computing for healthcare. *Electronics (Basel)*, *8*(7), 768. doi:10.3390/electronics8070768

Dasman, R. F. (1981). *Wildlife Biology* (2nd ed.). John Wiley & Sons, Inc.

Daugaard, S. B., Adler-Nissen, J., & Carstensen, J. M. (2010). New vision technology for multidimensional quality monitoring of continuous frying of meat. *Food Control*, *21*(5), 626–632. doi:10.1016/j.foodcont.2009.09.007

Daveis, J. L., & Gurr, T. R. (2010). *Preventive Measures: Building Risk Assessment*. Academic Press.

De Mello, L. H., & Sanderson, A. C. (1990). And/or graph representation of assembly plans. *IEEE Transactions on Robotics and Automation*, *6*(2), 188–199. doi:10.1109/70.54734

De, A., & Do, N. (2020). *Techniques to deal with imbalanced data in multi-class problems : A review of existing methods*. Mestrado Integrado Em Engenharia Informática e Computação.

Deisenroth, M., & Rasmussen, C. (2011). Pilco: A model-based and dataefficient approach to policy search. *Proceedings of the 28th International Conference on Machine Learning (ICML-2011)*, 465–472.

Del Vaglio, M. A., Nicolaou, H., Bosso, L., & Russo, D. (2011). Feeding habits of the Egyptian fruit bat Rousettus aegyptiacus on Cyprus island: A first assessment. *Hystrix*, *22*(2), 281–289.

Delcomyn, F. (1980). Neural basis of rhythmic behavior in animals. *Science*, *210*(4469), 492–498. doi:10.1126cience.7423199 PMID:7423199

Deng, J., Dong, W., Socher, R., Li, L. J., Li, K., & Fei-Fei, L. (2009, June). Imagenet: A large-scale hierarchical image database. In *2009 IEEE conference on computer vision and pattern recognition* (pp. 248-255). IEEE. doi:10.1109/CVPR.2009.5206848

Deng, J., Liu, S., Liu, Y., Wang, L., Gao, X., & Li, K. (2021). A 2-DOF Needle Insertion Device Using Inertial Piezoelectric Actuator. *IEEE Transactions on Industrial Electronics*.

Denning, P. J. (2007). Computing is a natural science. *Communications of the ACM, 50*(7), 13–18. doi:10.1145/1272516.1272529

Denning, P. J. (2017). Remaining trouble spots with computational thinking. *Communications of the ACM, 60*(6), 33–39. doi:10.1145/2998438

Dewey, J. (1975). *Interest and effort in education*. Southern Illinois University Press.

Di Martino, F., & Sessa, S. (2020, January). PSO image thresholding on images compressed via fuzzy transforms. *Information Sciences, 506*, 308–324. doi:10.1016/j.ins.2019.07.088

Dickson, B. (2020). *Neuroscience shows what's right and wrong with AI*. https://bdtechtalks.com/2020/01/20/neuroscience-artificial-intelligence-synergie/

Dick, T. E., Oku, Y., Romaniuk, J. R., & Cherniack, N. S. (1993). Interaction between central pattern generators for breathing and swallowing in the cat. *The Journal of Physiology, 465*(1), 715–730. doi:10.1113/jphysiol.1993.sp019702 PMID:8229859

Dietz, C., von Helversen, O., Nill, D., Lina, P. H., & Hutson, A. M. (2009). *Bats of Britain, Europe and Northwest Africa*. A & C Black.

Diez, M., & Raths, J. (2007). *Dispositions in teacher education*. Information Age Publishing, Inc.

Dingemans, L. M., Papadakis, V. M., Liu, P., Adam, A. J. L., & Groves, R. M. (2017). Quantitative coating thickness determination using a coefficient-independent hyperspectral scattering model. *Journal of the European Optical Society. Rapid Publications, 13*(1), 40. Advance online publication. doi:10.118641476-017-0068-2

Dini, G., & Santochi, M. (1992). Automated sequencing and subassembly detection in assembly planning. *CIRP Annals, 41*(1), 1–4. doi:10.1016/S0007-8506(07)61140-8

Disabato, S., Canonaco, G., Flikkema, P. G., Roveri, M., & Alippi, C. (2021, August). Birdsong Detection at the Edge with Deep Learning. In *2021 IEEE International Conference on Smart Computing (SMARTCOMP)* (pp. 9-16). IEEE. 10.1109/SMARTCOMP52413.2021.00022

Dissanayake, T., Rajapaksha, Y., Ragel, R., & Nawinne, I. (2019). An ensemble learning approach for electrocardiogram sensor based human emotion recognition. *Sensors (Basel), 19*(20), 4495. doi:10.3390/s19204495

Dji. (2021). *Matrice 100*. https://www.dji.com/matrice100/

Domhan, T., Springenberg, J. T., & Hutter, F. (2015, June). Speeding up automatic hyperparameter optimization of deep neural networks by extrapolation of learning curves. *Twenty-fourth international joint conference on artificial intelligence*.

Domingos, P., & Hulten, G. (2000). Mining high-speed data streams. *Proceedings of the sixth ACM SIGKDD international conference on Knowledge discovery and data mining*.

Dong, J., Gibson, P., & Arndt, G. (2007). Disassembly sequence generation in recycling based on parts accessibility and end-of-life strategy. *Proceedings of the Institution of Mechanical Engineers. Part B, Journal of Engineering Manufacture, 221*(6), 1079–1085. doi:10.1243/09544054JEM697

Dougherty, E. R. (Ed.). (2020). *Digital Image Processing Methods*. Dekker, Inc.

Dowd, B. (2020). *What are the Mating Habits of Bats?* Online available: https://www.skedaddlewildlife.com/blog/what-are-the-mating-habits-of-bats/

Du, C. J., & Sun, D. W. (2006). Learning techniques used in computer vision for food quality evaluation: A review. *Journal of Food Engineering, 72*(1), 39–55. doi:10.1016/j.jfoodeng.2004.11.017

Duysens, J., & Pearson, K. G. (1980). Inhibition of flexor burst generation by loading ankle extensor muscles in walking cats. *Brain Research, 187*(2), 321–332. doi:10.1016/0006-8993(80)90206-1 PMID:7370733

Dweck, C. S. (1999). *Self-theories: Their role in motivation, personality, and development*. Psychology Press.

Dzedzickis, A., Kaklauskas, A., & Bucinskas, V. (2020). Human emotion recognition: Review of sensors and methods. *Sensors (Basel), 20*(3), 592. doi:10.3390/s20030592

Edmund Optics Inc. (n.d.). *What is SWIR?* Retrieved November 30, 2019, from https://www.edmundoptics.com/knowledge-center/application-notes/imaging/what-is-swir/

Eisenberg, L. S., Martinez, A. S., & Boothroyd, A. (2007). Assessing auditory capabilities in young children. *International Journal of Pediatric Otorhinolaryngology, 71*(9), 1339–1350. doi:10.1016/j.ijporl.2007.05.017

Ekman, P. (1992). An argument for basic emotions. *Cognition and Emotion, 6*(3-4), 169–200. doi:10.1080/02699939208411068

El Daou, H., Salumäe, T., Ristolainen, A., Toming, G., Listak, M., & Kruusmaa, M. (2011, June). A bio-mimetic design and control of a fish-like robot using compliant structures. In *2011 15th International Conference on Advanced Robotics (ICAR)* (pp. 563-568). IEEE.

Elmasry, G., Barbin, D. F., Sun, D. W., & Allen, P. (2012). Meat Quality Evaluation by Hyperspectral Imaging Technique: An Overview. *Critical Reviews in Food Science and Nutrition, 52*(8), 689–711. doi:10.1080/10408398.2010.507908 PMID:22591341

ElMasry, G., Kamruzzaman, M., Sun, D. W., & Allen, P. (2012). Principles and Applications of Hyperspectral Imaging in Quality Evaluation of Agro-Food Products: A Review. *Critical Reviews in Food Science and Nutrition, 52*(11), 999–1023. doi:10.1080/10408398.2010.543495 PMID:22823348

ElMasry, G., Sun, D. W., & Allen, P. (2011). Non-destructive determination of water-holding capacity in fresh beef by using NIR hyperspectral imaging. *Food Research International, 44*(9), 2624–2633. doi:10.1016/j.foodres.2011.05.001

Elmasry, G., Sun, D. W., & Allen, P. (2012). Near-infrared hyperspectral imaging for predicting colour, pH and tenderness of fresh beef. *Journal of Food Engineering, 110*(1), 127–140. doi:10.1016/j.jfoodeng.2011.11.028

ElMasry, G., Wang, N., ElSayed, A., & Ngadi, M. (2007). Hyperspectral imaging for non-destructive determination of some quality attributes for strawberry. *Journal of Food Engineering, 81*(1), 98–107. doi:10.1016/j.jfoodeng.2006.10.016

ElMasry, G., Wang, N., Vigneault, C., Qiao, J., & ElSayed, A. (2008). Early detection of apple bruises on different background colors using hyperspectral imaging. *Lebensmittel-Wissenschaft + Technologie, 41*(2), 337–345. doi:10.1016/j.lwt.2007.02.022

ElSayed, A., Kongar, E., Gupta, S. M., & Sobh, T. (2012). A robotic-driven disassembly sequence generator for end-of-life electronic products. *Journal of Intelligent & Robotic Systems, 68*(1), 43–52. doi:10.100710846-012-9667-8

Emmons, R. (1986). Personal strivings: An approach to personality and subjective well-being. *Journal of Personality and Social Psychology, 51*(5), 1058–1068. doi:10.1037/0022-3514.51.5.1058

English, H. B., & English, A. C. (1958). *A Comprehensive Dictionary of Psychological and Psychoanalytical Terms.* Longmans Green.

Erikson, E. (1968). *Identity, Youth and Crisis.* Norton.

Esteva Fabregat, C. (2008). Follow-Up for a Complexity Theory [Acompañamientos a una teoría de la complejidad]. *Desacatos, 12*(28).

EUROPOL. (2002). *Strategic Intelligence Analysis Course.* Reading Material File No: 2520-47 Rev 1.

EWC. (2006). Developing Early Warning Systems: A Checklist. *EWC III Third International Conference on Early Warning, From concept to action,* Bonn, Germany.

Facione, P. A. (2000). The Disposition Toward Critical Thinking: Its Character, Measurement, and Relationship to Critical Thinking Skill. *Informal Logic, 20*(1), 61–84. doi:10.22329/il.v20i1.2254

Facione, P. A., Facione, N. C., & Sanchez, C. A. (1995). *Test Manual for the CCTDI* (2nd ed.). The California Academic Press.

Fahmy, A. A., Kalyoncu, M., & Castellani, M. (2012). Automatic design of control systems for robot manipulators using the bees algorithm. *Proceedings of the Institution of Mechanical Engineers. Part I, Journal of Systems and Control Engineering, 226*(4), 497–508. doi:10.1177/0959651811425312

Falkner, S., Klein, A., & Hutter, F. (2018). *BOHB: Robust and efficient hyperparameter optimization at scale.* arXiv:1807.01774v1 [cs.LG].

Fan, S. (2019). *Three Invaluable Ways AI and Neuroscience Are Driving Each Other Forward.* https://singularityhub.com/2019/08/08/three-invaluable-ways-ai-and-neuroscience-are-driving-each-other-forward/

Fan, J., Fang, L., & Wu, J. (2020). From brain science to artificial intelligence. *Engineering, 6*(3), 248–252.

Fankhauser, P., Bjelonic, M., Bellicoso, B. C., Miki, T., & Hutter, M. (2018). Robust rough-terrain locomotion with a quadrupedal robot. In *2018 IEEE International Conference on Robotics and Automation (ICRA)* (pp. 5761-5768). IEEE. 10.1109/ICRA.2018.8460731

Farroha, J. (2019). Security Analysis and Recommendations for AI/ML Enabled Automated Cyber Medical Systems. In F. Ahmad (Ed.), *Big Data: Learning, Analytics, and Applications* (Vol. 10989). Spie-Int Soc Optical Engineering. doi:10.1145/347090.347107

Fazel Zarandi, M. H., & Abdolkarimzadeh, M. (2018). Fuzzy rule based expert system to diagnose chronic kidney disease. *AISC, 648,* 323–328. doi:10.1007/978-3-319-67137-6_37

FDA. (2021). https://www.fda.gov/

Femenias, A., Gatius, F., Ramos, A. J., Sanchis, V., & Marín, S. (2020). Use of hyperspectral imaging as a tool for Fusarium and deoxynivalenol risk management in cereals: A review. *Food Control, 108,* 106819. doi:10.1016/j.foodcont.2019.106819

Feng, H., Golshan, M. H., & Mahoor, M. H. (2018). A wavelet-based approach to emotion classification using EDA signals. *Expert Systems with Applications, 112,* 77–86. doi:10.1016/j.eswa.2018.06.014

Fishbein, M., & Azjen, I. (1975). *Belief, attitude, intention and behaviour: An introduction to theory and research.* Addison and Wesley Pub.

Fleisher, C. S., & Bensoussan, B. E. (2003). *Why is analysis performed so poorly and what can be done about it?* Academic Press.

Fleisher, C. S., & Bensoussan, B. E. (2007). *Business and Competitive Analysis: Effective Application of New and Classic Methods*. Pearson Education, Inc.

Fleisher, C. S., & Blenkhorn, D. L. (Eds.), *(n.d.)*. *Controversies in Competitive Intelligence: The Enduring Issues*. Praeger Publishers.

Fletcher, R. R., Dobson, K., Goodwin, M. S., Eydgahi, H., Wilder-Smith, O., Fernholz, D., Kuboyama, Y., Hedman, E., Poh, M.-Z., & Picard, R. W. (2010). Icalm: Wearable sensor and network architecture for wirelessly communicating and logging autonomic activity. *IEEE Transactions on Information Technology in Biomedicine*, *14*(2), 215–223. doi:10.1109/TITB.2009.2038692

Flores, G., & Rakotondrabe, M. (2021). Robust nonlinear control for a piezoelectric actuator in a robotic hand using only position measurements. *IEEE Control Systems Letters*. Advance online publication. doi:10.1109/LCSYS.2021.3136456

Fogel, D. B. (2006). *Evolutionary computation: toward a new philosophy of machine intelligence* (Vol. 1). John Wiley & Sons.

Franch-Lage, F., Amigo, J. M., Skibsted, E., Maspoch, S., & Coello, J. (2011). Fast assessment of the surface distribution of API and excipients in tablets using NIR-hyperspectral imaging. *International Journal of Pharmaceutics*, *411*(1–2), 27–35. doi:10.1016/j.ijpharm.2011.03.012 PMID:21419207

Frick, W. F., Kingston, T., & Flanders, J. (2020). A review of the major threats and challenges to global bat conservation. *Annals of the New York Academy of Sciences*, *1469*(1), 5–25. doi:10.1111/nyas.14045 PMID:30937915

Friedrich, C., Csiszar, A., Lechler, A., & Verl, A. (2017). Efficient task and path planning for maintenance automation using a robot system. *IEEE Transactions on Automation Science and Engineering*, *15*(3), 1205–1215. doi:10.1109/TASE.2017.2759814

Frigon, A., & Rossignol, S. (2006). Experiments and models of sensorimotor interactions during locomotion. *Biological Cybernetics*, *95*(6), 607–627. doi:10.100700422-006-0129-x PMID:17115216

Frohm, J., Lindström, V., Winroth, M., & Stahre, J. (2006). The industry's view on automation in manufacturing. *IFAC Proceedings Volumes*, *39*(4), 453-458.

Fukuoka, Y., & Kimura, H. (2009). Dynamic locomotion of a biomorphic quadruped 'Tekken'robot using various gaits: Walk, trot, free-gait and bound. *Applied Bionics and Biomechanics*, *6*(1), 63–71. doi:10.1155/2009/743713

Gadziola, M. A., Grimsley, J. M., Faure, P. A., & Wenstrup, J. J. (2012). *Social vocalizations of big brown bats vary with behavioral context*. Academic Press.

Gagne, R. M., & Medsker, K. L. (1996). *The conditions of learning: Training applications*. Harcourt Brace.

Gambella, C., Ghaddar, B., & Naoum-Sawaya, J. (2021). Optimization problems for machine learning: A survey. *European Journal of Operational Research*, *290*(3), 807–828. doi:10.1016/j.ejor.2020.08.045

Gao, Y. (2006). *Research on Average Reward Reinforcement Learning Algorithms*. National Laboratory for Novel Software Technology, Nanjing University. Retrieved from https://pdfs.semanticscholar.org/a428/b91e4f13edd8e69ec9cc932f1d-084b8a2e5d.pdf

Gao, Z., & Yang, G. (2019). Insulator Segmentation for Power Line Inspection Based on Modified Conditional Generative Adversarial Network. Academic Press.

Gao, Z., Yang, G., Li, E., Shen, T., Wang, Z., Tian, Y., Wang, H., & Liang, Z. (2019). Insulator Segmentation for Power Line Inspection Based on Modified Conditional Generative Adversarial Network. *Journal of Sensors.*

Gao, L., Qian, W., Li, X., & Wang, J. (2010). Application of memetic algorithm in assembly sequence planning. *International Journal of Advanced Manufacturing Technology, 49*(9-12), 1175–1184. doi:10.100700170-009-2449-1

Garbarino , M., Lai, B. D. M., Picard, R., & Tognetti, S. (2014). Empatica e3 - a wearable wireless multi-sensor device for real-time computerized biofeedback and data acquisition. In 2014 EAI 4th International Conference on Wireless Mobile Communication and Healthcare (MOBIHEALTH) *(pp. 39-42). Academic Press.*

García-Martín, E., Lavesson, N., Grahn, H., Casalicchio, E., & Boeva, V. (2018). Hoeffding Trees with nmin adaptation. *2018 IEEE 5th International Conference on Data Science and Advanced Analytics (DSAA).*

Gatouillat, A., Badr, Y., Massot, B., & Sejdic, E. (2018, Oct). Internet of Medical Things: A Review of Recent Contributions Dealing With Cyber-Physical Systems in Medicine. *IEEE Internet of Things Journal, 5*(5), 3810-3822. doi:10.1109/jiot.2018.2849014

Genzel, D., Desai, J., Paras, E., & Yartsev, M. M. (2019). Long-term and persistent vocal plasticity in adult bats. *Nature Communications, 10*(1), 1–12. doi:10.103841467-019-11350-2 PMID:31358755

Ghandi, S., & Masehian, E. (2015). Review and taxonomies of assembly and disassembly path planning problems and approaches. *Computer Aided Design, 67,* 58–86. doi:10.1016/j.cad.2015.05.001

Gibson, J. L., Ivancevich, J. M., & Donnelly, J. H. (1991). *Organizations: Behavior, structure, processes* (7th ed.). Irwin.

Gilad, B. (2000). Industry Risk management: CI's next step. Competitive Intelligence Magazine, 4(3).

Gilad, B. (2003). Early Warning: Using Competitive Intelligence to Anticipate Market Shifts, Control Risk, and Create Powerful Strategies. AMACOM.

Gilad, B. (2004). *Early Warning.* AMACOM.

Gilbert, X. (2000). *From information to knowledge – How managers learn in Competing with Information.* Wiley.

Gilovich, T. (1991). *How We Know What Isn't So: The Fallibility of Human Reason in Everyday Life.* The Free Press.

Giri, R., & Kanthababu, M. (2015). Generating complete disassembly sequences by utilising two-dimensional views. *International Journal of Production Research, 53*(17), 5118–5138. doi:10.1080/00207543.2015.1005249

Gomez-Avila, J., Lopez-Franco, C., Alanis, A. Y., Arana-Daniel, N., & Lopez-Franco, M. (2018). Ground Vehicle Tracking with a Quadrotor using Image Based Visual Servoing. *IFAC Papers OnLine, 2nd IFAC Conference on Modelling, Identification and Control of Nonlinear Systems MICNON 2018, 51*(13), 344–349. 10.1016/j.ifacol.2018.07.302

Gonçalves, R. S., Souza, F. C, Homma, R. Z., Sudbrack, D. E. T., Trautmann, P. V., & Clasen, B. C. (2021). *Robots for Inspection and Maintenance of power transmission lines.* Academic Press.

Gonçalves, R. S., & Carvalho, J. C. M. (2013). Review and Latest Trends in Mobile Robots Applied in Power Transmission Lines. *International Journal of Advanced Robotic Systems.*

Gonçalves, R. S., & Carvalho, J. C. M. (2015). A Mobile Robot to be Applied in High Voltage Power Lines. *Journal of the Brazilian Society of Mechanical Sciences and Engineering, 37*(1), 349–359. doi:10.100740430-014-0152-0

Gonnuru, V. K. (2013). Disassembly planning and sequencing for end-of-life products with RFID enriched information. *Robotics and Computer-integrated Manufacturing, 29*(3), 112–118. doi:10.1016/j.rcim.2012.05.001

Gonuguntla , V., Shafiq, G., Wang, Y., & Veluvolu, K. C. (2015). Overlapping community detection via bounded non-negative matrix trifactorization. In 2015 37th Annual International Conference of the IEEE Engineering in Medicine and Biology Society (EMBC) *(pp. 2896-2899). IEEE.*

Gonzales, R. C., & Woods, R. F. (2007). *Digital Image Processing.* Prentice-Hall.

Gonzalez, B., & Adenso-Diaz, B. (2006). A scatter search approach to the optimum disassembly sequence problem. *Computers & Operations Research, 33*(6), 1776–1793. doi:10.1016/j.cor.2004.11.018

Google AutoM. L. (n.d.). https://cloud.google.com/automl/

Gordon, J., Rawlinson, D., & Ahmad, S. (2020). Long Distance Relationships Without Time Travel: Boosting the Performance of a Sparse Predictive Autoencoder in Sequence Modeling. In F. P. Schilling & T. Stadelmann (Eds.), Lecture Notes in Computer Science: Vol. 12294. Artificial Neural Networks in Pattern Recognition. ANNPR 2020. Springer. https://doi.org/10.1007/978-3-030-58309-5_4

Goud, N. (2020). *Malware and ransomware attack on Medical Devices.* Retrieved 28/4/2021 from https://www.cyber-security-insiders.com/malware-and-ransomware-attack-on-medical-devices/

Goulart, C., Valadao, C., Delisle-Rodriguez, D., Caldeira, E., & Bastos, T. (2019). Emotion analysis in children through facial emissivity of infrared thermal imaging. *PLoS One, 14*(3), e0212928. doi:10.1371/journal.pone.0212928

Gouverneur , P., Jaworek-Korjakowska, J., Koping, L., Shirahama, K., Kleczek, P., & Grzegorzek, M. (2017). Classification of physiological data for emotion recognition. In International Conference on Artificial Intelligence and Soft Computing *(pp. 619-627). Springer. doi:10.1007/978-3-319-59063-9_55*

Gowen, A. A., O'Donnell, C. P., Esquerre, C., & Downey, G. (2010). Influence of polymer packaging films on hyperspectral imaging data in the visible-near-infrared (450-950 nm) wavelength range. *Applied Spectroscopy, 64*(3), 304–312. doi:10.1366/000370210790918337 PMID:20223066

Gowen, A. A., Taghizadeh, M., & O'Donnell, C. P. (2009). Identification of mushrooms subjected to freeze damage using hyperspectral imaging. *Journal of Food Engineering, 93*(1), 7–12. doi:10.1016/j.jfoodeng.2008.12.021

Grabowski, K., Rynkiewicz, A., Lassalle, A., Baron-Cohen, S., Schuller, B., Cummins, N., Baird, A., Podgórska-Bednarz, J., Pieniążek, A., & Lucka, I. (2019). Emotional expression in psychiatric conditions: New technology for clinicians. *Psychiatry and Clinical Neurosciences, 73*(2), 50–62. doi:10.1111/pcn.12799

Gray, N. (2006). ABCs of ADCs. N. Semiconductor.

Greco, A., Lanata, A., Citi, V. N. L., Valenza, G., & Scilingo, E. P. (2016). Skin admittance measurement for emotion recognition: A study over frequency sweep. *Electronics (Basel), 5*(3), 46. doi:10.3390/electronics5030046

Greenhill, S., Rana, S., Gupta, S., Vellanki, P., & Venkatesh, S. (2019). Bayesian Optimization for Adaptive Experimental Design: A Review. *IEEE Access: Practical Innovations, Open Solutions, 8,* 2020.

Greeno, J. G. (1998). The stativity of knowing, learning and research. *The American Psychologist, 53*(1), 5–26. doi:10.1037/0003-066X.53.1.5

Greff, K., Srivastava, R. K., Koutník, J., Steunebrink, B. R., & Schmidhuber, J. (2016). LSTM: A search space odyssey. *IEEE Transactions on Neural Networks and Learning Systems, 28*(10), 2222–2232. doi:10.1109/TNNLS.2016.2582924 PMID:27411231

Grey, J. M., & Gordon, J. W. (1978). Perceptual effects of spectral modifications on musical timbres. *The Journal of the Acoustical Society of America, 63*(5), 1493–1500. doi:10.1121/1.381843

Griffiths, C. A., Giannetti, C., Andrzejewski, K., & Morgan, A. (2021). Comparison of a bat and genetic algorithm generated sequence against lead through programming when assembling a PCB using a 6 axis robot with multiple motions and speeds. *IEEE Transactions on Industrial Informatics.*

Grillner, S. (1975). Locomotion in vertebrates: Central mechanisms and reflex interaction. *Physiological Reviews, 55*(2), 247–304. doi:10.1152/physrev.1975.55.2.247 PMID:1144530

Grillner, S., & Zangger, P. (1979). On the central generation of locomotion in the low spinal cat. *Experimental Brain Research, 34*(2), 241–261. doi:10.1007/BF00235671 PMID:421750

Group, O. C. A. W. (2017). OpenFog reference architecture for fog computing. *OPFRA001, 20817,* 162.

Grover, S., & Pea, R. (2013). Computational thinking in K–12: A review of the state of the field. *Educational Researcher, 42*(1), 38–43. doi:10.3102/0013189X12463051

Gruber, F., Wollmann, P., Schumm, B., Grählert, W., & Kaskel, S. (2016). Quality control of slot-die coated aluminum oxide layers for battery applications using hyperspectral imaging. *Journal of Imaging, 2*(2), 12. Advance online publication. doi:10.3390/jimaging2020012

Guilford, J. P. (1970). Creativity: Retrospect and prospect. *The Journal of Creative Behavior, 4*(3), 149–168. doi:.1970.tb00856.x doi:10.1002/j.2162-6057

Gumuslu, E., Barkana Erol, D., & Kose, H . (2020). Emotion recognition using eeg and physiological data for robot-assisted rehabilitation systems. In Proceedings of the 2020 International Conference on Multimodal Interaction, *(pp. 379-387). Academic Press.*

Gungor, A., & Gupta, S. M. (1998). Disassembly sequence planning for products with defective parts in product recovery. *Computers & Industrial Engineering, 35*(1-2), 161–164. doi:10.1016/S0360-8352(98)00047-3

Gungor, A., & Gupta, S. M. (2001). Disassembly sequence plan generation using a branch-and-bound algorithm. *International Journal of Production Research, 39*(3), 481–509. doi:10.1080/00207540010002838

Guo, Y., Li, J. Y., & Zhan, Z. H. (2020). Efficient hyperparameter optimization for convolution neural networks in deep learning: A distributed particle swarm optimization approach. *Cybernetics and Systems, 52*(1), 36–57. doi:10.1080/01969722.2020.1827797

Gupta, S., Venugopal, V., Mahajan, V., Gaur, S., Barnwal, M., & Mahajan, H. (2020). *HIPAA, GDPR and Best Practice Guidelines for preserving data security and privacy-What Radiologists should know.* Academic Press.

Gupta, R., Tanwar, S., Tyagi, S., & Kumar, N. (2020). Machine learning models for secure data analytics: A taxonomy and threat model. *Computer Communications, 153,* 406–440.

Habib, M. K. (2011). Biomimetics: Innovations and robotics. *International Journal of Mechatronics and Manufacturing Systems, 4*(2), 113–134. doi:10.1504/IJMMS.2011.039263

Habib, M. K., Watanabe, K., & Izumi, K. (2007). The sociotechnical nature of mobile computing work: Evidence from a study of policing in the United States. *International Journal of Technology and Human Interaction, 1*(3), 1–14.

Habu, Y., Yamada, Y., Fukui, S., & Fukuoka, Y. (2018). A simple rule for quadrupedal gait transition proposed by a simulated muscle-driven quadruped model with two-level CPGs. In *2018 IEEE International Conference on Robotics and Biomimetics (ROBIO)* (pp. 2075-2081). IEEE.

Hadipour, M., & Shiran, M. A. (2017). Various Pollutions of Power Line Insulators. *Majlesi Journal of Electrical Engineering, 6*(1).

Hafner, D., Lillicrap, T., Norouzi, M., & Ba, J. (2021). *Mastering Atari with Discrete World Models*. In *Proceedings of The International Conference on Learning Representations (ICLR-2021), Poster*. Retrieved from https://iclr.cc/virtual/2021/poster/2742, https://openreview.net/pdf?id=0oabwyZbOu

Hagara, M., & Kubinek, P. (2018). About Edge Detection in Digital Images. *Wuxiandian Gongcheng, 27*(4), 1–11.

Hambrusch, S., Hoffmann, C., Korb, J., Haugan, M., & Hosking, A. (2009). A multidisciplinary approach towards computational thinking for science majors. *ACM SIGCSE Bulletin, 41*(1), 183–187. doi:10.1145/1539024.1508931

Hameed, S. S., Hassan, W. H., & Latiff, L. A. (2021). An Efficient Fog-Based Attack Detection Using Ensemble of MOA-WMA for Internet of Medical Things. In F. Saeed, F. Mohammed, & A. Al-Nahari (Eds.), Innovative Systems for Intelligent Health Informatics. Springer.

Hameed, S. S., Hassan, W. H., & Latiff, L. A. (2021). An Efficient Fog-Based Attack Detection Using Ensemble of MOA-WMA for Internet of Medical Things. In *Innovative Systems for Intelligent Health Informatics. IRICT 2020* (Vol. 72, pp. 774-785). Springer. doi:https://doi.org/10.1007/978-3-030-70713-2_70

Hameed, S. S., Hassan, W. H., Latiff, L. A., & Ghabban, F. (2021). A systematic review of security and privacy issues in the internet of medical things; the role of machine learning approaches. *PeerJ. Computer Science, 7*, e414.

Han, Yang, Zhang, Chen, Li, Lai, Xu, Xu, Wang, & Chen. (2019). *A Method of Insulator Faults Detection in Aerial Images for High-Voltage Transmission Lines Inspection*. Março.

Handa, H. (2009). Solving Multi-objective Reinforcement Learning Problems by EDA-RL -, Acquisition of Various Strategies. *Proceedings of the Ninth International Conference on Intelligent Systems Design and Applications*, 426-431. 10.1109/ISDA.2009.92

Han, H., Wang, W., & Mao, B. (2005). Borderline-SMOTE : A New Over-Sampling. *Methods*, 878–887.

Hanifah, F. S., Wijayanto, H., & Kurnia, A. (2015). SMOTE bagging algorithm for imbalanced dataset in logistic regression analysis (case: Credit of bank X). *Applied Mathematical Sciences, 9*(137–140), 6857–6865. doi:10.12988/ams.2015.58562

Han, J., Gondro, C., Reid, K., & Steibel, J. P. (2021). Heuristic hyperparameter optimization of deep learning models for genomic prediction. *G3 (Bethesda, Md.), 11*(7), jkab032. doi:10.1093/g3journal/jkab032 PMID:33993261

Han, J., & Seo, Y. (2017). Mechanism to minimise the assembly time with feeder assignment for a multi-headed gantry and high-speed SMT machine. *International Journal of Production Research, 55*(10), 2930–2949. doi:10.1080/00207543.2016.1229071

Han, J., Yang, Z., Zhang, Q., Chen, C., Li, H., Lai, S., Hu, G., Xu, C., Xu, H., Wang, D., & Chen, R. (2019). A Method of Insulator Faults Detection in Aerial Imagens for High-Voltage Transmission Lines Inspection. *Applied Sciences (Basel, Switzerland), 9*.

Hanneman, R. A., & Riddle, M. (2005). *Introduction to Social Network Methods*. University of California.

Han, Z., Wang, Y., & Tian, D. (2021). Ant colony optimization for assembly sequence planning based on parameters optimization. *Frontiers of Mechanical Engineering, 16*(2), 393–409. doi:10.100711465-020-0613-3

Hasanpour, S. H., Rouhani, M., Fayyaz, M., & Sabokrou, M. (2016). *Lets keep it simple, using simple architectures to outperform deeper and more complex architectures*. arXiv preprint arXiv:1608.06037.

Hassabis, D., Summerfield, C., & Botvinick, M. (2017). *AI and Neuroscience: A virtuous circle*. https://deepmind.com/blog/article/ai-and-neuroscience-virtuous-circle

Hassabis, D., Kumaran, D., Summerfield, C., & Botvinick, M. (2017). Neuroscience-Inspired Artificial Intelligence. *Neuron, 95*(2), 245–258.

Hassan, H., Ahmad, N. B., & Anuar, S. (2020). *Improved students' performance prediction for multi-class imbalanced problems using hybrid and ensemble approach in educational data mining.* doi:10.1088/1742-6596/1529/5/052041

Hassler Hallstedt, M., & Ghaderi, A. (2018). Tablets instead of paper-based tests for young children? Comparability between paper and tablet versions of the mathematical heidelbergerrechen test 1-4. *Educational Assessment, 23*(3), 195–210. doi:10.1080/10627197.2018.1488587

Hattori, H. (2008). Stereo Vision Technology for Automotive Applications. *IEEE Intelligent Vehicles Symposium, 63*(5), 48–51.

Hawkins & Maver. (2019). *Numenta, The Thousand Brains Theory of Intelligence.* https://numenta.com/blog/2019/01/16/the-thousand-brains-theory-of-intelligence

Hawkins, J. (2017). *What Intelligent Machines Need to Learn From the Neocortex.* https://spectrum.ieee.org/what-intelligent-machines-need-to-learn-from-the-neocortex

Hawkins, D. I., & Mothersbaugh, D. L. (2010). *Consumer behavior: Building marketing strategy* (11th ed.). McGraw-Hill Irwin.

Hawkins, J. (2021). *A thousand brains: A new theory of intelligence* (1st ed.). Basic Books.

Haya, A. (2019). *Handling Class Imbalance Using Swarm Intelligence Techniques, Hybrid Data and Algorithmic Level Solutions.* Academic Press.

Hayakawa, Y., Oonuma, T., Kobayashi, H., Takahashi, A., Chiba, S., & Fujiki, N. M. (2017). Feature Extraction of Video Using Artificial Neural Network. *International Journal of Cognitive Informatics and Natural Intelligence, 11*(2), 25–40. doi:10.4018/IJCINI.2017040102

Hay, G. J., Castilla, G., Wulder, M. A., & Ruiz, J. R. (2005). An Automated Object-Based Approach for the Multiscale Image Segmentation of Forest Scene. *International Journal of Applied Earth Observation and Geoinformation, 7*(4), 339–359. doi:10.1016/j.jag.2005.06.005

Hearst, M. A., Dumais, S. T., Osuna, E., Platt, J., & Scholkopf, B. (1998). Support vector machines. *IEEE Intelligent Systems & their Applications, 13*(4), 18–28. doi:10.1109/5254.708428

Heaven. (2021). *We'll never have true AI without first understanding the brain.* https://www.technologyreview.com/2021/03/03/1020247/artificial-intelligence-brain-neuroscience-jeff-hawkins/

Hecht-Nielsen, R. (1987). Kolmogorov's mapping neural network existence theorem. *Proceedings of the International Conference on Neural Networks.*

Hedin, H., & Kovero, J. (2006). *Does Your Business Radar Work?* Early Warning / Opportunity Systems for Intelligence, GIA White Paper 1/2006.

He, H., Bai, Y., Garcia, E. A., & Li, S. (2008). ADASYN. *Adaptive Synthetic Sampling Approach for Imbalanced Learning., 3*, 1322–1328.

Hei, X., Du, X., Wu, J., & Hu, F. (2010). Defending resource depletion attacks on implantable medical devices. *2010 IEEE global telecommunications conference GLOBECOM 2010.*

He, K., Zhang, X., Ren, S., & Sun, J. (2015). Delving deep into rectifiers: Surpassing human-level performance on imagenet classification. In *Proceedings of the IEEE international conference on computer vision* (pp. 1026-1034). IEEE. 10.1109/ICCV.2015.123

Heppner, P. P., & Petersen, C. H. (1982). The development and implications of a personal problem-solving inventory. *Journal of Counseling Psychology, 29*(1), 66–75. doi:10.1037/0022-0167.29.1.66

Herdman, S. J., Tusa, R. J., Blatt, P., Suzuki, A., Venuto, P. J., & Roberts, D. (1998). Computerized dynamic visual acuity test in the assessment of vestibular deficits. *Otology & Neurotology, 19*(6), 790–796

Herr, A., Klomp, N. I., & Atkinson, J. S. (1997). Identification of bat echolocation calls using a decision tree classification system. *Complexity International, 4*, 1–9.

Herrala, E., & Oy, S. I. (2020). *Textile identification and sorting using hyperspectral imaging*. Academic Press.

Herrmann, M. (2015). *RL 16: Model-based RL and Multi-Objective Reinforcement Learning*. University of Edinburgh, School of Informatics. Retrieved from http://www.inf.ed.ac.uk/teaching/courses/rl/slides15/rl16.pdf

Hertel, L., Baldi, P., & Gillen, D. L. (2020). *Quantity vs. Quality: On Hyperparameter Optimization for Deep Reinforcement Learning*. arXiv preprint arXiv:2007.14604.

Hesse, F., Care, E., Buder, J., Sassenberg, K., & Griffin, P. (2015). A framework for teachable collaborative problem-solving skills. In P. Griffin & E. Care (Eds.), *Assessment and teaching of 21st century skills: Methods and approach* (pp. 37–56). Springer.

Hessel, M., Modayil, J., van Hasselt, H., Schaul, T., Ostrovski, G., Dabney, W., Horgan, D., Piot, B., Azar, M., & Silver, D. (2018). Rainbow: Combining Improvements in Deep Reinforcement Learning. *Proceedings of the AAAI Conference on Artificial Intelligence, 32*(1). Retrieved from https://ojs.aaai.org/index.php/AAAI/article/view/11796

Heuer, J. R. (1999). *The Psychology of Intelligence Analysis*. Center for the Study of Intelligence.

Heuer, R. J., & Pherson, R. H. (2010). *Structured Analytic Techniques for Intelligence Analysis*. Washington DC CW Press College.

He, X., Zhao, K., & Chu, X. (2021). AutoML: A Survey of the State-of-the-Art. *Knowledge-Based Systems, 212*, 106622. doi:10.1016/j.knosys.2020.106622

Hilgard, E. R. (1980). The Trilogy of Mind Cognition, Affection and Conation. *Journal of the History of the Behavioral Sciences, 6*(2), 107–117. doi:10.1002/1520-6696(198004)16:2<107::AID-JHBS2300160202>3.0.CO;2-Y PMID:11608381

Hinz, T., Navarro-Guerrero, N., Magg, S., & Wermter, S. (2018). Speeding up the Hyperparameter Optimization of Deep Convolutional Neural Networks. *International Journal of Computational Intelligence and Applications, 17*(2), 1850008. doi:10.1142/S1469026818500086

Hiraoka, K., Yoshida, M., & Mishima, T. (2009). Parallel reinforcement learning for weighted multi-criteria model with adaptive margin. *Cognitive Neurodynamics, 3*(1), 17–24. doi:10.100711571-008-9066-9 PMID:19003453

Hofstede, G. H. (1991). *Cultures and Organizations: Software of the Mind*. McGraw Hill.

Hole, K. J., & Ahmad, S. (2021). *A thousand brains: toward biologically constrained AI*. doi:10.1007/s42452-021-04715-0

Holmes, G., Kirkby, R., & Pfahringer, B. (2005). Stress-testing hoeffding trees. *European conference on principles of data mining and knowledge discovery*.

Hou, W., Zheng, Y., Guo, W., & Pengcheng, G. (2021). Piezoelectric vibration energy harvesting for rail transit bridge with steel-spring floating slab track system. *Journal of Cleaner Production, 291*, 125283.

Ho, W., & Ji, P. (2005). A genetic algorithm to optimise the component placement process in PCB assembly. *International Journal of Advanced Manufacturing Technology, 26*(11), 1397–1401. doi:10.100700170-004-2132-5

Ho, W., & Ji, P. (2006). *Optimal production planning for PCB assembly*. Springer Science & Business Media.

Hoyt, D. F., & Taylor, C. R. (1981). Gait and the energetics of locomotion in horses. Nature, 292, 239–240.

Hoyt, D. F., & Taylor, C. R. (1981). Gait and the energetics of locomotion in horses. *Nature, 292*(5820), 239–240. doi:10.1038/292239a0

Hsu, H. P. (2016). Solving feeder assignment and component sequencing problems for printed circuit board assembly using particle swarm optimization. *IEEE Transactions on Automation Science and Engineering, 14*(2), 881–893. doi:10.1109/TASE.2016.2622253

Hsu, H. P. (2020). Printed Circuit Board Assembly Planning for Multi-Head Gantry SMT Machine Using Multi-Swarm and Discrete Firefly Algorithm. *IEEE Access: Practical Innovations, Open Solutions, 9*, 1642–1654. doi:10.1109/ACCESS.2020.3046495

Hu, J., Huang, W., Su, Y., Liu, Y., & Xiao, P. (2020, June). BatNet++: A Robust Deep Learning-Based Predicting Models for Calls Recognition. In *2020 5th International Conference on Smart Grid and Electrical Automation (ICSGEA)* (pp. 260-263). IEEE.

Huang, Q., Li, H., Zhao, J., Huang, G., & Chen, Q. (2015). Non-destructively sensing pork quality using near infrared multispectral imaging technique. *RSC Advances, 5*(116), 95903–95910. doi:10.1039/C5RA18872E

Huang, Y. M., & Huang, C. T. (2002). Disassembly matrix for disassembly processes of products. *International Journal of Production Research, 40*(2), 255–273. doi:10.1080/00207540110079770

Huang, Y. P., & Basanta, H. (2021). Recognition of Endemic Bird Species Using Deep Learning Models. *IEEE Access: Practical Innovations, Open Solutions, 9*, 102975–102984. doi:10.1109/ACCESS.2021.3098532

Hu, C., Shi, Y., & Liu, F. (2021). Research on Precision Blanking Process Design of Micro Gear Based on Piezoelectric Actuator. *Micromachines, 12*(2), 200. doi:10.3390/mi12020200 PMID:33672013

Huitt, W., & Cain, S. (2005). An Overview of the Conative Domain. In *Educational Psychology Interactive* (pp. 1–20). Valdosta State University.

Hui, W., Dong, X., & Guanghong, D. (2008). A genetic algorithm for product disassembly sequence planning. *Neurocomputing, 71*(13-15), 2720–2726. doi:10.1016/j.neucom.2007.11.042

Hull, R. (1999). *Aural rehabilitation serving children and adults* (4th ed.). Singular Publishing Group Inc.

Hunter, D., Yu, H., Pukish, M. S. III, Kolbusz, J., & Wilamowski, B. M. (2012). Selection of proper neural network sizes and architectures—A comparative study. *IEEE Transactions on Industrial Informatics, 8*(2), 228–240. doi:10.1109/TII.2012.2187914

Hunter, J. D. (2007). Matplotlib: A 2D graphics environment. *Computing in Science & Engineering, 9*(03), 90–95. doi:10.1109/MCSE.2007.55

Hunt, M. (1982). *The Universe Within*. Simon & Schuster.

Hussain, M. M., Farokhi, S., McMeekin, S. G., & Farzaneh, M. (2015). The Effects of Salt Contamination Deposition on HV Insulators Under Environmental Stress. *IEEE 11ᵗʰ International Conference on the Properties and Applications of Dielectric Materials.*

Hussain, M., Zhu, W., Zhang, W., Abidi, S. M. R., & Ali, S. (2018). Using machine learning to predict student difficulties from learning session data. *Artificial Intelligence Review, 52*(1), 381–407. doi:10.100710462-018-9620-8

Hussain, S., Dahan, N. A., Ba-Alwib, F. M., & Ribata, N. (2018). Educational data mining and analysis of students' academic performance using WEKA. *Indonesian Journal of Electrical Engineering and Computer Science, 9*(2), 447–459. doi:10.11591/ijeecs.v9.i2.pp447-459

Hutagaol, N. (2019).. . *Predictive Modelling of Student Dropout Using Ensemble Classifier Method in Higher Education., 4*(4), 206–211.

Hutter, F., Lucke, J., & Schmidt-Thieme, L. (2015). Beyond Manual Tuning of Hyperparameters. *Kunstl Intell, 29*(4), 329–337. doi:10.100713218-015-0381-0

Hyunho, L., Changhwan, K., Sunggi, P., Seok, L., Jaehun, K., & Kim Sun, J. (2013). *Vision Based Automatic Real Time Inspection of Power Transmission Line Inspection Metric.* Power Transmission Line.

I2 Group. (2010). *The Power of Social Network Analysis.* www.i2group.com

I2 Group. (2012). *i2 White Paper, Revealing Links.* IBM Software White Paper, i2 Analyst's Notebook.

Iandola, F. N., Han, S., Moskewicz, M. W., Ashraf, K., Dally, W. J., & Keutzer, K. (2016). *SqueezeNet: AlexNet-level accuracy with 50x fewer parameters and< 0.5 MB model size.* arXiv preprint arXiv:1602.07360.

Ibrahim, A. K., Zhuang, H., Erdol, N., & Ali, A. M. (2018, December). Detection of north atlantic right whales with a hybrid system of cnn and dictionary learning. In *2018 International Conference on Computational Science and Computational Intelligence (CSCI)* (pp. 1210-1213). IEEE. 10.1109/CSCI46756.2018.00232

IEEE Guide for Cleaning Insulators. (2005). IEEE Power Engineering Society, Transmission and Distribution Committee.

Ieracitano, C. (2020). Towards an automatic classification of SEM images of nanomaterial via a deep learning approach. Multidisciplinary approaches to neural computing. *Neural Approaches to Dynamics of Signal Exchanges*, 61-72.

Ijspeert, A. J., & Crespi, A. (2007, April). Online trajectory generation in an amphibious snake robot using a lamprey-like central pattern generator model. In *Proceedings 2007 IEEE International Conference on Robotics and Automation* (pp. 262-268). IEEE. 10.1109/ROBOT.2007.363797

Ilgin, M. A., & Gupta, S. M. (2010). Environmentally conscious manufacturing and product recovery (ECMPRO): A review of the state of the art. *Journal of Environmental Management, 91*(3), 563–591.

Ilievski, I., Akhtar, T., Feng, J., & Shoemaker, C. (2017, February). Efficient hyperparameter optimization for deep learning algorithms using deterministic rbf surrogates. *Proceedings of the AAAI Conference on Artificial Intelligence, 31*(1).

Incze, A., Jancsó, H. B., Szilágyi, Z., Farkas, A., & Sulyok, C. (2018, September). Bird sound recognition using a convolutional neural network. In *2018 IEEE 16th International Symposium on Intelligent Systems and Informatics (SISY)* (pp. 295-300). IEEE. 10.1109/SISY.2018.8524677

İnik, Ö., Altiok, M., Ülker, E., & Koçer, B. (2021). MODE-CNN: A fast converging multi-objective optimization algorithm for CNN-based models. *Applied Soft Computing, 109*, 107582. doi:10.1016/j.asoc.2021.107582

International Society for Technology in Education (ISTE). (2016). *ISTE standards for students.* Retrieved from: http://www.iste.org/docs/Standards-Resources/iste-standards_students-2016_onesheet_final.pdf

Iqbal, A., Sun, D. W., & Allen, P. (2014). An overview on principle, techniques and application of hyperspectral imaging with special reference to ham quality evaluation and control. *Food Control*, *46*, 242–254. Advance online publication. doi:10.1016/j.foodcont.2014.05.024

Iranfar, A., Zapater, M., & Atienza, D. (2021). Multi-Agent Reinforcement Learning for Hyperparameter Optimization of Convolutional Neural Networks. *IEEE Transactions on Computer-Aided Design of Integrated Circuits and Systems*, 1. doi:10.1109/TCAD.2021.3077193

Ishii, T., Masakado, S., & Ishii, K. (2004). Locomotion of a quadruped robot using CPG. In *2004 IEEE International Joint Conference on Neural Networks* (vol. 4, pp. 3179-3184). IEEE. 10.1109/IJCNN.2004.1381184

ISTE. (2015). *CT leadership toolkit*. Available at: http://www.iste.org/docs/ct-documents/ct-leadershipttoolkit.pdf?sfvrsn=4

Ito, S., Yuasa, H., Luo, Z., Ito, M., & Yanagihara, D. (1998). A mathematical model of adaptive behavior in quadruped locomotion. *Biological Cybernetics*, *78*(5), 337–347. doi:10.1007004220050438 PMID:9691263

Izard, C. E. (2009). Emotion theory and research: Highlights, unanswered questions, and emerging issues. *Annual Review of Psychology*, *60*(1), 1–25. doi:10.1146/annurev.psych.60.110707.163539

Izenman, A. J. (2013). Linear Discriminant Analysis. In *Modern Multivariate Statistical Techniques. Springer Texts in Statistics*. Springer. doi:10.1007/978-0-387-78189-1_8

Izyumskaya, N., Alivov, Y., Cho, S. J., Morkoc, H., Lee, H., & Kang, Y. S. (2007). Processing, structure, properties, and applications of PZT thin films. *Critical Reviews in Solid State and Material Sciences*, *32*(3-4), 111–202. doi:10.1080/10408430701707347

Jabid, T., & Ahsan, T. (2018). Insulator detection and defect classification using rotation invariant local directional pattern. *International Journal of Advanced Computer Science and Applications*, *9*(2), 265–272. doi:10.14569/IJACSA.2018.090237

Jaigirdar, F. T., Rudolph, C., & Bain, C. (2019). Can I Trust the Data I See? A Physician's Concern on Medical Data in IoT Health Architectures. *Proceedings of the Australasian Computer Science Week Multiconference.*

Jalan, U. (2020). Four-class emotion classification using electrocardiography (ECG) in virtual reality (VR). *International Journal of Advanced Science and Technology*, *29*(6), 1523–1529.

Jalota, C., & Agrawal, R. (2021). Feature Selection Algorithms and Student Academic Performance: A Study. In Advances in Intelligent Systems and Computing (Vol. 1165). Springer Singapore. doi:10.1007/978-981-15-5113-0_23

Jancovic, P., & Köküer, M. (2019). Bird species recognition using unsupervised modeling of individual vocalization elements. *IEEE/ACM Transactions on Audio, Speech, and Language Processing*, *27*(5), 932–947. doi:10.1109/TASLP.2019.2904790

Jang, J. R., Sun, C., & Mizutani, E. (2006). *Neuro-Fuzzy and Soft Computing*. Prentice-Hall of India.

Janik, V. M., & Slater, P. J. (2000). The different roles of social learning in vocal communication. *Animal Behaviour*, *60*(1), 1–11. doi:10.1006/anbe.2000.1410 PMID:10924198

Jin, J., Dundar, A., & Culurciello, E. (2014). *Flattened convolutional neural networks for feedforward acceleration*. arXiv preprint arXiv:1412.5474.

Jing, H. (2020). *Fascinating Relationship between AI and Neuroscience: How they inspire & advance together to benefit each other*. https://towardsdatascience.com/the-fascinating-relationship-between-ai-and-neuroscience-89189218bb05

Jin, G., Li, W., & Xia, K. (2013). Disassembly matrix for liquid crystal displays televisions. *Procedia CIRP*, *11*, 357–362. doi:10.1016/j.procir.2013.07.015

Jingjing, Z., Xingtong, L., Jixiang, S., & Lin, L. (2012), Detecting insulators in the image of overhead transmission lines. Lecture Notes in Computer Science.

Jin, X., Memon, H., Tian, W., Yin, Q., Zhan, X., & Zhu, C. (2017). Spectral characterisation and discrimination of synthetic fibers with near-infrared hyperspectral imaging system. *Applied Optics*, *56*(12), 3570. doi:10.1364/AO.56.003570 PMID:28430236

Jishan, S. T., Rashu, R. I., Haque, N., & Rahman, R. M. (2015). *Improving accuracy of students' final grade prediction model using optimal equal width binning and synthetic minority over-sampling technique.* 1–25 doi:10.1186/s40165-014-0010-2

Ji, Z., Liao, Y., Zheng, L., Wu, L., Yu, M., & Feng, Y. (2019). An Assembled Detector Based on Geometrical Constraint for Power Component Recognition. *Sensors (Basel)*, *19*(16), 3517. doi:10.339019163517 PMID:31405244

Johansson, R. S., & Vallbo, Å. B. (1983). Tactile sensory coding in the glabrous skin of the human hand. *Trends in Neurosciences*, *6*, 27–32. doi:10.1016/0166-2236(83)90011-5

Johnston, R. (2005). *Analytic Culture in the U. S. Intelligence Community*. The Center for the Study of Intelligence.

Jolliffe, I. (2005). *Principal component analysis*. Encyclopedia of statistics in behavioral science.

Jones, M. D. (1998). The Thinker's Toolkit: Fourteen Powerful Techniques for Problem Solving. Three Rivers Press.

Joshi, N. (2021). *Why Neuroscience and AI Need Each Other*. https://www.allerin.com/blog/why-neuroscience-and-ai-need-each-other

Jung, D. H., Kim, N. Y., Moon, S. H., Jhin, C., Kim, H. J., Yang, J. S., Kim, H. S., Lee, T. S., Lee, J. Y., & Park, S. H. (2021). Deep Learning-Based Cattle Vocal Classification Model and Real-Time Livestock Monitoring System with Noise Filtering. *Animals (Basel)*, *11*(2), 357. doi:10.3390/ani11020357 PMID:33535390

Kaelbling, L. P., Littman, M. L., & Moore, A. W. (1996). Reinforcement Learning: A Survey. *Journal of Artificial Intelligence Research*, *4*, 237–285. doi:10.1613/jair.301

Kafai, Y., & Burke, Q. (2013). The social turn in K-12 programming: Moving from computational thinking to computational participation. *Proceedings of the 44th ACM Technical Symposium on Computer Science Education, SIGCSE 2013*, 6–9. 10.1145/2445196.2445373

Kaiser, L., Babaeizadeh, M., Milos, P., Osinski, B., Campbell, R. H., Czechowski, K., Erhan, D., Finn, C., Kozakowski, P., Levine, S., Mohiuddin, A., Sepassi, R., Tucker, G., & Henryk Michalewski, H. (2020). Model-Based Reinforcement Learning for Atari. In *Proceedings of 2020 International Conference on Learning Representations (ICLR2020)*. Error! Hyperlink reference not valid.Retrieved from https://openreview.net/pdf?id=S1xCPJHtDB

Kaluri, R., & Pradeep, C. H. (2017). An enhanced framework for sign gesture recognition using hidden Markov model and adaptive histogram technique. *Int J Intell Eng Syst*, *10*(3), 11–19. doi:10.22266/ijies2017.0630.02

Kaluri, R., & Reddy, C. H. P. (2018). Optimized Feature Extraction for Precise Sign Gesture Recognition Using Self-improved Genetic Algorithm. *IACSIT International Journal of Engineering and Technology*, *8*(1), 25–37.

Kammies, T. L., Manley, M., Gouws, P. A., & Williams, P. J. (2016). Differentiation of foodborne bacteria using NIR hyperspectral imaging and multivariate data analysis. *Applied Microbiology and Biotechnology*, *100*(21), 9305–9320. doi:10.100700253-016-7801-4 PMID:27624097

Kamruzzaman, M., ElMasry, G., Sun, D. W., & Allen, P. (2012). Prediction of some quality attributes of lamb meat using near-infrared hyperspectral imaging and multivariate analysis. *Analytica Chimica Acta, 714*, 57–67. doi:10.1016/j.aca.2011.11.037 PMID:22244137

Kandpal, L. M., Tewari, J., Gopinathan, N., Boulas, P., & Cho, B. K. (2016). In-process control assay of pharmaceutical microtablets using hyperspectral imaging coupled with multivariate analysis. *Analytical Chemistry, 88*(22), 11055–11061. doi:10.1021/acs.analchem.6b02969 PMID:27731983

Kane, R. (1985). *Free will and values*. State University of New York Press.

Kang, J. G., & Xirouchakis, P. (2006). Disassembly sequencing for maintenance: A survey. *Proceedings of the Institution of Mechanical Engineers. Part B, Journal of Engineering Manufacture, 220*(10), 1697–1716. doi:10.1243/09544054JEM596

Karaboga, D., & Basturk, B. (2007). A powerful and efficient algorithm for numerical function optimization: Artificial bee colony (ABC) algorithm. *Journal of Global Optimization, 39*(3), 459–471. doi:10.100710898-007-9149-x

Karlik, B., & Olgac, A. V. (2011). Performance analysis of various activation functions in generalized MLP architectures of neural networks. *International Journal of Artificial Intelligence and Expert Systems, 1*(4), 111–122.

Katz, L. G. (1988). What Should Young Children Be Doing? *American Educator: The Professional Journal of the American Federation of Teachers, 12*(2), 28-33, 44-45.

Katz, L. G. (1993). *Dispositions: Definitions and implications for early childhood practices* (Perspectives from ERIC/EECE Monograph No. 4). ERIC Clearinghouse on Elementary and Early Childhood Education.

Kaur, D., & Kayr, Y. (2014). Various Image Segmentation Techniques: A Review. *International Journal of Computer Science and Mobile Computing, 3*(5), 809–814.

Kaur, P., & Gosain, A. (2018). ICT Based Innovations. Advance online publication. doi:10.1007/978-981-10-6602-3

Kazimoglu, C., Kiernan, M., Bacon, L., & MacKinnon, L. (2012). Learning programming at the computational thinking level via digital game-play. *Procedia Computer Science, 9*, 522–531. doi:10.1016/j.procs.2012.04.056

Kemel, G. (2020) *The logical reasoning in symbolic language and natural language* [El razonamiento lógico en el lenguaje simbólico y en el lenguaje natural]. UNIMAGDALENA.

Kenneth, H., Ohnishi, H. L., & Ohnishi, N. (1995). *FEDGE-Fuzzy Edge Detection by Fuzzy Categorization and Classification of Edge*. Fuzzy Logic in Artificial Intelligence.

Keras A. P. I. Applications. (n.d.). https://keras.io/api/applications/

Kerkeni, L., Ruano, P., Delgado, L. L., Picco, S., Villegas, L., Tonelli, F., . . . Masuelli, M. (2016). Understanding Color Image Processing by Machine Vision for Biological Materials. *Intech, 13*. Retrieved from https://www.intechopen.com/books/advanced-biometric-technologies/liveness-detection-in-biometrics

Keskar, N. S., Mudigere, D., Nocedal, J., Smelyanskiy, M., & Tang, P. T. P. (2017). On Large-batch Training for Deep Learning: Generalization Gap and Sharp Minima. *ICLR 2017*.

Khalsa, S. (2004). *Forecasting Terrorism: Indicators and Proven Analytic Techniques*. Scarecrow Press, Inc.

Khamy, E. L. (2000). Modified Sobel Fuzzy Edge Detection. *Proceedings of 17th National Radio Science Conference (NRSC 2000)*, 1-9.

Kheder, M., Trigui, M., & Aifaoui, N. (2017). Optimization of disassembly sequence planning for preventive maintenance. *International Journal of Advanced Manufacturing Technology, 90*(5), 1337–1349. doi:10.100700170-016-9434-2

Khezri, M., Firoozabadi, M., & Sharafat, A. R. (2015). Reliable emotion recognition system based on dynamic adaptive fusion of forehead biopotentials and physiological signals. *Computer Methods and Programs in Biomedicine*, *122*(2), 149–164. doi:10.1016/j.cmpb.2015.07.006

Khodabakhshian, R., Emadi, B., Khojastehpour, M., Golzarian, M. R., & Sazgarnia, A. (2017). Development of a multispectral imaging system for on-line quality assessment of pomegranate fruit. *International Journal of Food Properties*, *20*(1), 107–118. doi:10.1080/10942912.2016.1144200

Khoo, L. P., & Ng, T. K. (1998). A genetic algorithm-based planning system for PCB component placement. *International Journal of Production Economics*, *54*(3), 321–332. doi:10.1016/S0925-5273(98)00010-3

Khoshnoudi-Nia, S., & Moosavi-Nasab, M. (2019a). Non-destructive Determination of Microbial, Biochemical, and Chemical Changes in Rainbow Trout (Oncorhynchus mykiss) During Refrigerated Storage Using Hyperspectral Imaging Technique. *Food Analytical Methods*, *12*(7), 1635–1647. doi:10.100712161-019-01494-8

Khoshnoudi-Nia, S., & Moosavi-Nasab, M. (2019b). Prediction of various freshness indicators in fish fillets by one multispectral imaging system. *Scientific Reports*, *9*(1), 1–11. doi:10.103841598-019-51264-z PMID:31605023

Kienzler, R. (2017). *IBM Report, Developing cognitive IoT solutions for anomaly detection by using deep learning, Part 1: Introducing deep learning and long-short term memory networks: Detecting anomalies in IoT time-series data by using deep learning.* IBM.

Kikhia, B., Stavropoulos, T. G., Andreadis, S., Karvonen, N., Kompatsiaris, I., Sävenstedt, S., Pijl, M., & Melander, C. (2016). Utilizing a wristband sensor to measure the stress level for people with dementia. *Sensors (Basel)*, *16*(12), 1989. doi:10.3390/s16121989

Kim, H.-J., & Xirouchakis, P. (2010). Capacitated disassembly scheduling with random demand. *International Journal of Production Research*, *48*(23), 7177–7194. doi:10.1080/00207540903469035

Kim, J., Caire, G., & Molisch, A. F. (2015). Quality-aware streaming and scheduling for device-to-device video delivery. *IEEE/ACM Transactions on Networking*, *24*(4), 2319–2331. doi:10.1109/TNET.2015.2452272

Kimura, H., & Fukuoka, Y. (2004, September). Biologically inspired adaptive dynamic walking in outdoor environment using a self-contained quadruped robot: 'Tekken2'. In *2004 IEEE/RSJ International Conference on Intelligent Robots and Systems (IROS) (IEEE Cat. No. 04CH37566)* (Vol. 1, pp. 986–991). IEEE. 10.1109/IROS.2004.1389481

Kim, Y., Sa, J., Chung, Y., Park, D., & Lee, S. (2018). Resource-efficient pet dog sound events classification using LSTM-FCN based on time-series data. *Sensors (Basel)*, *18*(11), 4019. doi:10.339018114019 PMID:30453674

Kintzlinger, M., Cohen, A., Nissim, N., Rav-Acha, M., Khalameizer, V., Elovici, Y., Shahar, Y., & Katz, A. (2020). CardiWall: A Trusted Firewall for the Detection of Malicious Clinical Programming of Cardiac Implantable Electronic Devices. *IEEE Access: Practical Innovations, Open Solutions*, *8*, 48123–48140.

Klepac, G. (2010). Preparing for New Competition in the Retail Industry. In A. Syvajarvi & J. Stenvall (Eds.), Data Mining in Public and Private Sectors: Organizational and Government Applications (pp. 245-266). Hershey, PA: Information Science Reference. doi:10.4018/978-1-60566-906-9.ch013

Klepac, G. (2013). Risk Evaluation in the Insurance Company Using REFII Model. In S. Dehuri, M. Patra, B. Misra, & A. Jagadev (Eds.), *Intelligent Techniques in Recommendation Systems: Contextual Advancements and New Methods* (pp. 84–104). Information Science Reference. doi:10.4018/978-1-4666-2542-6.ch005

Klepac, G. (2014). Data Mining Models as a Tool for Churn Reduction and Custom Product Development in Telecommunication Industries. In P. Vasant (Ed.), *Handbook of Research on Novel Soft Computing Intelligent Algorithms: Theory and Practical Applications* (pp. 511–537). Information Science Reference. doi:10.4018/978-1-4666-4450-2.ch017

Koballa, T. R. (1989). *Changing and measuring attitudes in the science classroom, Research Matters to the Science Teacher.* National Association for Research in Science Teaching.

Koc, A., Sabuncuoglu, I., & Erel, E. (2009). Two exact formulations for disassembly line balancing problems with task precedence diagram construction using an and/or graph. *IIE Transactions, 41*(10), 866–881. doi:10.1080/07408170802510390

Kollins, S. H., DeLoss, D. J., Cañadas, E., Lutz, J., Findling, R. L., Keefe, R. S., & Faraone, S. V. (2020). A novel digital intervention for actively reducing severity of paediatric adhd (stars-adhd): A randomised controlled trial. The Lancet. *Digital Health, 2*(4), 168–178. doi:10.1016/S2589-7500(20)30017-0

Konda, T., Tensyo, S., & Yamaguchi, T. (2002). LC-Learning: Phased Method for Average Reward Reinforcement Learning - Preliminary Results. In *Proceedings of 7th Pacific Rim International Conference on Artificial Intelligence (PRICAI2002)*. Springer. 10.1007/3-540-45683-X_24

Kong, S. C., Chiu, M. M., & Lai, M. (2018). A study of primary school students' interest, collaboration attitude, and programming empowerment in computational thinking education. *Computers & Education, 127*, 178–189. doi:10.1016/j.compedu.2018.08.026

Kong, S.-C., Abelson, H., & Lai, M. (2019). Introduction to computational thinking education. In S.-C. Kong & H. Abelson (Eds.), *Computational thinking education* (pp. 1–10). Springer. doi:10.1007/978-981-13-6528-7_1

Kopal, R. & Korkut, D. (2011) *Kompetitivna analiza 2 – strukturirane i kreativne analitičke tehnike.* Zagreb: Comminus d.o.o. & Visoko učilište Effectus.

Kopal, R., Korkut, D., & Knežević, H. (2009). *Primjena analitičkih tehnika u poslovnim istraživanjima.* Zbornik Visoke poslovne škole Libertas, Zagreb, godina II.

Korkmaz, Ö., Cakir, R., & Ozden, M. Y. (2017). A validity and reliability study of the computational thinking scales (CTS). *Computers in Human Behavior, 72*, 558–569. doi:10.1016/j.chb.2017.01.005

Kouchaksaraei, H. R., & Karl, H. (2018). Joint orchestration of cloud-based microservices and virtual network functions. *Future Generation Computer Systems, 78*, 1–2.

Koutsoukas, A., Monaghan, K. J., Li, X., & Huan, J. (2017). Deep-learning: Investigating deep neural networks hyperparameters and comparison of performance to shallow methods for modeling bioactivity data. *Journal of Cheminformatics, 9*(1), 1–13. doi:10.118613321-017-0226-y PMID:29086090

Koziar, Y., Levchuk, V., & Koval, A. (2019). Quadrotor Design for Outdoor Air Quality Monitoring. *2019 IEEE 39th International Conference on Electronics and Nanotechnology (ELNANO)*, 736-739.

Kramer, O. (2013). K-nearest neighbors. In *Dimensionality reduction with unsupervised nearest neighbors* (pp. 13–23). Springer. doi:10.1007/978-3-642-38652-7_2

Krawczyk, B. (2016). Learning from imbalanced data: Open challenges and future directions. *Progress in Artificial Intelligence, 5*(4), 221–232. doi:10.100713748-016-0094-0

Krech, D., Crutchfield, R. S., & Ballackey, E. L. (1962). *Individual in Society.* McGraw Hill.

Krishnaraj, N., Elhoseny, M., Thenmozhi, M., Selim, M. M., & Shankar, K. (2020). Deel learning model for real-time imaage compression in Intern Underwater Things (IoUT). *J Real-Time Image PRoc*, *17*(6), 2097–2111. doi:10.100711554-019-00879-6

Krizhevsky, A., Sutskever, I., & Hinton, G. E. (2012). Imagenet classification with deep convolutional neural networks. *Advances in Neural Information Processing Systems*, *25*, 1097–1105.

Kukillaya, R., Proctor, J., & Holmes, P. (2009). Neuromechanical models for insect locomotion: Stability, maneuverability, and proprioceptive feedback. *Chaos (Woodbury, N.Y.)*, *19*(026107), 1–15. doi:10.1063/1.3141306 PMID:19566267

Kumari, P., Jain, P. K., & Pamula, R. (2018). *An Efficient use of Ensemble Methods to Predict Students Academic Performance*. Academic Press.

Kumar, P., Gupta, G. P., & Tripathi, R. (2021). An ensemble learning and fog-cloud architecture-driven cyber-attack detection framework for IoMT networks. *Computer Communications*, *166*, 110–124. https://doi.org/10.1016/j.comcom.2020.12.003

Kuo, F. Y., & Sloan, I. H. (2005). Lifting the curse of dimensionality. *Notices of the American Mathematical Society*, *52*(11), 1320–1328.

Kuo, H. (2004) Maximum entropy modeling for speech recognition. *International Symposium on Chinese Spoken Language Processing*, T-2. 10.1109/CHINSL.2004.1409569

Kurosawa, M., Sasaki, T., Usami, Y., Kato, S., Sakaki, A., Takei, Y., Kaneko, M., Uchikoba, F., & Saito, K. (2021). Neural networks integrated circuit with switchable gait pattern for insect-type microrobot. *Artificial Life and Robotics*, *26*(2), 297–303. doi:10.100710015-021-00678-y

Kurtgis, M. P. (1984). *Method for washing voltage transmission line insulators*. US4477289.

Kvsn, R. R., Montgomery, J., Garg, S., & Charleston, M. (2020). Bioacoustics data analysis–A taxonomy, survey and open challenges. *IEEE Access: Practical Innovations, Open Solutions*, *8*, 57684–57708. doi:10.1109/ACCESS.2020.2978547

Laili, Y., Tao, F., Pham, D. T., Wang, Y., & Zhang, L. (2019). Robotic disassembly re-planning using a two-pointer detection strategy and a super-fast bees algorithm. *Robotics and Computer-integrated Manufacturing*, *59*, 130–142. doi:10.1016/j.rcim.2019.04.003

Lalonde, M., Chapdelaine, C., Foucher, S., Team, I., Ave, O., & Qc, M. (2015). *Multispectral imaging: An application to density measurement in photographic paper manufacturing process control*. doi:10.1117/12.000000

Lambert, A. J. (2003). Disassembly sequencing: A survey. *International Journal of Production Research*, *41*(16), 3721–3759. doi:10.1080/0020754031000120078

Lampert, M. (1990). Connecting inventions with conventions: The teachers' role in classroom communication about mathematics. In L. Steffe & T. Wood (Eds.), *Transforming Early Childhood Mathematics Education* (pp. 253–265). Erlbaum.

Lampert, M. (2001). *Teaching problems and the problems in teaching*. Yale University Press.

Landau, O., Cohen, A., Gordon, S., & Nissim, N. (2020). Mind your privacy: Privacy leakage through BCI applications using machine learning methods. *Knowledge-Based Systems*, 105932.

Lang, P. J. (1995). The emotion probe: Studies of motivation and attention. *The American Psychologist*, *50*(5), 372–385. doi:10.1037/0003-066X.50.5.372

Lave, J., & Wenger, E. (1991). *Situated learning: Legitimate peripheral participation*. Cambridge University Press., doi:10.1017/CBO9780511815355

Lavoix, H. (2008). *Developing an early warning system for crises.* Academic Press.

Leadholm, Lewis, & Ahmad. (2021). *Grid Cell Path Integration For Movement-Based Visual Object Recognition.* arXiv preprint arXiv:2102.09076.

LeCun, Y., Boser, B., Denker, J. S., Henderson, D., Howard, R. E., Hubbard, W., & Jackel, L. D. (1989). Backpropagation applied to handwritten zip code recognition. *Neural Computation, 1*(4), 541–551. doi:10.1162/neco.1989.1.4.541

Lee. (2019). *How neuroscience enables better Artificial Intelligence design.* https://medium.com/swlh/how-neuroscience-enables-better-artificial-intelligence-design-5d254098470b

Lee, I., Martin, F., Denner, J., Coulter, B., Allan, W., Erickson, J., Malyn-Smith, J., & Werner, L. (2011). Computational thinking for youth in practice. *ACM Inroads, 2*(1), 32–37. doi:10.1145/1929887.1929902

Lee, J., Noh, B., Jang, S., Park, D., Chung, Y., & Chang, H. H. (2015). Stress detection and classification of laying hens by sound analysis. *Asian-Australasian Journal of Animal Sciences, 28*(4), 592–598. doi:10.5713/ajas.14.0654 PMID:25656176

Leevy, J. L., Khoshgoftaar, T. M., Bauder, R. A., & Seliya, N. (2018). A survey on addressing high - class imbalance in big data. *Journal of Big Data, 5*(1), 42. Advance online publication. doi:10.118640537-018-0151-6

Lee, W. Y., Park, S. M., & Sim, K. B. (2018). Optimal hyperparameter tuning of convolutional neural networks based on the parameter-setting-free harmony search algorithm. *Optik (Stuttgart), 172*, 359–367. doi:10.1016/j.ijleo.2018.07.044

Legg & Hutter. (2007). A collection of definitions of intelligence. *Frontiers in Artificial Intelligence and Applications, 157*, 17.

Leipälä, T., & Nevalainen, O. (1989). Optimization of the movements of a component placement machine. *European Journal of Operational Research, 38*(2), 167–177. doi:10.1016/0377-2217(89)90101-X

Lendasse, A., Wertz, V., & Verleysen, M. (2003). Model selection with cross-validations and bootstraps—application to time series prediction with RBFN models. *Artificial Neural Networks and Neural Information Processing—ICANN/ICONIP 2003*, 174-174.

Leu, M. C., Wong, H., & Ji, Z. (1993). Planning of component placement/insertion sequence and feeder setup in PCB assembly using genetic algorithm. *ASME. Journal of Electronic Packaging, 115*(4), 424–432. doi:10.1115/1.2909352

Li, B., Wu, D., Cong, Y., Xia, Y., & Tang, Y. (2012), A method of insulator detection from video sequence. *International Symposium on Information Science and Engineering*, 386–389.

Li, L. (2015). The UAV Intelligent Inspection of Transmission Lines. Atlantis Press. doi:10.2991/ameii-15.2015.285

Li, L., Jamieson, K., Rostamizadeh, A., Gonina, E., & Talwalkar, A. (2018). *Massively Parallel Hyperparameter Tuning.* arXiv:1810.05934.

Li, Su, & Liu. (2020). *Insulator Defect Recognition Based on Global Detection and Local Segmentation.* Academic Press.

Liang, F., Liu, H., Wang, X., & Liu, Y. (2018). Hyperspectral image recognition based on artificial neural network. *NeuroQuantology: An Interdisciplinary Journal of Neuroscience and Quantum Physics, 16*(5), 699–705. doi:10.14704/nq.2018.16.5.1244

Li, B., & Huang, Y. (2011). Study on the on-line monitoring method of insulator in the world. *Electrical Engineering*, (9), 1–5.

Li, D., & Yoon, S. W. (2017). PCB assembly optimization in a single gantry high-speed rotary-head collect-and-place machine. *International Journal of Advanced Manufacturing Technology*, 88(9-12), 2819–2834. doi:10.100700170-016-8942-4

Li, H. S., Qingxin, Z., Lan, S., Shen, C. Y., Zhou, R., & Mo, J. (2013). Image Storage Retrieval, Compression and Segmentation in a Quantum System. *Quantum Information Processing*, 12(6), 2269–2290. doi:10.100711128-012-0521-5

Li, J., Barwood, M., & Rahimifard, S. (2018). Robotic disassembly for increased recovery of strategically important materials from electrical vehicles. *Robotics and Computer-integrated Manufacturing*, 50, 203–212. doi:10.1016/j.rcim.2017.09.013

Li, J., Meng, X., Wang, W., & Xin, B. (2019). A novel hyperspectral imaging and modeling method for the component identification of woven fabrics. *Textile Research Journal*, 89(18), 3752–3767. doi:10.1177/0040517518821907

Li, L., & Goodchild, M. F. (2010). The Role of Social Networks in Emergency Management: A Research Agenda. *International Journal of Information Systems for Crisis Response and Management*, 2(4), 48–58. doi:10.4018/jiscrm.2010100104

Li, L., Jamieson, K., DeSalvo, G., Rostamizadeh, A., & Talwalkar, A. (2017). Hyperband: A novel bandit-based approach to hyperparameter optimization. *Journal of Machine Learning Research*, 18(1), 6765–6816.

Lim, J., Kim, G., Mo, C., Kim, M. S., Chao, K., Qin, J., Fu, X., Baek, I., & Cho, B. K. (2016). Detection of melamine in milk powders using near-infrared hyperspectral imaging combined with regression coefficient of partial least square regression model. *Talanta*, 151, 183–191. doi:10.1016/j.talanta.2016.01.035 PMID:26946026

Lin, C.-J., & Chen, C.-H. (2005). Identification and prediction using recurrent compensatory neuro-fuzzy systems. *Fuzzy Sets and Systems*, 150(2), 307–330. doi:10.1016/j.fss.2004.07.001

Ling, Qiu, Jin, Zhang, He, Liu, & Lei. (2018). *An Accurate and Real-time Self-blast Glass Insulator Location Method Based on Faster R-CNN and U-net with Aerial Images*. Janeiro.

Lin, S., & Kernighan, B. W. (1973). An effective heuristic algorithm for the traveling-salesman problem. *Operations Research*, 21(2), 498–516. doi:10.1287/opre.21.2.498

Li, Q., He, X., Wang, Y., Liu, H., Xu, D., & Guo, F. (2013). Review of spectral imaging technology in biomedical engineering: Achievements and challenges. *Journal of Biomedical Optics*, 18(10), 100901. doi:10.1117/1.JBO.18.10.100901 PMID:24114019

Liu, X., Miao, X., Jiang, H., & Chen, J. (2020), *Review of data analysis in vision inspection of power lines with an in-depth discussion of deep learning technology*. arXiv:2003.09802.

Liu , Y., & Sourina, O. (2014). Transactions on Computational Science XXIII: Special Issue on Cyberworlds (Lecture Notes in Computer Science, 8490) *(2014 ed.). Springer.*

Liu, C., Hao, G., Su, M., Chen, Y., & Zheng, L. (2017). Potential of multispectral imaging combined with chemometric methods for rapid detection of sucrose adulteration in tomato paste. *Journal of Food Engineering*, 215, 78–83. doi:10.1016/j.jfoodeng.2017.07.026

Liu, C., Wu, Y., Liu, J., & Sun, Z. (2021). Improved YOLOv3 Network for Insulator Detection in Aerial Images with Diverse Background Interference. *Electronics (Basel)*, 10(7), 771. doi:10.3390/electronics10070771

Liu, C., Xu, X., & Hu, D. (2015). Multiobjective Reinforcement Learning: A Comprehensive Overview. *IEEE Transactions on Systems, Man, and Cybernetics. Systems*, 45(3), 385–398. doi:10.1109/TSMC.2014.2358639

Liu, H., Jia, W., & Bi, L. (2017). Hopf oscillator based adaptive locomotion control for a bionic quadruped robot. In *2017 IEEE International Conference on Mechatronics and Automation (ICMA)* (pp. 949-954). IEEE. 10.1109/ICMA.2017.8015944

Liu, J., Zhou, Z., Pham, D. T., Xu, W., Ji, C., & Liu, Q. (2018). Robotic disassembly sequence planning using enhanced discrete bees algorithm in remanufacturing. *International Journal of Production Research*, *56*(9), 3134–3151. doi:10.1080/00207543.2017.1412527

Liu, S.-T., Yen, J.-Y., & Wang, F.-C. (2018). Compensation for the Residual Error of the Voltage Drive of the Charge Control of a Piezoelectric Actuator. *Journal of Dynamic Systems, Measurement, and Control*, *140*(7), 1–9. doi:10.1115/1.4038636

Liu, Y., Sun, Y., Xue, B., Zhang, M., Yen, G. G., & Tan, K. C. (2021). A Survey on Evolutionary Neural Architecture Search. *IEEE Transactions on Neural Networks and Learning Systems*, 1–21. doi:10.1109/TNNLS.2021.3100554 PMID:34357870

Li, X. (2020, March). Gecko-Like Adhesion in the Electrospinning Process. *Results in Physics*, *16*(102899). Advance online publication. doi:10.1016/j.rinp.2019.102899

Li, X., Wang, W., & Yi, J. (2016). Foot contact force of walk gait for a quadruped robot. In *2016 IEEE International Conference on Mechatronics and Automation (ICMA)* (pp. 659-664). IEEE. 10.1109/ICMA.2016.7558641

Li, Z. (2016). *Transmission line intelligent inspection central control and mass data processing system and application based on UAV*. IEEE.

Liz-Domínguez, M., Caeiro-Rodríguez, M., Llamas-Nistal, M., & Mikic-Fonte, F. A. (2019). Systematic literature review of predictive analysis tools in higher education. *Applied Sciences (Switzerland)*, *9*(24), 5569. Advance online publication. doi:10.3390/app9245569

Lizotte, D. J., Bowling, M., & Murphy, S. A. (2012). Linear Fitted-Q Iteration with Multiple Eeward Functions. *Journal of Machine Learning Research*, *13*, 3253–3295. PMID:23741197

Lombardo, R. (2011). Data Mining and Explorative Multivariate Data Analysis for Customer Satisfaction Study. In A. Koyuncugil & N. Ozgulbas (Eds.), *Surveillance Technologies and Early Warning Systems: Data Mining Applications for Risk Detection* (pp. 243–266). Information Science Reference. doi:10.4018/978-1-61692-865-0.ch013

López De Luise, D. & Azor, R. (2015). *Sound Model for Dialog Profiling*. Inderscience Publishers Ltd.

Lostanlen, V., Salamon, J., Farnsworth, A., Kelling, S., & Bello, J. P. (2018, April). Birdvox-full-night: A dataset and benchmark for avian flight call detection. In *2018 IEEE International Conference on Acoustics, Speech and Signal Processing (ICASSP)* (pp. 266-270). IEEE. 10.1109/ICASSP.2018.8461410

Lostanlen, V., Salamon, J., Farnsworth, A., Kelling, S., & Bello, J. P. (2019). Robust sound event detection in bioacoustic sensor networks. *PLoS One*, *14*(10), e0214168. doi:10.1371/journal.pone.0214168 PMID:31647815

Loussaief, S., & Abdelkrim, A. (2018). Convolutional neural network hyper-parameters optimization based on genetic algorithms. *International Journal of Advanced Computer Science and Applications*, *9*(10), 252–266. doi:10.14569/IJACSA.2018.091031

Lu, Z., Zhang, B., Sun, L., Fan, L., & Zhou, J. (2020, October). Whale-Call Classification Based on Transfer Learning and Ensemble Method. In *2020 IEEE 20th International Conference on Communication Technology (ICCT)* (pp. 1494-1497). IEEE. 10.1109/ICCT50939.2020.9295729

Luciana, M. (2003). Practitioner review: computerized assessment of neuropsychological function in children: clinical and research applications of the Cambridge Neuropsychological Testing Automated Battery (CANTAB). *Journal of Child Psychology and Psychiatry, and Allied Disciplines, 44*(5), 649–663. doi:10.1111/1469-7610.00152

Lungarella, M., Bongard, J., & Pfeifer, R. (Eds.). (2007). *What can Artificial Intelligence get from Neuroscience?* Springer-Verlag.

Luo, J., Liu, J., & Hu, Y. (2017). An MILP model and a hybrid evolutionary algorithm for integrated operation optimisation of multi-head surface mounting machines in PCB assembly. *International Journal of Production Research, 55*(1), 145–160. doi:10.1080/00207543.2016.1200154

Lu, T. C. (2020). CNN Convolutional layer optimisation based on quantum evolutionary algorithm. *Connection Science*, 1–13.

Lu, Z., Nagata, F., & Watanabe, K. (2017a). Development of iOS application handlers for quadrotor UAV remote control and monitoring. *2017 IEEE International Conference on Mechatronics and Automation (ICMA)*, 513-518. 10.1109/ICMA.2017.8015870

Lu, Z., Nagata, F., & Watanabe, K. (2018). Mission Planning of iOS Application for a Quadrotor UAV. *Artificial Life and Robotics, 23*(3), 428–433. doi:10.100710015-018-0432-3

Lu, Z., Nagata, F., Watanabe, K., & Habib, M. K. (2017b). iOS Application for Quadrotor UAV Remote Control – Implementation of Basic Functions with iPhone. *Artificial Life and Robotics, 22*(3), 374–379. doi:10.100710015-017-0372-3

Lye, S. Y., & Koh, J. H. L. (2014). Review on teaching and learning of computational thinking through programming: What is next for K-12? *Computers in Human Behavior, 41*, 51–61. doi:10.1016/j.chb.2014.09.012

Maas, A. L., Hannun, A. Y., & Ng, A. Y. (2013, June). Rectifier nonlinearities improve neural network acoustic models. In Proc. ICML (Vol. 30, No. 1, p. 3). Academic Press.

Mac Aodha, O., Gibb, R., Barlow, K. E., Browning, E., Firman, M., Freeman, R., Harder, B., Kinsey, L., Mead, G. R., Newson, S. E., Pandourski, I., Parsons, S., Russ, J., Szodoray-Paradi, A., Szodoray-Paradi, F., Tilova, E., Girolami, M., Brostow, G., & Jones, K. E. (2018). Bat detective—Deep learning tools for bat acoustic signal detection. *PLoS Computational Biology, 14*(3), e1005995. doi:10.1371/journal.pcbi.1005995 PMID:29518076

Ma, F., Yao, J., Xie, T., Liu, C., Chen, W., Chen, C., & Zheng, L. (2014). Multispectral imaging for rapid and non-destructive determination of aerobic plate count (APC) in cooked pork sausages. *Food Research International, 62*, 902–908. doi:10.1016/j.foodres.2014.05.010

Mahadevan, S. (1996). Average Reward Reinforcement learning: Foundations, Algorithms, and Empirical Results. *Machine Learning, 22*(1-3), 159–196. doi:10.1007/BF00114727

Mair, P. (2018). *Principal Component Analysis and Extensions*. doi:10.1007/978-3-319-93177-7_6

Mäkelä, M., Rissanen, M., & Sixta, H. (2020). Machine vision estimates the polyester content in recyclable waste textiles. *Resources, Conservation and Recycling, 161*(June), 105007. doi:10.1016/j.resconrec.2020.105007

Ma, L., & Fan, S. (2017). CURE-SMOTE algorithm and hybrid algorithm for feature selection and parameter optimization based on random forests. *BMC Bioinformatics, 18*(1), 1–18. doi:10.118612859-017-1578-z PMID:28292263

Mandelbrot, B. (1965). *Information Theory and Psycholinguistics* (B. B. Wolman & E. Nagel, Eds.). Scientific Psychology.

Mantovani, V. A., Franco, C. S., Mancini, S. D., Haseagawa, H. L., Gianelli, G. F., Batista, V. X., & Rodrigues, L. L. (2013). Comparison of polymers and ceramics in new and discarded electrical insulators: Reuse and recycling possibilities. *Revista Matéria*, *18*(04), 1549–1562. doi:10.1590/S1517-70762013000400015

Maraaba, L., Al-Hamouz, Z., & Al-Duwaish, H. (2014). Estimation of High voltage Insulator Contamination Using a Combined Image Processing and Artificial Neural Networks. *IEEE 8th International Power Engineering and Optimization Conference*.

Marder, E., & Bucher, D. (2001). Central pattern generators and the control of rhythmic movements. *Current Biology*, *11*(23), 986–996. doi:10.1016/S0960-9822(01)00581-4 PMID:11728329

Marin-Morales, J., Higuera-Trujillo, J. L., Greco, A., Guixeres, J., Llinares, C., Scilingo, E. P., Alcañiz, M., & Valenza, G. (2018). Affective computing in virtual reality: Emotion recognition from brain and heartbeat dynamics using wearable sensors. *Scientific Reports*, *8*(1), 1–15. doi:10.1038/s41598-018-32063-4

Matache, C. (2019). *Efficient Design of Machine Learning Hyperparameter Optimizers*. MEng Individual Project. Imperial College London. https://docs.microsoft.com/en-us/azure/machine-learning/concept-automated-ml

Ma, X., Liu, S., Hu, S., Geng, P., Liu, M., & Zhao, J. (2018). SAR Image Edge Detection Via Sparse Representation. *Soft Computing*, *22*(8), 2507–2515. doi:10.100700500-017-2505-y

Ma, Y., Wang, Y., Yang, J., Miao, Y., & Li, W. (2017). Big Health Application System based on Health Internet of Things and Big Data. *IEEE Access: Practical Innovations, Open Solutions*, *5*, 7885–7897. https://doi.org/10.1109/ACCESS.2016.2638449

Mayer, R. E. (1983). *Thinking, problem solving and cognition*. W. H. Freeman and Co.

McCune, V., & Entwistle, N. (2011). Cultivating the disposition to understand in 21st century university education. *Learning and Individual Differences*, *21*(3), 303–310. doi:10.1016/j.lindif.2010.11.017

McFee, B., Raffel, C., Liang, D., Ellis, D. P., McVicar, M., Battenberg, E., & Nieto, O. (2015, July). librosa: Audio and music signal analysis in python. In *Proceedings of the 14th python in science conference* (Vol. 8, pp. 18-25). 10.25080/Majora-7b98e3ed-003

McGeer, T. (1990). Passive dynamic walking. *The International Journal of Robotics Research*, *9*(2), 62–82. doi:10.1177/027836499000900206

McMahon, E., Williams, R., El, M., Samtani, S., Patton, M., & Chen, H. (2017). Assessing medical device vulnerabilities on the Internet of Things. *2017 IEEE International Conference on Intelligence and Security Informatics (ISI)*.

McMahon, T. A. (1985). The role of compliance in mammalian running gaits. *The Journal of Experimental Biology*, *115*(1), 263–282. doi:10.1242/jeb.115.1.263 PMID:4031769

Meece, J. L., Blumenfeld, P. C., & Hoyle, R. H. (1988). Students' goal orientations and cognitive engagement in classroom activities. *Journal of Educational Psychology*, *80*(4), 514–523. doi:10.1037/0022-0663.80.4.514

Mehrabi, D., Mohammadzaheri, M., Firoozfar, A., & Emadi, M. (2017). A fuzzy virtual temperature sensor for an irradiative enclosure. *Journal of Mechanical Science and Technology*, *31*(10), 4989–4994. doi:10.100712206-017-0947-x

Meinhold, W., Martinez, D. E., Oshinski, J., Hu, A.-P., & Ueda, J. (2020). A direct drive parallel plane piezoelectric needle positioning robot for MRI guided intraspinal injection. *IEEE Transactions on Biomedical Engineering*, *68*(3), 807–814. doi:10.1109/TBME.2020.3020926 PMID:32870782

Meissen, U., & Voisard, A. (2010). *Current State and Solutions for Future Challenges in Early Warning Systems and Alerting Technologies,* published. In E. Asimakopoulou & N. Bessis (Eds.), *Advanced ICTs for Disaster Management and Threat Detection: Collaborative and Distributed Frameworks* (pp. 108–130). Information Science Reference. doi:10.4018/978-1-61520-987-3.ch008

Menesatti, P., Costa, C., & Aguzzi, J. (2010). Quality Evaluation of Fish by Hyperspectral Imaging. *Hyperspectral Imaging for Food Quality Analysis and Control,* 273–294. doi:10.1016/B978-0-12-374753-2.10008-5

Mete, S., Çil, Z. A., Ağpak, K., Özceylan, E., & Dolgui, A. (2016). A solution approach based on beam search algorithm for disassembly line balancing problem. *Journal of Manufacturing Systems, 41,* 188–200. doi:10.1016/j.jmsy.2016.09.002

Meyer, L. H., Beyer, W. W., & Molina, F. H. (2013). Salt fog testing of glass insulators with different surface conditions. *2013 3rd International Conference on Electric Power and Energy Conversion Systems,* 1-4. 10.1109/EPECS.2013.6713083

Michael, J. (1991). A behavioural perspective on college teaching. *The Behavior Analyst, 14*(2), 229–239. doi:10.1007/BF03392578 PMID:22478107

Michael, M., Phebus, R. K., & Amamcharla, J. (2019). Hyperspectral imaging of common foodborne pathogens for rapid identification and differentiation. *Food Science & Nutrition, 7*(8), 2716–2725. doi:10.1002/fsn3.1131 PMID:31428359

Miller, A. (1991). Personality types, learning styles and educational goals. *Educational Psychology, 11*(3-4), 217–238. doi:10.1080/0144341910110302

Miller, G. A. (1959). The Magical Number Seven - Plus or Minus Two: Some Limits on Our Capacity for Processing Information. *Psychological Review, 63*(2), 81–97. doi:10.1037/h0043158 PMID:13310704

Miller, G. A. (2003). The cognitive revolution: A historical perspective. *Trends in Cognitive Sciences, 7*(3), 141–144. doi:10.1016/S1364-6613(03)00029-9 PMID:12639696

Minar, M. R., & Naher, J. (2018). *Recent advances in deep learning: An overview.* arXiv preprint arXiv:1807.08169.

Minase, J., Lu, T.-F., Cazzolato, B., & Grainger, S. (2010). A review, supported by experimental results, of voltage, charge and capacitor insertion method for driving piezoelectric actuators. *Precision Engineering, 34*(4), 692–700. doi:10.1016/j.precisioneng.2010.03.006

Minati, L., Frasca, M., Yoshimura, N., & Koike, Y. (2018). Versatile locomotion control of a hexapod robot using a hierarchical network of nonlinear oscillator circuits. *IEEE Access: Practical Innovations, Open Solutions, 6,* 8042–8065. doi:10.1109/ACCESS.2018.2799145

Ministery of Education of Spain. (2021). *Ministerio de educación de España.* https://www.educacionyfp.gob.es/

Miri, N., Mohammadzaheri, M., & Chen, L. (2015). An enhanced physics-based model to estimate the displacement of piezoelectric actuators. *Journal of Intelligent Material Systems and Structures, 26*(11), 1442–1451. doi:10.1177/1045389X14546648

Mirschel, G., Daikos, O., & Scherzer, T. (2019). In-line monitoring of the thickness distribution of adhesive layers in black textile laminates by hyperspectral imaging. *Computers & Chemical Engineering, 124,* 317–325. doi:10.1016/j.compchemeng.2019.01.015

Mirschel, G., Daikos, O., Scherzer, T., & Steckert, C. (2017). Near-infrared hyperspectral imaging of lamination and finishing processes in textile technology. *NIR News, 28*(1), 20–25. doi:10.1177/0960336016687949

Mirschel, G., Daikos, O., Scherzer, T., & Steckert, C. (2018). Near-infrared chemical imaging used for in-line analysis of functional finishes on textiles. *Talanta, 188*(February), 91–98. doi:10.1016/j.talanta.2018.05.050 PMID:30029452

Mirzaei, G., Majid, M. W., Jamali, M. M., Ross, J., Frizado, J., Gorsevski, P. V., & Bingman, V. (2011, July). The application of evolutionary neural network for bat echolocation calls recognition. In *The 2011 International Joint Conference on Neural Networks* (pp. 1106-1111). IEEE. 10.1109/IJCNN.2011.6033347

Mirzaei, G., Majid, M. W., Bastas, S., Ross, J., Jamali, M. M., Gorsevski, P. V., ... Bingman, V. P. (2012, November). Acoustic monitoring techniques for avian detection and classification. In *2012 Conference Record of the Forty Sixth Asilomar Conference on Signals, Systems and Computers (ASILOMAR)* (pp. 1835-1838). IEEE. 10.1109/ACSSC.2012.6489353

Mirzaei, G., Majid, M. W., Ross, J., Jamali, M. M., Gorsevski, P. V., Frizado, J. P., & Bingman, V. P. (2012, May). The BIO-acoustic feature extraction and classification of bat echolocation calls. In *2012 IEEE International Conference on Electro/Information Technology* (pp. 1-4). IEEE. 10.1109/EIT.2012.6220700

Mischel, W. (1996). From good intentions to willpower. In P. Gollwitzer & J. Bargh (Eds.), The psychology of action. *Guilford Press.*

Mishra, P., Asaari, M. S. M., Herrero-Langreo, A., Lohumi, S., Diezma, B., & Scheunders, P. (2017). Close range hyperspectral imaging of plants: A review. *Biosystems Engineering, 164*, 49–67. doi:10.1016/j.biosystemseng.2017.09.009

Mishra, P., & Nordon, A. (2020). Classifying green teas with near infrared hyperspectral imaging. *NIR News, 31*(1–2), 20–23. doi:10.1177/0960336019889321

Mishra, P., & Yadav, A. (2013). Of art and algorithms: Rethinking technology & creativity in the 21st century. *TechTrends, 57*(3), 11.

Mittal, M. (2019). *Efficient Edge Detection Approach to Provide Better Edge Connectivity for Image Analysis.* Academic Press.

Miyazaki, K., Yamamura, M., & Kobayashi, S. (1997). *k*-Certainty Exploration Method: An action selector to identify the environment in reinforcement learning. *Artificial Intelligence, 91*(1), 155–171. doi:10.1016/S0004-3702(96)00062-8

Mnih, V., Kavukcuoglu, K., Silver, D., Graves, A., Antonoglou, I., Wierstra, D., & Riedmiller, M. (2013). Playing Atari with Deep Reinforcement Learning. In *NIPS Deep Learning Workshop 2013.* Retrieved from https://arxiv.org/pdf/1312.5602.pdf

Mnih, V., Kavukcuoglu, K., Silver, D., Rusu, A. A., Veness, J., Bellemare, M. G., & Petersen, S. (2015). Human-level control through deep reinforcement learning. *Nature, 518*(7540), 529–533. doi:10.1038/nature14236 PMID:25719670

Moffaert, K. V., & Nowe, A. (2014). Multi-Objective Reinforcement Learning using Sets of Pareto Dominating Policies. *Journal of Machine Learning Research, 15*, 3663–3692.

Mohammadzaheri, M., Amouzadeh, A., Doustmohammadi, M., Emadi, M., Jamshidi, E., Ghodsi, M., & Soltani, P. (2021). Fuzzy Analysis of Resonance Frequencies for Structural Inspection of an Engine Cylinder Block. *Fuzzy Information and Engineering*, 1-11. https://www.tandfonline.com/doi/pdf/10.1080/16168658.2021.1908819

Mohammadzaheri, M., Akbarifar, A., Ghodsi, M., Bahadur, I., AlJahwari, F., & Al-Amri, B. (2020). *Health Monitoring of Welded Pipelines with Mechanical Waves and Fuzzy Inference Systems* [Paper presentation]. *International Gas Union Research Conference*, Muscat, Oman.

Mohammadzaheri, M., & AlQallaf, A. (2017). Nanopositioning systems with piezoelectric actuators, current state and future perspective. *Science of Advanced Materials, 9*(7), 1071–1080. doi:10.1166/sam.2017.3088

Mohammadzaheri, M., AlQallaf, A., Ghodsi, M., & Ziaiefar, H. (2018). Development of a Fuzzy Model to Estimate the Head of Gaseous Petroleum Fluids Driven by Electrical Submersible Pumps. *Fuzzy Information and Engineering, 10*(1), 99–106. doi:10.1080/16168658.2018.1509523

Mohammadzaheri, M., AlSulti, S., Ghodsi, M., Bahadur, I., & Emadi, M. (2021). Assessment of capacitor-based charge estimators for piezoelectric actuators. *2021 IEEE International Conference on Mechatronics (ICM)*.

Mohammadzaheri, M., Amouzadeh, A., Doustmohammadi, M., Emadi, M., Jamshidi, E., & Ghodsi, M. (2021). *Fault Diagnosis of an Automobile Cylinder Block with Neural Process of Modal Information*. Academic Press.

Mohammadzaheri, M., & Chen, L. (2010). Intelligent predictive control of a model helicopter's yaw angle. *Asian Journal of Control*, *12*(6), 667–679. doi:10.1002/asjc.243

Mohammadzaheri, M., Chen, L., & Grainger, S. (2012). A critical review of the most popular types of neuro control. *Asian Journal of Control*, *16*(1), 1–11. doi:10.1002/asjc.449

Mohammadzaheri, M., Emadi, M., Ghodsi, M., Bahadur, I. M., Zarog, M., Saleem, A. J. I. J. A. I., & Learning, M. (2020). Development of a Charge Estimator for Piezoelectric Actuators: A Radial Basis Function Approach. *International Journal of Artificial Intelligence and Machine Learning*, *10*(1), 31–44. doi:10.4018/IJAIML.2020010103

Mohammadzaheri, M., Emadi, M., Ghodsi, M., Jamshidi, E., Bahadur, I., Saleem, A., & Zarog, M. (2019). A variable-resistance digital charge estimator for piezoelectric actuators: An alternative to maximise accuracy and curb voltage drop. *Journal of Intelligent Material Systems and Structures*, *30*(11), 1699–1705. doi:10.1177/1045389X19844011

Mohammadzaheri, M., Emadi, M., Ziaiefar, H., Ghodsi, M., Bahadur, I., Zarog, M., & Saleem, A. (2019). Adaptive Charge Estimation of Piezoelectric Actuators, a Radial Basis Function Approach. *20th International Conference on Research and Education in Mechatronics Wels*, Austria.

Mohammadzaheri, M., Firoozfar, A., Mehrabi, D., Emadi, M., & Alqallaf, A. (2019). Temperature Estimation for a Point of an Infrared Dryer Using Temperature of Neighbouring Points: An Artificial Neural Network Approach. *Journal of Engineering Research*, *7*(4).

Mohammadzaheri, M., Ghodsi, M., & AlQallaf, A. (2018). Estimate of the Head Produced by Electrical Submersible Pumps on Gaseous Petroleum Fluids, a Radial Basis Function Network Approach. *International Journal of Artificial Intelligence Applications*, *9*(1).

Mohammadzaheri, M., Grainger, S., & Bazghaleh, M. (2012). Fuzzy modeling of a piezoelectric actuator. *International Journal of Precision Engineering and Manufacturing*, *13*(5), 663–670. doi:10.100712541-012-0086-3

Mohammadzaheri, M., Grainger, S., & Bazghaleh, M. (2013). A system identification approach to the characterization and control of a piezoelectric tube actuator. *Smart Materials and Structures*, *22*(10), 105022. doi:10.1088/0964-1726/22/10/105022

Mohammadzaheri, M., Grainger, S., Bazghaleh, M., & Yaghmaee, P. (2012). *Intelligent modeling of a piezoelectric tube actuator*. International Symposium on Innovations in Intelligent Systems and Applications (INISTA), Trabzon, Turkey. 10.1109/INISTA.2012.6246980

Mohammadzaheri, M., Mirsepahi, A., Asef-afshar, O., & Koohi, H. (2007). Neuro-fuzzy modeling of superheating system of a steam power plant. *Applied Mathematical Sciences*, *1*, 2091–2099.

Mohammadzaheri, M., Tafreshi, R., Khan, Z., Franchek, M., & Grigoriadis, K. (2016). An intelligent approach to optimize multiphase subsea oil fields lifted by electrical submersible pumps. *Journal of Computational Science*, *15*, 50–59. doi:10.1016/j.jocs.2015.10.009

Mohammadzaheri, M., Ziaeifar, H., Bahadur, I., Zarog, M., Emadi, M., & Ghodsi, M. (2019). *Data-driven Modelling of Engineering Systems with Small Data, a Comparative Study of Artificial Intelligence Techniques*. 5th Iranian Conference on Signal Processing and Intelligent Systems (ICSPIS), Semnan, Iran. 10.1109/ICSPIS48872.2019.9066058

Mohammed, R., Rawashdeh, J., & Abdullah, M. (2020). Machine Learning with Oversampling and Undersampling Techniques. *Overview Study and Experimental Results.*, (April), 243–248. Advance online publication. doi:10.1109/ICICS49469.2020.239556

Mohd, N., & Mahmood, T. F. P. T. (2011). The effects of attitude towards problem solving in mathematics achievements. *Australian Journal of Basic and Applied Sciences*, *5*(12), 1857–1862.

Moh, M., & Raju, R. (2018). Machine Learning Techniques for Security of Internet of Things (IoT) and Fog Computing Systems. *2018 International Conference on High Performance Computing & Simulation (HPCS)*.

Mok. (2017). *Why Artificial Intelligence Needs Neuroscience for Inspiration.* Academic Press.

Molnár, C., Kaplan, F., Roy, P., Pachet, F., Pongrácz, P., Dóka, A., & Miklósi, Á. (2008). Classification of dog barks: A machine learning approach. *Animal Cognition*, *11*(3), 389–400. doi:10.100710071-007-0129-9 PMID:18197442

Montgomery, D. C., & Runger, G. (2017). *Probability and Statistics for Engineers.* Wiley.

Moore, D. R., Cowan, J. A., Riley, A., Edmondson-Jones, A. M., & Ferguson, M. A. (2011). Development of auditory processing in 6- to 11-yr-old children. *Ear and Hearing*, *32*(3), 269–285. doi:10.1097/AUD.0b013e318201c468

Morishita, K., Kato, S., Sasaki, T., Takei, Y., & Saito, K. (2021, January). Development of receptor cell model converting sensor inputs into pulse waveforms. *The Twenty-Sixth International Symposium on Artificial Life and Robotics 2021.*

Mortazi, A., & Bagci, U. (2018, September). Automatically designing CNN architectures for medical image segmentation. In *International Workshop on Machine Learning in Medical Imaging* (pp. 98-106). Springer. 10.1007/978-3-030-00919-9_12

Moschella, M. (2019). Observable computational thinking skills in primary school children: How and when teachers can discern abstraction, decomposition and use of algorithms. *INTED2019 Proceedings*, *1*(March), 6259–6267. 10.21125/inted.2019.1523

Mosenia, A., & Jha, N. K. (2016). A comprehensive study of security of internet-of-things. *IEEE Transactions on Emerging Topics in Computing*, *5*(4), 586–602.

Moustafa, N. (2019). *TON_IOT Datasets.* doi:10.21227/fesz-dm97

Mršić, L. (2014). Widely Applicable Multi-Variate Decision Support Model for Market Trend Analysis and Prediction with Case Study in Retail. In P. Vasant (Ed.), Handbook of Research on Novel Soft Computing Intelligent Algorithms: Theory and Practical Applications (pp. 989-1018). Hershey, PA: Information Science Reference. doi:10.4018/978-1-4666-4450-2.ch032

Muallem, A., Shetty, S., Pan, J. W., Zhao, J., & Biswal, B. (2017). Hoeffding tree algorithms for anomaly detection in streaming datasets: A survey. *Journal of Information Security*, *8*(4).

Mulder, R., Radu, V., & Dubach, C. (2020). *Optimising the Performance of Convolutional Neural Networks across Computing Systems using Transfer Learning.* arXiv preprint arXiv:2010.10621

Mumtaz, J., Guan, Z., Yue, L., Zhang, L., & He, C. (2020). Hybrid spider monkey optimisation algorithm for multi-level planning and scheduling problems of assembly lines. *International Journal of Production Research*, *58*(20), 6252–6267. doi:10.1080/00207543.2019.1675917

Mushtaq, Z., & Su, S. F. (2020). Environmental sound classification using a regularized deep convolutional neural network with data augmentation. *Applied Acoustics*, *167*, 107389. doi:10.1016/j.apacoust.2020.107389

Mustafic, A., Jiang, Y., & Li, C. (2016). Cotton contamination detection and classification using hyperspectral fluorescence imaging. *Textile Research Journal, 86*(15), 1574–1584. doi:10.1177/0040517515590416

N., G. I. (2020). Eddy Currents in Multilayer Coils. *American Journal of Physics, 89*(284), 1-24. doi:10.1119/10.0002444

Naganathan, G. K., Grimes, L. M., Subbiah, J., Calkins, C. R., Samal, A., & Meyer, G. E. (2008). Visible/near-infrared hyperspectral imaging for beef tenderness prediction. *Computers and Electronics in Agriculture, 64*(2), 225–233. doi:10.1016/j.compag.2008.05.020

Nagata, F., Miki, K., Otsuka, A., Yoshida, K., Watanabe, K., & Habib, M. K. (2020). Pick and Place Robot Using Visual Feedback Control and Transfer Learning-Based CNN. *Procs. of the 2020 IEEE International Conference on Mechatronics and Automation (ICMA 2020)*, 850-855.

Nagata, F., Habib, M. K., & Watanabe, K. (2021). Design and Implementation of Convolutional Neural Network based SVM Technique for Manufacturing Defect Detection. *International Journal of Mechatronics and Automation, 8*(2), 53–61.

Nagy, K., Cinkler, T., Simon, C., & Vida, R. (2020, October). *Internet of Birds (IoB): Song Based Bird Sensing via Machine Learning in the Cloud: How to sense, identify, classify birds based on their songs? In 2020 IEEE Sensors*. IEEE.

Nakatani, K., Sugimoto, Y., & Osuka, K. (2009). Demonstration and analysis of quadruped passive dynamic walking. *Advanced Robotics, 23*(5), 483–501. doi:10.1163/156855309X420039

Nanayakkara, N., Halgamuge, M., & Syed, A. (2019). Security and Privacy of Internet of Medical Things (IoMT) Based Healthcare Applications. *RE:view*.

Nanda, A. (2018). Image Edge Detection Using Fractional Calculus with Features and Contrast Enhancement. *Circuits, Systems, and Signal Processing, 37*(9), 3946–3972. doi:10.100700034-018-0751-6

Narasimhan, R., Fern, X. Z., & Raich, R. (2017, March). Simultaneous segmentation and classification of bird song using CNN. In *2017 IEEE International Conference on Acoustics, Speech and Signal Processing (ICASSP)* (pp. 146-150). IEEE. 10.1109/ICASSP.2017.7952135

Natarajan, S., & Tadepalli, P. (2005). Dynamic Preferences in Multi-Criteria Reinforcement Learning. *Proceedings of the 22nd international conference on machine learning (ICML-2005)*, 601-60. 10.1145/1102351.1102427

Nazir, S., Patel, S., & Patel, D. (2018, July). Hyper parameters selection for image classification in convolutional neural networks. In *2018 IEEE 17th International Conference on Cognitive Informatics & Cognitive Computing (ICCI* CC)* (pp. 401-407). IEEE. 10.1109/ICCI-CC.2018.8482081

Neath, R. C., & Johnson, M. S. (2010). Discrimination and classification. International Encyclopedia of Education, 135–141. doi:10.1016/B978-0-08-044894-7.01312-9

Neetesh, M. (2017). The Connect between Deep Learning and AI. *Open Source for You*.

Nelson, K. M., & Wille, L. T. (1995, March). Comparative study of heuristics for optimal printed circuit board assembly. *Proceedings of Southcon, 95*, 322–327. doi:10.1109/SOUTHC.1995.516124

Neumann, M. M., & Neumann, D. L. (2019). Validation of a touch screen tablet assessment of early literacy skills and a comparison with a traditional paper-based assessment. *International Journal of Research & Method in Education, 42*(4), 385–398. doi:10.1080/1743727X.2018.1498078

Newaz, A., Sikder, A. K., Rahman, M. A., & Uluagac, A. S. (2020). *A Survey on Security and Privacy Issues in Modern Healthcare Systems: Attacks and Defenses*. arXiv preprint arXiv:2005.07359.

Nguyen, D., & Widrow, B. (1990). *Improving the learning speed of 2-layer neural networks by choosing initial values of the adaptive weights. International Joint Conference on Neural Networks*, San Diego, CA.

Nguyen, H. N., & Lee, C. (2018). Effects of Hyper-parameters and Dataset on CNN Training. *Journal of IKEEE, 22*(1), 14–20.

Nguyen, V. N., Jenssen, R., & Roverso, D. (2019). Intelligent Monitoring and Inspection of Power Line Components Powered by UAVs and Deep Learning. *IEEE Power and Energy Technology Systems Journal, 6*(1), 11–21. doi:10.1109/JPETS.2018.2881429

NLP. (2021). https://nlp.stanford.edu/software/tagger

Nooy de, W., Mrvar, A., & Batagalj, V. (2008). Exploratory Social Network Analysis with Pajek. Cambridge University Press.

Norris, S. P., & Ennis, R. H. (1989). *Evaluating critical thinking*. Midwest Publications.

Ntalampiras, S., Kosmin, D., & Sanchez, J. (2021, July). Acoustic classification of individual cat vocalizations in evolving environments. In *2021 44th International Conference on Telecommunications and Signal Processing (TSP)* (pp. 254-258). IEEE. 10.1109/TSP52935.2021.9522660

Öber, A. (2007). *Hayvan Davranışları (Temel Ögeler)*. Nobel Yayın Dağıtım Lt. Şti.

OECD. (2017). Collaborative problem-solving framework. *PISA 2015*.

Ollander , S. (2015). Wearable sensor data fusion for human stress estimation *[Ph.D. thesis]. Linköping University*.

Ong, N. S., & Khoo, L. P. (1999). Genetic algorithm approach in PCB assembly. *Integrated Manufacturing Systems, 10*(5), 256–265. doi:10.1108/09576069910280648

Ong, N. S., & Tan, W. C. (2002). Sequence placement planning for high-speed PCB assembly machine. *Integrated Manufacturing Systems, 13*(1), 35–46. doi:10.1108/09576060210411495

Ong, N., & Wong, Y. (1999). Automatic subassembly detection from a product model for disassembly sequence generation. *International Journal of Advanced Manufacturing Technology, 15*(6), 425–431. doi:10.1007001700050086

Onoyama, H., Ryu, C., Suguri, M., & Iida, M. (2013). Potential of hyperspectral imaging for constructing a year-invariant model to estimate the nitrogen content of rice plants at the panicle initiation stage. In *IFAC Proceedings Volumes (IFAC-PapersOnline)* (Vol. 4). 10.3182/20130828-2-SF-3019.00054

Osmanagić Bedenik, N. (2003). *Kriza kao šansa: kroz poslovnu krizu do poslovnog uspjeha*. Zagreb: Školska knjiga d.d.

Otri, S. (2011). *Improving the bees algorithm for complex optimisation problems* (Doctoral dissertation). Cardiff University.

Otsuka, H., Yajima, R., Nagatani, K., & Kubo, D. (2015). Localization of a Small Multi-Rotor UAV Using Dropping AR Markers. *Procs. of the 2015 JSME Conference on Robotics and Mechatronics*, 2A2-G02.

Owaki, D., & Ishiguro, A. (2017). A quadruped robot exhibiting spontaneous gait transitions from walking to trotting to galloping. *Scientific Reports, 7*(277), 1–10. doi:10.103841598-017-00348-9 PMID:28325917

Owaki, D., Kano, T., Nagasawa, K., Tero, A., & Ishiguro, A. (2013). Simple robot suggests physical interlimb coordination is essential for quadruped walking. *Journal of the Royal Society, Interface, 10*(78), 20120669. doi:10.1098/rsif.2012.0669 PMID:23097501

Ozaki, Y., Yano, M., & Onishi, M. (2017). Effective hyperparameter optimization using Nelder-Mead method in deep learning. *IPSJ Transactions on Computer Vision and Applications, 9*(1), 1–12. doi:10.118641074-017-0030-7

Ozceylan, E., Kalayci, C. B., Gungor, A., & Gupta, S. M. (2019). Disassembly line balancing problem: A review of the state of the art and future directions. *International Journal of Production Research, 57*(15-16), 4805–4827. doi:10.108 0/00207543.2018.1428775

Page, A. M. (1996). Providing effective early warning: Business Intelligence as a strategic control system. In The Art & Science of Business Intelligence Analysis. JAI Press.

Page, A. M. (1996). The Art & Science of Collection Management. In The Art & Science of Business Intelligence Analysis. JAI Press.

Pagnano, A., Höpf, M., & Teti, R. (2013). A Roadmap for Automated Power Line Inspection. *Maintenance And Repair. Procedia Cirp, 12*, 234–239. doi:10.1016/j.procir.2013.09.041

Pandey, P., & Litoriya, R. (2020). Elderly care through unusual behavior detection: A disaster management approach using IoT and intelligence. *IBM Journal of Research and Development, 64*(1/2), 15:11-15:11. doi:10.1147/JRD.2019.2947018

Pandeya, Y. R., Kim, D., & Lee, J. (2018). Domestic cat sound classification using learned features from deep neural nets. *Applied Sciences (Basel, Switzerland), 8*(10), 1949. doi:10.3390/app8101949

Panetta, K., Gao, C., Agaian, S., & Nercessian, S. (2014). Nonreference Medical Image Edge Map Measure. *International Journal of Biomedical Imaging, 2014*, 1–8. doi:10.1155/2014/937849 PMID:25132844

Panicker, S. S., & Gayathri, P. (2019). A survey of machine learning techniques in physiology based mental stress detection systems. *Biocybernetics and Biomedical Engineering, 39*(2), 444–469. doi:10.1016/j.bbe.2019.01.004

Pannu, A. (2015). Artificial intelligence and its application in different areas. *Artificial Intelligence, 4*(10), 79–84.

Papert, S. (1980). *Mindstorms: Children, computers, and powerful ideas*. Basic Books.

Park, J., & Sandberg, I. W. (1993). Approximation and radial-basis-function networks. *Neural Computation, 5*(2), 305–316. doi:10.1162/neco.1993.5.2.305 PMID:31167308

Park, J.-Y., Cho, B.-H., Byun, S.-H., & Lee, J.-K. (2009). Development of Cleaning Robot System for Live-line Suspension Insulator Strings. *International Journal of Control, Automation, and Systems, 7*(2), 211–220. doi:10.100712555-009-0207-7

Park, J.-Y., Lee, J.-K., Cho, B.-H., & Oh, K.-Y. (2012). An Inspection Robot for Live-Line Suspension Insulator Strings in 345-kV Power Lines. *IEEE Transactions on Power Delivery, 27*(2), 632–639. doi:10.1109/TPWRD.2011.2182620

Parsa, M., Mitchell, J. P., Schuman, C. D., Patton, R. M., Potok, T. E., & Roy, K. (2020). Bayesian multi-objective hyperparameter optimization for accurate, fast, and efficient neural network accelerator design. *Frontiers in Neuroscience, 14*, 667. doi:10.3389/fnins.2020.00667 PMID:32848531

Parsons, S., & Jones, G. (2000). Acoustic identification of twelve species of echolocating bat by discriminant function analysis and artificial neural networks. *The Journal of Experimental Biology, 203*(17), 2641–2656. doi:10.1242/jeb.203.17.2641 PMID:10934005

Passmore, J. (1967). Logical Positivism. In P. Edwards (Ed.), The Encyclopedia of Philosophy. Macmillan.

Pattanaik, A., Mishra, S., & Rana, D. (2015). Comparative Study of Edge Detection Using Renyi Entropy and Differential Evolution. *International Journal of Engineering Research & Technology (Ahmedabad), 4*(3), 1001–1005. doi:10.17577/IJERTV4IS031077

Paumen, Y., Mälzer, M., Alipek, S., Moll, J., Lüdtke, B., & Schauer-Weisshahn, H. (2021). Development and test of a bat calls detection and classification method based on convolutional neural networks. *Bioacoustics*, 1–12. doi:10.1080/09524622.2021.1978863

Pavan, G. (2008). Short field course on bioacoustics. Taxonomy Summer School, 1-15.

Pavo, J., Gasparics, A., Sebestyen, I., Vertesy, G., Darczi, C. S., & Miya, K. (1996). *Eddy Current Testing with Fluxset Probe*. Applied Electromagnetics and Mechanics.

Pea, R. D., & Kurland, D. M. (1984). On the cognitive effects of learning computer programming. *New Ideas in Psychology, 2*(2), 137–168. doi:10.1016/0732-118X(84)90018-7

Peng, B., Zhang, L., & Zhang, D. (2013). A Survey of Graph Theoretical Approaches to Image Segmentation. *Pattern Recognition, 26*(3), 1020–1032. doi:10.1016/j.patcog.2012.09.015

Peres, R. S., Jia, X., Lee, J., Sun, K., Colombo, A. W., & Barata, J. (2020). Industrial artificial intelligence in industry 4.0-systematic review, challenges and outlook. *IEEE Access: Practical Innovations, Open Solutions, 8*, 220121–220139. doi:10.1109/ACCESS.2020.3042874

Perez, A. (2018). A Framework for Computational Thinking Dispositions in Mathematics Education. *Journal for Research in Mathematics Education, 49*(4), 424–461. doi:10.5951/jresematheduc.49.4.0424

Perkins, D. (2008). Beyond understanding. In *Threshold Concepts within the Disciplines*. Sense Publishers.

Perkins, D. N. (1993). Person-plus: a distributed view of thinking and learning. In G. Salomon (Ed.), *Distributed cognitions: psychological and educational considerations*. Cambridge University Press.

Perkins, D. N., Jay, E., & Tishman, S. (1993). Beyond Abilities: A dispositional theory of thinking. *Merrill-Palmer Quarterly, 39*(1), 1–21.

Pernebayeva, D., Irmanova, A., Sadykova, D., Bagheri, M., & James, A. (2019). High voltage outdoor insulator surface condition evaluation using aerial insulator images. *High Volt., 4*(3), 178–185. doi:10.1049/hve.2019.0079

Pham, D. T., Castellani, M., & Ghanbarzadeh, A. (2007a). Preliminary design using the bees algorithm. In *Proceedings of eighth international conference on laser metrology, CMM and machine tool performance, LAMDAMAP* (pp. 420-429). Academic Press.

Pham, D. T., Koc, E., Lee, J. Y., & Phrueksanant, J. (2007b). Using the bees algorithm to schedule jobs for a machine. In *Proceedings Eighth International Conference on Laser Metrology, CMM and Machine Tool Performance, LAMDAMAP* (pp. 430-439). Academic Press.

Pham, D. T., Otri, S., & Darwish, A. H. (2007d). Application of the Bees Algorithm to PCB assembly optimisation. In *Proceedings of the 3rd virtual international conference on intelligent production machines and systems* (pp. 511-516). Academic Press.

Pham, D. T., Soroka, A. J., Ghanbarzadeh, A., Koc, E., Otri, S., & Packianather, M. (2006b). Optimising neural networks for identification of wood defects using the bees algorithm. In *2006 4th IEEE International Conference on Industrial Informatics* (pp. 1346-1351). IEEE. 10.1109/INDIN.2006.275855

Pham, D. T., Afify, A., & Koc, E. (2007c). *Manufacturing cell formation using the Bees Algorithm*. In *Innovative Production Machines and Systems Virtual Conference*, Cardiff, UK.

Pham, D. T., & Castellani, M. (2009). The bees algorithm: Modelling foraging behaviour to solve continuous optimization problems. *Proceedings of the Institution of Mechanical Engineers. Part C, Journal of Mechanical Engineering Science, 223*(12), 2919–2938. doi:10.1243/09544062JMES1494

Pham, D. T., Ghanbarzadeh, A., Koç, E., Otri, S., Rahim, S., & Zaidi, M. (2006a). The bees algorithm—a novel tool for complex optimisation problems. In *Intelligent production machines and systems* (pp. 454–459). Elsevier Science Ltd. doi:10.1016/B978-008045157-2/50081-X

Phan, H. V., Aurecianus, S., Kang, T., & Park, H. C. (2019). KUBeetle-S: An insect-like, tailless, hover-capable robot that can fly with a low-torque control mechanism. *International Journal of Micro Air Vehicles, 11*, 11. doi:10.1177/1756829319861371

Physiopedia. (2021). *Cerebral Cortex*. https://www.physio-pedia.com/Cerebral_Cortex

Piaget, J. (1971). The Stages of Intellectual Development of the Child. Readings in Child Development, 55(2), 178-204.

Piaget, J. (1936). *Origins of intelligence in the child*. Routledge & Kegan Paul.

Piczak, K. J. (2015, October). ESC: Dataset for environmental sound classification. In *Proceedings of the 23rd ACM international conference on Multimedia* (pp. 1015-1018). 10.1145/2733373.2806390

Pieplow, N. (2019). *Peterson Field Guide to Bird Sounds of Western North America*. Peterson Field Guides.

PiezoDrive. (2021). *Piezoelectric Actuators*. https://www.piezodrive.com/actuators/

Pinder, J. M. (2016). *Multi-Objective Reinforcement Learning Framework for Unknown Stochastic & Uncertain Environments* (Unpublished doctoral dissertation). Retrieved from http://usir.salford.ac.uk/id/eprint/39978/2/John%20Pinder%20PhD%20Thesis%20Complete.pdf

Pinheiro, C. A. R. (2011). *Social Network Analysis in Telecommunications*. John Wiley and Sons, Inc.

Pirouz, D. M. (2012). An Overview of Partial Least Squares. SSRN *Electronic Journal*. doi:10.2139/ssrn.1631359

Plaat, A., Kosters, W., & Preuss, M. (2020). *Deep Model-based Reinforcement Learning for High-Dimensional Problems, a Survey*. Retrieved from https://arxiv.org/pdf/2008.05598.pdf

Plutchik, R. (2001). The nature of emotions: Human emotions have deep evolutionary roots, a fact that may explain their complexity and provide tools for clinical practice. *American Scientist, 89*(4), 344–350. doi:10.1511/2001.4.344

Polat, K., & Alhudhaif, A. (2021). *Classification of imbalanced hyperspectral images using SMOTE-based deep learning methods*. doi:10.1016/j.eswa.2021.114986

Pont-Tuset, J., Arbelaez, P., Barron, J., Marquez, F., & Malik, J. (2017). Multiscale Combinatorial Grouping for Image Segmentation and Object Proposal Generation. *IEEE Transactions on Pattern Recognition, 39*(1), 128–137. doi:10.1109/TPAMI.2016.2537320 PMID:26955014

Porter, M. (1980). *Competitive Strategy*. Amacom.

Prabavathy, S., Sundarakantham, K., & Shalinie, S. M. (2018). Design of cognitive fog computing for intrusion detection in Internet of Things. *Journal of Communications and Networks (Seoul), 20*(3), 291–298.

Pradeep Kumar Reddy, R., & Nagaraju, C. (2019). Improved Canny Edge Detection Technique Using S-Membership Function. *International Journal of Engineering and Advanced Technology, 8*(6), 43–49. doi:10.35940/ijeat.E7419.088619

Prat, Y., Taub, M., Pratt, E., & Yovel, Y. (2017). An annotated dataset of Egyptian fruit bat vocalizations across varying contexts and during vocal ontogeny. *Scientific Data, 4*(1), 1–7. doi:10.1038data.2017.143 PMID:28972574

Prat, Y., Taub, M., & Yovel, Y. (2015). Vocal learning in a social mammal: Demonstrated by isolation and playback experiments in bats. *Science Advances, 1*(2), e1500019. doi:10.1126ciadv.1500019 PMID:26601149

Predić, B., Dimić, G., Rančić, D., Štrbac, P., Maček, N., & Spalević, P. (2018). Improving final grade prediction accuracy in blended learning environment using voting ensembles. *Computer Applications in Engineering Education*, *26*(6), 2294–2306. doi:10.1002/cae.22042

Probst, P., Wright, M. N., & Boulesteix, A-L. (2019). Hyperparameters and tuning strategies for random forest. *2019 WIREs Data Mining Knowl Discov.*

Puchale, L. H. B. (2019), *Metodologia para mitigação de desligamento intempestivos em linhas de transmissão correlacionados a umidade elevada* (Dissertation). Unisinos.

Puterman, M. L. (1994). *Markov Decision Processes: Discrete Stochastic Dynamic Programming*. John Wiley & Sons, Inc. doi:10.1002/9780470316887

Qasim, A. J., Din, R. E., & Alyousuf, F. A. (2020). Review on Techniques and File Formats of Image Compression. *Bulletin of Electrical Engineering and Informatics*, *9*(2), 602–610. doi:10.11591/eei.v9i2.2085

Qiao, J., Ngadi, M. O., Wang, N., Gariépy, C., & Prasher, S. O. (2007). Pork quality and marbling level assessment using a hyperspectral imaging system. *Journal of Food Engineering*, *83*(1), 10–16. doi:10.1016/j.jfoodeng.2007.02.038

Qin, J., Chao, K., Kim, M. S., Lu, R., & Burks, T. F. (2013). Hyperspectral and multispectral imaging for evaluating food safety and quality. *Journal of Food Engineering*, *118*(2), 157–171. doi:10.1016/j.jfoodeng.2013.04.001

Qu, G., & Yuan, L. (2014). *Design THINGS for the Internet of Things—An EDA perspective. In 2014 IEEE/ACM international conference on Computer-Aided Design*. ICCAD.

Qui, X., Li, K., Liu, P., Zhou, X., & Sun, M. (2020). Deep Attention and Multi-Scale Networks for Accurate Remote Sensing Image Segmentation. *IEEE Access: Practical Innovations, Open Solutions*, *8*, 146627–146639. doi:10.1109/ACCESS.2020.3015587

Rahmani, A. M., Gia, T. N., Negash, B., Anzanpour, A., Azimi, I., Jiang, M., & Liljeberg, P. (2018). Exploiting smart e-Health gateways at the edge of healthcare Internet-of-Things: A fog computing approach. *Future Generation Computer Systems*, *78*, 641–658.

Rahman, M. A., & Mohsenian-Rad, H. (2012). False data injection attacks with incomplete information against smart power grids. *2012 IEEE Global Communications Conference (GLOBECOM)*.

Raibert, M., Blankespoor, K., Nelson, G., & Playter, R. (2008). Bigdog, the rough-terrain quadruped robot. *IFAC Proceedings Volumes*, *41*(2), 10822-10825.

Raibert, M., Blankespoor, K., Nelson, G., & Playter, R. (2008). BigDog, the rough-terrain quadruped robot. In *IFAC Proceedings Volumes* (vol. 41, pp. 10822-10825). Elsevier. 10.3182/20080706-5-KR-1001.01833

Rambally, G. (2017). Integrating Computational Thinking in Discrete Structures. In P. Rich & C. Hodges (Eds.), *Emerging Research, Practice, and Policy on Computational Thinking. In Educational Communications and Technology: Issues and Innovations*. Springer. doi:10.1007/978-3-319-52691-1_7

Rashid, M. F. F., Hutabarat, W., & Tiwari, A. (2012). A review on assembly sequence planning and assembly line balancing optimisation using soft computing approaches. *International Journal of Advanced Manufacturing Technology*, *59*(1), 335–349. doi:10.100700170-011-3499-8

Rasley, J., He, Y., Yan, F., Ruwase, O., & Fonseca, R. (2017, December). Hyperdrive: Exploring hyperparameters with pop scheduling. In *Proceedings of the 18th ACM/IFIP/USENIX Middleware Conference* (pp. 1-13). ACM.

Rathore, H., Wenzel, L., Al-Ali, A. K., Mohamed, A., Du, X., & Guizani, M. (2018). Multi-layer perceptron model on chip for secure diabetic treatment. *IEEE Access: Practical Innovations, Open Solutions, 6*, 44718–44730.

Real Academia Española. (2021). https://www.rae.es/

Real, E., Moore, S., Selle, A., Saxena, S., Suematsu, Y. L., Tan, J., Le, Q. V., & Kurakin, A. (2017). Large-scale evolution of image classifiers. In *Proceedings of Int. Conf. Machine Learning*. ACM.

Rebolledo, R. (2018). Complexity and Chance [Complejidad y azar]. *Humanities Journal of Valparaiso*. doi:10.22370/rhv.2018.12.1322

Ren, Y., Yu, D., Zhang, C., Tian, G., Meng, L., & Zhou, X. (2017). An improved gravitational search algorithm for profit-oriented partial disassembly line balancing problem. *International Journal of Production Research, 55*(24), 7302–7316. doi:10.1080/00207543.2017.1341066

Ren, Y., Zhang, C., Zhao, F., Xiao, H., & Tian, G. (2018). An asynchronous parallel disassembly planning based on genetic algorithm. *European Journal of Operational Research, 269*(2), 647–660. doi:10.1016/j.ejor.2018.01.055

Repelianto, A. S., & Kasai, N. (2019). The Improvement of Flaw Detection by the Configuration of Uniform Eddy Current Probe. *Sensors (Basel), 19*(2), 1–13. doi:10.339019020397 PMID:30669390

Resnick, M., Maloney, J., Monroy-Hernández, A., Rusk, N., Eastmond, E., Brennan, K., Millner, A., Rosenbaum, E., Silver, J., Silverman, B., & Kafai, Y. (2009). Scratch. *Communications of the ACM, 52*(11), 60–67. doi:10.1145/1592761.1592779

Reynolds , C. R., Voress, J. K., Pearson, A., N. (2008). Developmental test of auditory perception. *Examiner's Manual, PRO-ED*.

Richter, Y., Yom-Tov, E., & Slonim, N. (2010). Predicting customer churn in mobile networks through analysis of social groups. *Proceedings of the SIAM International Conference on Data Mining*, 732-741.

Rickli, J. L., & Camelio, J. A. (2013). Multi-objective partial disassembly optimization based on sequence feasibility. *Journal of Manufacturing Systems, 32*(1), 281–293. doi:10.1016/j.jmsy.2012.11.005

Riggs, R. J., Battaïa, O., & Hu, S. J. (2015). Disassembly line balancing under high variety of end of life states using a joint precedence graph approach. *Journal of Manufacturing Systems, 37*, 638–648. doi:10.1016/j.jmsy.2014.11.002

Rim, B., Sung, N., Min, S., & Hong, M. (2020). Deep learning in physiological signal data: A survey. *Sensors (Basel), 20*(4), 969. doi:10.3390/s20040969

Rios, S., & Fleming, A. (2014). *Control of Piezoelectric Benders Using a Charge Drive*. Proc. Actuator.

Rish, I. (2001, August). An empirical study of the naive Bayes classifier. In IJCAI 2001 workshop on empirical methods in artificial intelligence (Vol. 3, No. 22, pp. 41-46). Academic Press.

Robles, M. M. (2012). Executive perceptions of the top 10 soft skills needed in today's workplace. *Business Communication Quarterly, 75*(4), 453–465. doi:10.1177/1080569912460400

Rodríguez Duch, M. F. (2016). Chaos, entropy and public health: Legal analysis from a multidimensional perspective [Caos, entropía y salud pública: Análisis desde una perspectiva jurídica multidimensional]. *Argentina Association of Administrative Law Magazine*.

Rodriguez Santos, A. (2011) *Epswiclas*. I.E.S. San Cristóbal de los Ángeles de Madrid.

Roijers, D. M., Vamplew, P., Whiteson, S., & Dazeley, R. (2013). A Survey of Multi-Objective Sequential Decision-Making. *Journal of Artificial Intelligence Research, 48*, 67–113. doi:10.1613/jair.3987

Roijers, D. M., Whiteson, S., Vamplew, P., & Dazeley, R. (2015). Why Multi-objective Reinforcement Learning? *Proceedings of the 12th European Workshop on Reinforcement Learning (EWRL 2015)*, 1-2.

Román-gonzález, M., Perez-Gonzelez, J. C., & Jimenez-Fernandez, C. (2016). Which cognitive abilities underlie computational thinking? Criterion validity of the Computational Thinking Test. *Computers in Human Behavior*, 72, 678–691. doi:10.1016/j.chb.2016.08.047

Romaniello, R., & Baiano, A. (2018, July). Discrimination of flavoured olive oil based on hyperspectral imaging. *Journal of Food Science and Technology*, 55(7), 2429–2435. Advance online publication. doi:10.100713197-018-3160-8 PMID:30042558

Romero, M., Lepage, A., & Lille, B. (2017). Computational thinking development through creative programming in higher education. *Int J Educ Technol High Educ*, 14(1), 42. doi:10.118641239-017-0080-z

Ronneberger, O., Fischer, P., & Brox, T. (2015). *U-Net: Convolutional Networks for Biomedical Image Segmentation.* MICCAI.

Rosario, J.R.B., Azarraga, E.J.C., Chiu, M.J.C., Del Rosario, A.J.C., Jarabelo, A.B.S., & Bandala, A.A. (2020). Development of a Vision Based Parking Monitoring System Using Quadrotor UAV. *Proc. Of the 2020 IEEE 12th International Conference on Humanoid, Nanotechnology, Information Technology, Communication and Control, Environment, and Management (HNICEM)*, 1-6.

Rosenberg, M. J., Hovland, C. I., McGuire, W. J., Abelson, R. P., & Brehm, J. W. (1960). *Attitude organization and change: An analysis of consistency among attitude components.* Yale University Press.

Rosenblatt, F. (1958). The perceptron: A probabilistic model for information storage and organization in the brain. *Psychological Review*, 65(6), 386–408. doi:10.1037/h0042519 PMID:13602029

Rostom, N. G., Shalaby, A. A., Issa, Y. M., & Afifi, A. A. (2017). Evaluation of Mariut Lake water quality using Hyperspectral Remote Sensing and laboratory works. *The Egyptian Journal of Remote Sensing and Space Sciences*, 20, S39–S48. Advance online publication. doi:10.1016/j.ejrs.2016.11.002

Rubin, L. (2000). *The Future of Power Line Inspection.* Electrical World T&D.

Ruiz, A. T., Jung, K., Tschapka, M., Schwenker, F., & Palm, G. (2017). *Automated identification method for detection and classification of neotropical bats.* Academic Press.

Rumelhart, D., Hinton, G., & Williams, R. (1986). Learning representations by back-propagating errors. *Nature*, 323(6088), 533–536. doi:10.1038/323533a0

Rungpichayapichet, P., Nagle, M., Yuwanbun, P., Khuwijitjaru, P., Mahayothee, B., & Müller, J. (2017). Prediction mapping of physicochemical properties in mango by hyperspectral imaging. *Biosystems Engineering*, 159(2011), 109–120. doi:10.1016/j.biosystemseng.2017.04.006

Russakovsky, O., Deng, J., Su, H., Krause, J., Satheesh, S., Ma, S., Huang, Z., Karpathy, A., Khosla, A., Bernstein, M., Berg, A. C., & Fei-Fei, L. (2015). ImageNet Large Scale Visual Recognition Challenge. *International Journal of Computer Vision*, 115(3), 211–252. doi:10.100711263-015-0816-y

Russell, S., & Norvig, P. (2020). *Artificial intelligence: A modern approach* (4th ed.). Pearson.

Russ, J. C., & Brent Neal, F. (2018). *The Image Processing Handbook.* CRC Press. doi:10.1201/b18983

Ryan, R., & Deci, E. (2000). Self-Determination theory and the facilitation of intrinsic motivation, *social development, and well-being. The American Psychologist*, 55(1), 68–78. doi:10.1037/0003-066X.55.1.68 PMID:11392867

Saari, M. (2018). *The effect of two hyper parameters in the learning performance of the convolutional neural networks* (Bachelor thesis). Tampere University of Technology.

Sabek, W., Al-mana, A., Siddiqui, A. R., Assadi, B. E., Mohammad-khorasani, M., Mohammadzaheri, M., & Tafreshi, R. (2015). Experimental Investigation of Piezoelectric Tube Actuators Dynamics. *2nd International Conference on Robotics and Mechatronics*, Madrid, Spain.

Sadykova, D., & James, A. P. (n.d.). *Quality Assessment Metrics for Edge Detection and Edge-Aware Filtering: A Tutorial Review.* doi:10.1109/ICACCI.2017.8126200

Saffran, J. R., Werker, J. F., & Werner, L. A. (2006). In D. Kuhn, R. S. Siegler, D. William, & R. M. Lerner (Eds.), *The infant's auditory world: Hearing, speech and the beginnings of language* (6th ed., pp. 58–108). Handbook of Child Psychology. John Wiley and Sons.

Sahoo, P. K., & Arora, G. (2004). A Thresholding Method Based on Two-Dimensional Reny's Entropy. *Pattern Recognition*, *37*(6), 1149–1161. doi:10.1016/j.patcog.2003.10.008

Saito, H., Takubo, T., Ueno, A., Cai, K., Miyamoto, R., & Hara, S. (2018). Recognizing Own UAV Position and Measuring Position of a Person Using Camera Image. *Procs. of the 2018 JSME Conference on Robotics and Mechatronics*, 1P1-C08. 10.1299/jsmermd.2018.1P1-C08

Saito, K., Ohara, M., Abe, M., Kaneko, M., & Uchikoba, F. (2017). *Gait generation of multilegged robots by using hardware artificial neural networks. In Advanced Applications for Artificial Neural Networks.* INTEC.

Sala Torrent, M. (2020). Trastornos del desarrollo del lenguaje oral y escrito. Congreso de actualización en Pediatría, 251 – 263.

Salamon, J., Bello, J. P., Farnsworth, A., & Kelling, S. (2017, March). Fusing shallow and deep learning for bioacoustic bird species classification. In 2017 IEEE international conference on acoustics, speech and signal processing (ICASSP) (pp. 141-145). IEEE. doi:10.1109/ICASSP.2017.7952134

Salamon, J., & Bello, J. P. (2017). Deep convolutional neural networks and data augmentation for environmental sound classification. *IEEE Signal Processing Letters*, *24*(3), 279–283. doi:10.1109/LSP.2017.2657381

Salomon, G. (1994). *Interaction of media, cognition, and learning.* Erlbaum.

Salomon, G. (Ed.). (1993). *Distributed cognitions: psychological and educational considerations.* Cambridge University Press.

Salovey, P., & Mayer, J. D. (1990). Emotional intelligence. *Imagination, Cognition and Personality*, *9*(3), 185–211. doi:10.2190/DUGG-P24E-52WK-6CDG

Samy, A., Yu, H., & Zhang, H. (2020). Fog-Based Attack Detection Framework for Internet of Things Using Deep Learning. *IEEE Access: Practical Innovations, Open Solutions*, *8*, 74571–74585. https://doi.org/10.1109/access.2020.2988854

Sands, P., Yadav, A., & Good, J. (2018). Computational think: In-service Teacher Perceptions of Computational Thinking. In *Computational thinking in the STEM disciplines.* Springer.

Sanes, D. H., & Woolley, S. M. (2011). A behavioral framework to guide research on central auditory development and plasticity. *Neuron*, *72*(6), 912–929. doi:10.1016/j.neuron.2011.12.005

Sanyal, S., Aslam, F., Kim, T., Jeon, S., Lee, Y-J., Yi, J., Choi, I-H., Son, J-A., & Koo, J-B. (2019). Deterioration of Porcelain Insulators Utilized in Overhead Transmission Lines: A Review. *Transactions on Electrical and Electronic Materials*.

Sasaki, T., Kurosawa, M., Usami, Y., Kato, S., Sakaki, A., Takei, Y., Kaneko, M., Uchikoba, F., & Saito, K. (2021). Development of neural networks chip generating driving waveform for electrostatic motor. *Artificial Life and Robotics*, *26*(2), 222–227. doi:10.100710015-020-00669-5

Satoh, K., & Yamaguchi, T. (2006). *Preparing various policies for interactive reinforcement learning.* Paper presented at the meeting of SICE-ICASE International Joint Conference 2006.

Sawka, K. (2006). *Intelligence Ostriches and Eagles: Why Some Companies Soar at Competitive Intelligence and Why Others Just Don't Get It.* Paper presented at the International SCIP Conference, Orlando, FL.

Schapire, R. E. (2013). Explaining adaboost. In *Empirical inference* (pp. 37–52). Springer. doi:10.1007/978-3-642-41136-6_5

Schiffman, L. G., Kanuk, L., & Hansen, H. (2012). *Consumer Behaviour: A European Outlook* (2nd ed.). Pearson Education Limited.

Schmidhuber, J. (2015). Deep learning in neural networks: An overview. *Neural Networks*, *61*, 85–117. doi:10.1016/j.neunet.2014.09.003 PMID:25462637

Schneeweis, D. M., & Schnapf, J. L. (1995). Photovoltage of rods and cones in the macaque retina. *Science*, *268*(5213), 1053–1056. doi:10.1126cience.7754386 PMID:7754386

Schunk, D., & Zimmerman, B. (2008). *Motivation and self-regulated learning: Theory, research, and applications.* Routledge.

Schwab, Pogrebnoj, Freund, & Flossmann, Vogl, & Frommolt. (2021). Automated Bat Call Classification using Deep Convolutional. *Neural Networks*.

Scott, J. (1991). *Social Network Analysis*. Sage.

Seeley, T. D. (2009). *The wisdom of the hive: the social physiology of honey bee colonies.* Harvard University Press. doi:10.2307/j.ctv1kz4h15

Sehatbakhsh, N., Alam, M., Nazari, A., Zajic, A., & Prvulovic, M. (2018). *Syndrome: Spectral analysis for anomaly detection on medical iot and embedded devices. In 2018 IEEE international symposium on hardware oriented security and trust.* HOST.

Seidl, T. (2009). Nearest Neighbor Classification. Encyclopedia of Database Systems, 1, 1885–1890. doi:10.1007/978-0-387-39940-9_561

Sekehravani, E. A., Babulak, E., & Masoodi, M. (2020). Implementing Canny Edge Detection Algorithm for Noisy Image. *Bulleting of Electrical Engioneering and Informatics*, *9*(4), 1404–1410. doi:10.11591/eei.v9i4.1837

Self, K. (2003). *Why do so many firms fail at competitive intelligence?* Academic Press.

Selverston, A. I., & Ayers, J. (2006). Oscillations and oscillatory behavior in small neural circuits. *Biological Cybernetics*, *95*(6), 537–554. doi:10.100700422-006-0125-1 PMID:17151878

Sen, P. C., Hajra, M., & Ghosh, M. (2020). Supervised classification algorithms in machine learning: A survey and review. In *Emerging technology in modelling and graphics* (pp. 99–111). Springer. doi:10.1007/978-981-13-7403-6_11

Serizawa, K., Ladig, R., & Shimonomura, K. (2019). Movable Camera and Stereoscopic Image System for Teleoperation of Aerial Robot Working in High Place. *Procs. of the 2019 JSME Conference on Robotics and Mechatronics*, 1P2-N08. 10.1299/jsmermd.2019.1P2-N08

Serranti, S., Palmieri, R., & Bonifazi, G. (2015). Hyperspectral imaging applied to demolition waste recycling: Innovative approach for product quality control. *Journal of Electronic Imaging, 24*(4), 043003. doi:10.1117/1.JEI.24.4.043003

Setser, A. L., & Waddell Smith, R. (2018). Comparison of variable selection methods prior to linear discriminant analysis classification of synthetic phenethylamines and tryptamines. *Forensic Chemistry (Amsterdam, Netherlands), 11*(October), 77–86. doi:10.1016/j.forc.2018.10.002

Shannon, C.E. (1948). A Mathematical Theory of Communication. *Bell System Technical Journal, 3*(27), 379–423 & 623–656.

Shao, L., Nagata, F., & Watanabe, K. (2019). Remote Control Application for a Quadrotor Supporting iOS and Android. *Procs. of the 2019 JSME Conference on Robotics and Mechatronics*, 1P1–N06.

Shao, L., Nagata, F., Ochi, H., Otsuka, A., Ikeda, T., Watanabe, K., & Maki, K. H. (2020). Visual Feedback Control of Quadrotor by Object Detection in Movies. *Procs. of 25th International Symposium on Artificial Life and Robotics*, 624–628. 10.100710015-020-00609-3

Sharir, O., Peleg, B., & Shoham, Y. (2020). *The cost of training NLP Models*. Available at: https://arxiv.org/pdf/2004.08900.pdf

Sharma, K., Papavlasopoulou, S., & Giannakos, M. (2019). Coding games and robots to enhance computational thinking: How collaboration and engagement moderate children's attitudes? *International Journal of Child-Computer Interaction, 21*, 65–76. doi:10.1016/j.ijcci.2019.04.004

Sharon, E., Brandt, A., & Basri, R. (2020). Fast Multiscale Image Segmentation. Computer Society Conference on Computer Vision nd. *Pattern Recognition, 1*, 70–77.

Shaziya, H., & Zaheer, R. (2021). Impact of Hyperparameters on Model Development in Deep Learning. In *Proceedings of International Conference on Computational Intelligence and Data Engineering* (pp. 57-67). Springer. 10.1007/978-981-15-8767-2_5

Shen, D., Wu, G., & Suk, H. I. (2017). Deep learning in medical image analysis. *Annual Review of Biomedical Engineering, 19*(1), 221–248. doi:10.1146/annurev-bioeng-071516-044442 PMID:28301734

Sheng, H., Shi, E., & Zhang, K. (2019). Image-Based Visual Servoing of a Quadrotor with Improved Visibility Using Model Predictive Control. *Procs. Of the 2019 IEEE 28th International Symposium on Industrial Electronics (ISIE)*, 551–556. 10.1109/ISIE.2019.8781212

Sheng, I. L., & Kok-Soo, T. (2010). Eco-efficient product design using theory of inventive problem solving (TRIZ) principles. *American Journal of Applied Sciences, 7*(6), 852–858. doi:10.3844/ajassp.2010.852.858

Shinomoto, S., & Kuramoto, Y. (1986). Cooperative phenomena in two-dimensional active rotator systems. *Progress of Theoretical Physics, 75*(6), 1319–1327. doi:10.1143/PTP.75.1319

Shinomoto, S., & Kuramoto, Y. (1986). Phase transitions in active rotator systems. *Progress of Theoretical Physics, 75*(5), 1105–1110. doi:10.1143/PTP.75.1105

Shute, V., Sun, C., & Asbell-Clarke, J. (2017). Demystifying computational thinking. *Educational Research Review, 22*.

Siddiqui, Z. A., Park, U., Lee, S.-W., Jung, N.-J., Choi, M., Lim, C., & Seo, J.-H. (2018). Robust Powerline Equipment Inspection System Based on a Convolutional Neural Network. *Sensors (Basel), 18*(11), 3837. doi:10.339018113837 PMID:30413123

Siderakis, Pylarinos, Thalassinakis, Vitellas, & Pyrgioti. (2011). *Pollution Maintenance Techniques in Coastal High Voltage Installations.* Academic Press.

Siegel, H. (1988). *Educating for reason: Rationality, critical thinking, and education.* Routledge.

Siegler, R. S. & Booth, J. L. (2004). Development of numerical estimation in Young Children. *Child Development, 2*(75), 428 – 444.

Sifaoui, A., Abdelkrim, A., & Benrejeb, M. (2008). On the use of neural network as a universal approximator. *Int. J. Sci. Tech. Control Comput. Eng, 2*, 386–399.

Silva, L. E., Senra Filho, A. C., Fazan, V. P., Felipe, J. C., & Murta Junior, L. O. (n.d.). Two-Dimensional Sample Entropy: Assessing Image Texture Through Irregularity. *Biomedical Physics & Engineering Express.* doi:10.10882057-1976/2/4/045002

Silva. (2019). *Neuroscience and artificial intelligence can help improve each other.* https://theconversation.com/neuroscience-and-artificial-intelligence-can-help-improve-each-other-110869

Simas. (2010), Kinematic Conception of a Hydraulic Robot Applied to Power Line Insulators Maintenance. *ABCM Symposium Series in Mechatronics, 4*, 739-748.

Simon, H. A. (1957). *Models of Man: Social and Rational.* John Wiley and Sons, Inc.

Simoni, M. F., Cymbalyuk, G. S., Sorensen, M. E., Calabrese, R. L., & DeWeerth, S. P. (2004). A multiconductance silicon neuron with biologically matched dynamics. *IEEE Transactions on Biomedical Engineering, 51*(2), 342–354. doi:10.1109/TBME.2003.820390 PMID:14765707

Simon, T. (1967). *Administrative Behaviour.* Free Press.

Simpson, E. J. (1972). *The classification of educational objectives in the psychomotor domain: The psychomotor domain.* Gryphon House.

Singhal, Y., Jain, A., Batra, S., Varshney, Y., & Rathi, M. (2018). Review of Bagging and Boosting Classification Performance on Unbalanced Binary Classification. *2018 IEEE 8th International Advance Computing Conference (IACC).* 10.1109/IADCC.2018.8692138

Singh, K., Sharma, S., Kumar, R., & Talha, M. (2021). Vibration control of cantilever beam using poling tuned piezo-electric actuator. *Mechanics Based Design of Structures and Machines,* 1–24. doi:10.1080/15397734.2021.1891934

Singh, P., Chaudhury, S., & Panigrahi, B. K. (2021). Hybrid MPSO-CNN: Multi-level Particle Swarm optimized hyperparameters of Convolutional Neural Network. *Swarm and Evolutionary Computation, 63*, 100863. doi:10.1016/j.swevo.2021.100863

Sinha, A., & Dolz, J. (2021). Multi-Scale Self-Guided Attention for Medical Image Segmentation. *Journal of Biomedical and Health Informatics, 25*(1), 121–130. doi:10.1109/JBHI.2020.2986926 PMID:32305947

Şişli, N. (1999). *Ekoloji (Çevre Bilim).* Gazi Büro Kitabevi Tic. Ltd. Şti.

Sivertsen, A. H., Kimiya, T., & Heia, K. (2011). Automatic freshness assessment of cod (Gadus morhua) fillets by Vis/Nir spectroscopy. *Journal of Food Engineering, 103*(3), 317–323. doi:10.1016/j.jfoodeng.2010.10.030

Snow, R. E., Corno, L., & Jackson, D. III. (1996). Individual differences in affective and conative functions. In D. C. Berliner & R. C. Calfee (Eds.), *Handbook of educational psychology* (pp. 243–310). Macmillan Library: Prentice Hall International.

Sollins, K. R. (2018). *IoT Big Data Security and Privacy vs. Innovation. IEEE Internet Things J.*

Somervuo, P., Harma, A., & Fagerlund, S. (2006). Parametric representations of bird sounds for automatic species recognition. *IEEE Transactions on Audio, Speech, and Language Processing, 14*(6), 2252–2263. doi:10.1109/TASL.2006.872624

Sondakh, D. E., Osman, K., & Zainudin, S. (2020). A pilot study of an instrument to assess undergraduates' computational thinking proficiency. *International Journal of Advanced Computer Science and Applications, 11*(11). Advance online publication. doi:10.14569/IJACSA.2020.0111134

Sondakh, D. E., Osman, K., & Zainudin, S. (2020). A Proposal for holistic assessment of computational thinking for undergraduate: Content validity. *European Journal of Educational Research, 9*(1), 33–50. doi:10.12973/eu-jer.9.1.33

Sonka, M. (2001). *Image Processing. Analysis and Machine Vision.* Brooks/Cole Pubisher.

Soon, F. C., Khaw, H. Y., Chuah, J. H., & Kanesan, J. (2018). Hyper-parameters optimisation of deep CNN architecture for vehicle logo recognition. *IET Intelligent Transport Systems, 12*(8), 939–946. doi:10.1049/iet-its.2018.5127

Sousa, R. O, Pontes, R. S. T., Aguiar, V. P. B, Luna, A. M., Andrade, C. T. C. (2009), Technique of dry washing of the insulators of the electrical nets of distribution. *11° Conferência Espanhola-Lusa de Engenharia Elétrica.*

Sousa, R. O. (2010). *A New Technique of Washing of Insulators of the Electric Distribution Grid.* Universidade Federal do Ceará – UFC.

SPAFE. (n.d.). *Simplified Python audio features extraction.* https://spafe.readthedocs.io

Spinadel, V. W. (2003). Fractal geometry and Euclidean thermodynamics [Geometría fractal y geometría euclidiana]. *Magazine Education and Pedagogy, 15*(1), 85-91.

Spinadel, V. M. (2008) Fractals [Fractales]. *Segundo Congreso Internacional de Matemáticas en la Ingeniería y la Arquitectura,* 113 - 123.

Spooncer, F. (1992). *Behavioural studies for marketing and business.* Stanley Thornes, Leckhampton.

Spyrelli, E. D., Doulgeraki, A. I., Argyri, A. A., Tassou, C. C., Panagou, E. Z., & George-John, E. N. (2020). Implementation of multispectral imaging (MSI) for microbiological quality assessment of poultry products. *Microorganisms, 8*(4), 1–14. doi:10.3390/microorganisms8040552 PMID:32290382

Srivastava, A. K., Singh, D., Pandey, A. S., & Maini, T. (2019). A Novel Feature Selection and Short-Term Price. *Energies,* 1–18.

Srivastava, N., Hinton, G., Krizhevsky, A., Sutskever, I., & Salakhutdinov, R. (2014). Dropout: A simple way to prevent neural networks from overfitting. *Journal of Machine Learning Research, 15*(1), 1929–1958.

Stowell, D., Benetos, E., & Gill, L. F. (2017). On-bird sound recordings: Automatic acoustic recognition of activities and contexts. *IEEE/ACM Transactions on Audio, Speech, and Language Processing, 25*(6), 1193–1206. doi:10.1109/TASLP.2017.2690565

Stowell, D., Wood, M. D., Pamuła, H., Stylianou, Y., & Glotin, H. (2019). Automatic acoustic detection of birds through deep learning: The first Bird Audio Detection challenge. *Methods in Ecology and Evolution, 10*(3), 368–380. doi:10.1111/2041-210X.13103

Sudqi Khater, B., Wahab, A., Bin, A. W., Idris, M. Y. I. B., Abdulla Hussain, M., & Ahmed Ibrahim, A. (2019). A lightweight perceptron-based intrusion detection system for fog computing. *Applied Sciences (Basel, Switzerland), 9*(1), 178.

Sugimoto, Y., Yoshioka, H., & Osuka, K. (2011). Development of super-multi- legged passive dynamic walking robot "Jenkka-III". In *SICE Annual Conference 2011* (pp, 576-579). IEEE.

Sulbarán Sandoval, J. A. (2016). Fractal as architectural paradigm: deconstruction vs vivid patterns language [El fractal como paradigma arquitectónico: deconstrucción vs lenguaje de patrones viviente]. *Procesos Urbanos*, (3), 79–88. doi:10.21892/2422085X.268

Su, M., Liang, B., Ma, S., Xiang, C., Zhang, C., & Wang, J. (2020). Automatic machine learning method for hyper-parameter Search. *Journal of Physics: Conference Series*, 1802.

Sun, Y., Gong, H., Li, Y., & Zhang, D. (2019). Hyperparameter importance analysis based on N-RReliefF algorithm. *International Journal of Computers, Communications & Control*, *14*(4), 557–573. doi:10.15837/ijccc.2019.4.3593

Sun, Y., Lo, F. P.-W., & Lo, B. (2019). Security and Privacy for the Internet of Medical Things Enabled Healthcare Systems: A Survey. *IEEE Access: Practical Innovations, Open Solutions*, 7, 183339–183355.

Supratak, A., Wu, D. H. C., Sun, K., & Guo, Y. (2016). Survey on feature extraction and applications of biosignals. In *Machine Learning for Health Informatics* (pp. 161–182). Springer., doi:10.1007/978-3-319-50478-0_8.

Sutton, R. S. (1990). Integrated Architectures for Learning, Planning, and Reacting Based on Approximating Dynamic Programming. *Proceedings of the Seventh International Conference on Machine Learning (ICML-1990)*, 216-224. 10.1016/B978-1-55860-141-3.50030-4

Sutton, R. S. (1991). Planning by Incremental Dynamic Programming. In *Proceedings Ninth Conference on Machine Learning (ICML-1991)*. Morgan-Kaufmann. doi:10.1016/B978-1-55860-200-7.50073-8

Sutton, R., & Barto, A. (1998). *Reinforcement Learning: An Introduction*. MIT Press.

System Overview — Benchtop Assembly for Spectronon Version 3.1.1. (n.d.). Retrieved November 25, 2020, from http://docs.resonon.com/spectronon/BenchtopAssemblyGuide/html/SystemOverview_include.html

Szegedy, C., Liu, W., Jia, Y., Sermanet, P., Reed, S., Anguelov, D., Erhan, D., Vanhoucke, V., & Rabinovich, A. (2015). Going deeper with convolutions. In *Proceedings of Conference on Computer Vision and Pattern Recognition* (CVPR). IEEE.

Szeremeta, W. K., Harniman, R. L., Bermingham, C. R., & Antognozzi, M. (2021). Towards a Fully Automated Scanning Probe Microscope for Biomedical Applications. *Sensors (Basel)*, *21*(9), 3027. doi:10.339021093027 PMID:33925843

Tabak, M. A., Murray, K. L., Lombardi, J. A., & Bay, K. J. (2021). Automated classification of bat echolocation call recordings with artificial intelligence. bioRxiv. doi:10.1101/2021.06.23.449619

Tabassum, A., Erbad, A., Mohamed, A., & Guizani, M. (2021). Privacy-Preserving Distributed IDS Using Incremental Learning for IoT Health Systems. *IEEE Access: Practical Innovations, Open Solutions*, 9, 14271–14283.

Tadepalli, P., & Ok, D. (1998). Model-based Average Reward Reinforcement Learning. *Artificial Intelligence*, *100*(1-2), 177–224. doi:10.1016/S0004-3702(98)00002-2

Tajmajer, T. (2017). *Multi-Objective Deep Q-learning with Subsumption Architecture*. Retrieved from https://arxiv.org/pdf/1704.06676v1.pdf

Takaya, K. (2019). Development of UAV System for Autonomous Power Line Inspection. *2019 23rd International Conference on System Theory, Control and Computing, Icstcc 2019 - Proceedings*, 762–767.

Takei, Y., Tazawa, R., Kaimai, T., Morishita, K., & Saito, K. (2021, January). *Dynamic simulation of non-programmed gait generation of quadruped robot* [Paper presentation]. The Twenty-Sixth International Symposium on Artificial Life and Robotics 2021.

Takei, Y., Morishita, K., Tazawa, R., Katsuya, K., & Saito, K. (2021). Non-programmed gait generation of quadruped robot using pulse-type hardware neuron models. *Artificial Life and Robotics*, 26(1), 109–115. doi:10.100710015-020-00637-z

Takei, Y., Morishita, K., Tazawa, R., & Saito, K. (2021). *Active Gaits Generation of Quadruped Robot Using Pulse-Type Hardware Neuron Models. In Biomimetics*. IntechOpen.

Tallon, A. (1997). *Head and heart: Affection, cognition, volition as triune consciousness*. Fordham University.

Tang, Y., Zhou, M., Zussman, E., & Caudill, R. (2002). Disassembly modeling, planning, and application. *Journal of Manufacturing Systems*, 21(3), 200–217. doi:10.1016/S0278-6125(02)80162-5

Tao, F., Bi, L., Zuo, Y., & Nee, A. Y. (2018). Partial/parallel disassembly sequence planning for complex products. *Journal of Manufacturing Science and Engineering*, 140(1), 011016. doi:10.1115/1.4037608

Tao, X., Zhang, D., Wang, Z., Liu, X., & Zhang, H., & Xu, D. (2018). Detection of Power Line Insulator Defects Using Aerial Images Analyzed with Convolutional Neural Networks. *IEEE Transactions on Systems, Man, and Cybernetics. Systems.*

Taylor, C. R. (1980). Force development during sustained locomotion: A determinant of gait, speed and metabolic power. *The Journal of Experimental Biology*, 115(1), 253–262. doi:10.1242/jeb.115.1.253 PMID:4031768

Tedre, M., & Denning, P. J. (2016). The long quest for computational thinking. In *ACM International Conference Proceeding Series* (pp. 120–129). Association for Computing Machinery. 10.1145/2999541.2999542

Tengfei, S., Ronghai, L., Xin, Z., Zhangqin, W., Xinliang, G., Yingchun, Y., & Hongwei, X. (2015). *Electrified insulator cleaning method based on unmanned aerial vehicle*. CN105170523A.

The College Board. (2012). *Computational thinking practices and big ideas, key concepts, and supporting concepts*. http://www.csprinciples.org/home/about-the-project

The MathWorks. (2020). Matlab (version (r2020a)) [computer software]. https://www.mathworks.com/

Thiebault, A., Charrier, I., Pistorius, P., & Aubin, T. (2019). At sea vocal repertoire of a foraging seabird. *Journal of Avian Biology*, 50(5), jav.02032. Advance online publication. doi:10.1111/jav.02032

Thurstone, L. L. (1931). The measurement of social attitudes. *Journal of Abnormal and Social Psychology*, 26(3), 249–269. doi:10.1037/h0070363

Tiantian, Y., Guodong, Y., & Junzhi, Y. (2017). Feature fusion-based insulator detection for aerial inspection. *2017 36th Chinese Control Conference (CCC)*, 10972-10977. 10.23919/ChiCC.2017.8029108

Tibbetts, J. H. (2018). The Frontiers of Artificial Intelligence. *Bioscience*, 68(1), 5–10. doi:10.1093/biosci/bix136

Tomaszewski, M., Ruszczak, B., & Michalski, P. (2018). The collection of images of an insulator taken outdoors in varying lighting conditions with additional laser spots. *Data in Brief*, 18, 765–768. doi:10.1016/j.dib.2018.03.063 PMID:29900234

Transmission and Distribution Committee. (2005). *IEEE Guide for Cleaning Insulators*. IEEE Std 957™.

Travers, R. M. W. (1977). *Essentials of learning* (4th ed.). Macmillan.

Triandis, H. C. (1971). *Attitude and Attitude Change (Foundations of Social Psychology)*. John Wileys & Sons Inc.

Trilling, B., & Fadel, C. (2009). *21st century skills: Learning for life in our times*. Jossey-Bass/Wiley.

Tripathi, M., Agrawal, S., Pandey, M. K., Shankar, R., & Tiwari, M. (2009). Real world disassembly modeling and sequencing problem: Optimization by algorithm of self-guided ants (ASGA). *Robotics and Computer-integrated Manufacturing*, *25*(3), 483–496. doi:10.1016/j.rcim.2008.02.004

Trisal, S. K., & Kaul, A. (2019). K-RCC: A novel approach to reduce the computational complexity of KNN algorithm for detecting human behavior on social networks. *Journal of Intelligent & Fuzzy Systems*, *36*(6), 5475–5497.

Truong, A., Walters, A., Goodsitt, J., Hines, K., Bruss, C. B., & Farivar, R. (2019, November). Towards automated machine learning: Evaluation and comparison of AutoML approaches and tools. In *2019 IEEE 31st international conference on tools with artificial intelligence (ICTAI)* (pp. 1471-1479). IEEE.

Tseng, H. E., Chang, C. C., Lee, S. C., & Huang, Y. M. (2018). A block-based genetic algorithm for disassembly sequence planning. *Expert Systems with Applications*, *96*, 492–505. doi:10.1016/j.eswa.2017.11.004

Tsitsiklis, J. N. (2007). NP-Hardness of checking the unichain condition in average cost MDPs. *Operations Research Letters*, *35*(3), 319–323. doi:10.1016/j.orl.2006.06.005

Tutorial, D. L. (2015). *Release 0.1, LISA Lab*. University of Montreal. http://deeplearning.net/tutorial/deeplearning.pdf

Uddin, M. A., Stranieri, A., Gondal, I., & Balasubramanian, V. (2018). Continuous Patient Monitoring With a Patient Centric Agent: A Block Architecture. *IEEE Access: Practical Innovations, Open Solutions*, *6*, 32700–32726. https://doi.org/10.1109/ACCESS.2018.2846779

Uluer, P., Kose, H., Landowska, A., Zorcec, T., Robins, B., Barkana Erol, D . (2021). Child-robot interaction studies during covid-19 pandemic. *Academic Press.*

Uluer , P., Kose, H., Oz, B. K., & Aydinalev, C. (2020). Towards an affective robot companion for audiology rehabilitation: How does pepper feel today? In 2020 29th IEEE International Conference on Robot and Human Interactive Communication (RO-MAN), *(pp. 567-572). IEEE.*

Umapathy, K., Krishnan, S., & Rao, R. K. (2007). Audio signal feature extraction and classification using local discriminant bases. *IEEE Transactions on Audio, Speech, and Language Processing*, *15*(4), 1236–1246. doi:10.1109/TASL.2006.885921

Utari, M., Warsito, B., & Kusumaningrum, R. (2020). Implementation of Data Mining for Drop-Out Prediction using Random Forest Method. *2020 8th International Conference on Information and Communication Technology, ICoICT 2020*. 10.1109/ICoICT49345.2020.9166276

Valdez, F., Melin, P., & Castillo, O. (2017). Comparative study of the use of fuzzy logic in improving particle swarm optimization variants for mathematical functions using co-evolution. *Appl. Soft Comput. J.*, *52*, 1070–1083.

Van Laarhoven, P. J., & Aarts, E. H. (1987). Simulated annealing. In *Simulated annealing: Theory and applications* (pp. 7–15). Springer. doi:10.1007/978-94-015-7744-1_2

Van Rossum, F. L., & Drake, G. (2009). *Python 3 reference manual*. Createspace.

Verma, O. P., & Parihar, A. S. (2017). An Optimal Fuzzy System for Edge Detection in Color Image using Bacterial Foraging Algorithm. *IEEE Transactions on Fuzzy Systems*, *25*(1), 114–127. doi:10.1109/TFUZZ.2016.2551289

Vernes, S. C., & Wilkinson, G. S. (2020). Behaviour, biology and evolution of vocal learning in bats. *Philosophical Transactions of the Royal Society B*, *375*(1789), 20190061.

Versaci, M., & Morabito, F. C. (2003, May). Fuzzy Time Series Approach for Disruption Prediction in Tokamak Reactors. *IEEE Transactions on Magnetics*, *39*(3), 1503-1506.

Versaci, M., Calcagno, S., & Morabito, F. C. (2015)Fuzzy Geometrical Approach Base on Unit Hyper-Cubes for Image Contrast Enhancement. *IEEE International Conference on Signal and Image Processing Applications.* 10.1109/ICSIPA.2015.7412240

Versaci, M., Jannelli, A., Morabito, F. C., & Angiulli, G. (2021). A Semi-Linear Elliptic Model for a Circular Membrane MEMS Device Considering the Effect of the Fringing Field. *Sensors (Basel)*, *21*(15), 5237. doi:10.339021155237 PMID:34372474

Versaci, M., La Foresta, F., Morabito, F. C., & Angiulli, G. (2018). A Fuzzy Divergence Approach for Solving Electrostatic Identification Problems for NDT Applications. *International Journal of Applied Electromagnetics and Mechanics*, *1*(2), 1–14. doi:10.3233/JAE-170043

Versaci, M., & Morabito, F. C. (2021). Image Edge Detection: A New Approach Based on Fuzzy Entropy and Fuzzy Divergence. *International Journal of Fuzzy Systems*, *23*(4), 918–936. doi:10.100740815-020-01030-5

Versaci, M., Morabito, F. C., & Angiulli, G. (2017). Adaptive Image Contrast Enhancement by Computing Distance in a 4-Dimensional Fuzzy Unit Hypercube. *IEEE Access: Practical Innovations, Open Solutions*, *5*, 26922–26931. doi:10.1109/ACCESS.2017.2776349

Vickers, W., Milner, B., Gorpincenko, A., & Lee, R. (2021, January). Methods to Improve the Robustness of Right Whale Detection using CNNs in Changing Conditions. In *2020 28th European Signal Processing Conference (EUSIPCO)* (pp. 106-110). IEEE. 10.23919/Eusipco47968.2020.9287565

Victoria, A. H., & Maragatham, G. (2021). Automatic tuning of hyperparameters using Bayesian Optimization. *Evolving Systems*, *2021*(12), 217–223. doi:10.100712530-020-09345-2

Vidal, M., & Amigo, J. M. (2012). Pre-processing of hyperspectral images. Essential steps before image analysis. *Chemometrics and Intelligent Laboratory Systems*, *117*, 138–148. doi:10.1016/j.chemolab.2012.05.009

Vidaña-Vila, E., Navarro, J., Alsina-Pages, R. M., & Ramirez, A. (2020). A two-stage approach to automatically detect and classify woodpecker (Fam. Picidae) sounds. *Applied Acoustics*, *166*, 107312. doi:10.1016/j.apacoust.2020.107312

Vollmer, M., & Mollmann, K. P. (2018). *Infrared Thermal Imaging.* Wiley-YCH Verlag GmbH.

Von Bertalanffy, L. (1984). *General System Theory; Foundations, Development, Applications* [Teoría general de los sistemas; fundamentos, aplicaciones]. Fondo de Cultura Económica.

Vongbunyong, S., Kara, S., & Pagnucco, M. (2015). Learning and revision in cognitive robotics disassembly automation. *Robotics and Computer-integrated Manufacturing*, *34*, 79–94. doi:10.1016/j.rcim.2014.11.003

Waidyanatha, N. (2010). Towards a typology of integrated functional early warning systems. *International Journal of Critical Infrastructures*, *6*(1), 31–51. Retrieved August 3, 2012, from. doi:10.1504/IJCIS.2010.029575

Wallace, M. B., Wax, A., Roberts, D. N., & Graf, R. N. (2009). Reflectance Spectroscopy. *Gastrointestinal Endoscopy Clinics of North America*, *19*(2), 233–242. doi:10.1016/j.giec.2009.02.008 PMID:19423021

Wang, L., Wang, H-G., & Song, Y-F. (2016), Development of a Bio-Inspired Live-Line Cleaning Robot for Suspension Insulator Strings. *International Journal of Simulation: Systems, 17*(48), 24.1-24.9.

Wang, T., Bao, X., Clavera, I., Hoang, J., Wen, Y., Langlois, E., Zhang, S., Zhang, G., Abbeel, P., & Ba, J. (2019). *Benchmarking model-based reinforcement learning.* Retrieved from https://arxiv.org/abs/1907.02057

Wang, K., Pu, H., & Sun, D. W. (2018). Emerging Spectroscopic and Spectral Imaging Techniques for the Rapid Detection of Microorganisms: An Overview. *Comprehensive Reviews in Food Science and Food Safety*, *17*(2), 256–273. doi:10.1111/1541-4337.12323 PMID:33350086

Wang, L., & Wang, H. (2016). A survey on insulator inspection robots for power transmission lines. *4th International Conference on Applied Robotics for the Power Industry*. 10.1109/CARPI.2016.7745639

Wang, L., Wang, H., & Chang, Y., (2015) Mechanism Design of an Insulator Cleaning Robot for Suspension Insulator Strings. *Proceedings of the 2015 IEEE Conference on Robotics and Biomometics*. 10.1109/ROBIO.2015.7419103

Wang, M., Liu, B., & Foroosh, H. (2017). Factorized convolutional neural networks. In *Proceedings of the IEEE International Conference on Computer Vision Workshops* (pp. 545-553). IEEE.

Wang, X., Wang, H., Niu, S., & Zhang, J. (2019). Detection and Localization of Image Forgeries uUsing Improved Mask Regional Convolutional Neural Network. *Mathematical Biosciences and Engineering*, *16*(5), 4581–4593. doi:10.3934/mbe.2019229 PMID:31499678

Wang, Z. J., Turko, R., Shaikh, O., Park, H., Das, N., Hohman, F., Kahng, M., & Chau, D. H. P. (2020). CNN explainer: Learning convolutional neural networks with interactive visualization. *IEEE Transactions on Visualization and Computer Graphics*, *27*(2), 1396–1406. doi:10.1109/TVCG.2020.3030418 PMID:33048723

Wasserman, S., & Faust, K. (1994). *Social Network Analysis: Methods and Applications*. Cambridge University Press. doi:10.1017/CBO9780511815478

Wei, K., Zhang, L., Guo, Y., & Jiang, X. (2020). Health Monitoring Based on Internet of Medical Things: Architecture, Enabling Technologies, and Applications. *IEEE Access: Practical Innovations, Open Solutions*, *8*, 27468–27478. https://doi.org/10.1109/ACCESS.2020.2971654

Weintrop, D., Beheshti, E., Horn, M., Orton, K., Jona, K., Trouille, L., & Wilensky, U. (2016). Defining computational thinking for mathematics and science classrooms. *Journal of Science Education and Technology*, *25*(1), 127–147. doi:10.100710956-015-9581-5

Wellman, B., & Berkowitz, S. D. (Eds.). (1988). *Social Structures: A Network Approach*. Cambridge University Press.

Wenger, E. (1998). *Communities of Practice: learning, meaning and identity*. Cambridge University Press. doi:10.1017/CBO9780511803932

Wheaton, K. J. (2001). *The Warning Solution – Intelligent analysis in the age of information overload*. AFCEA.

Widyarto, S., Syafrullah, M., Sharif, M. W., & Budaya, G. A. (2019). Fractals Study and Its Application. *6th International Conference on Electrical Engineering, Computer Science and Informatics (EECSI)*, 200-204. 10.23919/EECSI48112.2019.8977124

Wiering, M. A., Withagen, M., & Drugan, M. M. (2014). Model-Based Multi-Objective Reinforcement Learning. *Proceedings of the IEEE Symposium on Adaptive Dynamic Programming and Reinforcement Learning*, 1-6.

Wightman, A., & Bodger, P. (2011). Volcanic Ash Contamination of High Voltage Insulators. *EEA Conference & Exhibition*.

Wilensky, H. (1969). *Organizational Intelligence*. Basic Books.

Wing, J. M. (2006). Computational thinking. *Communications of the ACM*, *49*(3), 33–35. doi:10.1145/1118178.1118215

Wing, J. M. (2017). Computational thinking's influence on research and education for all. *Italian Journal of Educational Technology*, *25*(2), 7–14.

Woollard, J. (2016). CT driving computing curriculum in England. *CSTA Voice, 12*, 4–5.

Wright, R. E. (1995). *Logistic regression.* Academic Press.

Wu, Chen, Zhang, Xiong, Lei, & Deng. (2019). Hyperparameter optimization for machine learning models based on Bayesian Optimization. *Journal of Electronic Science and Technology, 17*(1).

Wu, D., Shi, H., Wang, S., He, Y., Bao, Y., & Liu, K. (2012). Rapid prediction of moisture content of dehydrated prawns using on-line hyperspectral imaging system. *Analytica Chimica Acta, 726*, 57–66. doi:10.1016/j.aca.2012.03.038 PMID:22541014

Wulder, M. A., Loveland, T. R., Roy, D. P., Crawford, C. J., Masek, J. G., Woodcock, C. E., Allen, R. G., Anderson, M. C., Belward, A. S., Cohen, W. B., Dwyer, J., Erb, A., Gao, F., Griffiths, P., Helder, D., Hermosilla, T., Hipple, J. D., Hostert, P., Hughes, M. J., ... Zhu, Z. (2019). Current status of Landsat program, science, and applications. *Remote Sensing of Environment, 225*, 127–147. doi:10.1016/j.rse.2019.02.015

Wu, Q., An, J., & Lin, B. (2012). A texture segmentation algorithm based on PCA and global minimization active contour model for aerial insulator images. *IEEE Journal of Selected Topics in Applied Earth Observations and Remote Sensing, 5*(5), 1509–1518. doi:10.1109/JSTARS.2012.2197672

Wynn, K. (1992). Addition and Subtraction by human infants. *Letters to Nature, 358*(6389), 749–750. doi:10.1038/358749a0

Xia, K., Gu, X., & Zhang, Y. (2020). Oriented grouping-constrained spectral clustering for medical imaging segmentation. *Multimedia Systems, 26*(1), 27–36. doi:10.100700530-019-00626-8

Xiao, L., Wan, X., Lu, X., Zhang, Y., & Wu, D. (2018). IoT security techniques based on machine learning: How do IoT devices use AI to enhance security? *IEEE Signal Processing Magazine, 35*(5), 41–49.

Xie, J., Hu, K., Zhu, M., Yu, J., & Zhu, Q. (2019). Investigation of different CNN-based models for improved bird sound classification. *IEEE Access: Practical Innovations, Open Solutions, 7*, 175353–175361. doi:10.1109/ACCESS.2019.2957572

Xie, L., & Yuille, A. (2017). Genetic cnn. In *Proceedings of the IEEE international conference on computer vision* (pp. 1379-1388). IEEE.

Xing, B., & Gao, W. (2014). Post-Disassembly Part-Machine Clustering Using Artificial Neural Networks and Ant Colony Systems. In *Computational Intelligence in Remanufacturing* (pp. 135–150). Information Science Reference., doi:10.4018/978-1-4666-4908-8.ch008

Xing, J., Bravo, C., Jancsók, P. T., Ramon, H., & De Baerdemaeker, J. (2005). Detecting bruises on "Golden Delicious" apples using hyperspectral imaging with multiple wavebands. *Biosystems Engineering, 90*(1), 27–36. doi:10.1016/j.biosystemseng.2004.08.002

Xing, K., Srinivasan, S. S. R., Jose, M., Li, J., & Cheng, X. (2010). Attacks and countermeasures in sensor networks: a survey. In *Network security* (pp. 251–272). Springer.

Xiong, D., Zhang, M., & Li, H. (2011, November). A Maximum-Entropy Segmentation Model for Statistical Machine Translation. *IEEE Transactions on Audio, Speech, and Language Processing, 19*(8), 2494–2505. doi:10.1109/TASL.2011.2144971

Xu, G., Lan, Y., Zhou, W., Huang, C., Li, W., Zhang, W., Zhang, G., Ng, E. Y. K., Cheng, Y., Peng, Y., & Che, W. (2019). An IoT-Based Framework of Webvr Visualization for Medical Big Data in Connected Health. *IEEE Access: Practical Innovations, Open Solutions, 7*, 173866–173874. https://doi.org/10.1109/ACCESS.2019.2957149

Xu, Y., Hu, X., Kundu, S., Nag, A., Afsarimanesh, N., Sapra, S., Mukhopadhyay, S. C., & Han, T. (2019). Silicon-based sensors for biomedical applications: A review. *Sensors (Basel)*, *19*(13), 2908. doi:10.339019132908 PMID:31266148

Yadav, A., Mayfield, C., Zhou, N., Hambrusch, S., & Korb, J. T. (2014). Computational thinking in elementary and secondary teacher education. *ACM Transactions on Computing Education*, *14*(1), 1–16. doi:10.1145/2576872

Yamaguchi, T., Nagahama, S., Ichikawa, Y., Honma, Y., & Takadama, K. (2020). Model-based Multi-Objective Reinforcement Learning by a Reward Occurrence Probability Vector. Advanced Robotics and Intelligent Automation in Manufacturing, 269-296.

Yang, L., Liu, Z., & Wang, X. (2019). A New Image-Based Visual Servo Control Algorithm for Target Tracking Problem of Fixed-Wing Unmanned Aerial Vehicle. *Procs. Of the 2019 Chinese Control Conference (CCC)*, 8142-8147. 10.23919/ChiCC.2019.8865341

Yang, B., Gao, Y., Li, H., Ye, S., He, H., & Xie, S. (2019). Rapid prediction of yellow tea free amino acids with hyperspectral images. *PLoS One*, *14*(2), 1–17. doi:10.1371/journal.pone.0210084 PMID:30785888

Yang, C., Li, C., & Zhao, J. (2017). A Nonlinear Charge Controller With Tunable Precision for Highly Linear Operation of Piezoelectric Stack Actuators. *IEEE Transactions on Industrial Electronics*, *64*(11), 8618–8625. doi:10.1109/TIE.2017.2698398

Yang, L., Jiang, X., Hao, Y., Li, L., Li, H., Li, R., & Luo, B. (2017). Recognition of natural ice types on in-service glass insulators based on texture feature descriptor. *IEEE Transactions on Dielectrics and Electrical Insulation*, *24*(1), 535–542. doi:10.1109/TDEI.2016.006049

Yang, L., & Shami, A. (2020). On hyperparameter optimization of machine learning algorithms: Theory and practice. *Neurocomputing*, *415*, 295–316. doi:10.1016/j.neucom.2020.07.061

Yang, S., Gao, Y., Bo, A., Wang, H., & Chen, X. (2016). Efficient Average Reward Reinforcement Learning Using Constant Shifting Values. *Proceedings of the Thirtieth AAAI Conference on Artificial Intelligence (AAAI-16)*, 2258-2264.

Yang, X., Li, Z., Fei, C., Liu, Y., Li, D., Hou, S., ... Zhou, Q. (2020). High frequency needle ultrasonic transducers based on Mn doped piezoelectric single crystal. *Journal of Alloys and Compounds*, *832*, 154951. doi:10.1016/j.jallcom.2020.154951

Yan, L., & Liu, Y. (2020). An Ensemble Prediction Model for Potential Student Recommendation using Machine Learning. *Symmetry*, *12*(728), 1–17. doi:10.3390ym12050728

Yao, C., Jin, L., & Yan, S. (2012). Recognition of insulator string in power grid patrol images. *Xitong Fangzhen Xuebao*, *24*(9), 1818–1822.

Yaseen, M. U., Anjum, A., Rana, O., & Antonopoulos, N. (2019). Deep learning hyper-parameter optimization for video analytics in clouds. *IEEE Transactions on Systems, Man, and Cybernetics. Systems*, *49*(1), 253–264. doi:10.1109/TSMC.2018.2840341

Yi Lee, M. & Prieto, F. R. (2010) Generation of fractals with akin transformations [Generación de fractales a partir de transformaciones afines]. *Trans. III REPEM*.

Yi, K. A., & Veillette, R. J. (2005). A charge controller for linear operation of a piezoelectric stack actuator. *IEEE Transactions on Control Systems Technology*, *13*(4), 517–526. doi:10.1109/TCST.2005.847332

Ying, H. (1998). *General Takagi-Sugeno fuzzy systems are universal approximators*. Academic Press.

Yin, Z., Zhao, M., Wang, Y., Yang, J., & Zhang, J. (2017). Recognition of emotions using multimodal physiological signals and an ensemble deep learning model. *Computer Methods and Programs in Biomedicine*, *140*, 93–110. doi:10.1016/j.cmpb.2016.12.005

Yoo, J., Joseph, T., Yung, D., Nasseri, S. A., & Wood, F. (2020). *Ensemble squared: A meta automl system*. arXiv preprint arXiv:2012.05390.

York, T. T., & York, T. T. (2015). *Defining and Measuring Academic Success*. Academic Press.

Yu, T., & Zhu, H. (2020). *Hyper-Parameter Optimization: A Review of Algorithms and Applications*. arXiv:2003.05689v1 [cs.LG].

Yuan, L., Yan, P., Han, W., Huang, Y., Wang, B., Zhang, J., Zhang, H., & Bao, Z. (2019). Detection of anthracnose in tea plants based on hyperspectral imaging. *Computers and Electronics in Agriculture*, *167*(June), 105039. doi:10.1016/j.compag.2019.105039

Yuasa, H., & Ito, M. (1990). Coordination of many oscillators and generation of locomotory patterns. *Biological Cybernetics*, *63*(3), 177–184. doi:10.1007/BF00195856

Yu, B., Wu, E., Chen, C., Yang, Y., Yao, B., & Lin, Q. (2017). A general approach to optimize disassembly sequence planning based on disassembly network: A case study from automotive industry. *Advances in Production Engineering & Management*, *12*(4), 305–320. doi:10.14743/apem2017.4.260

Yue-Hei Ng, J., Hausknecht, M., Vijayanarasimhan, S., Vinyals, O., Monga, R., & Toderici, G. (2015). Beyond short snippets: Deep networks for video classification. In *Proceedings of the IEEE conference on computer vision and pattern recognition* (pp. 4694-4702). 10.1109/CVPR.2015.7299101

Yu, P., Huang, M., Zhang, M., Zhu, Q., & Qin, J. (2020). Rapid detection of moisture content and shrinkage ratio of dried carrot slices by using a multispectral imaging system. *Infrared Physics & Technology*, *108*(May), 103361. doi:10.1016/j.infrared.2020.103361

Zahavi, A., Palshin, A., Liyanage, D. C., & Tamre, M. (2019). Influence of Illumination Sources on Hyperspectral Imaging. *2019 20th International Conference on Research and Education in Mechatronics (REM)*, *5*, 1–5. 10.1109/REM.2019.8744086

Zakaria, E., Haron, Z., & Daud, M. (2004). The reliability and construct validity of scores on the attitudes toward problem solving scale. *Journal of Science and Mathematics Education in South East Asia*, *27*(2), 81–91.

Zhai, Y., Cheng, H., Rui, C., Qiang, Y., & Li, X. (2018). Multi-saliency aggregation-based approach for insulator flashover fault detection using aerial images. *Energies*, *11*(2), 340. doi:10.3390/en11020340

Zhai, Y., Wang, D., Zhang, M., Wang, J., & Guo, F. (2017). Fault Detection of Insulator Based on Saliency and Adaptive Morphology. *Multimedia Tools and Applications*, *76*(9), 12051–12064. doi:10.100711042-016-3981-2

Zhang, X., An, J., & Chen, F. (2010). A simple method of tempered glass insulator recognition from airborne image. *2010 International Conference on Optoelectronics and Image Processing*, *1*, 127–130.

Zhang, X., Wang, Y., & Wu, L. (2019). Research on Cross Language Text Keyword Extraction Based on Information Entropy and TextRank. *2019 IEEE 3rd Information Technology, Networking, Electronic and Automation Control Conference (ITNEC)*, 16-19. 10.1109/ITNEC.2019.8728993

Zhang, X., Xue, R., Liu, B., Lu, W., & Zhang, Y. (2018). Grade Prediction of Student Academic Performance with Multiple Classification Models. *2018 14th International Conference on Natural Computation, Fuzzy Systems and Knowledge Discovery (ICNC-FSKD)*, 1086–1090.

Zhang, K., Zhang, Y., Wang, P., Tian, Y., & Yang, J. (2018). An Improvved Sobel Edge Algorithm and FPGA Implementation. *8th International Congress of Information and Comunication Technology, Procedia Computer Science*, 243-248.

Zhang, M., Li, H., Pan, S., Lyu, J., Ling, S., & Su, S. (2021). Convolutional neural networks based lung nodule classification: A surrogate-assisted evolutionary algorithm for hyperparameter optimization. *IEEE Transactions on Evolutionary Computation*, 25(5), 869–882. doi:10.1109/TEVC.2021.3060833

Zhang, M., Raghunathan, A., & Jha, N. K. (2013). MedMon: Securing medical devices through wireless monitoring and anomaly detection. *IEEE Transactions on Biomedical Circuits and Systems*, 7(6), 871–881. https://ieeexplore.ieee.org/document/6507636/

Zhang, S., Li, X., Zong, M., Zhu, X., & Cheng, D. (2017). Learning k for kNN Classification. *ACM Transactions on Intelligent Systems and Technology*, 8(3), 1–19. Advance online publication. doi:10.1145/2990508

Zhang, S., Ma, Z., Zhang, G., Lei, T., & Zhang, R. (2020). Semantinc Image Segmentation with Deep Convolutional Neural Networks and Quick Shift. *Symmetry*, 12(427), 1–21.

Zhang, X., & Wang, J.-L. (2016). From sparse to dense functional data and beyond. *Annals of Statistics*, 44(5), 2281–2321. doi:10.1214/16-AOS1446

Zhang, Y., Yun, Y., Dai, H., Cui, J., & Shang, X. (1755). Graphs Regularized Robust Matrix Factorization and Its Application on Student Grade Prediction. *Applied Sciences (Basel, Switzerland)*, 10(5), 1–19. doi:10.3390/app10051755

Zhao, Z., Xu, G., Qi, Y., Liu, N., & Zhang, T. (2016), Multi-patch deep features for power line insulator status classification from aerial images. *2016 International Joint Conference on Neural Networks*, 3187–3194.

Zhao, W., & Shute, V. J. (2019). Can playing a video game foster computational thinking skill? *Computers & Education*, 141, 103653. doi:10.1016/j.compedu.2019.103633

Zhong, B., Zhang, S., Xu, M., Zhou, Y., Fang, T., & Li, W. (2018). On a CPG-based hexapod robot: AmphiHex-II with variable stiffness legs. *IEEE/ASME Transactions on Mechatronics*, 23(2), 542–551. doi:10.1109/TMECH.2018.2800776

Zhong, Z., Yan, J., Wu, W., Shao, J., & Liu, C. L. (2018). Practical block-wise neural network architecture generation. In *Proceedings of the IEEE conference on computer vision and pattern recognition* (pp. 2423-2432). IEEE.

Zhou, G., Lim, Z. H., Qi, Y., & Zhou, G. (2020). Single-Pixel MEMS Imaging Systems. *Micromachines*, 11(2), 1–24. doi:10.3390/mi11020219 PMID:32093324

Zhou, L., Guo, H., & Deng, G. (2019). A fog computing based approach to DDoS mitigation in IIoT systems. *Computers & Security*, 85, 51–62. https://doi.org/10.1016/j.cose.2019.04.017

Zhou, Z., Liu, J., Pham, D. T., Xu, W., Ramirez, F. J., Ji, C., & Liu, Q. (2019). Disassembly sequence planning: Recent developments and future trends. *Proceedings of the Institution of Mechanical Engineers. Part B, Journal of Engineering Manufacture*, 233(5), 1450–1471. doi:10.1177/0954405418789975

Zhu, B., Sarigecili, M. I., & Roy, U. (2013). Disassembly information model incorporating dynamic capabilities for disassembly sequence generation. *Robotics and Computer-integrated Manufacturing*, 29(5), 396–409. doi:10.1016/j.rcim.2013.03.003

Zhu, G., & Zhu, R. (2020). Accelerating Hyperparameter Optimization of Deep Neural Network via Progressive Multi-Fidelity Evaluation. *Advances in Knowledge Discovery and Data Mining*, 12084, 752–763. doi:10.1007/978-3-030-47426-3_58

Zhu, X., Li, X., & Yan, F. (2018). Design and implementation for integrated UAV multi-spectral inspection system. *IOP Conference Series. Earth and Environmental Science*, *133*(1), 012006. doi:10.1088/1755-1315/133/1/012006

Zimmer, L., Lindauer, M., & Hutter, F. (2021). Auto-Pytorch: Multi-Fidelity MetaLearning for Efficient and Robust AutoDL. *IEEE Transactions on Pattern Analysis and Machine Intelligence*, *43*(9), 3079–3090. doi:10.1109/TPAMI.2021.3067763 PMID:33750687

Zipf, G. K. (1932). *Selected Studies of the Principle of Relative Frequency in Language*. Harvard Univ. Press. doi:10.4159/harvard.9780674434929

Zualkernan, I., Judas, J., Mahbub, T., Bhagwagar, A., & Chand, P. (2020, September). A Tiny CNN Architecture for Identifying Bat Species from Echolocation Calls. In *2020 IEEE/ITU International Conference on Artificial Intelligence for Good (AI4G)* (pp. 81-86). IEEE.

Zualkernan, I., Judas, J., Mahbub, T., Bhagwagar, A., & Chand, P. (2021, January). An AIoT System for Bat Species Classification. In *2020 IEEE International Conference on Internet of Things and Intelligence System (IoTaIS)* (pp. 155-160). IEEE.

Zuhair, H., Selamat, A., & Krejcar, O. (2020). A Multi-Tier Streaming Analytics Model of 0-Day Ransomware Detection Using Machine Learning. *Applied Sciences (Basel, Switzerland)*, *10*(9). https://doi.org/10.3390/app10093210

Zussman, E., & Zhou, M. (1999). A methodology for modeling and adaptive planning of disassembly processes. *IEEE Transactions on Robotics and Automation*, *15*(1), 190–194. doi:10.1109/70.744614

About the Contributors

Maki K. Habib obtained Doctor of Eng. Sciences in Intelligent and Autonomous Robotics, Univ. of Tsukuba, Japan. Selected research scientist at RIKEN Japan. Senior researcher at RISO-Labs Japan. Visiting researcher at EPFL, Switzerland. Visiting expert under ADB, Associate Prof. UTM, Malaysia. Senior Manager MCRIA Malaysia. Senior research scientist with GMD-Japan. Associate Prof. with Monash Univ. leading Mechatronics program. A full Prof. Robotics and Mechatronics at Swinburne Univ. Invited Prof. KAIST South Korea, Visiting Prof. at Saga Univ. Japan. Since Sept. 2007 he is full Professor of Robotics and Mechatronics at AUC. He also served consultant and technical adviser for Toyota group, ABB, etc. He published 10 books, 24 book chapters, more than 275 papers at international journals and intern. confs. His main research focus: Human and Friendly Mechatronics, Intelligent and Autonomous Robotics/Vehicles: Control, Mapping-Localization, Navigation and Learning. Service Robots for Humanitarian Demining, Biomimetic and Biomedical Robotics, Telecooperation Distributed Teleoperation, and Collaborative Control, Intelligent and Nonlinear Control, Wireless Sensor Networks, Industry 4, Flying Robots.

* * *

Liza Abdul Latiff is currently attached to Razak Faculty of Technology and Informatics in UTM. She obtained her B. Sc in Electrical Engineering from South Dakota State University USA, master's in electrical engineering (Data Communication) and PhD in Electrical Engineering from UTM. She is the Head of Ubiquitous Broadband Access Network (U-BAN) Research Group, an affiliate member of Wireless Communication Center (WCC), and serves as a Member of IMT & Future Networks Working Group in Malaysia Technical Standards Forum Berhad (MTFSB). Her research interests are computer networking and edge computing, routing protocols and quality of service, mobility management and IoT in Healthcare Industry.

Guilherme Agostini is a student in Mechatronics Engineering at the Federal University of Uberlandia. Extremely passionate for technology and challenges.

Luca Baronti is a Research Fellow at the School of Computer Science of the University of Birmingham, United Kingdom. He received his Master Degree in Computer Science at University of Pisa in 2015, and PhD at University of Birmingham in 2020. Amongst his research interests are Machine Learning and Intelligent Optimisation Techniques applied to industrial and biomedical problems. His recent work includes an analysis of the properties of the Bees Algorithm, an application of the Bees

Algorithm for the Primitive Fitting problem and an application of a Generative Adversarial Network for Data Augmentation in the context of macro-properties identification in manufactured surfaces. His current research focus is the combined application of Machine Learning and Topological Data Analysis approaches on biomedical images.

Vedat Beşkardeş, after graduating from the Biology Department of Trakya University in 1997, completed his MA in 2002 and PhD in 2010 in Forest Engineering Program at Istanbul University, Institute of Science and Technology . Currently, Vedat Beşkardeş works as a lecturer at Istanbul University - Cerrahpaşa, Faculty of Forestry.

Reinaldo A.C. Bianchi holds a Bachelor's degree in Physics from the Institute of Physics of the University of São Paulo (1994), master's and doctorate in electrical engineering from the Polytechnic School of the University of São Paulo (1998, 2004). He completed a postdoctoral internship at the Institute of Investigation in Artificial Intelligence, IIIA-CSIC, Barcelona, Catalunya, Spain. He is currently Full Professor at the Fei University Center, in São Bernardo do Campo. Having as main objective of his research work the creation of Autonomous and Intelligent Robotic Systems, he works mainly in the following areas: Robotics, Artificial Intelligence, Machine Learning, Computer Vision, Multi-Agent Systems and also in the Teaching and Dissemination of Engineering.

Marco Castellani is Senior Lecturer in Robotics and Automation at the Department of Mechanical Engineering of University of Birmingham. He studied Physics (Laurea) and Artificial Intelligence (MSc and PhD), and worked for over twenty years in a broad interdisciplinary field encompassing engineering, biology, and computer science. He published over 50 research papers in peer-reviewed international journals and conferences, on a wide range of topics including motor control, remote sensing, pattern recognition, optimisation, system identification, and ecological modelling. He has a keen interest in evolutionary and swarm intelligence, and is particularly active in the development and characterisation of the Bees Algorithm.

Dilara Demirpençe Seçinti is a child and adolescent psychiatrist in Şişli Etfal Research and Training Hospital and tutor in Clinical Psychology at Rumeli University. She received her residency in the Child and Adolescent Mental Health Department at Cerrahpaşa Faculty of Medicine. She has worked as a visitor researcher Trauma Center at JRI in the USA and observer at Maudsley Hospital in the UK. Her research interest lies in early childhood psychopathology, mother-infant relationship, emotional expression style of infant and toddler. She is working as a part of international and national research projects in these areas and she is actively working as a clinician in the hospital.

Siti Dianah received the B.S. degree in Science (Computer Science) and M.S degree in Science from Universiti Teknologi Malaysia (UTM) in 2006 and 2010, respectively. She is currently pursuing the Ph.D. degree in Software Engineering at Malaysia- Japan International Institute of Technology, UTM in Kuala Lumpur. Her thesis focuses on the application of predictive analytics on student grade prediction in a higher education institution. From 2010 to 2019, she was the senior lecturer of Information and Communication Technology Department at Polytechnic Sultan Idris Shah, Sabak Bernam, Selangor, Malaysia. She has experienced in developing the polytechnic curriculum for Diploma in Information Technology (Technology Digital) 2.5 years' program. She is one of the book authors that contribute for the Department of Polytechnic and Community College Education. Her research interests include data analytics, predictive analytics, learning analytics, educational data mining and machine learning.

Duygun Erol Barkana is a Professor in Electrical and Electronics Engineering at Yeditepe University, Istanbul, Turkey, and she is the director of the Robotics Research Laboratory at Yeditepe University. Her research interests include robot-assisted rehabilitation systems, social robotics, medical robotics, human-robot interaction, dynamical systems and control, emotion recognition, signal processing of sensory information, and deep/machine learning methods. She received her M.Sc. and Ph.D. degrees in Electrical Engineering and Computer Science from Vanderbilt University, Nashville, TN, USA, in 2003 and 2007, respectively. She has been honored with Career Award by the Scientific and Technological Research Council of Turkey (2009), Outstanding Young Scientists Awards by the Turkish Academy of Sciences (2018), and Research Incentive Award by Middle East Technical University Professor Mustafa Parlar Research and Education Foundation (2019). Her research, supported by the European Union, and the Scientific and Research Council of Turkey, has culminated in many publications.

Mojtaba Ghodsi is a Senior Lecturer of Instrumentation, and Measurement Systems at the School of Energy and Electronic Engineering at the University of Portsmouth, UK. He received his Ph.D. in Precision Engineering from the University of Tokyo (2007) and continued his research as a JSPS postdoctoral fellow (2009) at the University of Tokyo, Japan. He continued his academic career at Sultan Qaboos University in Oman up to 2019. His main research interests are around smart materials and structures to develop actuators, sensors, energy harvesters, vibration control, NDT, and mechatronics systems.

Rogério S. Gonçalves was born in Barretos, Brazil, in 1981. He received the mechanical engineering degree from the Federal University of Uberlândia in 2004, Master degree in 2006 and Ph.D. at the same University in 2009. Now he is Assistant Professor in Federal University of Uberlândia. He is member of RoboCup Brazil and ABCM (Brazilian Society of Engineering and Mechanical Sciences). He is author or co-author of about 60 papers, which have been presented in national and international conferences or published in national and international journals. His research interest includes kinematics and dynamics of serial and parallel structure, stiffness, cable-driven parallel structure, mobile robots, biorobotics and humanoid robots.

Shijie Guan, Doctor of Engineering, Associate Professor. He graduated from Northeastern University in 2014 and works at Shenyang Ligong University. His research interests include space information network, complex networks, and artificial intelligence.

Yoshihiro Ichikawa got Doctor of Engineering Degree from The University of Electro-Communications, Japan, in 2014. He joined the University of Tsukuba from 2014 to 2017 as a postdoctoral researcher. He moved to the National Institute of Technology (KOSEN), Nara College as an assistant professor in 2017. His research interests include multiagent system, artificial intelligence, and human-computer interaction.

Itır Kaşıkçı is a Neurosicence PhD currently lecturing at Istanbul Commerce University, Department of Psychology. She had previously worked in Istanbul University, Department of Neuroscience and

Stanford University, Laboratory of Behavioral and Cognitive Neurology as a research assistant. Her areas of interest are number cognition, emotion related brain electrical activation and emotion recognition.

Shinya Kato received his bachelor's degree from Nihon University in 2020. He is now a master course student of the Precision Machinery Engineering, Graduate School of Science and Technology, Nihon University, Tokyo, Japan. His current research interests are developing analog electronic circuit models that mimic biological neurons and hardware neural networks that mimic the nervous systems of animals for integration into autonomous robots.

Yuto Kawabchi is a student of the Faculty of Advanced Engineering, National Institute of Technology (KOSEN), Nara College, Japan. His research interests include reinforcement learning and multiple objective optimization.

Goran Klepac, Ph.D., Assistant prof., works as a director of big data analytics in Croatian Telecom, previously worked as director of Stretegic unit in Sector of credit risk in Raiffeisenbank Austria d.d., Croatia. In several universities in Croatia, he lectures subjects in domain of data mining, predictive analyitics, decision support system, banking risk, risk evaluation models, expert system, database marketing and business intelligence. As a team leader, he successfully finished many data mining projects in different domanins like retail, finance, insurance, hospitality, telecommunications, and productions. He is an author/coauthor of several books published in Croatian and English in domain of data mining.

Hatice Köse is an Associate Professor at Istanbul Technical University, Turkey, coordinating the Cognitive Social Robotics research group and GAMELab (Game and Interaction Technologies Lab). She is working on Social Assistive Robots, human-robot interaction, affective computing, and gamification, mostly in the domain of education, therapy and treatment of children with disabilities. She is part of several national and international projects in this field.

Ondrej Krejcar is a full professor in systems engineering and informatics at the University of Hradec Kralove, Faculty of Informatics and Management, Center for Basic and Applied Research, Czech Republic; and Research Fellow at Malaysia-Japan International Institute of Technology, University Technology Malaysia, Kuala Lumpur, Malaysia. In 2008 he received his Ph.D. title in technical cybernetics at Technical University of Ostrava, Czech Republic. He is currently a vice-rector for science and creative activities of the University of Hradec Kralove from June 2020. At present, he is also a director of the Center for Basic and Applied Research at the University of Hradec Kralove. In years 2016-2020 he was vice-dean for science and research at Faculty of Informatics and Management, UHK. His h-index is 20, with more than 1300 citations received in the Web of Science, where more than 100 IF journal articles is indexed in JCR index. In 2018, he was the 14th top peer reviewer in Multidisciplinary in the World according to Publons and a Top Reviewer in the Global Peer Review Awards 2019 by Publons. Currently, he is on the editorial board of the MDPI Sensors IF journal (Q1/Q2 at JCR), and several other ESCI indexed journals. He is a Vice-leader and Management Committee member at WG4 at project COST CA17136, since 2018. He has also been a Management Committee member substitute at project COST CA16226 since 2017. Since 2019, he has been Chairman of the Program Committee of the KAPPA Program, Technological Agency of the Czech Republic as a regulator of the EEA/Norwegian Financial Mechanism in the Czech Republic (2019-2024). Since 2020, he has been Chairman of the

Panel 1 (Computer, Physical and Chemical Sciences) of the ZETA Program, Technological Agency of the Czech Republic. Since 2014 until 2019, he has been Deputy Chairman of the Panel 7 (Processing Industry, Robotics, and Electrical Engineering) of the Epsilon Program, Technological Agency of the Czech Republic. At the University of Hradec Kralove, he is a guarantee of the doctoral study program in Applied Informatics, where he is focusing on lecturing on Smart Approaches to the Development of Information Systems and Applications in Ubiquitous Computing Environments. His research interests include Control Systems, Smart Sensors, Ubiquitous Computing, Manufacturing, Wireless Technology, Portable Devices, biomedicine, image segmentation and recognition, biometrics, technical cybernetics, and ubiquitous computing. His second area of interest is in Biomedicine (image analysis), as well as Biotelemetric System Architecture (portable device architecture, wireless biosensors), development of applications for mobile devices with use of remote or embedded biomedical sensors.

Yuanjun Laili received her B.S., M.Sc. and Ph.D. degrees in Automation Science and Electrical Engineering from Beihang University, Beijing, China, in 2009, 2012 and 2015 respectively. Her research interests include intelligent optimization theory and algorithms, modeling and simulation of complex system, robotic disassembly for remanufacturing and online incremental learning. She has managed 1 National Key Research and Development Program, 1 National Natural Science Foundation Project, and participated 2 National High-Tech Programs and 2 National Natural Science Foundation Project as a key researcher. She is very active in knowledge transfer to industry, making her research expertise available to multi-disciplinary companies. She has co-authored two books, and published more than 30 papers in international peer-reviewed journals or conferences. She is Member of SCS and the Commitee of Intelligent Networked Things (CINT) in China Simulation Federation (CSF), and serves as editor for the International Journal of Modeling, Simulation, and Scientific Computing.

Engin Masazade received his B.S. degree from the Department of Electronics and Communications Engineering, Istanbul Technical University, Istanbul, Turkey, in 2003, and M.S. and Ph.D. degrees from the Department of Electronics Engineering, Sabanci University, Istanbul, Turkey, in 2006 and 2010, respectively. He is currently an Assistant Professor in the Department of Electrical and Electronics Engineering, Marmara University, Istanbul, Turkey. His research interests include statistical signal processing, machine learning, distributed detection, localization, and tracking for wireless sensor networks, and dynamic resource management in sensor/communication networks.

Morteza Mohammadzaheri received his PhD from School of Mechanical Engineering, University of Adelaide, Australia in 2011. He has published/presented more than 120 peer-reviewed articles in technical journals and conferences. He is now a Senior Lecturer in Mechatronics at Birmingham City University, UK, and an Assistant Professor of Dynamic Systems and Control at Sultan Qaboos University, Oman.

Katsuyuki Morishita received his bachelor's degree from Nihon University in 2019. In 2021 he received his master's degree from Nihon University. He is now a doctor course student of the Precision Machinery Engineering, Graduate School of Science and Technology, Nihon University, Tokyo, Japan. His current research interests are developing analog electronic circuit models that mimic biological neurons and hardware neural networks that mimic the nervous systems of animals for integration into autonomous robots.

Leo Mrsic is a Scientist/Manager with proven experience in managing companies and teams of various sizes and a proven track record in innovation projects based on technical and business knowledge with the aim of increasing business efficiency. Holder of the diploma in the field of insurance of the Chair of Foreign Trade, the Master of Science in Business Economics of the Chair of Business Informatics, and the doctorate in the field of statistical models of the Chair of Information Science of the University of Zagreb. Permanent court expert in the fields of finance, accounting and computer science with about 50 expert assessments completed. The holder of the scientific title is Assistant Professor/Senior Research Associate, the teaching title University College Professor with Tenure. He is Vice-Dean for Research and Development at the Algebra College, Head of the Algebra LAB Research and Innovation Centre, Head of the Data Science study program at the Algebra University College in Zagreb. He is a member of the ESCO Maintenance Committee of the European Commission in Brussels in the third convocation (2018-2022).

Fusaomi Nagata is currently a Professor at the Department of Mechanical Engineering, Faculty of Engineering, Sanyo-Onoda City University, Japan. His research interests include 1. Intelligent control of industrial robot and its applications, 2. Design tool for AI-based visual inspection system using CNN (convolutional neural network), SVM (support vector machine) and CAE (convolutional auto encoder).

Sajid Nazir is a lecturer at Glasgow Caledonian University, Glasgow, UK. He received PhD degree in Electrical Engineering from Strathclyde University, Glasgow, UK, in 2012. He has worked on remote video monitoring projects as a Research Fellow at University of Aberdeen from 2012 to 2015. He worked on virtualization, CCTV and SCADA projects as a KTP Associate with the School of Engineering, London South Bank University, London, and Firstco Ltd., UK. He has authored one book and over 50 research publications. His current research interests include IoT, video communications, cyber security, machine learning, industrial systems, and cloud computing.

Kamisah Osman is a Prof at the Center for Teaching and Learning Innovation, Faculty of Education, Universiti Kebangsan Malaysia. She is currently the Head of Social and Economic Transformation Research Cluster at the Universiti Kebangsaan Malaysia.

Dilip Patel is Professor Emeritus at London South Bank University. His academic career in computer science spans over 30 years. He has published extensively in the areas of object technology, cognitive informatics, and data technologies.

Shushma Patel (BSc (H), PhD, FBCS, CITP, PFHEA, NTF) is Professor of Information Systems, Pro Vice Chancellor and Dean in the Faculty of Computing, Engineering and Media at De Montfort University. She studied Life Sciences as an undergraduate, before completing a PhD from the Faculty of Medicine, University of London. She has more than 30 years of teaching and research experience in Cognitive Informatics, and Qualitative Research. Professor Patel worked on many clinical research projects, in collaboration with, and funded by leading pharmaceutical and medical research councils. She has worked on many EU and commercially funded projects, exploiting innovative technologies for business solutions. Her current interest in cyber security is informed by her considerable experience working with industry and in particular her interest in user behaviours.

Marek Penhaker received the M.Sc. degree in measurement and control, in 1996, and the Ph.D. degree in technical cybernetics from the VSB - Technical University of Ostrava, in 2000. He has been an Associate Professor of biomedical engineering since 2016. He has also been a Professor of biomedical engineering since 2018. His research interests include biomedical engineering, especially medical devices and home telemetry and signal processing.

Duc Truong Pham, BE, PhD, DEng, holds the Chance Chair of Engineering at the University of Birmingham where he started his career as a lecturer in robotics and control engineering following undergraduate and postgraduate studies at the University of Canterbury in New Zealand. Until 2011, he was Professor of Computer-Controlled Manufacture and Director of the Manufacturing Engineering Centre at Cardiff University. His research is in the areas of intelligent systems, robotics and autonomous systems and advanced manufacturing technology. He has published over 600 papers and books and graduated more than 100 PhD students. He is a recipient of several awards including five prizes from the Institution of Mechanical Engineers, a Lifetime Achievement Award from the World Automation Congress and an IEEE Distinguished International Academic Contribution Award. He is a Fellow of the Royal Academy of Engineering, the Society for Manufacturing Engineers, the Institution of Engineering and Technology and the Institution of Mechanical Engineers.

Shukor A. Razak is currently an Associate Professor with the Universiti Teknologi Malaysia. He is the author or coauthor of many journals and conference proceedings at national and international levels. He is actively conducting several types of research in digital forensic investigation, wireless sensor networks, and cloud computing. His research interests include security issues for mobile ad hoc networks, mobile IPv6, vehicular ad hoc networks, and network security.

Ken Saito was born in Japan in 1978. He received the B.S. degree in electronic engineering, the M.S. degree in electronic engineering, and the Ph.D. degree in engineering from Nihon University in 2001, 2004 and 2010, respectively. He was a Research Assistant at Department of Physics, College of Humanities & Sciences, Nihon University from 2007 to 2010, Research Assistant at Department of Precision Machinery Engineering, College of Science and Technology, Nihon University from 2010 to 2011, Assistant Professor from 2011 to 2017, and Associate Professor from 2017 to 2021 in the same university. Also, he was a visiting scholar at the University of California, Berkeley. He is now a Professor at the Department of Precision Machinery Engineering, College of Science and Technology, Nihon University. His current research interests include hardware neural networks, and microrobots. Dr. Saito is a member of IEEE, IEICE, IEEJ, INNS and so on.

Shilan Sameen Hameed is a Ph.D. student at Malaysia-Japan International Institute of Technology (MJIIT), University Technology Malaysia (UTM). She obtained MSc in Computer Science from University Technology Malaysia (UTM) in 2017, where she has been granted the best student and pro-chancellor awards. During her Master study she has obtained champion award for CIMB Data Science Challenge 2017. She has published more than ten papers in peer-reviewed international journals. She has been reviewer for several papers from international journals. She is also a member in Women in CyberSecurity (WiCyS). Her current research interests include Machine Learning, Medical IoT, and Cybersecurity.

Ali Selamat has received a B.Sc. (Hons.) in IT from Teesside University, U.K. and M.Sc. in Distributed Multimedia Interactive Systems from Lancaster University, U.K. in 1997 and 1998, respectively. He has received a Dr. Eng. degree from Osaka Prefecture University, Japan in 2003. He is also a Dean at Malaysia Japan International Institute of Technology, Universiti Teknologi Malaysia, Malaysia. He was a Chief Information Officer (CIO) and Director of Computer and Information Technology, Universiti Teknologi Malaysia (UTM). He was the Dean of Research, Knowledge Economy Research Alliance, UTM. He is currently a Chair of IEEE Computer Society Malaysia Chapter. He is also the Editorial Boards of Knowledge Based Systems – Elsevier, International Journal of Information and Database Systems (IJJIDS), Inderscience Publications, Vietnam Journal of Computer Science. He is the Program Chair of International Conference on Software Engineering Tools, Methodologies (SOMET), 2019 to be held in Kanazawa, Japan. He has been a visiting professor at Hradec-Kralove University, Czech Republic, Kuwait University, and few other universities in Japan. His research interests include cloud-based software engineering, software agents, information retrievals, pattern recognition, genetic algorithms, neural networks and soft-computing, knowledge management, key performance indicators.

Melih Sen is studying his MS in Computer Engineering at Marmara University. Also, he received his BS in Electrical and Electronics Engineering from Marmara University in 2020. While studying for his BS, he was a team member at MUFE Robotics, a university student organization, to conduct research and apply them to robots. His research interests are autonomous robots, image processing, digital signal processing and low-cost deep learning systems.

Keiki Takadama received his M.E. degree from Kyoto University, Japan, in 1995 and got Doctor of Engineering Degree from the University of Tokyo, Japan, in 1998, respectively. He joined Advanced Telecommunications Research Institute (ATR) International from 1998 to 2002 as a visiting researcher and worked at Tokyo Institute of Technology from 2002 to 2006 as a lecturer. He moved to The University of Electro-Communications as associate professor in 2006 and is currently a professor from 2011. His research interests include evolutionary computation, reinforcement learning, multiagent system, autonomous system, space intelligent system, and health care system. He is a member of IEEE and ACM and a member of major AI- and informatics-related academic societies in Japan.

Shota Takahashi graduated the Faculty of Information Engineering, National Institute of Technology (KOSEN), Nara College, Japan in 2019. He currently works at ASTEC Co., Ltd., Japan. His research interests include reinforcement learning, parallel algorithm and distributed algorithm.

Yuki Takei received his bachelor's degree from Nihon University in 2017. In 2019 he received his master's degree from Nihon University. He is now a doctor course student of the Precision Machinery Engineering, Graduate School of Science and Technology, Nihon University, Tokyo, Japan. His current research interests are implementing bio-inspired methods in robots to enable them to unconsciously perform simple actions and estimate a system that animals use to generate gaits.

Elif Toprak is a researcher at the Robotics Research Laboratory and a PhD student in Electrical and Electronics Engineering at Yeditepe University, Istanbul, Turkey. She participated in research projects and studies including areas such as robot-assisted rehabilitation systems, social robotics, human-robot interaction, emotion recognition, processing and classification of physiological and EEG signals using machine learning and deep learning methods.

Lorna Uden is Emeritus Professor of IT systems in the school of Computing, Engineering and Technology at Staffordshire University. She published widely in conferences, journals, chapters of books and workshops. Her research interests include Learning Technology, Web Engineering and Technology, Human Computer Interaction, Activity Theory, big data, innovation, Knowledge management, big data, social media, Intelligent transport systems, Service Science, Ecosystems, Internet of Things(IOT), artificial intelligence, intelligence science, neuroscience and Problem-Based Learning (PBL). She is also the editor of IJLT and IJWET.

Mario Versaci received his degree in civil engineering from the "Mediterranea" University, Italy, where he also he received a PhD in electronic engineering. He also received the Diplome d'Etudes Approfondites at the Grenoble Electrotechnics Lab. In the "Mediterranea" university, he serves as both Associate Professor of electrical engineering and scientific head of the NDT/NDE Lab. He received a degree in mathematics from the University of Messina. His research focuses on soft computing, image processing, and MEMS/NEMS.

Tomohiro Yamaguchi received his M.E. degree from Osaka University, Japan, in 1987. He joined Mitsubishi Electric Corporation in 1987 and moved to Matsushita Electric Industrial in 1988. He worked at Osaka University from 1991 to 1998 as a research associate and got Doctor of Engineering Degree from Osaka University in 1996. He moved to Nara National College of Technology as associate professor in 1998 and is currently a professor from 2007. His research interests include interactive recommender system, music information retrieval, multiagent reinforcement learning, autonomous learning agent, human-agent interaction, learning support system, human learning process and mastery process. He is a member of The Japanese Society for Artificial Intelligence and The Society of Instrument and Control Engineers, Japan.

Selma Yılar is a Postdoctoral researcher in Pediatric Audiology. She is currently a doctor of an audiologist at the ENT Department at Istanbul University-Cerrahpasa Cerrahpasa Medical School, Turkey. Her research interests lie in the areas of emotion recognition in children with hearing loss, diagnostic assessment in the pediatric group with aided computer-based technology, and genetic hearing loss. She has participated in various research as a researcher and project coordinator.

Batuhan Yılmaz received his BSc. degree from Marmara University Electrical and Electronics Engineering. He is currently pursuing a Master's degree in the same domain at Boğaziçi University, while working as a software engineer for SmartIR Infrared Technologies. His main fields of interests are digital imaging systems and signal processing with deep learning.

Index

Become an Evaluator for IGI Global Authored Book Projects

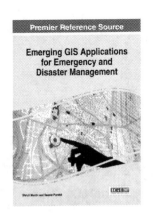

Premier Reference Source

Emerging GIS Applications for Emergency and Disaster Management

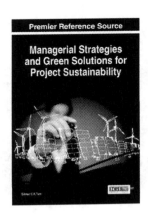

Premier Reference Source

Managerial Strategies and Green Solutions for Project Sustainability

Premier Reference Source

Comparative Approaches to Using R and Python for Statistical Data Analysis

Premier Reference Source

Solutions for High-Touch Communications in a High-Tech World

The overall success of an authored book project is dependent on quality and timely manuscript evaluations.

Applicants must have a doctorate (or equivalent degree) as well as publishing, research, and reviewing experience. Authored Book Evaluators are appointed for one-year terms and are expected to complete at least three evaluations per term. Upon successful completion of this term, evaluators can be considered for an additional term.

If you have a colleague that may be interested in this opportunity, we encourage you to share this information with them.

Printed in the United States
by Baker & Taylor Publisher Services